D0161105

e-Commerce

Jeffrey F. Rayport
Harvard University and
Marketspace, a Monitor Group Company

Bernard J. Jaworski
Marketspace, a Monitor Group Company

 **McGraw-Hill/ Irwin**
MarketspaceU

Boston   Burr Ridge, IL   Dubuque, IA   Madison, WI   New York   San Francisco   St. Louis
Bangkok   Bogotá   Caracas   Kuala Lumpur   Lisbon   London   Madrid   Mexico City
Milan   Montreal   New Delhi   Santiago   Seoul   Singapore   Sydney   Taipei   Toronto

McGraw-Hill Higher Education

A Division of The **McGraw-Hill** *Companies*

e-COMMERCE
Published by McGraw-Hill/Irwin, an imprint of The McGraw-Hill Companies, Inc.
1221 Avenue of the Americas, New York, NY 10020. Copyright © 2001 by Rayport and Jaworski. All rights reserved. No part of this publication may be reproduced or distributed in any form or by any means, or stored in a database or retrieval system, without the prior written consent of The McGraw-Hill Companies, Inc., including, but not limited to, in any network or other electronic storage or transmission, or broadcast for distance learning. Some ancillaries, including electronic and print components, may not be available to customers outside the United States.

This book is printed on acid-free paper.

2 3 4 5 6 7 8 9 0 QKP/QKP 0 9 8 7 6 5 4 3 2 1

ISBN 0-07-246521-2

Publisher: *David Kendric Brake*
Executive Editor: *Gary L. Bauer*
Developmental Editor: *Christine Parker*
Marketing Manager: *Kimberly Kanakes*
Production Supervisor: *Susanne Riedell*
Media Technology Producer: *Burke Broholm*
Project Management: *Proof Positive/Farrowlyne Associates, Inc.*
Cover Design: *Proof Positive/Farrowlyne Associates, Inc.*
Cover Photo: *Nora Good/Masterfile*
Compositor: *Black Dot Composition*
Typeface: *10/12 Minion*
Printer: *Quebecor Printing Book Group/Kingsport*

Library of Congress Card Number: 00-108389

www.mhhe.com

McGraw-Hill/MarketspaceU
Mission Statement

This text and companion casebook, *e-Commerce* and *Cases in e-Commerce,* are the first volumes produced for the McGraw-Hill/MarketspaceU learning series on e-commerce. McGraw-Hill/MarketspaceU was created to develop exceptional higher education teaching materials on the latest business practices and theories by leading thinkers in the field of e-commerce. McGraw-Hill/MarketspaceU is committed to providing the business instructor a comprehensive set of pedagogical tools with the most current materials in an easy-to-use learning system that includes textbooks, casebooks, video interviews, and Web support for teaching the state-of-the-art in e-commerce business practice and theory. We aim to equip present and future executives, managers, and strategists in becoming successful creators of value in the New Economy.

To accomplish this task, we offer a suite of cutting-edge tools to help you navigate the world of e-commerce:

- *e-Commerce* text
- *Cases in e-Commerce*
- McGraw-Hill Online Learning Center (OLC)
- MarketspaceU.com
- PowerWeb in e-Commerce

For more information about these tools, see page xviii.

ACKNOWLEDGMENTS

We are grateful to a team of outstanding colleagues who have made the preparation of this book possible. We acknowledge specific contributions chapter by chapter throughout the book, but we want to thank heartily and with great enthusiasm our colleagues in Marketspace, a Monitor Group Company, who constituted the core team for this work: Yannis Dosios, Leo Griffin, and Michael Yip. Yannis and Leo contributed extensively to many of the chapters in the book while Mike worked tirelessly over many months in a variety of capacities—content, editorial, and project management—to ensure we stayed the course.

We also wish to acknowledge the valuable contributions to portions of the manuscript from Jennifer Baron, Wendy Cholbi, Tom Copeland, Lisa Ferri, Sharon Grady, Ellie Kyung, Peter Meyers, Nancy Michels, Rafi Mohammed, Mark Pocharski, Marco Smit, and Toby Thomas. We also wish to thank Steve Libenson, John Trinidad, Yakir Siegal, Scott Daniels, and Alex Scherbakovsky for their advice, comments, and contributions. We thank Kim Bender for her work on the companion casebook. And we also thank JoAnn Kienzle and Jason Park for their valuable editorial and administrative work on the project.

This book also draws from the video production work of Lori Cohen and her crack team as well as the Web content under the direction of Josh Clark and Steve Szaraz. In managing the project, we are indebted to Rafe Sagalyn, our literary agent, and Alan M. Kantrow, our local knowledge management czar.

We also gratefully acknowledge the editorial support at McGraw-Hill/Irwin of Rob Zwettler, Vice President and Editor-in-Chief; David Brake, Publisher; Gary Bauer, Executive Editor; Christine Parker, Developmental Editor; and the production support of Lauren Woodrow and the staff at Proof Positive/Farrowlyne Associates, Inc.

Finally, none of this would have been possible without the generous support and enthusiasm of Mark Fuller, Joe Fuller, and Mark Thomas, cofounders and leaders of Monitor Group, a strategy consulting company and merchant bank based in Cambridge, Massachusetts.

ABOUT THE AUTHORS

Jeffrey F. Rayport, founder of Marketspace, a Monitor Group Company, is regarded as one of the most influential thinkers in the field of e-commerce. He launched the first e-commerce strategy course at the Harvard Business School nearly six years ago and to date has written nearly 100 case studies on e-commerce. His second-year elective course on this subject consistently enrolled nearly half of the Harvard Business School class of 800 students. From 1997–1999, he was voted "best professor" at Harvard Business School by the student body, and he was the first Harvard Business School professor to receive this award three years in a row.

Dr. Rayport's research has focused on the impact of information technologies on service management and on marketing strategies for business and has involved a wide array of high-tech and service firms, industry associations, and professional practices. In addition to his HBS case studies, he has written numerous articles on New Economy topics that have appeared in industry and popular business publications.

Dr. Rayport earned an A.B. from Harvard College, a M.Phil. in International Relations at the University of Cambridge (U.K.), and an A.M. in the History of American Civilization and a Ph.D. in Business History at Harvard University. His doctoral research examined diversification strategies among the regional Bell operating companies after the breakup of AT&T, with a focus on the transformation of high-tech companies from technology-driven to marketing-oriented firms.

Bernard J. Jaworski is a cofounder and senior advisor at Marketspace, a Monitor Group Company, and holds the Markets Chair within Monitor University. He has been the Jeanne and David Tappan Marketing Fellow and a tenured Full Professor of Marketing at the University of Southern California. He previously served on the faculty at the University of Arizona and was a visiting professor at the Harvard Business School. In 1997, he received the Golden Apple Award as the MBA teacher of the year at USC. Dr. Jaworski is one of a few two-time winners of the prestigious Alpha Kappa Psi award for best marketing practice article published in the *Journal of Marketing*. He currently serves on the review board of the *Journal of Marketing*, the *Journal of Marketing Research*, the *Journal of Business-to-Business Marketing*, the *Asian Journal of Marketing*, and other journals.

About MarketspaceU and the Contributing Authors

MarketspaceU is a community of award-winning academics and talented business practitioners dedicated to developing managers for the New Economy. We are part of Marketspace, a Monitor Group Company, founded in 1998 as a multimedia enterprise to provide advice on, research about, and analysis of the impact of new media and technology on businesses. Marketspace activities include consulting to freshly minted dot-coms, as well as to Global 1000 companies, and providing New Economy insights to the public through a variety of media that includes the Web, television, and print.

Drawing upon the resources at Marketspace and at other Monitor Group companies, as well as from a network of academic institutional partners and CEO visionaries, MarketspaceU.com brings together the diverse talents of practitioners, management consultants, academic experts, and writers.

WHAT LEADERS IN THE NEW ECONOMY ARE SAYING ABOUT *E-COMMERCE*:

In today's turbulent Internet-driven business environment, clear and understandable rules to the New Economy are hard to come by. Jaworski and Rayport have taken a dizzying amount of research and boiled it down to exactly that. The framework they present is not only clear and graspable, but also universal. Their new rules of business management are as applicable to General Motors as they are to Yahoo! Inc.

Tim Brady
Sr. Vice President of Network Services, Yahoo! Inc.

Finally someone has put it all together! These leading thinkers have put in one place a brilliant and comprehensive framework for thinking through, planning, teaching, and managing e-Business. And—beyond that—this book is a portal to a stream of the most complete set of online, video, and other resources for e-Business learning to date. Great insights. Powerful tools.

Ralph Oliva
Executive Director of the Institute for the Study of Business Markets and Professor of Marketing, Pennsylvania State University

This is a wonderfully designed pedagogical device. The chapters build foundationally, so as to empower the student to deal with unique New Economy concepts, like the DCF approach to valuation, etc., towards the end. The chapters are filled with case vignettes, viewpoints, and thought bytes that draw the self-selected readers in and engage them in a sophisticated debate regarding the Internet economy. The highlight of the book, for me, was the way linkages were provided to existing management concepts. Thus, the reader is not left wondering what the connection to the old paradigm is; in fact, the reader gets a working dose of those ideas in the book chapters. This makes the book a stand-alone, comprehensive text with cutting-edge tone and content.

Kastori Rangan
Eliot I. Snider and Family Professor of Business Administration
Harvard Business School

e-Commerce is the first textbook to show how firms gain competitive advantage in the New Economy. The authors introduce a number of new and innovative concepts, frameworks, and tools that benefit both students and managers. This book is destined to become the standard New Economy text in leading MBA programs.

John Quelch
Dean, London Business School

Of all the Internet textbooks I have seen, *e-Commerce* by Rayport and Jaworski does the best job making both an intellectual and practical contribution to electronic commerce. Students and managers alike will come away with a better understanding of the nature of electronic commerce, how it has changed the existing business model, and its likely impact in the future.

Particularly valuable are the chapters on Business Models (Chapter 3), the Customer Interface (Chapter 4), Implementation (Chapter 6), Metrics (Chapter 7), and Valuation (Chapter 8). Together with its companion casebook, *e-Commerce* will soon become the electronic commerce textbook of choice.

Russ Winer
J. Gary Shansby Professor of Marketing Strategy
University of California at Berkeley

PREFACE

To say that the Internet changes everything is, in some high-technology circles, almost a cliché. But this book makes a strong argument for the truth of that now familiar phrase. Or, put differently, the application of new media and information technology to business—which, of course, includes the Internet and the World Wide Web—has not only changed what we know about management, strategy, and business design, but also has assured us of a continuing and unfolding impact on what managers do and how businesses operate in the foreseeable future. All hype aside, there is truly a revolution here, and we have little choice but to embrace it.

We aim to equip present and future executives, managers, and strategists in becoming successful in this sweeping change. This book is the entry point into a learning system that includes this textbook, a companion casebook, video interviews, and integrated Web support for teaching the state-of-the-art in e-commerce business practice and theory.

The most succinct way of characterizing this revolution is to understand that we are operating today in what some call the New Economy. While there are many definitions of this term, New Economy businesses have several key traits in common. Successful New Economy firms must be able to accomplish each of the following tasks:

- Create value largely or exclusively through the gathering, synthesizing, and distribution of information. Success is predicated on creating value by tapping the power of electronic information networks and new media interfaces.

- Formulate strategy in ways that make management of the enterprise and management of technology convergent.

- Compete in real time rather than in "cycle time" and operate in a constantly responsive dialogue with their customers and markets.

- Operate in a world characterized by low barriers to entry, near-zero variable costs of operation, and, as a result, intense, constantly shifting competition.

- Organize resources around the demand side—e.g., customers, markets, trends, and needs—rather than around the supply side, as businesses have done in the past.

- Manage relationships with customers and markets often through "screen-to-face" channels and interfaces, meaning that technology rather than people manages these relationships.

- Use technology-mediated channels, which means that ongoing operations are subject to measurement and tracking in unprecedented and granular ways.

Taking these themes together does more than furnish a rigorous understanding of what business managers and pundits alike mean when they talk about doing business in the New Economy. Each of these statements implies significant changes in how New Economy practitioners determine strategy, deploy resources, operate firms, manage relationships with their markets, and measure results. This does not mean that everything we know about business up to this point becomes irrelevant and obsolete, but it does mean that significant changes in the environment of business justify—indeed, demand—radically new approaches to thinking about strategy and management.

As a result, we strongly argue in the following pages that the revolution in business is, in fact, larger than any one particular technology, including the Internet, and that it is more profound than any one innovation, including the World Wide

Web. We are entering a world in which a new array of considerations—issues that were once peripheral to management or completely outside its scope—have now taken center stage. These include technology, interface design, real-time market metrics, and deep understanding of customer attitudes and behavior. For anyone who is considering a career in business of any kind that impinges on these New Economy realities, a deep understanding of these themes is essential to business success, if not business survival.

In this sense, we have created this set of materials to be not only about technology but also about a world enabled by technology. Increasingly, the New Economy is built of businesses that exploit, at their core, a variety of technological innovations. These innovations have proven necessary, but not sufficient, in the creation of a viable business proposition. Rather, they have created a flood of new entrants in practically every sector of the economy, most with some kind of new technology-enabled approach to changing the way traditional industries work; this, in turn, has resulted in a flood of venture capital and private equity into the New Economy sector that has further fueled the pace of innovation and competition.

However, it would be a mistake to interpret these developments as a sign that technology is the new competitive weapon for business. Rather, it is the new definition of the minimum entry price—or what gamblers would call "table stakes"—of doing business. Put differently, technology is no longer the scarce resource. Indeed, it is ubiquitous in the New Economy. The scarce resources are the talented individuals with management, strategy, and executive skills tailored to doing business in the New Economy.

This constitutes the goal of the learning system that includes this textbook. Again, we are here to provide tools to present and future executives, managers, and strategists in becoming successful creators of value in the New Economy. While this involves a solid grasp of relevant technology and new media forms, it demands just as solid a grasp of how the functions of the manager and executive have changed in this new world.

It is no coincidence that today in Silicon Valley—easily "ground zero" of the Internet business revolution—there are no less than 400 CEO positions on offer with few if any candidates to fill them. The Valley is a place rife with ideas, entrepreneurs, and capital; it's a place where the idea of a shortage in *anything* seems almost a contradiction in terms. Yet there is truly a shortage of one critical skill set, and that is the ability to manage effectively at the highest levels in the world that the New Economy has wrought.

You, the reader, are the person with the potential to develop such skills. And this is an exciting notion. There could not be a better time in the history of business to have the skills for doing business in the New Economy. With these at your fingertips, the world will truly be your (high-technology) oyster.

Approach

This book is written for present and future practitioners in New Economy businesses. As such, it provides both a deep exploration of core concepts of New Economy management and strategy. It is also enriched by a wide variety of examples, case studies, and explanations culled directly from practice. We take this approach for a variety of reasons.

New Economy management and strategy are being invented in real time as we go to press. Every marketspace business we have studied—and our work is based on nearly 100 case studies completed at the Harvard Business School over the last six years—has been engaged in the creation of "new science" for doing business. The true insights will be generated at this stage by deep observation of both new and established businesses wrestling with New Economy challenges. Thus, we take a militantly field-based and practitioner-focused perspective on this work. This is not to say that management theory is irrelevant. Existing concepts and theories such as "network effects" and "increasing returns to scale" do apply. However, in general, that practice is far ahead of theory at this time in history.

The result presented in this book is a collection of rigorous concepts, frameworks, and approaches that represent an entire applications suite of tools for doing business in the New Economy. Observation of business practices, while often fascinating and instructive, is not enough. We have taken our knowledge of practice as developed through case studies and followed through with conceptualization. These tools represent a critical source of competitive advantage for companies and their managers, and we have tested them with our own students in MBA and executive education programs and with our consulting clients in the context of their own businesses. In other words, these are "road-tested" approaches to New Economy business, developed out of rigorous observation from the inside of such businesses and then tested in real firms.

Because New Economy businesses operate in rich media or new media environments, we have endeavored to make this book a rich information environment. We provide deeper exploration of topics that appear in the text through Drill-Down sidebars. Point-Counterpoints highlight the two sides to some of the unresolved debates in New Economy businesses. POVs are sidebar commentaries from leading practitioners in the New Economy. We transcribe excerpts from videotaped conversations with thought leaders in the New Economy into Sound Byte sidebars. And at the end of every chapter, Schwab serves as a living case study to which we apply the ideas and concepts presented in each chapter. We show exactly how these ideas apply, and we help you see the ideas in action in ways that have created substantial value for a company doing business in the real world.

You will see that every chapter has a variety of standard features that augment the text. You can count on these to enrich your understanding of the material covered, to introduce new and often controversial perspectives, and to provide greater detail on topics of current and future salience.

In addition, you will see that every chapter begins with a chapter overview to help you get a quick grasp on the topics discussed in that segment. In addition, we provide study questions to guide you in reading the material. And of course, context is important; we frame every chapter in the first few sections by consistently indicating each chapter's connection to the previous one, the overall purpose of the chapter, and an overview of its organization. This way, before you even think about reading any one section of this book, you will have all the information you need to judge its relevance and anticipate its approach.

Content and Organization

The book is organized around the decision-making process we propose for formulating New Economy enterprise strategy. There are six interrelated, sequential decisions to this strategy—market-opportunity analysis, business model, customer interface, market communications and branding, implementation, and evaluation. These decisions are made in the context of a changing market-level infrastructure. The infrastructure includes factors related to the network infrastructure and media convergence.

As such, the sequence and topics of chapters reflect the intellectual architecture of our approach to managing in this field. Chapters are organized to reflect the framework sequence of the decision-making process.

Chapter 1—Overview: Many students and clients constantly ask us what's different about managing in the New Economy. In this chapter, we set forth those differences in detail, attempting to frame the unique attributes of the New Economy and the implications for managers and strategists. In doing this, we present a working definition and framework for the study and practice of e-commerce. We also review the e-commerce landscape to provide context for discussions throughout the rest of the book. Notably, we divide the world of New Economy businesses into several key groups, including business-to-consumer, business-to-business, and consumer-to-consumer.

Chapter 2—Framing the Market Opportunity: In this chapter, we revisit the basics for any business to construct an original New Economy approach to formulating business strategy. In so doing, we focus on the players who make up the dynamics of any business—customers, competitors, and strategic partners. The goal here is to understand what market analysis becomes in this new world and to introduce a process not only to understand the market but also to identify those portions of the market that are unserved or underserved. This chapter identifies five conditions that must be carefully analyzed to determine if there is a market opportunity for the firm.

Chapter 3—Business Models: While many believe that Internet businesses in many cases do not have business models, we strongly disagree. There may be poorly articulated models out there, but a business-model definition is essential to competition in this new space. Here we introduce the four components of the marketspace business model. These are: (1) the value proposition or cluster, (2) the product offering that we call a marketspace offering, (3) the resource system that the firm selects to deliver the offering, and (4) a financial model that enables the business to generate revenues, cash flows, and, ultimately, profit margins or valuation potential. These four choices constitute the foundation of the strategy decisions that we explore throughout the book.

Chapter 4—The Customer Interface: The visible presence of most e-commerce businesses is a digital or rich media interface. While New Economy businesses may make substantial use of traditional offline interfaces—such as retail points of sale, printed catalogs, stand-alone kiosks, and call centers—they rely primarily on a virtual storefront connected to the Internet. In this chapter, we fully develop the set of design tools and elements that we refer to as the 7Cs of the customer interface. These elements include content, context, community, commerce, customization, communications, and connection. In particular, we focus on the levers management can use to create competitive advantage and generate customer value through these essential elements of interface design.

Chapter 5—Communications and Branding: In the demand-oriented world of the New Economy, there is nothing more valuable than mindshare or the ability to attract and hold the attention of markets and customers. The traditional tools of attention management are marketing communications. In this chapter, we explore the variety of traditional and new media communication approaches that provide competitive advantages to New Economy businesses. And we delve into the extraordinary power of brands in this new, information-enabled world. Many believed that the Web would create a world of downward price pressures and rapid commoditization of goods and services of all kinds. As we explain, the opposite has occurred. Brands are more important than ever—and some would argue that, at least in business-to-consumer ventures, they are essential to success.

Chapter 6—Implementation: If strategy is about "what to do," implementation is about "how to do it." In most management texts focused, as this one is, on strategy, implementation is often left to the last chapters. Indeed, in the management literature, it has constituted a "poor cousin" of fashion-forward fields such as strategy, marketing, and finance. Doing business in the New Economy demands a different approach. Because such businesses operate in constant dynamic dialogue with their markets, it is difficult—and unproductive—to approach strategy and implementation in a linear, sequential fashion. Rather, they are two elements in a real-time cycle, wherein each set of decisions pertaining to strategy and implementation must constantly be reevaluated, based on new data one from the other. In this chapter, we consider both the "delivery system" and innovation components of strategy implementation.

Chapter 7—Metrics: The dynamic relationship between strategy and market feedback demands new approaches to measurement and evaluation of business results. We know that e-commerce businesses offer unprecedented opportunities for capturing information on how markets operate and how customers engage in search and shopping behavior. Because this kind of data is available in rich granular forms and, as importantly, in real time, we introduce a new management tool called the Performance Dashboard. It is a set of metrics that reflect both the early warning indicators of the progress of an e-commerce strategy, as well as outcome measures, such as customer satisfaction and financial performance.

Chapter 8—Valuation: One of the more provocative aspects of the e-commerce revolution has been the extraordinary valuations that Web-based businesses have achieved in the capital markets around the world. These range from Yahoo!, the Web's leading search engine, which is worth more than General Motors, to America Online, which achieved a valuation so high that it acquired Time Warner, the world's largest media conglomerate. They also include phenomenal valuations outside the United States, such as the Hong Kong-based Pacific Century Cyberworks, a holding company of Internet business investments, which achieved a valuation at one point so rich that it threatened to acquire Hong Kong's national telecommunications giant, and the India-based Wipro, an Internet services firm that, after an offering on its country's national stock exchange, became the most highly valued company in India's history. We attempt to cut through the mystique and hype surrounding such valuations with the aid of one of the world's leading experts on corporate valuation, Tom Copeland. This chapter provides an overview of how to determine or project the valuation of an e-commerce business.

Chapter 9—Network Infrastructure: In traditional business, we all know what retail points of sale look like and how trucks transport raw and finished goods on the nation's highways. In the New Economy, the infrastructure of economic activity—primarily oriented around the processing and shipment of information—is both less visible and less familiar. In this chapter, we explore how the market-level dynamics that operate outside the formal boundaries of the organization provide the infrastructure for traditional and new business approaches. We provide an overview on hardware, software, servers, and the parts that make up the enabling "railroad" for the New Economy. The chapter also provides a brief overview of several notable public policy issues that have implications for business and society.

Chapter 10—Media Convergence: What rides on the "rails" of this new infrastructure is a wide variety of content and media. In this chapter, we examine media undergoing transformation from analog to digital and the consequences of value migration from old media to new media, media megamergers, and synergies.

Supporting Materials

To facilitate the teaching of the book content, we realize that instructors need teaching support materials. In an effort to assist instructors, we have developed a support package that includes: (1) an instructor's manual, (2) the McGraw-Hill/Irwin OLC for this book at *www.mhhe.com/marketspace* and its companion casebook, and (3) the website (*www.marketspaceu.com*) that includes advanced supplemental materials.

USER'S GUIDE
Textbook Navigation

Because New Economy businesses operate in rich media or new media environments, we have endeavored to make this book a rich information environment. You will see that every chapter has a variety of standard features that augment the text. You can count on these to enrich your understanding of the material covered, to introduce new and often controversial perspectives, and to provide greater detail on topics of current and future salience. Look for the following features as you read.

- **Drill-Downs:** These sidebars provide deeper explorations of topics that appear in the text by taking a focused approach to issues that some readers will find essential at a level of detail inappropriate to the main body of our work. For example, not every reader will want to explore the intricacies of collaborative filtering or viral marketing, but many will find these additional materials useful. Think of Drill-Downs as hypertext—there when you need them, out of your way when you don't.

- **Point-Counterpoints:** These segments acknowledge the reality that many debates in New Economy businesses—such as whether profits matter or whether Internet company valuations are rational—remain unresolved. Rather than take an artificial approach to these issues and present the "right" answers, we make the case for and against. Of course, we do have our points of view, and you will find these clearly indicated.

- **Sound Bytes:** The MarketSpace Center has invested heavily in new media and video products that lend unique insights into the New Economy. The interviews featured in the Sound Byte sections are transcribed excerpts from ongoing research and videotaped conversations with thought leaders in the New Economy such as Netscape cofounder Marc Andreessen, Ethernet inventor Bob Metcalfe, and the creators of ICQ instant messaging, Yair Goldfinger and Sefi Vigiser. These interviews represent fresh, up-to-date, and exclusive perspectives on the state of play in the field. Longer streaming video excerpts are available on the website at *www.marketspaceu.com* and full interviews are available on videotape for purchase.

- **POVs (Points of View):** Throughout the chapters, we have included sidebar commentaries from leading practitioners in the New Economy—people who have invented new business approaches, developed new network architectures, created major Web brands, and influenced policies in the field. These comments are excerpted from articles published in leading periodicals of the New Economy, such as the *Industry Standard, Upside,* and *Business 2.0.*

- **Schwab Case Study:** At the end of every chapter, we visit one company, broker Charles Schwab, that the world has come to admire as the leading example of a "clicks-and-mortar" player—an established business that led the way in developing Web-based brokerage services while maintaining its leading brick-and-mortar franchise throughout the United States. Despite a raft of competitors from the Internet world, such as E*Trade, Ameritrade, and Datek Online, Schwab has held its own as the category dominant competitor, forcing even an old-line wire house such as Merrill Lynch to enter the online fray, even as it continues to maintain 40,000 brokers on its payroll around the world. Schwab serves us as a living case study to which we apply the ideas and concepts presented in each chapter. We show exactly how these ideas apply, and we help you see the ideas in action in ways that have created substantial value for a company doing business in the real world.

Supporting Materials

To facilitate the teaching of this book's content, we realize that instructors need teaching support materials. In an effort to assist instructors, we have developed a comprehensive support package that includes materials available on the Web.

- *Cases in e-Commerce:* Available separately for purchase, a casebook complements our textbook and charts an educational course through the key practical issues in the New Economy business landscape. Case studies—long used in clinical psychology, medical, and business school programs—are designed to facilitate *a healthy debate* on the alternative solutions to a particular problem. Today, there are precious few case studies that illustrate "what works" in the New Economy, and in our casebook we have assembled a unique and comprehensive selection that is directly relevant to the New Economy.

  Qualified adopters of *e-Commerce* or *Cases in e-Commerce* will also have access to two unique supporting websites, McGraw-Hill's Online Learning Center (OLC) and Marketspace's *www.marketspaceu.com,* with a wide variety of additional materials available to support the text.

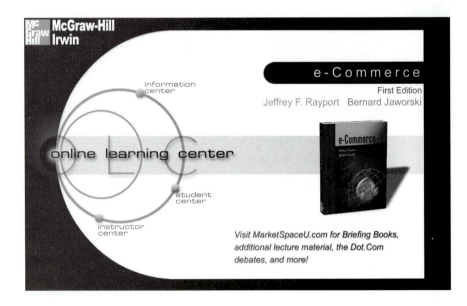

- **McGraw-Hill/Irwin OLC:** McGraw-Hill/Irwin continues its leading role in providing excellent support to instructors in higher education. Instructors using this textbook to teach an e-commerce course or module are able to access the McGraw-Hill/Irwin OLC at *www.mhhe.com/marketspace* for sample syllabi for different approaches to teaching the material; descriptions of how to use the various pedagogical features, such as the POVs, Point-Counterpoints, and videos; suggested test/discussion questions for each chapter; guidelines for different types of projects; and PowerPoint slides for each of the chapters—these vary from 10 to 15 slides per chapter.

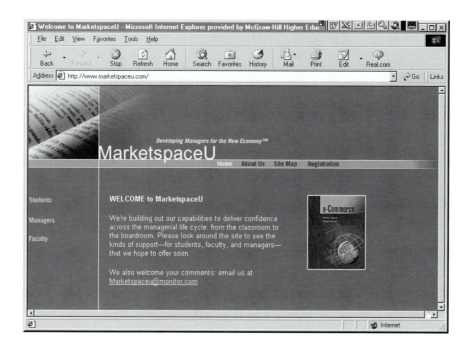

- **Instructor's Manual:** Available directly from the McGraw-Hill OLC at *www.mhhe.com/marketspace,* the instructor's manual is designed and written to help faculty using our textbook teach an e-commerce course or module. Our manual offers a concise summary of each chapter's key themes, classroom questions (and answers) that highlight those themes and spur lively classroom debates, and relevant student project assignments (and answers) designed to reinforce key learning points in each chapter. The instructor's manual provides teaching tips and suggestions for presenting each chapter, suggested test/discussion questions for each chapter, and suggested exercises and associated websites that illustrate the chapter content.

- **MarketspaceU Multimedia Materials:** We draw upon the extensive professional media capabilities of the Marketspace media group and of our partners at ENEN.com to let the New Economy speak for itself.

  - The MarketspaceU media archives contain over 100 focused broadcast-quality interviews with leading CEOs, investors, inventors, and implementers, conducted at leading New Economy conferences around the world. Streaming video excerpts are available on the website at *http://www.marketspaceu.com* and full interviews are available on videotape for purchase.

  - MarketspaceU.com has captured Professors Rayport and Jaworski in a series of "dot-com Debates" on live and lively issues in the New Economy. Does profit matter? Do the valuations make sense? Who's got it better, dot-com start-ups or dot-coms backed by brick-and-mortar giants? Does segmentation matter on the Web? Tune in by visiting us at *http://www.marketspaceu.com* as Dr. Rayport and Dr. Jaworski provide an educational—and entertaining—Point-Counterpoint discussion.

- **Cases:** Our library includes cases written for top business schools and our own cases written by our team of scholars and practitioners. Case studies—long used in clinical psychology, medical, and business school programs—are designed to facilitate a dialogue, or more appropriately, *a healthy debate* on the alternative solutions to a particular problem.

  The interesting challenge in crafting cases on New Economy firms is that the solution seems to be changing as rapidly as the practitioner is able to diagnose the problem. We use the term "seems" because there are some basic strategy principles that *do* last the test of time. Our intent in providing the following set of case studies is to challenge your thinking and to stir debate among your classmates, colleagues, or friends about the lasting principles that will emerge in the New Economy.

- **Teaching Notes:** We offer teaching notes to assist instructors that are using our cases in an e-commerce course or module. Our concise teaching notes help instructors understand the case and teaching themes and provide several helpful resources. Each teaching note offers a case synopsis, case teaching objectives, several case-analysis questions (and answers), potential problems with teaching the case, an endnote that provides a general update on what has happened to the company since the case was written, and several board plans that offer suggestions on how the classroom boards should be organized when teaching a case.

- **Briefing Books:** For each case we offer a briefing book, an enhanced multimedia teaching note to keep instructors informed on the cases and in control in the classroom. Each briefing book provides a quick summary of the case, key articles, teaching aids (e.g., a time line of company developments), discussion questions and focused point-counterpoint debates, and real-time updates powered by our sister site, tnbt.com. Designed by our unique combination of academics and practitioners, briefing books provide confidence in the classroom. They focus and enhance preparation time, reduce the chance for blindside surprises, and direct discussion to the most recent issues.

- **Lectures:** For each textbook chapter, we offer an expanded PowerPoint presentation designed to capture key chapter themes and insights. These slide decks offer visual aids to assist instructors who are using the textbook to teach an e-commerce course or module. Professors, managers, and students can also incorporate these slides into their PowerPoint presentations on various New Economy topics. Mini lectures generally offer 10–12 professional PowerPoint slides that provide an overview of the key themes in each textbook chapter. Enhanced lectures generally offer 23–27 professional PowerPoint slides that illustrate in greater depth the key themes of each textbook chapter.

- **Syllabi:** For instructors using our textbook to teach an e-commerce course or module, we offer three types of suggested syllabi (all case format, all lecture format, combination case/lecture format) to use for their course.

  - *All Case Teaching Format:* For instructors using an all case format, we offer a syllabus that outlines a 13-week course structure and specifies suggested course timing, class session summaries, recommended cases that illustrate important e-commerce themes, and class preparation questions.

- *All Lecture Teaching Format:* For instructors using an all lecture format, we offer a syllabus that outlines a 13-week course structure and specifies suggested course timing, class session summaries, and class preparation questions.

- *Combination Case/Lecture Format:* For instructors using a combination case/lecture format, we offer a syllabus that outlines a 13-week course structure and specifies suggested course timing, class session summaries, recommended cases to augment textbook-based lectures, and class preparation questions.

For Faculty

The changes taking place in real time in the New Economy have both energized the classroom and brought a new set of challenges to faculty teaching in this space. Students have unprecedented access to sources of information and data, they have had a greater range of experiences—from investments in New Economy companies to their own start-up battle scars—and support for teachers in the classroom has advanced from a blackboard or two to a multimedia tool kit to make lessons more immediate.

These developments make the job of staying on top of the New Economy and of effectively conveying its lessons more difficult. Given the speed of change, how can we prevent being blindsided by late-breaking developments? Because the "old warhorse" cases often no longer work, what *can* we repurpose, and where do we turn for new frameworks?

- *e-Commerce* provides a strong knowledge foundation to help chart your course through the New Economy.

- *Cases in e-Commerce* and the stand-alone cases raise the key issues to show how New Economy knowledge is applied in the business world and to drive productive discussions.

- Teaching support materials give you unequaled confidence in the classroom. Our teaching notes outline the issues and chart the questions. Our briefing books give you real-time intelligence on the case, time lines of case developments, key articles, and focused point-counterpoint questions.

- Articles and forums provide in-depth insights on what academic and New Economy business leaders are thinking and doing.

- An extensive media library of New Economy interviews provides the first— and the last—word on New Economy issues from the men and women who are driving them.

- And every day, our sister site, tnbt.com, provides New Economy news updates—knowledge to keep you on the cutting edge of the New Economy.

For Students

You are riding the wave of a technological revolution that is changing the way that economy operates. Businesses, entrepreneurs, governments, academic institutions, nonprofit organizations—they all are scrambling to hire students who understand, can operate in, and can lead in the New Economy. MarketspaceU provides you with the knowledge to harness, drive, and benefit from the opportunities brought on by the New Economy.

- *e-Commerce* provides a strong New Economy knowledge foundation.
- Case studies show how New Economy knowledge is applied in the business world.
- Articles and forums provide in-depth insight on what academic and New Economy business leaders are thinking and doing.
- A library of New Economy PowerPoint slide decks provides new ideas and professional slides to ensure that your next presentation is a rousing success.
- And every day, our sister site, tnbt.com, provides New Economy news updates—knowledge to keep you on the cutting edge of the New Economy.

BRIEF CONTENTS

CONTENTS

©Bill Frymire/Masterfile

Overview of e-Commerce Framework

This chapter provides an overview of the framework that organizes the managerial decision-making process for e-commerce strategy. We begin with a discussion of the scope of e-commerce strategy, the reasons why the study of this field is unique, and the types of e-commerce activity. After this background material, we will then introduce you to the organizing framework for the book.

The e-commerce strategy process is composed of six parts: framing the market opportunity, defining the business model, customer interface, market communications and branding, implementation, and evaluation. This strategy process rests on two key platforms: the network infrastructure that makes the Internet possible and the convergence of alternative forms of media such as radio, TV, magazines, and newspapers. The chapter concludes with a short synopsis of the nine remaining chapters.

QUESTIONS

Please consider the following questions as you read this chapter:

1. What is e-commerce?

2. What are the distinct categories of e-commerce?

3. How is e-commerce different from traditional commerce?

4. Why study e-commerce?

5. What is the e-commerce decision-making process?

The **Internet** is transforming the world's economy. It is radically changing how people live, learn, work, play, and consume. At the center of this revolution is technology. Technology has moved from the "back office" to the front line. Namely, the interface between the customer and the firm has changed dramatically. Increasingly, technology is shifting the firm's relationships with its customers from a "face-to-face" to a "screen-to-face" interaction.

The impact of the Internet on business is akin to previous innovations that transformed not just one business sector but every sector. Just as railroads, electric power, and the telephone brought disruption and opportunity to business—transforming it as these innovations swept the world—the Internet is having a similar impact. That's why it's affecting everything. The Internet is not an innovation that concerns only one or two sectors of the economy. Because it changes the way businesses should sensibly organize their activities and go to market, the Internet affects all economic activity.

Despite the uncertain competitive landscape, we have witnessed the emergence of thousands of new electronic commerce ventures that attempt to capitalize on the emerging digital New Economy. Furthermore, this electronic commerce, or "e-commerce," revolution has not gone unnoticed by traditional brick-and-mortar businesses. Now, physical world businesses must either adopt new digital strategies (e.g., Schwab.com), launch new digital businesses to complement their physical world models (e.g., iQVC.com), or be forced to completely revise their strategies (e.g., Egghead.com). Every company—large or small, profit or nonprofit, goods or services—is simultaneously vulnerable and empowered by the New Economy.

The purpose of this book is to provide a comprehensive description and definition of the e-commerce landscape to assist managers in crafting and implementing e-commerce strategy. We begin by reviewing the scope of e-commerce and the attributes that make it unique. Then we provide a framework that organizes the managerial decision-making process for e-commerce strategy.

WHAT IS E-COMMERCE?

Kevin Kelly describes the new business landscape in *New Rules for the New Economy.* "It is global. It favors intangible things—ideas, information, and relationships. And it is intensely interlinked. These three attributes produce a new type of marketplace and society, one that is rooted in ubiquitous electronic networks."[1] That is, the New Economy has been transformed by digital technology in the "postindustrial" period. Value creation for consumers has shifted from physical goods to an economy that favors service, information, and intelligence as the primary sources of value creation. E-commerce is characterized by several attributes:

- *It Is About Exchange of Digitized Information Between Parties.* This information exchange can represent communication between two parties, coordination of the flows of goods and services, or transmission of electronic orders. These exchanges can be between organizations, individuals, or both.

- *It Is Technology-Enabled.* E-commerce uses technology-enabled transactions. The use of Internet browsers in the World Wide Web to make these transactions is perhaps the best known example of technology-enabled **customer interfaces.** However, other interfaces such as ATMs, electronic data interchange (EDI) between business-to-business partners, and electronic banking by phone also fall in the general category of e-commerce. Businesses used to manage such transactions with customers and markets strictly through human or face-to-face interaction; in e-commerce, such transactions can be managed using technology.

- *It Is Technology-Mediated.* Furthermore, e-commerce is moving away from simply using technology-enabled transactions to a more technology-mediated relationship. Purchases in the "marketplace" at Wal-Mart are technology-enabled, in that we have a human using a cash register that is performing PC-based order processing. The difference now is that transactions in the "marketspace" are managed or mediated not so much through human contact but largely by technology—and, in that sense, so is the relationship with the customer. The place where buyers and sellers meet to transact is moving from the physical world "marketplace" to the virtual world "marketspace." Hence, the success of a business rests on how well screens and machines manage customers and their expectations. That's a big difference from the past, when transactions with human-human contact were the norm.

- *It Includes Intra- and Interorganizational Activities That Support the Exchange.* The scope of electronic commerce includes *all electronically based* intra- and interorganizational activities that directly or indirectly support marketplace exchanges.[2] In this sense, e-commerce affects both how business organizations relate to external parties—customers, suppliers, partners, competitors, and markets—and how they operate internally in managing activities, processes, and systems.

A Contemporary Definition

In summary, **e-commerce** can be formally defined as . . .

> . . . *technology-mediated exchanges between parties (individuals, organizations, or both) as well as the electronically based intra- or interorganizational activities that facilitate such exchanges.*

WHAT ARE THE DISTINCT CATEGORIES OF E-COMMERCE?

Four distinct categories of electronic commerce can be identified: business-to-business, business-to-consumer, consumer-to-consumer, and consumer-to-business (see Table 1–1).

- *Business-to-Business.* **Business-to-business (B2B)** refers to the full spectrum of e-commerce that can occur between two organizations. Among other activities, B2B e-commerce includes purchasing and procurement, supplier management, inventory management, channel management, sales activities, payment management, and service and support. While we may be familiar with a few B2B pioneers—e.g., Chemdex (*www.chemdex.com*), FastParts (*www.fastparts.com*), and FreeMarkets (*www.freemarkets.com*)—some other exciting new consortia are emerging. One recently announced venture is composed of the Big Three automakers working with Oracle and Commerce

Table 1-1

FOUR CATEGORIES
OF E-COMMERCE

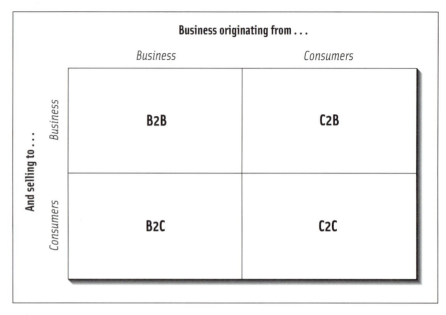

One to provide auto parts sourcing. This venture is forecasted to create a $250 billion market. Other similar initiatives are under way with industry groups including commercial real estate developers and manufacturers of pharmaceuticals and electronic subcomponents.

- *Business-to-Consumer.* **Business-to-consumer (B2C)** e-commerce refers to exchanges between businesses and consumers, e.g., Amazon.com, Yahoo.com, and Schwab.com. Similar transactions that occur in business-to-business e-commerce also take place in the business-to-consumer context. For instance, as with smaller business-to-business, transactions that relate to the "back office" of the customer (i.e., inventory management at the home) are often not tracked electronically. However, all customer-facing, or "front office," activities are typically tracked. These include sales activities, consumer search, frequently asked questions, and service and support.

- *Consumer-to-Consumer.* **Consumer-to-consumer (C2C)** exchanges involve transactions between and among consumers. These exchanges may or may not include third-party involvement as in the case of the auction-exchange eBay. Other activities include: classified ads (e.g., *www.numberoneclassifieds .com*), games (*www.heat.net*), jobs (*www.monster.com*), Web-based communications (*www.icq.com*), and personal services (e.g., Yahoo! Personals, *webpersonals.com*).

- *Consumer-to-Business.* Consumers can band together to form and present themselves as a buyer group to businesses in a **consumer-to-business (C2B)** relationship. These groups may be economically motivated as with the demand aggregator, Mercata.com, or socially oriented as with cause-related advocacy groups at voxcap.com.

HOW IS E-COMMERCE DIFFERENT FROM TRADITIONAL COMMERCE?

Each business-to-business and business-to-consumer company must make fundamental choices about how to compete in its chosen market. Some of these choices represent the traditional blocking and tackling of business strategy, as in: "How do we segment our market?", "Does our offering add value to these targeted customers?", and "How do we outperform competitors in our chosen markets?" A number of strategic choices are unique to the New Economy, such as which type of a technology-enabled customer interface to use. Prior to the further discussion of these key strategic decision areas, it is first important to consider what makes an e-commerce business unique or different from a traditional brick-and-mortar business.

Core Strategic Decisions Are Technology-Based

In the New Economy, strategic decisions—about the virtual storefront, customer service, the look and feel of the customer experience, the content of the site—are commingled with the technological decisions. These decisions relate to the selection of service providers, common business systems, approaches to Web design, and so on. In contrast to various brick-and-mortar businesses, digital businesses cannot extract technological choices from the strategic decision-making process. This observation is not to suggest that technology is unimportant to traditional businesses; rather their technological decisions are not as tightly linked to strategy.

A Real-Time Competitive Responsiveness

Recent strategy writers have introduced the notion of speed-based competition and "hyper-competition" to denote the increasing importance of speed in the brick-and-mortar world.[3] However, as the New Economy emerges, the speed of decision making has been reduced from months to minutes. In a virtual world, the business-to-consumer storefronts are frequently engaged in dynamic dialogues on the public platform of the Web. Hence, it is easier for companies to duplicate their competitors' success. This does not mean that the e-commerce marketplace will eventually evolve to commodity-like status, with price being the only consideration. Quite the contrary, speed of innovation, branding, ease of use, operational effectiveness, product assortment, affiliate agreements, and other levers can be used by companies to maintain or increase differentiation.

The Store Is Always Open

The Web storefront is expected to be open 7 days a week, 24 hours a day, and 365 days a year, now simply known as 24×7 (read "twenty-four seven"). This level of access has significant implications for both customers and the firm. On the customer side, the buyer is always able to gather information, conduct product searches, compare prices across multiple sites, and order products. As such, 24×7 has significantly altered customer notions of convenience and availability. On the firm side, the level of access has forced businesses to adjust both tactical responsiveness to competitive moves and strategic responsiveness; e.g., it is not possible to close the factory for retooling or the storefront for a strategic relaunch. When retooling or a relaunch has to occur, businesses must do so in real time and in ways that are immediately visible to the outside world.

A Technology-Based Customer Interface

In a brick-and-mortar business, customers conduct transactions either face-to-face or over the phone with store clerks, account managers, or other individuals. In contrast, the customer interface in the electronic environment is a "screen-to-face" interaction. This includes PC-based monitors, ATM machines, PDAs, or other electronic devices, not to mention the exploding field of wireless application protocol or WAP devices such as the DoCoMo iMode in Japan and the Nokia 7110 in Europe. Operationally, these types of interfaces place enormous responsibility on the organization to capture and represent the customer experience because there is often no opportunity for direct human intervention during the encounter. If the interface is designed correctly, the customer will have no need for a simultaneous or follow-up phone conversation. Thus, the "screen-to-customer" interface has the potential to both increase sales and decrease costs. In fact, a number of innovators are entering the e-commerce markets with solutions that reintroduce humans into the process, such as the service representatives available on demand for Web users at *www.liveperson.com*. When the interface does not work, not only is revenue lost but the organization also incurs the technology costs. Thus, a poorly designed customer interface has both negative revenue and cost implications.

The Customer Controls the Interaction

At most websites, the customer is in control during screen-to-face interactions, in that the Web largely employs a "self-service" model for managing commerce- or community-based interactions. The customer controls the search process, the time spent on various sites, the degree of price/product comparison, the people with whom he or she comes in contact, and the decision to buy. In a face-to-face interchange, the control can rest with either the buyer, seller, or community member. At a minimum, the seller attempts to influence the buying process by directing the potential buyer to different products or locations in the store, overcoming price objections and reacting in real time to competitive offerings. The virtual store can attempt to shape the customer experience with uniquely targeted promotions, reconfiguration of storefronts to reflect past search behavior, recommendations based on previous behavior of other similar users, and access to proprietary information. However, the seller has much less power in the online environment due to the control and information flows that the online world puts in customers' hands.

Knowledge of Customer Behavior

While the customer controls the interaction, the firm has unprecedented access to observe and track individual consumer behavior. Companies, through third-party measurement firms such as Vividence and Accrue, can track a host of behaviors: websites visited, length of stays on a site, page views on a site, contents of wish lists and shopping carts, purchases, dollar amounts of purchases, repeat purchase behavior, conversion rates of visitors who have completed transactions, and other metrics. This level of customer behavior tracking—as compared with tracking consumer attitudes, knowledge, or behavioral intentions—is not possible (or, when it is, cost-effective) in the brick-and-mortar world. Armed with this information, companies can provide one-to-one customization of offerings. In addition, companies can dynamically publish their storefronts on the Web to configure offerings to individual customers. In a tactical embellishment, electronic retailers can welcome a user back by name. In more strategic terms, an online business can actually position offers and merchandise in ways that uniquely appeal to specific customers.

Moreover, this ability to track behavior translates into real-time customer financial estimates using metrics such as acquisition costs, retention costs, lifetime value of customers, value of affiliate agreements, and behaviorally oriented communication pricing structures (e.g., payments for "click-throughs" or commissions on purchases). This turns conventional advertising on its head, by replacing proxies for anticipated customer behavior (e.g., reach, frequency, and impressions) with actual transactions. This is why native Web terms for media impact, such as "page views" or "hits," have become less salient to marketers than click-throughs and yields to purchase.

Network Economics

In information-intensive industries, a key competitive battleground centers on the emergence of industry standard products, services, components, and/or architectures. Network effects, as described by Metcalfe's Law,[4] can best be expressed as the situation where the value of a product or service rises as a function of how many other users are using the product. Classic examples are the fax machine and the telephone. The value to the customer is largely determined by the number of *other* people who adopt the technology.

A key characteristic of **network economics** is positive feedback. That is, as the installed base grows, more and more users are likely to adopt the technology *because* of the installed base. Many commercial wars in the digital economy revolve around setting a standard—growing the installed base and attempting to "lock-in" customers to the standard because of rising switching costs.[5] This applies to both hardware (e.g., cable modems versus DSL lines) and software (e.g., MP3 versus streaming audio).

A key result of network effects and positive feedback is "increasing returns" economics—as compared to the traditional decreasing returns model often associated with the brick-and-mortar world. This means, too, that traditional realities of marketing, such as the importance of word-of-mouth (WOM) among potential customers, become greatly magnified in this new environment. It is this turbocharged WOM phenomenon that makes viral marketing[6] a reality for consumer-oriented e-commerce businesses such as ICQ, an instant messaging system.

Nontraditional Performance Metrics and Emergent Valuation Models

At the time this book goes to press, there are no widely accepted methods to (1) evaluate and track the progress of e-commerce businesses, and (2) calculate the economic value of an e-commerce business. Historically, cash flow—or some derivative—has been the key metric to assess the financial performance of a business and, in the long run, to estimate the dollar value—or market capitalization—of the business. However, many of the highly valued Internet start-ups have negative cash flows and have no plans in the near term to reverse that trend.[7] Moreover, the standard metrics to judge basic business performance—whether financial or customer based—are clearly under debate in the financial analyst and market research communities.

In sum, each of these differences from traditional commerce makes e-commerce businesses unique. However, the power of these differences is magnified when they are considered collectively. The combination of screen-to-customer interfaces, network effects, real-time competitive responses, and one-to-one customization leads to "value increases" for both the customer and the firm. Both parties have increased access to unique, heretofore nonexistent information—the customer gets more availability, convenience, ease of use, and contextual information, while the firm obtains objective behavioral data on customers and competitors. This combination leads to a highly dynamic, new competitive marketspace.

WHY STUDY E-COMMERCE?

Uniqueness certainly is one important reason that validates the study of electronic commerce; however, it is equally important to ask how significant the study of e-commerce is. We believe it is significant in several respects, including economic and industry structure, wealth creation, and social structure considerations.

Exhibit 1-1
GROWTH IN NUMBER
OF INTERNET USERS

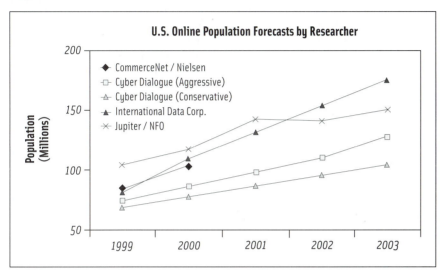

U.S. Online Population Forecasts by Researcher

- ◆ CommerceNet / Nielsen
- ◻ Cyber Dialogue (Aggressive)
- △ Cyber Dialogue (Conservative)
- ▲ International Data Corp.
- ✕ Jupiter / NFO

Exhibit 1-2
BUSINESS-TO-BUSINESS
E-COMMERCE PROJECTIONS

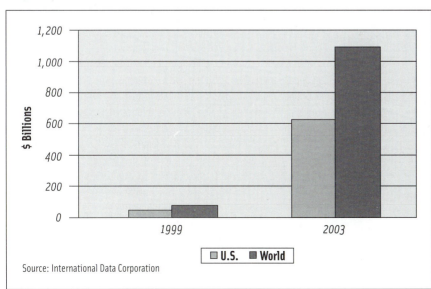

Source: International Data Corporation

U.S. ■ World

Economics of Growth

Exhibit 1-1 on page 9 illustrates the projected growth of Internet use through the year 2003. These figures suggest that at the end of that time approximately 50–60 percent of the United States will be online. Exhibit 1-2 on page 9 illustrates the projected growth rate in the business-to-business sector over the same period. Annual B2B revenue was $43 billion in 1998[8] and some forecasts suggest that it may be greater than $1 trillion in 2003.[9]

Other forecasts of Internet use in the business-to-consumer and business-to-business arena provide similar "speed of adoption" rates. Mary Meeker, a respected e-commerce analyst at Morgan Stanley Dean Witter (*www.msdw.com*), made an early and now famous observation about the rise of Internet usage.[10] She plotted the number of years it took the major media to reach 50 million users in the United States. While the telephone, radio, and TV took decades, the Internet took only about five years. In other words, the rate of growth of the Internet far outdistances the rate of adoption of any other popular technology—television, radio, cell phones, pagers—in the last half of the twentieth century (see Exhibit 1-3). This gives a sense for not only the scale but also the velocity of how e-commerce is reshaping the nature of economic activity. Data on cost savings suggest a similar rate of growth. Projections in Exhibit 1-4 show that the cost savings from e-commerce is expected to exceed $1 trillion by the year 2002.

Exhibit 1-3

INTERNET ADOPTION RATES
VERSUS OTHER MEDIUMS

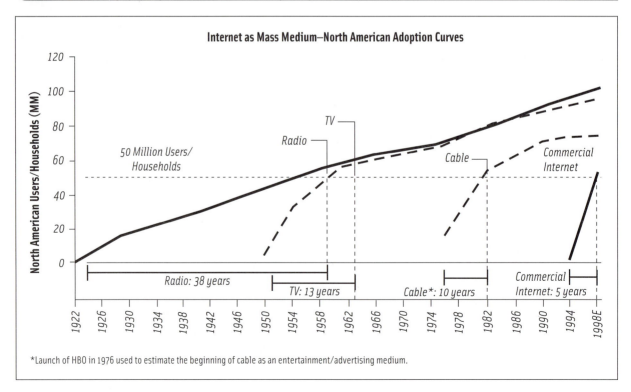

*Launch of HBO in 1976 used to estimate the beginning of cable as an entertainment/advertising medium.

Exhibit 1-4

ESTIMATED SAVINGS
FROM E-COMMERCE

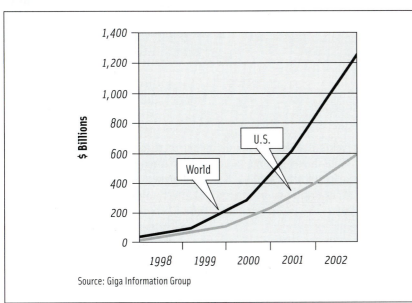

Source: Giga Information Group

Blurring of Industry Boundaries

Another significant impact of electronic commerce is observable in the blurring of the traditional industry boundaries of competition.[11] The NAICS codes (formerly SIC codes) applied to all business classifications for the traditional industrial and service economies. That being said, what's happening in content and infrastructure is a blurring of boundaries as the economy is reorganized around customer, or demand-side, needs instead of supply-side classifications. The old categories are breaking down.

Services for stock market quotes (e.g., news media—either paper or broadcast), bookkeeping and tax counsel (e.g., tax accountants), investment advice (e.g., stockbrokers), car insurance (e.g., insurance), home mortgages (e.g., mortgage brokers), and even sports scores are blended into the offerings of many online businesses (i.e., Schwab.com or Quicken.com). Even along the so-called "last mile" to consumers' homes, we are witnessing the blurring of alternate telecommunications networks (i.e., traditional phone lines, digital subscriber lines), cable TV, digital satellite, and wireless providers. We might say that the "blurring" is really occurring everywhere, with two key areas being the "content," or offerings to consumers, and the platforms, or technologies that deliver those offerings into markets.

Transformation of Social Structure and Society

A third impact of e-commerce is the transformative effect of the New Economy on how children learn, how work groups communicate across time zones, how scientific interchange occurs, and, more generally, how we function as a society. It is difficult to pass a billboard, read an advertisement, visit a store, watch a television ad,

(continued on page 12)

(continued from page 11)

Now that it's clear that the Internet is in its second phase, . . . , what is it there for? [The] Second phase [is] useful technology, [the] third phase [is] indispensable utility service. As we move into the indispensable utility service, the technology becomes more transparent and it touches everything. Meaning, that as we become a world where the Internet is an indispensable part of our lives, we'll no longer have an Internet industry just like we don't have an electricity division inside of a big corporation: it's an enablement for everything. And it means that . . . you can't escape it if you're a big traditional business-to-business company. . . . Therefore the power of the next wave of companies will come from the business partnerships that are put together by big companies who are doing the back end services and the newcomers who are doing the front end innovation.

Get the full interview at www.marketspaceu.com

or listen to the nightly news without seeing or hearing a reference to either a website address or an Internet start-up. Just about every school in America is now wired for access to the Internet, most public libraries have banks of PCs that can access the Web, and the political process, at sites such as election.com, could potentially become an information-enabled phenomenon that supports "town meetings."

Opportunities for Wealth Creation

The last few years have witnessed enormous market capitalizations for several New Economy players. This is true of all types of e-commerce businesses ranging from consumer products (e.g., Amazon.com, priceline), financial markets (e.g., E*TRADE, CharlesSchwab), portals (e.g., Yahoo!, Infoseek—now part of GO.com), service providers (e.g., excite@Home, RCN), infrastructure (e.g. Cisco, Broadcom, Global Crossing), middleware enabling commerce (e.g., Ariba, Vignette, CommerceOne) services (e.g., CMGI, Sterling Commerce, VeriSign), and advertising (e.g., DoubleClick, 24/7). At the same time, we are all aware of a number of initial public offerings in the past few years that did not fare as well as expected—or rapidly deflated in value following an initial run-up in share price and market capitalization.

The opportunities for wealth generation are largely due to the confluence of three factors: the number of people using the new medium, the blurring and aggregation of once disparate industries into a "winner-take-all" model, and the transformative nature of e-commerce impacting on the broader economy and society. While not every highly valued public company in the e-commerce world will justify its market capitalization over time, the ones that successfully deliver on the promise of these massive changes in how we conduct business and live our lives will easily sustain their value.

WHAT IS THE E-COMMERCE DECISION-MAKING PROCESS?

Assume for the moment that you are in charge of a new e-commerce business. Early on in the life cycle of the business, you must make a set of decisions related to the items below.

1. Which customer groups should I serve?

2. How do I provide a compelling set of benefits to my targeted customer? How do I differentiate my "value proposition" versus online and offline competitors?

3. How do I communicate with customers?

4. What is the content, "look-and-feel," level of community, and degree of personalization of the website?

5. How should I structure my organization? What business services and applications software choices do I need to consider?

6. Who are my potential partners? Whose capabilities complement ours?

7. How will this business provide value to shareholders?

8. What metrics should I use to judge the progress of the business? How do I value the business?

Who Will Win? Online Vs. Offline

Established offline players are joining the Internet race and competing against a plethora of pure online players. Who will win?

Proponents of an online-player victory primarily cite the archaic, inflexible systems and rigid corporate culture of offline companies. For example, offline companies tend to move slowly because decisions need to go through a complex organizational hierarchy. Offline companies often have difficulty accepting the cannibalization of their sales by a cheaper solution delivered online. At the same time, even though the stock market so far has been patient with online company losses, it will not tolerate established blue chip companies running loss-making businesses. For example, Schwab's launch of its online discounted offering, Schwab.com, in January 1998, led to an 18% stock price decline from $40 per share in January to $33 per share in June.

Furthermore, offline companies moving online may be faced with a channel conflict. A car manufacturer deciding to offer cars online can create a conflict with its dealers, who may see some of their car sales lost to the Internet. General Motors is trying to address this problem through its GMBuyerpower online offering. At GMBuyerpower.com, customers can specify the features and price range of their desired car. The website allows the customer to locate the most convenient GM dealer who can offer that vehicle, get the best possible quote, set up a test drive, and hold the vehicle for purchase. GM vehicle sales still occur through dealers; the Internet only facilitates the selling process.

Proponents of an offline victory can cite Charles Schwab as a good example of an offline company that put its business online. In its transition from offline only to a combination of offline and online, Schwab changed the rules of the online brokerage industry and became a leading player. The offline proponents can also point to the valuable assets of offline companies, such as access to funds, market leadership, deep industry knowledge and experience, relationships with key suppliers, an established and trusted brand name, and, very importantly, a large customer base. Most online companies are struggling to develop such assets, while they give offline companies a significant, initial competitive advantage.

Proponents of offline companies can further point out that established companies can overcome offline cultural and structural barriers by creating spin-out businesses with their own culture and organizational structure. For example, eSchwab (the predecessor to the Schwab.com site) was developed as an internal Schwab project that was quarantined from the rest of the organization and operated as a separate unit to protect eSchwab from a culture clash as well as a scramble for resources with the offline organization.

Finally, offline proponents can look back at history to note there have been other technological revolutions that initially gave rise to a plethora of new players but eventually lead to a shakeout and to the dominance of only a handful of established players. From 1894 to 1903, for example, 20,000 telephone companies were started in the United States. Today, only a few dominant players remain. Will history repeat itself with the Internet?

e-Commerce Strategy

Because this book is focused on the managerial task of crafting and implementing an e-commerce strategy, we provide an organizing framework to find the answers to the questions above. The task of crafting and implementing an online strategy can be divided into several interrelated, sequential decisions:

Framing the Market Opportunity. Market opportunity analysis answers the question "Where will I play?" While traditional market analysis focuses on customers (item 1 listed above) and competitors (item 2), the online environment places a significant amount of emphasis on potential business partners (item 6).

Business Model. Business model selection involves four choices: (1) the value proposition or "cluster" to offer to the segment (item 2), (2) the specific product offering, (3) the associated resource system to deliver the benefits, and (4) the financial model to pursue (item 7). Collectively, these choices should answer the question "How will I win?"

Customer Interface. The customer interface refers to the screen-to-customer interface. Among other dimensions, it includes the look-and-feel, content, transaction capability, and community building aspects of the screen-to-customer interface (items 3 and 4). These decisions address the question of "How will customers perceive my business?"

Market Communications and Branding. Market communications considers all of the online and offline methods that the firm uses to reach its customers. Branding captures all of the firm-level choices (e.g., logo, slogan, distribution outlet) that affect the meaning of the brand. Brand equity captures all of the assets linked to the brand, thus providing value for both customers (e.g., reassurance) and the firm (e.g., high margins). Marketing communications and branding answer the question "How do I attract and retain customers?"

Implementation. Once a strategy is agreed upon, the firm must decide "How do we go to market?" The answer to this question involves a discussion of the "delivery system" of the firm and how to continually innovate to serve customers (item 5).

Metrics. The establishment of metrics to chart the performance of the business answers the question "How are we doing?" (items 7 and 8). This involves a consideration of financial metrics as well as metrics that map onto the entire strategy formulation process. Hence, we consider customer, business model, branding, and implementation metrics as well.

Valuation. The New Economy presents new challenges and issues in "valuing," or estimating the market value of New Economy businesses (item 8). Valuation answers the question "How do we create value for stakeholders or shareholders?" Methods of valuation become increasingly important with an escalated pace of mergers and acquisitions among a mix of privately and publicly held firms in various stages of business development.

In sum, all of these interrelated decisions form the core of the e-commerce business strategy process. The strategy for how a company chooses to compete in the New Economy is comprised of these organization-level decisions.

One related theme of e-commerce strategy is also critically important to consider: We are witnessing the emergence of many companies that combine both online and offline capabilities to serve customers. Exhibit 1-5 provides a basic overview of the combination of choices that are available to firms. This figure is comprised of two dimensions: online/offline presence and customer interface/fulfillment systems. To understand this framework, we consider four companies. Amazon.com has an online customer interface—but no offline brick-and-mortar stores.

Exhibit 1-5

WHERE TO PLAY
ONLINE AND OFFLINE

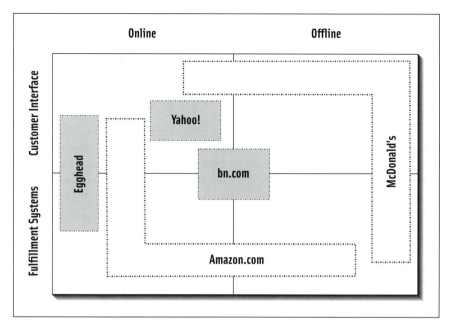

However, Amazon.com does employ both online and offline back office resources to support its virtual storefronts. For example, it uses a sophisticated network of online technology infrastructure (e.g., servers, data interchange between units) and offline physical warehouses (e.g., distribution centers in multiple regions of the United States as well as abroad). Hence, Amazon.com plays in three quadrants of the metrics. In contrast, Yahoo! plays exclusively in the online customer interface quadrant. BarnesandNoble.com plays in all four quadrants (if we include its sister company, Barnes & Noble, which operates superstores and mall stores in the brick-and-mortar world). Finally, the fast-food restaurant McDonald's is largely an offline enterprise with a "promotions" website.

Market Infrastructure

Underlying each e-commerce strategic decision is the general industry environment outside the boundaries and largely outside of the control of the specific business. This environment, which represents both opportunities and constraints, can be divided into two broad categories: network infrastructure and media infrastructure.

Network Infrastructure. **Network infrastructure** is the basic, underlying group of electronic devices and connecting circuitry designed as a system to share information. This infrastructure includes all of the various communications systems and networks now in use, such as telephones, cable television, broadcast radio and television, computer, satellite, and wireless telephone. Network infrastructure refers to the hardware and software used in communication.

In computer networks any two or more computers are connected for exchange and sharing of data and system resources. These networks can be characterized by topology (bus, star, or ring), spatial distances (LAN or WAN), network protocol (TCP/IP or SNA), type of signals (voice, data, or both), type of connection (dial-up, dedicated, or virtual connection), and type of physical link (fiber-optic, coax cable, or twisted-pair). Local area networks (LAN) connect PCs, usually over private communications lines within an office of a building, while wide area networks (WAN) connect many PCs over long-distance common carrier telephone lines. The Internet is a WAN that connects thousands of disparate networks worldwide and provides a resource for global communication between government, educational, and industrial computer networks.

Network infrastructure companies and service providers that enable the transport of digital information include network service providers (e.g., telephone companies, or telcos; cable-TV companies, known as multiple system operators, or MSOs; and direct-broadcast satellite, or DBS, firms, etc.); Internet service providers, or ISPs (EarthLink, ATT WorldNet, GTE); electronic subcomponent suppliers (Intel, Motorola); hardware providers (Dell, Compaq, IBM); and software companies (Microsoft, Oracle).

E-business application architecture includes software and service providers that facilitate the online buying and selling process: applications service providers, or ASPs (Marimba, Novell); and middleware or enterprise solution providers for e-commerce (SAP, PeopleSoft, Ariba).[12]

Media Infrastructure.

The **media infrastructure** is all the various communications companies and their channels of communication, such as radio, television, newspapers, and magazines, used in mass communication with the general public. Whereas the network infrastructure refers to the hardware and software used in communication, the media infrastructure refers to the content of the communication. Media companies produce the content for print media distribution chains or for programs that are broadcast over a chain or network of radio or television broadcast stations.

Media convergence is where the different types of media content (news, information, and entertainment) found across various types of media forms (text, images, audio, and video) are evolving into a single media platform through the Internet. Media convergence—and its expected synergistic benefits—has been the key driver behind several recent mega-mergers of media companies, including those of America Online and Time Warner, Viacom and CBS, The Walt Disney Company and Capital Cities/ABC, and the Tribune Company with the Times Mirror Company.

Two Forms of Convergence: Network and Media.

Both network and media infrastructures are independently converging due to the digitalization of information (see Exhibit 1-6). As we will see in Chapter 9, the network to deliver digitized content has converged, leading to massive cross-industry competition in the telecommunications, satellite, cable, and wireless industries. These heretofore indirect or noncompetitors now are all competing for the same customers. A second type of convergence—what we term as "media convergence"—is also unfolding. In Chapter 10, we explore how the major content players of the twentieth century—radio, TV, magazines, film, newspapers, and now the dot-coms—are competing to deliver content to the same target segments.

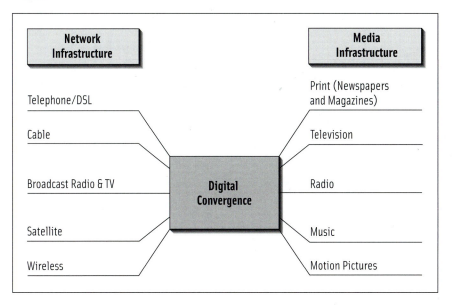

Exhibit 1-6 MEDIA CONVERGENCE TO A DIGITAL PLATFORM

Publics and Politics. A number of public policy and legal concerns have arisen concerning the Internet, including privacy, security, taxes, and public access. These concerns can play a significant role in shaping how a firm competes. Standards, regulations, and informal controls can all serve to impact the business strategy. These issues are considered at the end of Chapters 9 and 10.

A FRAMEWORK FOR E-COMMERCE

Exhibit 1-7 is a diagrammatic framework for the study of electronic commerce. As noted earlier in the chapter, there are six interrelated, sequential decisions to make to implement an e-commerce strategy—market-opportunity analysis, business model, customer interface, market communications and branding, implementation, and evaluation. These decisions are made in the context of a changing market-level infrastructure. The infrastructure includes factors related to the network infrastructure and media convergence.

There are two key points to keep in mind as one employs the framework. First, the vertical boxes in the framework are analyses and decisions that are inside the boundaries of the firm and, therefore, from a managerial point of view, are "controllables," while the horizontal boxes represent forces outside the boundaries of the firm and are "noncontrollables." In other words, there are things that managers in the business can affect, and there are things that are out of their control and must be worked with or around.[13] Second, e-commerce strategy decisions as well as market infrastructure conditions apply to all firms competing in the online world. All types of business players, including wholesalers, retailers, infrastructure, solutions, and service providers, as well as marketing firms, must confront basic e-commerce strategy decisions and market-level forces.

Exhibit 1-7 A FRAMEWORK FOR
ELECTRONIC COMMERCE

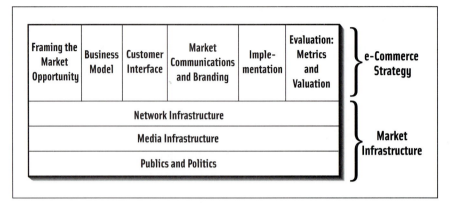

ORGANIZATION OF THE BOOK

The chapters in this text are organized to reflect the framework sequence of the decision-making process.

Chapter 1:
Overview

In the current chapter, we provide a working definition and framework for the study of e-commerce and a comprehensive view of the e-commerce landscape from where we can begin our discussion.

Chapter 2:
Framing the Market Opportunity

Here we focus on the players that have an immediate impact on the construction of the business strategy—customers, competitors, and partners. The goal of market analysis is not only to grow to understand the market; it also aims to locate portions of the market that are unserved or underserved. This chapter identifies five conditions that must be carefully analyzed to determine if there is a market opportunity for the firm.

Chapter 3:
Business Models

Chapter 3 details the four components of a business model: (1) value proposition, or "cluster," (2) the product offering—termed a "marketspace" offering, (3) the resource system that the firm selects to deliver the offering, and (4) a financial model that enables the business to earn revenues and margins. These four choices constitute the core of the business model decisions.

Chapter 4:
The Customer Interface

In Chapter 4, we fully develop the set of design tools and elements that we refer to as the 7Cs of the customer interface. In particular, we focus on the levers management can use to provide more customer value.

Chapter 5:
Market Communications and Branding

Chapter 5 covers both market communications and branding. Market communications are designed to build customer awareness and traffic, while branding conveys the brand meaning to target customers. Brand equity relates to both benefits to the customers as well as to the firm.

Chapter 6:
Implementation

Strategy is about "what to do" and implementation is about "how to get the job done." In Chapter 6, we consider the "delivery system" and innovation issues that both "glue the organization together" and facilitate the work flow.

Chapter 7:
Metrics

Chapter 7 introduces the "Performance Dashboard" as a set of metrics that reflect both the "early warning" indicators of the progress of an e-commerce strategy as well as outcome measures, such as customer satisfaction and financial performance.

Chapter 8:
Valuation

Chapter 8 provides an overview of how to determine or project the valuation of an e-commerce business.

Chapter 9:
Network Infrastructure

The market-level dynamics that operate outside the formal boundaries of the organization provide the infrastructure for traditional and new business approaches. Chapter 9 provides an overview on hardware, software, servers, and the parts that make up the enabling "railroad" for the New Economy. The chapter also provides a brief overview of several notable public policy issues that have implications for business and society.

Chapter 10:
Media Convergence

In Chapter 10, we examine how media is undergoing a transformation from analog to digital and the consequences of value migration from old media to new media, media megamergers, and media synergies.

SUMMARY

1. What is e-commerce?

E-commerce is characterized by the exchange of digital information, occurs between individuals, organizations, or both, and is technology-enabled. Electronic commerce also includes all intra- and interorganizational activities that directly or indirectly support marketplace exchanges. New classes of buying processes have emerged in e-commerce, in particular those originating from customers.

More importantly, the focus of e-commerce is moving away from technology-enabled to technology-mediated. Now transactions in e-commerce are managed or mediated largely by technology, as is the relationship with the customer.

Electronic commerce can be formally defined as technology-mediated exchanges between parties (individuals, organizations, or both) as well as the electronically based intra- or interorganizational activities that facilitate the exchanges.

2. What are the distinct categories of e-commerce?

Four distinct categories of electronic commerce can be identified: business-to-business, business-to-consumer, consumer-to-consumer, and consumer-to-business.

Business-to-business refers to the full spectrum of e-commerce that can occur between two organizations. Many of the same activities that occur in business-to-business also occur in the business-to-consumer context, except transactions that relate to the "back office" of the customer are often not tracked electronically. Consumer-to-consumer activities include auction-exchanges, classified ads, games, bulletin boards, instant messaging services, and personal services. Consumers can band together to form buyer groups in a consumer-to-business relationship.

3. How is e-commerce different from traditional commerce?

The following attributes make an e-commerce business unique and different from a traditional brick-and-mortar business: core strategic decisions are technology-based, competitive response must occur in real time, the store is always open, the customer interface is technology-mediated, the customer controls the interaction, online firms have an increased knowledge of customer behavior, players benefit from network economics, and nontraditional evaluation metrics and emergent valuation models apply.

The combination of screen-to-customer interfaces, network effects, real-time competitive responses, and one-to-one customization leads to value increases for both the customer and the firm. Both parties have increased access to unique, heretofore inaccessible information; the customer gets more availability, convenience, ease of use, and full information, while the firm obtains objective behavioral data on customers' and competitors' behaviors. This combination leads to a highly dynamic, new competitive marketplace.

4. Why study e-commerce?

The reasons to study e-commerce hardly require clarification. Significant points to consider are the phenomenal adoption rate for household use of the Internet along with the economics of growth, the blurring of industry boundaries, the transformation of social structure and society, and the opportunities for wealth generation.

5. What is the e-commerce decision-making process?

The task of crafting and implementing a business strategy can be divided into six interrelated, sequential decisions. These are market opportunity analysis, business model definition, customer interface, market communications and branding, implementation, and evaluation. These six interrelated decisions form the core of the e-commerce business strategy process.

However, the electronic commerce arena is made possible by a host of software and hardware that forms the infrastructure for e-commerce activities. This environment can be divided further into network infrastructure and media infrastructure.

Exhibit 1-7 provides a framework for the study of electronic commerce. It illustrates the six interrelated, sequential decisions—market opportunity analysis, business model definition, customer interface, market communications and branding, implementation, and evaluation as well as the market-level forces. The framework includes analyses and decisions that are inside the boundaries of the firm that are "controllables" as well as forces outside the boundaries of the firm that are "noncontrollables." In other words, there are things that managers in the business can affect, and there are things that are out of their control and must be worked around.

E-commerce strategy decisions as well as market infrastructure conditions apply to everyone. All types of business players, including offering-type, infrastructure, solutions and service providers, and marketing firms, must confront basic e-commerce strategy decisions and market-level forces.

KEY TERMS

Internet	consumer-to-consumer (C2C)
customer interfaces	consumer-to-business (C2B)
e-commerce	network economics
business-to-business (B2B)	network infrastructure
business-to-consumer (B2C)	media infrastructure

Endnotes

[1]See Kelly, Kevin. 1998. *New rules for the new economy: 10 radical strategies for a connected world*. New York: Penguin Group, p. 2.

[2]Kosiur, David. 1997. *Understanding electronic commerce*. Redmond, WA: Microsoft Press.

[3]Please see the following: Stalk, Thomas, Jr., & Thomas M. Hout. 1990. *Competing against time*. New York: The Free Press. D'Aveni, Richard A., & Robert Gunther. 1994. *Hypercompetition: Managing the dynamics of strategic maneuvering*. New York: The Free Press.

[4]Metcalfe's Law: The value of a network is "n" squared, with "n" being the number of nodes on the network.

[5]Shapiro, Carl, & Hal Varian. 1999. *Information rules*. Cambridge, MA: Harvard Business School Press.

[6]*Viral marketing* is a marketing technique where each participant in a highly networked environment is persuaded to pass on a marketing message to several other participants. The message spreads in the virulent manner that a flu virus successively passes from a single flu victim as he comes in contact with several new victims and each new victim, in turn, again comes in contact with several new victims. This term was coined by Jeffrey F. Rayport. 1996. The virus of marketing. *Fast Company,* no. 6 (December): 68.

[7]Regan, Keith. 2000. Forrester: most dot-coms will sink by 2001. *E-Commerce Times*, 12 April. URL: *http://www.ecommercetimes.com/news/articles2000/000412-7.shtml.*

[8]Davis, Jeffrey. 1999. B-2-B boom. *Business 2.0.* (September).

[9]URL: *http://www.thestandard.com/research/metrics/display/0,2799,11300,00.html.*

[10]Meeker, Mary. 1996. *The Internet advertising report*. Morgan Stanley, U.S. Investment Research, Technology: Internet/New Media (December): 1–5.

[11]Meyer, Christopher, & Stan Davis. 1998. *Blur: The speed of change in the connected economy*. New York: Warner Books.

[12]See Kalakota, Ravi, & Andrew B. Whinston. 1996. *Electronic commerce: A manager's guide*. 2nd ed. Reading, MA: Addison-Wesley Publishing Company, p. 15.

[13]Technically, there are opportunities for firms to influence the environment in which they compete. In the strategic management literature, this issue is addressed in such specialty literatures as "resource-dependence" and "population ecology" theory. In the marketing literature, this issue has arisen under the heading of environmental management or "market-driving" strategy. Finally, in the managerial or trade literature, we have witnessed the emergence of terms such as "coopetition" and "competing for the future" to signal that firms no longer have to take the environment as a "given." Rather, they can actively shape the future. Hence, it may be more appropriate to note that network and media infrastructure are comparatively less influenceable as compared to the e-commerce strategy choices noted in the vertical boxes of the framework.

Framing the Market Opportunity

In Chapter 1, we examined the impact of e-commerce and some of its distinguishing features. We also briefly reviewed the decision-making process that companies must go through in order to develop an e-commerce strategy. In this chapter we answer the first question a company must address: "Where will the business compete?" Ideally, a company would like to play in an area where customer needs are not fully met, there are few or no competitors, there is a large financial opportunity, and the company is well-positioned to fulfill the customer need either on its own or through partnerships. Obviously, this is very difficult to accomplish.

Hence, a firm needs to follow a rigorous approach—such as the one outlined in this chapter—to isolate market opportunities.

In this chapter, we introduce a five-step process that a company can go through to address this first question: (1) seeding an opportunity in an existing or new value system, (2) uncovering an opportunity nucleus, (3) identifying target segments, (4) declaring a company's resource-based opportunity, and (5) assessing the opportunity attractiveness. By following these five steps, a company can make an educated "go/no go" decision about pursuing the opportunity.

QUESTIONS

Please consider the following questions as you read this chapter:

1. **What is the framework to market-opportunity analysis?**

2. **Is market-opportunity analysis different in the New Economy?**

3. **What are two generic "value types"?**

This chapter was coauthored by Toby Thomas and Mark Pocharski. Substantive input was also provided by Robert Lurie, Leo Griffin, Yannis Dosios, Bernie Jaworski, and Scott Daniels.

4. How do we identify unmet and/or underserved needs?

5. What determines the specific customers the company is to pursue?

6. Who provides the resources to deliver the benefits of the offering?

7. How do we assess the attractiveness of the opportunity?

8. How do we prepare a "go/no-go" assessment?

In the last three years, we have seen an unprecedented launch rate of Internet-related start-up companies. For some, the risks associated with starting a new business will prove to be very rewarding, but in many cases these businesses will not prosper. The historical failure rate of start-up companies is over 80 percent.

Market-opportunity analysis is an essential tool for both entrepreneurs and senior managers who plan to launch new businesses. While good opportunity analysis will not guarantee a start-up's success, thinking through the conditions that define opportunity attractiveness increases the likelihood of pursuing an attractive idea. Poor or no opportunity analysis increases the chance that a new venture will fail.

This chapter examines the key question: "Where will the business compete?" and will also briefly touch upon the issue of "How will it succeed?" Regardless of the reasons a firm seeks online business opportunities, the successful company defines its marketspace early in the business development process. Here the term **marketspace** refers to the digital equivalent of a physical world marketplace. By defining the intended marketspace, the company identifies the customers it will serve and the competitors it will face. Over time a company's defined marketspace may change as both the company and the market evolve, but a clear, initial definition is necessary to develop the business model.

In this chapter, we propose a framework for **market-opportunity analysis** and review some of the tools that can be used to "frame" the market opportunity. A lot of this spadework will be deepened and refined as the company moves toward developing and launching a market offering. This is discussed in subsequent chapters.

WHAT IS THE FRAMEWORK TO MARKET-OPPORTUNITY ANALYSIS?

The framework for our market-opportunity analysis consists of five main investigative stages and a final "go/no go" decision. Exhibit 2-1 illustrates the five conditions that firms should satisfy in order to frame market opportunity. When they are taken together, these five conditions comprise the scope of a sound market-opportunity analysis:

Condition 1: Seed opportunity in an existing or new value system.

Condition 2: Uncover an opportunity nucleus, an unmet or underserved need(s).

Condition 3: Identify and choose priority customer segment(s).

Condition 4: Declare the company's resource-based opportunity for advantage.

Condition 5: Assess competitive, technological, and financial opportunity attractiveness.

Exhibit 2-1

FRAMEWORK FOR
MARKET OPPORTUNITY

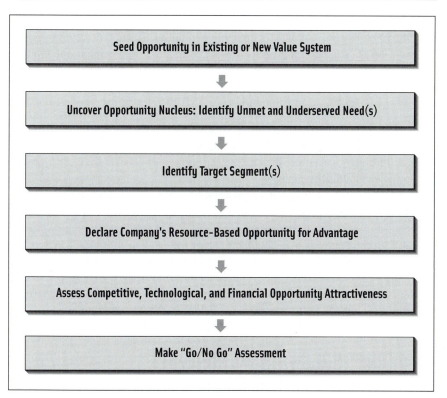

Seed Opportunity. Opportunity identification and analysis is anchored within an existing or new value system, or the "playing field." The **value system** can be thought of as the entire "chain" of suppliers, distributors, competitors, buyers, and intermediaries that bring an existing offering to market. In the New Economy, the starting point for opportunity identification often is someone with a belief about a value system that can be reinvented or transformed. This value system becomes the anchor for framing the opportunity. Then, economic activities can be identified to be harnessed, redirected, or created; customers and current market players can be identified.

Uncover Opportunity Nucleus. Once a rough definition of the playing field is set, the company can define the opportunity to increase customer satisfaction or create a new, highly valued customer experience. What do customers do today that frustrates them? What aren't they doing, consciously or unconsciously, while foregoing benefits? What can be fixed, even if customers don't know it's broken?

A key activity at this stage is the uncovering of either unmet needs (i.e., needs not currently being served) or underserved needs (i.e., needs being served but in an improvable manner).

Identify Target Customers. Identifying and choosing priority customers leads to a preliminary understanding of the potentially attractive customers the company could seek to serve. Who are they, and what makes them attractive to pursue? What experiences do they seek? What would the company need to offer them? What barriers would the company need to overcome to get these customers to participate in an offering? In identifying and selecting target segments, the company should develop an initial sketch of these customers to both shape the business concept and to estimate the size of the opportunity. This knowledge is essential as the company determines the nature of its offer and the size of the opportunity.

Declare the Company's Resource-Based Opportunity.

The fourth step is to examine the distinct capabilities and activities the company would bring to the offering to achieve advantage through its own resources and those of potential partner companies. In Chapter 3, we will examine the concept of a company's "resource system" in depth, but for now we will simply state that the firm must have a reason to believe it will be able to bring a set of distinct resources to win in the market. Without these resources, the company will not have the advantages it needs to build or sustain a highly profitable business and will fail to generate cash flow.

Assess Opportunity Attractiveness.

Finally, to assess opportunity attractiveness (step five), the company must assess the market's financial, technological, and competitive situations. Financial attractiveness focuses on segment size, growth rates, profitability, and other company-specific performance criteria. Technological assessment and a reality check ensures that available technology does or will enable the business's dream to be realized without being needlessly constrained by rapidly changing technologies. Checks on both underserved customer needs and the strength of prospective competition must also be made to satisfy this opportunity assessment condition. What competition would the firm face? Does the firm see ways to succeed versus this competition?

IS MARKET-OPPORTUNITY ANALYSIS DIFFERENT IN THE NEW ECONOMY?

Before exploring market-opportunity analysis in greater depth, we should consider whether this type of analysis should be any different from an analysis of opportunities in more traditional sectors of the economy. Some authors and analysts believe that opportunity analysis in the marketspace is unique and requires a different approach. We summarize this reasoning below.

Competition Occurs *Across* Industry Boundaries Rather than *Within* Industry Boundaries.

Web-enabled business models can operate across traditional industry boundaries because they lack the constraints of physical product manufacturing or service delivery. Consequently, these businesses can more accurately match value creation from the customer's perspective. For example, Cars.com (*www.cars.com*) allows customers to research and purchase new and used vehicles, finance them, insure them, and purchase parts, accessories, and even extended warranties through the site and its partners. Limiting opportunity assessment to traditional definitions of industry or value system could result in missed market opportunities.

Competitive Developments and Response Are Occuring at an Unprecedented Speed.

Advances in technology and the adoption of creative business models are occuring at a rapid pace. During the "browser wars" between Microsoft and Netscape, each firm introduced a new version of its product approximately every six months. Any market-opportunity assessment must be continually refreshed by keeping abreast of important trends or discontinous events that could redefine opportunity attractiveness.

Competition Occurs Between Alliances of Companies Rather than Between Individual Companies.

Many technology based products have a high degree of reliance on other related "complementary" products (for example, Web businesses are reliant on browser technology; browsers are dependent on operating systems, PCs, and modem technologies). Furthermore, the networked nature of the Web means that several companies can easily ally to create a seamless offer. Companies can often find themselves in "**co-opetition**"[1] with each other, i.e., they are both competitors and collaborators at the same time. For example Bizbuyer.com and Staples.com compete as suppliers of products such as computers and photocopiers to small- and medium-sized businesses, yet they are also partners. Staples customers can use Bizbuyer to source business services such as Web design and consulting from an extensive supplier network. In assessing the resources necessary to succeed, managers must examine both internal and external possibilities, rather than assume the company must perform all alone.

Consumer Behavior Is Still in the Early Stages of Being Defined, Thus It Is Easier to Influence and Change Consumer Behavior.

Most modern marketing textbooks emphasize the importance of being "customer focused." This means that businesses must analyze customer needs, define products that meet those needs, and implement defendable strategies. In the Old Economy, competitive battles are frequently fought over a well-defined set of consumer behavior patterns (e.g., consumers shopping in grocery stores). However, in the New Economy, new software and hardware tilt the landscape of consumer behavior. Companies introduce products leading to new behavior and new customer requirements. The challenge is to listen closely enough to today's customers to develop insights about opportunities without being lulled into simply meeting customers' stated needs. Stating the obvious, customers don't know what they don't know. The company's task is to define new experiences that customers will recognize and seek based on insights into how customers are acting today and why.

Take for example the recent emergence of Napster. Napster enables users to search, share, and copy MP3 song files across a distributed database of all the songs of all connected World Wide Web members. Introduced in the fall of 1999, Napster has revolutionized consumer behavior in the recorded music industry. Interestingly, in the spring of 2000, a new use of Napster emerged—the "wrapping" of not just MP3 files but any file format including games, movies, software, and spreadsheets. Again, this newly "hacked" version could revolutionize file sharing, having major impact on incumbent players.[2]

Industry Value Chains, or "Systems," Are Rapidly Being Reconfigured.

The Internet allows businesses to reconfigure their interactions with customers by such means as allowing 24×7 interactions, increasing the level of information throughout the value chain, and eradicating or significantly reducing the cost of stages in the value chain. Examples of this online "reengineering" are easy to find. Freemarkets.com (*www.Freemarkets.com*) constructed a reverse auction for B2B markets and, in doing so, eliminated many of the costly "process" steps for businesses to find product price quotes.

Obviously, many existing companies as well as start-ups begin opportunity framing from a base of experience about a market or a technology. This experience base may enable a management team to accelerate through meeting one or more of the five conditions. Regardless of where a company enters the opportunity-framing process, satisfying all five conditions should create a sufficient base of knowledge and

Which Is Better?
Analyses ("Ready, Aim, Fire")
Vs. No Analysis ("Fire, Ready, Aim")

An interesting debate is raging in the New Economy that is concerned with whether market-opportunity assessment is helpful, valueless, or, worse still, harmful. Many argue that speed, not precision, is critical. A basic economic force referred to as "network economics" is at work in many marketspace businesses. Businesses with network economics capitalize on "first mover momentum"—rapidly connecting with and locking in large numbers of customers. In situations such as these, it is extremely difficult for the competition to "catch up" with the first mover. A virtuous cycle is created in which the large customer base provides lower costs. This allows the first mover to win customers at a faster rate than their competitors.

Another argument supporting the "Fire, Ready, Aim" approach states that companies must take advantage of the high stock-market multiples. This argument often points out that the New Economy is nascent, a place where the old rules no longer apply and no one really understands the forces that drive the market. As a consequence, companies are better off learning by doing.

Finally, some argue even more vociferously that market analysis is a waste of time because, in the end, a company will be further behind having passed up major market opportunities during the time that it took to perform the analysis.

However, an alternate point of view is beginning to emerge that "Fire, Ready, Aim" approach outlined above actually limits a company's potential. While speed is important, the real goal is to reach critical mass with key customer segments in as short a time as practical. The sheer number of potential-channel blind alleys, time-intensive partner negotiations, and customer-complaint black holes inevitably bogs companies down if they don't sort out a clear opportunity path from the start. Although a company may feel it is moving fast without assessing its opportunity, it is in fact likely "generating more heat than light." Furthermore, in some cases second and third movers actually survive and perform better than first pioneers. They can capitalize on the mistakes and on the groundwork done by others and capture more mind and market share for less effort. At the time of this writing, Peapod, the first entrant into the online grocery market had been saved from bankruptcy by Ahold, a Dutch conglomerate. Webvan and Homegrocer.com, although much later entrants to the game, have merged and appear to be succeeding where Peapod failed, partly because they learned from their rival's mistakes.

perspective to frame a winning business model. In this chapter, we will move sequentially through the five opportunity-framing conditions. We will start by defining the opportunity space within a specific value system or a collection of linked activities.

Whether you choose to spend one day, one month, or one year examining a market opportunity, the framework laid out in this chapter provides a useful way to discuss whether and how to pursue an opportunity in the marketspace.

WHAT ARE TWO GENERIC "VALUE TYPES"?

The first step in framing the business opportunity is to broadly identify the business arena in which the new business will participate. The purpose is to declare both "what is in" and "what is out" of the business-model consideration set. For our purposes, the business arena is typically defined within or across an industry "value

Network Economics

Network economics[3] is a fundamental driving force in the New Economy. This law of economics states that users of "network" products tend to value those products more highly (because they get more utility from them) when there are a large number of users. In fact, the value of a product to each of its users increases with the addition of each new user. Telephones are an example of a product subject to network economics. The first purchaser of a telephone had no use for it—it was impossible to call anyone. The second purchaser made the telephone valuable for the first purchaser (they could now call each other!), and the third purchaser increased the utility of the telephones purchased by the other two (it was now possible to make conference calls!).

Named after Bob Metcalfe, the inventor of the network technology known as Ethernet, **Metcalfe's Law** states that the value of a network to each of its members is proportional to the number of other users (which can be expressed as $(n^2 - n)/2$). The near universal adoption of Windows as an operating system for PCs is a good example of network economics. The more users adopted Windows, the more software companies wrote Windows compatible products, making Windows more and more valuable to its users.

In many cases, however, computers with Windows are not connected to a network, so why does this product benefit from network economics? Windows users may or may not be physically networked together, but they do operate in a form of "community." They use software written for the Windows operating system, and they share files with each other. These activities make Windows subject to network economics.

Network economics has a profound impact on the equilibrium states of the markets in which it operates. Because users tend to prefer products that already have many users, strong companies tend to get stronger (this is known as "positive reinforcement") and weak companies weaker ("negative reinforcement"). As a result, markets with many competing technologies tend to converge on one product standard.

chain" or a "value system." Businesses are made up of discrete collections of individual and organizational activities that work together to create and deliver customer benefits via products or services. These integrated activities describe a "value chain." Value chains are linked within an industry or, in the New Economy environment, across industries to create a "value system." A value system is an interconnection of processes and activities within and among firms that creates benefits for intermediaries and end consumers.[4] Value is created from the first inputs through to the end: customer purchase, usage, and disposal activities.

We start our exploration by looking for a set of activities ripe for positive transformation, either within a firm or across activities conducted by multiple firms. Within a firm, there may be ways to create value. After all, a firm is made up of a series of connected activities that result in the creation of an end product or the delivery of a service from purchasing inputs to manufacturing to marketing and sales to product delivery to after-sales support. In addition, there are supporting activities necessary to ensure a company's viability, from financial planning and control to employee recruiting and training to research and development. Just as many of these activities are interconnected within one company, there are also connections with other companies or with consumers. Both the activities within a firm (the value chain) and those connecting firms with other firms and customers (the value system) are potential candidates for New Economy value creation. Furthermore, if we look across several related industries in the same manner as customers, we may find cross-value chain opportunities.

Firms should look at the value system with a lens that yields ideas about new business possibilities. Specifically, a firm looks for either: **trapped value** to be liberated, or **new-to-the-world value** to be introduced.

Trapped Value

New Economy companies often unlock four types of trapped value by creating more efficient markets, or creating more efficient value systems, by enabling easier access, or by disrupting current pricing power.

Create More Efficient Markets. By lowering search and transaction costs, the market is more efficient—customers can buy what's best for them at a lower net cost. Bizbuyer.com brings together suppliers and buyers of products and services for small and medium businesses. Customers submit a request for proposal, and qualified suppliers can provide their quotes. The entire transaction can be arranged over the Web.

Create More Efficient Value Systems. Compressing or eliminating steps in the current value system can result in greater efficiencies in time or cost. For example, Federal Express has been moving its customer interactions into the marketspace since 1982 (when the firm started equipping its major customers with dedicated terminals). Enabling customers through the Internet to request pick-ups, find drop-off points, and track shipments was a natural development. Today the company estimates that it would need an additional 20,000 employees to handle the tasks that customers handle themselves. By connecting directly with its customers, FedEx removed the duplication of tasks such as the reentry of shipping data.

Enable Ease of Access. Enabling ease of access entails enhancing the access points and the degree of communication between relevant exchange partners. Guru.com expedites access to hard-to-find professional experts across a wide range of fields. Another way in which ease of access increases is through the use of the Internet as a channel. J. Crew used to only sell clothes through offline stores and catalogs, but the company recently added JCrew.com as a new sales channel. The website offers the same products as its offline channels, but it also provides the added convenience associated with the online offering.

Disrupt Current Pricing Power. Beyond making markets more efficient, this value-unlocking activity changes current pricing-power relationships. Customers can gain greater influence over pricing and capture a portion of the vendor's margin when they have greater information about relative vendor performance, a deeper understanding of vendor economics, or insight into the vendor's current supply-demand situation. By providing customers with greater access to these types of information and demystifying vendor economics, a New Economy company can give customers greater negotiating power. For example, RUsure.com (*www.rusure.com*) informs its users when they are about to buy something which is priced lower elsewhere.

New-to-the-World Value

In addition to reconfiguring existing value chains to release trapped value, New Economy companies look to create new-to-the-world benefits. These new benefits can enhance an existing offer or be the basis for creating a new offer. There are at least five generic ways companies can create new value: customize offerings, radically extend reach and access, build community, enable collaboration among multiple people across locations and time, and introduce new-to-the-world functionality or experience.

Customize Offerings.

With both the digital flexibility and economic advantages of the Internet, companies can allow customers to customize the specific product or service they receive. Companies can also make their products more attractive to customers by *removing* features that customers do not value. Yahoo! exemplifies both dimensions. By adding personalization to news and stock quotes through its "my.yahoo" function, Yahoo! created value for customers who previously had to navigate through "one size fits all" news and information services over the Web. A my.yahoo page contains just a small subset of all available information, but it is information that is relevant to the user.

Radically Extend Reach and Access.

Companies may extend the boundaries of an existing market or create a new market by delivering a cost-effective reach. Keen.com created an entirely new market by building a virtual marketplace for advice. Anyone can advertise their services as an advisor on subjects such as "managing your lovelife" or "choosing a career." Customers log on to the site, choose an advisor, and are connected to the advisor on a per-minute fee basis. Keen.com and the advisor share these revenues.

Build Community.

The Internet enables efficient community building, as can be seen in the explosion of chat rooms addressing a myriad of topics. Beyond chat rooms, companies also foster the building of public and private communities. MyFamily.com seeks to bring together the far-flung modern family, enabling conversation, picture sharing, recipe exchange, etc. Natural communities can be leveraged in many ways that include enhancing the effectiveness and impact of viral marketing.

Enable Collaboration Among Multiple People Across Locations and Time.

In the networked world, people increasingly are working together more efficiently and more effectively than ever before. Construction portal Buzzsaw.com offers its users a place to buy or sell materials, create a shared project workspace, and review building plans.

Introduce New-to-the-World Functionality or Experience.

The convergence of communications, computing, and entertainment as well as the ever-changing form and functionality of access devices are making new experiences possible. The Internet fosters broad access and participation in these new experiences. Owners of the new iMac can use their computers to create and edit digital "iMovies™" which can then be uploaded (for free!) to an Apple webserver and shared with friends around the world.

An interesting question to consider is whether companies can both unlock trapped value and create new benefits at the same time. Companies such as Amazon.com appear to do both. Not only have they eliminated steps and reduced hassle from book shopping, Amazon has introduced extra services and functionality to enhance the experience. Through "collaborative filtering" technology from Net Perceptions, readers can browse conveniently while getting recommendations from other readers or based upon previous orders from Amazon. Amazon.com has changed how people think about shopping and purchasing in product categories such as books, music, and toys.

To define where in a value system or value chain a company should focus its development activities, there are two simple dimensions to first consider—horizontal versus vertical plays. In the business world, horizontal plays improve functional operations that are common to multiple industries and types of value systems. In the software world, horizontal players typically tackle improving functional areas such as accounting and control, customer service, inventory management, and standard CAD/CAM applications. In the consumer world, horizontal plays reflect common activities in which most consumers broadly engage (e.g., paying taxes).

Vertical plays, on the other hand, focus on creating value within or among activities that are central to a particular business (e.g., Chemdex in the chemicals industry). These vertical plays can often be thought of as industry-specific plays (e.g., steel industry, chemical industry, automotive industry). There are, of course, niches within each industry (e.g., specialty steel), so there may be vertical niches (e.g., automotive parts distributor site vs. supply chain site in automotive).

At its most extreme, a "white sheet" exercise (i.e., a thorough analysis beginning from a blank slate) could systematically look for and evaluate the trapped and new-to-the-world value potential across all functions and activities pursued by businesses and individual consumers. More typically, a group of managers will have some familiarity with or interest in a particular horizontal function or vertical activity. The challenge for this group is to map out the major sets of activities related to that horizontal function or vertical business at a high level. After mapping out the activities, the group should consider a series of questions designed to guide the knowledgeable manager to uncover trapped value or recognize the opportunity for new value creation.

The guiding questions the group should consider include the following:

- Is there a high degree of asymmetric information between buyers and sellers or colleagues at any step in the value system that traps value?
- Are significant amounts of time and resources consumed in bringing people together to make a transaction or complete a task?
- Do customers view activities as more collapsed than do industry participants (e.g., shopping across a variety of categories)?
- Are key participants in an activity able to collaborate effectively and efficiently at critical stages in a process?
- Do people have access to necessary advice and information to maximize their effectiveness or the ability to extract maximum benefits from a given activity?
- Are people foregoing opportunities to participate in an activity due to privacy or other concerns?

While identification of hot spots in a business or consumer value system is a necessary starting point, the process is not sufficiently developed to make the leap from identification to creation of the value proposition or to business model. At this point the manager has a sense of where the opportunity may lie in terms of business and customer activities. The next step is to specify the nature of that opportunity from a customer's perspective. As the manager begins to specify the opportunity, the potential associated with the opportunity should become more apparent.

HOW DO WE IDENTIFY UNMET AND/OR UNDERSERVED NEEDS?

New value creation is based on doing a better job of meeting customer needs. What customer needs will the new business serve? Are these needs currently being met by other companies in the market, and if so, why will customers choose your business over the competition? Customers will choose to switch from their old supplier only if the new company does a better job of meeting some set of needs. This condition of our opportunity-analysis framework describes the uncovering of an **opportunity nucleus,** a set of unmet or underserved needs.

Customer Decision Process

The **Customer Decision Process** is an organizing framework to look systematically for unmet or underserved needs. The Customer Decision Process maps the activities and the choices customers make in accessing a specific experience within a value system, then lays out the series of steps from awareness of the experience to the purchase experience and through the use experience. The process of generating a map of the customer decision process may help generate new ideas about unmet or underserved needs. For example, an examination of the process people go through to buy books might identify the fact that people rely on recommendations from others. Jeff Bezos of Amazon.com successfully identified this need and created a website where customers can read reviews and comments about a book being considered for purchase *while they are in the store,* an activity that customers in a brick-and-mortar bookstore can almost never do.

Before looking for unmet or underserved needs, senior management should map out the Customer Decision Process. When properly answered, the following questions will help you to structure a Customer Decision Process, such as the one illustrated in Exhibit 2-2.

- What are the steps that the typical customer goes through?
- Who gets involved and what role does he or she play?
- Are there any distinct and significant activities and paths that different customers go through?
- Where does the process take place?
- How much time does the overall process take? How much time is associated with individual steps? Does the customer move through the entire process at once or does he or she take breaks?
- What product category and competitors does the customer consider and choose along the way?
- What choices do customers not consider? What choices are they unaware of?
- Which customers are not participating in this Customer Decision Process for a specific value system? Why not?

Of course, not all businesses involve purchases just by users. Access to CNN Online is free to users, and is paid for by advertisers, so the business has two sets of customers. In this case it is worthwhile developing a Customer Decision Process cycle for both visitors (who use the site, but do not purchase, from it) and for advertisers (who purchase advertisement space from the site).

Exhibit 2-2 sets out the Customer Decision Process for document shipping in a consulting company. The illustration shows how consultants and their administrative assistants interact to make choices about shipping providers. Some decision processes are highly linear while others may have multiple pathways or loop backs. Each process is organized into three broad categories: "prepurchase," "purchase," and "postpurchase."

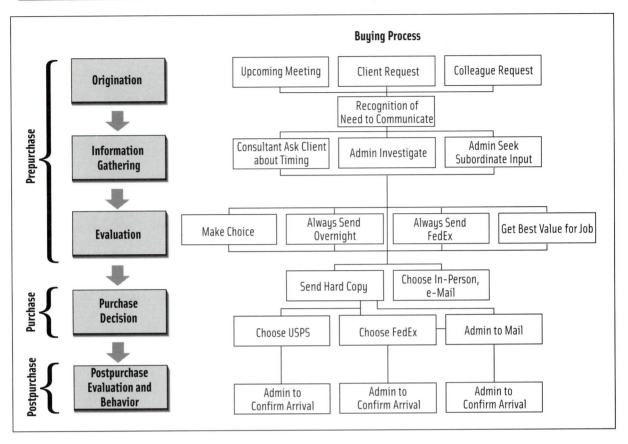

Revealing Unmet or Underserved Needs

(continued from page 35)

So we do that ourselves and we think we get it right. . . . we say no customer feedback is going to tell us to do this, we're going to go do it anyhow because we think it's right.

Get the full interview at www.marketspaceu.com

Having identified the steps in the Customer Decision Process, the management team can look to uncover unmet or underserved needs. The following questions can help identify these needs:

- What are the series of activities or steps of the Customer Decision Process in which a customer participates to receive an experience?

- What is the nature of the ideal experience the customer wishes to receive both functionally and emotionally? How does it vary step-by-step in the activity?

- How closely does the actual experience compare to the customer's view of the ideal? What are the key frustration points? What compensating behaviors do we observe (i.e., what actions does the customer engage in to overcome these frustrations)? How successful has the customer been and why? What underserved needs do you observe, regardless of whether or not the customer is conscious of them?

- Does the experience customers seek vary according to their environment (e.g., how often they participate in the activity, with whom they are working, where they are using the product or service, or their role in an organization)?

- What are customer beliefs and associations about carrying out this activity? How do they view their relative competence and role? How positively or negatively do they view the current set of company offerings?

- What barriers block some or all participation by potential customers? What would potentially block adoption of an online activity?

- What are the online opportunities to enhance or transform the customers' experience? What will be the most important drivers for getting customers to adopt an online activity in this value system?

- How do the customers define value for critical steps in the process? Would they be willing to pay for certain elements of that value?

Uncovering these needs may be as straightforward as having a conversation with a number of customers or may be as complex as creating observation opportunities to watch the customer in action and identifying things of which they may be unaware. Immersion in the Customer Decision Process is the most effective way to reveal opportunities for a better way of doing things.

Zaltman Metaphoric Elicitation Technique

 "Most of what influences what we say and do occurs below the level of awareness. That's why we need new techniques: to get at hidden knowledge—to get at what people don't know they know," says Harvard Business School professor Jerry Zaltman.[6] His revolutionary market research technique, the Zaltman Metaphoric Elicitation Technique (ZMET), tries to get to that hidden knowledge. The technique uses consumer metaphors to shed light into the consumer's subconscious, into the way he or she thinks.

In his book *Strategic Brand Management: Building, Measuring, and Managing Brand Equity*, Kevin Lane Keller identifies the following seven basic premises on which ZMET is based:[7]

1. Most human communication is nonverbal.
2. Thoughts often occur as nonverbal images.
3. Metaphors are essential units of thought and are the key mechanism for viewing consumer thoughts and feelings and understanding consumer behavior.
4. Sensory images provide important metaphors.
5. Consumers have mental models—interrelated ideas about a market experience—that represent their knowledge and behavior.
6. Hidden or deep structures of thought can be accessed.
7. Emotion and reason are forces that commingle in the minds of consumers.

So how does ZMET work? ZMET participants are asked the question: "What are your thoughts and feelings about this experience or that product?" They are then asked to collect pictures that capture these thoughts and feelings or display the exact opposite of these thoughts and feelings. Each participant returns 7 to 10 days later to discuss their pictures with a specially trained ZMET interviewer over a two-hour period. During that interview, the participant describes each picture as well as any pictures that he or she was looking for but was unable to obtain. Next, the participant organizes the pictures and describes the pic-

tures that portray the opposite of his or her thoughts and feelings. The participant then explains his or her reaction in sensory terms, such as color, sound, smell, taste, and touch. Finally, with the help of a graphic artist, the participant and the interviewer build a collage with the selected images. A careful examination of this collage can shed light into the participant's mind, thoughts, and associations.

To illustrate the output of ZMET, let us consider the results of ZMET in the panty hose industry.[8] Twenty panty hose–wearing women were selected to participate in a study. They were asked, "What are your thoughts and feelings about buying and wearing panty hose?" The pictures they selected included fence posts encased in plastic wrap, twisted telephone cords, and steel bands strangling trees. These images are relatively easy to interpret: panty hose are tight and inconvenient. However, other images were selected that shed a different light on the story. For example, one selected image showed flowers resting peacefully in a vase. The discussion with the ZMET interviewer eventually revealed that the flowers in a vase referred to the fact that wearing the product made a woman feel thin and tall. Further discussion revealed that panty hose made women feel they had longer legs and that this was important because men think long legs are sexy. Hence, a desired experience from wearing panty hose is to feel sexy around men. A traditional research method would have great difficulty revealing this type of finding.

Zaltman is currently working on expanding ZMET to new frontiers. Using brain scans, interviewers can see how people think and where thoughts take place inside the brain. Messages with a negative effect on respondents lead to activity in an area of the brain associated with negative feelings. In contrast, messages that lead to positive feelings stimulate activity in a different part of the brain. By massaging their marketing messages, companies may at some point be able to create messages that activate only areas of the brain associated with positive feelings. This technique is still in development but has great potential to further revolutionize the way market research is conducted.

Which Is Better?
Online Consumer Tracking Vs. Wholistic View

In the online world, there is no lack of data. Click-stream information reveals purchase patterns, online habits, basic demographics, and potentially a host of other consumer information. Is this information sufficient to define new business opportunities?

Many argue that studying past and real-time behavior will yield enough sufficient information about customers to make choices about the services they need at that time. The Web enables companies to watch customers interacting in real time with their product with a high degree of precision and allows them to intervene while the customer is still in the buying process—the marketing Holy Grail. Procedures like collaborative filtering allow real-time suggestive selling. An example of this is Amazon.com's success at cross-selling customers.

An alternative view is that click-through-based data provides an insufficient picture of the reasons customers behave the way they do. In other words, click-stream analysis explains what customers do but not why they do it. A total customer view brings together consumer behavior and insights about motivations for that behavior; this view considers the behavior plus the customer context and environment, the functional and emotional desired experiences of the customer, and the customer's beliefs and associations about the product, service, and current purveyors of the offering. Without a total customer view, managers are unlikely to generate real insight into key customer groups. Companies such as DoubleClick seem to have been responding to this concern by trying to merge their online data sets with behavioral data that has been gathered offline.

WHAT DETERMINES THE SPECIFIC CUSTOMERS THE COMPANY IS TO PURSUE?

So far we have talked about where a company is likely to play in the value system, how customers go through their decision-making process, and what are potential areas for value creation. Now we will discuss the specific customers whom the company plans to pursue. Companies need to develop a sense for the type(s) of customers they ultimately seek to serve. This understanding allows a company to assess opportunity attractiveness at a high level and to focus on crafting an offering that will appeal to the target customer.

To better understand customers engaged in the Customer Decision Process, companies are likely to find customer sets with very different patterns of behavior, underlying needs, and drivers of behavior. **Segmentation** is the process of grouping these customers based on their similarities. Once the different segments have been identified, the company must find the segments (or customers) it will target to further refine the type of opportunity the company will seek to capture. Of course, the digital play you have in mind may radically change how customers act in this value system. Hence, you would look both for segments that disproportionately benefit from some change in the status quo as well as those more predisposed to adopt a new product or service.

Approaches to Market Segmentation

There are many varied approaches to segmentation, and the best way to segment a market is an often debated topic. The best segmentation for the opportunity depends on the value system that the opportunity is centered upon, how the customer can and will make decisions within that value system, and what action your company is likely to take. Before we describe a practical approach to segmentation for the New Economy, it is important to briefly review the different ways a market (and customers) can be segmented. Academic literature and textbooks often cite the following segmentation approaches:[9]

- **Demographics (or Firmographics).** For individuals, the demographic approach includes grouping by age, gender, occupation, ethnicity, income, family status, lifestage, Internet connectivity, and browser type. In a firmographic approach, companies are segmented by categories including, for example, online/offline business, number of employees, company size, job function, and purchasing process.
- **Geographics.** Segmentation examples include: country/region/city, city size, density (urban, suburban, rural), ISP domain, etc.
- **Behavioral.** Examples: online shopping behavior, offline shopping behavior, web-page/site visited, website loyalty, prior purchases, site, etc.
- **Occasion (or Situational).** Occasional examples include, routine occasion, special occasion, time (time of day, day of week, holidays), location (from home, while on the road), event (while writing a business plan, when shopping), trigger (out of supply), etc.
- **Pyschographics.** Psychographics examples include, lifestyle (thrill seekers, fun lovers, recluses), personality (laid-back, Type A, risk takers), affinity (community builders, belongers, outcasts), etc.
- **Benefits.** Examples of benefits include: convenience, economy, quality, ease of use, speed, information, selection, etc.
- **Beliefs and attitudes.** Examples: brand beliefs (New Economy, old fashioned), attitudes toward the category, channel effectiveness beliefs, beliefs about themselves (technically savvy), etc.

Table 2-1 provides a more comprehensive listing of variables with illustrations. Over time, segmentation has evolved from the use of more actionable "observable" and "customer external" variables (e.g., age, income, geography) in the 1960s and 1970s to more "customer internal," highly meaningful variables (e.g., needs, attitudes) in the 1980s and 1990s. The fact remains that neither is sufficient on its own to fully define the segmentation. The difficulty is in selecting the segmentation approach and the variables that most effectively describe and reflect the nature of the New Economy opportunity being analyzed.

Actionable and Meaningful Segmentation

Unfortunately most segmentation efforts fail to deliver on the intended objective—to be both useful and insightful. The segments are often either easy to recognize but do not provide much insight into customer motivations (actionable, but not meaningful), or they generate real insight on customers but are difficult to address (meaningful, but not actionable). The goal of market segmentation is to identify

Table
2-1

SEGMENTATION APPROACHES

Segmentation Type	Description	Examples–Variables
Geographics	Divides market into different geographical units	Country, region, city
Demographics	Divides market on the basis of demographic variables	Age, gender, income
Firmographics	Divides market on the basis of company-specific variables	Number of employees, company size
Behavioral	Divides market based on how customers actually buy and use the product	Website loyalty, prior purchases
Occasion (Situational)	Divides market based on the situation that leads to a product need, purchase, or use	Routine occasion, special occasion
Psychographics	Divides market based on lifestyle and/or personality	Personality (laid-back, type A), lifestyle
Benefits	Divides market based on benefits or qualities sought from the product	Convenience, economy, quality

the *intersection or combination* of marketplace variables that will generate **actionable segmentation** and **meaningful segmentation** of customers.

Actionable Segmentation. To be *actionable*, segmentation must be consistent with how a company can go to market and be able to be sized and described. A segmentation is *actionable* if

- The segments are easy to identify.
- The segments can be readily reached.
- The segments can be described in terms of their growth, size, profile, and attractiveness.

Meaningful Segmentation. To be *meaningful*, segmentation must help describe and begin to explain why customers currently behave—or are likely to—in a specific way. A segmentation is *meaningful* if

- Customers within a segment behave similarly while customers across segments behave in different ways.
- It provides some insight into customers' motivations.
- It corresponds to the set of barriers customers face when they buy or use a product or service.
- It corresponds with how customers currently (or could) buy or use the product or service.

- It correlates to differences in profitability or cost to serve.
- The segments and/or their differences are large enough to warrant a different set of actions by your company.

Webvan, an online grocery service, provides a good illustration of the value of segmentation and how it can be both actionable and meaningful. The company looked at the market and determined that the core users of their service are likely to be affluent families who regularly use the Internet from their homes. In addition, the economics of delivering goods to customers is heavily dependent on how close they are to one another. They used income (affluent), family status (families), Internet connectivity (Internet from home), and density (close to one another) as categories to segment the market—variables you can readily find through available geo-targeting software. As a consequence, Webvan selected the San Francisco Bay area and the Atlanta metropolitan area as the locations to start offering its service to customers. These areas contain a large number of busy, high-income families with Internet access—characteristics that meaningfully influence customers' likelihood of using Webvan.

The Right Blend of Segmentation Variables

Finding the right blend of segmentation variables that are both actionable and meaningful is difficult to do in practice. One is often forced to trade off one variable for another. In the online world, this trade-off can be decided more easily than in the offline because firms can quickly collect data that is both actionable and meaningful. Through a registration form that asks customers for basic demographic information, such as income, gender, age, and zip codes, or through real-time tracking of customer click-streams on both search data and final purchase behavior, online companies have access to a rich source of segmentation data.

"Clickographics," the demonstrated behavior of an online customer using click-stream data, is an interesting example of a behavioral variable that often tends to be highly meaningful and actionable. Website server logs can capture every step the customer takes while surfing the company site. Using clickographics, a company can easily identify and communicate with their target customers. For example, launch.com is an online radio station that plays songs for users and asks them to rate each song they hear. Based on user response, launch.com builds a musical taste profile unique to each user and selects songs the user will like. The customer's song ratings are meaningful variables because the site is responding to the customer's musical tastes. The segment is also actionable because the site can at any moment reach each customer and communicate with him or her to offer a new album by one of his or her favorite artists.

In our experience, an intersection, or combination, of demographic, geographic, situational, and behavioral variables will create a market segmentation that is both actionable and meaningful. Typical variables to consider include intersections of user demographics, life-stage, purchase occasion, and online behavior. The end result is a segmentation scheme that tends to favor one factor or another; for example, "online holiday purchasers" (more occasion based), "first-time users" (more behaviorally based), or "graduating high-school seniors from affluent neighborhoods" (more demographic and geography based). We rarely recommend using pyschographic, benefits, or attitudinal variables *in isolation* as the basis for a segmentation. These approaches often maximize meaningful dimensions but are rarely actionable and, therefore, are often rejected by managers. It would be difficult for Ashford.com to identify a customer as a "high achiever" before or as he or she interacts with the website. Rather, you may need to look at prior purchase data (other luxury brands purchased on sale) and the path-in to the site (click-through from MySimon.com) to determine the likelihood this customer is shopping for a Rolex watch at a bargain price. The point is to use the more observable information to generate insight on the motivation, not the other way around.

Segmentation Variables About the Customers.
To gain some insight into what variables to use, ask yourself the following questions about the customers:

- Who are they? Where do they live? What do they do for a living? How busy are they? What else do they do? What do they like to do in their spare time? How much spare time do they have?

- What is their purchase process?

- When and where do they shop? What else do they buy? How much did they pay for the product? How often do they buy? What channels do they have ready access to?

- From where do they get their information? Is there anyone else who influences the purchase or use of the product? If so, who?

- What is their usage process? What external factors affect their product use? When do they use the product? How often do they use the product? For which occasions are the products purchased or used? Are these occasions frequent or episodic?

- Where do they use the product? What is the setting they are in? How often are they in this setting?

- Is the purchase or usage planned? What happens to them if they do not purchase the product?

Segmentation Variables About the Microeconomics.
To gain some insight into what variables to use, ask yourself the following questions about the microeconomics:

- What are the major cost drivers? Are they related to physical proximity? Are they affected by time?

- Are there major learning curve effects? Are they scale sensitive? Are they scope sensitive?

A good illustration of market segmentation can be seen by studying the strategy adopted by Priceline.com. Priceline.com saw the opportunity to use their reverse-auction technology to enable a buyer-driven model in the purchase of airline tickets. The company wanted to make the average air traveler a "price-setter," not a "price-taker." Under this model, customers "name their price" for a roundtrip flight between two cities on a certain date. This price request is then submitted to a group of airline "partners" that considers the offer and, the consumer hopes, accepts the bid.

Priceline.com saw the conventional process to buy discount tickets as cumbersome and frustrating for the consumer. The tiered-seat pricing structure is complex and confusing. Further, the process the consumer has to go through to check across airlines for schedule, availability, and pricing is convoluted. Moreover, discount ticket hunters are treated with little care by the airlines. In short, the budget airline ticket buyer had no power over the carriers. Priceline.com set out to change all that.

However, Priceline's service will not appeal to all travelers. The service has many constraints. For example, customers' bids may or may not be accepted, customers do not receive frequent flyer miles, and they cannot specify either the flight times, the routing, or the carrier.

If you were Priceline.com and suspected there was an opportunity, how would you make it concrete? How would you segment the market? Which of the consumer segments are most likely to be interested in the concept? How much opportunity is there likely to be?

Start by looking at the broad list of segmentation variables and identify the ones that, when combined with other variables, correlate to customer motivations, barriers, use habits, and profitability. Look for combinations of variables that generate insight. For Priceline.com, these would be

- **Occasion (or Situation):** The *reason for the trip* (business or personal) corresponds to a customer's likely willingness to be flexible on schedule and price-sensitivity. Furthermore, *lead time for a trip* (schedulable weeks in advance, event timing flexibility, or last minute) corresponds to the ability for customers to coordinate other elements of the trip around specific flight times.

- **Demographics:** The *lifestage* of a consumer (student, retiree, parent) corresponds to their price sensitivity, schedule flexibility, and tolerance for a less than efficient itinerary. *Income/occupation* (low to moderate income with an occupation that is not travel-intensive or moderate to high income with a travel-intensive occupation) corresponds to the customer's price sensitivity and their tolerance for a less-than-efficient itinerary.

- **Behavior:** The *number of flights* the customer takes a year (frequent flyer or infrequent flyer) will correlate to the customer's ability to use frequent flyer miles to secure a ticket, their airline brand loyalty, and their tolerance of inconvenience or of a less-than-efficient itinerary.

Combining these variables yields distinct, actionable, and meaningful segments of the market to whom Priceline.com can sell airline tickets. Exhibit 2-3 illustrates the segmentation for Priceline that emerges from this analysis. The vertical axis divides the population into different demographic groups (for example, students and families with children). The vertical axis also categorizes some groups by their behavior—whether or not they fly frequently. The horizontal axis shows "occasions," or reasons, for flying. These include business trips, family vacations, and last minute trips. Cross-tabulating the two axes and blocking some of the subsegments together creates a matrix of behaviorally distinct segments.

The Priceline.com example illustrates the value of going beyond simply using "price conscious" as a market-segmentation variable. First, "price conscious" does not help provide any clue into *who the consumer is* or *why* he or she may be price conscious. Is the consumer price conscious because he or she has no discretionary income? Or is the itinerary so flexible that the consumer feels no need to pay a premium for a specific time? Second, as companies extend their business concepts into new arenas, a "price conscious" customer in one arena may not be a "price conscious" customer in another. For example, Priceline.com also offers "name your price" mortgages. The target consumer in this arena is the middle/upper income individual who has a high degree of comfort with sophisticated financial instruments, not the cash-starved student or retiree, who is the target in the airline ticket business arena.

Exhibit
2-3

PRICELINE.COM SEGMENTATION

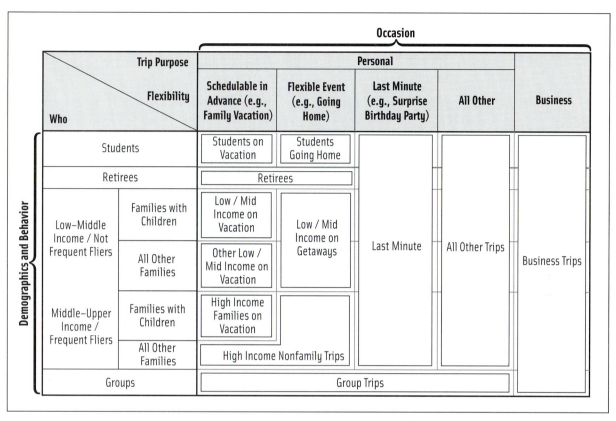

		Occasion				
Trip Purpose		**Personal**				
Flexibility		**Schedulable in Advance (e.g., Family Vacation)**	**Flexible Event (e.g., Going Home)**	**Last Minute (e.g., Surprise Birthday Party)**	**All Other**	**Business**
Who						
Students		Students on Vacation	Students Going Home			
Retirees		Retirees		Last Minute	All Other Trips	Business Trips
Low–Middle Income / Not Frequent Fliers	Families with Children	Low / Mid Income on Vacation	Low / Mid Income on Getaways			
	All Other Families	Other Low / Mid Income on Vacation				
Middle–Upper Income / Frequent Fliers	Families with Children	High Income Families on Vacation				
	All Other Families	High Income Nonfamily Trips				
Groups		Group Trips				

Left axis label: **Demographics and Behavior**

Market Mapping and Target Customers

With the set of actionable and meaningful dimensions identified, management can construct a basic marketing map to show the segment's size, growth rate, and financial attractiveness. For Priceline.com, several of the travel segments noted in Exhibit 2-3 are small. For example, several segments represent about 5 percent of the market (e.g., students on vacation, last minute), a few represent about 10 percent of the market (e.g., groups), while "business trips" represents about 40 percent of the market. Exhibit 2-4 is shaded to show the size of each segment.

These simple maps are important for several reasons. First, the map identifies the location of the money and the relative opportunities in the market. Second, a clear representation of the opportunity's location makes it easier to select initial target segments and to lay out a game plan for sequencing the approach to other segments in the future. Third, a map provides structure for synthesizing additional information and insight. Fourth, the segmentation shown in a map is a touchstone for identifying future shifts in market definition and opportunity.

Look at each segment, and identify those who are likely to find the service valuable. For Priceline.com, the high priority segments are "Students on Vacation," "Retirees," "Low/Middle Income Families on Vacation," "Low/Middle Income

Exhibit 2-4

PRICELINE.COM NUMBER
OF AIRLINE TRIPS

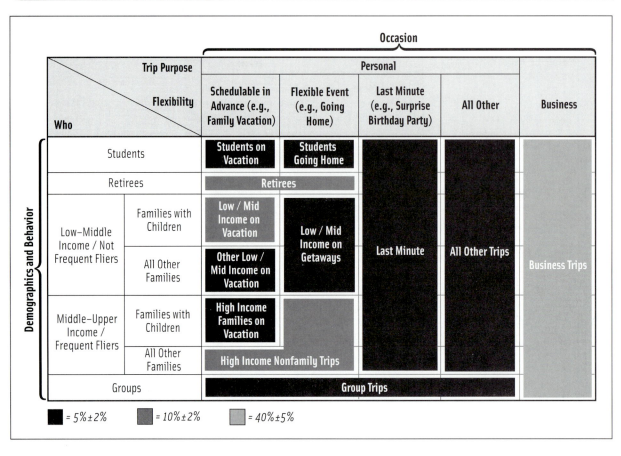

Trip Purpose / Who ⟍ Flexibility	Occasion				Business
	Personal				
	Schedulable in Advance (e.g., Family Vacation)	**Flexible Event (e.g., Going Home)**	**Last Minute (e.g., Surprise Birthday Party)**	**All Other**	**Business**
Students	Students on Vacation	Students Going Home	Last Minute	All Other Trips	Business Trips
Retirees	Retirees				
Low–Middle Income / Not Frequent Fliers — Families with Children	Low / Mid Income on Vacation	Low / Mid Income on Getaways			
Low–Middle Income / Not Frequent Fliers — All Other Families	Other Low / Mid Income on Vacation				
Middle–Upper Income / Frequent Fliers — Families with Children	High Income Families on Vacation				
Middle–Upper Income / Frequent Fliers — All Other Families	High Income Nonfamily Trips				
Groups	Group Trips				

■ = 5% ±2%   ■ = 10% ±2%   ■ = 40% ±5%

Families on Getaways," "Other Low/Middle Income on Vacation," "Last Minute." Exhibit 2-5 is shaded to show the priority segments for Priceline. Each of these segments are likely to find the Priceline.com buying constraints acceptable in order to get a lower price. Together these segments constitute 45–55 percent of the total number of trips taken—a very large opportunity.

As stated at the beginning of the chapter, it is often as important to identify both the segments who are likely candidates and those who are unlikely to find the idea attractive—who is in and who is out. It is also important to communicate who's in/out to potential collaborators to minimize the negative response that could otherwise ensue. The Priceline.com example also illustrates this concept well. For the "name your price" concept to work you need to have willing buyers and sellers. We just discussed the "buyers" perspective, now let's look at the opportunity from the airline's perspective. It is well known that most airlines make most of their money on customers traveling for business, customers who are brand-loyal (top-tier frequent fliers), and customers who cannot plan ahead. Airlines look to other customer segments as ways to make some contribution margin to the fixed cost of their highly "perishable" product—once the door of a plane closes, the carrier has forever lost the opportunity to sell an empty seat. Not only is Priceline.com not under-

Exhibit 2-5

PRICELINE.COM SEGMENT PRIORITIZATION

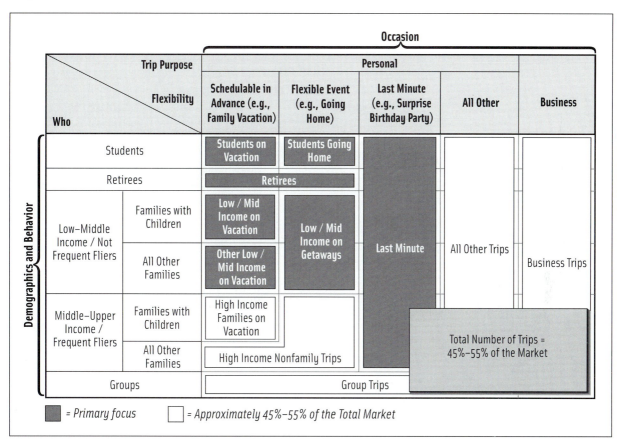

Who / Trip Purpose / Flexibility		Schedulable in Advance (e.g., Family Vacation)	Flexible Event (e.g., Going Home)	Last Minute (e.g., Surprise Birthday Party)	All Other	Business
Students		Students on Vacation	Students Going Home			
Retirees		Retirees				
Low–Middle Income / Not Frequent Fliers	Families with Children	Low / Mid Income on Vacation	Low / Mid Income on Getaways	Last Minute	All Other Trips	Business Trips
	All Other Families	Other Low / Mid Income on Vacation				
Middle–Upper Income / Frequent Fliers	Families with Children	High Income Families on Vacation				
	All Other Families	High Income Nonfamily Trips				
Groups		Group Trips				

Occasion — Personal

Total Number of Trips = 45%–55% of the Market

◼ = *Primary focus*   ☐ = *Approximately 45%–55% of the Total Market*

cutting any airline's bread-and-butter business, they are also providing airlines with a way to offload their unsold capacity quickly and cheaply. Priceline.com targets customers who are precisely the customers most airlines ignore because they are not attractive.

A final note is in order. Some analysts and faculty have argued that online businesses no longer need to focus on demographics or other traditional criteria because the online world enables the firm to track consumer behavior in real time. Hence, this behavior by itself combines both actionability and meaningfulness. To some degree, this argument is correct because behavior data (and the e-mail address) is sufficient information to interact with current customers. However, the standard demographic data is highly relevant in the online world for three reasons. First, the online firm can collect demographic data on their consumer set, then more effectively sell advertising to potential advertisers. Second, with the demographic data, the firm will, in turn, know where to place offline advertising to attract customers to its own site. Third, for companies with both brick-and-mortar and online operations, this picture of the customer will foster more effective activation of channels, product mix decisions, and other marketing mix decisions.

Does Segmentation Matter?

An interesting debate has surfaced in the online world. Namely, there are authors who have begun to question whether the segmentation concept applies in the online world. Because the online world enables consumers to customize products, services, and information specifically to their needs, the segmentation concept has been reduced to "segments of one."

Proponents of this approach have labeled the direct approach variously with terms such as "1:1," "segment-of-one," or "one-to-one-marketing." Furthermore, they argue Web businesses such as eBay often attract an exceptionally wide variety of customers who weigh buying criteria (e.g., "low price," "most convenient buying method," "best online information and reviews," or "broadest selection") quite differently. Hence, it is foolish to attempt to cluster these widely divergent groups. Rather, customization enables firms to uniquely meet the needs of each customer. Additionally, they argue that the back-office supply systems and infrastructure can easily accommodate every type of customer. Finally, multiple storefronts—even 1:1 store-

fronts—can be constructed in a real-time basis. (Amazon's homepage is an excellent example of this, since it is tailored to each customer who comes to the store. Exhibit 2-6 shows the Amazon.com homepage for two different customers who visited the site at exactly the same time.)

Conversely, the proponents of segmentation argue that all Web storefronts are, by definition, already segmenting the market. That is, if a given Web storefront simultaneously attracts selected customers and repels certain customers, it is segmenting the market. By disregarding these segments and focusing exclusively on 1:1 marketing, the company would miss the fundamental economics of which particular class of customer is most profitable or least profitable. For example, Buy.com offers some of the lowest prices on a wide variety of products. It is not clear that the store explicitly targets a particular customer segment; however, the store's focus on prices is likely to attract the most price-sensitive customers.

WHO PROVIDES THE RESOURCES TO DELIVER THE BENEFITS OF THE OFFERING?

Having determined the initial customer focus of the business, we are ready to make a first attempt at describing the business concept. At this step, the company should stake out what experience and benefits **the offering** will provide and what capabilities and technology will be needed to deliver the benefits of the offering. While the offering and the means to deliver its benefits will be revisited and refined many times, understanding these details will be a vital part of the company's rationale for success in this endeavor.

Company Resources

Before spending a great deal of time crafting a specific business model to support a concept, the management team should assess whether or not it can identify at least three or four resources or assets that it can leverage successfully into the selected online space. These resources should be central to delivering new benefits or unlocking trapped value, the core of the company's value story. These resources should also hold the promise for advantage, considering the current and prospec-

Exhibit 2-6

AMAZON.COM HOMEPAGE FOR
TWO DIFFERENT CUSTOMERS

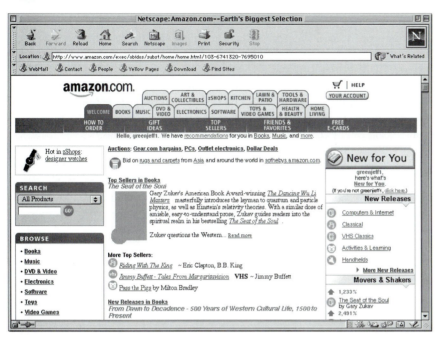

Amazon.com is the registered trademark of Amazon.com, Inc.

tive players in the targeted space. With three or four such resources, the management team will have the beginnings of a robust business.

In this step, the team will already have a strong understanding of the following:

- The selected value system in which the company will be participating

- The key stages of the target's Customer Decision Process and the benefits sought/value trapped at each stage
- The target customer segments

Looking across these insights, the management team should identify which winning resources it can bring to bear, create, or provide through business partnerships. In Chapter 3 we will introduce an analytical tool which we call the **resource system;** this is a useful framework for assessing the new business's resources. A resource system is a discrete collection of individual and organizational activities and assets that, when taken together, create organizational capabilities. These capabilities allow the company to serve customer needs. Resources that a company can bring to bear can be classified into the three following groupings:

- **Customer Facing.** Customer-facing resources include brand name, well-trained salesforce, and multiple distribution channels.
- **Internal.** These resources are associated with the company's internal operations. Examples include technology, product development, economies of scale, and experienced staff.
- **Upstream.** These resources are associated with a company's relationship to its suppliers. Examples include partnerships with suppliers and the degree of operational seamlessness between the company and its suppliers.

Partners

On its own, a company may not be able to bring to bear all of the resources necessary to deliver value to its target segments. In opportunity assessment, a company must be realistic about any missing capability gaps. If a gap is insurmountable, the company should not proceed. At this step, the company must seek a way to close any gaps. Partnering may be an effective alternative to building or acquiring the capability. New Economy companies find partnerships particularly relevant as their offerings span traditional value system boundaries. In fact, effective partnering can be an important source of advantage—for example, BarnesandNoble.com's exclusive marketing deal with AOL and Amazon.com's use of Netperceptions for collaborative filtering. The potential partners for a company can be grouped into two categories: complementors and traditional partners.

Complementor Partners. Complementor partners are companies that provide offerings that are complementary to the company's offerings. An increase in sales of a complementor offering is likely to lead to an increase in the company sales. For example, Intel is a complementor to PC manufacturers. An increase in sales of Intel's Pentium processor is likely to lead to an increase in PC sales.

Capability Partners. Capability partners are companies that give and receive value from partnering with the company. For example, Merrill Lynch is a traditional partner for works.com, a website that automates purchasing for small and medium businesses and gives them volume-purchasing power. Merrill Lynch provides financial assistance, management, and advice to works.com customers. By doing so, it is adding a financing resource to works.com's capabilities. In return, works.com offers additional volume by sending small and medium businesses that require financing to the Merrill Lynch site.

In Chapter 3 we will be considering in greater detail how the company can determine what capabilities it needs to develop and how to develop them.

Combining the benefits to be delivered along with the way in which the company will deliver them fills in the business concept. With this high-level business concept in mind, we can assess the attractiveness of the opportunity from financial, technical, and competitive points of view.

HOW DO WE ASSESS THE ATTRACTIVENESS OF THE OPPORTUNITY?

There is little point in targeting a new business concept, in general, or a meaningful and easy-to-reach segment, specifically, if the opportunity is not attractive. Here we review nine factors in four areas that we can assess to determine the character and magnitude of the opportunity.

- **Competitive Intensity.** Factors that relate to overall *competitive intensity* can be expressed in a competitors map that includes (a) the number and identity of competitors along with their respective (b) strengths and weaknesses at delivering benefits.
- **Customer Dynamics.** Elements that frame the overall *customer dynamics* of the market are (a) the level of unmet need/magnitude of unconstrained opportunity, (b) the level of interaction between major customer segments, and (c) the likely rate of growth.
- **Technology Vulnerability.** *Technology vulnerability* includes (a) the impact of the penetration of enabling technologies and (b) the impact of new technologies on the value proposition.
- **Microeconomics.** The *microeconomics* of the opportunity include (a) the size/volume of the market and (b) the level of profitability.

We later discuss how to look across these factors to assess the overall attractiveness of the opportunity and quantify the financial upside.

Competitive Intensity

Identify Competitors.
To measure competitive intensity, a company needs to identify the competitors it will face. In the value system discussion, key competitors would have been identified, and "white space" opportunities (i.e., those where there is no apparent competition) isolated. At this step, the task is to develop a better understanding of the threats and opportunities associated with various participants.

Identifying online competitors is at once both easier and more difficult than in the offline world. On one hand, the online firm can simply use search engines to begin identifying competitors (although generic searches may deliver thousands of "relevant" pages), visit the online businesses, and, as a result, obtain a very good understanding of their offerings. On the other hand, competition in the market-space typically occurs across traditional industry boundaries. No matter what online business you are in, there is a good chance that either Microsoft or AOL Time Warner (or both!) are your competitors.

The significance is that in the online world, companies that one would not consider **direct competitors** (in the sense of offering a similar or competing product) can become **indirect competitors** by reaching and attracting the same customers or by developing a technology, platform, or offering that can be swiftly geared to compete with your offering and for your customers.

Direct competitors are companies in the same industry and rivals to each other. In his book *Competitive Strategy,* Michael Porter defines these firms as offering products or services that are "close substitutes" for each other.[10] For example, Petsmart.com and Petopia.com are direct competitors; both offer pet supplies to customers. Direct competitors reach and compete for the same customers. However, Webvan and Streamline are not (at the time of writing) direct competitors, even though both offer grocery and pharmacy products ordered online and delivered to the customer's door. This is because Webvan serves San Francisco and Atlanta customers, while Streamline serves Boston customers.

Indirect competitors contain two categories of companies:

- **Substitute Producers.** Porter defines substitute producers as companies that, though in different industries, produce products and services that "perform the same function."[11] Keen.com and Britannica.com are substitutes. Keen.com is a switchboard that connects people with questions to individuals with the right knowledge to help them. Britannica.com offers answers to a wide range of questions through its online encyclopedia.

- **Adjacent Competitors.** Adjacent competitors do not currently offer products and services that are direct substitutes, but they have the potential to quickly do so. For example, adjacent competitors may hold relationships with a company's current customers. The free ISP Netzero had relationships with many customers who used Yahoo! or Excite frequently, but it did not compete directly with those companies (it was an adjacent competitor). Recently Netzero partnered with the search engine Looksmart to create MyZstart, a personalized portal site that directly competes with Yahoo!'s and Excite's personalized portal offers. Netzero automatically routes all users to its MyZstart page when signing on, transforming the company into a powerful direct competitor to other portals. Adjacent competitors might also use a similar technology or platform or have similar activity systems.

A useful tool for identifying direct and indirect competitors is the profiling approach in Exhibit 2-7. Exhibit 2-7 illustrates the "radar screen" for Kodak. It consists of three concentric circles. The innermost circle contains the set of customer activities that are central to the industry that we are examining (we will explore this concept more fully in Chapter 3). In Kodak's case, these include purchasing a camera, purchasing film, taking pictures, downloading and choosing pictures to print, printing and receiving pictures, sharing pictures, storing them on a CD, and purchasing accessories. Kodak faces competition in each of these areas. The middle circle contains Kodak's *direct competitors.* For example, in the purchase-camera step, Kodak competes with a number of companies that include Fuji, Sony, Nikon, and Olympus. In the downloading and choosing pictures to print stage, Kodak faces both offline and online players that include Ofoto, Photo Access, Seattle Filmworks, Shutterfly, and Snapfish. Finally, the outermost circle contains Kodak's indirect competitors. For example, in the purchase camera stage, HP and Intel do not offer cameras, but they provide accessory hardware products that are targeted to the same customer groups; the hardware products conceivably could be leveraged toward offering cameras in the future.

Competitor Maps. Current and prospective competitors can significantly shape the nature of a company's online opportunity. In previous steps, we identified the customer segments that the company wants to target and the competitors (direct and indirect) that a company may face. To assess competitive intensity, we need to

Exhibit 2-7

COMPETITOR PROFILING—
EASTMAN KODAK

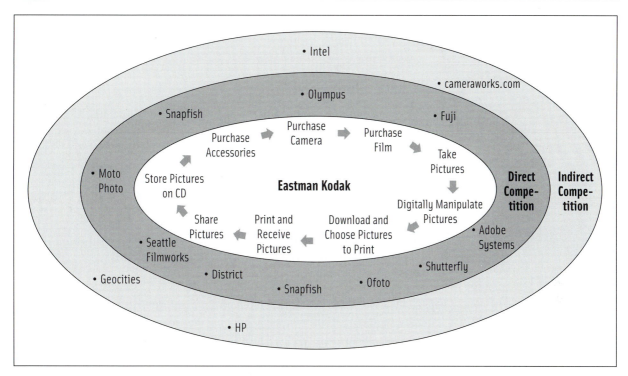

map the competitors to the target segments. In other words, we need to map out where current competitor companies are participating and their effectiveness in delivering benefits to our target customers. This analysis will help the company do the following:

- Demarcate any "white space," or underserved areas, in the market and, conversely, the most competitive areas.
- Identify companies against whom we will compete and provide an early indication of their strengths.
- Spot companies that could be potential "collaborators," i.e., offer a critical capability or unique access to customers at a specific stage of the Customer Decision Process.

The competitor mapping of segments also can be used to record the relative strengths and weaknesses of current competitors and their offerings at each relevant cell in the map. Ultimately, the customer seeks specific benefits. Assessing the current player performance in meeting the customer standard will provide an indication of the potential for you to move in and win. Understanding current competitor capabilities will also give you a sense of the height of competitive hurdles you may face in your selected space.

Exhibit 2-8 illustrates a mapping of Priceline's competitors to two of its target segments. The competitors considered are Travelocity and American Airlines E-Fares (the weekly discount fares offered by American). A closer study of the low-to-middle income families with children segment reveals that Priceline performs moderately. It offers low prices; however, the flight schedules can be inconvenient for families, and the quality of service on the Priceline.com site is low. In contrast, Travelocity seems to serve that segment well. It offers vacation planning tools, a large selection of destinations, and allows customers to select their schedule. Finally, American Airlines E-Fares perform very poorly on this segment. This site often does not give enough notice, has a poor selection of destinations, and offers a limited number of seats, which potentially makes it difficult for families to book tickets for all its members.

Customer Dynamics

Once we have described competitor vulnerabilities, we next need to turn our attention to the customer dynamics of the market and how they create, accelerate, and sustain unit demand. The following are three factors we consider central to understanding:

Unconstrained Opportunity. This is the amount of "white space" that is still apparent in the marketplace. Markets with a high degree of trapped or relatively untapped new-to-the-world value are extremely valuable. Note the explosive growth of eBay in the online auctions space. The number of goods that individuals want to buy and sell along with the relatively arcane auction markets and providers that existed signaled a massive opportunity.

Segment Interaction. This is the level of reinforcing activity that generates more purchase and usage. Companies that have member-influencing-member dynamics (viral) can quickly capture much of the opportunity. For example, MarketTools through Zoomerang.com, its self-serve customer feedback offering, has a geometric viral effect associated with it. Each member can write a customer feedback survey to 30 customers, who then experience the Zoomerang offering and decide whether to write their own survey and send it on in turn to 30 of their customers, and so on.

Exhibit 2-8 COMPETITOR MAPPING TO SELECTED SEGMENTS FOR PRICELINE

Target Segments	Priceline	Travelocity	AA E-Fares
• Students – Flexible Events	◔ • Low prices • Only 24% of bids get matched	◔ • Special deals • Fare watch	◑ • Often not enough notice • Poor selection
• Low/Middle Income Families with Children	◑ • Low prices • Inconvenient flight schedules	● • Vacation planning tools • Large selection	◔ • Often not enough notice • Limited seats
• Last-Minute Travelers	◕ • Last-minute prices • Considerably cheaper than consolidators	◔ • Typically very high last-minute prices • Large selections	◕ • Very low prices

● High Performance Level	◑ Medium Performance Level	○ Low Performance Level

Growth. Growth usually refers to the percentage of annual growth of the underlying customer unit market. Markets with high expected growth represent significant opportunities for players. For example, Onvia.com, which is a general services portal to small business, can benefit from the high rate of growth in the small business sector (including the Internet)—the fastest growing sector of the economy. Onvia benefits from a growth "three-fer," i.e., a growing number of small businesses that exist, penetration of these existing small businesses, and a growing number of services that small companies require.

Technology Vulnerability

Beyond the competitive arena, the company must make a high-level judgment on the concept's vulnerability to technology trends, both in the penetration of enabling technologies and in the impact of new technologies on the value proposition.

Technology Adoption. Is there sufficient penetration of the technologies (e.g., cable modems, scanners) that enable the customer to take advantage of or participate in the offering? What penetration is necessary to make the offering financially viable? When is the minimum penetration likely to be met? Is there an introductory version that could be upgraded as technology penetration increases?

Impact of New Technologies. What new technologies could radically alter the economics of delivering an offering or require adjustment of the actual features and functionality of an offering? How likely is it that your target population or competitors will use these technologies?

The pace and discontinuity of technological change make forecasting the future particularly challenging, and it is not our intent to provide an exhaustive treatment of the subject here.[12] Fortunately, several rules of thumb about technological development can guide entrepreneurs. One of them is that computers will continue to increase in power. Moore's Law (which we examine in greater depth elsewhere in the book) forecasts the pace at which processing power increases. Our definition of what a computer is will also probably change. Andy Grove of Intel predicts that by 2002 there will be 500 million computers in the world, yet already there are over 6 billion computer chips embedded in devices such as phones and cars.[13] Soon every device will be a computer. Many believe these devices will all be connected by a vastly larger Internet. George Gilder, a technology forecaster, has given his name to Gilder's Law, which predicts that total bandwidth of communications systems will triple every 12 months for the foreseeable future. The challenge for entrepreneurs is to understand what these macro trends will mean for their proposed businesses.

Microeconomics

So far in this section, we have assessed the magnitude of the opportunity from a competitive perspective (how easy it is to enter the space and to differentiate the company from competitor offerings), an understanding of customer dynamic (how unit demand is created, accelerated, and sustained), and the impact of technology. We now need to assess the level of financial opportunity. The following two factors should be considered to be of critical importance:

Market Size. This is the dollar value of all of the sales generated in a particular market. Opportunities with a large market size are very attractive since winning even a small piece of the pie may correspond to a significant revenue flow. For example, a large number of competitors in the online pet products industry have emerged in part due to the huge size of the pet food and supplies market, estimated at $23 billion.[14]

Profitability. This is the profit margin that can be realized in the market. Markets with high profit margins are highly attractive because they can generate high levels of profit with moderate sales volume. For example, eBay's auction market provides a highly attractive opportunity partly because it generates profit margins in excess of 80 percent.[15]

An important aspect of the assessment of market size and profitability is determining how the company will generate revenue. What are the opportunities for monetizing the value creation? Consider typical sources of revenue in the New Economy—advertising revenue, referrals, "affiliate program" fees[16], customer subscriptions, and the purchase of products and services.

To assess the overall opportunity attractiveness, managers must not only rate each factor separately but also rate them together as a whole. Whether a particular factor helps, is neutral, or hinders the overall market opportunity, the manager must try to gauge the magnitude of its impact. Look across all factors to see the overall effect (see Overall Opportunity Analysis Summary of Priceline.com in Exhibit 2-9). These effects may be multiplicative and not additive. The value of this exercise is to think about all the pluses and minuses encountered. In addition, we are merely trying to determine if this situation is a moderate, good, great, or gigantic opportunity.

HOW DO WE PREPARE A "GO/NO-GO" ASSESSMENT?

At this point, the management team should be able to describe the opportunity that lies before them. The team can describe the value system for the industry and has a strong sense for how intervention into this value system and the Customer Decision Process could either create new benefits, enhance existing ones, or unlock value trapped in the current system. The team should be able to clearly describe the market as a set of customer segments supported by data or strong hypotheses about the underserved or unmet needs of one or more of these customer segments. This understanding provides the basis to create a high-level value proposition and to determine capabilities the team can bring to bear to participate successfully in the business. The examination of potential competitors enhances the team's thinking about where to participate in the identified market and what to bring to the opportunity.

We suggest the management team craft an "opportunity story," which is really the first rough outline of the business plan. The story should accomplish all of the following tasks:

- Briefly describe the target segment(s) within the selected value system.
- Articulate the high-level value proposition (see Chapter 3).

Exhibit 2-9

PRICELINE.COM OVERALL
OPPORTUNITY ASSESSMENT

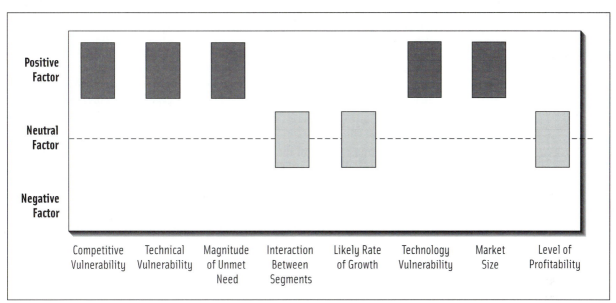

- Spell out the expected elements of customer benefits (we largely focused on functional benefits in this chapter; however, needs can be emotional or self-expressive).

- Identify the critical capabilities and resources needed to deliver the customer benefits.

- Lay out the critical "reasons to believe" that the identified capabilities and resources will be a source of advantage over the competition.

- Categorize the critical capabilities (and supporting resources) as "in house," "build," "buy," or "collaborate."

- Describe how the company will monetize the opportunity (i.e., how it will capture some portion of the value that it creates for its customers).

- Provide an initial sense for the magnitude of the financial opportunity for the company.

The team now must decide whether or not to proceed to defining the specific value proposition and designing a business model. This should be the first of several "go/no-go" decision gates. If it hasn't already done so, the team should define the criteria to be met before members will feel comfortable about proceeding to the next step of the business development process.

If uncertainty remains around one or more of the gating questions, the management team must judge whether or not additional analysis would remove uncertainty or if there are ways to proceed while revisiting the areas of greatest concern.

The team should not proceed too far down the path toward business model development if members cannot reach a consensus on passing these initial gates.

SCHWAB'S MARKET OPPORTUNITY

Let us now apply the market opportunity framework for Charles Schwab. On January 15, 1998, Schwab launched Schwab.com. In doing so, Schwab was able to provide brokerage services through an integrated online and offline offering of high quality service, information, and tools at lower prices. We will apply our framework to identify some of the market opportunities for Schwab at that time.

Our first step is to identify the business arena in which Schwab participated. For years, Charles Schwab was an established brand name in the brokerage services business. But within the brokerage services business, where could Schwab release trapped value or create new value?

Exhibit 2-10 illustrates some of the areas of potential value release or generation. One way Schwab made markets more efficient, or released trapped value, was by aggregating suppliers and buyers of mutual funds through its OneSource® program, initiated in 1992. This program aggregated mutual funds from a number of suppliers and allowed users to research and trade these funds free of charge. Schwab charged the mutual fund suppliers a small percentage fee. OneSource® released value for Schwab by providing an additional revenue source without charging its customers. It also released value for investors by providing them access to a wide selection of mutual funds that they could trade commission-free.

Schwab could also create new value for itself and its investors. For example, Schwab introduced new-to-the-world functionality through its after-hours trading program, launched in October 1999. After-hours orders could be placed on most Nasdaq and certain listed securities between 4:05 P.M. and 8 P.M. eastern standard time, Monday through Friday. This initiative created significant new value for Schwab by increasing transaction volumes and associated commissions. It also created new-to-the-world value to investors by providing an added convenience—the ability to trade even after markets closed.

 Exhibit 2-10 SCHWAB: DEFINING EXISTING OR NEW VALUE SYSTEM

	How?
Released Trapped Value	• Making markets more efficient
	• Compressing or eliminating steps in current value systems
	• Enabling ease of access
	• Disrupting current pricing power
Create New Value	• Customizing offerings
	• Extending reach/access
	• Building community
	• Collaborating across multiple people, locations, and time
	• Introducing new-to-the-world functionality or experience

Exhibit 2-11

SCHWAB: UNMET AND UNDERSERVED
NEEDS (1997 TIME FRAME)

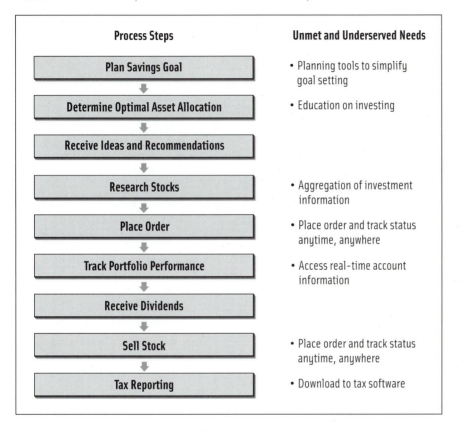

Process Steps	Unmet and Underserved Needs
Plan Savings Goal	• Planning tools to simplify goal setting
Determine Optimal Asset Allocation	• Education on investing
Receive Ideas and Recommendations	
Research Stocks	• Aggregation of investment information
Place Order	• Place order and track status anytime, anywhere
Track Portfolio Performance	• Access real-time account information
Receive Dividends	
Sell Stock	• Place order and track status anytime, anywhere
Tax Reporting	• Download to tax software

To attract customers from other providers in the brokerage services market, Schwab had to identify needs either unmet or underserved by competitors. As was discussed in stage 2 of the market opportunity framework, we can use the investment purchase process to identify such needs.

Exhibit 2-11 illustrates the purchase process for investors in late 1997 and indicates areas of unmet or underserved needs at that time. The purchase process is broken into three main areas: prepurchase (including steps such as determining optimal asset allocation and researching stocks), purchase (involving the order placement step), and postpurchase (including steps such as tracking portfolio performance and selling stocks). There were a number of needs that were not addressed or were served poorly by competitors. For example, there was a lack of effective and comprehensive tools that could help investors plan their investments based on their personal needs. Investors often made decisions without complete information, helpful investment strategies, or useful investment tips. A one-stop shop that would aggregate investment information as well as provide an investment education program (both online and offline) would help address these poorly met needs and would help investors make smarter investment decisions. Not surprisingly, Schwab's recent marketing message in 1999 centered around the motto: "We are creating a smarter kind of investor."

The next step in our analysis of Schwab's opportunities in late 1997 is to better understand its target customers, whose needs it would strive to serve. We can do this by breaking down the market into meaningful and actionable segments and then identifying the segments of highest priority. We have selected some key variables that, combined with each other, help segment the brokerage services market. These are as follows:

- **Demographics:** The *lifestage* of a consumer (single, married, with children, mature) corresponds to his or her willingness to take on risk and to the purpose of any investment (college education, retirement). *Income/occupation* (high net worth; professionals making less than or more than $150K; other white collar, blue collar, retiree, university student) corresponds to the investor's price sensitivity, the amount he or she is able to invest, as well as to his or her need for advice or complete fund management.

- **Behavior:** The *trading frequency* of investors (frequent traders versus investors who buy and hold) correlates to the investor's need for information versus advice, as well as his or her sensitivity to commission rates. The *current broker of choice* (current offline Schwab customer versus a non-Schwab customer) correlates directly to the priority target segments because Schwab would be targeting all of its existing customers but only some of its noncustomers.

Combining these variables can yield distinct, actionable, and meaningful segments of the market to which Schwab could offer its brokerage services. Exhibit 2-12 illustrates the market segmentation. It also indicates the target segments of primary, secondary, and tertiary priority for Schwab at the time (late 1997) as well as those segments that were not of priority. Over the medium term, Schwab want-

Exhibit 2-12

SCHWAB SEGMENTATION
(1997 TIME FRAME)

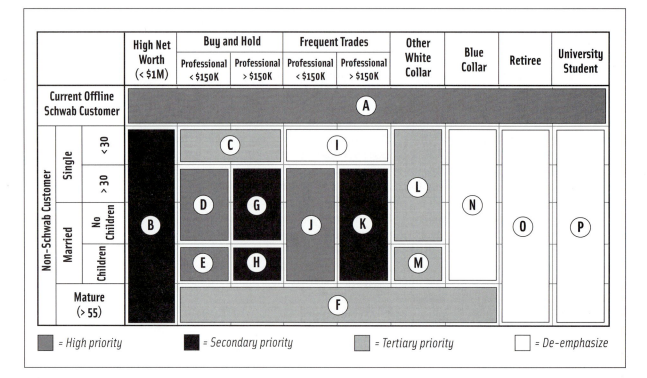

Exhibit 2-13

SCHWAB—COMPETITOR MAP TO SEGMENTS

Segments	Schwab	Merrill Lynch	Ameritrade	DLJDirect
B. High Net Worth	◕	●	○	◐
G. Buy and Hold (> $150K)	◕	◐	◕	◔
J. Frequent Traders (< $150K)	◕	○	◕	◔

● High performance level   ◐ Medium performance level   ○ Low performance level

ed to move all existing Schwab offline high priority customers (segment A) to its online offering to decrease related costs and to expand the number of services offered to them. Non-Schwab customers who were older professionals, married or single, making less than $150K, and performing frequent trades (segment J) were also of high priority. This segment required comprehensive and up-to-the-minute information as well as the ability to perform trades at any time through different channels. In addition, this segment was affluent enough to be willing to pay Schwab's moderately priced commissions in exchange for valuable information and services.

A secondary priority segment was the high net-worth individuals who were not Schwab customers at the time (segment B). They required comprehensive information, advice, and, potentially, complete fund management. To serve these customers, Schwab would need to develop a network of independent financial advisors.

Even though Schwab had developed AdvisorSource since June 1995, this referral service for fee-based advisors was not a core capability and would need time and resources to develop. Hence, Schwab first focused on providing comprehensive information and service to the primary priority segment and would gradually develop the independent advisor network to serve this segment. Finally, a no-priority segment for Schwab was non-Schwab customers who were university students (segment P). This segment was highly price-sensitive and invested small amounts, making them unattractive potential customers for Schwab.

Having identified the segments to target as well as the prioritization of these segments, the next steps are to determine Schwab's available resources to serve these segments and the magnitude of the opportunity. An essential component of assessing the opportunity magnitude is measuring competitive intensity. Exhibit 2-13 focuses on three of Schwab's key competitors in late 1997, Merrill Lynch (offering full brokerage), DLJDirect (offering quality information and service), and Ameritrade (offering trades at highly discounted rates). We should now examine the degree to which Schwab and each competitor were serving three of Schwab's target segments. For example, Schwab was serving the frequent-trader segment well through reduced prices for frequent traders as well as multiple channels for trading, including phone, online, and branches. Schwab would eventually be able to serve that segment even better in August 1999 by introducing its Velocity Software Program, which enabled very fast transactions for frequent traders.

By contrast, Merrill Lynch was not well positioned to serve the frequent-trader segment because its very high commission rates constituted a prohibitive cost. Ameritrade was also well positioned to serve frequent traders by offering one of the lowest commission rates in the market ($8 per trade). However, Ameritrade offered limited research, which made the company less attractive to long-term investors than it did to the short-term "momentum" traders. Ameritrade would eventually add free real-time quotes as well as a wireless channel for trading, thereby enhancing its offering to frequent traders. Finally, DLJDirect was poorly positioned to serve the frequent-trader segment. Its commission rates at $20 per trade, albeit lower than Merrill Lynch, were high for frequent traders and there were no commission discounts for high trade volume. Eventually, DLJDirect would increase the attractiveness of its offering to frequent traders. Its Marketspeed 3.0 software would allow for faster trade execution, and it would also offer real-time quotes and wireless alerts to its investors.

Competitive intensity is just one of the eight factors to consider while assessing overall opportunity attractiveness for Schwab. Exhibit 2-14 provides a preliminary rating of these factors for Schwab in late 1997. For example, the competitive vulnerability was a negative factor because of the high degree of competitive intensity in the brokerage services industry and because many new competitors were entering the market. The technology vulnerability was a neutral factor. Newly developed technologies did constitute a threat to Schwab, but they required significant investments over time in research and developing technologies. The probable rate of

 Exhibit 2-14 SCHWAB.COM OVERALL OPPORTUNITY ASSESSMENT

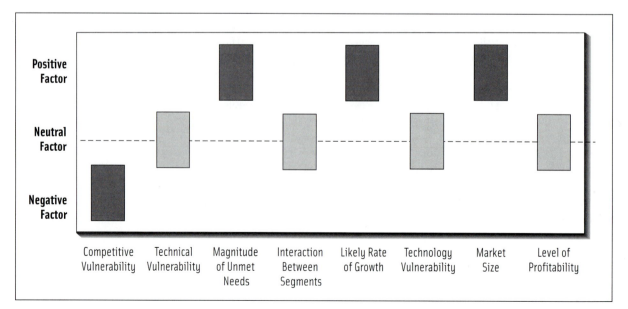

growth of the online brokerage industry was a positive factor because the migration from offline to online brokerage was likely to occur at a very fast pace. The combination and consideration of these factors leads to the conclusion that fully embracing the online brokerage market and targeting the segments outlined above was an attractive opportunity for Schwab to pursue in late 1997.

SUMMARY

1. What is the framework to market-opportunity analysis?

The market-opportunity analysis framework consists of five main investigative stages, a final assessment of the opportunity, and a final "go/no go" decision. The five stages are as follows: (1) seed opportunities in the existing or new value system, (2) uncover the opportunity nucleus, (3) identify the target customers, (4) declare the company's resource-based opportunity for advantage, and (5) assess competitive, technological, and financial attractiveness.

2. Is market-opportunity analysis different in the New Economy?

Market-opportunity analysis is distinctive in the following five areas: (1) competition occurs *across* industry boundaries rather than *within* industry boundaries, (2) competitive developments and responses are occurring at an unprecedented speed, (3) competition occurs between alliances of companies rather than between individual companies, (4) consumer behavior is still in the early stages of being defined; thus it is easier to influence and change consumer behavior, and (5) industry value chains or "systems" are rapidly being reconfigured.

3. What are two generic "value types"?

Firms should look at the value system as a lens that yields ideas about new business possibilities. Specifically, a firm is looking for either (1) trapped value to be liberated, or (2) new-to-the-world value to be introduced.

4. How do we identify unmet and/or underserved needs?

New value creation is based on doing a better job of meeting customer needs. Customers will switch from their old supplier only if the new company does a better job of meeting some set of needs. The Customer Decision Process is an organizing framework to look systematically for unmet or underserved needs. The process maps the activities and the choices customers make in accessing a specific experience within a value system. The Customer Decision Process lays out the series of steps from awareness of the experience to the purchase experience and follows on through the use experience. The process of generating a map of the Customer Decision Process may help to generate new ideas about unmet or underserved needs.

5. What determines the specific customers the company is to pursue?

To be effective and efficient, it is essential for the company to know which customer groups are most attractive, which groups the company should pursue, which groups the company should de-emphasize, and what offerings to present to which target segment. Customer segmentation, or the grouping of similar customers in order to better serve their needs, must be both actionable (consistent with how the company can take action in the market) and also meaningful (correlating to differences in how customers will behave). Simple market maps profiling the segments will identify "where the money is," how well competitors serve the segments, and where underserved customers reside.

6. Who provides the resources to deliver the benefits of the offering?

Having determined the initial customer focus of the business, the company should stake out the capabilities and technology needed to deliver the benefits of the offering. The management team should identify at least three or four resources or assets that make up the winning resource system that it can bring to bear, create, or provide through business partnerships. This resource system is central to delivering new benefits or unlocking trapped value, the core of the company's value story, and should hold the promise for an advantage when compared with the current and prospective players in the targeted marketspace. A resource system is a discrete collection of individual and organizational activities and assets that, when combined, create organizational capabilities. These capabilities allow the company to serve customer needs.

On its own, a company may not be able to bring all the necessary resources to deliver value to its target segments. In opportunity assessment, a company must be realistic about any missing capability gaps. Partnering may be an effective alternative to building or acquiring the capability. The potential partners for a company can be grouped into two categories—complementors and traditional partners.

7. How do we assess the attractiveness of the opportunity?

There are eight factors in four areas that we can assess to determine the character and magnitude of the opportunity: competitive intensity with a (1) map of direct and indirect competitors; customer dynamics with levels of (2) unconstrained opportunity, (3) segment interaction, and (4) the likely rate of growth; technology vulnerability with the impact of (5) the penetration of enabling technologies and (6) new technologies on the value proposition; and microeconomics with an estimate of the (7) size/volume of the market and (8) level of profitability.

8. How do we prepare a "go/no-go" assessment?

An opportunity story may be thought of as the first draft of a business plan. The story should articulate the value proposition and the target customers. It should demonstrate the benefits to these customers and the way in which the company will "monetize" the opportunity. It should estimate the magnitude (in financial terms) of the opportunity, identify the key capabilities and resources, and then, finally, discuss the "reasons to believe." In other words, the story should tell why the company's capabilities will create a competitive advantage for the new business in serving its target customers.

The management team must decide whether or not to proceed to defining the specific value proposition and designing a business model. This should be the first of several "go/no-go" decision gates. The team should define the criteria to be met in order to feel comfortable in proceeding to the next step of the business development process. If uncertainty remains around one or more of the gating questions, the management team must judge whether or not additional analysis would remove uncertainty or if there are ways to proceed while revisiting the areas of greatest concern. The team should not proceed too far down a path toward business model development if they cannot reach a consensus on passing these initial gates.

KEY TERMS

marketspace	**Customer Decision Process**
market-opportunity analysis	**segmentation**
value system	**actionable segmentation**
"co-opetition"	**meaningful segmentation**
Metcalfe's Law	**the offering**
trapped value	**resource system**
new-to-the-world value	**direct competitors**
opportunity nucleus	**indirect competitors**

Endnotes

[1] Brandenburger, Adam M. and Barry J. Nalebuff. 1996. *Co-opetition*. New York: Currency Doubleday.

[2] Web: Napster's program, which raised copyright issues, has been adapted to search and copy other types of files without a firm's OK. Hufstutter, P. J. and Greg Miller. 2000. Hackers find new uses for song-swap software. *Los Angeles Times*, 24 March, Home edition, Business section.

[3] Shapiro, Carl and Hal R. Varian. 1999. *Information rules*. Boston: Harvard Business School Press. This book contains an excellent and detailed examination of network economics.

[4] Interested readers could learn more about value chains and value systems in the following cited reference: Porter, Michael E. 1985. *Competitive advantage: Creating and sustaining superior performance*. New York: The Free Press; London: Collier Macmillan.

[5] This sidebar is summarized from the following article: Leonard, Dorothy, and Jeffrey F. Rayport. 1997. Spark innovation through empathic design. *Harvard Business Review* 75, no. 6 (Nov–Dec): 102–13.

[6] This sidebar is partly drawn from an article authored by the following individual. Pink, Daniel H. 1998. Metaphor marketing. *Fast Company*, issue no. 14 (April): 214.

[7] Keller, Kevin Lane. 1998. *Strategic brand management: Building, measuring and managing brand equity*. Upper Saddle River, NJ: Prentice Hall, Inc., pp. 317–8.

[8] Pink, Daniel H. 1998. Metaphor marketing. *Fast Company,* issue no. 14 (April): 214.

[9] Kotler, Philip. 2000. Chapter 9 in *Marketing management*. 10th ed. Upper Saddle River, NJ: Prentice Hall.

[10] Porter, Michael E. 1980. *Competitive strategy*. New York: The Free Press, p. 5.

[11] *ibid.*, p. 23.

[12] Interested persons should refer to these references for further reading: Foster, Richard N. 1986. *Innovation: The attacker's advantage*. New York: Summit Books. Christensen, Clayton M. 1997.

The innovator's dilemma: When new techniques cause great firms to fail. Boston: Harvard Business School Press.

[13]Kelly, Kevin. 1998. *10 new rules for the new economy.* New York: Viking, p. 11.

[14]Stone, Brad. 1999. Amazon's pet projects: Start-Ups jump when the online giant comes calling. *Newsweek,* 21 June.

[15]Simons, David. 1999. What's the deal: The true cost of marketing. *Industry Standard,* 2 December.

Zacks Investment Research, Inc. 2000. EBAY INC annual income statement, 14 May. URL: *http://www1.zacks.com/cgi-bin/JMFR/Free Report?ref=DEF&ticker=EBAY&hist=1.*

[16]For more information on affiliate programs see Chapter 4.

Business Models

The previous chapter on market-opportunity analysis answered the question "Where will the business compete?" In this chapter we turn our attention to the question "How will the business win?" Certainly, winning is relative to the goals of the business. A business may choose to define victory in terms of revenue targets, gross margin, number of unique visitors, or other criteria.

Regardless of the goals of the enterprise, the business must first specify its business model. In this chapter, we introduce the concept of a business model for the New Economy. A New Economy business model requires four choices on the part of senior management. These include the specification of (1) a value proposition or a value cluster for targeted customers, (2) a marketspace offering—which could be a product, service, information or all three, (3) a unique, defendable resource system, and (4) a financial model.

QUESTIONS

Please consider the following questions as you read this chapter:

1. What is a business model?

2. Do firms compete on value propositions or value clusters?

3. How does a firm develop an online offering—whether product, service, or information?

4. What is a successful, unique resource system? What are characteristics of good resource systems?

This chapter was coauthored by Bernie Jaworski, Jeffrey Rayport, Leo Griffin, and Yannis Dosios. Substantive input was also provided by Yakir Siegal, Sharon Grady, and Lisa Ferri.

5. **What are the financial models available to firms?**

6. **What business classification schemes seem most appropriate for the New Economy?**

In order to understand the four components of a business model, we will apply the framework to the highly competitive, rapidly changing flower industry. The domestic retail flower business is a $15 billion industry. The industry is highly fragmented, with no national brand, multiple layers of distribution, and uneven product quality. Given the complexity of the supply chain, flowers are typically sold 10 to 12 days after they are harvested. On the customer side, approximately 60 percent of all flower sales are made by walk-in customers. When flowers are delivered, 80 percent are local—that is, they remain in the same place as where they were ordered.

The online flower market was approximately $350 million in 1999. Industry experts predict that the online flower industry will be a $2.5 billion market by the year 2004. However, who will eventually win in this space is unclear at the current time. The value propositions of the major online retailers are quite similar. Hence, one would expect some consolidation and industry fallout.

A recent *Los Angeles Times* article noted that FTD.com has lost 75 percent of its value since it went public in fall 1999.[1] Equally important, FTD.com and the other major flower sites are experiencing a significant cash drain. In particular, the article noted the following:

- FTD is spending $6.1 million per month to stay in business but is taking in only $2.2 million in gross revenues for a $3.9 million deficit per month. With $37.9 million in cash and current assets, it will run out of cash by the end of 2000.

- 1-800-flowers is running a monthly deficit of $22.4 million and can hold out for 8.4 months.

- Gerald Stevens is losing $17.7 million a month and will last less than 2 months.

- PC Flowers & Gifts is losing $326,000 a month and can hold on for 13 months with its current cash and assets.

Therefore, the prediction is that the number of online flower retailers will "shrink dramatically." Indeed, FTD.com's CEO noted that by the end of the year 2000 there will be only two remaining players, FTD.com and 1-800-flowers. While it is difficult to forecast the future, it is entirely possible that 1-800-flowers could be one of the casualties of this consolidation.

In this chapter, we will consider components of the business models of key players in this industry (see Exhibit 3-1). As discussed in Chapter 2, we observe significant cross-industry competition emerging in this product category. Flowers are sold online by conventional brick-and-mortar flower merchants (e.g., FTD.com connects approximately 21,000 North American local retail florists to exchange orders for out-of-town deliveries), new online flower merchants (e.g., proflowers.com), and cross-industry players in the gift, card, and crafts markets and in other categories (e.g., Hallmark.com). With this backdrop, firms must make critical decisions concerning how to win in the online world.

Exhibit 3-1. COMPONENTS OF A BUSINESS MODEL

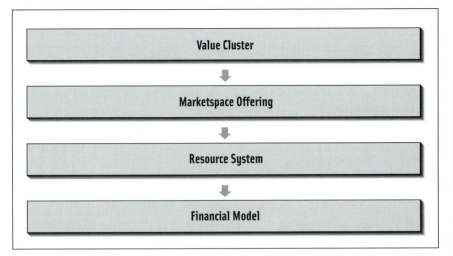

WHAT IS A BUSINESS MODEL?

The New Economy **business model** requires four choices on the part of senior management that include the specification of (1) a value proposition or a value cluster for targeted customers, (2) a marketspace offering—which could be a product, service, information, or all three, (3) a unique, defendable resource system, and (4) a financial model.

In this chapter, we consider each of the components of the business model. While each component is considered sequentially, it is likely that the senior management team "iterates," reexamining the various steps as they consider these critical decisions. Our most important message in this chapter is the need to base all of these decisions on the forces that are unfolding in the marketplace. That is, each step in the proposed process is fundamentally based around the benefits that matter most to customers. All else being equal, firms that are able to understand both current and future customer needs are likely to be the long-term winners in their respective industries.

Do Firms Compete on Value Propositions or Value Clusters?

The first step in the articulation of the business model is to clearly specify the **value proposition** for the business. Construction of a value proposition requires management to specify the following three items: (1) choice of target segment, (2) choice of focal customer benefits, and (3) rationale for why the firm can deliver the benefit package significantly better than competitors in the same space.

A value proposition can be considered a basic or baseline case. However, a recent alternate view, which we term a value-cluster approach, argues that because of the customization capabilities available to online businesses, multiple segments of customers can be addressed with a variety or combination of benefits offered. The value proposition is no longer singular but is a **value cluster** composed of these three parts: (1) the choice of target customer *segments,* (2) a particular focal *combination* of customer-driven benefits that are offered, and (3) the rationale for why this firm and its *partners* can deliver the value cluster significantly better than competitors can.

Choice of Segments. The first decision in the construction of a value cluster (or proposition) is the selection of target segments. A careful market-opportunity analysis, as reviewed in Chapter 2, should reveal the segments in which a particular firm can be competitive. While a number of classical frameworks exist to assess the segment-choice decision, most reduce the analysis to two basic dimensions: the attractiveness of the market and the firm's ability to compete in the market. Market attractiveness is a function of many variables,[2] but the key decision variables frequently reduce to the following:

- **Market Size and Growth Rates.** The overall dollar size of the market and percentage growth rates of the market segments.
- **Unmet or Insufficiently Met Customer Needs.** Customers are either not being served or not being served well by existing players.
- **Weak or Nonexistent Competitors.** Obviously, it is best to enter markets where competition is either not evident, performing poorly, or does not have sufficient resources to win the market.

The firm's ability to compete in a particular segment can be assessed by examining how well their business strengths (relative to competitors) match the customer benefits sought in a segment. For example, if a particular online flower retailer has unique strengths (e.g., such as exclusive sourcing of fresh flowers) and the target segment highly desires that strength (e.g., freshness of flowers), then there would be a strong match between the *relative* business strength and the desires of this segment.

In addition to the traditional market attractiveness and the firm's ability dimensions, one important factor strongly enters into the online segment-choice decision—degree of fit (or conflict) with existing channels. The 1-800-flowers.com and proflowers.com offline businesses are very compatible, indeed synergistic, with the new online businesses because their order fulfillment processes, payment services, and supply chain are the same.

In Chapter 2 we discussed alternative ways that a given firm can segment the online market. Within the context of the flower industry, this can translate into demographic segments, benefit segments, or some combination of the two. Thus, firms such as 1-800-flowers.com must decide which particular portion or segment of the market they will attempt to dominate or own. Segmentation-approach options are many, including such demographic approaches as (1) the under-30 segment and (2) the upper-income segment. Benefit segment options include selecting those who are looking for the (1) freshest flowers, (2) most convenient buying method, or (3) the lowest priced flowers. As shown in Chapter 2, we believe that it is critical to select a segmentation approach that maximizes both actionability and meaningfulness.

Choice of Focal Customer Benefits. The second step in the articulation of a value proposition or cluster is the specification of the key benefits that are to be delivered to the target segment. Conventional offline marketing and business strategy textbooks often recommend that firms must focus on one or two critical benefits. The examples often cited include Volvo (i.e., the safety benefit), Southwest Airlines (i.e., convenience and low-price benefits), or the Four Seasons (i.e., outstanding service). Consistent with the segment focus argument above, authors argue that firms that attempt to compete on more than one benefit create two basic problems. The first, on the demand-side, is that customers will be confused by the messages sent by the company. The second, on the supply-side, is that systems must be uniquely constructed to deliver certain benefits. Choosing two highly conflicting benefits (e.g., fast delivery and low price) will lead to compromises in the development of strategy—the classic "stuck in the middle"—providing average performance on two benefits while other firms focus on delivering high performance on only one of the benefits.

Now let us turn to the online world. The question as we begin to examine various online businesses is whether they focus on one, two, or multiple benefits. Most of the well-respected flower sites seem to focus on providing the freshest flowers.

However, after providing this core benefit they tend to differ somewhat in their other benefit offerings. Some tend to focus on "complementary gifts," some on "fast delivery," and others on "low prices." For example, FTD is emphasizing both "fresh flowers" and "complementary gift offerings."

Some authors argue that the Internet will lead to the commodization of products, whereby all products are viewed equally and the customer selects products based solely on price. For example, these proponents argue that products, such as the Palm VII, can be comparatively shopped across the Internet using "bots," such as mySimon.com. Once the product is located, these authors would argue that customers would select the lowest priced site, and no other criteria would matter.

However, we would argue that this search process results in more customer information but does not necessarily lead to the choice of the lowest priced site. Emergent research suggests that price sensitivity can actually decrease when usability of quality information increases. Moreover, even when consumers have access to competitive price information, the quality of information on the site can actually increase customer retention.[3]

In Exhibit 3-2, we provide the results of a study that was reported in a J.P. Morgan report on retailing.[4] This study illustrated that price is indeed an important decision criteria (e.g., 19 percent reporting cared about that attribute). However, a host of other services that imply different benefits were significantly more likely to influence the purchase decision. These included such attributes as customer support, on-time delivery, shipping and handling, and privacy concerns.

Thus, a strong argument could be made that the Internet will lead to much more differentiation as compared with the traditional brick-and-mortar business world.

| Exhibit 3-2 | SHATTERING THE MYTH THAT CONSUMERS CARE ONLY ABOUT PRICES ONLINE |

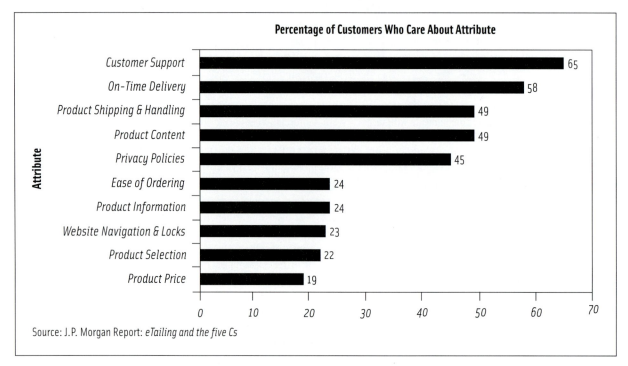

Source: J.P. Morgan Report: *eTailing and the five Cs*

Firms that are better able to offer services and the associated benefits than the competition will continue to compete and win on attributes other than price. Thus, to return to our example, customers who use shop bots such as mySimon.com may find the lowest priced Palm VII on a largely unknown site and the next lowest priced PalmVII on the Palm.com site (i.e., the designers and manufacturers of the Palm VII). Will customers choose the lowest priced Palm VII on the unknown site or use other criteria? Our view is that some customers will buy the product from the unknown site; however, the vast majority of customers will use other criteria and buy from dealers who they perceive to deliver other attributes such as customer support, on-time delivery, and so on. That is, customers will choose to buy from direct dealers such as Palm.com.

Choice of Unique and Differentiating Capabilities.

The third component of the value proposition is the compelling rationale why a particular online firm can provide a single benefit (or multiple benefits) significantly better than competitors. Thus, in contrast to segment choice and benefits, this third component focuses on factors inside the firm (or with partners) that lead to the superior delivery of targeted benefit(s). These have variously been termed "core competencies," "business strengths," "strategic control points," "unique resources," and "unique capabilities."[5]

The key issue is whether these unique capabilities can be linked directly to the core benefit or benefits that form the value proposition. Here we broadly define capabilities to include tangible assets (e.g., location), intangible assets (e.g., brand name), and capabilities/skills of the organization (e.g., supply chain management).[6] That is, firms can have superior performance of selected capabilities but these capabilities can be unrelated to the delivery of the critical benefit. A litmus test for the unique capability is whether it can be directly tied to customer benefits that matter most. We more fully elaborate on the capability concept in the resource-system portion later in the chapter.

Value Propositions or Clusters.

Given our discussion above, we now have a good understanding of the three concepts needed to construct a value proposition or cluster. Below we have constructed sample value propositions for four of the major dot-com flower competitors.[7] Keep in mind that we are not suggesting that these are defendable value propositions; rather, our intent is to illustrate how a proposition can be constructed.

- PC Flowers & Gifts serves the "special occasions" segment (*the target segment*) with "fresh flowers, complementary gifts, and lower prices" (*the three key benefits*) because of their accumulated online experience and knowledge since 1989 and their unique, broad product line of complementary gifts (*the two key differentiating capabilities*).

- proflowers serves the "price-sensitive and convenience-oriented customers" with the "freshest cut flowers at a competitive price" because of their unique sourcing and FedEx shipping arrangements.

- FTD.com serves "the mid- to high-end market" by providing the "easiest way to send flowers and gifts" because of their strong brand name, market communications, and supplier network.

- 1-800-flowers.com serves the "mid- to high-end market" with a broad gift assortment, fresh flowers, reasonable prices, and easy access because of their strong brand name, product and media partnerships, and brick-and-mortar network of franchises (i.e., Bloomnet).

The question that should be asked at this point is how differentiated are these value propositions—not simply the desired position, but the firm's ability to uniquely "own" this position in the minds of customers. Three specific classes of criteria should be used to assess the quality of the value proposition or cluster of a company:

- **Customer Criteria.** Multiple criteria can be employed to assess to what degree the target customer values the position. Do target customers understand the proposition or cluster? Is it relevant to their needs? Is it believable? Is it perceived as unique or as "me too," or indistinguishable from other propositions or clusters? Will it provoke action on the part of the target customer?
- **Company Criteria.** Will the organization "rally around" the proposition or cluster? Does the company have the resources or capabilities to own this cluster? Will it block or facilitate the eventual move to additional vertical markets?
- **Competitive Criteria.** Are other competitors attempting to hold a similar proposition or cluster? Will competitors allow the focal company to own the stated cluster in the market? Can current competitors match this cluster? How easy is it for future competitors to match this cluster?

A casual review of many of the principal flower sites reveals that several competitors are attempting to own similar segments with similar benefits. Equally significant, one could argue that few of the sites have unique capabilities that cannot be replicated by others. Collectively, this suggests that the markets are likely to be intensely competitive with no clear indication of who has the unique capabilities or activities needed to win in this segment.

How Does a Firm Develop an Online Offering?

Once the value proposition has been articulated, the next step is to fully articulate the online product, service, and information offering. Keep in mind that at this stage, we are not designing the content and "look-and-feel" of the website (this will be the focus of Chapter 4—Customer Interface), rather we are providing a broad description of the actual product or service that will be provided online.

In particular, the senior management team must complete three sequential tasks: (1) identify the scope of the offering, (2) identify the Customer Decision Process, and (3) map the offering (product, services, and information) to the consumer decision process.

Scope of Offering.
The scope refers to the number of categories of products and services that are offered in the site. There is a continuum of scope that exists from a firm focusing on one product category (termed a "category killer") as compared to a firm focusing on a large number of categories. Secondspin.com, Reel.com, and Dealtime.com illustrate the various levels of scope. Secondspin.com, at one end of the spectrum, focuses principally on the selling of used CDs ("category killer"); Dealtime.com, at the other end of the spectrum, sells a wide variety of electronics and other goods; and Reel.com, somewhere in the middle of the spectrum, focuses on multiple video products including DVDs and VHS videotapes. Below, we describe two specific types of scope.

- **Category-Specific Dominance.** Category-specific dominance refers to companies that focus exclusively on one product category, such as flowers, candy, or gifts. However, from observation, it is increasingly difficult to isolate firms that are focusing only on one category. Within the online flowers category, firms seem to be focusing on a combination of flowers, gifts, and other complementary goods, such as candy.

- **Cross-Category Dominance.** One of the most interesting developments in the online world is the extension of product offerings from a single category to additional product categories as an attempt toward achieving cross-category dominance. The most well-known example, of course, is Amazon's initial domination of the book market and subsequent extension to CDs, videos, toys, home improvement, and auctions. Amazon is an interesting example of "supply-side" cross-category dominance. That is, Amazon offers products that naturally group together from a logistics and distribution point of view. Their products (1) are physical goods, (2) can be stored in inventory, (3) cannot be digitized, and (4) are consumer-focused, as opposed to being business-to-business focused. However, the products do not naturally cluster together around specific themes. In short, in contrast to websites such as BabyCenter.com and Chemdex.com, these particular product combinations do not necessarily make sense from the customer's point of view.

Recently, the term "metamarkets" has been used to refer to those sites that group naturally clustering categories of goods and services. According to Northwestern University marketing professor Mohanbir Sawhney, this new breed of "metamediaries" is significant since it is based on a simple insight—products and services are grouped based on how customers engage in activities rather than being based on a categorization of products and services from the physical world. Sawhney notes:

> *"Customers think in terms of activities, while firms think in terms of products. Activities that are logically related in 'cognitive space' may be spread across very diverse providers in the marketplace. Metamarkets, then, are clusters of markets in the minds of customers. Their boundaries are derived from activities that are closely related in the minds of customers, and not from the fact that they are created or marketed by related firms in related industries."*[8]

Interestingly, this observation by Sawhney has a parallel in academic literature. Consumers naturally group together products or services based upon the goals that the products help the consumers achieve.[9] For example, consumers may classify a wide variety of disparate products under an entertainment category. Do consumers categorize entertainment in terms of favorite sports, clubs/organizations, food, shows, art, or dining out? Or do they categorize based on things to do with the family or things to do when the weather is problematic? The answer is that consumers categorize products and services in a variety of ways. By implication, therefore, online businesses can be organized in a variety of goal-derived ways.

If you consider citysearch.com, you will see that consumer classification can provide significant challenges. Its homepage has two broad categories of search—complete city guides and arts and entertainment guides. Once you have searched for a destination, you then are able to choose from a broad selection of activities. For Los Angeles, you arrive at the calendarlive.com site that is supported by the *Los Angeles Times*. This site is organized by date, topic, best bets, events and entertainment updates, check traffic, buy tickets, restaurants, and other categories.

In effect, one can first make a selection on the options for evening (by date or venue choice), purchase the ticket for the event (for example, Dodgers baseball), read a review of the players, read a review of a nearby restaurant, book reservations (offline), check the various traffic reports, choose a route, and take the directions with you. These activities cross a wide range of industries—entertainment, automotive, travel, literature, and so on.

A good example of another goal-derived metamarket is BabyCenter.com. BabyCenter.com involves a wide variety of products, information, and a support community that is based on one overarching goal—the raising of a healthy baby. The site is packed with reference information, links to other online destinations, helpful hints and checklists, and ways to connect with other parents. The site also provides a search engine to research by topic, or the user can personalize the site to get information customized to the user's pregnancy or parenting stage. The site provides high-quality, medically reviewed information; a community of supportive, helpful fellow parents; and a store that sells baby and maternity items as well as offers advice on products best suited for particular lifestyles and needs.

Identify Customer Decision Process. The second step in the construction of an online offering entails articulating the consumer decision process for the various product categories. Table 3-1 provides a simplified version of the Customer Decision Process. The *Customer Decision Process* can be divided into three stages: prepurchase, purchase, and postpurchase. Within the prepurchase stage, consumers go through a number of steps, including recognizing a problem or need, searching for ideas and offerings, and evaluating the alternatives. In the purchase stage, the consumer decides to purchase and goes through the process of purchasing. The postpurchase stage involves the postdecision evaluation of levels of satisfaction and eventually the consideration of becoming a loyal customer. Finally, when the consumer is done with the product, he or she may or may not choose to dispose of the goods.

Table 3-1 provides an overview of actions that a consumer in the flower category might engage in at each step of the process. The recognition of a need for flowers may be triggered by a holiday (e.g., Valentine's Day), a personal life event (e.g., anniversary), or a more everyday event (e.g., a first date). The consumer makes an

Table 3-1 CUSTOMER DECISION PROCESS— FLOWER PURCHASE EXAMPLE

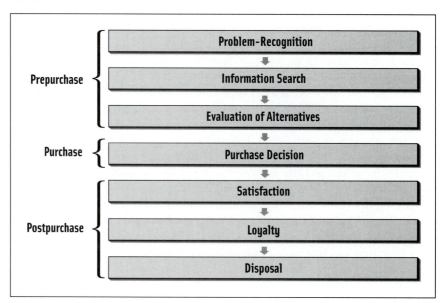

information search for ideas and offerings across whatever is available from online or offline flower vendors. After gathering gift ideas, recommendations, and advice, the consumer makes an evaluation of alternatives using a number of criteria including price, appeal, availability, convenience, and other measures. After considering and evaluating the alternatives, the consumer may make a purchase decision and choose to enclose an appropriate note or message along with the flowers. After the purchase has been made, the consumer may gain satisfaction if he or she learns that the flower order has been successfully and properly delivered. After the transaction has been completed, the consumer may want to learn more about flowers and arrangements, and the vendor may want to give additional incentives to gain customer loyalty.

The third step in the construction of the offering involves mapping products and services onto the Customer Decision Process. The idea is that the website should "walk the consumer through" the entire purchase-decision cycle and should encourage the consumer to continually revisit the cycle. Importantly, this decision cycle should be repeated for each of the product categories that are included on the site. Thus, for 1-800-flowers.com, the cycle should be completed for flowers, speciality foods, garden hardware, and other gift categories.

Exhibit 3-3 provides an illustration of the mapping exercise. We refer to this process as the mapping of an **Egg Diagram.** The process begins by first articulating the steps of the Customer Decision Process that the consumer passes through for a particular product category. Next, one identifies the products, services, and information that will aid the consumer in moving through these various stages.

Returning to the flower purchase example, we can identify site activities that assist the consumer through each step of the Customer Decision Process. To match need recognition, we might have a gift reminder service or holiday specials, for example. To aid in the information search, we could provide ideas across various categories, a store locator, recommendations by budget, a gift guru, lists of favorite gifts, or lists of best-sellers. During the evaluation of alternatives, we may provide product price, description, availability, and special delivery information. To support the purchase decision, we would accept credit cards over the phone or online, provide a "shopping basket," and show an assortment of cards and notes with appropriate messages to be delivered with the flowers. For customer satisfaction and loyalty, we could provide exceptional customer support, various free benefits or incentives, and special flower events and workshops to induce customers to return to our stores.

What Is a Successful, Unique Resource System?

The Resource System. The value proposition and offering specification are critical steps in the business model formulation because they dictate the resource system of the company.[10] The resource system shows how a company must align its internal systems (and partners) to deliver the benefits of the value proposition or cluster. Conventional wisdom suggests that the factor that sets highly successful companies apart from lesser companies is not simply the value proposition but the choice of actions and assets that are used to deliver the value proposition. These actions include the selection of capabilities and activities that uniquely deliver the value proposition.[11]

We agree with the logic that unique activities, tied to the value proposition, lead to a competitive advantage. However, we make four important modifications to the

Exhibit 3-3

EGG DIAGRAM FOR 1-800-FLOWERS.COM

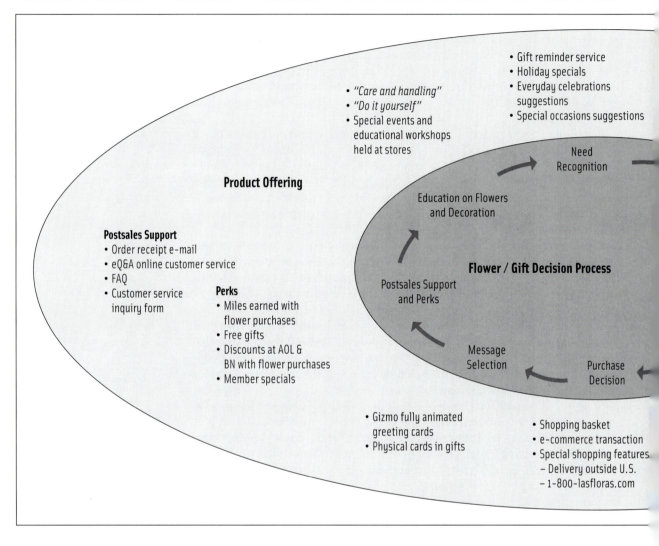

activity system logic in order to make it applicable to the online marketplace. The actions to take now not only include the selection of capabilities and activities to deliver the value proposition uniquely; they also involve the supply of all the resources needed to make the capabilities and activities a reality. Briefly, the four modifications are as follows:

- **Shift from Physical World to Virtual-and-Physical World.**[12] The first key modification is to shift from activities and capabilities in the physical world to a combination of marketplace and marketspace capabilities. Resource systems, for many companies, are a combination of the physical and virtual asset bases.

- **Shift from a Supply-Side Focus to a Demand-Side Focus.** Many activity systems focus heavily on the internal capabilities of the firm. This certainly may

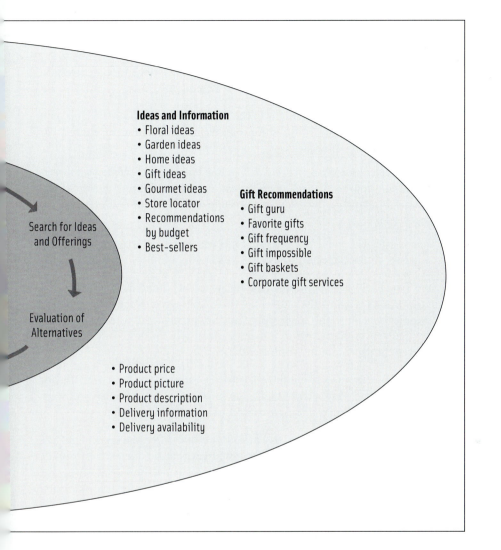

Ideas and Information
- Floral ideas
- Garden ideas
- Home ideas
- Gift ideas
- Gourmet ideas
- Store locator
- Recommendations by budget
- Best-sellers

Gift Recommendations
- Gift guru
- Favorite gifts
- Gift frequency
- Gift impossible
- Gift baskets
- Corporate gift services

Search for Ideas and Offerings

Evaluation of Alternatives

- Product price
- Product picture
- Product description
- Delivery information
- Delivery availability

seem reasonable; however, what is more appropriate is the initial focus on the benefits desired by targeted customers. The desired benefits should largely dictate the choice of capabilities.

- **Shift from Activities to Capabilities.** Capabilities are the higher order skills and assets of the company. Capabilities are typically supported by a cluster of resources which help to build and differentiate one or more of a company's capabilities. Resources[13] may take various forms; they might be *physical* assets (such as warehouses or server farms) or *intangible* assets, such as Yahoo!'s brand name or Priceline's patents on its business model. Activities might also be considered resources; for example, the incubator Idealab might argue that it is better at launching new companies than a competitor.

- **Shift from Single to Multifirm Systems.** A key aspect of the online environment is the need for partnerships. Resource systems require capabilities that must be in place and ready to use in order to win various markets. These capabilities may be resident in the firm, need to be developed in-house, acquired in the open market, or accessed through strategic partnerships and alliances.

Specifying a Resource System. With these four modifications in mind, we turn in this section to the construction of a resource system.

- **Step One: Identify Core Benefits in the Value Cluster.** The core benefits have been identified in the construction of a value proposition or cluster. For 1-800-flowers the value proposition is as follows:

  1-800-flowers.com serves the "mid to high-end market" with a broad gift assortment, fresh flowers, reasonable prices, and easy access because of their strong brand name, product and media partnerships, and brick-and-mortar network of franchises (i.e., Bloomnet).

Thus, their cluster of benefits includes fresh flowers, broad assortment, reasonable prices, and easy access. Aspects of the cluster of benefits are shown in Exhibit 3-4.

- **Step Two: Identify Capabilities That Relate to Each Benefit.** The second step in the process is to link the capabilities that are required to deliver a particular customer benefit. At this stage, we are not concerned about whether the company can deliver the capability, rather, we are simply concerned about the link between the capability and the benefit.

Exhibit 3-4 identifies the capabilities that deliver each of the four benefits. For example, "widespread, easy access" is linked to four capabilities: popularity of website, wide reach to customers, multiple contact points, and brand name.

- **Step Three: Link Resources to Each Capability.** After the capabilities are identified, the firm can identify the resources that deliver each capability. These are the key assets, activities, actions, and partnerships or alliances that create the firm's capability. For example, signed partnerships with Snap.com, AOL, MSN, and Starmedia provide media partnerships that, in turn, provide widespread points of access. The capability of multiple contact points is driven by the choice to use as many contact points as possible including telephone, online, retail stores, and affiliate programs.

- **Step Four: Identify to What Degree the Firm Can Deliver Each Capability.** The fourth step entails a close internal look at the company. Does this particular company, 1-800-flowers, contain all the necessary capabilities or must the company outsource and/or partner with others to gain missing capabilities? It is clear from the resource system chart that this firm does not hold all of the needed capabilities on its own. In particular, both product and media partnerships are required in order to make the system operate effectively.

- **Step Five: Identify Partners Who Can Complete Capabilities.** The final step is to identify key players who can fill out the resource system. For 1-800-flowers this would principally include product partnerships, such as those with Gardenworks.com, Plow and Hearth, and Greatfoods.com, and media partnerships with some of the major online sites. Exhibit 3-4 represents our best approximation of the complete resource system of 1-800-flowers.com.[14]

Exhibit 3-4

1-800-FLOWERS.COM
RESOURCE SYSTEM

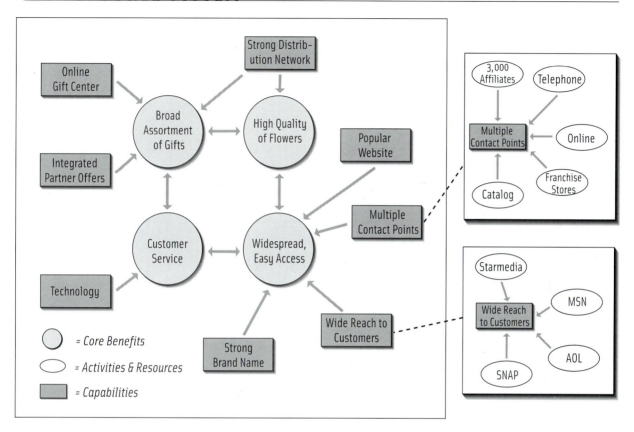

To continue our 1-800-flowers example, we have crafted an egg diagram that reflects both online and offline components. Exhibit 3-5 provides an overview of the types of offline and online products and services that are offered by 1-800-flowers. You will notice that many of the offline products and services integrate both the telephone reps as well as the in-store personnel.

We would also need to adjust our resource system model to integrate online and offline activities and assets in various combinations. For example, the capability of "wide reach to customers" might need to be supported by four online partnerships. The capability of "multiple contact points" may need to be supported by three offline (i.e., telephone, franchise stores, catalog) and two online (i.e., affiliates, online store) assets.

Criteria to Assess the Quality of a Resource System.
A number of criteria can be used to assess the quality of the resource system.

- **Uniqueness of the System.** Uniqueness refers to the extent to which the organization provides benefits, capabilities, and activities that are different relative to competitors. Are there capabilities unique to the 1-800-flowers.com activity system? That is, which themes have not been copied by FTD.com, PCFlowers.com, and proflowers? One could argue that the PC Flowers & Gifts

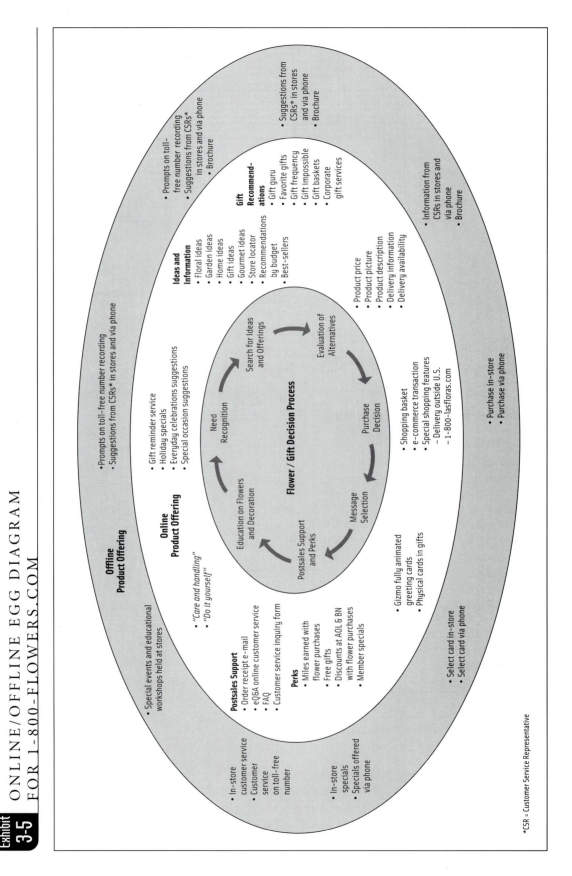

ONLINE/OFFLINE EGG DIAGRAM
FOR 1-800-FLOWERS.COM

Exhibit 3-5

*CSR = Customer Service Representative

An Integrated Online and Offline Business Model

 One of the decisions firms must confront is whether to provide both an online and offline interface to customers. The benefits of using a hybrid strategy include a persistent connection with customers, new value for customers, access to new customers, and scalability. The challenges of hybridization include cannibalization, channel conflict, customer confusion, and investor confusion.

The potential benefits for a company that uses both an online and offline strategy such as the Gap, Williams-Sonoma, or Wal-Mart are many. First, there is a persistent connection with customers—24 $\times$ 7. Also, there are new value possibilities for customers because the firm is now able to provide new-to-the-world offerings that would not be possible if they pursued only an online or an offline strategy. For example, it is now possible to place an online order anytime of day but return the merchandise to the brick-and-mortar store. Third, it is also possible to increase the size of the customer base. Wal-Mart can now reach customers that are hundreds of miles from the nearest brick-and-mortar store. Finally, the approach is "scalable" in the sense that the new integrated strategy can be replicated across regions of the world.

There are, however, potential drawbacks for the firm that does not carefully manage the integration.

Many writers are concerned that the opening of an online store will cannibalize, or draw down sales revenues, from the brick-and-mortar stores. Here they frequently cite a study conducted in fall 1999 that purportedly showed that online ventures did not provide significant new revenue increases. Rather, some 94 percent of sales were simply transfers of sales that normally would have occurred offline.[15] On the other hand, in the year 2000, we have witnessed a number of players who have gone online, and have seen a sales rise in offline products. A good example is the well-known Zagat restaurant guide. Zagat placed the entire contents of the book online and discovered that offline sales actually increased by 35 percent.[16]

One potential drawback of going online includes channel conflicts. For example, at one point in their online strategy, Compaq was forced by the dealer network to shut down their online store due to potential offline sales decreases expected by the dealers. There is also the potential for customer confusion. If the online and offline interfaces are not tightly linked, customers can become confused and frustrated. For example, if customers purchase products online but cannot return them to the brick-and-mortar stores, the customers may decide not to frequent either the online or offline store. Finally, investors may not understand how to value the online/offline integrated enterprise.

---

model is similar to the 1-800-flowers model at the benefit level, but a counter argument could show that these competitors differ at the activity level. In particular, only 1-800-flowers.com has AOL as a partner. Moreover, and perhaps more troubling to competitors in this industry is the fact that most of the competitors look very similar—nationwide florist network, combined offline and online presence, clear fit between offline and online systems, strong brand names, excellent order fulfillment, and integrated technologies.

- **Links Between Capabilities and Benefits.** Do each of the capabilities support the delivery of a customer benefit? Is the support strong or weak?

- **Links Among Capabilities in the System.** How well do the capabilities and activities complement and support one another? Are there tight linkages between the capabilities and activities? Are they consistent with the overall value cluster?

- **Links Among Resources.** Are the specific resources mutually reinforcing? Are they complementary? Are they consistent with the various benefits?

- **Links Between Virtual World and Physical World Business Systems.** Does the online resource system support or conflict with the offline system?
- **Sustainable Advantage.** Is the resource system difficult to replicate? Possessing a unique, but easily copied resource system will only deliver a fleeting advantage to a firm. Sustained high profits will only come from a sustainable competitive advantage. The ease with which a resource system can be imitated may depend on a number of factors.[17]

The Role of Partnerships.

One of the most important features of the online world is the use of partnerships. While partnerships are important in the offline world, they take on added significance in the online world as firms compete with partners to lock-in customer relationships. Often firms will look for exclusive partnerships to prevent competitors from accessing a customer base, critical technology, or key competencies that are necessary to gain competitive advantage in a particular sector. The types of partnerships that 1-800-flowers.com has pursued include the following:

- **Portal Agreements:** Portals such as AOL, Yahoo!, and Microsoft Network (MSN) provide significant brand exposure for 1-800-flowers. The AOL agreement is particularly significant given that it is an exclusive agreement through 2003.

  America Online: First agreement signed in 1994; exclusive marketer of fresh-cut flowers across key AOL brands until 2003; one-year exclusive agreement to market gardening products commencing November 1999.

  Microsoft Networks: Premier floral partner and anchor in the MSN Home and Garden Department; products, advertising and links featured on MSN Shopping Channel.

  Yahoo! Inc.: Will run banner advertisements throughout the Yahoo! Network, with additional presence in shopping area.

  Excite@Home: Markets flowers and other gifts through Excite.com and webcrawler.com websites; products, advertisments, and links featured in the Excite Shopping Channel; entered second year of marketing relationship in October 1999.

  StarMedia Network: Developing Spanish and Portuguese language versions of 1-800-flowers.com website.

- **Anchor Tenant Agreements:** Similar to other flower sites, 1-800-flowers has arranged to be the exclusive provider of flowers for retail sites such as Snap.com and Sears, Roebuck and Company.

  Snap.com: One of the 45 premier merchants in Snap shopping service (online e-superstore); anchor tenant in Snap.Com Flower Shop; to be spotlighted in select Snap.com on-air promotions, scheduled to run on the NBC Television Network during the Valentine's Day and Mother's Day time periods.

  Sears, Roebuck and Company: Licensing relationship which enables Sears customers to use their store charge cards when shopping with 1-800-flowers.com.

Proponents of activity (or resource) systems have clashed with advocates of core competencies in recent years. A core competency is a unique, enduring capability or resource of a firm that forms the basis for a long-term competitive advantage. Honda's small engine capability or Wal-Mart's supply-chain management systems are examples of core competencies in the physical world.

People who support the activity system point of view argue that it is inappropriate to reduce an organization to a few competencies or resources. Rather, the key to competitive advantage rests in the organization's ability to (1) select and critically manage core activities, and (2) simultaneously manage the "fit" between activities. From this point of view, it is systems of activities that compete with systems of activities. It is not a question of simply executing on a small set of core competencies.

Core competency advocates counterargue that the large activity systems can lead to a management mind-set that everything needs to be done well. As a result, the organization is unable to distinguish between the capabilities that can be considered "tablestakes" or "price of entry" and the capabilities that truly allow the organization to be differentiated.

- **Promotion Agreements:** Agreements have also been signed with various airlines (e.g., American Airlines, Delta) and MCI WorldCom.

> **American Airlines® Advantage®, Delta Airlines SkyMiles®, United Airlines Mileage Plus:** Earn frequent flier miles with 1-800-flowers.com purchases.
>
> **MCI Worldcom:** Receive 1-800-flowers.com gift certificates with long distance sign-up; receive 10 percent off every 1-800-flowers.com purchase with MCI WorldCom membership.
>
> **PeoplePC:** Signed one-year agreement to become key floral and gift-provider for 1-800-flowers.com that commenced October 1999.
>
> **Zapa.com:** Offers selection of online greeting cards on 1-800-flowers.com website; greeting cards never deleted by Zapa.com; users will be able to personalize greetings with their own photos, clip-art, or other multimedia creations.

What Are the Financial Models Available to Firms?

In this section, we review the financial model that follows from the resource system. We have divided this section into three parts: (1) a review of the **revenue models** that are typically practiced by online businesses, (2) a discussion of 10 approaches to **shareholder value models,** and (3) a description of **growth models** and how firms can pursue revenue growth.

Who Is Making Money on the Web?

by Alex Scherbakovsky and Yakir Siegal

 Hardly a day goes by without an Internet company having a hot IPO. It seems difficult not to do well in the lucrative Internet space. But are these companies actually making money? And, if so, which ones?

Study Methodology. Seeking an answer to these questions in the fall of 1999, we analyzed 190 public Internet companies that we grouped into the seven categories as follows: 1) Portals: companies such as Yahoo! that seek to be the user's entry point to the World Wide Web; 2) Transaction: companies that take a cut of transactions conducted on their sites, such as online brokerages and auction companies like eBay; 3) Commerce: e-tailers such as Amazon.com and Etoys.com; 4) Content: information providers such as About.com and TheStreet.com; 5) Internet Service Providers (ISPs): companies, such as Earthlink and Juno, that provide customers with access to the Internet; 6) Enablers: companies such as Cisco and Ariba that provide the hardware and software that enable communication and commerce over the Internet; and 7) Advertising: companies such as DoubleClick that sell Internet advertising.

We evaluated each company on four financial metrics: gross profit (revenue minus cost of goods sold), EBIT (earnings before interest and taxes, or operating profit), net income, and EBITM (operating profit before marketing expenses). The last metric shows whether Internet companies make money before they invest in the marketing expenses necessary to participate in the "land grab" of establishing brand identity and winning market share.

Results. The clear winners on all four metrics are the Transaction companies. Eight of the 11 stocks in this category had positive earnings, and nine had achieved operating profits. Transaction companies enjoy favorable financial performance because of their solid revenue model—they make money by taking a cut of every transaction conducted on their site. Unlike companies that focus on building a large audience with hopes to monetize those eyeballs in the future, most transaction companies extract immediate profits from their customer base.

Content providers and ISPs posted the worst numbers. Out of 34 Content stocks, only four had positive net incomes. Even after adding back the amount these companies spent on marketing, only nine showed positive EBITM. Indeed, nine of the Content stocks could not muster positive gross profits, showing that the cost of providing their content exceeded the revenues they were able to generate from their services. Most of these companies built their financial models around advertising revenue, which currently does not cover these companies' costs. Simply put, Content companies must find alternate revenue streams—or unlock new differentiation—if they hope to achieve profitability. Even C/Net, one of the few profitable Content providers, derives some of its revenues from referral fees and its television programming.

ISPs struggled to show positive operating numbers. Of the 34 companies we analyzed, all but two had net losses and negative EBIT. Although 71 percent posted positive gross profits, most of these profits were spent on marketing and infrastructure investments. The ISP field is very fragmented and is ripe for consolidation. In a few years, we are likely to see most of these money-bleeding players either go out of business or get consumed by their larger peers. Even as the winners achieve economies of scale, however, they will have to adjust their business model to address the threat of free ISP services. It is unclear when, and if, the ISP companies will start making money.

Commerce companies are also struggling, with none of the 26 showing positive earnings, and only eight achieving positive EBITM. Four Commerce players even failed to generate enough revenue to cover the cost of their merchandise. Most Commerce companies justify their poor financial performance by claiming that they are investing in infrastructure and building their customer base. Only time will show which of these players will succeed in garnering a loyal customer base that will enable them to achieve profitability.

The performance in the rest of the categories is more varied. Portals are divided into two camps—the established brands like Yahoo! are profitable, while

(continued on page 89)

(contined from page 88)

newcomers Ask Jeeves and Looksmart are bleeding money. Enablers tend to do well–like the shovel vendors during the Gold Rush. Companies such as Cisco and Check Point are making money by selling products to customers who hope to strike it rich. The Advertising companies all post positive gross profits, but spend most of those profits on marketing.

Our study of the Internet stocks concludes that, for the most part less than one in five of the companies that met the necessary requirements to go public had positive earnings. While most of the Transaction companies are making money, firms in other categories are investing heavily in building their brands and customer bases. As only a fraction of these companies will eventually succeed in monetizing their customer assets, most will realize that not everyone is making money on the Web.

Types of Revenue Models.

Firms can pursue a variety of revenue models. The following are the most frequently mentioned sources of revenue.

- **Advertising.** A particular site can earn advertising revenues through the selling of ads (i.e., banner, interstitial), site sponsorships, event underwriting, or other forms of communication.
- **Product, Service, or Information Sales.** This refers to income that is generated from the sales of goods on the site.
- **Transaction.** This refers to revenue that accrues from charging a fee or taking a portion of the transaction sum for facilitating a customer-seller transaction (e.g., Schwab, eBay).
- **Subscription.** This refers to subscriber fees for magazines, newspapers, or other information/service businesses.

Types of Shareholder Value Models.

While the revenue models clearly identify the flow of cash into the organization, they do not indicate how a company plans to generate cash flow or shareholder value—for either the long or short term. Profit and/or high margins originate from customers' perceptions that a given online business has provided better than competitors in a given marketspace. Recent writings have suggested that there are well over 20 alternative profit models that can be pursued in offline businesses.[18]

For example, a so-called "blockbuster" profit model is pursued by Disney. Profit does not originate from all of the Disney movies. However, if a blockbuster movie does emerge, Disney will aggressively pursue all potential sources of revenue including franchising, transactional revenue, licensing, merchandising, and other revenue sources. Therefore, profit in the Disney world is based upon the exploitation of selected blockbuster movies.

A second profit model is the "base and follow-on" model that is most easily understood through an example, such as razors and razor blades. That is, the base product (razors) is a "loss leader" while the real profit is extracted from follow-on products (razor blades).

Below we extend on this seminal work by identifying 10 shareholder value models for the online world. It is important to note that for Internet company discussion, we differ from traditional commerce theories on profit models in the following three ways:

- **Shift from Profit to Shareholder-Value Focus.** Many of the currently successful online businesses have yet to turn a profit. Significant energy is allocated to building a customer base, brand name, scaleable operations, and human resource base. The idea is to lock in the customer base and, then later, as the business matures, focus on profit. In our view, shareholder value is a more appropriate metric because it considers the market capitalization of the company—that is, the share price times the number of shares outstanding.

- **Shift from Supply-Side Language to Demand-Side Language.** A second key feature of the current approach is the shift to demand-side rather than supply-side terms and concepts. Significant financial gain (either price of offering or price of shares) is a result of what a company does in response to a market need. Companies, or at least successful companies, focus on the core benefits that customers are looking for and respond accordingly. Hence, demand comes first, supply second.

- **Introduce New Ways to Create Value.** Finally, this section introduces several new value-creation models that reflect the evolution of the New Economy.

In this section, we describe the models, illustrate the sources of profit or value for shareholders, and discuss key success factors. As firms begin to craft and build their business model—and associated value model—they also need to consider how other firms are likely to respond to their moves in the marketplace. Thus, we not only introduce the new value models, but we also discuss the threats to the chosen model (see Table 3-2). As you read this section keep in mind that a given company can pursue more than one model at a time.

We first consider three "company and user derived" value models that are based on the bringing together of large numbers of buyers and sellers. Later, we describe value models that are largely built on products and services that are provided by companies with significantly less "value added" input from customers.

Company and User Derived.
We term these models "company and user derived" since both the company and the user provide content and value added services to the site. eBay is an example of a "company and user derived" site where customers provide the products, information, service, and seller ratings. The users are the ones who largely provide the content.

- **Metamarkets Switchboard.** A metamarkets switchboard model brings together many buyers and sellers based upon the activities that customers engage in to meet particular goals (see Table 3-2).[19] Examples include BabyCenter.com, VerticalNet.com, and CarPoint.com. The revenue model may include transactions, product sales, and advertising. Value comes primarily from leveraging the brand name to provide value-added services that include product information, community events, and product sales.

  Consider BabyCenter.com. It is a website that sells all of the standard baby-related products—maternity clothing, toys, music, videos, and books—but also provides a gift center, baby-related expert advice from preconception through toddler stages, and community bulletin boards. It aggregates many different product providers with nonexclusive arrangements.

  Success Factors: Key success factors for this profit model include the building and sustaining of a large number of buyers and sellers. Frequently this model results in a single, clear-winning company with multiple second-tier players. It is possible that niche markets could also emerge. Constant innovation in value-added services is necessary to sustain the customer base. Enhancing user-to-user community formation may also create switching costs.

Threats: The key threats to this model include the formation of an alternative switchboard at a higher level of aggregation (e.g., children of all ages), the same level of aggregation (e.g., planet-baby.com), or a niche market. Innovative value-added services on the part of competitors who offer alternative switchboards can also threaten the profit stream.

- **Traditional and Reverse Auctions.** Traditional auctions such as eBay are designed to bring together large numbers of buyers and sellers. Buyers bid prices up to a point where no further bidding is offered. The buyer with the highest bid takes title to the item. Reverse auctions such as Freemarkets.com, a business-to-business site, allow suppliers to bid prices down until no further bids are received. The supplier with the lowest bid is to supply the goods to the buyer. Sites that act as hubs in these situations typically take a portion of the transaction revenue. The result is often a very high margin (i.e., eBay margins are reported to be in the neighborhood of 75 percent).

  Success Factors: Key success factors are similar to those of the metamarkets switchboard. That is, one needs to build a large base of buyers and sellers. The current thinking is that these types of markets are often winner-take-all, with no room for the second or third players. Another critical success factor is a strong brand name—one that signals both credibility and trust. Finally, these models are most effective when there is strong back-office support.

  Threats: Key threats to the model are similar to the metamarkets switchboard. Alternative switchboards can emerge in the market. The brand can lose credibility due to any negative factor such as site downtime, security breaches, privacy concerns, or questionable product assortments. In the case of business-to-business markets, the auction site could lose a few large suppliers and the overall model could be threatened. The auction model could also be threatened by the emergence of a pure low-price player in a particular product category. Hence, a key for firms in this market is continued innovation on value-added services.

- **Category Switchboard.** The category-specific switchboard, or a category-killer type site, is somewhat similar to the metamarkets switchboard except the focus is on one particular product category. Brands are aggregated in the product category, but there is much more focus that is typically not organized by the customer activities. Indeed, it tends to be more supply-side than demand-side driven. The revenue and profit sources tend to be similar to the metamarkets switchboard.

  Examples include Chemdex, eToys, and PlanetRx. eToys has managed to focus heavily on the toy category in the face of many competitors (such as Amazon) who have entered into the toy category. Toys are broadly defined to include games, puzzles, dolls, electronic games, and a host of other entertainment products. They also offer a variety of innovative valued-added services including toys for children with special needs, site organization by age, brand names associated with different age levels, and a gift center.

  Success Factors: Similar to the metamarkets switchboard, the key success factors relate to the leveraging of network economics. Namely, the building of a supplier and customer base and their subsequent "lock-in" due to switching costs such as an increasingly useful user profile, inter-user communication, and experience with the site.

(continued from page 90)
Our lifetime tenure for our customers, because our churn is slow, is somewhere around two and a half [to] three years. So we are running a fundamentally viable business. Now we're losing money currently because we're adding customers at such a fast clip that those hundred dollar chunks are bigger than our contribution margin on our existing base . . . It's very simple, easy to explain, easy to understand. But once we get to a certain scale . . . I mean EarthLink has . . . [gone] from . . . adding 20,000 customers a quarter, . . . [to] adding 50, . . . [to] adding 80, . . . [to] adding two hundred plus thousand customers per quarter. And pretty soon hopefully a lot more than that.

Get the full interview at
www.marketspaceu.com

Table
3-2

ALTERNATIVE SHAREHOLDER VALUE MODELS (COMPANY AND USER DERIVED)

Alternative Models	Company and User Derived		
	Metamarket Switchboard	**Auctions (Traditional & Reverse)**	**Category Switchboard**
Description	• Hub for many buyers and sellers; multiple categories	• Competitive bid hub for buyers and sellers	• Aggregates brands in product category
Examples	• BabyCenter.com • VerticalNet.com	• eBay • Amazon auctions • Freemarket	• Chemdex • PlanetRX
Revenue Model	• Transactions • Product sales • Advertising	• Transactions	• Transactions • Advertising • Product sales
Value Source	• Perceived value-added services • Brand name credibility	• % of transactions	• Perceived value-added services • Brand name credibility
Key Success Factors	• Build buyer database • Build seller database • Value-added services	• Build buyer database • Build seller database • Credible "hub" brand • Efficient back-office support	• Build brand • Critical mass of buyers and sellers
Key Threat Factors	• Alternative switchboard emerges • Niche switchboard emerges • Fundamental shift in care technologies	• Alternative auction • Niche auctions • Price of switchboard offering equal to auction • Value-added services differentiate competitors	• Emergence of metamarket • Niche category switchboard • Brand name strength of market leaders

Threats: The threats are, however, a bit distinct relative to the metamarkets switchboard. In particular, the key threat to a category-killer type site is the emergence of a metamarket player who rolls multiple-user activities into a single site (e.g., eToys can be challenged by Amazon toys, Wal-Mart.com, or BlueLight.com). At the other extreme, it may be possible that niche players will chip away at the overall category-killer. That is, a toy site that specializes in learning or development toys, a pure dot-com game site (e.g., Gamesville.com), or electronic games site (e.g., PlayStation.com). Finally, the brand name strength of market leaders in the offline world may challenge the dot-com pure play business models (e.g., ToysRUs.com).

Company Derived Value Creation.

The previous set of value models relied heavily on a combination of supply-side and demand-side forces to launch and defend the online competitive space. In this section, we focus on value models that are driven largely by "best of class" excellence on a key customer need or benefit (see Table 3-3). Also, as noted in the previous section, most of these models derive their value from company initiatives and products rather than from user-generated content. The exception is perhaps the model termed "broadest user network." In the following pages, we describe six such models.

- **Best Information.** This value model is based on providing customers with the most timely, "freshest," and most credible information product or service in the online environment. Examples exist across a variety of industries including industry research (e.g., Jup.com, Forrester.com), newspapers (e.g., NYTimes.com, latimes.com), magazines (e.g., salon.com), business reporting (e.g., TheStandard.com), and entertainment (e.g., Zagat.com, citysearch.com).

  Revenue for the players comes from a mix of sources including products, services, information, and advertising revenue. Profit originates from the customer's perception that the particular site has the more accurate, credible, and timely information. Consider for example, Jup.com. Jupiter Communications is positioning itself as the leading provider of information and research on online commerce. A key feature of this model is the ability to hire the right analysts and staff and, in turn, provide the most up-to-date, accurate estimates of the evolution of this industry. Their news must be "fresh" in the sense that their predictions for the online shopping behavior for 1999 are now worthless. However, their views of the online shopping prediction for 2001 are highly valuable. Similarly, real-time stock quotes are much more valuable than stock quotes that are delayed 15 minutes. Hence, there is a price premium associated with real-time, fresh information.

  Success Factors: The key success factors for this model include the hiring of the best personnel, providing the most timely and accurate information, and extracting the margins from the freshest product lines.

  Threats: Threats to the model include customers' perceptions that other firms have similar timeliness, the price sensitivity to the freshest information is too great, and the costs associated with providing the most timely information are prohibitive.

- **Widest Assortment.** Assortment value originates from the breadth of product, service, and information coverage or inventory in the chosen product category. Within the music category this could include CDNow.com, ArtistDirect.com, or SecondSpin.com. For example, SecondSpin positions itself as the Internet's largest buyer and seller of used CDs, videos, and DVDs. Consumers visit the site because they expect to find the largest assortment of used CDs relative to other competitor sites.

  Revenue is derived from product sales, however, the real source of profit lies in the selective premium pricing of the most desired products. Thus, used CDs for the best selling artists, rare CDs, classic CDs, and other hard-to-find music is likely to be charged premium prices.

  Success Factors: Key success factors involve reducing consumer uncertainty, building a strong brand presence, whether customers repeatedly buy and spread word of mouth, and the quality of additional information and services. For example, one feature of the SecondSpin site is the automatic notification of preferred artists or music. With the site's "personal favorites" feature you can choose up to 15 of your favorite artists. Every time you visit the site, you click on personal favorites and all titles currently in stock by those artists will appear. Thus, the inventory itself must be complemented with value-added services.

  Threats: Threats to the profit model include further specialization in the product category. For example, Furniture.com can be out-specialized by kitchen-specific sites. At the other extreme, megabrands such as Wal-Mart

Table 3-3 ALTERNATIVE SHAREHOLDER VALUE MODELS (COMPANY DERIVED)

Alternative Models	Company Derived					
	Best Information	**Widest Assortment**	**Lowest Prices**	**Broadest User Network**	**Best Experience**	**Most Personalized**
Description	• Timely, high value-added information	• Widest assortment within the category	• Lowest prices within category	• Aggregation of users around standard	• Highest quality merchandise as perceived by target customers	• Highest level of customization
Examples	• Forrester.com • Zagat.com • NYTimes.com • Jup.com	• ArtistDirect.com • SecondSpin.com	• Buy.com • Lowestfares.com	• ICQ • MP3 • Mercata • Accompany	• FAOSchwatz.com • Ashford.com	• Reflect.com
Revenue Model	• Product sales • Subscriptions	• Product sales	• Product sales	• Varied	• Product sales	• Product sales
Value Source	• Premium pricing based on perception of best information	• Selective premium pricing	• Unclear	• Users drive traffic • Standard emerges • Price premium follows	• Level of luxury premium drives prices	• Level of customization drives premium pricing
Key Success Factors	• Timeliness of information • Perceived quality of information	• Reduce uncertainty in offering • Quality of information and value-added services	• Operational excellence • Supply-chain management	• Establish standard • Grow user network • Network economics	• Ability to spot symbolic brands • Ability to judge quality	• Deep customer knowledge • Ability to "mine" customer database
Key Threat Factors	• Customers do not perceive sufficient gap in timeliness with generic offerings • Competitors match market leaders • Cost of "freshness" becomes prohibitive	• Specialization within the category • Emergence of dominant brands	• Shopbots • Lack of profit imperative • Shifting investor confidence • Re-engineer total process not price • Niche markets	• Alternate standard emerges • Technology shift • Backward or forward integration of complementary players	• Subniche markets emerge by category • Symbolic brand loses appeal	• Technology advances lead to "me too" products • Customers want control of personalization

and Amazon could attempt to aggregate consumers at a higher level with a metamarket switchboard.

- **Lowest Prices.** This model promises the customer the lowest prices online. This model may be specific to a product category (e.g., Lowestfare.com, AllBooks4Less.com) or a broader, mall-like approach (e.g., buy.com). Revenues originate principally from product sales and advertising.

  A good example of this approach is buy.com. Buy.com positions itself as the lowest-priced superstore on the Internet. It provides products in a wide range of product categories including computers, software, electronics, golf, books, videos, games, music, and "clearance" items.

  Success Factors: Margins are often minimal or even nonexistent; hence, the key is often to be exceptionally strong on back-office systems and leverage scale economies. In order to sustain its strategy, lowest-price sites must have outstanding supply-chain management, procurement, and overall operational excellence.

  Threats: Key threats to the value model include the emergence of shop bots. Shop bots such as mySimon.com search the Web for the lowest-priced items in a variety of product categories. A quick book search on the J.K. Rowling book, titled *Harry Potter and the Sorcerer's Stone,* revealed a wide range of prices—a range from approximately $8.50 to $30.00, including shipping costs. Interestingly, while buy.com was toward the lower end of this continuum, it was not the lowest-priced player.

  Other threats include the emergence of strong, branded players who create uncertainty in the low-priced brand, the lack of profit imperative, shifting investor confidence in low-priced business models, and the emergence of niche players who further specialize the market.

- **Broadest User Network.** A pure demand-based model is one that relies on the fast buildup of a user network. Examples include software and hardware standards that are emerging in a variety of Internet spaces (e.g., ICQ, RealNetworks) as well as demand aggregation models (e.g., Mercata.com, MobShop.com). The revenue models are varied including product sales, transactional fees, and advertising. Profits begin to appear after building the user base (largely through user initiated activities such as viral marketing). If a standard emerges, premium pricing can follow.

  A good example is Mercata.com. Mercata is a demand aggregation model that entails aggregating potential buyers into larger buyer groups and then leveraging their increased buying power for lower prices. Mercata engages in this activity across a wide range of product categories, including appliances, baby goods, gifts, electronics, lawn and garden goods, and jewelry.

  Success Factors: Key success factors include the building of a strong customer base, the customers' extent of viral marketing, and, potentially, trademarked software or patents to protect the core technology (e.g., "We-Commerce" is trademarked by Mercata).

  Threats: Threats to the model include the emergence of alternative standards, a fundamental technology shift, and backward or forward integration of complementary players.

- **Best Experience.** Within every product category, it is apparent that there is room for someone who can provide the best experience, regardless of price. Within the toys category, this could be FAOSchwartz.com or, within the jewelry category, this could be Ashford.com. Revenue is expected to originate from products, services, or information, while profit is maintained by premium prices across the entire range of products.

Success Factors: Key success factors include the sourcing of the best products, outstanding online service, and a comprehensive customer experience.

Threats: Key threats include the emergence of lower-priced offerings that offer similar benefits, the lack of a perceived value in the higher-priced goods, and a shift in customer preferences to emergent brand labels, as compared with the historical favorites.

- **Most Personalized.** This model is based on the best customization of the consumer experience. A good recent example is Reflect.com. Its website noted that they offer "products created by you, delivered free of charge in under a week." Its products are designed to give people the power to create their own beauty care experience. Here customers can create their own skin care, hair care, and makeup products.

  Success Factors: The key success factors for this business include deep customer knowledge and the ability to continually refresh and mine their customer database. Users must feel that they have the complete ability to customize the experience. Ultimately, the customer must feel in control of the level of personalization.

  Threats: Key threats include the emergence of new players who offer a richer, more personalized experience. Other threats include the emergence of new technologies that displace the incumbent or the use of older technologies that allow other companies to "catch up" and match the experience.

Because the business model pursued by the firm must be tightly integrated, we now consider how the previous section on resource system is tied to the shareholder value models. Consider once again, the 1-800-flowers resource system. At the center of the system would be the four key benefits of its offering. Each of these benefits would be tied directly to one of the shareholder value models. For example, the high quality flowers can be directly tied to the "best experience" value model while the "wide assortment of gifts" can be tied to the "wide assortment" value model. The important point is that the central benefits of the resource system should be tied directly to the type (or types) of value models pursued.

Financial Growth Models

A third component of a financial model is the firm's revenue growth strategy or **growth model.** A classic framework to understand how a company may drive revenue growth is exemplified by the Ansoff product/market matrix. Exhibit 3-6 illustrates that new revenue growth can come from deeper penetration into the current product market, new product development (i.e., new products for existing markets), new market development (e.g., existing products for new markets), or completely new products and markets. We have expanded this framework to include both online and offline activities. As a result, we will discuss eight options that a firm has to grow revenue.

Consider, once again, 1-800-flowers. Our first observation is that 1-800-flowers is attempting to grow revenue in a variety of ways—both online and offline. Their acquisition of Plow & Hearth (plowhearth.com and Gardenworks.com) has been focused on providing new products in new offline markets. Gardenworks.com

| Exhibit 3-6 | REVENUE GROWTH CHOICES: 1-800-FLOWERS |

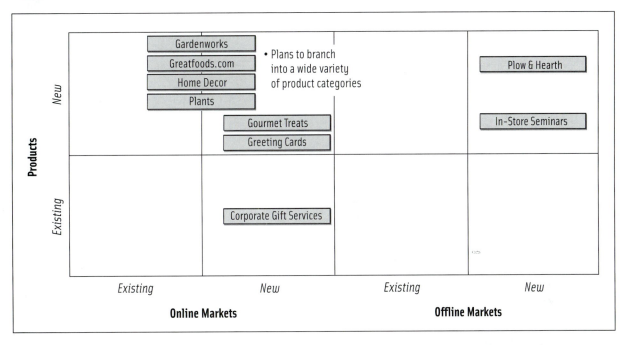

Online Markets · **Offline Markets**

Products: New / Existing

Gardenworks
Greatfoods.com
Home Decor
Plants

• Plans to branch into a wide variety of product categories

Plow & Hearth

Gourmet Treats
Greeting Cards

In-Store Seminars

Corporate Gift Services

Existing / New (Online Markets) · Existing / New (Offline Markets)

targets both the existing flower segment (e.g., existing online segment) and a new segment (e.g., those interested in garden products) for revenue growth. Overall, however, it appears that most growth is targeted in the area of new products for the online market (see Exhibit 3-6).

WHAT BUSINESS CLASSIFICATION SCHEMES ARE APPROPRIATE FOR THE NEW ECONOMY?

In recent years, authors have attempted to classify "generic" business frameworks or taxonomies. A good taxonomy or framework does two things. First, it makes the world simpler. That is, if the taxonomy is a good one, a reader should be able to read a case study or story about a business and easily categorize the business using the framework. Second, the classification should be meaningful. Meaningful refers to the fact that the classification should have business-model-choice implications. That is, placing a firm in one quadrant of the classification scheme should imply that its downstream business-model choice will be different than if it was placed in a different quadrant.

Below we describe three business-classification schemes. We begin with one of the most important classification schemes in strategy—the Porter Model. We then discuss its strengths and limitations in the New Economy. Later, we describe the Sawhney and Kaplan taxonomy and the Rayport, Jaworski, and Siegal model.

(continued from page 97)

this problem of trying to understand what is the business model. The truth of the matter is that I provided this funding, they went and disappeared for . . . six weeks, and after six weeks they called me to see the first demo, which was done in one of the homes of one of the young founders . . . When I saw the product, and I'm in business and in startups for the last 30 years, I really was completely, how do you say, flabbergasted . . . I literally sat on the sofa, I went back home, I told my wife, I saw something which is bigger than any business opportunity I saw in . . . my life. So much I was impressed, I told her it's not . . . a question of a few weeks until it will put all the telephones out of business . . . and then we went into a quest for a business model.

Get the full interview at www.marketspaceu.com

Porter Generic Strategy Model

Using a simple classification scheme, Porter argued that there are three basic generic strategies: differentiation, cost, and niche. Each strategy implied a different business model. For example, differentiation strategy required constant innovation and leadership on the benefits that matter most to customers while maintaining a competitive cost position. Cost strategy, on the other hand, focused on gaining competitive advantage on costs while maintaining some level of parity on "differentiation-type" customer benefits. The niche strategy involved "focusing" the business in a particular segment of the market and then pursuing either a differentiation or cost approach.

This is an important baseline model for us to consider given the wide-ranging impact that it has had on business academics and practitioners. Some believe that his model translates quite well into the New Economy. They believe it is possible to isolate players in a variety of vertical industries who pursue one of the three generic strategies. For example, Travelocity.com is pursuing a differentiation strategy and Lowestfare.com is pursuing a low-cost strategy. A niche strategy is being implemented by Lastminute.com in that it focuses on travelers who are looking for good deals but who also have the flexibility of traveling on very short notice.

At the same time, Porter's model has come under attack by New Economy thinkers for a variety of reasons. First, it has been argued that many Internet firms compete on both differentiation and low cost. Due to the technology capabilities of the Internet, one no longer has to make tradeoffs in strategy choices. Rather, a single company can compete in the low-cost, highly differentiated, and niche segments—all at the same time. Second, opponents argue that the Porter model focuses too heavily on "within industry" competition when the great business stories of the Internet involve the companies that are competing across industries based on customers' needs, goals, and activity choices.

Sawhney and Kaplan Model

Sawhney and Kaplan recently introduced the concept of electronic hubs (eHubs) and made a distinction between business-to-consumer (B2C) and business-to-business (B2B) hubs. They define the B2B eHub as "neutral Internet-based intermediaries that focus on specific industry verticals or specific business processes, host electronic marketplaces, and use various market-making mechanisms to mediate any-to-any transactions among businesses."[20] Sawhney and Kaplan argue that B2B hubs are the new middlemen that can create value by aggregating buyers and sellers, creating marketplace liquidity, and lowering transaction costs.

Further, Sawhney and Kaplan classify B2B hubs as either **vertical hubs** or **functional hubs.** Vertical hubs serve either vertical markets or a specific narrow industry focus while functional hubs provide common business functions or automate the same business processes horizontally across different industries. Exhibit 3-7 illustrates the relation of vertical hubs to functional hubs. Vertical hubs include PlasticsNet.com (plastics), e-Steel (steel), and Chemdex (chemicals). Examples of functional hubs are Celarix (logistics management), Adauction (media buying), and YOUtilities (energy management).

Generally, vertical hubs possess deep industry-specific knowledge but tend to lack business-process expertise. On the other hand, functional hubs possess business-process expertise, but tend to lack deep industry-specific knowledge.

Does Profit Matter?
Build Profit or Build User Base

An interesting debate is currently unfolding around Internet firms that are completely focused on increasing their number of users. The idea is that, based upon the principles of network economics, large pools of users will eventually translate into a huge revenue source in a variety of ways that include: (1) product sales and associated margins, (2) sale of customer information, and (3) potential sale of the entire business (e.g., Hotmail acquired by Microsoft). Firms that pursue these strategies frequently are not concerned about profit in the short run. Their point of view is that there will be only one winner—the one who builds the largest user base. All efforts should be laser focused on building the user base through offline advertising, online partnerships, viral marketing, customer interface improvements, and product innovation. Indeed, a recent Forrester study noted that only 18 percent of online retailers noted that profitability was a top goal for 2000, while 86 percent noted that they wanted to grow their business.[21]

Recently, however, there has been increasing pressure on companies to show profitability, not just revenue growth. Proponents of this view frequently turn to basic financial valuation models for their support. Stock prices and, thus, market capitalization are driven by estimates of current and future cash flow. Many of the Internet business model valuations are based on the belief that successful firms will have huge cash flows in future years.

The Point-Counterpoint debate that follows from these two paths of reasoning is quite straightforward. At what point do investors (or, more generally, Wall Street) begin to put pressure on firms to translate the growing user base into profitable, positive-cash-flow businesses? As this book goes to press, there is increasing pressure on Amazon.com to turn a profit, despite its escalating user base and rapidly growing top-line revenue stream. Similarly, as we go to press, CDNow, DrKoop, and eToys are under a great deal of pressure to show how the business can continue without positive cash flow in sight. It is difficult to forecast how this debate will unfold.

Unless vertical hubs find closely related domains where they can leverage their assets, they find it difficult to diversify into other vertical markets. Horizontal hubs, because of their low ability to deliver industry-specific content, run the risk of becoming back-end service providers to vertical hubs. Eventually, vertical hubs will probably form patchwork alliances with horizontal hubs or, alternatively, "metahubs" may emerge where multiple vertical hubs will share common back-ends and functional services.

Rayport, Jaworski, and Siegal Model

Table 3-4 provides a 2×2 categorization scheme proposed by Rayport, Jaworski, and Siegal (RJS Model). Along the top axis are sources of content origination. Content in this context may refer to products, services, and/or information. The business can focus on content from a single source (e.g., Landsend.com sources only its own brands) or multiple sources (e.g., Bluefly.com carries a variety of brand name apparel). On the side axis is the focus of the business strategy, whether it is principally focused on the back-office or on supply-chain improvement, and hence,

Exhibit 3-7
SAWHNEY AND KAPLAN—
CLASSIFICATION OF B2B MODELS

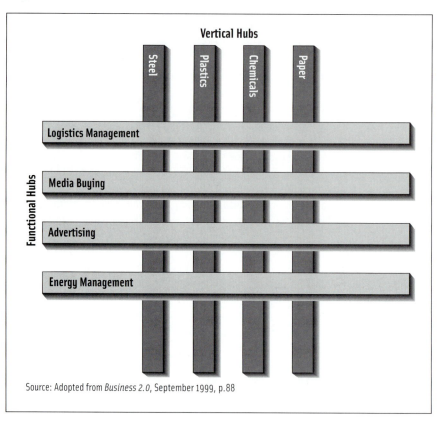

Source: Adopted from *Business 2.0*, September 1999, p.88

categorized as supply-side, or whether it is focused on a better customer experience and, therefore, demand-side focused. As we will describe below, the options included in the taxonomy are *not* mutually exclusive.

Pure Play. Given these two axes, we can now describe alternative, "pure play" generic approaches.

- **Forward-Integrated Producers.** Forward-integrated producers refer to single company initiatives that focus on enhancing the effectiveness or efficiency of the supply channel. We term these forward-integrated producers because they frequently refer to companies that have decided to pursue an Internet strategy to enhance their relationships with suppliers or to reduce supply-chain inefficiencies.

   A good example would be Wal-Mart. Its online business model is designed to bring the products to market in a more efficient and effective way. The model is efficient in the sense of shorter delivery time and lower operational costs and effective in the sense that Wal-Mart has the potential to increase revenues, and potentially, margins.

Table
3-4

RJS MODEL SUMMARY

| | **Sources of Content Origination** | |
	Single Brand	**Multiple Brands**
Supply-Side	*Forward-Integrated Producer* (Wal-Mart.com)	*Supply-Side Aggregator* (Surplusdirect.com)
Demand-Side	*Backward-Integrated User* (Dellonline.com)	*Demand-Side Aggregator* (Accompany.com)
	Hybrid Integrator (Cisco.com)	*Hybrid Aggregator* (Amazon.com)

(Left axis label: **Focus of Strategy**)

- **Supply-Side Aggregators.** Supply-side aggregators are similar to forward-integrated producers in their focus. That is, they enhance the effectiveness or efficiency of the supply chain. However, supply-side aggregators do so by aggregating multiple players in the supply chain. This means they do not offer their own products, but rather, they aggregate many suppliers. A good example is the recent decision by the "Big Three" automakers to create a supply chain for their industry.

- **Backward-Integrated User.** Backward-integrated user refers to a situation where a single company attempts to better serve its clients through a Web interface. The entire intent is to better serve existing or new clients through a single company site. An example is Forrester.com. Forrester provides market-level reports on the evolution of technology and e-commerce. It provides a series of standard reports online for its subscription customers. It also provides custom analysis. It does not provide reports of competitors such as Jup.com.

- **Demand-Side Aggregators.** Demand-side aggregators pull together many potential buyers on a single site. MobShop.com aggregates groups of buyers to enhance their purchasing power and lower the prices of each individual consumer.

Again, an important point in the classification scheme is that these choices are not mutually exclusive. Rather, many businesses pursue hybrid approaches. Through a hybrid model, a given firm can choose to aggregate many sources of

Table 3-5

IMPLICATIONS OF "PURE PLAY" BUSINESS APPROACHES

Business Implications	Forward-Integrated Producer	Backward-Integrated User	Supply Aggregator	Demand Aggregator
Potential Sources of Competitive Advantage	• Streamlined outbound logistics • Producer brand • Producer customer base	• Streamlined inbound logistics	• Strong brand identity • Relevant strategic alliances	• Strong brand identity • Relevant customer scale
Potential Benefits to Producer	• Lower cost for delivery of products, services, or information • Efficiencies which translate into cost savings	• Lower cost for delivery of products, services, or information • Efficiencies which translate into cost savings	• More targeted access to customers	• Expanded access to customers • More targeted access to customers
Potential Benefits to User	• Lower price for products, services, or information • Efficiencies which translate into cost savings	• Lower price for products, services, or information • Efficiencies which translate into cost savings	• Time savings • Privacy	• Connection to others who are like-minded • Access to relevant information/advice

supply and many sources of demand and thus combine the supply-side aggregation and demand-side aggregation cells of the matrix (e.g., the classic metamarkets switchboard). Similarly, a firm may decide to aggregate all of its suppliers and buyers into a single hub that is firm-specific (e.g., Cisco.com).

With respect to the meaningfulness dimension, we can turn to the business implications of this taxonomy by referencing Table 3-5. This table illustrates the potential implications of the "pure play" business approaches. In particular, the focus is on the potential sources of competitive advantage, potential benefits to producers, and potential benefits to users.

SCHWAB'S BUSINESS MODEL

In Chapter 2, we reviewed and analyzed five conditions that directly impacted the business-model choice of Schwab. In particular, we noted a fundamental shift in the buying behaviors of certain customer groups that favored innovative products in an online environment. However, this customer "sweet spot" alone could not fully explain the opportunity. It was also necessary to note that competitors were offering financial services both at low-price points (e.g., Ameritrade.com, E-TRADE.com) and high-price points (e.g., ML.com) and that Schwab had the first-mover advantage in securing key partnerships. Finally, through its continual focus on technology, innovation, and leadership, Schwab was constantly able to stay a clear step ahead of other firms in spotting new technology trends. Below we illustrate how the four components of Schwab's business model "fit" the evolution of the market.

Value Cluster

As noted earlier in this chapter, the value proposition or cluster consists of three components: (1) the target segment(s), (2) the key benefit(s), and (3) the supportive rationale for why these benefits can be delivered better than the competition can deliver them. Schwab's value cluster entails the use of technology to lower costs and offer superior service at lower prices to investors unwilling to pay for investment advice.[22]

From this statement, it is clear that Schwab *primarily* targets consumers who are unwilling to pay for investment advice. However, because this statement is very meaningful but lacks actionability, we return to our Chapter 2 segmentation scheme (Exhibit 2-10). From this analysis, it was clear that the highest-priority segment was transitioning the current customer base from offline to online. However, we also noted in Chapter 2 that we would argue that the key-priority segment was professionals who had incomes less that 150K and were trading frequently (recall this was segment J). Two other priority segments were also noted. Thus, the three components of the value cluster are as follows:

- **Target Segments:**
  Existing offline customers
  Professionals, incomes < 150K, trade frequently
  Professionals, incomes < 150K, buy and hold

- **Key Benefits:**
  Innovative products
  Superior service
  Lower prices

- **Supportive Rationale:**
  Superior ("cutting edge") technology
  Innovation

The Marketspace Offering (Egg Diagram)

Once the value proposition is specified, we can turn to the crafting of the offering—that is, the particular combination of products, services, and information. The first step is the articulation of the scope. Schwab had decided to focus on category dominance in the financial services with only a handful of services outside the traditional boundaries of financial services.

Next, we consider the Egg Diagram (see Exhibit 3-8). In the inner circle of the diagram, we have articulated the stages in the Online Investment Process. These include education, investment planning, research, investment decision, acting on the investment, and postinvestment support. In the outside circle, we have specified the specific products, services, and information that are "mapped onto" the investment decision process.

To match consumer education needs, Schwab provides various live events, courses through their online learning center, and online investment basics that cover the principles of investing and understanding market cycles. For the investment planning stage, planning tools, alternative comparison charts, and services are provided across four broad investment goals of retirement, estate, college, and tax planning. In the consumer's research phase, Schwab provides broad and

Exhibit 3-8

SCHWAB EGG DIAGRAM

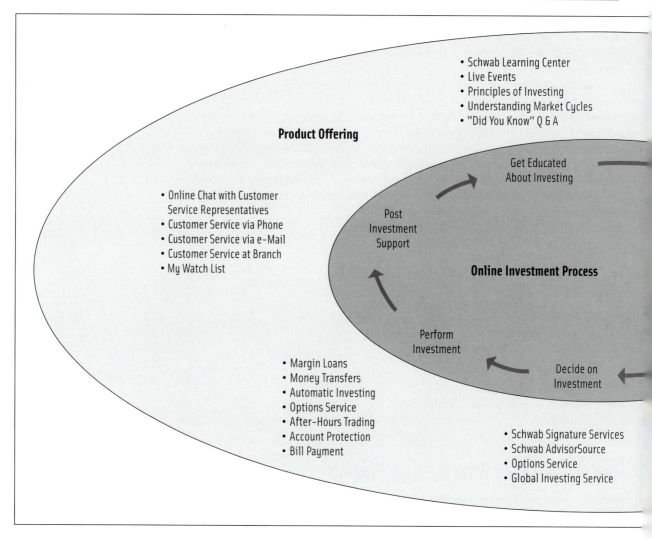

Product Offering

- Schwab Learning Center
- Live Events
- Principles of Investing
- Understanding Market Cycles
- "Did You Know" Q & A

- Online Chat with Customer Service Representatives
- Customer Service via Phone
- Customer Service via e-Mail
- Customer Service at Branch
- My Watch List

Get Educated About Investing

Post Investment Support

Online Investment Process

Perform Investment

Decide on Investment

- Margin Loans
- Money Transfers
- Automatic Investing
- Options Service
- After-Hours Trading
- Account Protection
- Bill Payment

- Schwab Signature Services
- Schwab AdvisorSource
- Options Service
- Global Investing Service

extensive information across all domestic and many international financial instruments. Consumers can receive equity online quotes and charts through the Analyst Center. Rates and yields of fixed income instruments can be viewed online as well.

To support the investment decisions, various levels of personal service and benefits are provided to customers for varying levels of investment. Through the Schwab Signature Services, customers can receive deeper transaction fee discounts, better research materials, and priority treatment on phone calls. To support the investment transaction, the customer can place orders over the telephone or online. Schwab also provides margin loans, money transfers, automatic investing, options services, and after-hours trading—all online. For customer postinvestment support, Schwab provides capabilities for online chats with customer service representatives and customer service at local branches, via phone or e-mail.

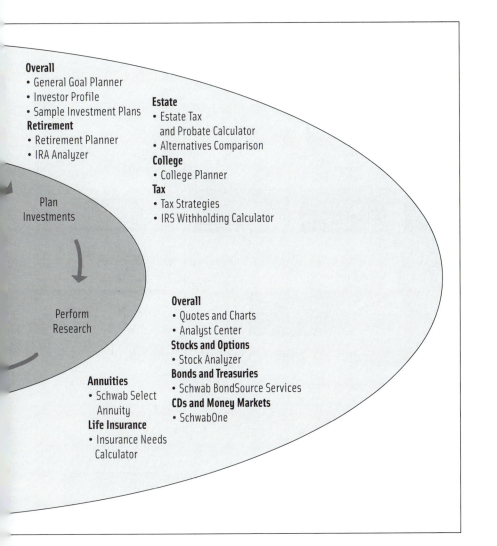

Overall
- General Goal Planner
- Investor Profile
- Sample Investment Plans

Retirement
- Retirement Planner
- IRA Analyzer

Estate
- Estate Tax and Probate Calculator
- Alternatives Comparison

College
- College Planner

Tax
- Tax Strategies
- IRS Withholding Calculator

Plan Investments

Perform Research

Overall
- Quotes and Charts
- Analyst Center

Stocks and Options
- Stock Analyzer

Bonds and Treasuries
- Schwab BondSource Services

CDs and Money Markets
- SchwabOne

Annuities
- Schwab Select Annuity

Life Insurance
- Insurance Needs Calculator

The Schwab Resource System

The resource system builds on the value proposition and Egg Diagram. Exhibit 3-9 illustrates our interpretation of the resource system of Schwab. We begin by articulating the three benefits that relate directly to the value proposition.

- Low prices
- Innovative products
- Superior service

Next, we map the capabilities that drive these benefits. For example, superior service is driven by well-trained customer service representatives (CSRs), partnerships with content providers, and a fully synergistic set of access points (e.g., Web, phone, and branches working together).

Exhibit
3-9
SCHWAB RESOURCE SYSTEM

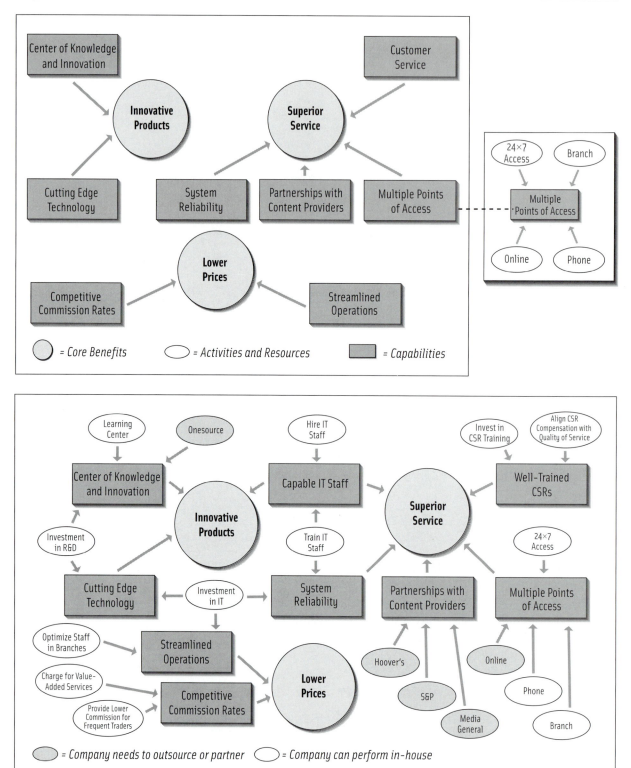

= Core Benefits   = Activities and Resources   = Capabilities

= Company needs to outsource or partner   = Company can perform in-house

The bottom diagram in Exhibit 3-9 takes the resource system illustrated in the top diagram of the exhibit and shows where the company can perform the service in-house and where partnerships will be necessary to deliver the service. Furthermore, Table 3-6 shows the "give/get" analysis for the partners of Charles Schwab.

For an example, consider the superior-service benefit once again. It is clear that well-trained CSRs can largely be the responsibility of Schwab. However, partnerships with content providers can only occur with outside vendors such as Hoover's, Standard & Poor's, and Media General. Turning to Table 3-6, we can begin to obtain some understanding of the "give/get" matrix for the content providers. Content providers would receive revenues, exposure, and click-throughs. Schwab would get access to best-of-class content.

The Financial Model

Finally, we consider the financial model of Schwab.

Revenue Model. Revenues are generated from trading and nontrading related activities. Trading revenues include commissions and principal transaction fees. Nontrading revenues come from mutual fund service fees, net interest revenue, interest on balances, and margins on lent funds.

Value Model. Profits are generated mainly from Schwab establishing themselves as the provider of the best information by supplying customers with a Stock Analyzer, an Analyst Center, planning advice services, as well as a category switchboard through their OneSource mutual funds program.

Growth Model. Growth will come through the continued development of advanced online software tools and after-hours online trading (see Exhibit 3-10). They plan to add new in-branch seminars as well as a new online Learning Center. Schwab is creating a new online investment bank and plans to expand its operations internationally both online and offline.

Table 3-6

PARTNERS "GIVE/GET" MATRIX

Partners	Benefits to Partner: "Give"	Benefits to Schwab: "Get"
Content Partners (e.g., Hoover's, S&P, Media General, H&Q)	• Partners receive revenues from Schwab • Exposure and branding on a major site • Click-throughs	• Best-in-class content essential for Schwab to differentiate itself from other discount brokers
Onesource Partners: Mutual Fund Managers	• Access to a large flow of business from Schwab customers • Significant reduction in marketing costs	• Cement the relationship with the customer by acting as a valuable "switchboard" • Schwab receives transaction fees from funds
Website Partners: Razorfish	• Opportunity to work with high profile client • Ongoing fee-based relationship	• Access to highly creative site designers • Consistent customer experience and look-and-feel • Makes internal resources available

Who Would You Rather Be: A Dot-Com or a Brick-and-Mortar Business?

A debate that is currently unfolding in the market is whether a particular firm is better off starting out as a pure "dot-com" business or whether a firm is better off starting out with brick-and-mortar assets.

Proponents on the pure dot-com side argue that dot-com businesses are not constrained by physical world assets because those assets do not translate into the New Economy. They argue that firms in this space need to operate differently—fast, with flat organizational structures, no functional boundaries, and a senior management team that understands the New Economy. Furthermore, dot-com proponents point to a number of successful companies that have followed this approach, such as Amazon.com, Yahoo.com, and AOL.

On the brick-and-mortar side, proponents counter that there are basic business issues that still apply in the New Economy. Firms must be businesses—not simply customer-acquisition organizations. Furthermore, the key assets that dot-coms are attempting to build (e.g., consumer awareness, traffic, strong brands) are already possessed by the incumbent traditional businesses. Indeed, as Jack Welch recently noted, "Digitizing a company and developing e-business models is easier—not harder—than we ever imagined.[23]

Exhibit 3-10 SCHWAB REVENUE GROWTH CHOICES

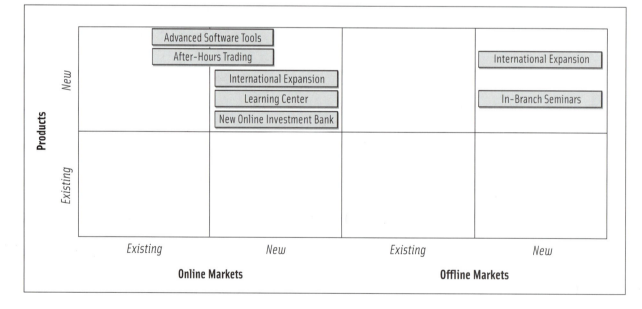

SUMMARY

1. What is a business model?

A business model is comprised of four parts: a value proposition or "cluster" of value propositions, a marketspace offering, a unique and defendable resource system, and a financial model. The value proposition defines the choice of target segment, the choice of focal customer benefits, and a rationale for why the firm can deliver the benefit package significantly better than competitors. The offering entails a precise articulation of the products, services, and information that is provided by the firm. The resource system supports the specific set of capabilities and resources that will be engaged in by the firm to uniquely deliver the offering. The financial model is the various ways that the firm is proposing to generate revenue, enhance value, and grow.

2. Do firms compete on value propositions or value clusters?

Firms can compete on either or both. While offline firms may have difficulty competing with value clusters, their online counterparts can compete on either value proposition or value clusters. Firms in the online world can address consumers specifically to their individual needs as "segments of one." Web businesses often attract multiple segments at the same time and compete with other firms on multiple benefits that are delivered by a single tightly conceived and implemented set of capabilities. Firms can choose to focus and primarily emphasize one critical benefit or provide multiple "storefronts" and clusters of benefits to multiple segments within the context of a single URL.

3. What are the approaches to developing an online offering, whether the business is providing a product, service, or information?

Development of an online offering requires completion of three sequential tasks: (1) identify the scope of the offering, (2) identify the Customer Decision Process, and (3) map the offering (product, services, and information) to the Customer Decision Process. The scope refers to the breadth or number of categories of products and services that are offered in a website. The Customer Decision Process can be divided into three broad stages: prepurchase, purchase, and postpurchase processes. The process of mapping the offering to the Customer Decision Process (i.e., mapping the Egg Diagram) involves the systematic matching of product, services, and information onto each stage of the Customer Decision Process.

4. What is a successful, unique resource system? What are characteristics of good resource systems?

The resource system shows how a company's value proposition is contained in a set of tailored capabilities that uniquely deliver the benefits of the proposition. A number of criteria can be used to assess the quality of the resource system, such as the uniqueness of a system and whether there are links between capabilities and benefits, links among capabilities in the system, links among resources, and links to physical world business systems.

5. What are the revenue models available to firms?

Firms can pursue a variety of revenue models that include the following: advertising, product, service, or information sales, transaction fees, and subscription fees.

6. What business classification schemes seem most appropriate for the New Economy?

Some have argued that the Porter model does not take into consideration the technology capabilities of the Internet, and, hence, does not allow for simulanteous pursuit of multiple "generic" strategies. Also, the model focuses too heavily on "within industry" competition while competition among Internet-based companies is across several industries and based on customers needs, goals, and activity choices.

The Sawhney and Kaplan model primarily concentrates on the burgeoning area of business-to-business hubs and whether these hubs are vertical or functional in nature. While this model captures important aspects of the business-to-business hubs, it fails to describe the broad landscape of the various business models that have emerged.

The RJS classification accounts for sources of content origination as well as the focus of business strategy whether the strategy is focused on supply-side or demand-side improvements. The model options in the taxonomy are not mutually exclusive and, therefore, can accommodate "pure play" as well as "hybrid form" business approaches. The flexibility of the RJS taxonomy accommodates both business-to-consumer and business-to-business metamarkets where the new focus is on customer needs, goals, and activity choices. While this model captures all of the Internet plays, it can be criticized for its complexity.

KEY TERMS

business model	shareholder value models
value proposition	growth models
value cluster	vertical hubs
Egg Diagram	functional hubs
revenue models	

Endnotes

[1] Kaplan, Karen. 2000. DOT-GONE? An occasional look at firms struggling in the online world: FTD.com hoped to flower on Web, but prospects are wilting. *Los Angeles Times*, 17 April, Home edition, Business section, p. C-1. URL: *http://www.latimes.com/archives/, searchword: ftd.*

[2] Market attractiveness is a function of the size of the market, growth rates of the market, weakness of competitors, strong consumer needs, supportive technology, and other forces.

[3] Lynch, John G. Jr. and Dan Ariely. 1999. Electronic shopping for wine: How search costs affect consumer price sensitivity, satisfaction with merchandise, and retention. *Marketing Science Institute Report*, pp. 99–104. URL: *http://www.msi.org/msi/publication_summary.cfm?publication=99-104.*

[4] Wyman, Tom. 1999. eTailing and the five Cs. *J.P. Morgan Industry Analysis*, 9 December.

[5] Each of these terms are independent but highly related. Interested readers may wish to consider the following sources: Prahald, C.K. and Gary Hamel. 1990. The core competence of the corporation. *Strategic Management Journal* 15 (May–June): 79–91. Collis, David J. and Cynthia A. Montgomery.

1995. Competing on resources: Strategy in the 1990s. *Harvard Business Review* 73, no. 4 (July–August): 118–28. Wernerfelt, Birger. 1994. A resource-based view of the firm. *Strategic Management Journal* 5: 171–80. Barney, Jay. 1991. Firm resources and sustained competitive advantage. *Journal of Management* 17, no. 1: 99–120. Dickson, Peter Reid. 1992. Toward a general theory of competitive rationality. *Journal of Marketing* 56 (January): 69–83. Hunt, Shelby D. 1995. The comparative advantage theory of competition. *Journal of Marketing* 59 (April): 1–15.

[6]See Collis, David J. and Cynthia Montgomery. 1995. Competing on resources, pp. 119–21.

[7]We are inferring these propositions from the websites' tag lines and communications.

[8]Sawhney, Mohanbir. 1999. Making new markets. *Business 2.0* (May): 116–21.

[9]Hoyer, Wayne and Deborah MacInnis. 1997. *Consumer behavior*. Boston: Houghton Mifflin Company, pp. 98–100.

[10]Value chains are company-specific activities that range from raw materials acquisition through to after-sale customer service (see Porter, Michael E. 1985. *Competitive advantage*. New York: The Free Press, p. 37). Activity systems are largely derived from the value chains but focus on the key "themes" and associated activities that are the most important in the delivery of a differentiated value proposition. Additionally, activity systems focus heavily on the links between activities, reflecting the need to interweave the activities as a network rather than a linear chain. This work was an important influence on the evolution of our resource system perspective.

[11]Porter, Michael E. 1996. What is strategy? *Harvard Business Review* 74, no. 6 (November–December): 61–78.

[12]Rayport, Jeffrey F. and John J. Sviokla. 1995. Exploiting the virtual value chain. *Harvard Business Review* 73, no. 6 (November–December): 75–85.

[13]For an excellent discussion of the resource-based view of the firm, read the article by Collis, David J. and Cynthia A. Montgomery. 1995. Competing on resources.

[14]This resource system is derived largely from the Securities and Exchange Commission S1-A filing on August 2, 1999. The online version can be found at the following URL: *http://www.sec.gov/cgi-bin/srch-edgar?flowers*.

[15]Thompson, Maryann J. 1999. Net steals billions from offline retailers. *The Standard*, 4 August. URL: *http://www.thestandard.com/article/display/0,1151,5744,00.html*.

[16]Meland, Marius. 2000. Zagat takes a big byte. *Forbes.com*, 8 February. URL: *http://www.forbes.com/tool/html/00/Feb/0208/mu2.html*.

[17]Imitability of resources is discussed in the following: Collis, David J. and Cynthia A. Montgomery. 1995. Competing on resources.

[18]Slywotzky, Adrian J. and David J. Morrison. 1998. *The profit zone: How strategic design will lead you to tomorrow's profits*. New York: Times Business. We strongly recommend that readers review this well-regarded book on alternative profit models in the offline world. The work provided an important input into the models that are illustrated in this section.

[19]Sawhney, Mohanbir. 1999. Making new markets. *Business 2.0* (May): 116–21.

[20]Sawhney, Mohanbir and Steven Kaplan. 1999. Let's get vertical. *Business 2.0* (September). URL: *http://www.business2.com/articles/1999/09/content/models.html*.

[21]Regan, Keith. 2000. Forrester: Most dot-coms will sink by 2001. *E-Commerce Times*, 13 April. URL: *http://www.ecommercetimes.com/news/articles2000/000412-7.shtml*.

[22]Maggioncalda, Jeff and Robert A. Burgelman. 1997. The Charles Schwab corporation in 1996. Case study no. SM-35 (August). Graduate School of Business of Stanford University, p. 2.

[23]Moore, Pamela L. 2000. GE's cyber payoff. *BusinessWeek*, 13 April. URL: *http://www.businessweek.com/bwdaily/dnflash/apr2000/nf00413f.htm?scriptFramed*.

4

Customer Interface

The purpose of this chapter is to introduce the concept of a technology-mediated customer interface. This interface can be a desktop PC, subnotebook, personal digital assistant, cell phone, WAP device, or other appliance. Within a technology-mediated customer experience, the user's interaction with the company shifts from the "face-to-face" encounter in a traditional retail environment to a "screen-to-face" interface. As this shift from people-mediated to technology-mediated interfaces unfolds, it is important to consider the types of interface design available to the senior management team. What is the "look-and-feel," or context, of the website? Should the site include commerce activities? How important are communities in the business model? To capture these design considerations, we will later introduce the 7Cs Framework. It is a rigorous way to understand the interface design choices that confront senior managers as they implement their business models.

QUESTIONS

Please consider the following questions as you read this chapter:

1. What are the seven design elements to the customer interface?

2. What are the alternative "look-and-feel" approaches to design?

3. What are the five content archetypes?

4. Why be concerned with community?

5. What are the levers used to customize a site?

This chapter was coauthored by Bernie Jaworski, Jeffrey Rayport, Leo Griffin, and Yannis Dosios.

. . . I think that what has happened is those who have spent some time on ergonomics and on a nice user interface and the aesthetics have seen some benefit from that. I think the more and more you get away from the desktop computer and towards the consumer devices, the more you'll have to pay attention to that and I think we're going to see it naturally evolve. The more you bring different demographics into the market—noncomputer user, consumers, women, children, different age demographics, different economic demographics—you are going to see different types of machines become important.

Get the full interview at www.marketspaceu.com

6. What types of communication can a firm maintain with its customer base?

7. How does a firm connect with other businesses?

8. What are alternative pricing models of commerce archetypes?

In Chapter 3, we detailed the four business model choices that confront senior managers: the value cluster, marketspace offering, resource system, and financial model. This set of strategy decisions significantly informs the type of customer interface choices that will confront a senior management team. For example, a decision to be a no-frills discount retailer of functional goods, such as electronics, would have very different customer interface implications compared to a high-end, trend-oriented fashion site.

Consider, for example, the different approaches of two well-regarded sports sites: Quokka.com and Gear.com. Quokka.com is concerned with immersion into sports categories such as sailing, auto racing, surfing, and the Olympics. The site focuses on the experiences that one can enjoy in each sports category, including the purchase of memorabilia, identifying event dates, and even experiencing a "sports digital network" for broadcasts. Features that encourage a sense of community are a significant portion of the site, because the primary goal is to gather sports fanatics together in one environment. Commerce is a very small portion of the site.

In sharp contrast, Gear.com is billed as "name brand sporting goods at closeout prices." In effect, it is similar to specialty mall outlets in the offline world. The entire site is focused on product offerings with a particular emphasis on low prices and good deals. No effort is made to build community or to provide "deep immersion" in the product category.

Given their distinct value propositions and associated marketspace offerings, it is not surprising that Quokka.com's and Gear.com's interfaces differ in content of the sites, look-and-feel of the layouts, degrees of commerce activity, emphases on community, and connections to other sites.

The purpose of this chapter is to introduce, describe, and provide examples for each of the 7Cs of customer interface design. The chapter is organized as follows. In the first section, we provide an overview of the 7Cs Framework. In addition, we also discuss two higher-order design principles to be considered when constructing a customer interface—fit and reinforcement. In the later sections, we provide a more thorough examination that includes discussion of the features or dimensions of each C along with respective sample archetypes. We conclude the chapter with an application of the framework to Schwab.

WHAT ARE THE SEVEN DESIGN ELEMENTS TO THE CUSTOMER INTERFACE?

The 7Cs Framework

Exhibit 4-1 provides a simple representation of the **7Cs Framework** for customer-interface design. The interface is the virtual (and, to date, largely visual) representation of a firm's chosen value proposition. Similar to a retail storefront, the virtual website provides significant information to current and prospective target-market customers. If designed effectively, the site quickly answers a number of basic questions that confront such users. Is this site worth visiting? What products or services does it sell? What messages does the site communicate: Exclusivity? Low price? Ease of use? Consistent with a tightly constructed business model, well-designed sites should simultaneously attract target segment customers and repel nontargeted customers. Compelling sites communicate the core value proposition of the company and provide a compelling rationale for buying and/or visiting the site.

Definitions and Simple Illustration. How then does the senior management team structure choices to enable the implementation of an effective site? Below we briefly describe the seven design choices that form the basis for an effective interface. After this brief review, we provide a more detailed explanation of each of the Cs.

Context. The **context** of the website captures its aesthetic and functional look-and-feel. Some sites have chosen to focus heavily on interesting graphics, colors, and design features, while others have emphasized more simple utilitarian goals, such as ease of navigation. Exhibit 4-1 contains a webpage from landsend.com. Lands' End balances both aesthetic (i.e., pastel colors; simple, warm visuals) and functional (e.g., crisp, uncluttered) design elements to communicate its core benefits—traditionally designed clothing, great service, and moderate prices. In sharp contrast, Luckyjeans.com is a more hip, nontraditional brand; its website is comparatively more edgy, with bolder colors, humor (i.e., the "get lucky" slogan), and a more focused product line. Landsend.com customers might not find the Luckyjeans.com site appealing, purely because of its look-and-feel. Luckyjeans.com suggests a younger, more urban, and fashion-forward target segment.

Content. **Content** is defined as all digital subject matter on the site. This includes the form of the digital subject matter—text, video, audio, and graphics—as well as the domains of the digital subject matter, including product, service, and information offerings. While context largely focuses on the "how" of site design, content focuses on "what" is presented. Consider once again, the Landsend.com site in Exhibit 4-1. The Landsend.com site includes content pertaining to its product offerings (e.g., overstocks, kids, luggage, gifts), services, and offline support (i.e., 1-800 phone number). In terms of media, the site uses a combination of text, photographs, and graphics to convey its content.

Community. **Community** is defined as the interaction that occurs between site users. It does not refer to site-to-user interactions. User-to-user communication can occur between two users (e.g., e-mails, joint game-playing) or between one user and many (e.g., chat rooms). Landsend.com has an innovative community feature that allows two users to shop simultaneously on its site. This trademarked service termed "Shop with a Friend™" enables two users to view the site at the same time, browse together, and purchase the product. It is a virtual shopping experience.

Customization. **Customization** is defined as the site's ability to tailor itself or to be tailored by each user. When the customization is initiated and managed by the firm, we term it *tailoring*. When the customization is initiated and managed by the user, we term it *personalization*. Let us consider two examples. On Landsend.com, the user is able to personalize the site to a limited degree, using a feature called the personal shopping account. Here, the user can enter basic personal information, complete an address book for potential recipients of purchases, and enter key dates in the reminder service. In turn, once personal profile data is entered and consumers begin to use the site, the site uses this data to tailor e-mail messages, banner ads, and the content of the site to the individual.

Communication. **Communication** refers to the dialogue that unfolds between the site and its users. This communication can take three forms: site-to-user communication (e.g., e-mail notification), user-to-site (e.g., customer service request), or two-way communication (e.g., instant messaging). Landsend.com has introduced a communication feature called "Lands' End Live," which enables the user to talk directly with the customer service representative while shopping on the site. Clicking on the Lands' End Live button results in two options: (1) connection by phone (this assumes the user has two phone lines), a direct Internet connection by DSL, or by cable modem or (2) connection by live text chat.

Connection. **Connection** is defined as the extent of the formal linkages between the site and other sites. Landsend.com does not have any connections to other sites; however, it does have an affiliates program that allows other sites to connect to Lands' End. In particular, Landsend.com supplies the affiliate site with banner ads to link visitors from the site to the Landsend.com store. The affiliate partner earns 5 percent on every sale that occurs on a click-through from the site. If a customer is a first-time Lands' End buyer, the affiliate earns an additional finder's fee.

Commerce. **Commerce** is defined as the sale of goods, products, or services on the site. The Landsend.com site obviously has transactional capability. It has the typical "shopping basket" feature along with shipping (i.e., to home, to someone else's home, or to the office) information. The shopping basket can be viewed at any

Exhibit 4-1

THE 7Cs OF THE
CUSTOMER INTERFACE

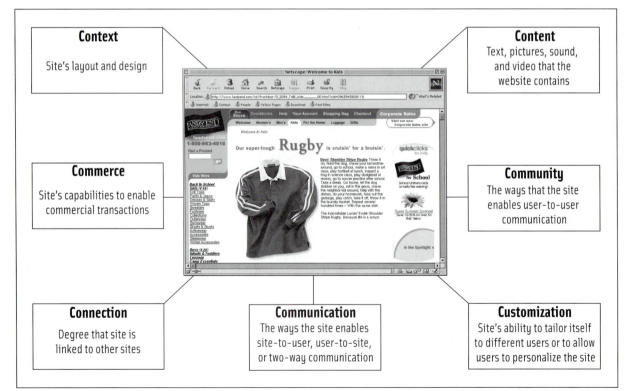

Context

Site's layout and design

Content

Text, pictures, sound, and video that the website contains

Commerce

Site's capabilities to enable commercial transactions

Community

The ways that the site enables user-to-user communication

Connection

Degree that site is linked to other sites

Communication

The ways the site enables site-to-user, user-to-site, or two-way communication

Customization

Site's ability to tailor itself to different users or to allow users to personalize the site

point in the shopping experience. It includes such information as quantity, description, size, prices, and availability, and it also provides options to "delete the item" and "order more of this." As a summary feature, the site displays the total price of items, extra services, taxes (if applicable), shipping costs (if the shipping choice has been already selected), and the grand total. The customer can choose to check out if everything in the shopping basket is acceptable. The acceptance step accesses a secure server where the customer inputs billing information (e.g., shipping address, e-mail contact address, and daytime phone number). Finally, the customer inputs the choice of credit card along with credit-card details and submits the final order.

Building Fit and Reinforcement

In the previous section, we provided a basic overview of each of the 7Cs. However, the success of a particular business such as Landsend.com depends on the extent that all of the Cs work together to support the value proposition and business model. Two concepts—fit and reinforcement—are particularly helpful in explaining how it is possible to gain synergy among the 7Cs.[1]

Fit refers to the extent to which each of the 7Cs individually support the business model. This is illustrated in Exhibit 4-2 as links between each of the Cs and the business model. Reinforcement refers to the degree of consistency between each of the Cs. This is illustrated in Exhibit 4-2 as the links between each of the Cs.

Consider, once again, Landsend.com. It largely targets the middle-class consumer, with its traditionally designed clothing, great service, and moderate prices. The content of the site "fits" this value proposition by providing mainstream and conservative fashion. Its innovative live chat "fits" with great service, and the price points of regularly priced clothing "fit" the moderate pricing strategy.

Exhibit 4-2   FIT AND REINFORCEMENT OF Cs

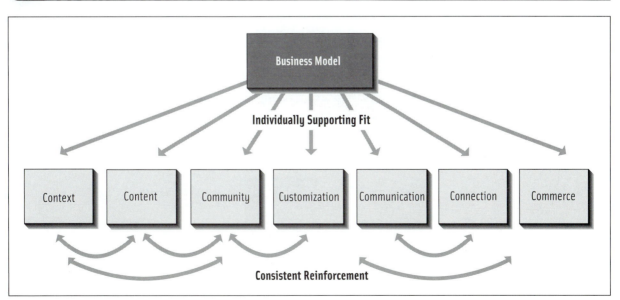

With respect to **reinforcement,** the aesthetic context of the site, the Lands' End site works well. The site's picture of a smiling customer-service representative, light-blue tones, and "soft sell" approach helps to focus the customer on the ease of product searches and navigation and on the clean and clear visual displays of clothing. The elements of context, content, customization, and commerce all work well together to provide a clear, reinforcing statement of the value proposition.

Lands' End's performance ratings by third-party evaluators also suggest that they would score high on both fit and reinforcement. In Exhibit 4-3 we provide a summary of the performance of the Lands' End's site according to five criteria. These criteria and the ratings were performed by Forrester Research (*www.forrester.com*).

WHAT DETERMINES THE LOOK-AND-FEEL OF THE DESIGN?

Context

Context is defined as the look-and-feel of a screen-to-face customer interface. The look and feel of a website, PDA, or cell phone can be categorized by both aesthetic and functional criteria. A functionally oriented site focuses largely on the core offering—whether that is product, services, or information. A good example is

Exhibit 4-3 PERFORMANCE OF THE LANDS' END SITE

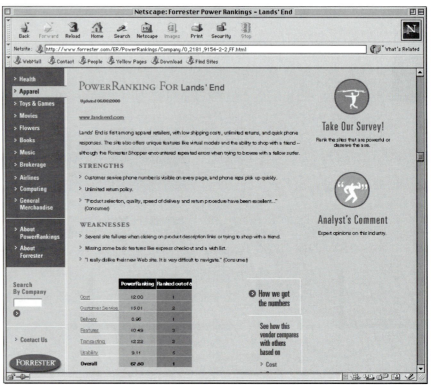

©Forrester Research, Inc.

CEOExpress.com (*www.ceoexpress.com*). CEOExpress is an information portal that aggregates magazine, newspaper, television, and other media sites into a single destination. Its design features are simple, clean, and straightforward. The site allows for quick, no-nonsense access to information that would be relevant to CEOs—stock quotes, business periodicals, news magazines, and other content-oriented sites.

In contrast, Reflect.com (*www.reflect.com*) is a more aesthetically oriented site. This does not mean that function is unimportant. The site has a very distinct look-and-feel that is artistic, visually appealing, and surprising in its blend of text, graphics, and photographs.

Nordstrom.com (*www.nordstrom.com*) combines both aesthetic and functional dimensions. On the aesthetic side, Nordstrom.com is a highly visual site with large photographs of products and fashion models. The fashion models not only communicate the product offering but also the type of woman who would purchase the Nordstrom product and the environment in which she resides. Recently, the Nordstrom site featured a model seated on the floor of what appeared to be an exclusive home with Spanish-influenced design. Clearly, this photograph attempted to set the tone for the kind of person who would be expected to shop at Nordstrom.

Dimensions to Context.
In this section, we elaborate on the two key context dimensions: function and aesthetics. In particular, we define the subdimensions of function and aesthetics and provide examples of how these dimensions are evidenced in Bluefly.com (*www.bluefly.com*). Bluefly.com is a retail store positioned as "the outlet store for your home." It has a wide variety of high-end, symbolically oriented retail goods that include clothing, household items, and gifts.

Function. Most sites contain much more information than can be usefully presented on a single computer screen, or "page." This vast amount of information must be presented to the customer in a coherent fashion, and the customer must be able to move from interest to interest within the website. A well-designed site organizes all resident information into sets of pages and provides customers with a means to navigate from page to page. Three factors are critical in the layout of the site:

- **Section Breakdown.** The section breakdown is the way the site is organized into subcomponents. Bluefly has a top-level tab structure that includes search, shopping bag, my account, flypaper, and help. Beneath this general tab structure are the categories of goods—men's, women's, kid's, house, and gifts. The homepage also includes clear directions to the following sections: bluesale, top designers, flybuys, mycatalog, and selected gift items.

- **Linking Structure.** The linking structure is the site's approach to linking its alternative sections. Clicking on the Prada brand on the Bluefly homepage enables one to visit the Prada fashion section. At the same time, the Prada fashion section is framed by the top-level tab structure and general categories that we noted earlier. This linking structure enables the users to move easily back and forth between sections of the site.

- **Navigation Tools.** The navigation tools are the site tools that facilitate how the user moves throughout the site. Navigation tools for Bluefly include mycatalog and two types of search (i.e., by price or by style number).

Another aspect of function relates to the performance of the site. As of this writing, the limited speed of most commonly available connections to the Internet presents a constraint to website design. Generally, with all else being equal, sites with limited graphics or multimedia features load in less time; i.e., at higher speeds, while sites with streaming video or large, richly detailed graphics take more time. We will now explore five dimensions of performance: speed, reliability, platform independence, media accessibility, and usability.

- **Speed.** Speed is described in terms of the time required to display a site page on the user's screen. For example, the Bluefly site is fast in that it has very short download times due to its straightforward design and limited use of complex graphics or sophisticated multimedia applications.

- **Reliability.** Reliability can be defined two ways. First, reliability is based on how often the website experiences periods of "downtime." Downtime is any time the website is unable to allow users access to the site, including periods of planned maintenance and unplanned system crashes. A second aspect of reliability is the percent of times that the site correctly downloads to the user. Even if the site is "up," it may not download correctly to the users' screens.

- **Platform Independence.** Platform independence is a measure of how well the site can run on multiple platforms that include previous versions of browsers and hardware (e.g., slower modems) and other access software. Most designers construct sites to perform on previous generation platforms.

- **Media Accessibility.** As Internet-enabled devices or Web appliances proliferate, browser-based PCs will become only one of many formats to be accommodated in the design of the website. Media accessibility (the ability of a site to download to various media platforms) may become increasingly complex. Websites may need to be simplified and designed specifically for multiple platforms until standards are established and accepted by a broad audience of users. The recent introduction of XML, a meta language for describing data, has greatly improved the Web's media accessibility. XML documents contain information about their own content that allows interface devices (such as a browser) to interpret how the content will be used. For example, Tellme networks has used XML to develop an interface that allows websites to tag content for delivery through Tellme's voice-based portal. Users can simply call Tellme from any phone to access Web-based information such as stock quotes, sports news, and flight information. Tellme promises to make the rich information of the Web accessible to everyone who has a phone.

- **Usability.** Usability is the ease with which a site can be used and navigated by users. Even if the content or the community of a site is wonderful, poor usability will make the site unappealing to users. Usability is affected by many elements of a website. For example, the speed that a site loads, the way that a site's multiple pages are structured, and the graphical design of the site all affect usability. Designing highly usable websites is part art, part science. Authors such as Jakob Nielsen have become recognized experts on usability.[2] Several sidebars in this chapter examine how some companies are working to improve the usability of their sites.

While these five performance dimensions may initially seem inappropriate for a discussion on context or the look-and-feel of a site, performance can greatly affect the user's perception and judgment of the look-and-feel of a site, especially when that site provides slow and unreliable downloads of graphic information.

Aesthetic. The aesthetic nature of the site is created by visual characteristics such as colors, graphics, photographs, font choices, and other visually oriented features. Over time, as bandwidth constraints ease for consumer use of the Web, largely visual experiences will expand into so-called rich media sites enabled by broadband services and including full use of one-way and interactive video and audio as well as text. Below we describe two aesthetic features and apply them to Bluefly.com.

- **Color Scheme.** The color scheme refers to the colors used throughout the site. As you might guess, Bluefly has emphasized a blue background for the site. It is a very light, pastel blue that conveys softness, freshness, and youthfulness.
- **Visual Themes.** Visual themes help to tell the story or stories portrayed across the site. The Luckyjeans.com site emphasizes the theme "get lucky" across many of the site pages. While the "get lucky" message is clearly a tag line, it also conveys a consistent story line throughout the site. The Bluefly brand does not appear to carry a theme or story line throughout its site.

A Visit to the Lycos Usability Lab

by Wendy Cholbi, staff writer for tnbt.com

"OK, keep your head steady . . . now look at the dot in the upper left corner of the screen," says the voice to my right. I do so, and hear a click. The voice continues: "Now look at the dot on the upper right . . ."

No, this isn't an optometrist's office. It's the laboratory of the User Experience Group at Lycos, where a video camera is being trained on my eyeballs in preparation for my introduction to Web usability testing.

When I'd heard that Lycos had eyeball-tracking equipment in its usability lab, I had had visions of a bizarre Clockwork Orange–type setup. I was secretly disappointed to find that the lab is a small, bare room furnished only with a desk, a computer, and some video and audio recording equipment—nary a lab coat or one-way mirror in sight.

Bill Albert, a soft-voiced researcher in khakis and tennis shoes, opens up the Lycos homepage and asks me to find a page where I can read discussion groups. My first task as a usability guinea pig! Will I be able to do it?

"Remember, we're not testing you, we're testing the site," Albert reminds me. "There's no way you can do anything wrong, and in fact we'll probably learn more from things you can't do." I can do no wrong! I jiggle the mouse with glee. He continues, "Now, try to talk out loud as much as you can, to describe your actions."

OK, here goes. "Well, I'm clicking on 'Boards' because . . . it sounds like a good place to find discussion boards." Duh. I wonder if all the user guinea pigs sound this lame. Though I can't see them, I know that in the next room, the other usability researchers, product managers, and Web designers are huddling around a TV screen showing exactly what I'm seeing—and where I'm looking. It's an odd feeling.

I'm attempting to reply to an item on the message board when I experience what the usability folks call a "critical instance." I mouse over the words "Post a Reply," but discover that it's not a hyperlink.

Dutifully, I narrate: "This doesn't seem to be a link. I guess I have to go somewhere else . . . do I have to sign in?" But Albert isn't allowed to answer questions, so it takes me a few clicks to discover that I do need to sign in first—a few clicks that in the real world might have cost Lycos a user.

When we discuss the test a few minutes later, the head of the usability lab takes my side. "'Post a Reply' should obviously be a link," says reed-thin, bespectacled David Hendry, in a slight Canadian accent. It turns out that two other users tested that day found the same problem, proving that it wasn't me playing dense.

"But we have to have people sign in to each discussion group—it would be impossible to have every visitor be a member of all clubs," counters Mark Staton, who is on the Lycos Clubs product team.

"Here we have a product person who's making logistics excuses for a bad design," David says to me, grinning at Mark. "We're obviously going to have to come up with a solution that's a compromise."

I like to think I've done my bit to make the Web a better place.

Read more articles about The Next Big Thing at *www.tnbt.com*

Context Archetypes

Context archetypes refer to broad, generic approaches to context design. There are two broad dimensions of context: function and aesthetics, which can be arrayed in a two-by-two matrix (see Exhibit 4-4). Some argue that there is an inherent trade-off between **form** and **function.** However, with the introduction of new technological capabilities, some feel that trade-offs are not fixed but are changing; i.e., new technologies introduce new techniques that then introduce new aesthetics. However, even given these varying points of view, we consider three context archetypes: aesthetically dominant, functionally dominant, and integrated.

Exhibit 4-4

FORM VS. FUNCTION—THE DESIGN CONTEXT FRONTIER

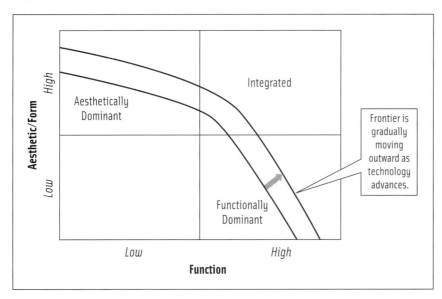

Aesthetically Dominant. The aesthetically dominant archetype is categorized by high form, or aesthetics, but low function. The primary emphasis is on the look-and-feel of the website. This type of site makes heavy use of multimedia or visual elements, even though this use may lead to poor performance. These sites contain pages that are visually composed with careful use and placement of the multimedia. Various art forms are frequently used to make these sites a pleasant escape for the user.

A good example of the aesthetic archetype is KMGI (*www.kmgi.com;* see Exhibit 4-5). KMGI is an online advertising agency specializing in effective online advertising. It offers a variety of services ranging from Web design to advice on ways to attract audiences to a site. KMGI uses text, graphics, sound, and top-notch animation in its "Webmercials" to create a highly aesthetically pleasing product that is comparable to television commercials in quality. However, the site is slow to load, limited in information for users, and has less evident function than most sites on the Web.

Functionally Dominant. As Exhibit 4-4 illustrates, the functionally dominant context archetype has low form but high function. The assumption is that users care little about visual elements or themes on the site, but they care much about information. This type of site focuses on the display of textual information and limits the visual design to the bare minimum required to keep the site operational.

An example of a functionally dominant context archetype is Brint.com (see Exhibit 4-6). Brint.com is all about content (*www.brint.com*). This site is a knowledge source for people in business. It contains sections for different business areas (e.g., E-biz & Internet Commerce Portal, Knowledge Economy Portal, and General Business Portal). Brint.com derives its success from the plethora of knowledge it makes available to people with questions related to business practices.

The site is pure text—no graphics, sound, or animation. The website is organized by areas of interest. It has a cluttered feel with an abundance of hyperlinks arranged closely to each other on each page. Although our example with Brint.com

Exhibit 4-5

AESTHETICALLY DOMINANT
EXAMPLE—KMGI.com

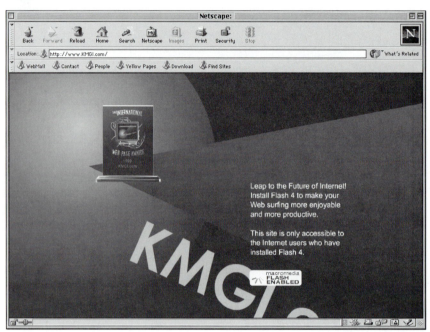

Design by Nikolai Mentchoukov, KMGI.com, Inc.

Exhibit 4-6

FUNCTIONALLY DOMINANT
EXAMPLE—Brint.com

Reprinted with the permission of "@Brint.com The BizTech Network," the Premier Business and Technology Portal and Global Community Network for E-Business, Information Technology and Knowledge Management. http://www.brint.com

is almost exclusively composed of textual links, many comparable sites contain content that is user-generated text in the form of chats, ratings, and reviews.

Integrated. The integrated archetype is a balance of form and function that creates an attractive and easy-to-use interface (see Exhibit 4-4). This type of site provides navigational tools as visual cues to allow users one-click access to any part of the site. Many times these sites have a clear and appealing theme or themes that support the underlying graphics or color schemes.

A good example of the integrated approach is Patagonia.com (*www.patagonia.com*). Patagonia.com is an online counterpart of the high-quality outdoor clothing and gear retailer (see Exhibit 4-7). Patagonia knows its athletic customers often seek

Exhibit 4-7 INTEGRATED APPROACH EXAMPLE—*patagonia.com*

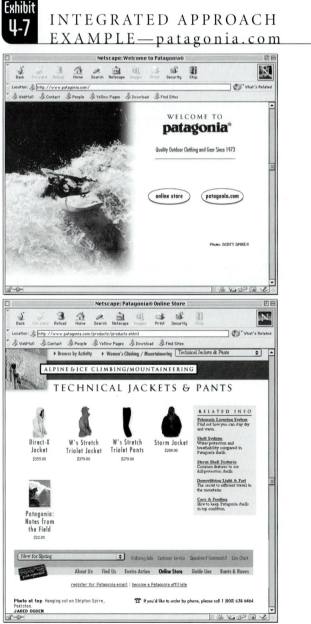

Form Vs. Function

Prior to our discussion of content, it is important to note that our suggested context archetype is not fully representative of prevailing views of design. Jeffrey Veen, Executive Interface Director for Wired Digital, the Web-based publisher of Hotwired, categorizes sites along two dimensions: form and function.[3] The form dimension is similar to our aesthetic dimension. Veen argues that there is a clear trade-off between form and function. According to Veen, it is impossible to create a site that combines both high function and elegant form. Thus, any attempt to design a site with high form or high function always results in a compromise—resulting in a suboptimal site.

While Veen's point of view frames the context question, it does not accommodate the constant evolution toward higher function in conjunction with higher form driven by technological advances and increasing bandwidth. We could argue that designers can move sites away from a suboptimal area of low form and low function by increasing form or function or both. Hence, successful sites can be identified along a form versus function frontier. This frontier expands outward with the advent of new technology and new understandings of how to use design in the Web medium, while providing new options to include new techniques and new aesthetics as new forms and new functions.

gear for a specific purpose and have provided a website that features three different areas: activity (e.g., skiing), product type (e.g., jackets), and special sale items.

The site is visually pleasing and inviting with its array of outdoor pictures. Each photo tells a story of outdoor adventure and provides the customer a degree of excitement in shopping for gear. Product pages are similarly evocative with photos depicting the beauty of the outdoor activities that the products are designed for, hopefully increasing the user's desire to actively participate.

The site combines the use of a simple design theme, small images (for rapid download), and plenty of white space. Zoom-in photos and further product information are only one click away.

WHAT ARE THE FIVE CONTENT ARCHETYPES?

Content

Content refers to all digital information included on the site. This is broadly conceived to include audio, video, image, and text content.

Dimensions to Content. In this section, we consider four dimensions of content: the offering, appeal, and multimedia mixes and content type. As we consider these dimensions, we will apply the concepts to a now familiar example, Gear.com.

Offering Mix. The content of the site can include product, information, and/or services. Frequently, sites include a mix of these three elements. Gear.com focuses almost exclusively on product content with significantly less emphasis on information or services. Product offerings include items in the outdoor shop, team sports, cycling shop, snow sports, golf shop, and others.

Appeal Mix. The appeal mix refers to the promotional and communications messaging projected by the company. Naturally, one would expect the appeal mix to be strongly linked to the value proposition. The academic literature has identified two broad types of appeals: cognitive and emotional. Cognitive appeals focus on functional aspects of the offering, including such factors as low price, reliability, availability, breadth of offerings, customer support, and degree of personalization. Emotional appeals focus on emotionally resonant ties to the product or brand. These include humor, novelty, warmth, or stories. Turning again to Gear.com, their tag line is "brand name sporting goods at closeout prices." This tag line suggests a very functionally or cognitively oriented appeal—good brands at low prices.

Multimedia Mix. The multimedia mix refers to the choices of media, including text, audio, image, video, and graphics. Gear.com is largely composed of pictures of products, product information, and pricing. There is very limited use of audio, video, and graphics.

Content Type. Information that has been collected and presented on a website has a degree of time-sensitivity. Current content is highly time-sensitive information with a very short shelf life. Bloomberg and Reuters are examples of proprietary sources of real-time financial market data. Week-old stock data has limited value, except for archival and research purposes, as compared with stock information that is instantaneous. On the other hand, reference content is less time-sensitive information with a longer shelf life. Often it is historical in nature. This type of content is used as supporting or related factual material. NYTimes.com is an online publication with an archive of articles published in the past and available for reference. Gear.com provides a great deal of current content (e.g., special deals in a product category, brand, and season) but very little reference content.

Content Archetypes

In this section, we describe five content archetypes: superstore, category killer, specialty (offering-dominant), information-dominant, and market-dominant. These archetypes are largely derived from the first content dimension, offering mix. We first describe each archetype and then provide a brief description of various sites that are representative of the archetype.

Offering-Dominant.
Offering archetypes are store sites that sell physical goods and have analog equivalents in the physical world marketplace. In this section, we consider three store types—the "superstore," the "category killer," and the "specialty store." In Exhibit 4-8, we classify these stores on two dimensions: number of product categories (multiple versus single) and depth of product line (narrow versus broad).

Superstore. A superstore is a one-stop shop where the customer can find a wide range of goods in multiple product categories. The site is commonly organized by product category and subcategory. The superstore may also offer price comparisons with additional incentives such as price discounts, coupons, and specials.

Exhibit 4-8 A FRAMEWORK TO UNDERSTAND OFFERING-DOMINATE ARCHETYPES

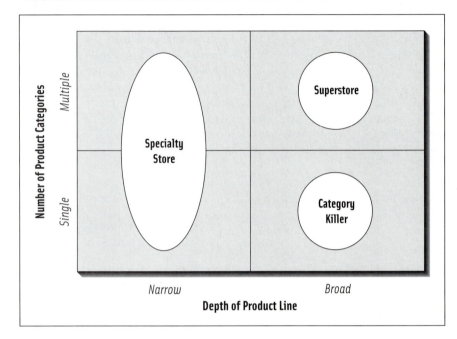

Amazon.com began as an online store for books but gradually extended its offerings to include a number of product categories including CDs, DVDs and videos, electronics, and toys (*www.amazon.com*). Navigation is simplified for the customer through a tab structure at the top of the screen that allows easy movement from store to store. A row of subtabs situated below each store tab provides immediate access to subcategories within the selected store (see Exhibit 4-9).

In addition to product categories, Amazon.com introduced the concept of zShops. For a low monthly fee, any user can set up their own store online in Amazon.com's zShops category and start selling goods. Sellers specify asking price and shipping terms while buyers can accept or reject the deal but are not provided any ability to counteroffer (i.e., no haggling). Upon buyer acceptance of a deal, Amazon.com contacts the seller and completes the transaction for the buyer.

Category Killer. A category killer exclusively provides products and services by specific product or by a customer-needs category. These sites offer a comprehensive selection of products and services but only within the specific category. Category killers also provide extensive product descriptions and recommendations along with additional incentives of price discounts and specials.

Petsmart.com (see Exhibit 4-10) is all about pets. It serves as a one-stop shop for all needs of almost all pet owners. Pets of interest are categorized as dogs, cats, birds, fish, reptiles, and small animals. Users can choose from a variety of products for each pet category. The site also provides chat rooms for interactions with licensed veterinary professionals, message boards for pet owners in each pet category, and responses to frequently asked question in an Answers section.

Exhibit 4-9	SUPERSTORE EXAMPLE— Amazon.com

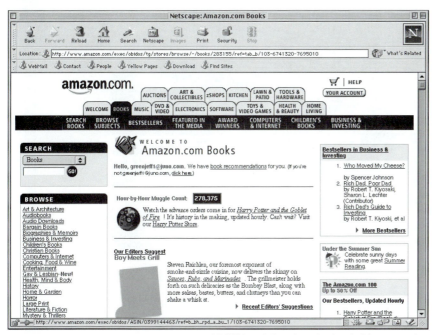

AMAZON.com is the registered trademark of Amazon.com, Inc.

As the user selects a pet category, the content of the site is adjusted and the website becomes the comprehensive pet store for that particular pet. Any product that the user can think of (for the dog owner, products range from dog apparel and 11 different types of dog food to dog vitamins and supplements) is categorized to the left of the site. The layout of the page makes it easy for customers to find what they need while unobtrusively presenting additional items to encourage impulse buying. The feeling one gets is, "If it's not here, it's probably not out there."

Specialty Store. A specialty store focuses on exceptional quality and exclusivity while selling single or multiple categories of products. Winespectator.com (*www.winespectator.com*) is an example of a single-category specialty store. An example of a multiple-category specialty store is frontgate.com (*www.frontgate.com*). These sites commonly provide high-quality imagery, photographs, and graphics. In addition, they provide extensive descriptions and background information on the products offered. Just as in the physical world, specialty stores tend to offer products or services that cater to customers shopping to fulfill part of a lifestyle need or consideration.

Frontgate (*www.frontgate.com*) is a good example of a specialty store that focuses on lifestyle positioning (see Exhibit 4-11). Frontgate carries a wide variety of home-related products, but the products have an air of traditional quality, high standards, and exclusivity. This is true across a wide range of product categories for the home, including "gourmet kitchen" goods, bath and outdoor furnishings, and grills.

CATEGORY KILLER EXAMPLE—
Petsmart.com

Exhibit 4-11

SPECIALTY STORE EXAMPLE—
Frontgate.com

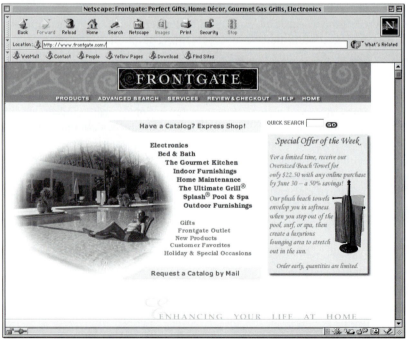

Information-Dominant. Information-dominant content archetypes focus heavily on information, but a subset of these sites focuses on entertainment as well. Information-dominant sites organize and house vast archives of information and provide tools to the customer to explore areas of interest and to find answers to specific questions. These sites can be generators of content, sources of content, or aggregators of content from other sources.

Fast Company.com (*www.fastcompany.com;* see Exhibit 4-12) is an example of an information-dominant site that focuses on providing information on cutting edge business ideas. From Old to New Economy, Fast Company puts its readers on the frontier of how strategy is being implemented in dynamic marketplaces. In addition to original content staff writers and guest columnists, Fast Company reinforces its reputation as a strategy information-dominant site by offering live events, monthly book-club chats, local discussion groups, and online discussion forums. Fast Company creates content that generally falls into one of the following themes: new ways of working, the digital domain, new logic of competition, learning, change, leadership, social justice, innovation and creativity, coping, design, and neoleisure.

Market-Dominant. Market-dominant archetype sites do not directly offer goods or services for sale but create a market where buyers and sellers congregate to conclude transactions. These sites serve as brokers and act as catalysts for business transactions. A vertical hub is a market site that addresses products and services associated with a single industry, while a horizontal hub serves a functional area across a number of industries. Market sites often provide product comparison tools and industry information, as well as links to supplier sites.

Exhibit 4-12 INFORMATION DOMINANT EXAMPLE— Fast Company.com

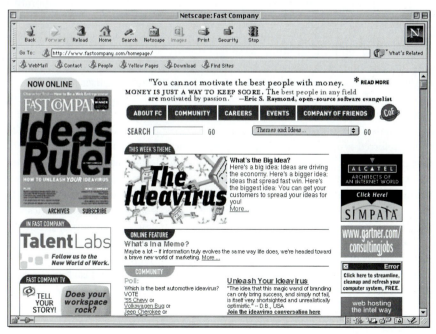

From www.fastcompany.com. All rights reserved.

Exhibit 4-13

MARKET-DOMINANT EXAMPLE—
Commerx PlasticsNet.com

Courtesy of Commerx, Inc.

Founded in 1995, Commerx PlasticsNet (see Exhibit 4-13) is a vertical hub for the plastic products industry developed by Commerx, a provider of collaborative e-commerce solutions. It brings together more than 90,000 monthly visitors with over 200 suppliers. The site is not only a marketplace for plastics, it also provides support for an online community as well as resources that include a supplier directory, material data sheets, an industry publication, job postings, and an Education Center. The Education Center is a search engine that allows the user to find a variety of educational programs, books, and seminars specific to their industry segment with one simple search.

Customers are guided through a process to select products of interest as well as their preferred type of transaction (catalog or auction). Customers can create "My Custom Catalogs" by specifying products they prefer to buy and the suppliers from whom they prefer to buy. In the Catalog sales, the site presents a detailed list of product options with set or negotiated contract prices, and the customers can proceed to complete the transaction. Commerx Global Xchange, accessed through PlasticsNet, provides auction-style pricing where customers can bid on limited-supply products. In most cases, prices drop continually and new products sell quickly. Customers must set their preferences and check back often to complete transactions.

Content archetypes cross all offering types. Table 4-1 shows that each of the content archetypes can be illustrated with a product, information, or service example. Thus, while one has a tendency to think about physical product superstores, the reality is that there are also information superstores (e.g., *www.ceoexpress.com*) and

Table
4-1

CONTENT ARCHETYPES VS. OFFERING TYPES

	Physical Product	Information	Service
Superstore	Walmart.com	CEOExpress.com	IBMSolutions.com
Category Killer	Petsmart.com	DowJones.com	Schwab.com
Specialty	Frontgate.com	Tnbt.com	Tradex.com
Information-Dominant	Census.gov	IFilm.com	Digitalthink.com
Market-Dominant	PlasticsNet.com	VerticalNet.com	Monster.com

service superstores (e.g., *www.ibmsolutions.com*). Most sites seem to offer a hybrid of these three offering types.

WHAT MAKES A COMMUNITY?

Community

Community includes a feeling of membership in a group along with a strong sense of involvement and shared common interests with that group. A group of people can create strong, lasting relationships that may develop into a sense of community through an engaged and extended exchange of views focused on their shared common interests. However, community not only contains elements of common interest and group acceptance. It also contains individual involvement. This sense of community can help encourage users and customers to return to a website.

Community is based on user-to-user communication. This communication can be one-to-one or one-to-many. Several authors have recently investigated community formation and maintenance within e-commerce sites. There are several ways to categorize communities including elements of a community, types of communities, degrees of participation, and member benefits. Exhibit 4-14 illustrates how these components of a community can be integrated.

Elements of a Community

The degree of community formation can be assessed along six criteria:[4]

- **Cohesion.** Sense of group identity and individual sense of belonging to the group.
- **Effectiveness.** Impact of the group on members' lives.
- **Help.** Perceived ability to ask for and receive help.
- **Relationships.** Likelihood of individual interaction and friendship formation.
- **Language.** The prevalence of specialized language.
- **Self-Regulation.** The ability of the group to police itself.

Is Content King?

There is considerable debate concerning the role of content in the success of online businesses. There are a number of pundits who argue that content is king and that the design interface and infrastructure are significantly less important. The argument has merit. Websites must have excellent content to compete in the targeted segment. Evidence suggests that even within a given product category (e.g., clothing), there are multiple strong content plays (e.g., Nordstrom vs. Lands' End vs. Bluelight). Users are able to discern inferior content due to negative word of mouth and network effects. This information disseminates quickly and drives out inferior content players.

Opponents of this point of view argue that content is certainly important, but it is not the only game in town. First, content is necessary for success, but it is not sufficient in its own right. Second, Web businesses appear to win more often on numbers of users rather than amount of content. Hence, some large dominant players leverage their brand names to drive out better-content competitors. Third, the most recent information sources, even if not the best content, can win out over the best content providers if the content is not current. Thus, news headline sites can be dominated by content players like the *New York Times* because NYTimes.com updates on a regular but not constant basis. However, for a segment of news junkies who want the freshest content, the Associated Press newswire may be the best source. Finally, *content* is a word that is misused and abused. If content means "just about everything" on the Web, then it loses precision and managerial relevance. Thus, content will always win because "everything is content." This circular argument results in little value.

Types of Communities

Several types of groups have been identified. In a later section on archetypes, we provide a complementary classification scheme.

- **Just Friends.** People who want to meet and socialize.
- **Enthusiasts.** People who share a special interest.
- **Friends in Need.** Support groups.
- **Players.** People who participate in game playing.
- **Traders.** People who trade possessions with one another.[5]

Degree of Member Participation

Users can choose different levels of participation in an online community. In the book *Virtual Reality Case Book*, Randall Farmer describes the four levels of participation.[6]

- **Passives.** Individuals who do not actively engage in but attend virtual communities.
- **Actives.** Those who participate in activities and topics created by others.
- **Motivators.** Those who create topics and plan activities of interest to other community members.
- **Caretakers.** Those who serve as intermediaries between community members.

Exhibit 4-14	COMMUNITIES—ELEMENTS, TYPES, AND BENEFITS

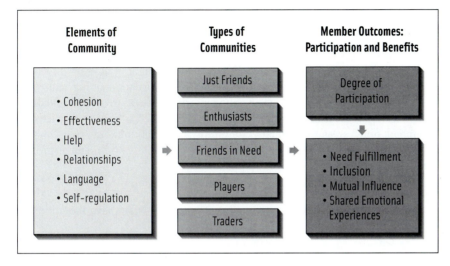

Elements of Community

- Cohesion
- Effectiveness
- Help
- Relationships
- Language
- Self-regulation

Types of Communities

- Just Friends
- Enthusiasts
- Friends in Need
- Players
- Traders

Member Outcomes: Participation and Benefits

Degree of Participation

- Need Fulfillment
- Inclusion
- Mutual Influence
- Shared Emotional Experiences

Member Benefits

Participants can derive a number of benefits from participation in the community that include the following:

- **Need Fulfillment.** The degree to which a participant's needs are satisfied.
- **Inclusion.** The extent to which participants are open and encouraged to participate in each other's plans and activities.
- **Mutual Influence.** The extent to which participants openly discuss issues and affect one another.
- **Shared Emotional Experiences.** The extent to which participants include each other in sharing events that specifically arouse feeling and are typically memorable.[7]

Dimensions of Community

Interactive Communication. Users or customers can directly and continually exchange responses with each other as interactive communication. Sites can provide facilities to support real-time or near real-time user-to-user interactive communication as electronic conversation in several forms that include the following:

- **Chat.** Asynchronous chat allows users to consider their response and formulate a response in nonreal time.
- **Instant Messaging or Instant Chat.** This form allows messages to happen quickly, because each participant sees the message within seconds of when it is sent. Examples include ICQ.com and AOL Instant Messenger. (ICQ is now a subsidiary of AOL.)
- **Message Boards.** Message boards allow a user to communicate with another by posting messages on a specific location on the website.

- **Member-to-Member e-Mail.** e-mail is the "killer app" of the Web—acting as a virtual post office for digitized messages.

Noninteractive Communication.
Noninteractive communication does not involve the direct and continual exchange of responses between users. Many times, noninteractive communication is supported by a structure that gives the user a sense of permanence and place rather than a continuous stream of conversation.

Sites or areas of sites can present static information and only allow unidirectional communication with users. Frequently, the site information only needs to be updated periodically. Users can view online information but are not provided any means to respond. Also, users may be controlled and access may be restricted to "members only" areas that contain community information. Some users may be allowed access only to public areas that contain community and member profiles that are made available to the general public.

Members make noninteractive contributions to community in two ways:

- **Public Member Webpages.** Community members may have the option of crafting their own webpages on a particular site.
- **Member Content.** Similar to public member webpages, this is content that is generated by members.

Community Archetypes

In this section, we consider several broad types of communities that have emerged on the Internet. As noted earlier, there are alternative classification schemes to categorize members (e.g., recall the approach noted earlier that included "just friends"). However, it is often helpful to consider multiple ways to conceive of Web communities. Again, we borrow names from the brick-and-mortar world to help us understand their counterparts in the digital world. In this spirit, we introduce six types of virtual communities: bazaar, theme park, club, shrine, theater, and café.[8] The first three communities are distinguished by the number of "interest areas," while the last three vary on the level of interactivity built into the site. We conclude this section with a discussion of ways these two dimensions—interest area focus and interactivity—can be combined.

Bazaar.
A bazaar is defined as a community that allows users to wander through a vast number of interest areas but does not provide any means for users to interact with each other in any meaningful way. This virtual space is lined with virtual shops and stalls where users can browse and wander through huge areas. The bazaar can be similar to a portal in that many times the user arrives here only to be presented with links to many other destinations. Here, users have no specific common interest to share or to focus upon. This place offers the user an unstructured sense of exploration but only unengaged or limited interactions with other users. No sense of community can easily be planted in the bazaar.

Yahoo! Games is a typical example of a bazaar. Yahoo! Games is a play world for Web wanderers (see Exhibit 4-15). The site is a wide collection of free, Java-based games. These are games that can be played alone or with multiple players connected to the Internet. Users wander through any of the available open play rooms and invite other room participants to play with them. Although friends might invite each other to play a game online or players might be able to comment on game results, community is not a high priority. The goal here is to have fun playing the games that the site provides.

Theme Park. A theme park is defined as a community that focuses on a finite number of interest areas that are organized by categories and subcategories. These sites commonly host a large number of communities. Members interact with each other, but few strong bonds are formed. VoxCap.com (see Exhibit 4-16) is an interactive community where individuals, organizations, and businesses interact with each other to take action concerning political, civic, and social issues. It enables users to create communities around issues that include education, family, health, environment, society, economics, and the world. Users are encouraged to share information, speak out on issues, and connect with others who have common interests to build and mobilize support for causes. Members can get informed, contribute text to newsletters and clubs, or start their own discussion group or newsletter. The site also allows members to reach out to their communities by providing e-mail links to local politicians and newspapers.

Club. A club is defined as a community that is highly focused on only one area of interest and promotes a considerable amount of interaction among members. These sites typically provide large volumes of information about the targeted area or the areas of interest. Gillette Women's Cancer Connection site (*gillettecancercon nect.org;* see Exhibit 4-17) provides a community where women can discuss all of the issues associated with any form of women's cancer. Community activities include chats, message boards, and special events. This community has a single point of focus—women learning about and living with cancer.

Exhibit 4-15

BAZAAR EXAMPLE—
Games.Yahoo.com

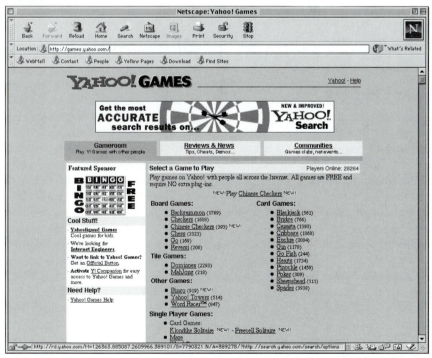

Reproduced with permission of Yahoo! Inc. ©2000 by Yahoo! Inc.
YAHOO! and the YAHOO! logo are trademarks of Yahoo! Inc.

Exhibit 4-16 · THEME PARK EXAMPLE—VoxCap.com

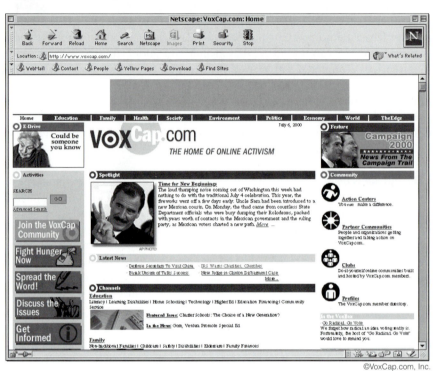

©VoxCap.com, Inc.

Shrine. A shrine is defined as a highly focused community with minimal interaction between members. The essence of the shrine is evidence of member activities that exhibit extreme enthusiasm toward a common person or object of interest. Although these sites many times provide chat opportunities and message-board facilities, only a minimal amount of interaction occurs among members. However, the greater part of the community content is member-contributed. These communities have high membership involvement, highly focused subject matter, and capabilities for interactive communication, but member-to-member exchanges are in the form of offering icons rather than conversation. The sense of community is muted by an intensely personal rather than public site experience.

An example is the Unofficial Dawson's Creek Web-Site (*http://dawsonsite.cjb.net*). It is composed of a number of areas that include biographies of the TV show's characters, an episode guide, still photographs, an unofficial newsletter, and links to other Dawson's Creek sites. There is also a news and rumors section. This site does encourage some level of interaction by including a message board and chat room.

Many shrine websites are unofficial in that the people operating the sites are not affiliated in any way with the sites' featured persons or objects of adoration. These sites often contain unauthorized copyrighted materials, but because the sites are operated by fans and do not have any commercial aspect, copyright holders have tended not to prosecute.

Theatre. A theatre is a community that is focused in a particular area but allows for moderate interaction among members. These sites present provocative and com-

Exhibit 4-17 CLUB EXAMPLE—GILLETTE WOMEN'S CANCER CONNECTION

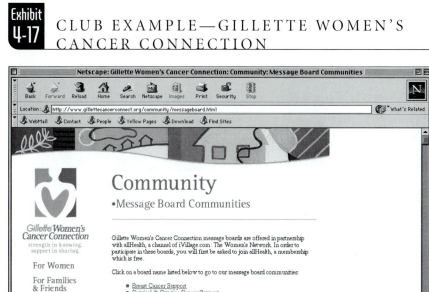

Illustration appears with permission of The Gillette Company

pelling content to trigger member interactions and to drive membership involvement in the form of conversation or reviews that are then used to further drive site content. iFilm.com (see Exhibit 4-18) is a film portal site that hosts independent films free of charge and provides filmmakers a previously unreachable audience. Site users download posted movies and view them online. Hosted films can receive immediate online reviews and ratings by online viewers. Although additional community-building tools are provided on the site (e.g., message boards and chat rooms), the online reviews and ratings are considered highly valuable community content. Because they are generated as a result of the original content on the site, they reinforce membership.

Café. A café is defined as a community that focuses on a common area of interest but also provides for considerable interaction among members. At this site, the primary focus is on conversation among members. These sites present an easily accessible and appropriately configured platform that supports the interaction. These sites also have the highest amount of interaction among community members. Typically, users are highly active in both receiving and creating content. Bolt (see Exhibit 4-19) is a popular online destination for high-school and college students. The main reason users come to the site is to communicate with their peers and voice their opinions. Bolt provides a variety of communication tools to encourage community participation by including chat rooms, message boards, instant messaging, polls, free e-mail, and homepage hosting. Ninety-five percent of site content is created by site users. Topics of discussion range from classes to music to parents to dating.

Exhibit 4-18

THEATER EXAMPLE—
iFilm.com

©IFILM Corp.

At the outset of this section, we noted that community archetypes could be divided into two dimensions. The first dimension is the degree of focus—from a single area to multiple areas of interest. The second dimension is the degree of member interactivity related to the site. In Exhibit 4-20, we cross these two dimensions to create nine possible community types. Most interestingly, this chart illustrates that a number of hybrid communities can form by combining interactivity and focus in unique ways.

WHAT ARE THE LEVERS USED TO CUSTOMIZE A SITE?

Customization

Customization refers to a site's ability to tailor itself to each user or be tailored by each user. To better address individual user needs, a site can be designed to be altered by the user or by the organization. Customization can be initiated by the user, a process we term "personalization," or by the organization, a process we term "tailoring."

Exhibit 4-19

CAFE EXAMPLE—
Bolt.com

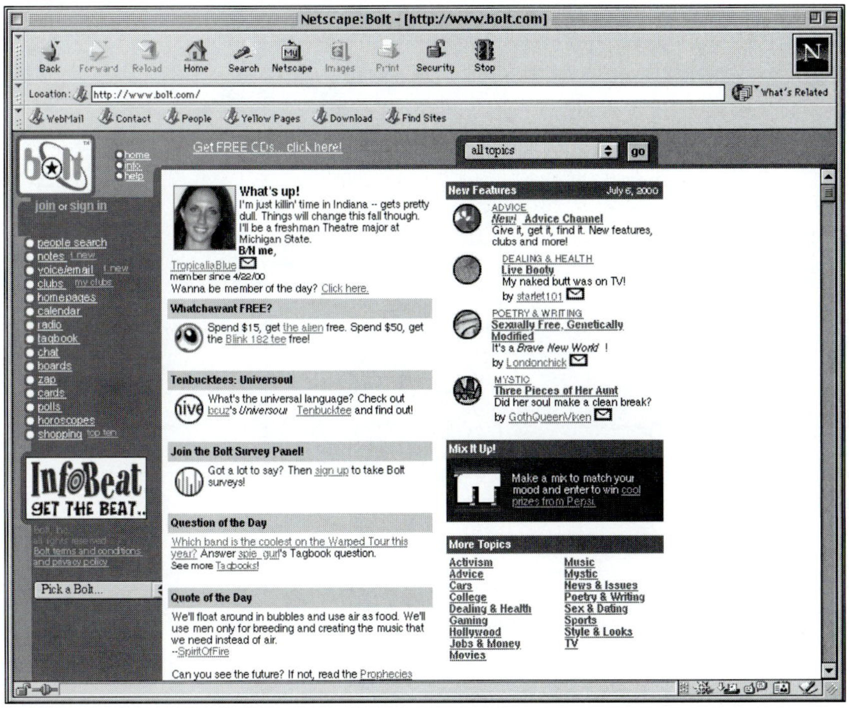

Dimensions of Customization.

Personalization. Some websites allow users to specify their preferences in content selection, context selection, and personalization tools. Once personal preferences have been entered by the user and saved, the site uses a log-in registration or "cookies" to match each returning user to his or her respective personal setting. The site then configures itself to these preferences accordingly. To attract users and to keep them returning, the site provides a variety of features that include personalized e-mail accounts, virtual hard-disk storage, and software agents to perform simple tasks.

- **Log-in Registration.** Having previously registered on a site, the user returns and enters the requisite identification information. The site then recognizes the returning user and configures itself to the preset preferences accordingly.

- **Cookies.** Most website owners want to identify and understand the users of their sites and the use of their sites. These sites frequently attempt to track and gather data about the returning users' behavior by quietly saving identifying and tracking information on the users' local disk storage in temporary files called "cookies."

- **Personalized e-Mail Accounts.** Many sites provide e-mail accounts free of charge to the user. Users may send and receive e-mail from the site, using a unique e-mail address.

- **Content and Layout Configuration.** Users can select site screen layout and content sources based on their interests.

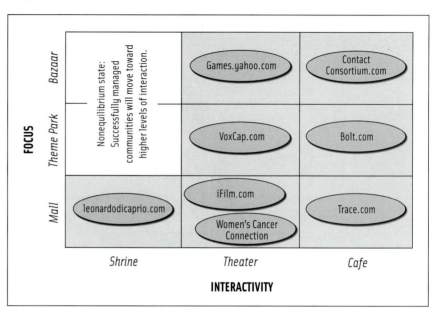

Exhibit 4-20

FOCUS VS. INTERACTIVITY

Storage. Sites provide virtual hard-disk storage space. Users can store e-mail, URLs, and other interesting content on these sites.

Agents. Users can initiate computer programs, also known as agents, that are designed to perform specific simple tasks (e.g., notify them via e-mail when a product is in stock).

Tailoring by Site. Many sites have the ability through their software to dynamically publish unique versions of the site to address a specific user's interests, habits, and needs more appropriately. This tailoring of a site can be designed to reconfigure and present different contents with various design layouts to individual users, depending on each user's responses and/or profile. A site can use a recommendation engine (e.g., collaborative filtering as developed by Firefly or NetPerceptions) to adapt automatically to each user's behavior and to vary the site's offering mix of products, information, and services. The site can also further recommend content or products that the user is likely to find of interest. Recommendations can be made based on past purchases by the user or based on purchases by other users with similar purchase profiles. A site can be automated to offer each user more suitable price and payment terms. Marketing messages can also be developed for the individual user based on exhibited behavior or declared preferences.

Tailoring Based on Past User Behavior. Many sites adjust themselves dynamically, based on a user's past behavior and preferences. Examples of automated adjustments include price, payment terms, and marketing messages.

Tailoring Based on Behavior of Other Users with Similar Preferences. Some sites make recommendations to the user based on preferences of other users with similar usage profiles (e.g., collaborative filtering).

Customization Archetypes

Customization archetypes are websites grouped by the source of customization that is either personalization by the user or tailoring by the site.

Personalization by User.
This form of customization (**personalization by user**) enables the user to modify site content and context based on consciously articulated and acted-upon preferences. The user can make layout selections and content source selections. Users of mylook.com (see Exhibit 4-21) can toggle-off or toggle-on presentation of headlines from a list of news sources as well as images from a list of webcams. Configurations for four layouts are offered. Depending on the layout selected, four to six webcam images can be viewed simultaneously.

Tailoring by Site.
This form of customization (**tailoring by site**) enables the site to reconfigure itself based on past behavior by the user or by other users with similar profiles. These sites can make recommendations based on past purchases, filter marketing messages based on user interests, and adjust prices and products based on user profiles. The Amazon.com site (see Exhibit 4-22) uses collaborative filtering to compare each user's purchases with the purchases of other users with similar preferences to create a list of additional purchase recommendations. Amazon also makes recommendations across product categories. For example, based on a user's history of book purchases, the site recommends CDs or DVDs that others with similar book interests have bought.

WHAT TYPES OF COMMUNICATION CAN A FIRM MAINTAIN WITH ITS CUSTOMER BASE?

Communication

Communication refers to dialogue that is initiated by the organization. The dialogue may be unidirectional (one-way from the organization to the user) or more interactive.

Dimensions of Communication.
Below we describe and provide examples of three dimensions of communication: broadcast, interactive, and hybrid.

Broadcast. Broadcast communication is a one-way information exchange from organization to user. With this unidirectional transmission of information, organizations provide no mechanism for the user to make a return response. In general, broadcast is a "one-to-many" relationship between the website and its users. Below, we describe the alternative forms of broadcast communication.

- **Mass Mailings.** Mass mailings are the broadcast transmissions of large volumes of e-mail targeted at relatively large audiences.
- **FAQ.** Organizations post webpages with clear answers to Frequently Asked Questions (FAQs) about the site, goods, or services.
- **e-Mail Newsletters.** Regular newsletters are sent by e-mail to inform site subscribers of new features or changes to a site, special offers, letters from other subscribers, corporate news, etc.

PERSONALIZATION BY USER
EXAMPLE—my look.com

Exhibit 4-21

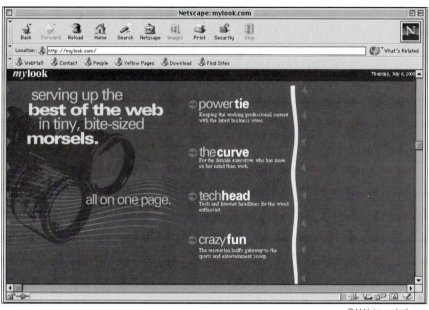

TAILORING BY SITE EXAMPLE—
Amazon.com

Exhibit 4-22

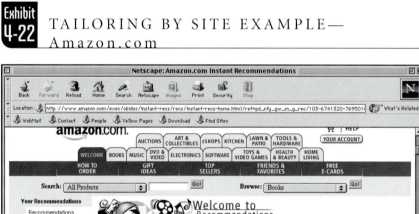

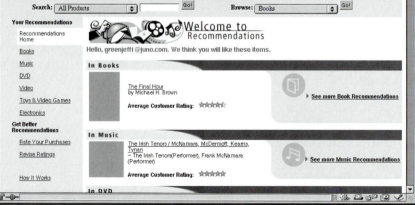

- **Content-Update Reminders.** E-mail messages can be further tailored to reflect each subscriber's interests and serve as a content-update reminder of relevant new content now available.
- **Broadcast Events.** Also, events can be broadcast (or sometimes referred to as webcast) from a website that allows limited user control over variables such as camera view.

Interactive. Interactive communication is two-way communication between the organization and a user. Below we describe alternative forms of interactive communication.

- **e-Commerce Dialogue.** Organizations use two-way communication as part of the e-commerce dialogue. Organizations and users regularly trade e-mail messages regarding order placement, tracking, and fulfillment.
- **Customer Service.** Organizations can provide customer service through the swapping of e-mail or through live online dialogue.
- **User Input.** Another two-way communication occurs when user input is an integral part of the content of a site (e.g., user-generated articles on topics of interest, user ratings of suppliers, and user feedback to the site).

POINT OF VIEW

Karman Parsaye's Methodology for Measuring Personalization

In his published article "PQ: The Personalization Quotient of a Website," Kamran Parsaye attempts to develop a methodology for calculating a site's degree of personalization. According to Parsaye's article, the Personalization Quotient (PQ) has three components:

- Customization (PQ1) measures the system's ability to customize items by allowing individual users to set their own preferences.
- Individualization (PQ2) measures the system's ability to customize itself to the user based on the user's exhibited behavior.
- Group-characterization (PQ3) measures the system's ability to customize itself to the user based on the preferences of other users with similar interests.

Parsaye then takes the average of these three quotients to derive the Personalization Quotient of a website: $PQ = (PQ1 + PQ2 + PQ3)/3$

The following presents ways to calculate each of these three quotients:

- Customization (PQ1) can be measured by taking the ratio of all the options that the user is allowed to change (call that Allowed) over all the options that could possibly be changed (call that Possible).
- Individualization (PQ2) can be measured by calculating the percentage of times that the item the site selects for a user is an item of maximum interest to them. If U is a user and Nj is item j on a site and match (U, Nj) gives the level of interest of item Nj to user U, then PQ2 = % times match (U, Nj) is maximized.
- Group Characterization (PQ3) can be measured by calculating how often similar users get shown similar pages. If $\delta U = \delta(U1, U2)$ is the difference between User 1 and User 2 and $\delta P = \delta(P1, P2)$ is the difference between Page 1 (viewed by User 1) and Page 2 (viewed by User 2), then $PQ3 = 100/\text{maximum}(\delta U/\delta P, \delta P/\delta U)$.

Hybrid. Hybrid communication, as its name indicates, is a combination of broadcast and interactive communications. These sites offer software tools as "freeware" that users can download and use at no charge for their work or entertainment. Users often pass this free software to friends and, in essence, provide free marketing to the originating site. Companies use this technique of viral marketing with the hope of rapid, broad distribution and immediate creation of brand recognition.

Communication Archetypes

Communication archetypes are grouped by types of site-to-user communication and user-to-site communication.

One-to-Many, Nonresponding User. This type of site communicates with users through mass mailings targeted at defined audiences. Communications typically are in the form of e-mail newsletters or broadcast events. Site messages are announcements that users receive without needing to respond. Site content is presented with no means for customer response. A site called TheStandard.com (see Exhibit 4-23) provides site-generated content and some is also available in the *Industry Standard* publication. Site newsletters, 19 at the time of this writing, are broadcast to registered users. Users can select from newsletters based on their interests. However, newsletters are broadcast to readers with no one-to-one or tailored messages.

One-to-Many, Responding User. This type of site communicates with a mass of users who have logged-on as registered users or through e-mailings targeted at specific users. Site messages are invitations to users to submit their comments and responses. BizRate.com (*www.bizrate.com;* see Exhibit 4-24) is a good example of this type of communication. Customers rate their experience with online merchants on multiple dimensions and provide comments regarding their performance. BizRate.com places a banner on the receipt page of member online stores and independently invites actual online buyers to participate in the BizRate.com survey. BizRate.com uses a two-part survey not only to help consumers make better online purchases but also to help merchants better understand what online consumers want and need. The survey's first part is delivered immediately after a purchase is completed and the second is e-mailed shortly after the scheduled product delivery date.

One-to-Many, Live Interaction. This type of site allows users to interact with the site live, with information exchanged back-and-forth in real time. This exchange is often in the form of live chat. Accrue Software Inc. (see Exhibit 4-25), a leading software provider to online businesses, recently hosted a Web seminar that was broadcast live to users. Users were able to register, dial in for live audio streaming, and participate in real time in this Web seminar. Users could submit questions either online or via phone.

One-to-One, Nonresponding User. This type of site sends personalized messages to users to address specific user interests or needs. This information can be in the form of real-time updates or reminders. The site provides no means for customer response, and users receive site messages without any need to respond. As part of its online offering, the American Greetings site extended services from simple online cards and shopping to provide a group of tools that became a vehicle through

Exhibit
4-23

ONE-TO-MANY, NONRESPONDING
EXAMPLE—TheStandard.com

Reprinted by permission of the Industry Standard, www.TheStandard.com

Exhibit
4-24

ONE-TO-MANY, RESPONDING USER
EXAMPLE—BizRate.com

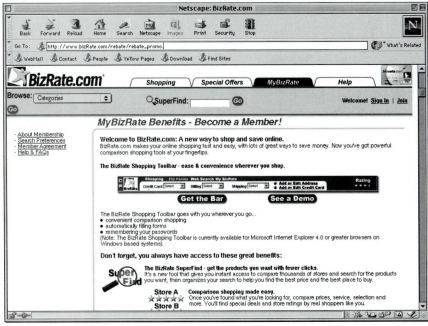

©BizRate.com

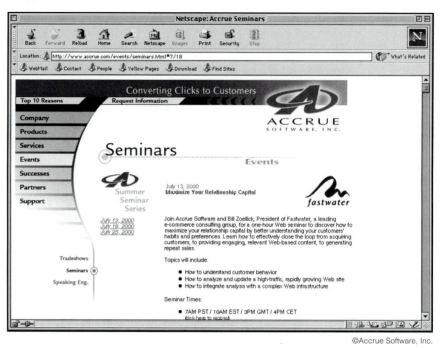

©Accrue Software, Inc.

which users could express themselves, manage their important dates and events, and manage their relationships. Users can create and print greeting cards, enter important dates and events into a personal list, and keep track of personal contacts in an address book. Americangreetings.com now offers a feature in which the user provides details surrounding important events (birthday, anniversary, etc.), and the American Greetings site then later sends an e-mail reminder to the user at a user-determined time prior to each event. Apart from entering information required to enable American Greetings' personalized tools, users do not enter content or inputs to the site.

One-to-One, Responding User. This type of site sends users personalized messages that address specific user interests or needs. This information can be real-time updates, reminders, or site tailoring of information to the user. Users respond to the site by submitting content of interest or specifics to transactions. Amazon.com is a hybrid communication archetype that uses one-to-one, responding-user communication. The zShops feature provides a broadcast platform that allows users to create their own storefront. For a low monthly fee, users post all information associated with their offerings and sell through the popular Amazon site. As an interactive site, Amazon.com allows users to check the status of their orders through queries to the site as well as automatic site transmission of e-mails. Upon order submission, Amazon.com sends a personal e-mail message to the customer confirming receipt of the order. Upon order shipment, Amazon.com sends a second e-mail message to the customer notifying him or her of the outbound order (see Exhibit 4-26).

Exhibit 4-26

ONE-TO-ONE, RESPONDING USER
EXAMPLE—Amazon.com

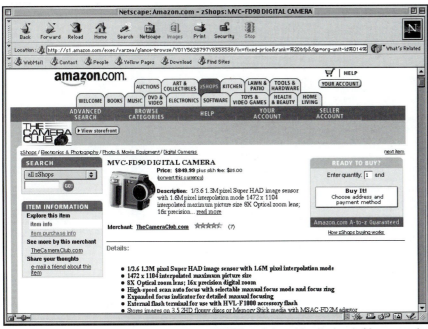

AMAZON.com is the registered trademark of Amazon.com, Inc.

One-to-One, Live Interaction. This type of site sends and receives personalized user messages or carries on chat sessions that address specific user interests or needs. Users interact live at the site with information exchanged in real time. LivePerson provides websites with a software tool that allows live customer service and sales. The software utilizes real-time text dialogue to enable sites to interact with visitors. LivePerson's intent is to help sites provide consumers a level of personal service that is at least equal to that of traditional retailers. The goal is to make e-commerce more user-friendly and more profitable. LivePerson enabled sites present a button or pop-up window to allow the visitor to begin the dialogue. The user enters his or her name and selects from a list of available customer service representatives. This personalized chat experience allows the user to choose a familiar person. During the LivePerson chat, the user and representative exchange information in real time on a one-to-one basis (see Exhibit 4-27).

HOW DOES A FIRM CONNECT WITH OTHER BUSINESSES?

Connection

Connection is the degree to which a given site is able to link to other sites through a hypertext jump or hyperlink from one webpage to another. These links are embedded in a web page and are most commonly presented to the user as underlined and highlighted words, a picture, or a graphic. The user's click on the link initiates the

Exhibit 4-27 ONE-TO-ONE, LIVE INTERACTION
EXAMPLE—LivePerson.com

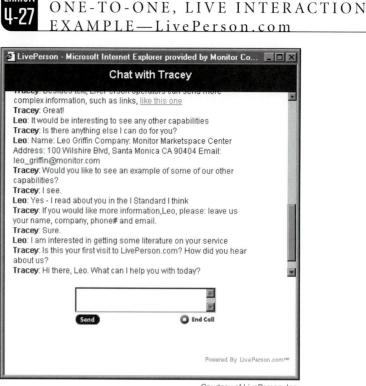

Courtesy of LivePerson, Inc.

immediate delivery of a text, graphic, or sound file or a webpage that can be a combination of all these types of files. Files may reside on the local server or on a server that might be anywhere in the world.

Dimensions of Connection. Connections vary in type, magnitude, and direction. Below we describe five dimensions of connection.

Links to Sites. This refers to links that take the user completely outside the home site and into a third-party site. For example, users of nytimes.com may access book reviews; in that section, a link to BarnesandNoble.com appears, as it does in other parts of the site, with an offer relating to its online retail bookstore. Users who click on the bn.com logo wind up on the bn.com site, where they can then pursue their shopping interests in a new environment.

Home Site Background. This refers to a situation where the link takes the user to a third-party site, but the home site is noticeable in the background. Users of ditto.com, a search engine for images on the Web, can click on any thumbnail image and examine the site from where the image was retrieved. This site opens over the ditto.com page in a smaller frame that "hovers" above the full-size browser window.

Outsourced Content. This refers to when the site content is derived from third parties, with the source of that content labeled clearly. The user remains in the home site environment. Many sites use stock quotes and news feeds to augment their appeal to users, even as these content "plug-ins" are identified by their sources (e.g., Associated Press, CNN.com, *www.weather.com*).

Percent of Home Site Content. This refers to the percentage of content that originates from the home site. Like newspapers that make use of wire-service stories, not all the content on any given site is generated, owned, or controlled by that site. As a result, it is important to understand how content is insourced or outsourced with respect to a given site's content strategy.

Pathway of Connection. The pathway of the connection can lead a user outside the environment of the site as a "pathway-out." It can also lead a user to retrieval from other sites, but not by formally leaving the site, as a "pathway-in." More specifically, pathway-out is where links are absolute in the sense that the user's click causes the absolute exit from the website. Pathway-in refers to situations where links are hybrid and the user's click causes the retrieval of material from the same or other sites without an exit from the current website.

Connection Archetypes

In this section, we consider six alternative connection approaches. We begin with a discussion of three instances of pathway-out approaches and conclude with overviews of three pathway-in designs.

Destination Site.
Destination sites almost exclusively provide site-generated content with very few links to other sites. These sites frequently are valued by users for integrity and trustworthiness of content and, therefore, disclose extensive information about the providers of their content. Many times, these destination sites license their content to other sites as third-party providers. NYTimes.com, the *New York Times* site, not only includes the daily contents of the newspaper but also publishes exclusive feature stories (see Exhibit 4-28) that appear on the site only. The site provides news updates every 10 minutes. As with the physical newspaper, content is almost exclusively site-generated. Links to other websites are very limited.

Hub Site.
Hub sites provide a combination of site-generated content and selective links to sites of related interests (see Exhibit 4-29). Many times, external links are to "expert" or related sites on specific topics of interest. For example, IndustryCentral (*www.industrycentral.net*), a motion picture and television industry site, is a hub that provides external links to various local film commissions, production studios, and other production-related resources, as well as to film festivals. IndustryCentral serves as the primary portal to Crew-List.net, an industry resume service that offers film and television cast and crew building and interaction features to employees. IndustryCentral also provides information concerning the production and distribution of film and television products to industry professionals. In addition, the site supplies industry news content through links to third parties such as hollywood.com and PR Newswire, as well as to Reuters, *Rolling Stone,* and *Entertainment Weekly* through iSyndicate.com.

Portal Site.
Portal sites consist almost exclusively of absolute links to a large number of other sites (see Exhibit 4-30). Portals usually provide a vast array of links to provide the widest possible reach to other sites but present very little or no site-generated content. Yahoo.com is one of the most well-known and established portals (*www.yahoo.com*). Yahoo.com users can easily reach thousands of sites, although, as impressive as this sounds, this constitutes only a small fraction of all available sites. Yahoo! has little or no original site-generated content on the site.

Exhibit 4-28

DESTINATION EXAMPLE—
NYTimes.com

Exhibit 4-29

HUB EXAMPLE—
IndustryCentral.net

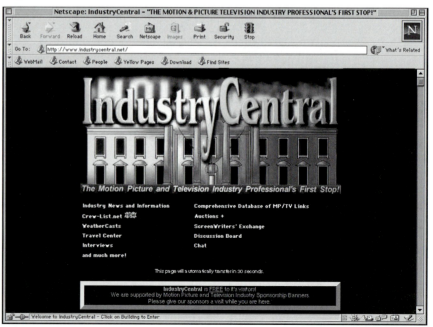

Exhibit 4-30

PORTAL EXAMPLE—
Yahoo.com

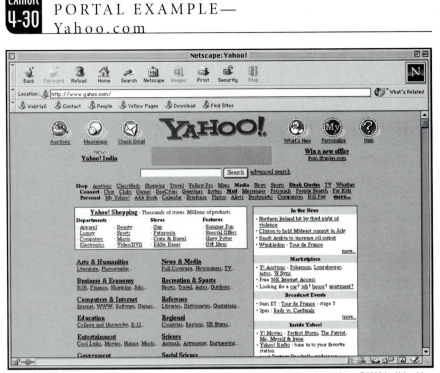

Reproduced with permission of Yahoo! Inc. ©2000 by Yahoo! Inc.
YAHOO! and the YAHOO! logo are trademarks of Yahoo! Inc.

Affiliate Programs. Websites with **affiliate programs** direct users to affiliated web-sites through links or through links embedded in site banners or other advertising materials (see Exhibit 4-31). Users of OnHealth Shopping (*www.onhealth.com*) can choose from a variety of products, some from providers other than OnHealth. For example, users who click on the Proflowers.com icon on this site get transferred to the Proflowers.com shopping environment where the user can make flower pur-chases. Although users are now shopping at Proflowers.com, they remain in the Onhealth Shopping environment and can easily move back to the Onhealth site by clicking on the prominent Onhealth band at the top of the page.

Outsourced Content. Websites often contain **outsourced content,** i.e., content that has been generated by third parties. Many times, third-party suppliers can create content of higher quality, greater appeal, or at a lower cost than the website opera-tion can. Outsourced content can be well integrated within a website. Often, the content provider is displayed clearly with a link to their site (see Exhibit 4-32). Real.com is an established player in streaming-media technology for the Internet. The RealSystem software (including the RealPlayer) delivers content on more than 85 percent of all streaming-media–enabled webpages (*www.realplayer.com*). Real.com presents outsourced broadcast content from established content sources that include CNN Interactive, BBC News Online, and National Public Radio. By outsourcing content, Real.com focuses on its core competency to further develop software while still maintaining a stimulating and appealing site.

Exhibit 4-31

AFFILIATE PROGRAM EXAMPLE—
Onhealth.com and Proflowers.com

Meta-Software. **Meta-software** consists of utility and plug-in software applications created to assist users in narrowly defined tasks. These applications may reside as "stand alone" on the user's desktop or as plug-ins to the Internet browser. Applications can be set to pop up and appear without the user requesting assistance (see Exhibit 4-33). R U Sure's goal is to make online shopping less burdensome, more efficient, and more economical for the shopper (*www.rusure.com*). Users download and install a free Shopping Agent that allows the user to easily conduct comparative shopping on the Internet for any requested product. While the user browses a supported site, the comparative shopping search engine searches other sites and notifies the user, within seconds, of any available lower prices. This task is done before the user completes a purchase and without requiring the user to leave the particular site being browsed. The R U Sure site also provides product reviews, classified ads, message boards, shop reviews, directories, auctions, e-shopping advice, and consumer comments.

WHAT ARE ALTERNATIVE PRICING MODELS OF COMMERCE ARCHETYPES?

Commerce

Commerce capabilities are those features of the customer interface that support the various aspects of trading transactions. In the next section, we focus on functional tools and conclude with a discussion of alternative pricing approaches.

Exhibit 4-32 OUTSOURCED CONTENT EXAMPLE—Real.com

Dimensions of Commerce. Functional tools are any commerce-enabling features of a website. For a site to have e-commerce capabilities, a number of features must be present. These include, but are not limited to, the following:

- **Registration.** User registration allows a site to store credit-card information, shipping addresses, and preferences.

- **Shopping Cart.** Users can place items into their personal, virtual shopping cart. Items can be purchased immediately or stored and purchased when the user returns on another visit to the site.

- **Security.** Sites attempt to guarantee the security of transactions and related data through encryption (e.g., SSL) and authentication technologies (e.g., SET).

- **Credit-Card Approval.** Sites can have the ability to receive instant credit approval for credit-card purchases through electronic links to credit-card clearance houses.

Exhibit 4-33

META-SOFTWARE EXAMPLE— RUSure.com

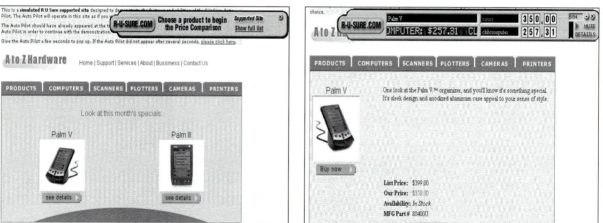

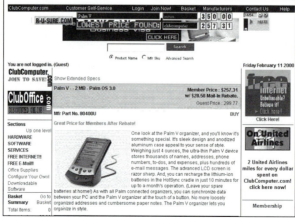

- **One-Click Shopping.** Amazon.com uses a patented feature that allows users to place and order products with a single click. Current delivery default settings are applied automatically.
- **Orders Through Affiliates.** Sites with affiliate programs must be able to track orders that originate from affiliate sites as well as determine affiliate fees for business generation.
- **Configuration Technology.** Users can put products and services together in a variety of permutations with the aid of configurator software, thus allowing analysis of performance/price trade-offs, interoperability among complex components within a system, and substitution of generic for branded products.
- **Order Tracking.** Users are provided with the ability to check the delivery status of products that they have ordered.
- **Delivery Options.** Users are presented with a choice of options to specify their desired speed and cost of delivery (e.g., next day, 2-day shipping, or 5-day shipping).

Commerce Archetypes

In this section, we review a number of prototypic examples of contrasting commercial transaction models.

Catalog Pricing. With **catalog pricing,** the price of goods and services is preset by the seller. Users select items from displayed catalogs and pay the associated prices. These sites provide detailed pictures and other product specifications. BarnesandNoble.com provides a large variety of books at heavily discounted prices. However, product prices are set and negotiation is not allowed. Customers can only affect the total price by varying the speed and associated cost of delivery.

Auction Pricing. With **auction pricing,** buyers bid against each other, and the highest bid wins the supplier's products or services. The auction site provides details to each auctioned product: product description, starting bid price, bid start-time, and bid end-time. Frequently, the performance of both suppliers and buyers is rated, and the ratings are presented by the site as a benefit to current and prospective customers. Adauction.com provides an environment where ad-space buyers and sellers interact and conduct business. Buyers bid against each other for a variety of available ad spaces, including some at premium locations.

Reverse Auction Pricing. With **reverse auction pricing,** sellers bid against each other, and the lowest bid wins the buyer the business. In many cases, suppliers (sellers) must be prequalified before their bids are considered. These sites generally will have links to prospective sellers. Many times, supplier performance is rated, and these ratings are presented by the site as a benefit to current and prospective buyers. Freemarkets.com conducts online auctions of industrial parts, raw materials, commodities, and services. Suppliers bid lower prices in real time until the auction is closed to fill the purchase orders of large buying organizations. In 1999 this site auctioned off more than $1 billion worth of purchases and saved buyers between 2 and 25 percent.

Demand Aggregations Pricing. With **demand aggregations pricing,** buyer demand for specific products is aggregated in order to achieve economies of scale.

Commerce Origination Vs. Facilitation

Table 4-2 provides a more detailed review of two general approaches to generate commerce. The first approach involves commerce that originates at the site. New customer acquisition tools include online advertising, viral marketing, and offline advertising (to be discussed in Chapter 5). Commerce can also be facilitated through third-party intervention to deliver traffic to a site. This can be achieved through affiliate network relationships, "distribution deals" for ad banner and icon placement, and partnerships with related groups and third-party associations.

Table 4-2 COMMERCE ORIGINATION VS. FACILITATION

Commerce Origination	Commerce Facilitation

• Commerce originating at a site. It is achieved through acquisition of new customers and loyalty building among existing customers.
• New Customer Acquisition Tools include
  – *Online advertising*
    – Banner ads at other sites
    – URL listing in industry catalogs
    – Sponsorships of online events or of other site activities
  – *Viral marketing*
    – Marketing with the assistance of existing customers, who pass marketing messages along to friends or colleagues
    – Examples include marketing footers at the end of user e-mail messages and prompts inviting users to send the site URL or the output of their activity on the site to others
  – *Offline advertising*
    – Advertisements on radio, television, and in movie theaters
    – Sponsorships of offline events, such as conferences on the New Economy
	• Commerce facilitated through the intervention of a third party directing traffic to a site. It can be achieved through affiliations and partnerships
	• Affiliations/Partnerships
	  – *How they work*
	    – Home site signs up other sites in a partnership/affiliation program
	    – Affiliate sites place a link on their site that directs users to the home site
	    – In some cases, a user gets directed to a site through an affiliate while remaining in the affiliate's URL space
	    – Participating affiliate sites receive a percentage cut (typically 5–10%) on all sales generated at the home site as a result of clickthroughs from the affiliate sites
	  – *Incentives to affiliates*
	    – Financial: Affiliate sites receive a percentage of the sales they generate
	    – Brand building: Being an affiliate to a well-known brand increases visibility
	    – Improved capabilities: By linking users to additional sites, affiliates can increase their breadth of offerings

Prospective buyers submit product orders by a set time, at which point price is negotiated. Community tools (such as message boards) enable ordering users to encourage other users to also submit orders. Mercata.com aggregates consumer demand in order to build bargaining power and to achieve lower prices for participating customers. In addition to product specifications, Mercata.com allows users to exchange messages about product purchases in the PowerTalk text box. Messages may include positive or negative views on particular products as well as encouragements to other users to place a product order to gain further price concessions.

Haggle Pricing. With **haggle pricing,** users and the site can negotiate over price. Users select products and exchange offers and counteroffers with the site until a deal is reached or refused. Hagglezone.com allows users to haggle online with sales representatives. The user and sales representative make offers and counteroffers, but this is not a live interaction. The sales representative is actually a programmed response to user-based bid inputs. Frequently, agreements on price are reached. However, if the difference between the bid and asking price is unlikely to be reached, the sales representative can back off and end the haggling. Users can choose among six representatives to find the one that best matches their negotiating style.

SCHWAB'S CUSTOMER INTERFACE

In this section, we apply the 7Cs Framework to Schwab.com.

Context

Exhibit 4-34 on page 162 shows the homepage for Schwab.com. Schwab.com's highly functional look-and-feel pays little attention to aesthetics. The site is designed to enable the user to quickly locate and process information needed to make investment decisions. For example, the Stock Analyzer provides three different ways to research any chosen stock: Company Fundamentals, Price History, and Comparison to Other Companies. The user can click any link and immediately find the desired information. Even charts are used sparingly and only when they clearly enhance user understanding of company economics.

In this way, the context of the site "fits" the Schwab value proposition by providing easy access to high-quality investment information without slow downloading of complex graphics to distract the user.

Content

The Schwab.com site strives to be a category killer in online investment by providing online investors all the needed products, information, and services. In terms of products, Schwab offers a large variety of investment instruments that include stocks, bonds, and mutual funds. Schwab.com also offers a suite of analytical tools to assist users with any investment decision (examples include the IRA Analyzer or the Retirement Planner) as well as innovative applications that increase the level of service and facilitate transactions (e.g., After Hours Trading). In terms of information, Schwab provides investors comprehensive information on companies and industries and up-to-the-minute content for many of its products (e.g., stock quotes).

The site content "fits" Schwab's value proposition. First, by providing information that is current and specifically addressing user investment needs, the site takes another step to improve the already high-quality investment information. Second, site features such as After Hours Trading add to the already superior service offered to users.

Online and Offline Integration
of the Customer Interface

 We have applied the 7Cs Framework to the online customer interface, but all the elements of the online interface also can be replicated offline. The design of mutually reinforcing online and offline interfaces provides a consistent offering and brand message to the customer. In this section, we explore how each of the 7Cs might be implemented offline and study examples of the successful integration of online and offline interfaces.

Context in the offline world is the look-and-feel of the physical store. Context is comprised of, among other things, the store architecture, the appearance and demeanor of the store's staff, the openness of the retail environment, the openness to light, the color, and the style selection. J. Crew stores provide a sense of spaciousness and lightness by the use of open space and abundant natural and artificial light. Store colors match store to store—and match the colors of the clothing offered in the store. The stylish and uncluttered look-and-feel of the physical store match the look-and-feel of the jcrew.com site. This look-and-feel reinforces the company's positioning as a relaxed shopping place that offers stylish and casual clothes. On the other hand, Gap stores have a consistent design to help shoppers navigate the store and to maximize sales. Customers know they can find new fashionable items at the front of the store, core lines (such as chinos and jeans) in the middle of the store, and sale items at the very back.

Content in the offline world includes all the products, services, and associated information about products and services offered at physical store locations. Barnes and Noble bookstores contain a very large selection of books and magazines. Customers can get large discounts on some book categories, such as best-sellers. Customers get information on books by searching through catalogs or by using in-store computer terminals. Customer service is readily available through the many customer service representatives at most stores. The Barnes and Noble physical store offering of easily accessible information on a large selection of books at discount prices complements a nearly identical virtual offering at the bn.com website. The website provides the same easy access to information and prices but through powerful search software.

Community in the offline world is communication between customers. Community can be encouraged through store events or through store participation in and sponsoring of community activities. Borders bookstores often host events at select stores for author readings and book signings. At these events, readers can interact with each other and meet people with similar book tastes. Evite.com, an online event invitation site, recently hosted a pool bar gathering for local members in Santa Monica. The event provided users an opportunity to physically meet and build relationships. Each year in Los Angeles, Revlon sponsors the Walk for Breast Cancer to increase breast cancer awareness, raise research funds, and bring together customers and noncustomers alike.

Customization in the offline world comes in a number of different ways. A store can personalize products and services that customers purchase. Credit-card holders can have their pictures and signatures imprinted on the face of their credit cards and thus personalize the cards as well as reduce the risk of credit-card fraud. Levis customers can order jeans made-to-order just for them. To some degree, stores can also customize customer experience based on exhibited customer needs. Local restaurants recognize loyal customers by automatically seating them at their favorite tables. Airlines can automatically assign customers to their preference of aisle or window seating each time they travel. Stores can also send targeted marketing messages to users based on exhibited purchase behavior. Many catalog retailers send customers customized catalogs based on individual purchase history.

Communication in the offline world is the one-way (store-to-customer) or two-way interaction between store and customer. One-way store-to-customer communication can be in the form of newsletters or catalogs that stores send to customers. Stores can

(continued on page 161)

(continued from page 160)
also provide personalized alerts to customers. For example, investors using Merrill Lynch full brokerage services can arrange for an alert by broker phone call whenever market conditions warrant. Customers can participate in two-way communications with stores by filling out and submitting surveys generated by the store. Furthermore, customers can ask for live assistance either in person (when physically in the store) or via phone. Nordstrom is widely know for excellent customer service. Nordstrom customer service representatives have been known to deliver purchased products directly to customer homes.

Connection in the offline world is the degree to which a store is connected to other stores. Stores in large shopping malls are closely located to a number of other stores, and customers can quickly move out of one store and into another. A retailer can rent concession space in large department stores to provide an additional sales channel, to be associated with other nearby concessions, and to allow customers to easily move back and forth between concessions. Stores can also provide links to a large number of suppliers who offer products or services of interest to customers. Travel agencies provide links to a large number of travel providers that include airlines, hotels, and cruise-line operators. Furthermore, stores can increase their number of customers through partnerships. Coca-Cola partners with McDonald's to increase sales by making Coca-Cola available at all McDonald's locations.

Commerce in the offline world is the transaction capabilities of a store. Stores provide transaction capabilities such as shopping carts, security, credit-card and personal-check verification, custom gift wrapping, and delivery options. In addition, stores can offer a number of price determination options. Most offline stores provide products and services at catalog (predetermined) prices. However, Sotheby's, an auction house, offers members Dutch-style or English-style auctions to determine the price offered for pieces of art, jewelry, and other collectors' items. Also, haggling remains a popular way of determining price in industries. Purchasing a car at your local dealer generally involves a lengthy negotiating process where dealer and customer make offers and counteroffers and may or may not reach an agreed-upon price. Demand aggregation also occurs occasionally in the offline world. Travel agents sometimes prepurchase large blocks of airlines seats and pass through some savings to buyers of package vacations.

Community

Schwab does not offer community features on its site. This "fits" well with the company's aspiration to provide all the necessary information and tools to enable users to invest on their own without outside assistance. The idea here is that an investor who has access to all the necessary information and who can analyze that information using the tools provided will not need to chat with other investors or post messages on a message board.

Customization

Schwab offers a selection of personalization tools for the user. After log-in, the Schwab user accesses his or her personal account page that contains information on all of his or her investments and investment plans. Schwab also offers the MySchwab feature that is enabled through Excite. In MySchwab, users can personalize the content, the layout, and the color scheme of their personal page. Users can choose between a variety of content types (e.g., news, business, entertainment, sports) as well as personal tools (e.g., MyPlanner, reminders, and a notepad).

7Cs OF SCHWAB

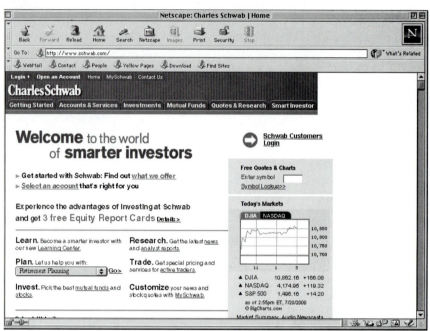

The site customization "fits" with Schwab's superior service by providing a user-friendly platform that supplies investors all the information and tools they need when they need them.

Communication

Schwab.com offers a number of communication venues between the user and the site. Schwab's investment forums are an example of a one-to-many communication that occurs live. Schwab's Learning Center is a one-to-many communication where the user can respond without necessarily engaging in a live interaction. Schwab's Quarterly Investment Magazine is an example of a one-to-many interaction where the user simply receives and does not respond. And finally, the e-mail customer service can be classified as a one-to-one interaction where the user can respond.

Schwab's live investment forums and Learning Center provide a "fit" with Schwab's technology leadership and innovative products by enhancing the perception that Schwab is at the cutting edge of research and thinking in this space. Furthermore, the purpose of both initiatives is to arm the investor with the most comprehensive and up-to-date tools and information and, again, enhance the notion that Schwab is a provider of high-quality investment information.

One might expect Schwab to offer live online customer service (as opposed to customer service e-mails) in order to strengthen the "fit" to superior customer service. A possible explanation is that Schwab offers several alternatives for investors to receive real-time customer service—both over the phone and in-branch.

Connection

The Schwab site also provides a number of connection venues to and from other sites. In terms of pathways-out of the site, Schwab.com functions as a hub for mutual funds through the OneSource program, which links to a number of mutual-fund providers. Furthermore, to a large extent, Schwab.com is a destination site for investors because it provides original content and tools to help investors with their decisions. In terms of pathways-in to the site, Schwab.com enhances the quality of the information by outsourcing some content, e.g., part of the Stock Analyzer content is provided by Hoover's Online. Also, Schwab.com increases traffic to the site through affiliate programs. An example is the partnership with Excite, where users can click to Schwab through a prominent link on the Excite homepage.

Schwab's ability to complement its original content with content outsourced from established providers (such as Hoover's Online) strengthens the "fit" with Schwab's high-quality investment information. Furthermore, Schwab's ability to aggregate a large number of mutual-fund providers through OneSource builds users' confidence that they will get the best price for a given quality fund by looking through the available funds.

Commerce

Pricing at Schwab is set through a catalog model. However, commission discounts are available to traders who perform more than a specified number of trades per year. In addition to basic elements of commerce functions (e.g., registration, security, and credit approval), Schwab.com offers advanced software applications that enable transactions. Examples include BillPay, which allows users to make payments online without writing checks, and Velocity Trading Software, which greatly reduces transaction processing time.

Schwab's unique commerce-enabling tools provide a "fit" with its position as a technology leader and an innovative products provider. Furthermore, decreased commission rates to heavy traders stress that Schwab strives to provide low prices to its dedicated users.

Reinforcement Among Schwab's 7Cs

The Schwab site context reinforces its content. By designing a highly functional layout with minimal distractions, Schwab has created a site context that sends the message that this site provides nothing short of useful and to-the-point investment content to the user.

Similarly, the site's connection reinforces its content. By supplying links to a large number of mutual-fund providers through the OneSource program, Schwab positions the site as a place where one can find everything one needs in terms of mutual funds, thus reinforcing the site's content position as a category killer.

Finally, communication and commerce reinforce each other by enhancing the notion that Schwab is a technology leader providing innovative products. Examples include the community investment forums and Learning Center as well as the advanced software tools that facilitate commerce transactions.

SUMMARY

1. What are the seven design elements to the customer interface?

The seven design elements are context, content, community, customization, communication, connection, and commerce. Each of the 7Cs needs to fit and reinforce the others while satisfying the business model.

2. What determines the look-and-feel of the design?

The look-and-feel of websites can be arrayed on two dimensions: form, or aesthetic, and function. Aesthetic designs focus on the artistic nature of the site. Function, on the other hand, involves the pragmatic usability of the site. Some argue that these are opposing design aspects with unavoidable trade-offs, while others argue that advancing technologies lead to new techniques and new aesthetics and, therefore, fewer trade-off decisions, such that both aesthetic and functional dimensions continue to expand.

3. What are the five content archetypes?

The five content archetypes are superstore, category killer, specialty, information-dominant, and market-dominant. The first three content archetypes are defined by the offering mix. The information-dominant specifically relates to information goods (although physical products can be purchased as a complement). Market-dominant provides a place for transactions and bring together buyers and sellers.

4. Why be concerned with community?

Community entails a feeling of membership in a group along with a strong sense of involvement and shared common interests with that group. A group of people can create strong, lasting relationships that may develop into a sense of community through an engaged and extended exchange of views focused on their shared interests. However, community contains not only elements of common interest and group acceptance but also individual involvement. This sense of community can help encourage users and customers to return to a website.

5. What are the levers used to customize a site?

Users can personalize the site, or the site can tailor itself to users. The levers for personalization include log-in registration, personalized e-mail, content and layout configuration, storage, and agents. An organization can design its site to tailor itself to users based on either past user behavior or the behaviors of other users with similar preferences.

6. What types of communication can a firm maintain with its customer base?

There are three forms of communication: broadcast, interactive, and a broadcast/interactive hybrid.

7. How does a firm connect with other businesses?

There are two generic approaches to form connections: pathways-in and pathways-out. The pathway of the connection can lead a user outside the environment of the site ("pathway-out") or can retrieve materials from other sites without necessitating the user to formally leave the site ("pathway-in"). More specifically, pathway-out refers to situations in which links are absolute and the user's click causes an exit from the website. Pathway-in refers to situations in which links are hybrid and the user's click causes the retrieval of material from the same or other sites without an exit from the current website.

8. What are alternative pricing models of commerce archetypes?

There are five alternative pricing approaches: catalog, auction, reverse auction, demand aggregation, and haggle.

KEY TERMS

7Cs Framework	tailoring by site
context	destination sites
content	hub sites
community	portal sites
customization	affiliate program
communication	outsourced content
connection	meta-software
commerce	catalog pricing
fit	auction pricing
reinforcement	reverse auction pricing
form vs. function	demand aggregations pricing
personalization by user	haggle pricing

Endnotes

[1]Park, Choong Whan, and Gerald Zaltman. 1987. *Marketing management*. Chicago: Dryden Press. Park and Zaltman introduced the concepts of consistency and complementarity to refer to the degree to which various marketing management concepts resulted in synergy. Complementarity is equivalent to reinforcement and fit is equivalent to consistency. Given the number of concepts that begin with the letter *C* in this chapter, we have chosen to use the terms *fit* and *reinforcement*.

[2]Interested readers should consult the following literature: Nielsen, Jakob. 2000. *Designing web usability*. Indianapolis, IN: New Riders Publishing.

[3]Veen, Jeffrey. 1997. *Hotwired style: Principles for building smart web sites*. San Francisco: Hardwired.

[4]Adler, Richard P., and Anthony J. Christopher. 1999. Virtual communities. In *Net Success*. Holbrook, MA: Adams Media, p. 42. The elements of community categorization was constructed by Teresa Roberts of Sun Microsystems.

[5]Stark, Myra. 1998. A fly on the virtual wall: Cybercommunities observed. *Digitrends Quarterly* (summer): 26.

[6]Farmer, Randall. 1994. Social dimensions of habitat's citizenry. In *Virtual Reality Case Book*. New York: Van Nostrand Reinhold, pp. 87–95.

[7]Adler, Richard P., and Anthony J. Christopher. 1999. Virtual communities. In *Net Success*. Holbrook, MA: Adams Media, p. 42. The sense of community or member benefits is based on research conducted by researchers at the Annenberg School.

[8]See: Figalo, Cliff. 1998. *Hosting web communities: Building relationships, increasing customer loyalty and maintaining a competitive edge*. New York: John Wiley & Sons, Inc.

Photography: Nicole Nelson. Computer illustration: J.W. Burkey/D2 Studios

5

Market Communications and Branding

In Chapter 4, we discussed the screen-to-customer interface that brings to life the value proposition and associated business model introduced in Chapter 3. In this chapter, we turn our attention to two key levers that a firm uses to motivate consumer traffic and, ultimately, consumption—market communications and branding. Market communications can be categorized into a simple two-by-two framework based upon the audience focus (broad versus individual) and communications media (offline versus online). In particular, we describe several alternative approaches in each of these quadrants. Next, we turn our attention to branding. In particular, we discuss (1) branding basics, (2) a framework for brand equity, (3) a 10-step process to build brands, and (4) two case studies of successful online branding. We conclude with a discussion of branding choices.

QUESTIONS

Please consider the following questions as you read this chapter:

1. What are the four categories of market communications?

2. What is a good brand?

3. What is the Ten-Step Branding Process?

4. How does online branding compare between American Airlines and Continental Airlines?

5. What are the Point-Counterpoint arguments for leveraging an offline brand into the online environment?

This chapter was coauthored by Bernie Jaworski, Jeffrey Rayport, Nancy Michels, Ellie Kyung, Jennifer Barron, Marco Smit, and Rafi Mohammed. Substantive input was also provided by Robert Lurie, Yannis Dosios, and Leo Griffin.

Chapter 4 focused on the types of interface design choices that confront the senior management team. Once these design choices are made, the team must turn its attention to building customer traffic, strengthening the brand, and locking in target customers. In this chapter, we consider how the online company communicates with its target customers and attempts to build strong brands.

We begin this chapter by introducing the link between communications and branding. Next, we introduce a simple marketing communications framework. This framework considers both online and offline media approaches as well as individualized and broad audiences. We review a number of new online approaches as well as traditional media approaches. Once we complete this discussion, we consider the question of how to build superior, lasting brands. This requires some basic discussion of brand equity as well as a methodology for the branding processes. After introducing this methodology, we apply it to two case studies: American Airlines (*www.aa.com*) and Monster (*www.monster.com*). In contrast to many pundits who thought the Internet would lead to pure commoditization of products, this mini-case study discussion reveals the potential for highly differentiated, unique brands.

As in prior chapters, we conclude our discussion of the chapter with an application of the market communications and branding concepts to Schwab.

INTEGRATING COMMUNICATIONS AND BRANDING

Regardless of the source of differentiation, **branding** is about the consumer's perception of the offering—how it performs, how it looks, how it makes one feel, and what messages it sends. These perceptions are nurtured by a combination of **market communications** in the marketplace—one's interaction with the brand, others' experiences with the brand, and, more generally, mass marketing approaches. In the offline world, these communications tend to be one-way, from the firm to the customer, while in the online world, we begin to see much more interactive, two-way communications.

Communications and brands are actually the media of which the Web is made. In other words, it is a world enabled by information technology, made of information, and limited largely to information. That means that the old marketing notions such as "shelfspace equals marketshare" in retail or "mindshare leads to marketshare" in entertainment apply with a vengeance here. Mental space is marketspace, so it should come as no surprise that e-commerce or New Economy markets are realms in which we have seen an explosion in innovation in communications techniques for business and a dramatic rise in the power and impact of strong brands.

If brands are real estate owned by companies in the minds of consumers, then communications and brands on the Web represent real estate competing to attract eyeballs that direct the scarcest resource, which is attention, in the New Economy. This is the critical challenge for businesses on the Web, and it links the two themes of this chapter.

Finally, it should be no surprise that approaches to claiming the real estate of the mind are varied and must take place in both the physical and virtual worlds. But the opportunity to reinforce online with offline and vice versa is a profound value-creation machine for business. It's the virtual cycle of the flight simulator in which you play a video game in virtual reality to fly a real plane better, but flying a real plane makes you better equipped to operate the simulator. This back-and-forth human experience between the two worlds is what we're talking about when we introduce the hybrid approaches to marketing communications involving both offline and online worlds.

WHAT ARE THE FOUR CATEGORIES OF MARKET COMMUNICATIONS?

Market communications refers to all the points of contact that the firm has with its customers. This includes the obvious offline communications such as television advertising, promotions, and sales calls, as well as the emergent advertising approaches on the Internet. It is important to stress that any chapter on marketing communications in the New Economy must include a blended discussion of both offline and online approaches.

Consider the case of Amazon. In its quest to develop (and retain) its customer base, Amazon.com has been losing large sums of money. In 1999, Amazon lost $390 million, compared to the $74 million that it lost in 1998. However, its marketing investments (broadly defined) have been paying off. Sales have increased 169 percent from $610 million in 1998 to $1.64 billion in 1999. In addition, its customer base grew from over 6.2 million accounts in 1998 to over 17 million in 1999.[1] Amazon is a good example of a company that has invested significantly in all four types of marketing communications, namely: (1) **general online,** (2) **personalized online,** (3) **traditional mass media,** and (4) to a much more limited extent, **direct communications.**

The Customer Decision Process and Market Communications

Prior to our discussion of these four media choices, we will reflect upon the objectives of the marketing communications effort and examine the so called hierarchy of the effects communications model. Put differently, it is difficult to think about the choice of marketing communications without first considering the objectives that one wants to accomplish (e.g., increase brand awareness, increases sales). At the same time, one also needs to consider a structured approach to moving the customer through the buying process—from early awareness of the brand through to purchase.

In Exhibit 5-1, we illustrate the buying process—which mirrors the hierarchy of effects. In traditional "big ticket" product categories, consumers are thought to pass through multiple decision stages. Each stage is a prerequisite for the next stage. That is, one cannot move through the buying process to purchase without first forming a preference for the brand. It should be noted that this buying process is a simple illustration of the egg diagram buying process illustrated in Chapter 3.

In the middle portion of Exhibit 5-1, we show the types of traditional marketing communications that are used to move the customer through the buying process. For example, television ads may create brand awareness, while point-of-sale promotions tend to trigger purchase.

Exhibit 5-1

EVOLUTION OF CUSTOMER
BUYING PROCESS

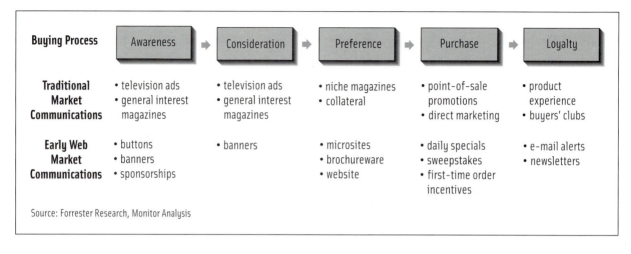

Buying Process	Awareness	Consideration	Preference	Purchase	Loyalty
Traditional Market Communications	• television ads • general interest magazines	• television ads • general interest magazines	• niche magazines • collateral	• point-of-sale promotions • direct marketing	• product experience • buyers' clubs
Early Web Market Communications	• buttons • banners • sponsorships	• banners	• microsites • brochureware • website	• daily specials • sweepstakes • first-time order incentives	• e-mail alerts • newsletters

Source: Forrester Research, Monitor Analysis

The lower portion of Exhibit 5-1 shows the early Web market communications that can be linked to the buying process. For example, banner ads can make target customers aware of the product or service while "daily specials" tend to be most associated with purchase.

It is important to reflect on how the marketing communications process has changed as one moves from traditional to online communications. Perhaps the most important shift is from the acquisition mindset of the traditional world to the experience, retention, and interactive (two-way) mindset of the New Economy. In the next section, we introduce a simple framework for marketing communications that provides a backdrop to our more detailed explanation of both offline and online communications tools.

A Framework for Online Marketing Communications

This section describes marketing communications that online companies use to attract new customers. These marketing strategies are clustered into four major categories: (1) personalized, online communications, (2) general online approaches, (3) traditional mass marketing, and (4) direct communications (see Table 5-1). In Table 5-2 we list some of the market communications options in each category.

The Four Categories of Communications
General Online Approaches.

Banner ads. **Banner ads** are the boxlike ads that are displayed on webpages. These ads usually display a simple message that is designed to entice viewers to click the ad. In general, this "click-through" leads to buying opportunities or to a company's

Table 5-1

FRAMEWORK FOR MARKETING COMMUNICATIONS

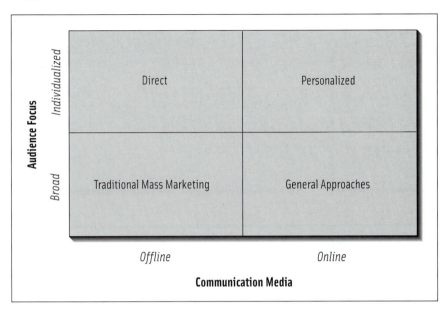

website. Banner ads can be used for multiple purposes with success being measured in several different manners.

- **Impressions.** Impressions (also termed gross exposures or ad views) is the total number of times an ad is seen by viewers. Ads are often sold based on cost per thousand impressions (CPMs). Based on the attractiveness of a site's customer base, ad CPMs range in price from $3 to $250.

- **Leads.** When a viewer takes an action (i.e., an information request).

- **Sales.** Firms can easily track whether click-throughs result in sales, and they can pay commissions to the site that referred the customer (we discuss associate programs later in this section). A general trend in structuring banner advertisement fees is to use performance-based deals. Forrester Research estimates that by the year 2004, performance-based deals will account for more than 50 percent of Web advertising dollars.

- **Click-throughs.** Click-throughs are the number of times viewers click on a banner ad. Clicking takes them to the advertiser's website or any other advertiser-specified location. Marketers try to increase the click-through rate by making banners more colorful and by adding interactivity (e.g., games, quick surveys, questions). Playing a banner game often results in a click-through, although these click-throughs are generally less effective relative to a click-through generated from a surfer's genuine interest.

In a related approach, John Hancock recently ran banner ads that targeted Web surfers concerned about retirement. John Hancock's banner ad asked viewers the enticing question, "I'm _ years old and I make _ a year. What will I need to retire?" Survey participants instantly received a response to this important question. Survey takers then had the option to learn more about

Table 5-2

THE FOUR CATEGORIES
OF COMMUNICATIONS

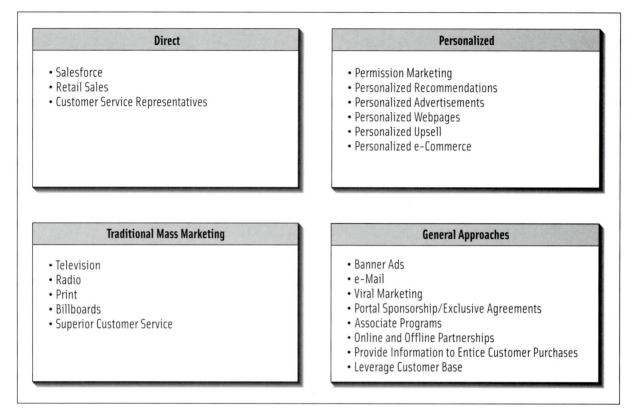

Direct	Personalized
• Salesforce • Retail Sales • Customer Service Representatives	• Permission Marketing • Personalized Recommendations • Personalized Advertisements • Personalized Webpages • Personalized Upsell • Personalized e-Commerce

Traditional Mass Marketing	General Approaches
• Television • Radio • Print • Billboards • Superior Customer Service	• Banner Ads • e-Mail • Viral Marketing • Portal Sponsorship/Exclusive Agreements • Associate Programs • Online and Offline Partnerships • Provide Information to Entice Customer Purchases • Leverage Customer Base

retirement and John Hancock products. For these types of innovative banner ads, John Hancock reaped a click-through rate of almost 5 percent, which is 10 times the national average.[2]

e-Mail. The use of **e-mail** as a marketing vehicle is attractive to e-commerce players due to its low production costs and simplicity. In 1999, spending on e-mail marketing was $97 million and is expected to jump to $2 billion by the end of 2003.[3]

An early form of e-mail advertising applied a typical offline advertising method: junk e-mails (otherwise known as spam). Junk e-mails are mass unsolicited e-mail mailings that contain the same advertising message as one would find in a traditional mass mailing in the offline world. Junk e-mails were labeled spam as a homage to a famous Monty Python "viking SPAM restaurant" sketch, in which SPAM (a smoked ham luncheon meat) was pushed onto every diner regardless of whether he or she wanted it or not. At the end of the sketch, members of the Monty Python troupe repeatedly screamed "SPAM, SPAM, SPAM!", overwhelming the normal conversation of restaurant patrons. Ever since, annoyed junk e-mail recipients have referred to junk e-mails as spam.

The company most credited with starting the spam craze is Cyber Promotions. As Cyber Promotions soon found, Web users treat their personal e-mail accounts with greater sanctity than their postal addresses. Cyber Promotions "spammed" e-mail addresses, and Web users revolted, making it very clear that they did not like spam. Cyber Promotions was sued by large Internet service providers claiming that the onslaught of spam overtaxed their systems and annoyed their users. By 1997 (three years after it started), Cyber Promotions was unable to find a company willing to supply it with the Internet connections that it needed to send spam.[4]

Viral Marketing. The term **viral marketing** was introduced into the business lexicon in 1996 when Mountain Dew created an immediate word-of-mouth phenomenon by offering a deal for cheap pagers to its young customers, and then by sending weekly marketing messages to these same users of those pagers.[5] Viral marketing is defined as company-developed products, services, or information that are passed from user to user. It is analogous to a viral infection passed between two people. Viral marketing gained mass-scale fame when it turned Hotmail from a tiny upstart company into one of the first online companies with a huge valuation at the time of its sale to Microsoft. Hotmail provided customers free e-mail service but also included in each sent message an invitation to e-mail recipients to obtain a free e-mail account at Hotmail.[6]

Many media related websites allow viewers to send news items of interest to friends. The *Washington Post* online offers such a service, which has proven to be the next step in viral marketing. This form of viral marketing is effective because marketing messages are sent between friends—consumers are more receptive to these subtle marketing messages. Readers can mail a specific article to their online friends. They simply type in their friend's e-mail address and the article is instantly e-mailed to them. The *Washington Post* benefits because new viewers will be exposed to their site at the suggestion of a friend. These new visitors may be transformed into regular users. The *Washington Post* also benefits because its loyal reader has filtered select articles from its wide product offering to a topic of exact interest to their friends. This educated filtering allows new viewers to be directed to information that is most relevant to them.

Universal Studios theme park has created an innovative viral marketing strategy. Universal set up three user-controlled webcams for patrons to use. Using the webcams, visitors can take pictures from various park vantage points and send them to friends. The average user has sent four Web picture postcards to friends resulting in over 6 million park images having been sent to potential visitors. This strategy is a unique version of viral marketing. Park visitors can easily send images of themselves enjoying Universal Studios with the studio prominently featured in the image to friends. People enjoy receiving Web postcards of their friends enjoying themselves, and Universal's brand image is formed or reinforced in people's minds.[7]

Sponsorship and Exclusive Partner Agreements. Many portals offer e-commerce companies the opportunity to become a sponsor or an exclusive partner. Companies have found these types of agreements to be valuable. In exclusive partnerships, portals aggressively feature and push their partner company's products. For instance, Talk.com's exclusive agreement to provide discount long distance to AOL's members has been AOL's most successful e-commerce partner program to date. In less than two years after its launch, Talk.com sold over 1.5 million long-distance lines to AOL members. This marketing relationship enabled Talk.com to achieve the fastest market share shift in the long-distance market's history.[8]

Affiliate Programs. Various forms of **affiliate programs** have been used by online firms for years. Affiliate programs refer to situations where a particular site (e.g., AOL) directs users to an e-commerce site (e.g., Amazon) and in turn receives a

Fifty Ways to Build Your Brand

by Leo Griffin

As online and offline companies increasingly look to the Web as a platform for building and sustaining brands, the market for Internet advertising is forecasted to explode. According to Forrester Research, U.S.-based Internet advertising will grow from approximately 1.3 percent of total advertising in 1999 to 8.1 percent, or $22.2 billion, in 2004. By that year, the global Internet advertising market will be worth $33 billion. It's not surprising that analysts expect such dramatic growth in Web advertising. In a survey by Jupiter Communications, 42 percent of respondents reported that they were spending less time watching television as a result of the Internet. As the number of Internet users rises and the average amount of time spent accessing the Internet by users increases, advertisers will need to spend an increasing proportion of their money on Internet advertising in order to capture the attention of their target audience.

Internet advertising extends three promises to advertisers:[9] accurate one-to-one targeting of ads, rich media, and interactivity (for example, banners that allow users to configure a product) and real-time detailed feedback on campaign performance, in turn allowing for adjustments to the campaign on the fly.

Despite these promises, the impact of Internet advertising has frequently proved to be a disappointment. The most common form of advertising on the Web is the banner ad, those little rectangular boxes (usually 468 pixels wide by 60 high) that contain messages from advertisers, but, in fact, there are dozens of different marketing tools on the Web. Here, we briefly examine some of the pros and cons of each.

Banner Ads. As users have grown more experienced with using the Web, it appears that they have become more reluctant to click on Web banners. The attached data from Nielsen-NetRatings (Exhibit 5-2) shows that banner click-through rates continued to decline through 1999, and that they currently stand at

Exhibit 5-2 BANNER CLICK-THROUGH RATES (APRIL 1999–JANUARY 2000)

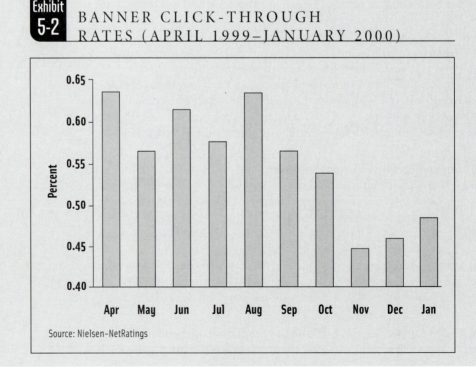

Source: Nielsen-NetRatings

less than half of one percent (in other words 1 in every 200 banners is clicked on). This does not speak well for the abilities of marketers to accurately target banners at people who will be interested in them, but are there other reasons for these low numbers?

Part of the problem is probably due to the cognitive mode that people are in when they are surfing the Web. Typically, we're sitting at a desk and we have a mission. We are looking to perform a particular task or find a piece of information. So, when a banner pops up asking us to drop what we're doing and turn our attentions to something else, we're not very likely to click on it. Contrast this to the experience of watching television, where we sit back in a comfortable chair and watch what appears on the screen in front of us. This experience requires no navigation beyond choosing a channel, and we're typically much more receptive to advertising messages that temporarily interrupt our program.

Advertisers have attempted to improve click-through rates by creating interactive banners (a famous banner developed for HP by Red Sky Interactive [*www.redsky.com*] allowed users to play "Pong" in the banner). Increasingly, banners will offer the richness of television and the interaction of the Web. Free ISP Netzero recently acquired a technology that will allow it to serve televisionlike streaming media banners.

Interstitials. Visit *Fortune* magazine on the Web (*www.fortune.com*), and when you click away from the site, a new window will open in your browser inviting you to subscribe to the magazine. These windows are called interstitials, and they demand your attention because you must click on them, if only to close the window. Click-through rates are as high as 5 percent[10] (10 times the average for banners), but costs are higher too. Furthermore, research by Keith Pieper (*www.keithpieper.com*) shows that most publishers and advertisers have experienced complaints or negative responses from customers who feel that interstitials are intrusive.

Sponsorships. Sponsorships can vary from a simple sponsorship of an e-mail list to much more sophisticated site-sponsorship deals. For example, e-retailer 800.com (*www.800.com*) sponsored a list of the top 10 videos which appeared alongside the 800.com logo on the Hollywood Stock Exchange (*www.hsx.com*). By clicking on one of the video titles, visitors were transported to the 800.com site where they could purchase the video. The advantage of sponsorships is that they can help to build a sponsor's brand by presenting it within the context of the sponsored site and by creating value for visitors to that site.

e-Mail. Junk mail, or spam, is an extremely common marketing tool since e-mail lists can be readily available and cheap. More recently, opt-in mail has become popular. It is offered by companies such as Yesmail (*www.yesmail.com*) which allow advertisers to send e-mail messages to a group of people who have indicated an interest in receiving e-mails about that type of product or service. Yesmail has built a database of 8 million users, all of whom have opted to receive e-mails about topics of interest to them. Yesmail claims that its e-mails result in a response rate between 10 and 15 percent.

Coupons. Companies such as Cool Savings (*www.coolsavings.com*) offer their members discount coupons which they can print out and then use for both online and offline retailers. Coupons can be an attractive marketing mechanism because they encourage product trial, and they are a way of selectively discounting prices to the most price-sensitive customers (those that are willing to go to a website and print out a coupon).

Pay-Per-Advertising View. Companies such as CyberGold "pay" customers to view advertisements. The approach uses the accountability of the Web to reward consumers for processing the "right" kind of information (e.g., targeted ads as opposed to generalized Web content).

Loyalty Programs. Companies such as Clickrewards (*www.clickrewards.com*) offer their members the chance to earn a currency, such as airline miles, by shopping at their network of partner sites (see also NetCentives, MyPoints). The economics of customer retention are well known; an existing, loyal customer is much more profitable than a new one, so rewarding existing customers to encourage them to remain loyal can be a good tactic. Beenz (*www.beenz.com*) employs a slightly different approach. It offers its members "beenz" currency in return for them registering at a site or signing up for a mailing list (as well as making purchases). This can help sites to reduce their customer-acquisition costs, but it poses the risk that beenz members will sign up just for the reward and never return to the site.

commission for sales generated by the user (usually in the 5–15 percent range). A reason for the popularity of associate programs is ease of implementation. With no more than a few clicks, websites can register, create an associate banner ad/icon, and start collecting associate commissions from their viewers. In addition to this ease of implementation, there is a virtually unlimited number of potential associates.

Although CDNow is credited with inventing this program, Amazon is often seen as the most innovative and successful. Amazon calls their affiliate program an associates program. Their associates program allows virtually any website to promote Amazon products that are relevant (or even irrelevant) to their viewers by creating a link to Amazon. Associates receive a commission of 5 percent to 15 percent for sales received from customers who connect through their site to Amazon. Thus, a music related site can promote Amazon's music inventory to its viewers and receive referral commissions. An enterprising family member with a family-related website can encourage family members to order all of their books through their Amazon link, so that he or she will reap commissions. Currently, there are over 400,000 Amazon associates including such well known sites as Yahoo!, Excite, AOL, Motley Fool, and MSN.

An affiliate program can offer a number of advantages to e-commerce companies. Amazon used its associate program to build over 400,000 new distribution avenues (i.e., sites that offer easy access to Amazon). Whether customers buy or not, they are exposed to Amazon banner advertising on associates' websites, which builds awareness about Amazon. In addition, while an affiliate reaps commissions from viewers linking to Amazon through their site, as consumers become more familiar with Amazon, they may decide to deal directly with Amazon (as opposed to clicking through the associate). Thus through time, Amazon ends up owning the customer and associates lose future commissions.

Partnerships. While many offline companies arrange partnerships, the use of partnerships is more pervasive in the New Economy. Similar to the manner in which complementary companies often collaborate to push a new technology (i.e., Microsoft's and Intel's partnership is often termed Wintel), Web companies often partner with complementary sites to quickly provide a more value-enhanced service to site visitors. One prevailing strategy is to select a customer niche and provide services that encompass the customer's entire needs in that area (recall our category switchboard discussion in Chapter 3).

Consider a retirement planning site seeking to offer a full range of information related to retirement strategy. Complementary information (and services) could be provided on topics including aging health care, Social Security, stocks and mutual funds, insurance, and elder law. For a site whose competitive advantage is providing retirement information, it can require too much in resources and time to provide all of these services and information. Thus, it is in the retirement site's interest to collaborate with complementary sites. Complementary sites benefit from collaboration in two primary ways: (1) receiving exposure and business from the retirement site's customers and (2) reciprocating by promoting the full service retirement site with banner ads or information.

Innovative Customer Acquisition. As the Internet market becomes more competitive, competitive advantage will be derived from innovative marketing. One form of innovative marketing is to ally with groups (or associations) and provide a complementary service that benefits the group's membership. By creating such an alliance, a new site can launch with a large customer base without incurring expensive and risky marketing fees. In such an arrangement, a site generally pays the group a fee for access to its membership.

Such an innovative marketing concept is being used by MyTeam.com. One focus of MyTeam is to provide Web-based services to support Little League baseball. MyTeam provides webpages for each team. These pages profile the team, scheduling, player information, and other information. This benefits Little League's membership and saves time for coaches. Instead of calling each team player about a scheduling change or to provide some other type of information, each member simply logs on to the team's site for updated information. Players benefit because they receive a personalized webpage that lists information such as their career highlights and statistics. In a version of viral marketing, Little League's brand is enhanced because players tell their friends and family to regularly check their personal Little League homepage. By teaming up with Little League, MyTeam benefits by gaining instant access to a large group of loyal users and their family and friends. MyTeam can capitalize on this large viewer base by selling targeted banner advertising and e-commerce opportunities (i.e., selling baseball equipment, team pictures, and uniforms).

Providing Information. The Web allows sites to instantly offer information that is relevant to their customer base. Many sites provide instantly accessible information to their customers as a form of marketing and product differentiation. The e-commerce market for travel (airlines, hotels, etc.) is very competitive with many well-funded players. Sites try to differentiate themselves by offering vast amounts of information to their customers. Travel information can range from top restaurant and hotel information targeted toward expense account business travelers to time-sensitive travel information (e.g., day-only specials, airfare updates) to budget-minded leisure travelers. Customers evaluate the information they receive and establish a relationship with the site that best meets their needs. Sites try to capitalize on this relationship by offering e-commerce opportunities like travel reservation services.

Leverage the Customer Base. As we have discussed, a primary goal of e-commerce businesses today is to invest heavily in creating a large customer base and establishing a relationship of trust with their customers. Many firms are trying to establish a reputation that conveys to its customer base that they are a solid company that is good at fulfilling e-commerce orders. Eventually, as a company establishes a large and loyal customer base, the goal is to leverage this relationship by offering an expanded product/service selection to its customers. Amazon has successfully leveraged its customer base. Within four months of offering CDs and six weeks of offering videos, Amazon was the top-selling site for both products.[11]

Personalized Online Communications.
Online companies have the opportunity to reduce mass-marketing expenses and increase response rates by developing marketing strategies that center around each individual customer. The manner in which transactions occur on the Net provides e-commerce companies with detailed information on their customers. Information derived from customers registering preferences and demographic information, as well as firms analyzing past purchases and Web surfing habits, provides e-commerce companies the opportunity to create a one-to-one marketing relationship with each of their customers. In addition to this information, many e-commerce companies use their sites to establish a two-

way dialogue with their customers. This dialogue provides additional information regarding product desires and avenues to better market to them. We categorize personalized marketing into five primary forms: (1) *permission marketing,* (2) *personalized recommendations,* (3) *personalized advertisements,* (4) *personalized webpages,* and (5) *personalized e-commerce stores.*

Permission Marketing. Seth Godin coined the term **permission marketing** to describe how successful e-mail campaigns can result from creating relationships with customers. Permission marketing has become the current rage of online marketers and has led to increases in marketing response rates.[12]

Permission marketing presumes successful marketing campaigns can be created by establishing a mutually beneficial and trusting relationship between the firm and its customers. In exchange for some offered benefit, customers volunteer information about themselves and, in essence, ask to be marketing targets. Once customers initiate this relationship, they anticipate e-mail messages because they know that these messages will be on relevant topics. By using the permission marketing philosophy, online firms create a valuable database of customers who have given the firm permission to market to them and are receptive to marketing messages.

Permission marketing e-mails must be relevant to the consumer. Relevance can range from general interest to very specific interest. Response rates and trust can increase by sending permission marketing e-mails that are highly specific to customers' interests. Many online firms ask their permission marketing customers for detailed personal information when they sign up for e-mails. This information allows them to send more targeted e-mails to specific segments of the firm's customer base. Customers appreciate these targeted e-mails and this increases their relationship level with the firm. The associated increased trust level may also induce customers to reveal additional information about themselves.

Estee Lauder's recent marketing campaign for its Clinique Stop Signs of Visible Anti-Aging Serum reveals the effectiveness of targeted e-mail campaigns. Clinique has a database of over 600,000 people who have registered to be updated via e-mails. To register, customers have to fill in a brief survey that provides Clinique with opportunities to send them more personalized e-mails. The company sends a monthly newsletter that contains beauty tips and information on new products.

In March 1999, Clinique introduced its Stop Signs of Visible Anti-Aging Serum with a two-tiered offline/online marketing strategy. By using data from its e-mail registration survey, Clinique initially sent a sample of its new product to every registered woman who was over 35 and/or had listed that she was worried about wrinkles. A few weeks after the sample was sent out, Clinique followed up with an e-mail message inviting the recipient to purchase the product. About 8 percent of the targeted customers proceeded to buy the product online. This is a very high response rate, and we note that this response rate does not include customers who purchased the product from retail outlets.[13]

Personalized Recommendations. Many e-commerce sites have personalized services that make specific merchandise recommendations for each user based on past purchases, site pages viewed, and survey information that the user has provided. As noted earlier in the book, the recommendations that work best rely on collaborative filtering technologies sold by NetPerceptions and Firefly (now a unit of Microsoft). These services use sophisticated algorithms that utilize information specific to each customer to find the best matches of additional products that may be of interest to the customer. Without this information, customers may not otherwise have known about these recommended products. This can increase revenues and loyalty from the all-important repeat customer. When Music Boulevard test marketed its personalized recommendation service, they found that the recommendations prompted customers to buy CDs 10 percent to 30 percent of the time. This purchase rate is much higher than the 2 percent to 4 percent general purchase rate realized on the rest of their site.[14]

Personalized Advertisements. Websites increasingly are using personalized technology software to determine dynamically, in real time, which Web advertisements should be exposed to viewers. ZDNET uses personalization technology that is based on an analysis of five user profile and impression environment variables. Variables used include the user's past click behavior, time of day, the page, recency/frequency of visits, and search keywords. Based on these variables, users are given a relevancy score (i.e., indicator of the probability of a click) and ads that are most likely to be of interest to the viewer are displayed. During a test run of this technology, ZDNET realized an impressive 20 percent to 100 percent increase in click-through results.[15] Yahoo! collects 400 billion bytes of information a day (the equivalent of a library with 800,000 books) on how its customers use the Yahoo! site.[16] This personalized information helps Yahoo! better understand each customer's needs. By using this information to target ads to individual customers, Yahoo! has realized higher ad rates and e-commerce sales.

Personalized Webpages. Many portals and e-commerce sites allow users to create their own personalized webpage. This allows users to create a webpage that caters exactly to their interests. Personalization encourages users to return more often and increases the user's familiarity and trust with the webpage. This leads to users spending more time on the website, thereby increasing advertising exposure time. Since a creator/user of a personalized webpage reveals detailed personal information, the site sponsoring the personalized webpage can deliver more targeted consumers to advertisers. This results in an opportunity to charge increased ad rates to reach specific customer groups. At portal site Excite, users can create a personalized portal page using Excite's MyExcite service. Excite found that users who create a MyExcite personal page come back five times as often as others and view twice the number of pages compared to Excite users who do not have a personal page. This has allowed Excite to reap higher advertising revenues.[17] In addition, personalization increases users' switching costs.

Personalized e-Commerce Stores. One of the goals of online merchants is to use Internet technology and their knowledge about individual consumers to tailor their products and services for each of their customers. Jeff Bezos, Amazon's chairman, has stated that one of his goals is to have his "store redecorated for each and every customer."[18] However, he cautions that it could take up to 10 years to achieve such individual customization. Office Depot offers its small-business customers personalized catalogs, allowing businesses to create real-time unique catalogs for their employees—based on their buying authority.[19] In addition to making their customers' shopping experience more pleasant, personalization is a key tool for increasing switching costs. If a customer is satisfied and becomes dependent on a site that offers personalized services, it will be more costly to switch sites. Even if a competing site offers superior services, there is a certain inertia that often slows users from switching sites.

Traditional Mass Media Communications. As the online environment is becoming more competitive, it has become increasingly difficult for Web companies to make (cost effectively) a marketing splash. Online companies increasingly turn to the primary advertising forum of brick-and-mortar companies: television advertising. In their quest to rapidly attract customers and stake out their niche, a growing number of online companies seem to feel that, while expensive, television advertising can quickly transmit their marketing message to a large scale audience. Moreover, in many cases, the offline media is necessary to bring new customers onto the Internet or, for existing Internet users, to make them aware of the brand.

According to Competitive Media Reporting, in 1998 Internet companies accounted for $323 million in television advertising spending. In 1999, Internet companies were expected to spend in excess of $1 billion on television advertising. In part due to increased demand from Internet companies, the cost of 30-second ads for top-rated programs has strongly increased. For example, 30-second ads for the 1999 Super Bowl averaged $1.6 million, but for the 2000 Super Bowl, the average 30-second ad sold for $2.0 million.[20] This 25 percent average increase has been attributed in part to the strength of demand from Internet companies.

Today, the general opinion is that online advertising is becoming less effective. In the early days of e-commerce, it was easier for a company to make a big splash by doing low-cost, innovative online advertising. As often happens in business, many saw the opportunities of the New Economy and jumped into the market. As more e-commerce companies inundated surfers with heaps of (innovative) online ads, online advertising effectiveness dropped. In response to this decrease in effectiveness, Internet companies are trying to better leverage more traditional marketing channels (e.g., television, radio, print).

Priceline believes that radio is the most effective medium to reach its potential customers. In 1999, Priceline targeted two-thirds of its $60 million marketing budget on radio. Jay Walker, Priceline's founder, claims that the radio campaign has helped Priceline increase sales by 5 percent a week.[21]

Many cite eToys success as an example of the effectiveness of television advertising. In eToys first year of business (the site was launched in October 1997), its total revenues were $2 million dollars. During the 1998 holiday season, VISA USA ran a co-branded television ad that featured eToys. The television ad featured parents using the eToys site to purchase holiday presents for their children. Due in large part to the effectiveness of these television ads, eToys' fourth quarter revenues skyrocketed to $23 million![22] In the first and second quarters of 2000, the stock price suffered a severe downturn and, hence, demonstrated that strong marketing communications only provide input to an overall strategy process and the overall strategy must be sound.

Monster.com found that using traditional television marketing fueled explosive growth of its business. In its quest to establish a brand for job seekers as being the best place to get their resume seen online as well as a brand for employers of being the easiest way to find people online, Monster.com has invested heavily in television advertising. Despite having 1998 estimated profits of $1.2 million, 1999 advertising spending was estimated at $60 million.

Direct Communications. *Direct communications* can take many forms including the use of the classical business-to-business sales rep calling on accounts, retail sales clerks, and telephone customer sales reps as well as the use of direct marketing and telemarketing.

Sales Reps. One of the most interesting developments on the Web is the reemergence of the **traditional sales rep.** When properly managed, the Web can paradoxically lead to increased effectiveness of sales reps rather than making sales reps obsolete. Dell Online found that sales leads increased in quality. As a result, sales reps could make more efficient use of their time, and their satisfaction increased after the new online channel was added.

Direct Marketing. A second form of offline marketing communication is **direct marketing** through the mail system. Of course, a key difference is, with the new information gained online, firms are able to target and customize the mailings to a much more significant degree.

Telemarketing. A third option is the use of a **telemarketing** salesforce. We have all received these wonderful sales pitches near the dinner hour. Their aim is clearly to increase sales—it is not intended to strengthen brand awareness or image. Rather, the entire aim is to entice the customer to purchase the goods or services.

DRILL-DOWN

Quotes on Online Branding

"E-branding is more important [than e-commerce]. And it must come first. Because few people will buy your stuff—online or off—unless you are top-of-mind."
—Annette Hamilton, Executive Producer, ZDNet

"Brand is the price of entry [to the Internet], not the winning strategy."
—Dylan Tweney, InfoNet

"By the time your potential customers log on, they already know what they're looking for, and they often know from whom they want to buy it. . . . They're just not listening to branding messages anymore."
—Michael Fischler, Principal, The Pubs Group

"Brands stand as comfort anchors in the sea of confusion, fear, and doubt. In dynamic markets, strong brands have more value than ever, precisely because of the speed with which these markets move."
—Chuck Pettis, Technobranding

"It took more than 50 years for Coca-Cola to become a worldwide market leader, but only five years for online search engine Yahoo! to gain market dominance. The role of the brand has changed dramatically and has created a vacuum between offline and online brands."
—Mark Lindstrom, Executive Director, ZIVO

"A company's website IS the brand. It's the hub of consumer experience, the place where all aspects of a company, from its annual report to its products to its support, intersect. It's the company in a nutshell, all there in a way that just is not possible in the analog world."
—Sean Carton, Carton Donofrio Interactive

A fascinating development of the Internet has been the importance of branding. Perhaps due to the limited "real estate" that a screen-to-customer interface provides, or to a desire to build consumer goods companies quickly, or to the perception that this is a winner-take-all environment. Regardless of the reason, it is abundantly clear that branding in the e-commerce arena is receiving a great deal of management attention.

Several key concerns are apparent in these quotes:

- Branding is a necessary but not sufficient condition for success.
- Branding may be more important in the online than the offline environment.
- Brands serve to add value in each step of the decision process—at prepurchase (e.g., driving traffic to the site), purchase (e.g., erasing doubt), and postpurchase (e.g., assurance).

What Is an Advertising Network Manager?[23]

by Leo Griffin

Advertising network managers such as DoubleClick, L90, Engage, and 24/7 aggregate and represent websites, selling (either to individual advertisers or to the media buying arms of advertising agencies) banner impressions on websites belonging to their network members. Typically these firms keep 35 to 50 percent of the sales revenues for ads that they serve, passing the balance on to the site on which the banner actually appeared. The advantages for advertisers being able to buy from an aggregator are considerable—rather than making hundreds of phone calls and purchase decisions, media buyers can make just one. DoubleClick, which has one of the most extensive networks, has operations in over 20 countries and represents over 1,500 sites; 24/7 represents over 3,500 small and medium traffic websites.

Network managers do much more than just aggregate websites. They also provide technology and systems that allow advertisers to accurately target advertisements to relevant customer segments, to track click-through rates, and to monitor where and when and to whom their ads are being displayed.

DART (Dynamic Advertising Reporting and Targeting) is DoubleClick's ad serving and reporting system. It is used by sites in the DoubleClick network as well as by websites that manage their own banners (such as Ask Jeeves *www.ask.com*) but contract with DoubleClick to use the application. The technology uses cookies (small data files placed on the hard disks of visitors to a DoubleClick network website) to individually identify each user whenever he or she visits a DoubleClick affiliate, and to record where he or she goes and what he or she does. DART has the ability to track people's click-stream and ad-viewing behavior across the DoubleClick network (sites such as Autobytel [*www.autobytel.com*], MTV [*www.mtv.com*], and Comedy Central [*www.comedycentral.com*], and to date DoubleClick has built up over 50 million user profiles. The software allows advertisers to show their ads across the whole network, or on specific sites or categories of sites (e.g., entertainment sites). They can also target users based on variables such as their computer operating system, their zip code, and even their business name. Companies can also serve customized ads to users who have, for instance, visited their site but not made a purchase, or who have viewed a specific page on their website. So don't be surprised if you visit an e-commerce site, check out albums by your favorite artist, and the next day you see an ad on a different site offering you a discount on CDs for that very same artist.

DoubleClick has recently made moves to expand its tracking capabilities beyond online clickstream data to include offline purchase data. In June 1999 DoubleClick announced the acquisition of Abacus Direct Corporation, which manages the largest database of catalog purchasing behavior in the United States. This database contains purchase information taken from 1,500 catalogs and 3.5 billion transactions and contains information such as name, address, and the dates, amounts, and categories of purchases for 90 million U.S. households. DoubleClick's original intention was to merge the Abacus database with its own data to create an incredibly powerful database on people's online and offline behavior, however public outcry over privacy concerns has caused it to agree to suspend its matching efforts, pending the agreement of industry standards.

L90 has taken a different approach to the advertising market. It focuses primarily on selling sponsorship-based advertising rather than banner ads. Sponsorships are attractive to advertisers and content creators alike. Advertisers like them because they can often create a more effective ad by integrating the message into the site's content. Websites like this approach because an advertising success does not automatically mean that the user will be transported away from the host's website. Sponsorship deals can also result in higher CPMs, which translates into more revenue for website owners.

Do Strong Online Brands Matter?

As the discussion in the previous section implies, a strong brand can be viewed as essential to the growth of an online business. In particular, with the introduction of so many brands, a strong brand name provides a clear presence in the market. Furthermore, strong brands attract customers, and, hence, in the long run, firms may be able to decrease marketing expenditures once the brand is established. In effect, a strong brand is an instant message that contains a wide variety of associations on the part of target customers. Clear brands are also associated with higher conversation rates. Finally and most importantly, all current online "winners" have strong brands.

Opponents of the strong brand line of reasoning argue that history will prove this argument to be limited. Opponents argue that alliances are the key to locking up a market—and these alliances can be accomplished with strong venture backing. Second, third party evaluators such as Gomez Advisors and BizRate will increasingly influence consumption—much like *Consumer Reports* does today. However, unlike *Consumer Reports*, the BizRate data is easily available, easy to access, and, hence, can drive consumption behavior during the purchase process. Third, speed to market may be more important than branding. Also, the meaning of brands is changing. Because all experiences are increasingly becoming customized, the meaning of a "mega-brand" is no longer relevant. Finally, while it is true that all winners have strong brands, a number of "big losers" also have strong brand names.

As noted at the beginning of this section, online companies must consider how to manage their entire mix of communications (as implied in Table 5-1) to influence both consumer behavior and the brand-building process. In the next section, we turn our attention to the building of strong brands.

WHAT IS A "GOOD" BRAND?

According to the American Marketing Association, a *brand* is a "name, term, sign, symbol, or design, or a combination of them intended to identify the goods and services of one seller or group of sellers and to differentiate them from those of competition." The term *product* simply describes the general category of the good (e.g., books), while the brand (e.g., Amazon.com) refers to both the product and the additional "wrap-arounds" (e.g., easy customer interface, one-click shopping, collaborative filtering) that differentiate it from other products in the category.

Branding Basics

Exhibit 5-3 provides a few key insights into what constitutes good online branding. At the center of the exhibit is the core product or service. In the case of American Airlines (*www.aa.com*), this means "safe, on-time" transportation from location A to location B. The "wrap-arounds" for American Airlines include superior service, the AADVANTAGE frequent flier club, the Admirals club, in-flight service, and the comfort of the environment. The market communications emphasize the benefits of membership including functional (e.g., arrive at location on-time), symbolic (e.g., communicates your social status versus Southwest Airlines), and experiential (e.g., comfort of chairs) benefits.[24]

Good brands provide a clear message to the market about the core offering, the wrap-around, and the communications. All provide not only a signal about the functional offering, but they are simultaneously differentiated by their emotional, symbolic, and experiential benefits—for both the firm and target customers. Below we construct a simple model of branding that extends these ideas.

A Simple Conceptual Model of Brand Equity. Exhibit 5-4 provides a simple framework by which to understand the effects of the brand (e.g., core, wrap-around, and communications) and brand equity. The exhibit has three basic parts: the brand, customer responses, and benefits (both firm and customer). **Brand equity** has a wide variety of definitions in the academic literature.[25] According to David Aaker, brand equity is a combination of assets that can be viewed from both the firm's and the customer's perspectives. Put differently, he views brand equity as a combination of consumer responses and benefits (firm and customer). In particular he notes that brand equity is "a set of assets (and liabilities) linked to a brand's name and symbol that add to (or subtract from) the value provided by a product or service to a firm and/or that firm's customers."[26]

Other authors tend to focus heavily on the customer responses only: "Customer-based brand equity is defined as the differential effect that brand knowledge has on consumer response to the marketing of that brand."

Others tend to focus only on financial criteria such as the dollar value of the brand. Similar to Aaker, we tend to divide brand equity into two key components: (1) intermediate customer responses and (2) the benefits—to both the customer and the firm. Thus, the framework has three basic parts: the brand, customer

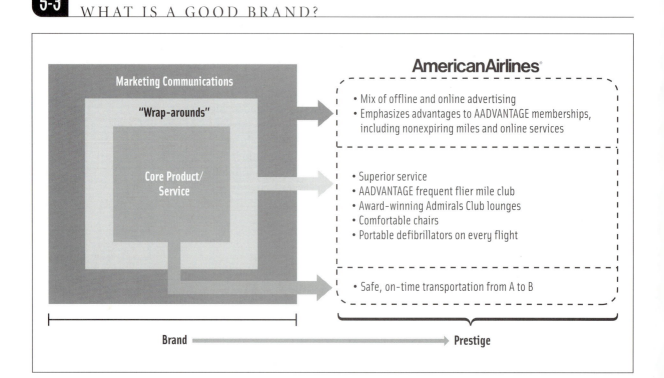

Exhibit 5-3 WHAT IS A GOOD BRAND?

Exhibit
5-4

A SIMPLE CONCEPTUAL MODEL OF BRAND EQUITY

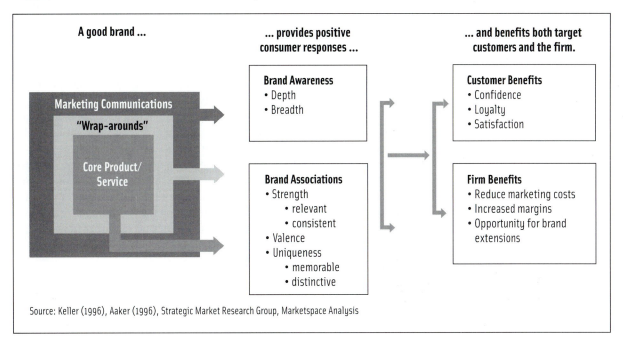

A good brand ...

... provides positive consumer responses ...

... and benefits both target customers and the firm.

Marketing Communications

"Wrap-arounds"

Core Product/ Service

Brand Awareness
• Depth
• Breadth

Brand Associations
• Strength
  • relevant
  • consistent
• Valence
• Uniqueness
  • memorable
  • distinctive

Customer Benefits
• Confidence
• Loyalty
• Satisfaction

Firm Benefits
• Reduce marketing costs
• Increased margins
• Opportunity for brand extensions

Source: Keller (1996), Aaker (1996), Strategic Market Research Group, Marketspace Analysis

responses to the brand (awareness and associations), and benefits (to both the firm and the target customers). We will first review customer responses and then benefits.

Consumer Responses. Consumer responses can take two broad forms: brand awareness and brand associations. Brand-name awareness refers to the strength of a brand's presence in the consumer's mind. A brand with high brand awareness (e.g., Monster) is more likely to be recalled—either prompted by an advertisement or unaided by the firm.

Brand associations refer to the connections that consumers make to the brand. These associations can be categorized in terms of (1) strength, (2) valence, and (3) uniqueness. Consider for example the brand Amazon. **Strength of association** refers to the intensity with which the target consumer links a particular word, phrase, or meaning to a particular brand. Thus, if one were to cue the customer to reflect on the meaning of Amazon, the customer might say "big company," "Jeff Bezos," "They sell books," "It was my first Internet purchasing experience," "It is easy to use," or "They are unprofitable." Strong associations tend to be those that are "top of mind" for the customer. Measures of strength include: number of times an association was mentioned, rank order of the association, and speed of recall. Our hypothesis is that "Jeff Bezos" would be a strong association to the Amazon brand name relative to it being a "Seattle-based" company.

Valence refers to the degree to which the association is positive or negative. Again, consider the Amazon associations above. "Easy to use" is a positive association, "unprofitable" is a negative association, and "they sell books" is a neutral association. **Uniqueness** captures the degree to which the association is distinct, relative to other brands. "Jeff Bezos" is an association that is unique to the Amazon brand.

Consider, for example, the American Airlines site once again. A given customer may have strong associations to the brand name (e.g., large carrier, the AA slogan). Strength of the association is often divided among two criteria: relevance and consistency. Relevance is defined as the degree to which the brand is perceived as meeting the needs of the target customer. Is the tag line relevant to the needs of the airline's key target segment—the business traveler? Consistency is the degree to which each element of the brand reinforces the brand intent. Does the AA symbol reinforce the airline's positioning as an airline for the business traveler? This is, of course, debatable. All else being equal, brands that are highly relevant and highly consistent tend to produce strong associations.

These associations are hopefully positive (e.g., "I had a great time flying American Airlines." versus "That is the airline that always is late."). Hence, associations can be rated on the degree to which they produce positive or negative associations—that is, their valence. Finally, associations can be rated on their uniqueness. Uniqueness also can be subdivided into distinctiveness and memorability. Distinctiveness captures the degree to which the brand is differentiated from competitors (e.g., Jeff Bezos is distinctive) while memorability captures the brand's ability to provide a lasting communication effect (e.g., does the tagline create memorability?). A memorable brand association leaves an impression in the mind of the customer, which enables easy recall.

Firm and consumer benefits. Returning to Exhibit 5-4, positive consumer responses in turn produce benefits for both customers and the firm. Customer benefits include the increased confidence in the purchase decision, loyalty to the brand, and satisfaction with the experience. Firm benefits translate into top line revenue growth, increased margins, and lower marketing costs. The firm also has the opportunity to extend the brand into new categories—such as Amazon's expansion into home improvement.

Types of Brands.

Pure Offline and Online Brands. Early in the evolution of the Internet, brands were categorized as pure offline or online brands. Table 5-3 provides a sampling of these brands. Classic offline brands included the Gap, UPS, OfficeMax, and Disney. New to the world online brands included Amazon, Yahoo!, Geocities, and Priceline. However, as the Internet expanded, we began to observe the crossover of offline brands into the online world, and the transition of online brands into the offline world (e.g., Yahoo! Magazine).

Blurring of the Distinction. The end result is a blurring of the distinction between pure offline and pure online brands. Consider the following developments:

- Brands such as Yahoo! were established as online brands but use offline promotional activities to grow their brand awareness.
- Brands such as Yahoo! Magazine are "traditional brands" in the sense that the product is established in the physical world, but they are extensions of the online brands—and thus a mixture of the two.
- Brands such as Egghead.com have completely shifted their product by moving from a traditional, offline brand to a purely online brand.
- Brands such as Wingspanbank are online brands in the sense that the product is established in the virtual world but by a traditional brand.

Table
5-3
TYPES OF BRANDS

Traditional Brands	Online Brands
• The product/service with which the brand is associated was established offline in the bricks-and-mortar world.	• The product/service with which the brand is associated was established in the online world.
Examples:	*Examples:*
• The Gap • UPS • Dell • JCrew • McDonald's • OfficeMax • Ragu • Coca-Cola • Disney	• Amazon • Yahoo! • Chemdex • ZDNet • AOL • Priceline • CDNow • WingspanBank • E*Trade

- Brands such as Schwab have successfully bridged the gap between online and offline activities.
- Brands such as Ragu were established offline but use online promotional activities to grow their brand awareness and loyalty.

Exhibit 5-5 provides a simple diagram to capture the movement of brands. In particular, the figure has two basic dimensions: mix of promotion (online versus offline) and initial product establishment (online brand versus offline brand). This figure illustrates that Schwab was initially a traditional brand—and has now moved toward the center of the figure to reflect its hybrid nature. Also, Schwab is doing both online and offline promotion—hence, the circle is quite wide. Egghead.com initially was a traditional, offline brand but has moved to an online brand with heavily online promotion activities.

What Is the Ten-Step Branding Process?

There are a number of well-known frameworks to build brands. In this section, we provide a simple, managerially relevant **Ten-Step Branding Process** (see Exhibit 5-6). In addition to the broad review of each step, we also discuss how the branding process may need to differ in the online environment. Broadly, these steps include the following:

Step 1: Clearly Define the Brand Audience. In Chapter 2, we discussed the need to clearly specify the target audience for the offering. Here we are simply reiterating the importance of having a clear picture of the target customer segment.

As noted in Chapters 2 and 3, it could be argued that a larger number of segments can be effectively addressed in the online environment as compared to the offline environment. This is due to a number of factors including the firm's ability to reconfigure its storefront in a real-time fashion for each customer.

Exhibit 5-5

BRAND PRESENCE

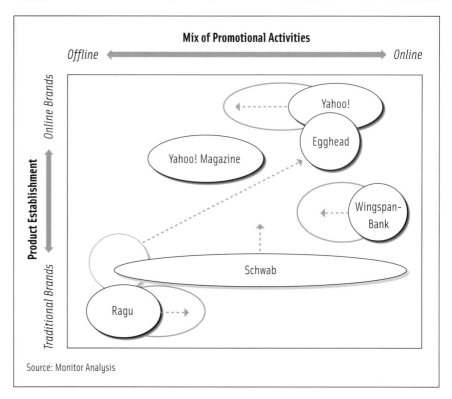

Source: Monitor Analysis

Step 2: Understand the Target Customer.
From the broad description of the target customer, it is frequently useful to describe a composite "prototypic" customer that can bring the target segment to life.

Both online and offline environments require deep understanding of customer behavior. Indeed, firms building brands exclusively in one environment still need to be aware of consumer behavior in the other environment. As noted in Chapter 2, it is clear that a great deal of information can be collected by click-stream data in the online environment; however, this information is not sufficient to infer the process of consumption (e.g., attitudes, knowledge, brand image). Hence, a blending of traditional and online research is often necessary.

Step 3: Identify Key Leverage Points in Customer Experience.
While target customers may share many of the same behavioral characteristics, this step forces the firm to consider the key organizational levers—prices of products, customer interface, mix of online versus offline communications—that will activate the customer to behave in a manner that is consistent with the objectives of the firm. Consumer research should focus heavily on these key organizational levers that can motivate consumption.

The Customer Decision Process involves prepurchase, purchase, and postpurchase decisions in both the online and offline environments. In the offline environment, it is the retail salesperson or the telephone customer service representative

Exhibit 5-6

BUILDING AN ONLINE BRAND

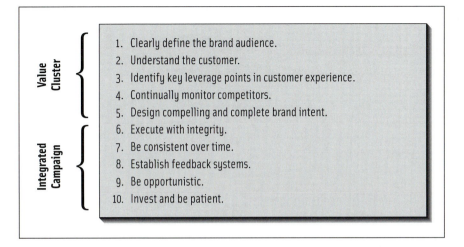

Value Cluster	1. Clearly define the brand audience.
	2. Understand the customer.
	3. Identify key leverage points in customer experience.
	4. Continually monitor competitors.
	5. Design compelling and complete brand intent.
Integrated Campaign	6. Execute with integrity.
	7. Be consistent over time.
	8. Establish feedback systems.
	9. Be opportunistic.
	10. Invest and be patient.

who guides the customer through the buying process. In the online environment, the store can be reconfigured—much like a chess match—to guide or direct consumers. It is a more subtle, less obvious form of selling.

Step 4: Continually Monitor Competitors.
The entire brand experience is tough enough if no competitors are in your space. However, competition in the online world is incredibly intense. It is not unusual for a firm to develop a clear business plan only to have new competitors emerge prior to the launch date. Hence, it is critical that new, emerging, and existing competitors are constantly monitored.

Competitors must be monitored in both online and offline environments. The online environment is distinctive in two respects. First, the degree of competitive intensity is different from the offline world. Here we are specifically referring to the number of new competitors that are emerging both within the product category and across product categories. Second, it is much quicker to analyze competitors given the emergence of sources such as Hoover's Online (*www.hoovers.com*), the securities and exchange commission (*www.sec.gov*), and financial sites (e.g., Yahoo! finance).

Step 5: Design Compelling and Complete Brand Intent.
The brand intent brings to life the value proposition or cluster. Value propositions or clusters tend to focus on the high-level customer benefits. Here we are looking for a more customer-friendly description of how the brand should be interpreted from the customer's viewpoint. The intent should be both compelling (e.g., provide the positive brand associations) and comprehensive.

While the brand intent is important in both environments, we believe that there is more of an opportunity to customize the brand intent in the online environment. In general, the brand intent tends to be more segment-focused in the offline environment, while the online environment allows individuals within the segment to customize the offering to exactly respond to their needs.

Step 6: Execute with Integrity. Executing with integrity refers to the quality of the implementation choices. Namely, the extent to which the firm provides a clear, trustworthy message.

In the offline environment, brands historically took consistent long-term investment. Most of the well-known Internet brands have been introduced since 1995.

Step 7: Be Consistent over Time. Strong brands take time to develop. Of course, on Internet time this may be weeks rather than decades. However, regardless of the time line, the key is that the message must be consistent.

While it is important to be consistent with brand message, it is also clear that each consumer can have a slightly modified experience with the brand—given the interactive nature of the Internet. Hence, while both environments attempt to be consistent, the interactivity of the Internet allows customers to experience the brand in unique ways.

Step 8: Establish Feedback Systems. Market communications and reactions in the marketplace rarely work out exactly as planned. Hence, it is important to have regular feedback systems in place.

The effects of branding can be experienced more quickly and more precisely in the online environment. Sophisticated tools exist to track customer responses to the brand, marketing communications, and marketing.

Step 9: Be Opportunistic. Opportunities present themselves to firms to build their brands in unexpected ways. Monster.com always attempts to be one of the first to try particular types of communications (e.g., Super Bowl advertising, blimps) in its category.

Opportunism typically occurs at the segment level in the offline environment and at the individual level in the online environment.

Step 10: Invest and Be Patient. While the stock market may vary considerably in their valuation of selected dot-coms, it is also evident that brands need to be nurtured and managed over time. Careful investment, long-term patience, and the ability to focus on the long run are critical.

Both environments require long-term investments in a consistent, compelling message. While it could be argued that online brands have the potential to generate loyalty more quickly—due principally to the newness of the experience for many consumers—both environments require significant long-term investment (see Table 5-4).

A Framework for Branding

Table 5-5 illustrates a simple categorization scheme for brands. On the top row, we divide brands into two categories according to whether the brand was established as a traditional brand or as an online brand. We further subdivide the traditional category into branding online and branding and selling online. For online brands, we classify them into two categories: intermediaries and e-commerce sites. Along the column, we have noted that these categorizations can apply to both business-to-business and business-to-consumer sites.

Table 5-4

SIMILARITIES AND DIFFERENCES IN OFFLINE VS. ONLINE BRANDING

Branding Element	Offline	Online
1. *Clearly define the brand audience*	• Limited to manageable number of segments to prevent inconsistent messaging	• Could include larger number of segments, with customer-driven messages
2. *Understand the customer*	• Requires understanding of environment, desired purchase and usage experience	• Requires more thorough understanding of desired purchase and usage experience in an interactive environment
3. *Identify key leverage points in customer experience*	• Buying process is typically a simplified representation of customer segment behavior with static leverage points	• Buying process tends to be more dynamic and flexible
4. *Continually monitor competitors*	• Requires monitoring of competitor advertisements and activities	• Competitor advertisements & activities can be monitored online
5. *Design compelling and complete brand intent*	• Brand intent (desired positioning) is designed to address the needs and beliefs of target segments	• Greater opportunity for customization of key messages
6. *Execute with integrity*	• Strong, positive brands are built up over time	• Online interactions bring in added concerns of security and privacy • Limited familiarity with online brands makes fostering trust more difficult
7. *Be consistent over time*	• Brand intent guides marketing communications • Image reinforced through variety of offline media	• Brand intent guides marketing communications • With the ability to customize, one customer's brand image may be different than another customer's brand image
8. *Establish feedback systems*	• Collecting and analyzing customer feedback is more time-consuming	• Sophisticated tools exist for tracking online; allow for anonymous, interactive, quick feedback
9. *Be opportunistic*	• Marketing strategy includes plan for sequenced growth and adjustment of brand based on changing customer needs	• Customization for multiple segments and opportunity for early recognition of the changing customer requires a corresponding tailoring of brand intent
10. *Invest and be patient*	• Building brand awareness requires significant investment • Building brand loyalty takes time offline, especially because early customer receptivity to brands is difficult to assess (and usually involves market research)	• Building brand awareness requires significant investment, especially for those competitors who are not first in their category online • Brands have the potential to generate loyalty more quickly, especially if customers are targeted effectively

Branding Choices

A firm's online branding choices depend upon its communication objectives. Exhibit 5-7 on page 196 illustrates the types of decisions that influence the ultimate choice of communication mix elements. In the middle of Exhibit 5-7, we note that a firm can have at least six different communications objectives.

Should Offline Firms Create New Brands or Use Their Existing Brands?

There is considerable debate in the practitioner community on the value of leveraging an existing brand name into the online environment. Simply put, should companies such as Lands' End, Wal-Mart, American Airlines, and K-Mart use their existing brand name in the online environment, or should they create a new-to-the-world brand name? Consider the following examples:

Wal-Mart Vs. K-Mart. Wal-Mart has decided to use its existing brand name to launch walmart.com (*www.walmart.com*) while K-Mart, a clear brick-and-mortar competitor, has decided to use a new brand name (*www.bluelight.com*). BlueLight.com is using a brilliant approach that involves the offer of free ISP service available to all through its site. If that isn't a direct pitch to Middle America, we don't know what is. And it's worked. After just a few months in the market, they have apparently attracted more than a million registrations for the service, which is fast and easy to download.

American Airlines Vs. Travelocity. Until this year, American Airlines owned SABRE. SABRE, in turn, owned over 80% of Travelocity. Hence, American was able to see the clear advantage of using a different brand name in an attempt to be the dominant company providing travel destinations in the entire category of travel.

Proponents of the "keep-the-same-brand" school argue that it takes an enormous amount of time and money to build a strong brand name. People in the

venture-capital community claim that it costs $50 to $100 million to launch a new consumer brand on the Web. Hence, it makes a great deal of sense to continue using the offline brand name for the online brand. Second, customers who decide to purchase online can be assured that services can occur offline (e.g., the ability to return product to a physical store, phone calls can be made to service centers). Third, it is difficult to uncover interesting new brand names. Fourth, the online and offline brand can have a synergistic effect—one that is greater than either brand operating alone. Finally, target customers will not be confused by brand offerings that appear on new sites (e.g., K-mart brands appearing on BlueLight.com).

Opponents argue that using an existing brand limits the growth of the user base. That is, it is easier for customers to believe that Travelocity or Expedia is the most comprehensive travel site as compared to their majority stockholders (i.e., American Airlines and Microsoft, respectively). Second, existing offline brands "don't get the Net." Hence, their user interfaces are likely to be less useable, hip, and interesting as compared to true dot-com brands. Third, it is possible to sign up more partners—potential competitors, collaborators, and others—when a third-party name is used (e.g., General Motors, Ford, and Chrysler selected a new brand name for their announced B2B exchange).

Brand Creation. The objective may be to build a new-to-the-world brand name. Under such a scenario, it is more likely to be the case that the firm will initially be focused on brand awareness as compared to brand loyalty. This choice, in turn, would lead to mix choices that emphasize the brand-name awareness as compared to communications that provide detailed information on the brand—such as comparative advertising.

Sales Leads. The company may decide that the Internet will be used to facilitate the sales lead process. Dell Online and others have found that their Web presence actually builds qualified leads in a quicker, more effective way than traditional sales approaches. Hence, in sharp contrast to the view that the sales force will decrease as

Table 5-5	CASE STUDIES OF SUCCESSFUL ONLINE BRANDING EFFORTS			

	Established as Traditional Brand		Established as Online Brand	
	Branding Online	**Branding and Selling Online**	**Intermediary/ Vertical Portal**	**e-Commerce**
Business-to-Consumer	Ragu	American Airlines	Monster.com	CDNow
Business-to-Business	FedEx	Cisco Systems	Healtheon	Ventro

the Web expands, this finding suggests that the roles of the sales force will change from lead generation to "closing the sale."

Store Traffic. The principal objective for some sites is store traffic. That is, the effectiveness of the campaign will be judged relative to the increase in unique visitors.

Product Trial. A fourth objective may be the actual "trial usage" of the product. Recently, the *Wall Street Journal* interactive edition provided two weeks free usage to Palm VII users to encourage trial adoption of the newspaper.

Product Sales. The company may also measure the success of a campaign based upon the actual increase in product or service sales.

Brand Reinforcement. Finally, it is possible that the communications effort is focused largely on reinforcing the brand image that is already widely accepted in the marketplace.

These communications objectives, in turn, can produce effects on the brand awareness, brand recognition, and firm/customer benefits. Finally, the particular choice of brand equity that is targeted will naturally lead to the selection of certain communication mix elements.

HOW DOES ONLINE BRANDING COMPARE BETWEEN AMERICAN AIRLINES AND CONTINENTAL AIRLINES?

In the discussion below, we more fully develop two case studies of online branding—one for American Airlines and one for Monster. In order to understand the branding process and to show how branding can be differentiated on the Internet (an equally important topic), we compare these to brands of so-called average performers in the product category.

Exhibit 5-7

ONLINE BRANDING CHOICES

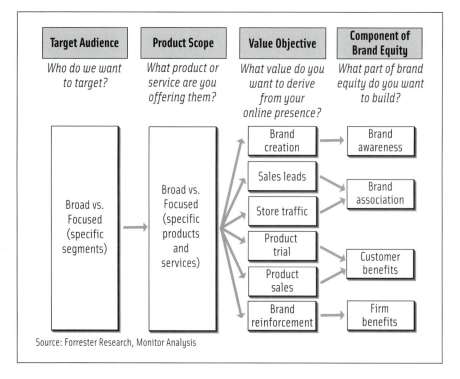

Target Audience	Product Scope	Value Objective	Component of Brand Equity
Who do we want to target?	What product or service are you offering them?	What value do you want to derive from your online presence?	What part of brand equity do you want to build?

Broad vs. Focused (specific segments) → Broad vs. Focused (specific products and services)

Brand creation → Brand awareness

Sales leads → Brand association

Store traffic → Brand association

Product trial → Customer benefits

Product sales → Customer benefits

Brand reinforcement → Firm benefits

Source: Forrester Research, Monitor Analysis

Case Study: American Airlines

American Airlines provides an excellent example of a brick-and-mortar company that was able to increase brand recognition and cement customer loyalty by successfully bringing its brand online. American historically had been a pioneer in the industry since developing the SABRE computer reservation system in the 1960s and initiating the first frequent flyer program in the 1980s.

Overview of Online Branding Efforts. American Airlines was the first airline to establish a website on May 17, 1995. It has grown to be one of the top airline sites—in terms of unique visitors and awards. As of February 2000, it was logging over 1.9 million unique visitors per month. It receives upwards of 300,000 visits on peak days with 25 million page views per month. It has 2.1 million subscribers to its weekly Net SAAver Fares™ e-mail list (the most popular e-mail travel product on the Web). Gross sales were $575 million in the 1999 calendar year.

A key to American's success in creating an online brand has been its ability to differentiate itself from competitors by consistently being first. Examples include the following:

- First to have a service-oriented website (May 1995)
- First to launch an e-mail service of discounted fares–Net SAAver Fares™ (March 1996)
- First to offer real-time flight information (Spring 1996)
- First to offer flight information on competitors (Spring 1996)

**Exhibit
5-8**   WWW.AA.COM

Courtesy of AA.com and American Airlines, Inc. (www.aa.com)

- First to offer airline reservation systems online (June 1996)
- First to offer paperless upgrade coupons and stickers (Spring 1997)
- First to send e-mail confirmation of itinerary and ticket purchase (Fall 1997)
- First to offer high personalization for consumers (June 1998)
- AOL AADVANTAGE Rewards Program (Fall 2000)

American's online strategy and brand are tightly aligned with its offline objectives: to provide the best possible product to the consumer and, in turn, increase the profitability of the company. Online resources not only provide an additional customer base and an additional medium for branding but also reduce the need for costly phone transactions.

Several other features of the American effort are worth noting. American's online initiative was set up as a separate entity with its own profit-and-loss statement to allow for flexibility and speed of responsiveness. They constantly attempt to anticipate and fulfill the needs of customers—to the point of offering competitor information and fares. They develop and adopt new technologies to respond to customers' needs, including such innovations as database synchronization to provide a single, integrated consumer database; a combined BookSmart and SABRE system; and new design features that stress an interactive, visual appearance.

Comparison to "Average Performer."
In Exhibit 5-9 we compared the American Airlines site to Continental Airlines on the Ten-Step Process of Brand Building.

Again, keep in mind that Continental is by no means the worst performer in the category. Indeed, Forrester ranked the site eighteenth in terms of reach, books, and revenue and first in its travel category ratings (i.e., Forrester Power Ratings). However, it is not in the Media Metrix top 10 travel sites. So, on balance, one could argue that it is an average performer.

In order to interpret this exhibit, it is first necessary to understand the key at the bottom of the exhibit. One can think of the circles as a visual way to express a five-point scale by which a clear circle (one-point score) is a rating of poor performance and a completely black circle is our highest rating (five-point score).

It takes a very lengthy discussion to highlight each and every point illustrated in Exhibit 5-9. Hence, we focus only on the most important lessons. A quick visual scan of the exhibit illustrates that American Airlines systematically outperforms Continental on almost all of the relevant elements. On seven of the elements, we have given American a "very high" score, while Continental received this score for only one element.

By examining particular elements, it becomes clear that American substantially outperforms Continental in several respects. With respect to the target audience, the *www.aa.com* site targets its frequent flier group, while the targeting of the client base for Continental is much less clear (appears to be three target groups). While American tends to be an innovator—as per our discussion above—Continental is a consistent laggard. One key leverage point for American is the Net SAAver Fares™ program. Their early entry into the last minute, discount fare e-mail newsletter enabled them to grow their user base very quickly. While Continental eventually followed with a similar e-mail discount program, the late entry led to significantly lower subscription rates.

Overall, American is providing a more consistent brand image over time when compared to Continental. Continental appears to have three distinct URLs for each group. In contrast, American has invested in a steady way with a similar message to their key constituent base—the business traveler. They have provided consistent technology and customer-facing innovation for well over 20 years. Finally, with respect to brand recognition, the American site receives high marks for relevancy, distinctiveness, consistency, and memorability (see Exhibit 5-10).

Case Study: Monster

Monster.com (see Exhibit 5-11) is a great example of an online company that has succeeded by branding itself in both online and offline environments. Monster is a metamarket switchboard that offers employment services to both job seekers and employers. For job seekers, Monster aims to serve as a "lifelong career network," offering not only job and resume postings but also chats, message boards, and expert advice on career management. For employers, Monster provides value-added solutions including resume skills screening, resume routing, and real-time recruiting in addition to access to its database of over 4 million job seekers.

Overview of Branding Efforts. Launched in 1994 as the 454th website in the world, Monster was a true "early entrant" into the commercial world of the Internet. According to Media Metrix, it has well over 50 percent of the online

Exhibit 5-9

ASSESSMENT OF KEY BRANDING ELEMENTS

Key Elements	Online Branding Best-in-Class American Airlines		Comparison Continental	
	Rating	Rationale	Rating	Rationale
1. Clearly define the brand audience	●	• Specifically targets AADVANTAGE members—highly profitable and loyal customers familiar with travel (and thus more likely to buy tickets online)	◑	• Targets both high-spending business customers as well as Onepass members and non-Onepass members
2. Understand the customer	●	• Constantly anticipates and innovates to meet the needs of the customer	◕	• Tends to be a "follower" in the industry, late in launching its website (6/97)
3. Identify key leverage points in customer experience	●	• Net SAAver Fares™ and new customization program leverage consumers' desire for finding cheap fares into transaction by sending out e-mails each week	◑	• Sends C.O.O.L. e-mails similar to Net SAAver Fares™ and added a personalization feature to site, but late identification of this leverage point resulted in significantly lower subscription rates
4. Continually monitor competitors	●	• In one of the few cases a competitor adopted a technology before American; was quick to follow	◑	• Tends to follow what competitors are doing at a slower pace, launching "copy-cat" initiatives many months after competitor roll-out
5. Design compelling and complete brand intent	◔	• Focus, streamlining, and ease of use of website all convey American's message of customer needs first	◑	• Unclear target segment (business travelers? OnePass members?) causes lack of clarity with brand intent
6. Execute with integrity	◕	• Trust fostered in the offline world carries over into the online world	◕	• Trust fostered in the offline world carries over into the online world, with extensive information for members on privacy and use of provided information
7. Be consistent over time	●	• Although constantly innovating new technologies and features, stays true to its tag line	◑	• Different URLs for different portions of the site do not convey message of consistency
8. Establish feedback systems	◑	• Customer service offered as a service at the top of each page in small letters but is not labeled as a specific menu item	●	• Very easy to access, prominent feature for obtaining customer feedback on the website
9. Be opportunistic	●	• Leader in its industry in innovation and development	◔	• Follower in the industry
10. Invest and be patient	●	• Invests significantly in technology for the future	◑	• Has a tendency to wait too long to make changes to its site

○ = Very Low ◔ = Low ◑ = Moderate ◕ = High ● = Very High

Exhibit 5-10

ASSESSMENT OF KEY BRAND ATTRIBUTES

		Online Branding Best-in-Class *American Airlines*		Comparison *Continental*
Key Attributes	**Rating**	**Rationale**	**Rating**	**Rationale**
1. Relevant	●	• Up-to-date flight and gate check information • Personalized information based on AAdvantage profiles • PDA applications with flight information	◕	• Offers only information for Continental Airlines, but does not offer bookings for rental cars and hotels • Allows travel preferences to be saved in profiles
2. Distinct	●	• Availability of competitor information • Offers highly personalized experience • First to offer tie-in with PDA applications	◕	• Offers extensive online customer service options • Offers customized services for the business traveler
3. Consistent	●	• Portrays a consistent online image throughout the site	◔	• No key messages online associated closely with the offline campaign
4. Memorable	●	• Provides a unique service others cannot offer (in terms of personalization) • Net SAAver Fares™ is the most well-known and effective e-mail marketing tool	◑	• Multiple URLs associated with the site and lack of online/offline message association fail to create a cohesively memorable brand for the consumer

○ = Very Low   ◔ = Low   ◑ = Moderate   ◕ = High   ● = Very High

recruitment advertising market.[27] Revenue increased from $6.9 million in 1996 to $133.5 million in 1999.[28] The site's traffic—averaging overall 3.6 million unique visitors in January 2000—translated into a reach of over 5 percent of all U.S. Internet users.

Some have argued that a large part of Monster's success was its ability to brand itself in both the online and offline environments. Its offline advertising and associated Monster logo provided a very unique, distinctive branding message. Its Super Bowl advertising showed young children discussing their desired futures: "I want to file all day," "I want to claw my way up to middle management," and "I want to have a brown nose." These provided a clear message as to what Monster could deliver—good jobs, challenging careers, and rapid advancement.

These somewhat risky ads produced immediate results. The 24 hours immediately following the February 1999 ads generated 2.2 million job searches—a 450 percent increase in traffic from the previous week. A considerable jump in job searches also followed the Super Bowl 2000 ad. Over 4.4 million job searches were conducted within a 24-hour period—twice the number of job searches that Monster received the day after the 1999 Super Bowl.

Monster's goal is to pursue an "Intern to CEO" strategy, providing recruiting solutions globally in a wide range of industries at all levels of experience. To pursue this strategy, it has formed alliances to expand its online career service offerings to include health care, technology, telecommunications, temporary work, and,

Exhibit 5-11

WWW.MONSTER.COM

courtesy monster®.com

more recently, free-agent talent markets. Advertising targets a wide array of individuals, attracting the largest and most diverse pool of job seekers for employers using the site.

To further its branding efforts, it has also signed alliances with Yahoo! as well as a recent $100 million four-year agreement with AOL to be the online service provider's exclusive career information provider.

Comparison to "Average Performer." Exhibit 5-12 provides a comparison of Monster versus Hotjobs on the 10 elements of branding. At first glance, it is apparent that Monster is outperforming Hotjobs on a number of elements—although the gaps in performance are not as wide as the American versus Continental gaps. Indeed, Hotjobs is strong in a number of areas, including a strong customer focus, specialization by entry-level positions, and privacy screens/policy. It is comparatively weaker on the interactive nature of the site, the compelling nature of its brand intent, and opportunity for feedback. Similar to Monster, they are clearly willing to take advertising risks—both with Super Bowl placement and with its various ad copy (e.g., "all the hottest jobs at all the hottest companies").

Exhibit 5-13 shows a comparison of Monster versus Hotjobs on four brand recognition criteria. Our analysis reveals that both brands are similar on relevancy and distinctiveness; however, Monster outperforms Hotjobs on consistency and memorability.

Exhibit
5-12

ASSESSMENT OF KEY BRANDING ELEMENTS

		Online Branding Best-in-Class *Monster.com*		Comparison *Hotjobs.com*
Key Elements	**Rating**	**Rationale**	**Rating**	**Rationale**
1. Clearly define the brand audience	◔	• Within the employer market, targets all types of companies, from start-ups to large corporations	◔	• Appeals to a wide range of job seekers, but specializes in the intern and entry-level positions
2. Understand the customer	●	• Offers highly personalized services for job seekers, addresses security concerns, and offers value-added services (resume help, advice, interactive communication with other job seekers)	●	• Only site to offer privacy feature that allows job seekers to select which companies have access to their resumes
3. Identify key leverage points in customer experience	●	• Provides interactive career information for customers who are not necessarily "looking," thus increasing the probability that they will become job seekers	●	• Allows recruiting process to become internal through Hotjobs.com and its proprietary Softshoe technology, eliminating concerns about adding an additional venue for recruiting
4. Continually monitor competitors	◕	• Currently a leader in providing unique services to its consumers, but lacks some features that competitors have	◑	• Adopts successful features of the Monster.com site, but usually on a lesser scale
5. Design compelling and complete brand intent	●	• Message of "there's a better job out there" combined with diversified strategic alliances and "intern-to-CEO" strategy to convey the idea that Monster.com can find you that better job	◑	• Message of "all the hottest jobs at all the hottest companies" was overshadowed in spring 2000 with controversy over tastefulness of ads that were rejected by networks
6. Execute with integrity	◕	• Offers password and ID protection, as well as some ability to selectively decide when and where your resume can be seen	◑	• Offers most specialized security measures for individual users (prevents current employers from viewing resume)
7. Be consistent over time	●	• In the short time since "there's a better job out there" messaging	◑	• Recent "Hottest Hand on the Web Campaign" different from past branding messages
8. Establish feedback systems	●	• Offers extensive feedback system for users, allowing users to even select categories of information/feedback	◕	• Also offers feedback mechanism for users, although less specialized
9. Be opportunistic	●	• Partners with firms that could potentially be competitors rather than trying to eliminate competition	◕	• Took a risk with Super Bowl advertising, even without a compelling ad campaign, to raise brand awareness
10. Invest and be patient	◔	• Willing to invest heavily in the offline world to gain brand recognition	◔	• Also willing to invest in the offline world to gain brand recognition

○ = Very Low   ◔ = Low   ◑ = Moderate   ◕ = High   ● = Very High

Exhibit 5-13

ASSESSMENT OF KEY BRAND ATTRIBUTES

		Online Branding Best-in-Class *Monster.com*		**Comparison** *Hotjobs.com*	
Key Attributes	**Rating**	**Rationale**	**Rating**	**Rationale**	
1. Relevant	●	• For job seekers: Provides information for individuals regardless of whether they are actively pursuing a new position, including career information and chats with other members on various career topics	●	• For job seekers: Provides information geared more specifically for those individuals who are seeking positions	
2. Distinct	●	• For job seekers: Aids in resume building, personalization with "My Monster" pages and enhanced privacy options; also offers opportunity for interactive communication with other members	●	• For job seekers: Allows selection of companies that view your resume	
3. Consistent	●	• Recent partnerships have been consistent with Monster.com's aim to provide the most diverse set of individuals with the most diverse set of employment opportunities	◑	• New "Hottest Hand on the Web" campaign, although new and catchy, has not been consistent since the company's beginning	
4. Memorable	●	• Witty and award-winning offline advertising has allowed Monster.com to cement itself as the best-known online career site on the Web	◑	• Although also one of the most well-known online career services on the Web, has not been as successful as Monster.com in creating a uniquely memorable advertising campaign and message	

SCHWAB MARKETING COMMUNICATIONS AND BRANDING

Schwab Marketing Communications

Schwab communicates its marketing message to its customers in a number of different ways. Table 5-6 uses the marketing communications framework discussed earlier in the chapter in order to classify the methods Schwab uses into the four framework categories: general approaches, personalized, traditional mass marketing, and direct.

In terms of *general online approaches,* in addition to banner advertisements and traffic driven from affiliate sites, Schwab has a partnership agreement with Excite that drives traffic from the popular portal to the Schwab site. A very popular way of communicating Schwab's value is by providing free information on securities (including company history and financial data and analysis) to Schwab customers and noncustomers alike through the Stock Analyzer tool. Customers who find this information useful in making investment decisions are more likely to decide to register with Schwab to perform trades. In another venue, Schwab has begun to lever-

Brand Loyalty

by Elizabeth Millard, staff writer for tnbt.com

Shot in gritty black and white, the scene is bleak: a young child, his expression blank and humorless, stares into the camera and declares, "I want to be forced into early retirement."

Remember the ad? Even though it first aired during the 1999 Super Bowl, Monster.com is betting that you do: Like many Internet players, Monster.com has embraced old-school branding for its new e-commerce model, investing heavily (to the tune of $60 million) in the notion that name recognition will translate into page hits, revenue, and ultimately, staying power as a powerhouse online brand. But despite the commercial's success—it was seen by some 100 million people, and still enjoys buzz as a best-of-breed dot-com ad—Monster.com is hardly home free. According to a pair of intriguing new studies, when it comes to establishing and maintaining dominant brands on the Web, many companies—even ones that break fast out of the branding gate—may face a bleak scenario of their own.

The first problem: The vast majority of Internet branding initiatives to date seem to have left consumers distinctly underwhelmed. A recent Harris Interactive poll revealed that while consumers are well-acquainted with a few New Economy superbrands—Amazon, eBay, and Egghead topped the name-recognition list—respondents were unable to name a single Web retailer in the insurance, fitness, or online electronics categories, despite the slew of advertising for Buy.com, Netmarket, and other companies that fit the bill.

"The sheer lack of penetration in the minds of most Americans is really stunning," says Ben Black, director of business development at Harris Interactive.

Still, Julia Resnick, product manager for the company's eCommercePulse division, says, "From our perspective, we look at unaided brand awareness among websites and there seems to be a correlation between brand awareness and high performance. It's kind of a chicken and egg thing, though. I don't think branding alone is what's causing the success, but it's really interconnected with performance."

If a company establishes its brand successfully, that means they've conquered the branding problem and are here to stay, right? Maybe not. A study done by Peter Golder, a marketing professor at New York University's Stern School of Business, re-examines a 1923 benchmark NYU study of top brands in 100 product groups and shows that only 23 were still leaders in 1997.

"I'm not here to bash brands, I certainly agree that they're important," Golder says. "What my study suggests is that the staying power of brands is a lot less than what people may believe." In the dot-com world, he says, the lack of staying power is particularly relevant as Internet companies try to build brand awareness quickly in a busy marketplace. Golder suggests an alternative tack: "In the Internet environment, there's confusion over brand awareness vs. brand equity. I think the primary emphasis of too many Internet companies is on just getting people to be aware of their name, but it's the equity that resides in the brand that insures success."

So, if you can get consumers to your site, but have difficulty filling orders or providing customer service, you can kiss those branding dollars good-bye. Golder says, "If the customer's experience at the site is consistent with your advertising message, then branding works, but if it's inconsistent, it'll ruin whatever efforts you've made."

If awareness is bolstered with equity, it's time and money well spent. "With branding, people build associations. If the entire usage experience for the customer reinforces those good associations, then you'll have staying power in an Internet environment that's constantly evolving."

Read more articles about The Next Big Thing at *www.tnbt.com*

Table 5-6

SCHWAB MARKETING COMMUNICATIONS

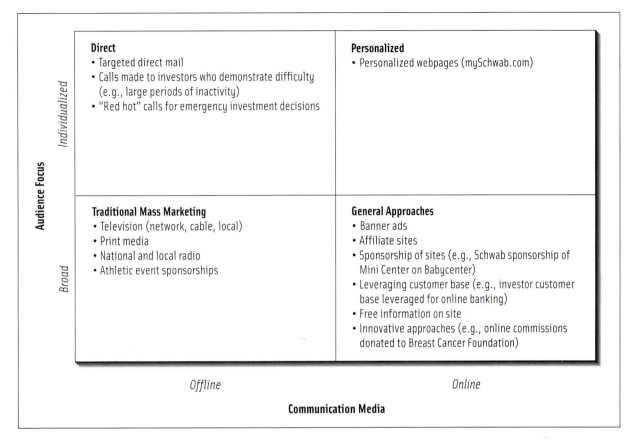

Audience Focus

Individualized

Direct
- Targeted direct mail
- Calls made to investors who demonstrate difficulty (e.g., large periods of inactivity)
- "Red hot" calls for emergency investment decisions

Personalized
- Personalized webpages (mySchwab.com)

Broad

Traditional Mass Marketing
- Television (network, cable, local)
- Print media
- National and local radio
- Athletic event sponsorships

General Approaches
- Banner ads
- Affiliate sites
- Sponsorship of sites (e.g., Schwab sponsorship of Mini Center on Babycenter)
- Leveraging customer base (e.g., investor customer base leveraged for online banking)
- Free information on site
- Innovative approaches (e.g., online commissions donated to Breast Cancer Foundation)

Offline   *Online*

Communication Media

age its existing customer base by making new offerings. For example, Schwab is developing online banking services, and the large existing investor customer base can be leveraged to adopt the new offering. Furthermore, Schwab is using innovative approaches to extend its customer base. On Mother's Day 1999, all commissions from online equity trading went to the Susan G. Komen Foundation for the fight against breast cancer. This move, in addition to serving a noble cause, generated goodwill among existing and potential Schwab customers. In terms of *personalized online communications,* Schwab was the first online broker to allow investors to create their own personalized site. The MySchwab site (powered by Excite) features customized investment information such as Watch Lists and access to breaking news, business and technology news, and other types of content such as sports, travel, and shopping.

Schwab also uses *traditional mass-marketing media* extensively for its communications. Schwab advertisements appear frequently on television (network, cable, and local), print media (including high-circulation newspapers and magazines) and national and local radio. In addition, Schwab frequently sponsors athletic events. These events tend to draw an audience that fits well with the Schwab target segments and associates Schwab with the broad theme of success. Schwab also uses *direct offline communications* with its customers. Examples include monthly statement inserts and special targeted mailings, or telephone calls made to investors who could potentially be having difficulty (e.g., investors who have been inactive for long periods of time). The combination of all the methods discussed above provides a diverse and far-reaching channel for Schwab's marketing message.

Key Branding Elements and Brand Attributes for Schwab Vs. E*Trade

Earlier in the chapter, we introduced a 10-step process for building a successful brand. In Exhibit 5-14, we assess the performance of Schwab versus E*Trade, a key

Exhibit 5-14 ASSESSMENT OF KEY BRANDING ELEMENTS FOR SCHWAB AND E*TRADE

		Schwab.com		etrade.com
Key Elements	**Rating**	**Rationale**	**Rating**	**Rationale**
1. Clearly define the brand audience	◔	• Primarily targets investors who are willing to invest on their own	◔	• Primarily targets investors who wish to make their own investment decisions
2. Understand the customer	●	• Understood need for both quality of information and service and lower price • Understood need for specific investment purposes and developed corresponding tools (retirement, estate, college, etc.)	◖	• Apart from information and analysis, did not offer tools that would help investors plan their investments • Did not grasp that some E*Trade customers would value advice for part of their portfolio
3. Identify key leverage points in customer experience	●	• Performed surveys and on-site testing with 500 individuals to understand desired investor experience and investors purchase process • Identified investors planning investments as a springboard to performing trades • Understood time limitations of investors and offered after-hours trading	●	• Was one of the first companies to offer online trading • Understood importance of speed in opening an account and offered Account Express, allowing new members to trade within minutes of applying
4. Continually monitor competitors	●	• Was a pioneer in many of the technologies and services it developed, usually was ahead of competition	◖	• Some services competitors offer are not matched at E*Trade, for example Schwab's planning tools or independent financial advisors
5. Design compelling and complete brand intent	◔	• Message of "we are creating a smarter kind of investor" in advertisements captures a large part of the value that Schwab offers to investors—high-quality information and service as well as tools for informed investment decisions	◔	• Message of "it's time for E*Trade," signaling "it's time to take control of your investments," captures a large part of E*Trade's offering, but does not focus as much on the additional financial services E*Trade offers, such as online banking

○ = Very Low   ◔ = Low   ◐ = Moderate   ◕ = High   ● = Very High

206 ▼ Chapter 5

online competitor, for each one of those steps. We will focus only on the most important lessons from this analysis. A quick overview of the figure indicates that Schwab is generally outperforming E*Trade on most of the branding elements. In particular, Schwab gets rated with top performance in six elements as compared with just two elements for E*Trade.

- With respect to *understanding the customer*, Schwab understood the need not only for quality information and service, but also for tools to help investors plan their investments and for investment advice, when appropriate. By contrast, even though E*Trade wants to make investors more empowered to make investment decisions, it does not offer tools to help investors, nor does it offer advice.
- With respect to *continually monitoring competitors*, Schwab was not only a pioneer in most of the technology and services that it developed but also

		Schwab.com		*etrade.com*
Key Elements	**Rating**	**Rationale**	**Rating**	**Rationale**
6. Execute with integrity	◕	• The Schwab Customer Care Center provides a private and secure Web environment—requires a personal account number and a password individually selected by each user, any order or personal information entered while in the Customer Center is encrypted with SSL technology	◑	• E*Trade attacked by cyber-hackers in early 2000, disrupting site operations • Offers investors protection for up to $100 million from online fraud
7. Be consistent over time	●	• Schwab's marketing message highly consistent over time—"create a smarter kind of investor," advertisements have similar feel, depicting very different types of people (such as athletes and musicians), exhibit a high level of knowledge on investing	◑	• Marketing message has changed considerably over time—initial message more passive: "Someday, we will all invest this way"; then came more aggressive marketing message: "Someone will win the lottery . . . just not you . . . It's time for E*Trade"
8. Establish feedback systems	◔	• In April 1999, Schwab unveiled a new customer website based largely on 500 hours of interviews and testing with investors, focusing on their desired purchase behavior • Customer service representatives are available 24 hours a day, 7 days a week	◔	• In July 1999, redesigned site based on surveys and testing with customers • Site allows members to provide feedback, can also offer feedback through the Live Customer Service Forum
9. Be opportunistic	●	• Invited competitor mutual funds to participate in the OneSource program, even though this could have jeopardized sales of Schwab mutual funds	●	• Took risk by changing to an aggressive and non-traditional marketing message in April 1999 • Undertook original marketing initiatives, such as the "on the Road to Atlanta 2000" tour with the E*Mobile (a vehicle allowing users to test online investing)
10. Invest and be patient	●	• Was willing to take the initial revenue and profitability hit from moving online, patiently betting on growth through the online channel eventually driving revenue growth	◔	• Invested in online brokerage very early on (E*Trade securities have offered online trading through AOL and Compuserve since 1992), betting on growth through the online channel

○ = Very Low ◔ = Low ◑ = Moderate ◕ = High ● = Very High

was sure to respond to new competitor offerings. For example, in response to other online brokers offering stock in IPOs to their investors, Schwab joined forces with other venture capital firms and banks to create an online investment bank that will distribute securities it underwrites to Schwab investors. By contrast, even though E*Trade does provide many of the same types of services offered by its competitors, there are also services that E*Trade fails to provide, such as Schwab's planning tools or advice or portfolio management services.

- With respect to a *consistent brand message,* Schwab has kept a highly consistent brand message over time: "Creating a smarter kind of investor." By contrast, E*Trade's message has changed considerably over time, starting with "Someday, we will all invest this way," moving to the more aggressive "Someone will win the lottery . . . just not you . . . It's time for E*Trade," to the more recent marketing messages focusing on all the things one can do with the gains from investing with E*Trade.

In terms of key brand attributes, both Schwab and E*Trade have very distinct brands. Furthermore, both of their brands are highly relevant, because their offerings are directly addressing investor needs. In addition, E*Trade is also offering online financial services and Schwab is in the process of developing its online bank. As we discussed earlier, Schwab's brand consistency is considerably higher than E*Trade's. Finally, E*Trade marginally outperforms Schwab on memorability because E*Trade has pursued a more aggressive marketing message and more original marketing events than Schwab's attractive but more traditional message (see Exhibit 5-15).

Exhibit 5-15 — ASSESSMENT OF KEY BRAND ATTRIBUTES FOR SCHWAB AND E*TRADE

Key Attributes	Rating (Schwab.com)	Rationale (Schwab.com)	Rating (etrade.com)	Rationale (etrade.com)
1. Relevant	●	• Provides investors with high-quality information, service, and sophisticated technologies and tools that help them make educated decisions about their investments	●	• Offers investors high-quality information and service and technology that empowers them to take more control of their investments
2. Distinct	●	• Well-known as an established brokerage services provider whose primary focus is on customers	●	• Distinct entrepreneurial feel to brand message, achieved through aggressive marketing strategy and innovative marketing events
3. Consistent	●	• Consistent message: "We are creating a smarter type of investor"	◐	• Marketing message has changed from "Someday, we will all invest this way" to "it's time for E*Trade," to help investors think about what they can do with the money earned through E*Trade
4. Memorable	◕	• Popular public figures featured in Schwab advertisements (e.g., Anna Kournikova) spike interest and memorability	●	• Aggressive one-liner marketing quotes that grasp attention and make an impression • Catchy E*Trade logo

○ = Very Low   ◔ = Low   ◐ = Moderate   ◕ = High   ● = Very High

SUMMARY

1. What are the four categories of market communications?

Market communications can be categorized into a simple two-by-two framework based upon the audience focus (broad versus individual) and communication media (offline versus online). The four categories of communications are direct, personalized, traditional mass marketing, and general online approaches.

2. What is a "good" brand?

Good brands provide a clear message to the market about the core offering, the wrap-around, and communications. All provide not only a signal about the functional offering, but are simultaneously differentiated by their emotional, symbolic, and experiential benefits—for both the firm and target customers.

3. What is the Ten-Step Branding Process?

The Ten-Step Branding Process can be broken down into two general stages: building the value cluster and the integrated campaign (see Exhibit 5-6 on page 191). The steps are as follows:

1. Clearly define the brand audience.
2. Understand the customer.
3. Identify key leverage points in customer experience.
4. Continually monitor competitors.
5. Design compelling and complete brand intent.
6. Execute with integrity.
7. Be consistent over time.
8. Establish feedback systems.
9. Be opportunistic.
10. Invest and be patient.

4. How does online branding compare between American Airlines and Continental Airlines?

Exhibit 5-9 illustrates that American systematically outperforms Continental on almost all of the relevant elements. On seven of the elements, we have given American Airlines a "very high" score, while Continental received this score for only one element.

5. What are the Point-Counterpoint arguments for leveraging an offline brand into the online environment?

Arguments for the use of existing brands are (1) known, (2) less costly to develop, (3) provide assurance to the target segment, and (4) provide an integrated online and offline experience. Opponents argue that using an existing brand limits the growth of the user base. Second, existing offline brands "don't get the net." Third, it is possible to sign up more partners—potential competitors, collaborators, and others—when a third-party name is used.

KEY TERMS

branding

market communications

general online

personalized online

traditional mass media

direct communications

banner ads

e-mail

viral marketing

affiliate programs

permission marketing

traditional sales rep

direct marketing

telemarketing

brand equity

strength of association

valence

uniqueness

Ten-Step Branding Process

Endnotes

[1] SEC Form 10-K for Amazon.com, Inc. filed on March 5, 1999, and March 29, 2000.

[2] Petersen, Andrea. 1999. You can have the greatest e-commerce site on the Web; The trick is to get people to come to it. *Wall Street Journal*, 12 July.

[3] Anderson, Diane. 2000. E-Mail or me-mail. *Industry Standard*, 6 March.

[4] Weber, Thomas E. 1999. The Spam king is back, and his new recipe clicks on changing net. *Wall Street Journal*, 13 December.

[5] Rayport, Jeffrey. 1996. The virus of marketing. *Fast Company*, issue no. 6 (December-January): 68.

[6] Jurvetson, Steve. 2000. Turning customers into a sales force. *Business 2.0*, March.

[7] Butt, Joseph L., Jr. 1999. Universal Escape Webcams turn images into marketing. In *The Forrester Report* (October): p. 18.

[8] Talk.com Investor Relations. 1999. America Online and Tel-Save.com announce extension of AOL Telecommunications Marketing Agreement. Press release newswire, 5 January. The URL for this citation is as follows: http://www.corporate-ir.net/ireye/ir_site.zhtml?ticker=talk&script=410&layout=-6&item_id=22775.

[9] Segrich, J. 2000. *L90 Inc.: Initiating coverage*. Analyst report. CIBC Worldmarkets Corporation, 25 February, p. 5.

[10] Sourced from the following online article: Cavoli, Brian. What really is beyond the banner. URL: http://adsonline.about.com/aa062199.htm

[11] Economist. 2000. Amazon's amazing ambition, 26 February, E-Commerce Survey, p. 24.

[12] For further information, see: Godin, Seth. 1999. *Permission Marketing: Turning strangers into friends, and friends into customers*. New York: Simon & Schuster.

[13] Petersen. 1999. You can have the greatest e-commerce site. *Wall Street Journal*, 12 July.

[14] Hof, Robert D., Heather Green, and Linda Himelstein. 1998. Now it's your web: The Net is moving toward one-to-one marketing—and that will change how all companies do business. *Business Week*, 5 October.

[15] For further clarification, please go to the following URL for the January 4, 2000 press release from Net Perceptions entitled: Net Perceptions to provide realtime ad targeting to ZDNET. http://www.netperception.com/press/indiv/0,1032,163,00.html.

[16] Green, Heather. 1999. The information gold mine: New Software—and the Net's legions of cybersurfers and shoppers—are starting to hand companies opportunities they've only dreamed of. *Business Week*, July 26.

[17] Hof, Green and Himelstein. 1998. Now it's your web. *Business Week*, 5 October.

[18] Green. 1999. The information gold mine. *Business Week*, 26 July.

[19] Hof, Green, and Himelstein. 1998. Now it's your web. *Business Week*, 5 October.

[20] Kaufman, Leslie. 1999. Web retailers empty wallets on advertising. *New York Times*, 2 November.

[21] Petersen. 1999. You can have the greatest e-commerce site. *Wall Street Journal*, 12 July.

[22]Kaufman. 1999. Web retailers empty wallets. *New York Times*, 2 November.

[23]This sidebar draws from data presented in several analysts' reports including an ING Barings report on DoubleClick dated March 31, 2000 and CIBC World Market's report on L90 dated 25th February 2000.

[24]Functional benefits capture the intrinsic advantages of the product. They tend to be correlated with the features or attributes of the product. Symbolic benefits relate to social approval and personal expression. Experiential benefits relate to what the product feels like to use, and tends to capture various sensory pleasures. See the following article for further elaboration: Park, Choong W., Bernard J. Jaworski and Deborah J. MacInnis. 1986. Strategic brand concept-image management. *Journal of Marketing* 50, no. 4 (October): pp. 135–45.

[25]Keller, Kevin Lane. 1998. *Strategic Brand Management.* Upper Saddle River, NJ: Prentice-Hall, Inc., p. 43.

[26]Aaker, David. 1996. *Building Strong Brands*. New York: The Free Press, pp. 7–8.

[27]*Media Metrix*. 2000. January. Cited in Dickson L. Louie and Jeffrey Rayport, *Monster.com* (Boston: Harvard Business School Publishing, 2000), p. 1. Fifty percent market share refers to percentage of eyeball minutes among career sites.

[28]As of December 1999. *Brean Murray Institutional Research Report*, 2 December. Cited in Dickson L. Louie and Jeffrey F. Rayport, *Monster.com* (Boston: Harvard Business School Publishing, 2000), p. 1. "Revenue increased from $6.9 million in 1996 to $133.5 million in 1999."

6

Implementation

This chapter provides a review of two key components of implementation—the delivery system and the innovation process. Implementation answers the general question "How do we go to market?" The delivery system is defined as the people, systems, assets, processes, and supply chains that enable the company to bring to market its offering and the associated customer interface. However, the delivery system alone is not sufficient to guarantee successful implementation. Rather, a comprehensive view of implementation must also consider innovation, because the Internet requires continual revision of strategies, offerings, and interfaces. Later in the chapter, we illustrate the differences between innovation in the online and offline domains as well as introduce several new frameworks for innovation.

QUESTIONS

Please consider the following questions as you read this chapter:

1. What is online implementation?

2. Why does implementation matter?

3. What is the delivery system?

4. What are the categories of offline innovation?

5. What is the offline innovation process?

6. What is the new logic behind New Economy innovation?

This chapter was coauthored by Marco Smit and Rafi Mohammed. Substantive input and supervision was provided by Bernie Jaworski. Sharon Grady and Lisa Ferri provided considerable substantive input on the online/offline integration issues.

7. What are the New Economy innovation frameworks?

8. What are the New Economy innovation processes?

In Chapter 4, we considered the Web interface choices that brought to life the firm's business model. In the previous chapter, we discussed the market communications and branding decisions designed to draw customers to the site. However, a highly usable interface and a strong brand are not sufficient to deliver the brand to target customers. Rather, the firm must develop a strong organization, hire and train the right human-resource talent, and build an infrastructure (e.g., structures, systems, processes) that will move the physical (or digital) products from suppliers through to the end customer.

The purpose of this chapter is to introduce the firm-specific infrastructure that must be created and configured to go to market and to achieve the firm's strategic goals. In particular, we discuss two broad categories of infrastructure—the delivery system and the innovation process. The delivery system is defined as the sum of the people, systems, assets, processes, and supply chains that enable the company to bring to market its offering and the associated customer interface. In addition to the delivery system, the firm must develop a clear point of view on how innovation related to offerings as well as to the infrastructure itself will unfold in the organization.

WHAT IS ONLINE IMPLEMENTATION?

We begin our discussion by introducing the general implementation framework. Then we consider the reason implementation is important and the consequences of poor implementation. Following this discussion, we turn to the five key components of a delivery system: people, systems, assets, processes, and supply chains. We conclude with a discussion of offline and online innovation and an application of the concepts to Schwab.

A Framework for Implementation

Exhibit 6-1 provides an overview of the connection between the communication and branding concerns of top management and implementation. In particular, this exhibit illustrates that implementation follows from and is informed by branding, communication, and the customer-interface choices. The **online implementation process** can be divided into two phases. First, the firm is concerned with the delivery of the offering. In the second phase, the firm is concerned with the extent to which the offerings and infrastructures are modified to fit the evolution of the market.

Once the customer interface has been developed, the company must configure the infrastructure to deliver on the site's brand promise. In particular, we consider two broad categories of infrastructure: the configuration of structure, systems, and processes that form the basis of company organization and the supply chain.

Supply chain models in the New Economy focus on rapidly changing structures in B2C, B2B, C2B, and C2C markets. These new supply chain options have significantly changed the manner that customers and suppliers interact with manufacturers.

The fast pace of change in the marketspace is driven by the evolution of technology, changes in customer preferences (and demographics), new competitors, and

Exhibit 6-1

MARKETSPACE EVOLUTION AND NEED
FOR CONTINUOUS INNOVATION

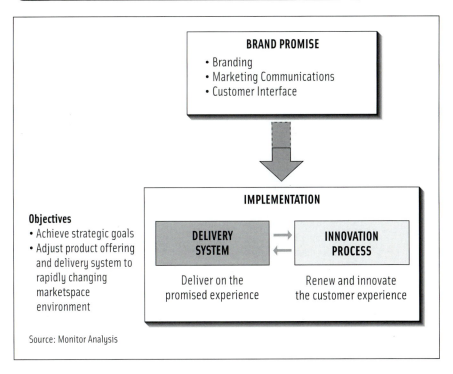

BRAND PROMISE
- Branding
- Marketing Communications
- Customer Interface

IMPLEMENTATION

DELIVERY SYSTEM	INNOVATION PROCESS
Deliver on the promised experience	Renew and innovate the customer experience

Objectives
- Achieve strategic goals
- Adjust product offering and delivery system to rapidly changing marketspace environment

Source: Monitor Analysis

new collaborators. To continue to execute and adapt strategy in this fast-changing, competitive environment, firms can no longer separate innovation from implementation. In this section, we contrast the different innovation categories and processes in New Economy and Old Economy companies and discuss archetypes of processes and organizations for innovation emerging in the online domain.

WHY DOES IMPLEMENTATION MATTER?

Exhibit 6-2 (on page 216) provides a simple illustration of the importance of solid implementation. On the horizontal axis, we observe two conditions: appropriate and inappropriate strategy. On the vertical axis, we consider both good and poor implementation. When crossed, we can view four conditions that can be experienced by firms in the marketplace: success, roulette, trouble, and failure.

In this chapter, we are particularly concerned with conditions that lead to experiences that fall into the trouble quadrant. In the trouble quadrant, the firm has made all the right strategy choices related to the business model, interface, brand, and marketing communications, but its implementation is poor. The result is not only the likelihood of poor performance in the marketplace but a situation in which senior management will be unable to distinguish low performance due to an inappropriate strategy or poor implementation.

Exhibit 6-2 WHY DOES IMPLEMENTATION MATTER?

Strategy

	Appropriate	*Inappropriate*
Good	**Success** • All that can be done to ensure success has been done	**Roulette** • Good execution can mitigate poor strategy, forcing management to success *or* • Same good execution can hasten failure
Poor	**Trouble** • Poor execution hampers good strategy • Management may never become aware of strategic soundness because of execution inadequacies	**Failure** • Difficult to diagnose—bad strategy masked by poor execution • More difficult to fix—two things are wrong

Implementation

Source: Modified version of materials in *The Marketing Edge* by Thomas V. Bonoma. 1985. New York: The Free Press

Implementation Challenges for Online Firms

Exhibit 6-3 provides an overview of the implementation challenges that confront online businesses. In particular, it has been argued that increased speed and intensity of competition in the online environment means that implementation mistakes will be punished much more severely and quickly than in the offline world. Below, we articulate six implementation challenges exemplified by online firms.

Higher Visibility to Errors. Due to investors' infatuation with the New Economy, the media closely monitors and reports on Internet firms. The Web also offers consumers a wide variety of easily accessible sources of information on e-commerce companies. Many rating services have been established to help consumers find reputable companies. In addition, Web bulletin boards allow forums for disgruntled customers to vent their feelings and experiences to a large audience. Some consumers become so frustrated with their experiences of failed implementation by specific companies that they create websites to share (and invite others to share) their experiences.

Lower Switching Costs. It can be argued that **switching costs** for consumers who shop on the Internet are significantly lower than for consumers who shop at brick-and-mortar firms. Should a consumer have an unsatisfactory experience shopping at a brick-and-mortar company and decide to shop elsewhere, switching costs could include additional driving, new constraints on method of payment, and time spent learning about a new retailer. In another scenario, a switching cost of conven-

Exhibit 6-3

CHALLENGES OF ONLINE IMPLEMENTATION

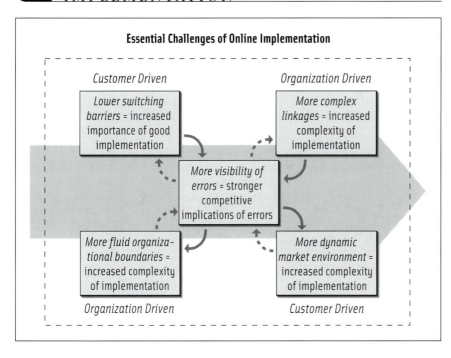

Essential Challenges of Online Implementation

Customer Driven

Lower switching barriers = increased importance of good implementation

Organization Driven

More complex linkages = increased complexity of implementation

More visibility of errors = stronger competitive implications of errors

More fluid organizational boundaries = increased complexity of implementation

More dynamic market environment = increased complexity of implementation

Organization Driven

Customer Driven

ience to a consumer could arise if a consumer became dissatisfied with only a particular shop in a shopping mall, while other satisfying and often-used shops were located in the same mall.

As the Internet further evolves, there will be a wider variety of competitive offerings in each product category. A recent survey revealed low switching costs in the Web retail book market. This market is relatively mature and has two well-funded companies (Amazon and Barnes & Noble) aggressively vying for customers. This survey found that more than 73 percent of online book shoppers indicated no retail brand preference for their next purchase.[1]

Switching costs involves a simple click of the mouse. If a retail site disappoints, there are several other sites offering similar goods or services that can be accessed by a simple click. This lack of loyalty reflects low switching costs and a willingness to switch online retailers for any reason, no matter how trivial the implementation error.

More Dynamic Competitive Environment. Due to the low barriers to entry, poor implementation by incumbent firms provides opportunities to potential entrants as well as to current competitors. It can be relatively easy for new entrants and competitors to gain advantage from a company's implementation errors and problems.

More Fluid Organizational Boundaries. The lack of clear dividing lines between parties partnering and collaborating creates fluid organizational boundaries. While this fluidity increases contact and community between partners, it also increases the complexity of interactions.

More Dynamic Market Environment. The speed of change in the market places a significant burden on firms to quickly respond to changing developments. Netscape went from the absolute dominator of the Web-browser market to becoming an also-ran and to struggling to be a significant player in the market over a period of barely three years. The speed of evolution and the implications for strategy implementation are clear. Even the best company cannot afford to implement too slowly or in a fashion that will inhibit it from adjusting to changing marketspace conditions.

More Complex Linkages. Complexity of linkages refers to the number of linkages among various partners. The more linkages, the more likely that decisions will be slowed, become prone to miscommunication, or become more bureaucratic. In his infamous book *The Mythical Man-Month*, Fred Brooks illustrates the implications for the organization of an increase in the number of communication linkages. He uses an example of a team writing software: "If each part of the task must be separately coordinated with each other part, the effort increases as $n(n-1)/2$. Three workers require three times as much pairwise intercommunications as two; four require six times as much as two." In the online world, the number and nature of the linkages (partnerships) frequently change, adding another layer of complexity.[2]

The Effects of Poor Implementation

The 1999 holiday season overwhelmed many e-commerce businesses. Late deliveries of gifts created unsatisfied customers. This led customers to question the ability of e-commerce companies to deliver on their promises. For e-commerce businesses, product fulfillment is one of the top consumer complaints. Reflecting the poor state of fulfillment, only 74 percent of all e-commerce deliveries were made on time in 1999.[3] Below, we consider two high-profile implementation breakdowns.

eBay's Network Shutdown. eBay is the world's largest personal online trading community. Individuals use its online auction site to buy and sell goods. eBay has over 2,900 auction item categories and offers over 400,000 new items for auction every day. eBay created value by developing the most-visited online personal item auction site. This reputation provides confidence to both sellers and bidders. Sellers gain confidence to list their items on eBay because they feel high volumes of user traffic will translate to a higher probability of selling their items through the site. Likewise, buyers feel confident that high volumes of user traffic ensure a robust marketplace and will increase the likelihood of finding items of interest relative to visiting other auction sites. eBay reaps a small commission from every sales transaction on its site.

In June 1999, eBay suffered a 22-hour site shutdown due to technical difficulties. When this shutdown occurred, investors panicked and eBay's stock immediately lost over 20 percent of its value. In addition to this market capitalization loss, eBay lost significant revenues. To appease angry sellers, eBay waived all listing fees for items offered during the service outage. eBay officials estimated that this resulted in $3 to $5 million of foregone revenues, a sizable loss considering the company's first quarter 1999 revenues were $34 million. Also, this service shutdown affected the confidence of auction sellers in eBay's abilities. Rival auction sites operated by Yahoo!, Amazon, and Auction Universe reaped significant additional business and gained media exposure as a result of eBay's troubles.[4]

Buy.com Pricing and Fulfillment. Buy.com is a retail website that primarily sells computer equipment. Buy.com attempts to attract a large customer base by selling goods at extremely low, sometimes negative, gross margins. Demonstrating this point, in the first nine months of 1999, Buy.com's net revenues were $3 million less

Built to Last or Built to Rebuild?

In 1995, Collins and Porras published *Built to Last*, an analysis of visionary companies in the offline world that were more successful than peer-group companies over a period of more than a century. This book drew a number of very strong conclusions about key factors differentiating these visionary companies from their peers. It is now interesting to see that the current online population of companies is marked by characteristics that are opposite to the key characteristics of the visionary companies from Collins and Porras's book. A hefty debate continues in the press around the question of whether these characteristics are temporary or sustainable phenomena.[5]

For advocates of "built to last," the argument is that growth is largely organic—coming from careful and systematic analysis of chosen markets. The firm scales up over a period of years and repeatedly leverages its brand in the marketplace. Brand assets and equity take many years to build and must be carefully nurtured over a long period of time. Finally, these companies are often not led by visionary leaders with strong personalities.

In sharp contrast, in the online world, there is frequently no time for elaborate planning and analysis. Rather, firms act very quickly. Often, growth comes from acquisitions that include the purchase of competitors or complementors. Growth can be organic but is equally likely to be from acquisitions. Opportunities are often not constrained by market opportunities—indeed, there are frequently too many opportunities. Finally, the successful companies are frequently launched by visionary leaders with big ideas.

---

than the $401 million worth of goods that it sold.[6] The goal of Buy.com is to attract a lot of eyeballs to its site by offering discounted goods and monetizing these eyeballs by selling advertising targeted at its customer base.

Buy.com utilizes a business model that outsources most of its infrastructure services (e.g., customer support, fulfillment). While outsourcing can be advantageous by requiring a relatively low capital structure, it has a crucial implementation downside. Buy.com does not control elements critical to its brand promise. It has developed a poor reputation of advertising products that become back-ordered for weeks. Further compounding this poor image, Buy.com faces a class action lawsuit in Orange County, California, that charges that it intentionally mispriced products and charged for orders while knowing the orders could not be filled. A similar class action was filed in Camden, New Jersey. A Securities Exchange Commission (SEC) filing by the company even acknowledges that the methods it uses to update its prices may result in future pricing errors, which may result in significant future litigation.[7] Buy.com's implementation problems have created negative publicity and shaken both consumers' and Wall Street's confidence in the company. Buy.com's February 2000 Initial Public Offering (IPO) was initially encouraging, with shares reaching as high as $33 per share. Less than two months later, Buy.com was trading in the $10 range, significantly below its initial offering price of $13.

WHAT IS THE DELIVERY SYSTEM?

In this section, we discuss how each online company must configure its delivery system to create an infrastructure that can effectively serve online customers. We first provide a framework for and then define and describe each of the components of the delivery system. In the next section, we focus on the evolution of the delivery system. The final section concludes with specific issues of online/offline integration that can be particularly challenging for many online companies.

A Framework for the Delivery System

Once the company has succeeded in attracting customers to its website, the delivery system must actually deliver the total customer experience the brand communication has promised. Not only must the customer experience satisfying interactions through the customer interface, but the company must be able to correctly execute transactions initiated through the customer interface.

That is to say, if a customer has ordered flowers through the company's website to be delivered to a certain address on Valentine's Day, then the company cannot make any mistake in the actual delivery of the flowers. Potential execution mistakes could be in the form of incorrect processing of payment, delivering to the wrong person or on the wrong date, delivering the flowers with the incorrect accompanying note, or delivering the wrong flowers. In short, the delivery system has a very direct bearing on the total experience that the customer equates with his or her beliefs about the brand. This in turn has major impact on customer retention and, thereby, on the lifetime value of the customer base.

A company's **delivery system** is the most detailed and concrete expression of the company's value proposition. The value proposition, product offering, and business model, each in turn, determine the requirements for the resource system's construction. The delivery system translates the resource system from a conceptual structure into a concrete configuration of resources, processes, and supply chains. In short, once the strategy has been defined and necessary capabilities identified, it becomes a matter of defining the structures, processes, reward systems, and human-resource practices that will produce the needed competencies and capabilities.[8]

In short, it is at this stage of the strategy process that strategic intent is turned into a configuration that produces actual consumer and financial results.

Exhibit 6-4

THE DELIVERY SYSTEM NEEDS TO SUPPORT AND REINFORCE THE RESOURCE SYSTEM

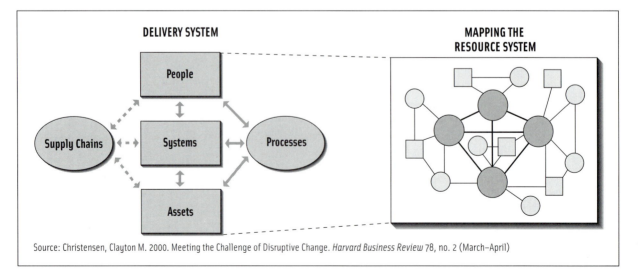

Source: Christensen, Clayton M. 2000. Meeting the Challenge of Disruptive Change. *Harvard Business Review* 78, no. 2 (March–April)

The Five Components of the Delivery System

The five components of a delivery system include people, systems, assets, processes, and supply chains (see Exhibit 6-4).

1. *People.* A key characteristic of many successful Internet companies is a human-resource system and an associated culture that places exceptionally high value on the recruitment, selection, training, development, and evaluation of key personnel.

2. *Systems.* Systems are defined as routines or established procedures for the organization. The systems can be related to any aspect of the organization. In the current context, there is an obvious emphasis on information technology (IT) systems (see DRILL-DOWN: The Changing Role of IT Implementation, page 223). These include database systems, website support systems, management information systems, and other digital data-based approaches.

3. *Assets.* Assets can be divided into physical and information-based assets. Physical assets are the assets that are so often found in the offline world: buildings, warehouses, offices, and equipment. Information-based assets, on the other hand, are assets constructed from data including databases, digital content, and customer-behavior data. As so much recent literature has pointed out, one of the most influential developments in the New Economy has been the replacement of physical assets as value generators by information-based assets.

4. *Processes.* Processes are defined as the patterns of interaction, coordination, communication, and decision making that employees use to transform resources into customer value. The online firm can potentially play a number of roles, including a pure manufacturer and distributor of products, a mere facilitator (e.g., AOL was originally a pure facilitator of chat among community members), or anything in between. The following processes must be configured by online firms during implementation:

   - **Resource Allocation Process.** With the vast areas of opportunity still to be developed in the online environment, there are often more opportunities available than a company can pursue in a sustainable manner. The resource allocation process is the formalization of the trade-offs and the prioritization that the company uses when making choices about which opportunities to pursue. It goes without saying that this process needs to be very tightly aligned with the value proposition and the business model.

   - **Human-Resource Management Processes.** Online companies need to scale up and adjust quickly to keep growing with the market. Upgrading the human-resource capabilities in a manner which is in line with the value proposition, resource system, and market evolution is essential in such an environment.

   - **Manufacturing and Distribution Processes.** This has been defined as the supply chains and is the subject of a later section in this chapter.

   - **Payment/Billing Processing.** It is clear that without proper functioning of the payment and billing processes the online company will have difficulty producing anything other than virtual profits. However, billing processes are not equally important for all online companies. For ISPs, it can be a strong strategic advantage to produce one integrated bill for the customer's telecom, (cable) television, online services, and other services it delivers. For most online companies, however, these processes are more of a minimum performance requirement and can have a mainly *negative* impact if they are not functioning properly. For example, B2C payment processes are typically credit-card based, and many online companies seem to experience problems with smooth, comprehensive billing.[9] B2B payments take place in more complex manners, and enabler companies have recently launched new billing products focusing specifically on this market.

- **Customer Support/Handling Processes.** The customer can have questions when he or she is on the website as well as when a transaction has been completed. This could be a simple request for tracking the delivery progress of the order (e.g., Amazon), a change of the order in process, or help with problems once the product has been received. CreativeGood describes on its website how as many as four customer support calls (and a lot of persuasion from the customer's side) were required to conclude an order for an Apple G3 Tower that CreativeGood wanted to buy from the Apple website. It is hard to imagine that such a customer handling process actually reinforces the resource system. It is more likely to hamper the system and cause loss of transactions and customers in the longer term.

5. *Supply Chains.* The online environment has radically changed the structure of business supply chains and options available to retailers and manufacturers. We first focus on B2C supply chains and several different **supply-chain models** that have arisen to serve B2C companies. Next, we review B2B supply chains and reveal how the online environment is creating significant efficiencies and opportunities in the B2B market. Finally, we discuss developments in the C2C and C2B markets (see Exhibit 6-5).

Business-to-Consumer (B2C) Supply Chains.

One reason for the many supply-chain options available in the **Business-to-Consumer (B2C)** market is that online retailers (or e-tailers) do not need to have products physically in stock in a network of physical retail outlets to sell directly to consumers. Unlike brick-and-mortar retailers, which must maintain stock on hand in retail outlets, as long as the e-tailer fulfills its promise to deliver goods in a specified time period, consumers do not care how the order is fulfilled. This provides the e-tailer significant flexibility in designing its supply chains.[10] On the other hand, the B2C supply chain for marketspace companies is significantly more complex than for offline companies. Many Web-based deliveries often are small, time-sensitive (overnight, 2 to 3 days) deliveries to individuals about whom the company might have very limited information. This is very different from periodically delivering to an established network of shops with which the company has long-term relationships. In addition, a physical outlet network provides the outlet supplier with a predictable expectation of needed routes and volumes. Such a predictability is certainly absent when it comes to delivering goods to a changing volume of both new and existing consumers every day.

One of the weakest links in the B2C implementation chain is fulfillment. Late or unfulfilled online orders are the leading source of e-commerce complaints. A recent Forrester study found that half of the customers who had an unsatisfactory online buying experience stopped doing business with the offending company. With high customer-acquisition costs and the knowledge that disgruntled customers will relay their poor experiences to friends, B2C firms must master fulfillment. Poorly

The Changing Role of IT Implementation—
Microsoft FrontPage

 In the offline world, IT played mainly a technical or tactical role in an organization. Often, IT departments managed IT systems and provided support services to other departments in the organization. Frequently, the scope of IT activities was limited to ensuring the smooth operation of an organization's PCs, modems, and servers. As such, IT normally did not play a significant role in strategy development in the offline world.

But with the combined online and offline aspects of the New Economy, the product offering and the customer interface are elements that drive customer value and also have a strong technological component. Consequently, IT and IT implementation are at the core of the new strategy process.

A close examination of Microsoft FrontPage, one of the first development tools that allowed users to design websites, offers useful insights into the changing role of IT in the online world. In *High Stakes, No Prisoners: A Winner's Tale of Greed and Glory in the Internet Wars* (Times Books, Oct. 18, 1999), author Charles Ferguson, the founder of Vermeer Technologies (the developer of FrontPage, later acquired by Microsoft), explains the company's IT use in its strategy implementation:

Create Customer Lock-In by Separating Front and Back End of the Customer Experience. The strategic objective for the developers of FrontPage was to make their software the standard tool for website development. Website software development tools tend to be built around client-interfacing and server-facing modules. When FrontPage launched, the Web-server market was fragmented among a small number of operating systems (e.g., Apache's freeware, Microsoft IIS, Netscape), each with a significant market share. To achieve their strategic goal, the developers created special software to allow FrontPage to function identically on any of the Web-server operating systems. Ferguson wrote, "So by adopting our technology, we could argue that our customers gained freedom from lock-in [to server standards]; of course what we were really doing was commoditizing Web-servers and transferring proprietary lock-in from Web-server vendors to us."

Ensure Appropriate Scalability. IT implementation needs to not only deliver today's customer value but also must provide the platform for future growth. The complexity of the Netscape browser went from 100,000 lines of code to four million lines of code in a mere three years. Ferguson delayed the FrontPage market launch to build a more robust and transparent IT architecture with the explicit purpose of maximizing ease of scale-up in the future.

Enable Fast Tactical and Strategic Adjustments to an Evolving Market. Evolution in the online world is fast and unpredictable. IT architecture must accommodate regular hardware and software upgrades as well as incorporate the latest innovations, all of which can be difficult if the IT architecture has not been designed for a future of change. Navisoft had intended to launch a product very similar to FrontPage and at one point seemed likely to launch its product several months earlier than FrontPage. Ferguson describes IT architecture compromises that Navisoft made in their rush to get to market first. Navisoft's IT architecture choices proved to hamper its abilities to quickly adjust to such an extent that they could not launch in the same time frame as Microsoft FrontPage.

Enable User-Driven Customization to Serve Niches Cost-Effectively. Because the emerging demand for website development tools was unpredictable, the developers of FrontPage designed their IT architecture to allow third-party programmers to easily add software plug-ins because they "wanted to use, and in fact used, a considerable number of other people's components rather than develop them ourselves," according to Ferguson. This strategy facilitates the entire scale-up process. The developers also introduced bots that allowed third-party programmers and corporate users to develop unlimited customized functions (text-search functions, navigation bars, etc.) on their own websites. The IT architecture also allowed FrontPage to serve niche markets very cost-effectively, because users could now develop what they needed to serve their own niche without a major investment in resources from FrontPage.

Exhibit 6-5

FOUR TYPES OF SUPPLY CHAINS FOUND IN MARKETSPACE

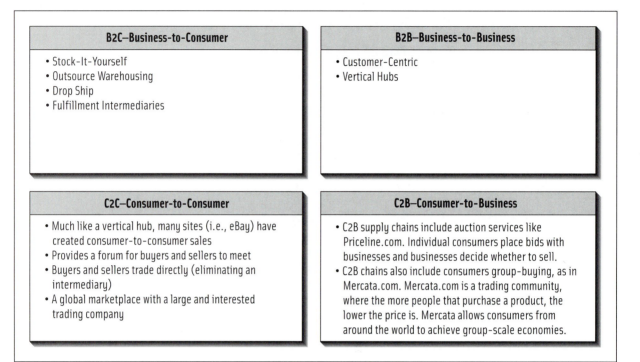

B2C—Business-to-Consumer

- Stock-It-Yourself
- Outsource Warehousing
- Drop Ship
- Fulfillment Intermediaries

B2B—Business-to-Business

- Customer-Centric
- Vertical Hubs

C2C—Consumer-to-Consumer

- Much like a vertical hub, many sites (i.e., eBay) have created consumer-to-consumer sales
- Provides a forum for buyers and sellers to meet
- Buyers and sellers trade directly (eliminating an intermediary)
- A global marketplace with a large and interested trading company

C2B—Consumer-to-Business

- C2B supply chains include auction services like Priceline.com. Individual consumers place bids with businesses and businesses decide whether to sell.
- C2B chains also include consumers group-buying, as in Mercata.com. Mercata.com is a trading community, where the more people that purchase a product, the lower the price is. Mercata allows consumers from around the world to achieve group-scale economies.

executed orders are costly to firms. The cost to handle returns generally is three to four times the cost to ship a product. In addition to refining fulfillment processes to satisfy customers, many firms are beginning to use expedited fulfillment as a means to product differentiation. In an effort to prove its superior fulfillment capabilities in 1999, Amazon guaranteed Christmas delivery to its customers if orders were received by December 22.

In today's B2C market, there are four primary supply-chain models: stock-it-yourself, outsource warehousing, drop ship, and fulfillment intermediaries.

- **Stock-It-Yourself.** For a brick-and-mortar company that also sells online, this model typically involves maintaining an integrated warehouse that is able to handle shipments to stores as well as shipments to Web customers. This is often very difficult, if not impossible, to implement. Systems and processes must handle both large deliveries to physical stores and small, individual orders to online customers.

  For purely online companies, the **stock-it-yourself** model generally involves an automated warehouse that can directly fulfill online orders. A primary benefit of this model is that it gives the online firm control over its fulfillment process. Control over fulfillment is a major concern for online companies. The primary reason Barnes & Noble recently tried to purchase the Ingram Book Group, the nation's largest book wholesaler, was to improve its book distribution system. This purchase was ultimately not completed due to antitrust concerns, but if the purchase had gone through, 80 percent of Barnes & Nobles' online and offline customers would have been within overnight delivery distance from the combined companies' 11 distribution centers.[11] The only disadvantage of this model is that the whole supply chain is likely to no longer be a strategic asset that the firm can shape in a proprietary way. Hence, it could be argued that such a structure commoditizes the supply chain.

- **Outsource Warehousing. Outsourcing warehousing** generally involves the use of logistics specialists like Federal Express (FedEx) or UPS to stockpile and ship Web orders. Hewlett Packard (HP) uses FedEx to handle all of its fulfillment orders from its retail website. FedEx warehouses HP inventory in Memphis, Tennessee (one of its hubs). Once an order comes in through HP's site, it is automatically transmitted to FedEx's Memphis facility. Orders are packaged at its warehouse and directly shipped to the customer via FedEx.[12] HP thereby has a very efficient distribution system to handle fulfillment to its distributors. However, its distribution system is simply not configured to handle small, individual shipments. It is not a trivial task to reconfigure its system to be able to handle both distributor and individual order fulfillment. FedEx also handles all of the fulfillment duties for ProFlowers.com. When orders come into ProFlowers, the order is routed directly to flower growers using FedEx technology. These growers create the arrangement, and FedEx picks it up and delivers it directly to the customer. In this case, ProFlowers.com's role is strictly focused on marketing, assembling a network of quality growers, and overseeing the production process.[13]

- **Drop Shipping. Drop shipping** requires e-commerce companies to depend on its manufacturers or distributors to pack and ship its retail Web orders. Drop-shipper specialists even go so far as placing the e-tailer's name and logo on all shipped orders. Direct-mail catalog companies are benefiting from the growth of e-tail drop shipping. Direct-mail catalog companies are experienced in fulfilling individual mail-order catalog purchases and are applying this experience to e-commerce fulfillment. The general design of a drop-shipping fulfillment warehouse is one by which shipments from manufacturers are unloaded at one end, merchandise is organized throughout the warehouse, and individual customer orders are shipped out via U.S. Mail or by an overnight service through the other end of the warehouse. One reason Federated Department Stores purchased Fingerhut, a mail-order house, was to help Federated with its e-commerce supply-chain strategy. In addition to working on Federated fulfillment orders, Fingerhut does order fulfillment for other well-known companies such as eToys and Wal-Mart. Fingerhut has strongly benefited from the drop-shipping boom. Fingerhut's revenues in 1999 were expected to be $40 million and are forecasted to increase to $100 million in 2000.[14]

- **Fulfillment Intermediaries. Fulfillment intermediaries** take care of all back-office operations for e-commerce companies. They handle order processing, direct orders to suppliers, keep customers updated on their order progress, handle order cancellations, and process product returns. These types of systems provide e-commerce entrepreneurs with the opportunity to focus on developing their business as well as reducing the initial set-up costs. One fulfillment intermediary, OrderTrust, estimates that it would cost the average e-commerce firm at least $1.5 million a year to build and operate an order-processing system. OrderTrust claims to sell the same fulfillment capabilities for between $25,000 to $100,000 a year.[15] Fulfillment intermediaries allow e-commerce companies to start operating almost immediately.

Outsourcing order fulfillment also minimizes risk. In the rapidly changing online environment, e-commerce companies that outsource do not have to commit to a specific type of supply chain. Shipper.com hopes to capture business from this growing trend of providing same-day service by investing $150 million to build fulfillment warehouses in 10 markets. It plans to focus its business on becoming an e-commerce facilitator rather than an e-commerce retail business. The core of Shipper.com's business will be to fulfill orders for e-commerce companies. Innovative fulfillment companies like Shipper.com may give firms without a proprietary supply chain an advantage over rivals that have invested resources in a supply chain that cannot provide same-day service.[16]

Example: Dell Online. When Dell moved to sell personal computers over the Internet, it identified two primary areas in which it could achieve cost savings: **salesforce efficiency** and **service efficiency.**[17]

- **Salesforce Efficiency.** By allowing consumers to order directly over the Internet, fewer transactions needed to be routed through the salesforce, which resulted in salesforce efficiencies. Also, salesforce personnel that handled calls originating from the website had a higher "close" rate. Dell found that the website sales team could handle 1.5 times the quota of the traditional salesforce.
- **Service Efficiency.** Dell saved considerably because its consumers used the Web to check on their order status, seek technical service FAQs, and download files. In a typical quarter, Dell Online's website had 200,000 order status checks, 500,000 technical service inquiries, and 400,000 file downloads. Had these inquiries been handled by telephone, each of these transactions would have cost between $5 and $15.

Business-to-Business (B2B) Supply Chains. Buyers reduce costs by creating an environment in which sellers are more competitive. Sellers can use **Business-to-Business (B2B)** sites to instantly advertise their products to potential customers. Gartner Group estimates the worldwide B2B Internet trade was $109 billion for last year. Gartner predicts that by 2004, the worldwide B2B Internet trade will be a $7.29 trillion market.[18] The potential B2B market is estimated to be 3 to 10 times the size of the B2C market.[19] B2B customers generally spend more than B2C customers. The average order for chemicals and supplies at Chemdex's B2B site is approximately $500. A typical Chemdex registered user orders over $20,000 of supplies a year.[20]

The B2B supply chains in the online space are somewhat different from the other supply chains. The key reason is that, whereas the other supply chains are truly new to the industry, B2B supply chains are rooted in more than a decade of enterprise-level expenditures in various technology, including computing, networking, and client servers.[21] Thus, companies may have had existing supplier relationships, and the parties simply converted the relationship into an electronic format.

Goldman Sachs, an investment bank, refers to an evolution from EDI (Electronic Data Interchange) via VPN (Virtual Private Networks) to intranets and, finally, to the Internet itself:

Prior to the existence of e-markets, large (buyer) businesses had 1:1 relationships with other (seller) businesses, using EDI or other mechanisms (like VPNs, ed.). These were primarily focused on direct materials and production goods. (For many suppliers, ed.) [. . .] the costs of doing business electronically was prohibitive and it was difficult enough to get the attention of the large buyers (Hubs).[22]

The five main reasons why big buyers (e.g., automobile companies) push such systems on their suppliers are as follows:

- Lower costs compared to offline management of suppliers and transactions
- Improved transaction speed and control (allowing for dependable global production of cars, for example)
- High security of the system, as it was purely proprietary and often supervised by the buyer
- Proprietary nature of the system created a strong switching barrier for participating suppliers
- Good reliability of capacity to process the transaction volume as the buyer was the key driver behind capacity management of the system

The evolution of computing and communications technology has made the Internet an increasingly attractive alternative to these proprietary, expensive systems due to the following advances:

- Improved security
- Increased transaction-handling capacity (hardware and software)
- Based on open standards, it allows for a much broader supplier-base to participate in network

Business-to-Business (B2B) sites are revolutionizing manufacturers' supply chains by allowing manufacturers the opportunity to realize lower input prices, reduced inventory, reduced transaction costs, faster delivery, and improved customer service.

- **Lower Input Prices.** Manufacturers use B2B sites to conduct auctions from prequalified bidders for their supply-chain inputs. The ease of bidding expands the universe of potential supplier bidders and takes human favoritism out of the buying equation. Increased competition coupled with decreased supplier overhead push suppliers to offer lower prices. One negative effect from the use of the auction process for procurement is that suppliers may become less inclined to invest in customizing products for a manufacturer if they have to bid against others for contracts at purchasing time. In many dynamic industries, it is necessary for manufacturers to create partnerships with suppliers to achieve fast product-development cycles.

- **Reduced Inventory.** B2B supply chains establish a closer communication process with suppliers regarding input needs and procurement time frames. This allows manufacturers to reduce their inventory stock, warehousing costs, and inventory carrying costs and to increase return on assets. At 3COM, in an effort to make their inventory process more efficient, expanded product production automatically triggers additional orders for input supplies like cardboard boxes.

- **Reduced Transaction Costs.** By using the Internet to announce order requests and to receive bids, both manufacturers and suppliers reduce the transaction costs associated with supply procurement. AMR Research reports that buyers in the B2B market can expect to realize a 15 to 20 percent drop in maverick purchases, $50 to $100 transaction savings per order, and a 2.5 to 10 percent price savings due to competition brought on by B2B sites.[23]

- **Faster Delivery.** Because procurement transactions are no longer processed through multiple internal departments or entered in several different data systems, the time between date of supply request to date of delivery can be greatly reduced.

- **Better Customer Service.** General Motors (GM) is trying to use B2B supply chains to provide better service to its customers. The current order-to-delivery time of a new car takes up to eight weeks. GM is trying to connect its factories and suppliers via the Internet. This connection will provide real-time notification to suppliers of materials needed and delivery deadlines. Prequalified suppliers can instantly submit a bid to provide supplies. This system allows GM to better coordinate with suppliers and GM hopes to reduce the order-to-delivery time of new cars to four to five days.[24]

GM will be insisting that all of its suppliers transact online through its TradeXchange site. By the end of 2001, GM intends to do all of its purchasing over this site. This translates into significant B2B purchase revenues as GM now orders over $500 billion in supplies worldwide per year.[25]

Example: Boeing's B2B Site. Until recently, 90 percent of Boeing's spare-parts customers had to go through a tedious and time-consuming process to order aircraft parts. Customers ordering spare parts were required to search through a catalog, find the spare part order number, relay requests to their purchasing departments, make phone calls to check part availability, and, finally, send the order by fax. Once Boeing received the fax, an employee would have to input the order into Boeing's order system (occasionally causing delays and mistakes). Boeing now uses a Web-based spare-parts ordering system that customers can use to instantly check part availability and simply click to order a part. Customers benefit because the Web-based process reduces transaction costs and the time needed to process and deliver each order. In the airline industry, this speed of order delivery can result in significant overall cost savings; it is very expensive to have an out-of-service aircraft awaiting a part. Boeing benefits because this new process lowers transaction costs and provides better service to its customers.

Consumer-to-Business (C2B) Supply Chain.
The concept of **Consumer-to-Business (C2B)** is well illustrated by the Mercata.com business model. Mercata.com tries to organize consumers together to gain group buying power when dealing with suppliers. Mercata aggregates customers who are interested in buying in volume and reaping lower prices. Mercata then negotiates with its suppliers to provide discounts on its merchandise based on the volume of goods sold. Mercata offers goods for sale on its website with a group buying incentive—as more purchases are made—the selling price that all customers receive decreases. By creating an online group of customers interested in gaining group buying power, Mercata allows both consumers and suppliers to win. Consumers benefit by receiving lower prices and sellers win by quickly selling a large amount of merchandise with a low transaction cost.

While group buying is common in the brick-and-mortar world, it is often very cumbersome to organize online. Mercata.com eliminates many of the obstacles associated with Old Economy group buying. Since Mercata has established a large and varied group of buyers interested in participating in group deals, suppliers simply offer their merchandise to Mercata's price-conscious group-buying crowd and the crowd participates without costly negotiations. Mercata receives a small fee for each product sold over its site.

Consumer-to-Consumer (C2C) Supply Chain. The eBay business model clearly illustrates a **Consumer-to-Consumer (C2C)** supply chain. eBay's mission is to help people trade practically anything on earth—it is a platform to facilitate person-to-person trading. eBay is a personal auction site that allows sellers to place individual items up for sale, and interested buyers then bid on these items. eBay has created the largest online community of individual buyers and sellers as well as an efficient platform for this community to interact and complete business. This platform provides a forum for buyers and sellers to meet, allows them to trade directly (as opposed to hiring an intermediary), uses the Internet to create a global marketplace, and offers convenience to the community. Each day eBay offers over 450,000 new items for sale. On each auction sale, it reaps a sliding scale fee of 5 percent to 1.5 percent of the final sales price of each auction item.

Online and Offline Integration

As noted earlier, many companies in the online environment not only have significant difficulty creating a smooth integration between the front end of the customer experience and the delivery system but with integrating online and offline front ends as well (e.g., retail outlets and website). This integration is most complex for hybrid companies. Exhibit 6-6 provides a simple matrix that illustrates the formation of hybrid companies. A pure online or pure offline company is not considered a hybrid. Hybrid companies combine both online and offline systems, whether it be customer interface, fulfillment, or both. For example, Borders, Inc. (*www.borders.com*) is a hybrid. The book retailer started as an offline firm whose brick-and-mortar bookstores served as its primary interfaces with customers. Later, it created a website to allow customers to shop and buy books online. Another example, Gazoontite.com (*www.gazoontite.com*), is also a hybrid. Gazoontite provides specialty products to allergy sufferers online via its website and offline through brick-and-mortar retail stores.

For brick-and-mortar–based sites, the mix of products offered on the Web may significantly differ from the product selection offered at retail stores. For example, consider drugstores. Many of the items bought at a physical drugstore are impulse or convenience items. Therefore, retail stores stock many items targeted toward convenience-related demand. Because shopping over the Web is not very conducive to the purchase of impulse convenience items, drugstore websites stock items not normally sold at drugstores that are nonetheless important to their Web customers. In addition, the economics of shopping on the Web or shopping in a retail store are very different due to the low prices of many items in drugstores, vis-à-vis the shipping costs of delivering Web-ordered goods to customers. Consequently, the average sale to customers at Drug Emporium's website is two and a half times the average sale at its retail stores.[26] Also, brick-and-mortar based companies must consider the demographic composition of their online customer base. The motive or

Exhibit 6-6

WHERE TO PLAY ONLINE AND OFFLINE

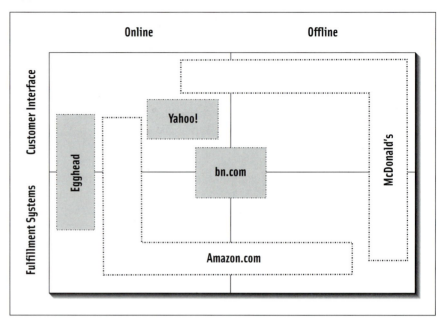

occasion for a purchase may significantly differ between their online customers and offline retail customer base. Online and offline product mix and the selling approach need to reflect the differences between customer bases as well as the customers' reasons for purchase.

Due to their dual-interface nature, hybrid firms face issues that do not concern pure online firms. One key choice the hybrid firm must confront is the form of organization. Should the online and offline parts of the business be housed in the same organization as its parent, or should it be spun out as a separate firm or operating unit?

Single-Organization Hybrid—Advantages. There are a number of advantages to housing the online and offline interfaces in the same organization.

- **Customer Benefits.** Tightly coupled online/offline back-office support systems benefit the customer as well as the firm. The more integrated the two interfaces, the more likely customers are able to migrate back and forth between the online and offline platforms during their interactions with the company. For instance, the planned Home Depot website hopes to make it easy for customers to interact with the company when they want and as they want. Website visitors will be able to browse online listings of Home Depot products, assemble a shopping list, pay for their purchases online, and have the merchandise shipped to their home. Alternatively, they can choose to send the order to their nearest Home Depot store, where it will be packaged and left for them at a checkout station where they can pay for it.

  Contrast the flexibility offered by Home Depot to that offered by bn.com, the online operation of Barnes & Noble. Customers who order books from bn.com must receive the books at home; they cannot pick up their purchases at a Barnes & Noble store. Should they decide to return books, these must be shipped back to bn.com; books purchased online cannot be returned to the physical stores.

The difference between the fluidity of the customer experiences offered by Home Depot and bn.com is due in part to the different organizational structures of the two firms. Home Depot's online operation is part of the parent firm. bn.com, in contrast, is a separate operation from Barnes & Noble. The two entities maintain separate inventory and cost-accounting systems, and revenues and sales are tracked separately as well. Thus, a book purchased from bn.com and returned to a brick-and-mortar store would pose a number of difficulties. First, the physical store would record the return against sales it had not made. As a result, its profit would be understated. Meanwhile, the online operation would have made the sale but not recorded the return and would appear to be more profitable than it really was.

- **People.** The single-organization structure can be a recruiting advantage for firms that begin offline and expand to the online platform. Because e-commerce is a very attractive field at present, offline firms become more attractive to many candidates when they add an online interface.

- **Taxes.** In cases in which one interface is operating at a loss and the other is profitable, combining the operations in a single entity can provide significant tax benefits. The profit of one venture is reduced by the loss of the second, immediately lowering the tax liability of the profitable venture. As a separate organization, the unprofitable venture would amass its losses for application against future profits, in effect postponing the benefit that could be gained immediately in a single organization.

- **Valuation.** At the time this book went to press, Wall Street was placing extraordinary values on select online ventures. In an online firm, a company's ability to lock-in alliance partners, acquire competitors, and attract the best talent is strongly related to its market capitalization. Shareholders of offline firms stood to gain when their firms built or bought online capabilities and housed the two interfaces in the same organization.

- **Systems.** The ability of any interface, online or offline, to deliver value to a customer depends in large part on the back-office infrastructure (i.e., IT infrastructure, order processing and fulfillment systems, inventory control, etc.) that supports it. Online and offline interfaces that are housed in a single organization have the potential of relying on a single set of back-office systems. This is particularly true for firms that start out as hybrids and so can design their back-office systems specifically to support two different types of interfaces.

  When the online and offline interfaces are housed in different organizations, it is unlikely that they will be supported by a single set of back-office systems. At best, the two organizations may attempt to link their systems at critical points—an endeavor that can be costly and is not always successful.

Single-Organization Hybrid—Disadvantages. The principal challenges associated with single-organization hybrids are as follows:

- **Coordination and Cooperation Processes.** Achieving the cost savings and customer benefits that derive from a single set of back-office systems requires considerable coordination between the online and offline operations. If managers of the two interfaces do not work cooperatively, they will be unable to leverage a single set of back-office systems. As a result, the firm will not realize the potential cost efficiencies and customer benefits of the single-organization structure.

- **People.** While some workers will be attracted to a single-organization hybrid, others may be repelled. In an interview with *Fortune* magazine, Jim Tuchler, a project manager working on Sears' website, conceded that recruiting New Economy workers to an Old Economy employer can be difficult. "Telling people you work at Sears doesn't elicit oohs and ahhs," he explained.[27]

- **Allocations.** When both interfaces are housed in the same organization, they compete for critical resources such as funding, staffing, and mind share with senior management. Managers of the new interface may find themselves spending as much time negotiating for resources as applying them. Given the interdependencies between the offline and online parts of the organization as well as the potential difference in drivers of competition, unambiguous resource-allocation processes may be very complex to design and difficult to manage.

Dual-Organization Hybrid—Advantages.

A dual-organization structure has its own advantages.

- **Coordination Processes.** Here there is no need for the company to simultaneously grow two organizations driven by very different skills and evolution speeds. Women.com is one of many online companies that experienced significant problems with the coordination of such different types of organizations under one roof. Women.com opted for the dual organization structure. Women.com quietly closed its online store for women's clothing and accessories just three months after launching. Instead of adding to its revenues, Women.com found that its e-commerce site was detracting from other revenue sources, especially banner-ads. Women.com decided that its new partner for women's books e-tailing, Harlequin Enterprises, would handle the customer service and fulfillment of orders placed on eHarlequin: "It is an integrated partnership in which they do what they do best, and we [Women.com] do what we do best: driving traffic and sales."

- **License to Cannibalize.** A cannibalistic strategy is easier to execute when the new interface is housed in a separate organization. Few organizations have the will or strength of leadership to cannibalize themselves.

- **People.** Housing the interfaces in two separate organizations can be a recruiting advantage for the online operation; some New Economy workers prefer a pure online environment.

- **Allocations.** When the new interface is housed in a separate organization, it does not have to fight with the offline interface for senior management time, funding, or staff.

- **Taxes.** As this book goes to press, online sales are exempt from sales tax. If the online and offline interfaces are legally separate entities, sales on the offline interface are subject to sales tax, but sales on the online interface are exempt. If the two interfaces are housed in a single corporation, sales on both interfaces are taxed.

- **Valuation.** Investors may prefer to see the online interface incorporated as a separate organization and valued at e-commerce multiples rather than risk having its value diluted by merging with an online firm.

Dual-Organization Hybrid—Disadvantages. The principal challenges associated with dual-organization hybrids are as follows:

- **Avoiding Customer Confusion.** A lack of consistency between online and offline interfaces can create confusion for customers. One author of this book is an executive platinum member of the American Airline system. He is quite satisfied with the offline interface—namely, the phone operations, service personnel, gate attendants, and Admirals Club staff. However, he was quite dissatisfied with the aa.com website prior to 1999 site modifications. First attempts to visit the site during a major site relaunch often failed and required multiple attempts to access. Second, there was no password storage, hence, one needed to remember the password on each occasion. Third, there was no clear integration of the offline and online services. This is despite the fact that we have identified the site as a Best of Class brand site in Chapter 5!

- **Consistent Integration of Online and Offline Customer Service.** Good customer service can build customer trust in the company managing the website. Customer service can be a significant portion of the customer experience if you look at the numbers: eBay receives between 40,000 and 75,000 customer support e-mails per week.[28] However, a survey by the *Industry Standard* of the top 10 e-commerce sites found that the average customer service response time (of surveyed companies on the Internet) was over a day and a half. The quickest response time was a speedy, 34-minute personalized response from Amazon.[29]

  A particularly illustrative example of the potential backlash of insufficient integration between online and offline customer service is offered by CreativeGood's review of the Apple website (*store.apple.com*). After the checkout process accidentally terminated the site evaluator's attempt to buy a G3 Tower, the evaluator called the Apple customer-service department to get their order processed. CreativeGood's summary of the interaction is as follows:

  We eventually were able to complete the buying process, after we called the Apple's 800 number no fewer than four times trying to figure it out. During the phone conversations, it became clear that the Apple [customer service] staff had little knowledge of the customer experience on the web site.[30]

Such a lack of integration between the online and offline customer interfaces and service can easily damage the company brand and hinder its ability to implement its strategy successfully.

- **Managing a Consistent Brand.** Maintaining a consistent brand image across interfaces requires cooperation and communication between managers of the online and offline interfaces. Together, managers must answer questions such as the following: How similar should the look and feel of the two interfaces be? How much consistency should there be between the online and offline versions of customer activities such as product selection, purchase, and returns? Coming to an agreement on such decisions is enough of a challenge when online and offline managers are part of a single organization. It is especially difficult in dual-organization hybrids, in which managers may have less contact with colleagues, less mutual trust, and fewer incentives to cooperate. Even when managers of the two interfaces share a common vision, their ability to execute it may be hampered by separate back-office systems with differing capabilities and limitations.

3M's Research Paradigm				Key Takeaways
Laboratories	**Primary Activities**	**Time Frame**	**Innovation Type**	
Division Laboratories	• Product development • Product control • Technical service	• Today's business 0–3 years	• Line extension	• Traditional offline innovation took years and empha-sized sustainable/gradual innovation • Marketspace still offers room for incremental innova-tion, but emphasizes shifts to more drastic innovations • High information content of innovation objects increases speed of innovation from years to months or even shorter • Short history of marketspace means new collaborators/complementors become available frequently
Sector Laboratories	• Sector technology development	• 3–10 years	• Changing the basis of competition	
Central Research	• New technology development	• 10+ years	• New industries	

Source: Gundling, Ernest. 2000. *The 3M Way to Innovation.* Tokyo: Kodansha Int. Ltd. And New York, New York: Kodansha America, Inc.

WHAT ARE THE CATEGORIES OF OFFLINE INNOVATION?

In this section, we explore the different ways in which offline and online firms produce **innovation.** First, we discuss innovation categories and the innovation process in the offline world. Then, we discuss how the online environment has impacted the drivers underlying the offline approach to innovation. Finally, we review new classifications of innovation categories and processes online.

Long considered a leading innovator in the off-line world, 3M has classified types of innovation into three categories: **line extensions, changing the basis of competition,** and **new industries** (see Table 6-1). Each of these developmental categories has a different research process and product time frame. Most offline companies use a similar categorization of innovation.

Line Extensions

Line extensions are innovations that are incremental advances to an existing product. An example of this may be the offering of a new and improved version of an existing product (i.e., an advanced release of a software package). To create line extensions, 3M established research units called Division Laboratories. These research units work closely with customers to determine their needs and develop variants of current products to meet these needs within a zero- to three-year project time frame.

Changing the Basis of Competition

These are innovations that create a new competitive position or niche in a market. In their rush to gain overnight service market share, UPS and FedEx constantly offer service innovations. Both services offer 8 A.M. service between select cities. FedEx offers Saturday and Sunday service. Each innovation does not need to be a profit center. The fact that one service offers delivery in one category that the other doesn't (i.e., weekend delivery) may sway a client company to give all its business (including lucrative overnight service) to the more innovative service. Thus, these types of incremental innovations have the ability to change the basis of how delivery services compete. 3M set up Sector Laboratories to develop this type of innovation in order to change the basis of competition. The goal of Sector Laboratories is to create innovations within a 3- to 10-year time frame.

New Industries

New industry innovations are innovations that can create a new industry. These types of innovations are quite common in the pharmaceutical industry. For example, Upjohn's introduction of Rogaine, a medical advance in growing scalp hair, created a lucrative new market—medicine that can grow real human hair. At 3M, Central Research Labs were established to develop this type of major innovation. Central Research Labs take a 10+ year time frame in order to create new industry type products.

WHAT IS THE OFFLINE INNOVATION PROCESS?

An underlying reason for the significant time required to innovate in the offline world is the complexity of the standard "funnel process." 3M has described three distinct and successive phases in the **innovation funnel process** (see Exhibit 6-7): **innovation by doodling, innovation by design,** and **innovation by direction.** This three-stage process functions like a funnel in that an increasing number of innovations are eliminated during each phase until only the most promising remain and are brought to market.

This funnel process is also sometimes referred to as the **waterfall concept of new product innovation.** The purpose of the funnel is to make internal choices about innovations that the company should pursue and to launch only the innovations with the highest chance of succeeding. 3M's three phases reflect the initial supportive focus on the generation of a host of ideas and the following shift toward consecutive screening of the ideas. The screening of the innovation ideas tightens as the innovation ideas move through phases of the funnel. The process becomes complex because these screenings are done within the organization, screenings are based on expected customer behavior, and the perspective of the screening criteria are very broad in nature. Indeed, as Gundling points out, "Full-scale innovation-success—the proverbial hit product—requires streetwise market acumen and staying power to select the right application, accurately forecast demand, and implement a sales strategy that gets the product into the hands of paying customers."[31]

Exhibit 6-7

THE OFFLINE INNOVATION PROCESS WAS INTERNAL TO THE FIRM

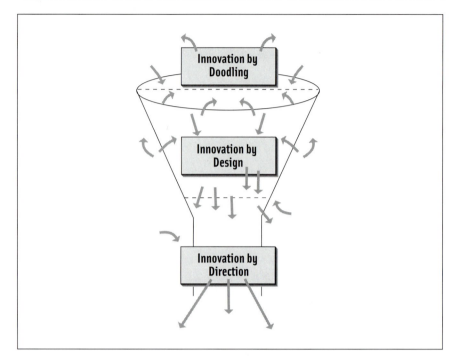

Innovation by Doodling

The enterprising manager knows that his staff has a great deal of experience, knowledge, and interesting ideas. He gathers them into a conference room for an afternoon meeting. He announces he wants to learn from his staff and wants to create a free-form brainstorming session during which no idea is dumb. At the end of the brainstorming session, the manager has several pages of innovative marketing ideas.

Innovation by Design

The manager and a subset of his staff cull ideas from the brainstorming session for those ideas that are cost effective and show promise in consumer acceptance. As a team, they reduce the initial set of ideas into a smaller, commercially viable set.

Innovation by Direction

Working from the commercially viable set, the staff undertakes market research, test runs, and further tests implementation viability. After reviewing the results of these tests, the staff further narrows the commercially viable idea set into a final set of marketing concepts to fully implement in the market.

WHAT IS THE NEW LOGIC BEHIND THE NEW ECONOMY INNOVATION?

The fundamental logic behind the offline innovation process is impacted significantly by the dynamic nature of online business. This is the topic of the first subsection. In the second subsection we illustrate how new innovation frameworks try to incorporate the new focus on coevolution of technology and customers. Finally, we consider new innovation processes that are emerging as applied versions of these new innovation frameworks.

Innovation in the New Economy shares a similarity to the 3M innovation funnel process. However, key differences between the nature of New and Old Economy innovations affect the innovation process. These differences change several crucial trade-offs underlying the offline (funnel-based) innovation process (see Table 6-2). Below we describe several of these differences.

High Investment Costs as Key Constraint in Innovation Selection Process

In general, the size of investments required to launch innovative services and products are significantly higher in the offline world relative to the online world. The implication is that the offline focus of "picking the big hit" loses its relevance as smaller innovations requiring lower investments can be just as effective in implementing the strategy.

Table 6-2 OFFLINE INNOVATION PROCESS VS. ONLINE INNOVATION PROCESS

Offline Trade-Offs/Principles Supporting Funnel Approach	Online Principles
• Investments required to launch new innovation are high	• Investments required to launch new products and services are moderate
• Limited resources force trade-offs/choices of which innovations to pursue or not	• Choices about future of new innovations can easily be made by markets, no need to make these choices internally
• Trade-offs/choices are made inside the organization before product hits the market	• First mover imperative can be aligned with gathering (more) customer input
• Time-to-market/first mover imperative needs to be traded off with extensive time required to gather customer input	• Launching beta-versions allows for revisioning/customization, actually benefiting innovator
• Launching early increases risk of flops, and flops need to be avoided at all times: – Costs of flops very high – Significant damage to brand equity	• Key drivers determining success of innovation/implementation are: – Customer base – Customer data analysis – Knowledge management

Innovation No Longer an Optimization Within Given Constraints

For many offline companies, the innovation process focused on an intense screening of innovation options. The main reason was that the company only had limited resources (capital, human resources) and, hence, had to optimize the potential use of these limited resources. The fluid nature of online companies and the (temporary?) abundance of external capital sources means that online companies do not need to focus on such an optimization. Instead, online companies can experiment much more and rapidly increase or decrease investments to launch marketing innovations.

Locus of Innovation Selection Moving Outside the Firm's Boundaries

As described above, in the offline world, all trade-offs regarding innovation were generally made internally. The management of the company/business unit would decide which innovations to pursue, how to market them, when to launch, and how to extract revenue. These decisions would be based on expectations about likely customer behavior gathered from testing prototypes or other forms of market research. In the online environment, the locus of innovation decision making moves outside the boundaries of the organization and into the market. That is to say, the organization can launch a series of innovations or versions of innovations, and customers provide direct feedback by either adopting it or not. The online company can actually gain customer buy-in by adjusting its innovation based on adoption behavior.

Adaptive Innovation Instead of Trying to "Guess It Right the First Time"

Online commerce is relatively young. As such, many online companies have developed a process of innovating and serving customers by means of a "sense and respond" approach.[32] This means that online companies toss into the marketplace many early versions of products and innovations (so-called beta-versions), which are then rapidly improved based on measured customer feedback. It certainly helps that online customers are much more open to this form of innovating/marketing than traditional offline customers.

As a result, it could be argued that innovation is fundamentally different in the online world. Offline firms tend to be risk averse because of the high cost of launching innovations. But also, once an innovation is launched, Old Economy companies do not have the infrastructure in place to immediately fix glitches and incorporate feedback ideas in real time—further exacerbating the potential downside of an early launch. These constraints, coupled with concern over the potential negative impact of a failed innovation on a well-established Old Economy brand name (e.g., Cherry Coke) limit offline firms' appetites for rapid-cycle innovation launches.

In contrast, online companies are eager to launch new innovations and are more tolerant of imperfections that can be quickly fixed. If the innovation proves ineffective, it is often very easy to undo the innovation. In addition, some have argued that online customers are more understanding of innovation glitches and derive some satisfaction in helping fix glitches and providing insights to sites for future evolution.

WHAT ARE THE NEW ECONOMY INNOVATION FRAMEWORKS?

In the New Economy, several factors are thought to speed up the innovation process. These factors include the observation that innovation decisions are cheaper and easier to implement, the market is actively seeking innovation, customers are willing to tolerate glitches and provide feedback, and online firms are well suited to immediately incorporate findings from customer feedback. This leads to rapid innovation in the New Economy and an innovation cycle that is measured in months, compared to years in the Old Economy.

The need to rapidly and continuously adapt and improve has led to frameworks for innovation that focus more on the coevolution of technology and customers. New models of innovation have emerged in attempts to address these challenges. Two frameworks are particularly useful to understanding in this context.

Disruptive Technologies

Clayton Christensen frames **disruptive technologies** as innovations that create an entirely new market through the introduction of a new kind of service or product. Though these disruptive technologies initially can be inferior to established technologies, their performance levels progress faster than market demands and more fully fulfill consumer expectations later in the product's lifecycle.[33]

> *Most technologies foster improved performance. I call these sustaining technologies. [. . .] What all sustaining technologies have in common is that they improve the performance of established products, along dimensions of performance that mainstream customers in major markets have historically valued. Disruptive technologies [. . .] result in worse performance, at least in the near-term. Generally disruptive technologies underperform established products in mainstream markets. But they have product features that a few fringe (and generally new) customers value.*"[34]

As examples of disruptive offline-world technologies, Christensen lists sectors that were surprised or upset by disruptive technologies: DEC was surprised by the rise of personal desktop computers; Sears did not anticipate the rise of discount retailing; and conventional health insurers were surprised by the rise of HMOs.

The Internet has proven to be a disruptive innovation for many companies and industry sectors. Yahoo!, Schwab.com, and Amazon.com are examples of organizations whose very reason for existence is a disruptive innovation. In the early days of the Internet, portals like Yahoo! were mainly extended search engines that served as an entry onto the World Wide Web. These search engines were an innovation to the buying process and were initially difficult and inconvenient to use with very specific input formats that must have made more sense to programmers than users. Also, search engines had limited reach as the universe of online users was small and consisted mainly of hobbyists. However, the sophistication of search engines has evolved to a level at which natural language words can be used and searches can be tailored much more precisely. And in turn, Yahoo! has kept innovating to not only benefit from search-engine evolution but also redefine its portal to be much more than a search engine surrounded by advertisements.

The same evolution goes for Amazon.com. At its launch, Amazon only sold books online at a discount without many frills or value-added services. As such, it was a relatively simple innovation in the world of the traditional book-buying market. Over time, Amazon upgraded its bookselling product offering by adding the following:

- Reviews by customers

- Easier purchase process (OneClick Buying)

- Personalized recommendations for new book purchases based on the customer's previous purchases

- Opportunity for customers to personalize their own account page

In addition, Amazon used its strong position in bookselling to initiate additional buying process innovations in a host of other categories (e.g., music, electronics, and even lawn and patio) as well as other forms of commerce (e.g., zShops and auctions).

However, an additional challenge arises for players in the online environment. Because so much of the online product offering is technology-driven, increased technological innovation can set expectations and affect performance levels demanded by consumers. It could be argued that there is a tighter link between technological innovations and performance demanded by online customers than in the offline world. The continual upgrading and changing of sites by Amazon.com, MP3, and, to a lesser extent, My Yahoo! are examples of this.

 Exhibit 6-8

NEW INNOVATION FRAMEWORKS ADDRESSING COEVOLUTION HAVE EMERGED

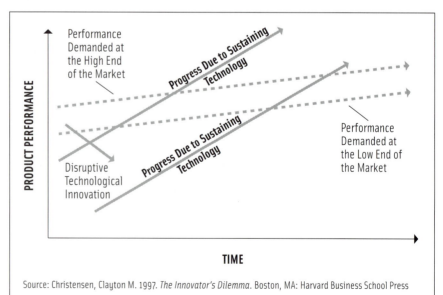

Source: Christensen, Clayton M. 1997. *The Innovator's Dilemma.* Boston, MA: Harvard Business School Press

Exhibit
6-9
NEW INNOVATION FRAMEWORKS ADDRESSING COEVOLUTION HAVE EMERGED

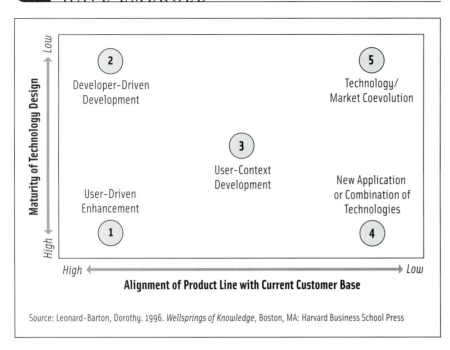

Source: Leonard-Barton, Dorothy. 1996. *Wellsprings of Knowledge*, Boston, MA: Harvard Business School Press

Dorothy Leonard Innovation Framework

Next, we consider the **Dorothy Leonard innovation framework.**[35] While this framework was developed in an offline context, many of the principles apply in the online environment. First, we review Leonard's five distinct categories of innovation: (1) **User-Driven Enhancement,** (2) **Developer-Driven Development,** (3) **User-Context Development,** (4) **New Application or Combination of Technologies,** and (5) **Technology/Market Coevolution.**

User-Driven Enhancement. Innovations of this type are generally features that are no-risk improvements to a product. Common types of user-driven enhancements include lowering product price, adding low-cost, high-value feature enhancements, and cost-efficient quality improvements. Crest has a long-standing reputation of offering high-quality toothpaste products. In recent years, competitors have created a new line of toothpaste products specializing in teeth whitening. These products often use baking soda as a whitener and have been very popular. Crest's entry into the premium whitening toothpaste market by offering a baking soda and peroxide whitening product is an example of a user-driven enhancement.

Developer-Driven Development. This type of innovation occurs when a firm develops a new way of meeting an existing consumer need. Palm Pilots are a great example of developer-driven development. There has been a long-standing need for personal organizers. For the most part, paper-based companies produced pocket diaries and desktop rolodexes to meet these needs. While simple hand-held organizers did exist, Palm revolutionized the market by finding a new way to meet consumers' organizing needs. Palm produced a hand-held device that incorporated more (if not all) of the important features that users need to organize themselves. As a result, Palm products have fueled the worldwide market for electronic personal companions and, as of May 1999, hold 68 percent of the worldwide market share.

User-Context Development.
This type of innovation occurs when firms develop products to meet a previously unexpressed need. In many cases, careful market research revealed these needs and firms have built products to meet these needs. A good example of user-context development is the positioning and further development of sport utility vehicles (SUVs) as spacious family vehicles. In today's SUV market, very few purchasers actually use SUVs for off-road travel or utilize their four-wheel-drive features. Although consumers apparently don't use many of the original design functions of SUVs, producers discovered that SUVs clearly meet personal expressive needs of many consumers buying large, family-sized vehicles. These expressive needs of SUV drivers clearly differ from those of station wagon or minivan drivers.

New Application or Combination of Technologies.
This type of innovation occurs when an established technology is applied to a new industry. Broadcast Data Systems (BDS) is a radio monitoring service that implemented this type of innovation. Music companies are always interested in learning when music from their artists is being played on the radio (to monitor airplay success, channel marketing promotions, etc.). Prior to BDS entering the market, radio airplay information was compiled by survey companies that called radio stations and asked what songs they played. There has always been a general concern over data integrity and frustration over the amount of play list detail; the best result survey takers could get was a top 40 list. To meet the needs of the music industry, BDS retooled existing technology to revolutionize the music reporting business. BDS uses a sophisticated monitoring system that involves feeding snippets of record samples into a computer. Every few seconds, this computer scans thousands of radio stations in the United States to make song matches. Every 24 hours, BDS provides clients detailed lists of the titles and exact playing times of songs played on specific radio stations. The BDS monitoring service is based on a version of advanced technology used during the Vietnam War to monitor troop movements along the Ho Chi Minh Trail.

Technology/Market Coevolution.
This type of innovation can be considered at the very frontier of innovation. The customer base is not clearly known, nor is the technology well-established. These products sometimes appear to have a more or less accidental growth path, but they can be the beginning of entire new markets. Post-it Notes is an offline example of Technology/Market Coevolution. This form of coevolution innovation is quite common in the online domain for the following three reasons:

- **Marketspace Is Undeveloped.** To a large extent, the online domain is still undeveloped with much "white space," new players emerging, and industry boundaries blurring.
- **User Behavior Is Not Well-Defined.** User-behavior is still in a much more embryonic stage than in the offline world.
- **Large Influence by Technology.** Product offerings in the marketspace are heavily influenced by technological evolution and content.

WHAT ARE THE NEW ECONOMY INNOVATION PROCESSES?

The erosion of traditional constraints on innovation does enable a faster, cheaper, and more adaptive innovation process. At the same time, the need for the innovation process to be adaptive increases sharply because uncertainty surrounding innovation has intensified dramatically as new innovation frameworks have tried to capture. Two fundamentally different process models that attempt to accommodate this additional uncertainty are emerging in the online world.

Flexible Development Process

In discussing product development on the Internet, professors Iansiti and MacCormack of Harvard Business School introduced a model that emphasizes the integration of technology with customer preferences.[36] In Exhibit 6-10, we illustrate their model.

DRILL-DOWN

Napster as an Example of Technology and Market Coevolution

Napster is an example of recent technology and market coevolution in the online music arena. Until fairly recently, the cost of the necessary computer hardware capacity that would allow easy downloading and playing of music files was prohibitive. Music buyers relied on traditional offline distribution channels to fulfill their music-buying needs.

By filtering out all humanly inaudible sounds from the music track, Layer 3 technology increased the ability to compress music files by a factor of 10. In 1988, Layer 3 was adopted as an international standard by MPEG (Moving Pictures Expert Group). In 1995, Windows-compatible Winplay was released and enabled users to download music files easily and quickly from the Internet. In 1999, MP3 was so successfully adopted that it overtook *sex* as the most-searched-for term on the Internet. [*The Men Behind MP3, Industry Standard, April 24, 2000*]

The Napster proposition is simple: Users download free software that indexes MP3 files on the user's hard drive and makes the hard drive visible to other Napster users when connected to the Internet. From there, a simple title or artist search results in locating the requested MP3 file on other users' hard drives from which to download. [*Napster Grows Up, RED HERRING.com, March 10, 2000*]

Napster's technology was not intended to be a major commercial product. Because the central concept is to allow users to share files with each other, pay-for-your-files is not currently required or possible. The technology was introduced into the online world, much like 3M's Post-It Notes, and has been adopted exponentially by the sheer demand of enthusiastic end-users. According to Jupiter-research, in 1999 (the year Napster was inadvertently launched), an estimated 1 million of the 10 million online music buyers were Napster users!

There are two final notes the reader should keep in mind on co-innovation of technology and markets. First, the behavior of music buyers changed as a result of this new technology. According to the same Jupiter research, music retailers saw a spike in album sales for artists like Beck and the Beastie Boys, who often release music in MP3 form. This could create a new form of advertising or promotional revenue opportunity for online music providers like MP3 or Napster. Second, the Napster indexing technology was originally developed for MP3 files but has already been extended to other applications. Recently, Scour.net offered the same type of functionality for all media-related files: pictures, music files, or any other media files.

Exhibit 6-10 INTEGRATING NEW TECHNOLOGY WITH CUSTOMER PREFERENCES

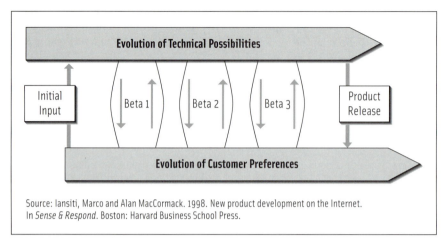

Source: Iansiti, Marco and Alan MacCormack. 1998. New product development on the Internet. In *Sense & Respond*. Boston: Harvard Business School Press.

The key point is concept development and implementation of the ideas in the field need to overlap and be tightly integrated. Beta testing begins shortly after the product is developed and continues well into the implementation phase. The benefits that have been associated with the **flexible development process** include the following:

- **Reduced Time-to-Market of Innovations Cut from Years to Months.** This simultaneous development and feedback process reduces the time to launch.

- **Multiple Versions of an Innovation Can Be Launched Without Significant Risk or Additional Cost.** As customer feedback is received, new versions of the product can be launched.

- **Increased Flexibility to Adjust Direction of Innovation.** The Netscape 3.0 product innovation process, illustrated in Exhibit 6-11, is a good example of the flexible development process. Netscape began the process of developing Netscape 3.0 shortly after Netscape 2.0 was released in January 1996. As Iansiti and MacCormack note, the first two beta version releases were made internally in February and March. The first public release was in March. From this point on, Netscape was able to gather a tremendous amount of user feedback for the revision of the interface.

Distributed Innovation Model

The flexible development process can be considered a dramatically improved version of the traditional funnel process. The **distributed innovation model** (see Exhibit 6-12) is an additional step away from the classical funnel process. This process model puts the purpose of continuously maintaining a fit between the organization and the evolution of the online domain at the very heart of the innovation process. In order to do this successfully, the organization tries to tap into the sources of online evolution: technology, collaborators, customer preferences, new entrants, and even competitors. The organization can be viewed as the center of the (innovation) web or like an octopus with its tentacles connecting the inside of the organization with the sources of online evolution.

The innovation process is therefore no longer a funnel process with a fixed beginning and end. The innovation process becomes a fluid, organic process. This innovation process is the ultimate expression of the "sense and response" concept of New Economy strategies. The benefits that have been associated with the distributed innovation process include the following:

- Maximizes use of both internal and external experts/sources
- Minimizes chances of the organization being surprised by external changes
- Highly interactive and much more flexible process than funnel process
- Reduced time-to-market

Red Hat Linux is an example of a company that adopted the distributed innovation process. The innovation of the Linux product is driven by an explicit interaction between market evolution and Red Hat's interactions with and reactions to these evolutions. The main drawback of this innovation process is that its fluidity can make it more difficult to manage. As we said, it links the competitive environment and the inside of the organization tightly together. The innovation process is partly steered by forces outside the boundaries of the firm, which makes it difficult to control. Also, participants outside the boundaries of the firm know more about what is going on inside the firm than in the usual (internal) innovation process. The firm must find a way to work effectively with this new fluidity. Which model proves to be most effective is likely to depend on the difficulty of consistently

Exhibit 6-11 THE DEVELOPMENT OF NAVIGATOR 3.0

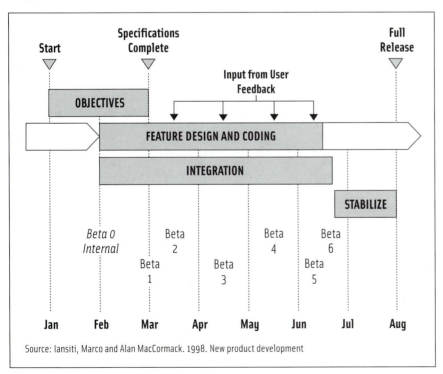

Source: Iansiti, Marco and Alan MacCormack. 1998. New product development

Exhibit
6-12

DISTRIBUTED INNOVATION

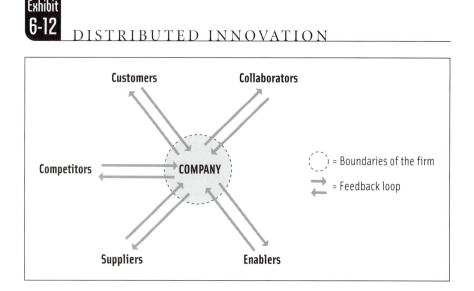

implementing the process models. So far, neither model has proven to be more effective than the other, although the flexible development process currently seems to be more widely adopted.

SCHWAB'S IMPLEMENTATION

We now examine the use of technology and innovation in the implementation of Schwab's delivery system and the integration of Schwab.com with Schwab's offline operations.

Schwab's Delivery System

As was discussed earlier, the five components of the delivery system include people, systems, assets, processes, and supply chains. Here we examine the first three components for Schwab at the time when it decided to migrate its products and services from offline to online by launching Schwab.com (1997).

Assets. Schwab's physical assets consisted primarily of 272 branches located across 47 states in the United States, Puerto Rico, and the United Kingdom. In late 1997, 70 percent of the U.S. population was located within 30 miles of a Schwab branch, allowing investors to easily reach a Schwab representative. Furthermore, Schwab invested $15 to $20 million in four regional customer service telephone centers. All calls (including calls to branches) were routed 24 hours a day through these call centers. This call processing aggregation led to high efficiency, with nearly all customer calls being answered within three rings and with hold times of less than one minute.[37] In intangible or information assets, by late 1997 Schwab had 1.2 million online and 3 million offline investor accounts. Schwab also continuously captured investor information in its mainframe database. This growing database provided invaluable information to build investor profiles, predict customer needs, and target marketing messages.

People. In October 1995, prior to the launch of its website, Schwab had launched eSchwab as a dial service to give customers access to the Schwab system to execute and track trades. eSchwab was an experiment and was not large enough to merit its own separate organization. To protect the new enterprise from a culture clash as well as a scramble for resources with the offline organization, Schwab's co-CEO David Pottruck decided to quarantine the new operation and have it report directly to him. Pottruck put the unit under the joint leadership of Schwab's CIO and an executive hired from IBM. Apart from the CIO, the entire IT team was recruited from outside Schwab. Unlike its parent company, eSchwab operated very much like a dot-com company with long hours, informal meetings, and no strict dress code.

With the launch of Schwab.com in January 1998, Schwab and eSchwab were replaced with a completely integrated hybrid. Unifying the organization also meant unifying the culture and knowledge base. To make the offline employees more technologically savvy, Schwab provided Internet access and training throughout the organization. By the end of 1998, all of Schwab's branches had Internet access. An intranet, "schWeb," was installed to promote internal communications among employees. And the two very different dress codes at Schwab and eSchwab were abandoned in favor of a company-wide, business-casual standard.

Exhibit 6-13 SCHWAB IT INFRASTRUCTURE

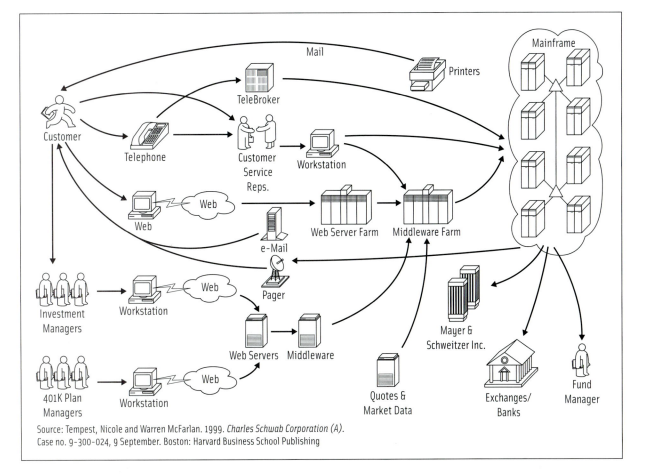

Source: Tempest, Nicole and Warren McFarlan. 1999. *Charles Schwab Corporation (A)*.
Case no. 9-300-024, 9 September. Boston: Harvard Business School Publishing

Exhibit
6-14

TIME LINE FOR SCHWAB INNOVATIONS

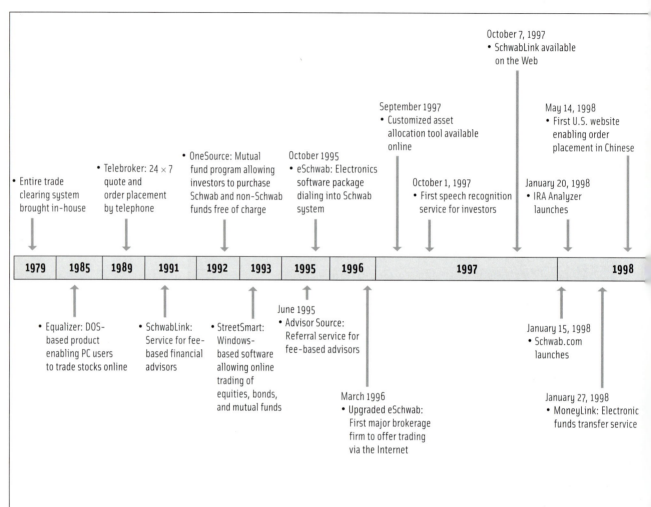

Systems. In late 1997, Schwab's IT systems infrastructure was three tiered with mainframes, middleware servers, and Web servers. Schwab had three mainframes for transaction processing and back office operations, one mainframe for reporting, and three other mainframes for backup, development, and disaster recovery.[38] The transaction processing and back office mainframes were located in Phoenix in two data centers located 20 miles apart that were connected with high-speed fiber lines. This allowed transactions to be quickly rerouted from one mainframe to the other in case of any catastrophic problem at either data center. Furthermore, the two centers were on separate power grids and flood plains and were routed through different telecommunication switching facilities to prevent simultaneous downtime in both locations. Schwab also had eight middleware servers that allowed Web servers to invoke transactions on Schwab's mainframe. One of the main functions of the middleware servers was to validate user passwords. Finally, Schwab had 48 Web servers to handle

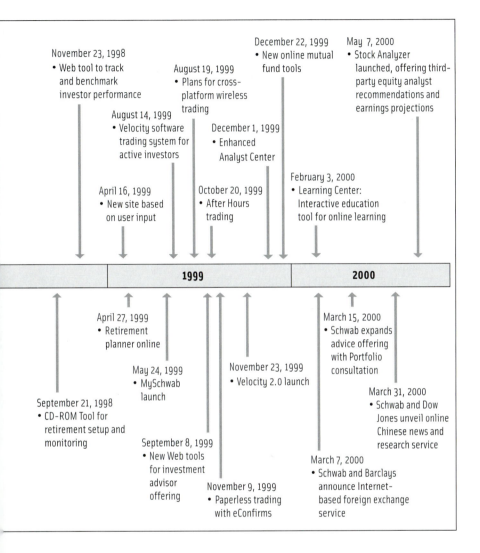

all of the interfaces with customers over the Web and to process all of the data obtained from the middleware servers and mainframes. Exhibit 6-13 illustrates Schwab's IT architecture.

SCHWAB'S INNOVATION

Schwab distinguishes itself by its high investment in technology and its strong performance in innovation. Since the 1980s, Schwab has invented new products and services that no other competitor has addressed. This positioning at the bleeding edge of innovation has played a key role in Schwab's ability to implement its online strategy and to integrate its online and offline operations.

Exhibit 6-14 illustrates the time line of Schwab innovations from 1979 until early 2000. In 1979, Schwab spent $500,000 (its entire net worth at the time) to bring its back office software in-house. In this way, it made sure that it did not have to depend on a third party for technology or innovation. From the mid-1980s through the mid-1990s, Schwab introduced new technology and products that allowed investors to execute and track trades in ways other than physically going to a Schwab branch office and interacting with a customer service representative. In 1989, Schwab launched Telebroker to allow investors to place orders by phone 24 hours a day, 7 days a week. Typically, these innovations offered new convenience to customers while reducing Schwab's overall service costs. In 1992, Schwab pioneered the purchase of Schwab and non-Schwab mutual funds free of charge through its OneSource mutual fund program. Although the mutual fund aggregator model originally faced skepticism and lack of cooperation by mutual fund providers, OneSource proved itself successful and enjoyed participation by more than 40 mutual fund suppliers. In October 1995, Schwab launched eSchwab to become the first major brokerage firm to offer trading via the Internet. The path toward online brokerage had just been opened.

eSchwab was revolutionary, but it was a source of frustration and confusion for customers. Customers were required to open a separate eSchwab account and could not be assisted by Schwab branch office representatives since they would not have access to online account information. These customers received unlimited free customer service via e-mail but could only make one call per month to a live customer service representative. They could get unlimited phone access to customer service representatives, but only if they were willing to open an offline Schwab account and pay $64 per trade rather than the $29.95 for online trades. Investors felt they were forced to make a trade-off between price and service when they wanted both.

Schwab.com was launched on January 15, 1998, to offer high-quality investment information and service at low prices to all investors. The website launch was followed by a suite of newly developed technologies and tools. The new tools helped investors manage their portfolios better and make smarter investment decisions. They included the IRA Analyzer (introduced in January 1998), the online Retirement Planner (launched in April 1999), as well as new tools for independent investment advisors (introduced in September 1999). These products made trading online easier, faster, and more convenient. In January 1998, Schwab introduced MoneyLink to allow investors to transfer funds online. In August 1999, Schwab released the Velocity software, allowing frequent investors to perform trades faster than ever before. In October 1999, Schwab introduced its wireless alert service to contact any individual investor at any time through his or her cell phone to make urgent investment decisions. In November 1999, the eConfirms product enabled paperless trading with e-mail confirmations of executed trades. Schwab's goal with these and future innovations is to expand a platform that allows investors to be well informed while they quickly, securely, conveniently, and seamlessly execute trades through Schwab's online and offline channels.

SUMMARY

1. What is online implementation?

The online implementation process can be divided into two phases. In the first phase, the firm is concerned with the delivery of the offering through the five key components of a delivery system—people, systems, assets, processes, and supply chains. In the second phase, the firm is concerned with the extent to which the offerings and infrastructures are innovative and modified to fit the evolution of the market.

2. Why does implementation matter?

It has been argued that increased speed and intensity of competition in the online environment means implementation mistakes are punished much more severely and quickly than in the offline world. Six implementation challenges are exemplified by online firms: (1) higher visibility to errors, (2) lower switching costs, (3) more dynamic competitive environment, (4) more fluid organizational boundaries, (5) more dynamic market environment, and (6) more complex linkages.

3. What is the "delivery system"?

The delivery system of a company is the most detailed and concrete expression of the company's Value Proposition. The Value Proposition, the Product Offering, and the Business Model each determine the requirements for the construction of the delivery system. The delivery system translates the resource system from a conceptual structure into a concrete configuration of resources, processes and supply chains. Once the strategy has been defined and necessary capabilities identified, it becomes a matter of defining the structures, processes, reward systems, and human resource practices that will produce the needed competencies and capabilities. It is at this stage of the strategy process that strategic intent is turned into a configuration that produces actual consumer and financial results. The five components of a delivery system include: people, systems, assets, processes, and supply chains.

4. What are categories of offline innovation?

Most offline companies classify types of innovation into three categories: (1) Line Extensions, (2) Changing the Basis of Competition, and (3) New Industries. Each of these developmental categories has a different research process and product time frame.

5. What is the offline innovation process?

The offline world typically views innovation in a funnel process with three distinct and successive phases: (1) Innovation by Doodling, (2) Innovation by Design, and (3) Innovation by Direction (see Exhibit 6-7 on page 236). This three-stage process functions like a funnel in that an increasing number of innovations are eliminated during each phase until only the most promising remain and are brought to market.

6. What is the new logic to New Economy innovation?

New Economy innovation shares a similarity with the innovation funnel process but key differences affect the innovation process: 1) high costs make offline firms risk averse but online innovation costs can be dramatically lower; 2) the fluid nature of online companies and the abundance of external capital allow online companies to experiment much more; 3) online organizations can launch innovations and have customers provide direct feedback; 4) online companies can launch early versions of innovations, which are then rapidly improved based on measured customer feedback.

7. What are the New Economy innovation frameworks?

The ability to rapidly and continuously adapt and improve has led to frameworks for innovation that focus more on the coevolution of technology and customers. Christensen frames disruptive technologies as innovations that create an entirely new market through the introduction of a new kind of service or product. Though these disruptive technologies initially can be inferior to established technologies, their performance levels progress faster than market demands and more completely fulfill consumer expectations later in the product's lifecycle.

Dorothy Leonard developed a framework in the offline context, but many of the principles apply in the online environment as well. Leonard categorizes innovation into five groups: (1) User-Driven Enhancement, (2) Developer-Driven Development, (3) User-Context Development, (4) New Application or Combination of Technologies, and (5) Technology/Market Coevolution.

8. What are the New Economy innovation processes?

The erosion of traditional constraints on innovation enables a faster, cheaper, and more adaptive innovation process, but intensified uncertainty also increases the demand to innovate. Two fundamentally different process models attempt to accommodate this additional uncertainty: 1) the flexible development process is one in which the key point is concept development, and implementation of the ideas in the field need to overlap and be tightly integrated; 2) the distributed innovation model is one in which the company tracks the evolution of each source of uncertainty and uses this to guide innovations while bringing all sources of market evolution inside the organization to maintain a continuous fit between the current online offering and the latest innovations.

KEY TERMS

online implementation process

switching costs

delivery system

resource allocation process

human-resource management
    processes

manufacturing and distribution
    processes

payment/billing processing

customer support/handling
    processes

supply-chain models

Business-to-Consumer (B2C)

stock-it-yourself

outsource warehousing

drop shipping

fulfillment intermediaries

salesforce efficiency

service efficiency

Business-to-Business (B2B)

Consumer-to-Business (C2B)

Consumer-to-Consumer (C2C)

innovation

line extensions

changing the basis of competition

new industries

innovation funnel process

innovation by doodling

innovation by design

innovation by direction

waterfall concept of new product
    innovation

disruptive technologies

Dorothy Leonard innovation framework	New Application or Combination of Technologies
User-Driven Enhancement	Technology/Market Coevolution
Developer-Driven Development	flexible development process
User-Context Development	distributed innovation model

Endnotes

[1]Butt, Joseph, L., Jr. 1999. Empowered consumers. In *The Forrester Report* (October): 12.

[2]Brooks, Fred. 1995. *The Mythical Man-Month*. Reading, MA: Addison-Wesley Publishing, p. 18.

[3]Lawrence, Stacy. 2000. E-Commerce spotlight: Hard numbers on e-Christmas in 1999. *Industry Standard*, 24 January.

[4]Anders, George. 1999. eBay struggles to repair image after big crash. *Deseret News*, 16 June, Business section.

[5]Collins, James. 2000. Built to flip. *Fast Company* (March): 131–43.

[6]*Economist.* 1999. Playing i-ball, 6 November, p. 65.

[7]Securities and Exchange Commission. 1999. BUY COM INC. S-1 filing, 27 October. For those who are not within close proximity of Washington D.C., please consider the convenient online version of this document, located at the following URL: *http://www.sec.gov/Archives/edgar/data/1097070/0001017062-99-001796-index.html.*

[8]Morhman, Susan A., Jay R. Galbraith, Edward E. Lawler III et al. 1998. *Tomorrow's organization: Crafting winning capabilities in a dynamic world.* San Francisco: Jossey-Bass Publishers.

[9]Please see the following article that provides a singular exemplification of a B2C complication: large-scale credit-card frauds by customers of an online company. Helft, Miguel. 2000. The real victims of fraud. *Industry Standard*, 6 March.

[10]Technically, many of these retailers such as Amazon do have large warehouses with stock on hand. However, companies such as Amazon are able to take advantage of significant cost differences relative to other retailers since they do not need to maintain expensive retail locations.

[11]Piller, Charles. 1999. Most net retailers all sale, no service. *Los Angeles Times*, 28 June, Home edition, Business section.

[12]Goldman, Abigail. 1999. E-Commerce gets an F without the 'D' word retailing. *Los Angeles Times*, 25 July, Home edition, Business section.

[13]*ibid.*

[14]*ibid.*

[15]Dorsey, David. 1999. The people behind the people behind e-commerce. *Fast Company*, issue no. 25 (June): 184.

[16]Li, Kenneth. 1999. Instant delivery. *Industry Standard*, 10 September.

[17]For further information, please see: Rangan, V. Kasturi and Marie Bell. 1999. *Dell on-line*. Case no. 9-598-116, 26 March. Boston: Harvard Business School Publishing.

[18]King, Julia. 2000. How to do B2B. *Computerworld*, 28 February.

[19]Hill, Miriam. 2000. A new net craze is on the way: Business-to-Business firms hold tremendous potential, but the investing risks are steep. *Philadelphia Inquirer*, 18 January.

[20]Schonfeld, Erick. 2000. How much are your eyeballs worth? *Fortune*, 21 February.

[21]As the following recent Goldman Sachs report on B2B put it: Goldman, Sachs and Co. 1999. *B2B: 2B or not 2B? Version 1.1*, 12 November.

[22]Goldman, Sachs and Co. 1999. *B2B: 2B or not 2B? Version 1.1*, 12 November, p. 14.

[23]Grygo, Eugene. 2000. A buy-sell revolution. *InfoWorld*, 6 March.

[24]Gerdel, Thomas W. 2000. Industry takes to the web; internet fast reshaping traditional supply chain. *Plain Dealer Reporter*, 27 February, final edition.

[25]Tait, Nikki, Louise Kehoe and Tim Burt. 1999. US car monoliths muscle in on the internet revolution: Ford and GM plans to buy from suppliers online may reduce costs further. *Financial Times*, 8 November, International Companies & Finance section.

[26]*Drug Store News.* 1999. The burgeoning e-retail frontier, 25 October, Technology section.

[27]Brown, Eryn. 1999. Big Business meets the e-world. *Fortune*, 8 November.

[28]Rafter, Michelle. 1999. Customer disservice. *Industry Standard*, 10 May.

[29]*ibid.*

[30]Hurst, Mark. Chapter 2: Apple store. In *In search of e-commerce*. This article exists in online form, and can be accessed at the following URL: *http://www.goodexperience.com/reports/isoe/apple/index.html.*

[31]Gundling, Ernest. 2000. *The 3M way to innovation: Balancing people and profit.* Tokyo, Japan: Kodansha Int. Ltd.; New York, USA: Kodansha America, Inc., p. 180.

[32]Bradley, Stephen P., and Richard L. Nolan. 1998. *Sense and respond.* Boston: Harvard Business School Press.

[33]Christensen, Clayton. 2000. Meeting the challenge of disruptive change. *Harvard Business Review* 78, no. 2 (March-April): 72.

[34]Christensen, Clayton. 1997. *The innovator's dilemma.* Boston: Harvard Business School Press, p. xv.

[35]Leonard-Barton, Dorothy. 1998. *Wellsprings of knowledge.* Boston: Harvard Business School Press, pp. 180–212.

[36]See: Iansiti, Marco, and Alan MacCormack. 1998. Product development on Internet time. In *Sense & respond.* Boston: Harvard Business School Press. See also: Iansiti, Marco and Alan MacCormack. 1999. *Living on Internet time: Product development at Netscape, Yahoo!, NetDynamics, and Microsoft.* Case study, no. 9-697-052, 30 June. Boston: Harvard Business School Publishing. URL: *http://www.hbsp. harvard.edu/hbsp/prod_detail.asp?697052.*

[37]Maggioncalda, Jeff and Robert S. Burgelman. 1997. *The Charles Schwab Corporation in 1996.* Case study, no. SM-35 (August). Graduate School of Business, Stanford University, p. 6.

[38]Tempest, Nicole, and Warren McFarlan. 1999. *Charles Schwab Corporation (A).* Case no. 9-300-024, 9 September. Boston: Harvard Business School Publishing, pp. 9–10.

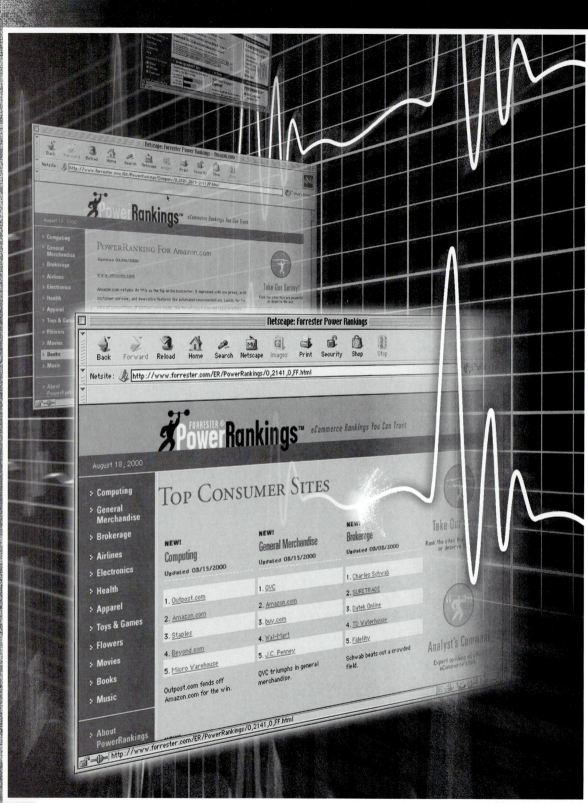

7

Metrics

This chapter focuses on ways companies can assess the progress and health of their online businesses. To determine the financial progress of their company, most companies routinely analyze benchmarks such as sales, margins, profit, and market share. However, to judge the strategic health of the company, senior executives must analyze metrics that reflect the entire strategy of the company—how customers perceive the value proposition, the market-place offering, and the effectiveness of implementation. In this chapter, we introduce the concept of a Performance Dashboard that

senior managers can use to assess the overall strategic health of the company. The Performance Dashboard is composed of five categories of metrics: (1) opportunity, (2) business model, (3) branding and implementation, (4) customer interface and outcomes, and (5) financial metrics. We conclude the chapter with an overview of the firms that provide metrics services for the New Economy. These metrics can be used to make a comprehensive assessment of the strategic as well as the financial health of individual companies.

QUESTIONS

Please consider the following questions as you read this chapter:

1. Should senior managers be concerned about metrics?

2. How can we assess the health of New Economy firms?

3. What are the steps to implement the Performance Dashboard?

4. What are three sources of metrics information that firms can use to chart their progress?

This chapter was coauthored by Bernie Jaworski, Jeffrey Rayport, Leo Griffin, and Yannis Dosios.

In Chapter 6, we analyzed the key components of business model implementation. In this chapter, we turn our attention to the **metrics** that senior managers can use to evaluate the progress of their businesses. This is not a straightforward issue. First, senior and stock market analysts tend to have a bias toward financial metrics. Clearly, this emphasis is important. However, focusing only on financial measures is limited in two fundamental respects. First, financial measures reflect the performance history of the company in the marketplace but do not provide managers with an early warning system by which to take corrective action before financial disappointing returns are realized.[1] Financial results are essentially a measure of the success of past strategies.

Second, financial measures are output measures that do not reflect the strategy of the company. In order to assess the progress of an online company, one needs to develop company-specific metrics that precisely track the strategy of the company.[2] To return for a moment to our flower example from Chapter 3, the value proposition of 1-800-flowers focused on freshness of flowers and reasonable prices. Hence, one of the early warning metrics for 1-800-flowers would be the degree to which customers in the company's target segment perceive that 1-800-flowers is outperforming competitors on freshness and reasonable prices. Because the value proposition is only one component of the overall strategy, other metrics would also need to be developed for each strategy component, such as the offering, resource system, and implementation.

The purpose of this chapter is to provide a framework by which one can assess the health of an online business. The framework is composed of five categories of metrics—opportunity, business model, branding and implementation, customer, and financial. Opportunity metrics focus on the conditions in the customer and competitor environments. Business-model metrics include topics related to the value cluster, marketspace offering, resource system and capabilities, and partnerships. Branding and implementation metrics focus on supply-chain performance, organizational dynamics, and marketing communication effectiveness (including branding). Customer metrics focus on output measures that relate to the customer experience (e.g., overall satisfaction, average dollar amount of purchases, stickiness) as well as metrics that relate to the customer interface. Finally, financial metrics capture the financial performance of the company, including such measures as sales, profit, and margins.

The chapter is organized as follows. In the first section, we address the question of why metrics matter. In the second section, we introduce the Balanced Scorecard as a reference framework, discuss its potential limitations in the New Economy, and introduce the Performance Dashboard. In the third section, we focus on a five-step process by which to implement the Performance Dashboard. In the fourth section, we apply this five-step implementation process to Schwab. We then conclude with an overview of the alternative sources of information that firms can use as inputs to the metrics process.

SHOULD SENIOR MANAGERS BE CONCERNED ABOUT METRICS?

Before we discuss alternative metric frameworks, it is important to consider whether metrics are significant to an organization. On one hand, we could argue that organization metrics are always important, because they represent the performance targets of the company. That is, each month any particular dot-com company might look at a handful of metrics to guide its progress with such measures as percent increase in revenue, percent increase in unique visitors, length of time that visitors remain on the site, and cost of customer acquisition.

However, it is vital that we stress that metrics only matter to the extent that they are used by senior management to either reward employees or take strategic action (e.g., change processes, strategy, product offerings). In other words, metrics devoid of follow-through action by senior management are of limited value.

Metrics Drive Behavior in a Number of Ways

Metrics can produce very positive results for an organization. In this section, we isolate five ways in which metrics can have a positive effect on the growth and vitality of an organization.[3]

Help Define Business Model.
The act of specifying concrete goals with precise measurement can help senior management refine the business model of a company. Companies often struggle with their choice of value proposition or cluster. Focusing attention on measurement can help increase the precision of the value proposition.

A good example is Dell Online Premier. Users from large accounts can access their password-protected company-specific site on Dell Online Premier to search, select, purchase, track shipping, and receive service. Moreover, the entire process is electronically enabled through interorganization applications (e.g., order tracking, funds transfering, and shipping).

Should Dell's value cluster focus on price, speed of delivery, level of custom configuration of the PC, customer service, or assurance of reliability? Certainly, one could implement metrics that reflect all five of these benefits. At the same time, one could ask which is the most important in rank order. Our point is simply to note that focusing on the measurement of key targets helps management clarify their strategic priorities.

Help Communicate Strategy.
Clearly documented performance targets can go a long way toward communicating the particular goals and strategy of a company. Once performance metrics are specified, they should be communicated as widely as possible within the organization. This not only communicates the strategy to the workforce, but also helps employees buy in to the metric-setting process.

Help Track Performance.
One of the unique features of the online world is the availability of instantaneous feedback concerning site performance. Metrics concerning usage, visitors, length of time on site, average sales, page views, and so on are constantly available. Thus, in sharp contrast to traditional offline models, firms are able to track performance in real time and make appropriate modifications in tactics or strategy.

Help Increase Accountability.
Firmwide metrics need to be linked to the performance appraisal system. If the metrics are tied to the reward system, then the metrics have weight behind them. Importantly, individual performance appraisals can be tied to companywide, team-specific, and individual metrics. That is, general performance measures such as sales growth and amount of sales are likely to have firmwide accountability. On the other hand, specific measures related to site usability can be tied to the interactive design function while customer service metrics can be tied directly to the customer service department.

Help Align Objectives. Finally, clear, precise metrics can help align individual objectives, departmental functional goals, and companywide strategic activities as a whole. For example, understanding that one's firm has made it a priority to increase its look-to-book ratio, e.g., the number of customers who buy relative to the number who visit, often expressed as a ratio of 100 visitors (a site with a look-to-book ratio of 5:100 has 5 buyers per 100 visitors), enables various departmental functional groups and individual employees to adjust their behaviors accordingly.

Current Challenges to Specifying Metrics for Online Businesses

While it is clear that there are important benefits in articulating metrics that link to business strategy, many online firms do not have a systematic approach to develop, assess, and apply metrics. In this section, we explore the reasons why some firms have not made an explicit commitment to metrics.

Companies' Strategies Change Rapidly. One classic argument against the use of metrics relates to doing business on "Internet time." It is now common for business models to change often and quickly, given the emergence of new competitors and rapidly evolving customer tastes. In this environment, it is difficult to think of a long-term commitment to a strategy, much less the metrics that follow. Free PC is a recent example. Initially, the revenue model was to give away PCs for free—in exchange for the forced-viewing advertisements. However, as Bill Gross, founder of IdeaLabs, admitted, the growth of new users could not sustain the business model. Hence, the business was sold and a new strategy emerged.

Measurement Is Resource-Intensive. While the Internet has made customer data much more available, making the data usable and actionable remains a significant issue. In many cases, capturing metrics data requires the setup and maintenance of systems and procedures that require significant capital investment and human resources. Moreover, once the data is mined, management must set aside time to review the data closely and then react accordingly. Each of these issues—data capture, data mining, and information use—requires the time and commitment of senior executives.

Online Measurement Systems Are Vulnerable. There is some evidence to suggest that online data capture (e.g., page views, usage data, demographics) can be compromised. Examples include sites that artificially boost their number of unique users (e.g., employees' access to sites), users submitting false demographic data, and hackers tampering with system data.

Soft Metrics Are Not Valued by the Investment Community. Generally, the investment community is most comfortable with the reporting of hard numbers related to revenues, margins, number of visitors, length of time on site, customer acquisition costs, and other easily quantifiable measures. Not as highly valued are the softer metrics of customer perception such as ease of use of site versus that of competitors' sites, belief that the site provides the best value, and other market research measures. But, curiously, these softer measures that reflect customers' perceptions of the site are frequently the best early warning indicators of site performance.

Meaningful Metrics Change on Internet Time. Metrics considered relevant and appropriate to use in tracking a site's success often change. Less than two years ago, companies used hits as the basic metric of success. The basic metric then shifted to page views. Now conversion rates are considered the appropriate measure. The point is, while traditional financial metrics remain timeless, customer metrics tend to change as firms learn to interpret the data.

One small case in point, the concept of stickiness, or length of visitor time on the site, makes perfect sense as a measure of success for eBay. However, the same measure would not be true for American Airlines (*www.aa.com*). Indeed, frequent travelers want to book tickets, cash in travel stickers, and check mileage. The last thing these travelers want is to stay on the site for an extended period of time. Moreover, the number of page views would probably be a measure of a frustrated consumer rather than an interested one. Our point is that even well-regarded customer metrics need to be carefully assessed when applied to the particular site.

HOW CAN WE ASSESS THE HEALTH OF NEW ECONOMY FIRMS?

In this section, we introduce the Performance Dashboard as a framework to judge the progress and health of an online business. We use the dashboard metaphor to describe the real-time navigation task that confronts the management team of a dot-com enterprise. Analogous to an automotive dashboard, the framework provides vital business performance feedback to the firm, which enables quick confirmation of success or the immediate identification of corrective actions needed. We begin our discussion by reviewing Kaplan and Norton's seminal work on the Balanced Scorecard.

The Balanced Scorecard

Kaplan and Norton introduced the **Balanced Scorecard** in response to their perception that managers overwhelmingly focus on short-term financial performance. To address this concern, they argued that firms must balance their financial perspective by analyzing other domains of the business, including internal business processes and customer responses. In particular, they introduced four categories of metrics that they believed more accurately captured the performance of companies (see Exhibit 7-1): financial, customer, internal business systems, and learning and growth. This approach not only added perspective to a restricted financial focus but also provided managers with an early warning system that allowed for corrective measures to be taken before poor financial results were realized. A key feature of the Kaplan and Norton approach was to start with the strategy of the firm and then derive the metrics in the four areas. Below we describe in detail each of the four areas.

Financial Metrics. **Financial metrics** are designed to assess the financial performance of the company. Typical financial measures include revenue, revenue growth, gross margins, operating income, net margin, earnings per share, and cash flow. Financial measures reflect strategic choices from the most recent planning period and, to some degree, an accumulation of all previous planning periods. Hence,

Exhibit
7-1

THE BALANCED SCORECARD
STRATEGY IN OPERATIONAL TERMS

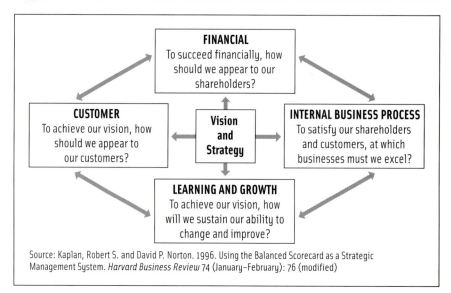

Source: Kaplan, Robert S. and David P. Norton. 1996. Using the Balanced Scorecard as a Strategic Management System. *Harvard Business Review* 74 (January–February): 76 (modified)

Amazon's recent financial performance in 2000 is a function not just of the past 12 months but of the previous five years, since its launch in 1995. Finally, financial measures are used by all stakeholders of the company, including employees, customers, and partnerships. However, these metrics are the most heavily weighted and analyzed by the investment community.

Customer Metrics. **Customer metrics** are intended to assess the management of customer relationships by the firm. With the Kaplan and Norton scheme, these measures typically focus on a set of core measurements including market share, customer acquisition, customer satisfaction, and customer profitability. These are general measures that reflect the overall health of the customer base. Kaplan and Norton also point out that these measures need to be customized to the target segment. To return to our Dell example, a large client such as Boeing would likely have fairly large customer acquisition costs but high profitability if the relationship is solidified. In contrast, smaller clients may have lower acquisition costs but also a lower total lifetime value of the customer.

Internal Business Process Metrics. **Internal business process metrics** focus on operations inside the company. In particular, this set of metrics focuses on the critical value-adding activities that lead to customer satisfaction and enhanced shareholder value. Kaplan and Norton divide these metrics into three broad groups: innovation, operations, and postsale service.

- *Innovation.* Innovation metrics measure how well the company identifies customer needs and creates associated new products. Innovation measures could include customers' perceptions of the innovativeness of the company or quantitative measures of innovativeness (e.g., percent of product sales from new products, percent of new products versus competitors).

- *Operations.* Operations metrics measure the quality of the entire supply-chain process through to delivery of products to the customer. This could include measures that reflect customer order processing, order cycle time, delivery time, and order error percent.
- *Postsale Service.* Postsale service metrics measure the quality of the service the company is offering to their customers. This includes return processing, warranty processing, turnaround time for e-mail questions, and payment processing.

Learning and Growth Metrics.

Learning and growth metrics broadly capture the employee, information systems, and motivation. Employee metrics relate to selection, training, retention, and satisfaction. Information system metrics capture the quality of the infrastructure that must be built to create long-term growth and improvement. Measures would include timeliness, accuracy, and utility of data. Motivation broadly captures employee motivation, empowerment, and alignment. Metrics would relate to alignment of company goals and incentives with personal employee goals.

Limitations to the Balanced Scorecard in the New Economy

The Balanced Scorecard has become a classic tool for senior managers. However, the Balanced Scorecard becomes less useful as one attempts to apply its framework to the online world. Below are some identified shortcomings.

- **No Clear Definition of Strategy or Business Models.** A key theme of the Balanced Scorecard is that the entire scorecard is based on the strategy of the firm. However, Kaplan and Norton do not clearly define the strategy or business model. Without this definition, it is difficult to assess whether the four categories of metrics accurately capture the critical aspects of the business strategy or the business model.
- **Unclear Location of Organizational Capabilities or Resources in the Framework.** Organizational capabilities and resources span a variety of domains, including internal business processes, customer relationships, partnerships, and the unique selection of markets (e.g., market-sensing capabilities).[4] Thus, capabilities often extend beyond internal business processes. It is unclear where capabilities are located in the framework.
- **Unclear Where Partnerships Reside in the Framework.** Strategic partnerships are a critical measure of a firm's ability to compete in the New Economy. However, partnerships are not addressed in the Balanced Scorecard framework.

In sum, the Balanced Scorecard has taken the important first step toward the development of a set of metrics to assess the effectiveness and efficiency of New Economy businesses. In the next section, we introduce a framework that resolves the issues noted above.

The Performance Dashboard

Similar to the Balanced Scorecard, the **Performance Dashboard** is intended to reflect the health of a business. We discussed the Balanced Scorecard and now address each of its limitations through features of the Performance Dashboard. We also review the five categories of metrics that reflect the strategy framework of this book.

The Strategy Framework Drives the Necessary Metrics. While the Balanced Scorecard has no clear definition of the strategy or business model, the Performance Dashboard utilizes the strategy framework to derive the necessary metrics. In Chapters 2 through 6, we articulated a strategy process that is captured in an organizing framework for the textbook (see Exhibit 1-7). In the proposed framework, there are six critical steps to the strategy process: (1) opportunity assessment, (2) business-model specification, (3) customer-interface design, (4) market communications and branding, (5) implementation, and (6) evaluation.

These six steps represent a strategy process for New Economy businesses and can be used to identify the categories that map onto and directly link to the strategy. Relevant metrics categories include: (1) opportunity metrics, (2) business-model metrics, (3) customer-interface and outcome metrics, (4) branding and implementation metrics, and (5) financial metrics (see Exhibit 7-2).

Capabilities Are Featured in the Resource System of the Business Model. While the Balanced Scorecard is unclear in specifying the location of organizational capabilities or resources, the Performance Dashboard identifies the capabilities featured in the resource system of the business model. Firm-level capabilities are defined during the third step of the business model. Hence, capabilities of the firm are highlighted and integrated into the Performance Dashboard metrics. Recall that the isolation of these capabilities is essential and key to determining the drivers of the customer benefits.

Partnerships Are Featured in the Resource System of the Business Model. While the Balanced Scorecard is unclear about where partnerships reside in its framework, partnerships are featured in the resource system of the business model in the Performance Dashboard. It explicitly includes partnership measurements in the business-model metrics. Recall that in Chapter 3 we isolated the firm-level

 Exhibit 7-2 THE PERFORMANCE DASHBOARD

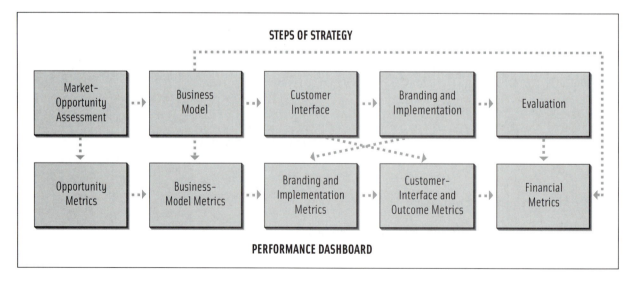

capabilities that related to the various benefits. We also noted that it is at this step that partnerships need to be considered to fill in where the firm does not have the requisite capabilities. Hence, partnerships are explicitly considered in the Performance Dashboard measures.

Components of the Performance Dashboard

The Performance Dashboard is composed of five categories of metrics: opportunity, business model, customer interface and outcomes, branding and implementation, and financial.

Opportunity Metrics.
Recall that we defined market-opportunity analysis as the firm's ability to discern an unfulfilled need in the marketplace. The ability to discern unserved needs is critical to the strategy process. This is not a one-time event within the strategy process, but rather a continual process, because market conditions ceaselessly evolve. For example, by constantly expanding its offerings to include complementary gifts, the 1-800-flowers site extended its segment focus beyond the core offerings.

Market-opportunity metrics assess the degree to which the firm can accurately gauge the market opportunity. Generic indicators include the ability of the firm to target the most attractive segments, the ability of the firm to understand and map competitors' strategy evolution, and the ability of the firm to track the evolution of target-segment needs.

Business-Model Metrics.
Business-model metrics capture the subcomponents of the business model: the value proposition, Egg Diagram, resource system, and financial metrics. In this section, we review the metrics that would capture the value proposition, Egg Diagram, and resource system. The financial metrics are critically important to the firm and, as such, represent an entire category of metrics in their own right (see discussion below).

Value Proposition or Cluster Benefits Metrics. The value proposition is composed of three parts: the target segment, benefits offered, and capabilities that drive the benefits. Metrics for this assessment would focus on customer perceptions of the benefits that a given site offers relative to competitors. Capabilities in the value proposition will be addressed in our discussion of the resource system.

Thus, to return to 1-800-flowers, the key customer benefits are: lower prices, fresh flowers, a broad assortment of gifts, and widespread access. Here, management would be concerned about the firm's performance relative to the competitors' on these four benefits, as perceived by target customers.

Marketspace-Offering Metrics. This phase of the business model is captured in the Egg Diagram reviewed in Chapter 3. Metrics should capture all phases of the customer decision process as well as the features and attributes of the offering.

Customer-decision-process metrics would reflect the entire decision process from prepurchase (e.g., customer acquisition costs, satisfaction with selection), purchase (e.g., satisfaction, site usability), and postpurchase (e.g., loyalty, customer response rates, percent of returns, percent of shopping carts filled versus products purchased, lifetime value of the customer). Offering metrics focus more on the

SOUND BYTE

Which Metrics to Look For;
Lise Buyer, Director and Senior
Analyst, Credit Suisse First
Boston Technology Group

Every month I put together a chart that looks at a bunch of different measures, looking for one that will correlate with the actual valuation of the stock. I care a lot about revenue per customer. I don't care about page views and I don't care about reach because unless you pay your employees with page views they're not going to matter at the end of the day. Here, take 59 page views and you knock yourself out.

So, I care about revenue per customer, I care about gross profitability per customer. And eventually, I will be doing the operating. At AOL, I can do the lifetime value of a customer. I can at least attempt to do that, and that's how I value that company. With most of the Internet stocks, particularly those that are advertising supported, for now I'll calculate the gross margin per customer less the customer acquisition cost.

(continued on page 267)

nuts-and-bolts features, attributes, and functionality of the site. Thus, to return to our Egg Diagram, the offering metrics would capture performance on the products and services ring of the Egg Diagram. For 1-800-flowers, this would include customer evaluations of the gift recommendations section, FAQs, ease of commerce transaction, and member specials.

Resource-System Metrics. The resource system is based on the benefits offered to consumers. From these benefits, the firm would analyze the capabilities that are necessary to supply the benefits. These benefits can be offered by the firm or its partners.

In this phase of metrics building, the firm should track its performance on the most critical capabilities and associated activities. In the context of 1-800-flowers (see Exhibit 3-3 on page 80), the capabilities include logistics, sourcing, brand name, multiple contact points, media partnerships, product partnerships, and an online gift center. At this stage, the firm would want to track performance on each of these key capabilities. Also, recall that capabilities are provided by both the firm and partners and, therefore, the firm would also want to consider performance metrics for these critical partnerships.

Financial-Model Metrics. Given the significance of financial measures, we address them as a separate category in the dashboard.

Customer-Interface and Customer-Outcome Metrics. Customer-interface and customer-outcome metrics capture two forms of metrics. The first class of metrics measures the customer's experience with the technology interface; that is, the customer's response to the 7Cs of the interface. The second class of metrics captures output metrics such as the overall levels of satisfaction, average order size, and customer profitability. Below we review each class of metric.

Customer-Interface Metrics. In Chapter 4, we provided a detailed review of the 7Cs of the customer interface. In this chapter we are concerned with customer perception of the firm's performance on each of the seven characteristics. For example, how would customers rate the level of customization on the firm's site versus the levels of competitors' sites in the category? Is the content adequate? Is the level of community adequate? Obviously, a host of specific measures could be created for each C. The challenge for managers is to select a subset of the most critical interface metrics. A starting point for this winnowing exercise is at the value proposition of the firm.

Customer-Outcome Metrics. The customer-interface metrics capture the process measures that the firm believes will produce favorable customer responses such as satisfaction and loyalty. Thus, a great community site will lead to more favorable overall levels of satisfaction with the site. Here, we focus attention on both the subjective and objective customer-outcome metrics. Subjective measures include customer satisfaction and, in regards to the site, an overall evaluation of the customer's experience at the site. Objective, quantitative measures include customer acquisition costs, average order size, customer profitability, and number of visits per month. These latter metrics can be aggregated into an overall lifetime value of the customer measure.

Branding and Implementation Metrics. Branding and implementation metrics focus on the supply-chain performance, organizational dynamics, and marketing-

communication effectiveness (including branding). In Chapter 5, we introduced approaches to developing branding; while in Chapter 6, we discussed implementing the plan through developing the delivery system and by creating an organization capable of continuous innovation. Fulfillment of the brand promise could include metrics related to the brand's strength, for example, widespread customer awareness of the brand. Delivery-system metrics track business processes, internal organization, and supply-chain management. Finally, innovation metrics could capture the firm's ability to rapidly innovate, even in a potentially discontinuous fashion.

Financial Metrics.

Financial metrics capture the revenues, costs, profits, and balance-sheet metrics of the firm. These are the most critical metrics for the long-term success of the firm. However, as noted at the outset, these results are a function of the accumulated strategy decisions of the firm. Hence, while they focus management attention on what results need to be correct, they offer no guidance to factors that can influence their correction.

Life Cycle of a Company

Exhibit 7-3 illustrates that online firms pass through four stages of development in the **life cycle of a company.** These stages are identified as **startup, acquisition of customers, monetization,** and **maturity.** Some authors have argued that the relative weight of the metrics vary by the stage of the business. For example, in the startup phase, the market-opportunity metrics and the articulation of the business model are critical. In the customer acquisition stage, customer acquisition is critical and financial metrics are not as critical. However, at the maturity stage, customer retention and cost control become comparatively as important as customer acquisition costs.

(continued from page 266)

So what do you have left over to actually build the infrastructure of your business? And there is actually significant correlation. If you look for instance at Yahoo!, Yahoo! on an annualized basis generates about six dollars per customer in this personal profitability, gross margin minus sales and marketing expense per customer. Lycos generates about a dollar per customer after sales and marketing expense.

Interestingly, if you then look at the market caps on those stocks, more often than not, the value that the market places on each Yahoo! customer is six times [what] they place on Lycos. So there is some rationality out there. Does it work all the time? No. But it's a step in the right direction.

Get the full interview at www.marketspaceu.com

Exhibit 7-3

LIFE CYCLE OF A COMPANY

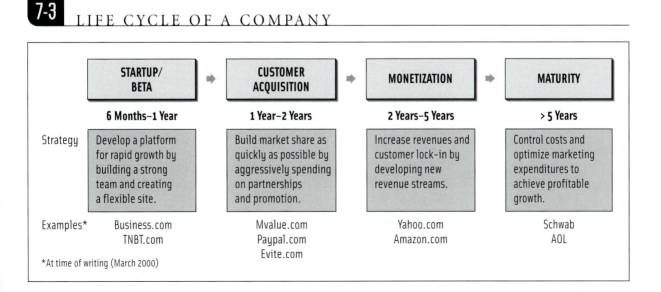

	STARTUP/ BETA	CUSTOMER ACQUISITION	MONETIZATION	MATURITY
	6 Months–1 Year	1 Year–2 Years	2 Years–5 Years	> 5 Years
Strategy	Develop a platform for rapid growth by building a strong team and creating a flexible site.	Build market share as quickly as possible by aggressively spending on partnerships and promotion.	Increase revenues and customer lock-in by developing new revenue streams.	Control costs and optimize marketing expenditures to achieve profitable growth.
Examples*	Business.com TNBT.com	Mvalue.com Paypal.com Evite.com	Yahoo.com Amazon.com	Schwab AOL

*At time of writing (March 2000)

POINT OF VIEW

Gurley on Customer Conversion Rates

Bill Gurley, a well-respected venture capitalist at Benchmark Capital, believes that the single most important metric of website performance is the "conversion rate".[5] Conversion rate is defined as the number of visitors who come to a website and take action (i.e., make a transaction) as a proportion of the total number of visitors to the site. This number has also been termed the look-to-book ratio.

According to Gurley, average conversion rates are in the 3 to 5 percent range. The very best websites achieve conversion rates of 10 percent or more. Gurley argues that the conversion rate captures information on many qualitative aspects of the sites (i.e., in our terminology, on effectiveness and efficiency of the 7Cs). He believes that "no other single metric captures so many aspects of the quality of the website in a single number."

In particular, Gurley asserts that five variables affect the conversion rate: user interface, performance, convenience, advertising, and word of mouth. When a user interface is easy to use, conversion rates increase. Gurley's performance variable is similar to our Chapter 4 performance dimension, namely, sites that

are extremely slow will tend to have lower conversion rates. Convenient functionality, such as Amazon's patented single-click shopping, also increases conversion. Finally, two key forms of marketing communication, standard online and offline advertising and word of mouth (both viral and offline), are particularly important in enhancing the conversion rate.

The impact of conversion rates on customer acquisition costs can be enormous. Table 7-1 shows the impact that increasing the conversion rate from 2 percent to 4 percent and 8 percent can have on marketing costs for a typical e-commerce site.

Consider the following example. A successful advertising campaign costing $10,000 might result in 5,000 unique visitors to a company's website. A site with a conversion rate of 2 percent will make 100 transactions as a result of these visits, while a site with an 8 percent conversion rate will make 400 transactions from the same number of visits. The site with a 2 percent conversion rate spends 100 percent of its revenues on marketing, while a site with 8 percent conversion spends a much more sensible 25 percent of its revenues on marketing.

Table 7-1 BILL GURLEY ON THE POWER OF CONVERSION RATES

	Conversion Rate		
	2%	4%	8%
Advertising Costs	$10,000	$10,000	$10,000
Visitors	5,000	5,000	5,000
Transactions	100	200	400
Cost/Transaction	$100	$50	$25
Revenue	$10,000	$20,000	$40,000
Marketing/Revenue (%)	100%	50%	25%
Average transaction size = $100			

Source: Gurley, J. William. 2000. The Most Powerful Metric of All. CNET News.com, 21 February

URL: http://www.news.com/Perspectives/Column/0,176,403,00/html?tag5st.ne

WHAT ARE THE STEPS TO IMPLEMENT THE PERFORMANCE DASHBOARD?

In this section, we provide an overview of how a company would implement the Performance Dashboard. As noted above, it is important to develop these metrics based on the strategy of the firm. The strategy, however, is likely to be influenced by the life cycle of the company.

Exhibit 7-4 provides a blueprint or road map to the metric development process. The five steps of the process are illustrated on the top row of the figure. Next, we show a more detailed flow of the types of questions, sample metrics, leading indicators, and specific performance targets. Keep in mind that this is simply an illustration and any metrics that followed would need to be tied specifically to the strategy. The following is a five-step process to implementing the Performance Dashboard.

Step One: Articulate Business Strategy

The first step in the process is to articulate the business strategy. The business strategy is composed of six stages: market-opportunity assessment, business model, customer-interface design, branding, implementation, and evaluation. The business strategy was the focus of Chapters 2 through 6.

Step Two: Translate Strategy into Desired Outcomes

The second step in the process is to specify key actions and desired outcomes in specific performance areas. For example, we have identified five areas where desired outcomes can be targeted. Consider, for example, the customer-interface design and the outcomes area. Here we may target increased levels of customer conversion, retention, and customer profitability. Note, we are not setting the performance target levels (e.g., increase conversion rates from 2 to 4 percent), rather we are simply specifying the outcome that we want to affect.

Step Three: Devise Metrics

Step three takes the outcome areas and identifies specific metrics that reflect the desired outcomes. Thus, during this step, one would specify the exact measurement (or often a set of metrics) that one would use to track the desired outcome. Again, we are not specifying the exact level of the metric that we desire (that will occur in step five) but rather isolating the metrics that can be gathered, measured, and tracked over time.

Take, for example, the conversion rate. We noted earlier that the conversion rate is typically measured in terms of look-to-book ratios. That is, how many customers buy, relative to the number of visitors? This is seemingly straightforward in that it entails tracking the log files of the website and simply calculating how many people conducted e-commerce transactions relative to the number of site visitors.

However, this conversion rate metric can be complicated in several ways. First, does the firm want to separate completely new users from previous users and buyers? What is a reasonable look-to-book ratio of all completely new visitors versus a look-to-book that includes all visitors? Should this look-to-book vary by sections of the site? For example, should the look-to-book ratio be the same for each product

Exhibit 7-4

BLUEPRINT TO THE PERFORMANCE DASHBOARD

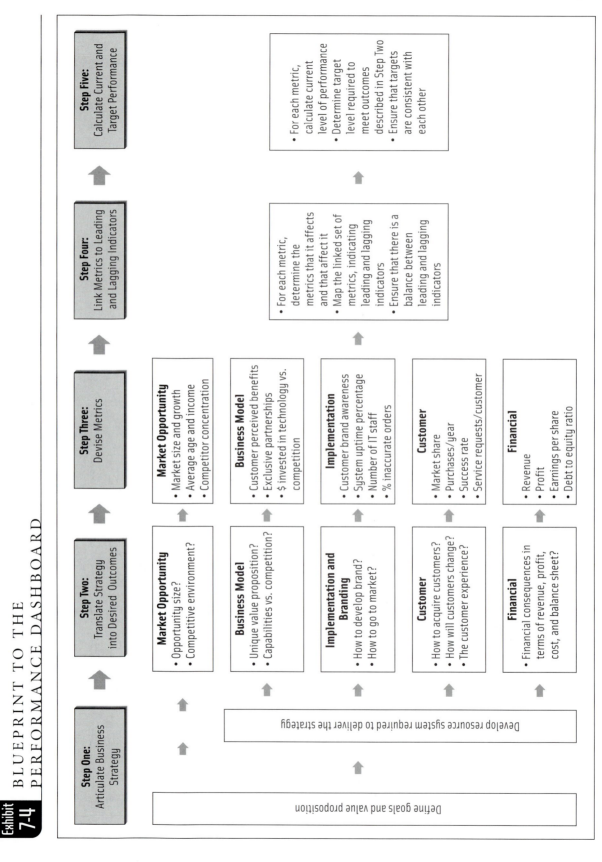

Step One: Articulate Business Strategy

Step Two: Translate Strategy into Desired Outcomes

Step Three: Devise Metrics

Step Four: Link Metrics to Leading and Lagging Indicators

Step Five: Calculate Current and Target Performance

Market Opportunity
- Opportunity size?
- Competitive environment?

Market Opportunity
- Market size and growth
- Average age and income
- Competitor concentration

Business Model
- Unique value proposition?
- Capabilities vs. competition?

Business Model
- Customer perceived benefits
- Exclusive partnerships
- $ invested in technology vs. competition

Implementation and Branding
- How to develop brand?
- How to go to market?

Implementation
- Customer brand awareness
- System uptime percentage
- Number of IT staff
- % inaccurate orders

Customer
- How to acquire customers?
- How will customers change?
- The customer experience?

Customer
- Market share
- Purchases/year
- Success rate
- Service requests/customer

Financial
- Financial consequences in terms of revenue, profit, cost, and balance sheet?

Financial
- Revenue
- Profit
- Earnings per share
- Debt to equity ratio

- For each metric, determine the metrics that it affects and that affect it
- Map the linked set of metrics, indicating leading and lagging indicators
- Ensure that there is a balance between leading and lagging indicators

- For each metric, calculate current level of performance
- Determine target level required to meet outcomes described in Step Two
- Ensure that targets are consistent with each other

Define goals and value proposition

Develop resource system required to deliver the strategy

category? Does the firm need to target different look-to-book ratios depending upon the level of site traffic?

Note that look-to-book is a rather straightforward metric. It gets more complicated when one looks at qualitative measures, such as employee or customer satisfaction. Let's say a company targets an increase in customer satisfaction from 80 to 95 percent. How does the firm translate this desired outcome into metrics that everyone in the organization buys into? Should it be a general measure of "how satisfied are you with the site?" Or should it ask a series of questions about satisfaction with the site's usability, content, products, ease of use, and so on, and then aggregate these measures into a customer satisfaction index?

Our point is not to make this process more complex. Rather, while it seems straightforward to link outcomes with desired metrics, the selection of metrics requires a great deal of management attention. Metrics must be established for all the desired outcomes targeted across the stages of business strategy.

Step Four: Link Metrics to Leading and Lagging Indicators

Step four is to determine the leading indicators of a particular metric and to map the entire set of metrics, including focal and leading indicators. Thus, if conversion rates is the target metric, one also needs to identify leading indicators such as levels of advertising expenditure and degree of positive (and negative) word of mouth. More often than not, the financial measures are lagging measures of business performance.

Step Five: Calculate Current and Target Performance

Step five is to calculate the current level and the target level of performance for selected metrics. Thus, the firm identifies the current conversion rates, advertising expenditure, and degree of positive word of mouth. At this stage, one also attaches specific numeric levels with each of the key desired outcomes. For example, one might state that the customer conversion rate should move from 2 to 4 percent, that customer retention or repeat use should increase from 15 to 20 percent, and that one should move from 10 to 30 percent customer profitability in the ensuing time period.

WHAT ARE THREE SOURCES OF METRICS INFORMATION THAT FIRMS CAN USE TO CHART THEIR PROGRESS?

We now continue on to discuss sources of industry standard metrics and benchmark values. As noted earlier, traditional financial metrics are common and easy to acquire while more qualitative metrics can be more difficult to obtain. Firms are often in a position to collect metrics on many of the targeted areas noted above. That is, firms are likely to track their value proposition versus competition, customer satisfaction with the site, site usability, and financial outcomes. However, it is also useful for the firm to complement these internal data sources with market-level data from third-party sources. Acquisition of external industry data allows the firm to compare its performance relative to the performance of other sites. For example, Forrester publishes detailed ratings on all the flower websites. Each flower site can obtain this objective data that compares its site to others on ratings devised and scored by Forrester, an objective third-party information provider.

In this section, we review three types of data sources for the metrics assessment. Following this discussion, we map the available Internet research sources to the various metric categories. Finally, we conclude with an overview of a firm in each of the three data source categories.

Online Information

Market Research.
Online **market research** firms collect primary customer data through online surveys or customer submissions. These firms tend to have a strong emphasis on site usability, customer satisfaction, and traffic level. Examples include Bizrate (*www.bizrate.com*), Media Metrix (*www.mediametrix.com/landing.jsp*), and AC Nielsen (*www.acnielsen.com*).

Table 7-2 is an example of the type of market-level findings produced by Media Metrix. The table shows the top 25 websites ranked according to the number of unique visitors to the site in a given month (unique visitors are counted only once). AOL is the top site with over 56 million unique visitors each month. NBC Internet is the most visited site excepting such ISPs and portals as Lycos, Yahoo!, and the Go Network.

Analyst Reports.
Analyst reports are data sources that blend primary market data on a particular topic with an analyst's view of the market. Thus, for example, Jupiter Communications (*www.jup.com*) produces a series of reports on various topics related to the Internet. These reports cover topics such as network infrastructure (e.g., broadband applications report), media convergence (e.g. AOL Time Warner Alliance), and trend data on Internet use (e.g., European use of online banking). Typically, analyst-report organizations conduct primary research and/or use site traffic information to produce an analyst report. Firms in this space include the Aberdeen Group, Forrester, Frost & Sullivan, and IDC.

Financial Information.
These data sources principally provide statutory filings of **financial information** on particular companies or aggregated financial data across industries. Reports may appear with or without accompanying analyst commentary. The data collected generally includes income statement, balance sheet, and statement of cash flow information. Among the providers are Hoover's Online (*www.hoovers.com*), Edgar Online (*www.edgar-online.com*), and broker/analyst reports from leading brokerage houses (e.g., DLJ Direct [*www.dljdirect.com*]).

To provide a richer feel for available Internet data services, we turn to a more detailed look at three companies. Here, we focus on Bizrate.com. Bizrate.com bills itself as the "people's portal" to e-commerce. Bizrate.com rates e-businesses by asking tens of thousands of customers about their shopping experiences. This is accomplished by asking every customer at participating online stores to take part in a survey, immediately after completing a purchase, to provide input on the quality of the experience. Follow-up queries ensure that the customer received the order as scheduled and that the overall experience met expectations.

In particular, Bizrate.com asks consumers to rate the performance of an online store on its "ten dimensions of service." Briefly, these are noted in Exhibit 7-5 and include ease of ordering, product selection, product information, website navigation and looks, and on-time delivery.

Table 7-2 U.S. TOP 25 WEB AND DIGITAL MEDIA PROPERTIES (MARCH 2000)

Rank	Digital Media/Web	Unique Visitors
1	AOL Network	59,858
2	Yahoo! Sites	48,336
3	Microsoft Sites	46,581
4	Lycos	32,899
5	Excite @ Home	28,571
6	Go Network	23,006
7	NBC Internet	17,169
8	Amazon	15,217
9	Time Warner Online	13,636
10	Real.com Network	13,482
11	Go2Net Network	13,041
12	Alta Vista Network	12,557
13	About.com Sites	12,329
14	Ask Jeeves	12,269
15	eBay	11,155
16	LookSmart	10,557
17	ZDNet Sites	10,226
18	CNET Networks	10,023
19	eUniverse Network	9,198
20	JUNO/JUNO.COM	9,177
21	EarthLink	8,526
22	Infospace Impressions	8,305
23	Viacom Online	8,139
24	FortuneCity Network	7,809
25	CitySearch-TicketMaster Online	7,689

Source: Media Metrix (*www.mediametrix.com/usa/press/releases/20000424.jsp*) March 31, 2000

Forrester (*www.forrester.com*) provides some of the most well-regarded reports on the e-commerce industry. It offers comprehensive coverage of a wide range of markets. Similar to our market-opportunity analysis chapter, Forrester's reports tend to cover the competitors, consumers, and technology evolution in a particular segment of the industry. More recently, it has teamed with Greenfield OnLine (*www.greenfieldonline.com*) to offer "power ratings" for various sites. These ratings

Exhibit 7-5

MARKET RESEARCH SOURCE— BIZRATE.COM

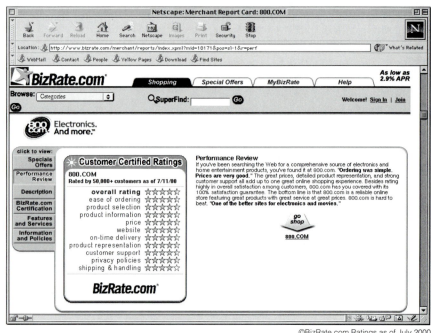

Exhibit 7-6

ANALYST SOURCE— FORRESTER

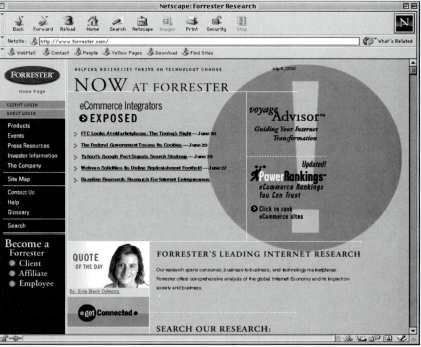

are based on six factors: cost, customer service, delivery, features and content, transacting ability, and usability. Forrester ratings are based on expert reviews and customer surveys as opposed to the pure user reviews of Bizrate.com (see Exhibit 7-6).

Hoover's Online is a leading provider of financial and market information for a variety of offline and online companies. Hoover's covers all major companies to provide company profiles, financials, and industry research.

Exhibit 7-7 provides a quick overview of the products and services of Hoover's. Company profiles include company overviews, history, press releases, products and operations, competitors, financial information, and research reports. Company financial data include annual and quarterly financial data, SEC filings, stock market data, and comparison data by industry and market. Finally, industry-wide information is provided to put the entire analysis in proper context.

Mapping Internet Research onto the Performance Dashboard

In Exhibit 7-8, we provide a mapping of the Internet research sources onto the business strategy framework for this book. This analysis reveals that each data source specializes in a different type of data. That is, Media Metrix and AC Nielsen tend to emphasize market information and traffic while Hoover's Online specializes in financial information. It is rare that a single source covers all types of data. However, Forrester captures a large number of the data categories.

FINANCIAL INFORMATION SOURCE— HOOVER'S ONLINE

Exhibit 7-7

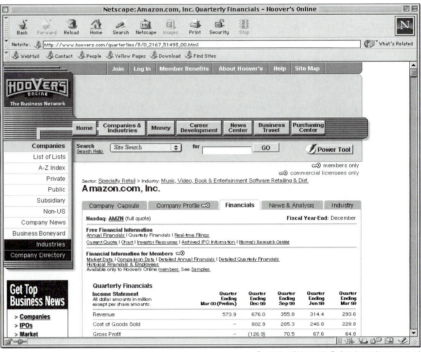

Courtesy of Hoover's Online (*www.hoovers.com*)

POINT-COUNTERPOINT

Which Is Better? User-Based or Expert-Based Research Content?

A second interesting debate in this area concerns the sources of research information. Of the sources noted earlier in the chapter, some focus on user responses while others focus on analysts' viewpoints.

User-based data sources rely on the input of consumers. Consumer-oriented data sources are often very up-to-date, may have a large customer base for input, and tend to be viewed as trustworthy by other users. In contrast, when experts rate a site, they tend to be more episodic in their reviews, can offer the

input of only one expert, and provide information often viewed as objective. On the other hand, expert sites typically are reviewed by people whose responsibility is to know how to evaluate the features and functionality of a site, who have deep knowledge of competitor sites, and whose annual performance reviews are based on the soundness of their analysis. Hence, they have an enormous incentive to provide the best information to their customer base.

Exhibit 7-8 MAPPING INTERNET RESEARCH ONTO THE PERFORMANCE DASHBOARD

		Market Research			Analyst				Financial Information
		Media Metrix	AC Nielsen	Bizrate	Forrester	Gomez	Jupiter	Creative Good	Hoover's
Market	Market Info	●	●		●		●		●
	Traffic	●	●						
Implementation	Fulfillment			●	●				
	Implementation				●		●		
	Privacy			●					
Customer	Usability			●	●	●	●	●	
	Content			●	●	●	●		
	Customer Satisfaction			●	●	●			
	Customer Service			●	●				
Financial	Financial Performance				●				●

DRILL-DOWN

Online and Offline Integration Metrics

Thus far, the metrics described refer primarily to a firm's online strategy and operations. We can also use the Performance Dashboard, with its five areas of market opportunity, business model, branding and implementation, customer interface and outcome, and financial, to determine appropriate measures of performance for offline company operations. Obviously, metrics must be adjusted to reflect a change of focus from the digital to the physical world. An extensive body of literature exists on the subject; in particular, Kaplan and Norton's Balanced Scorecard provides a comprehensive approach for offline companies. We find no need

to go into further detail concerning that subject. Instead, we focus on metrics that measure the successful integration of online and offline presence and operations.

A well integrated online and offline operation exhibits two major attributes: a seamless customer experience (front end) and a seamless set of internal business processes and operations (back end). We examine each of these in greater detail.

Seamless Customer Experience. A seamless customer experience refers to the customer's ability to have a consistent experience while moving between online and offline channels. The customer purchase

(continued on page 278)

(continued from page 277)

process framework (introduced in Chapter 2) is a useful tool for identifying metrics for a seamless customer purchase experience.

Exhibit 7-9 outlines steps of the customer purchase process and lists associated metrics to measure the consistency between the online and offline channels at each step. As discussed in Chapter 2, the customer purchase process has three stages: the prepurchase stage (includes brand awareness, knowledge, and evaluation of alternatives), the purchase stage, and the postpurchase stage (includes satisfaction, loyalty, and disposal).

In the step to evaluate alternatives, a consistent availability and selection of products through the online and offline channels would provide the customer access to the same pool of offerings regardless of channel. Wal-Mart, the world's leading retailer, offers nearly the same selection of products and services through its offline stores and its website, walmart.com. However, differences exist. For example, travel planning services are available to customers through the online offer but not though the offline offer.

In the purchase step, consistent security and privacy standards in offline and online stores allow users to feel equally comfortable in providing sensitive information when purchasing online and offline. ToysRUs, one of the largest toy retailers, offers a consistent level of security through its stores and its toysrus.com site. To prevent unauthorized viewing, toysrus.com uses the "secure socket layers" technology to encrypt all order-related information in transit to the company server. If a user's browser does not support this encryption technology or if the user does not want to send their credit-card information over the Web, the site urges customers to call its guest relations department to complete the order securely over a phone line.

(continued on page 279)

Exhibit 7-9 METRICS FOR SEAMLESS ONLINE/OFFLINE CUSTOMER PURCHASE PROCESS

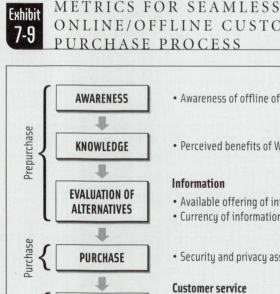

Prepurchase

AWARENESS
- Awareness of offline offer vs. awareness of online offer

KNOWLEDGE
- Perceived benefits of Web vs. offline offer

EVALUATION OF ALTERNATIVES

Information
- Available offering of information online vs. offline
- Currency of information online vs. offline

Purchase

PURCHASE
- Security and privacy associated with purchasing

Postpurchase

SATISFACTION

Customer service
- Response time online vs. offline

LOYALTY
- Customer loyalty incentive programs online vs. offline

DISPOSAL
- Exchange policies online vs. offline

(continued from page 278)

In the satisfaction step, consistent response time to a customer service request through online and offline channels allows customers to get assistance online or offline promptly and equally. 1-800-flowers provides live customer service seamlessly, regardless of channel. Customers can receive live assistance through a private online customer service eQ&A chat with a representative at 1800flowers.com or through a toll-free telephone call or through a visit to one of over 1,500 stores in the 1-800-flowers retail network.

Seamless Internal Business Processes and Operations. Seamless internal business processes and operations refer to a company's ability to perform all internal processes and operations, regardless of whether a customer is interacting with the company through its online or offline channel.

Table 7-3 outlines metrics that can be used to assess seamless internal business processes and operations. Most metrics refer to capabilities that are clearly "available" or "not available" and, therefore, the metric value will be either a "yes" or a "no." We can group these metrics into two categories: information sharing and fulfillment systems.

Information-sharing metrics measure the site's ability to collect and analyze collected information on customers or products seamlessly between online and offline channels. For example, a company's ability to have customers access their accounts online and offline is an essential part of a company's integrated back-office operations. Merrill Lynch customers can open and access their accounts through the ml.com site. Alternatively, they can access their account by calling a customer service representative or by visiting one of the Merrill Lynch branches.

Fulfillment-systems metrics refer to a company's ability to deliver seamlessly on a customer order, regardless of whether that order was placed online or offline. For example, a company's ability to provide seamless order tracking allows customers to check their order status online or offline, regardless of which channel they used to place their order. Federal Express customers can get information about the delivery status of a package by logging on to the fedex.com site and entering the package delivery confirmation code. Alternatively, they can call a Federal Express customer service representative and get the same information over the phone.

Table 7-3 METRICS FOR SEAMLESS INTERNAL BUSINESS PROCESSES AND OPERATIONS

Information Sharing	• Ability to open accounts online and offline • Ability to access accounts online and offline • Integrated customer databases
Fulfillment Systems	• Seamless order processing • Seamless order tracking • Integrated inventory keeping

SCHWAB METRICS

Let us now apply the five-step process used in implementing the Performance Dashboard to Schwab. As was discussed, strategy can change very quickly as a company moves through its different life stages. Hence, it is important that we specify a particular stage in Schwab's life cycle. In 1997, Schwab had launched its website and was focused on delivering this service to both existing and new customers. At that time, Schwab was in the customer acquisition stage.

In order to successfully apply the methodology, we use outcomes of the Schwab analysis that were performed in previous chapters. This is consistent with the proposed approach because the Performance Dashboard for Schwab reflects aspects of Schwab's performance at each step in the strategy process.

Step One: Articulate Schwab Strategy

The first step is to clearly articulate Schwab's business strategy. As was discussed in Chapter 3, a company's business strategy requires four choices: (1) a value proposition (or cluster) for targeted customers, (2) an offer (Egg Diagram), (3) a unique, defendable resource system, and (4) a financial model. At this first step, we will use the first three of the four choices (the financial model choice will be reflected in steps two and three).

Value Proposition. The stated value proposition of Schwab was to "use technology to offer innovative products and superior service at lower prices to investors unwilling to pay for investment advice."

Schwab's Offer. The Egg Diagram contains a wide variety of information and services aimed at delivering four key benefits to investors: innovative products, high-quality information, superior service, and low prices.

Resource System. Schwab's resource system consists of three layers. The first layer is the benefits delivered to customers, as they are described in the marketspace offering. The second layer is the capabilities that must be in place for Schwab to be able to deliver its benefits to investors. Such capabilities include cutting-edge technology, system reliability, multiple points of access, partnerships with content providers, capable IT staff, and competitive commission rates. The third layer is the resources that need to be retained to deliver these capabilities. For example, to offer 24×7 user access to customer service through online, phone, and branch channels, Schwab must provide a multiple-point-access capability. Other actions for Schwab include hiring and training IT staff; investing heavily in technology and in research and development; partnering with Hoover's, Standard & Poor's, Media General, and investment banks; and optimizing staffing in their branches. (For a more detailed description of the Schwab resource system, please see Figure 3-9 on page 106 in Chapter 3.)

Steps Two and Three: Translate Strategy into Outcomes and Metrics

The next two steps are easier to perform concurrently because they are very closely related. For each of the five categories of the Performance Dashboard, we need to translate the strategy defined in step one to a set of actions and associated metrics. This set of actions can be derived by specifying key questions and themes for each area.

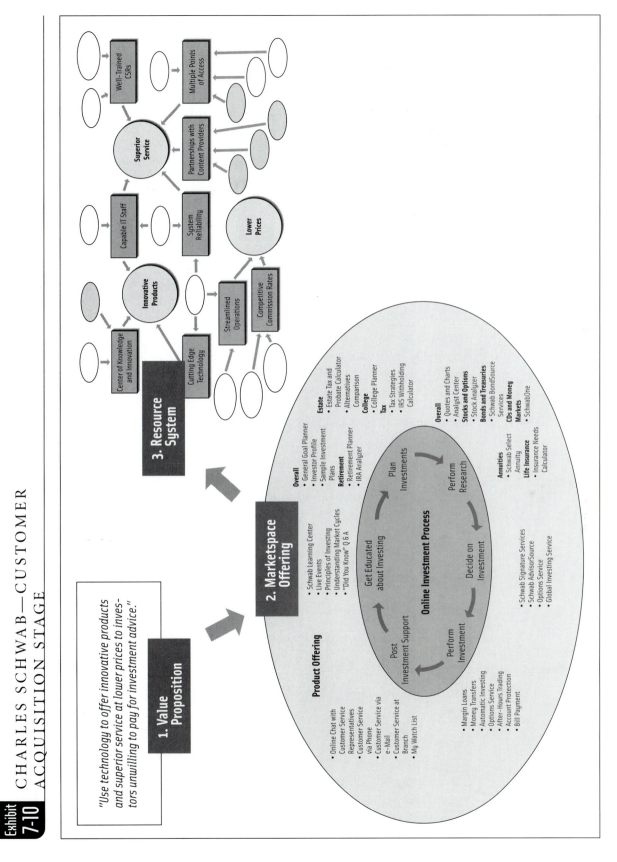

Exhibit
7-10

CHARLES SCHWAB—CUSTOMER
ACQUISITION STAGE

"Use technology to offer innovative products and superior service at lower prices to investors unwilling to pay for investment advice."

1. Value Proposition

2. Marketspace Offering

3. Resource System

Online Investment Process

- Plan Investments
- Perform Research
- Decide on Investment
- Perform Investment
- Post Investment Support
- Get Educated about Investing

Overall
- General Goal Planner
- Investor Profile
- Sample Investment Plans

Retirement
- Retirement Planner
- IRA Analyzer

Estate
- Estate Tax and Probate Calculator
- Alternatives Comparison

College
- College Planner

Tax
- Tax Strategies
- IRS Withholding Calculator

Overall
- Quotes and Charts
- Analyst Center

Stocks and Options
- Stock Analyzer

Bonds and Treasuries
- Schwab BondSource Services

CDs and Money Markets
- SchwabOne

Annuities
- Schwab Select Annuity

Life Insurance
- Insurance Needs Calculator

- Schwab Signature Services
- Schwab AdvisorSource
- Options Service
- Global Investing Service

Product Offering

- Schwab Learning Center
- Live Events
- Principles of Investing
- Understanding Market Cycles
- "Did You Know" Q & A

- Online Chat with Customer Service Representatives
- Customer Service via Phone
- Customer Service via e-Mail
- Customer Service at Branch
- My Watch List

- Margin Loans
- Money Transfers
- Automatic Investing
- Options Service
- After-Hours Trading
- Account Protection
- Bill Payment

Resource System boxes:
- Center of Knowledge and Innovation
- Capable IT Staff
- Well-Trained CSRs
- Innovative Products
- Cutting Edge Technology
- System Reliability
- Superior Service
- Partnerships with Content Providers
- Multiple Points of Access
- Streamlined Operations
- Lower Prices
- Competitive Commission Rates

Market Opportunity. In market-opportunity analysis, we establish metrics for the attractiveness of the opportunity for Schwab and the degree of market competition. We begin by specifying the relevant theme, identifying the desired outcome, and articulating the right set of metrics that will measure the outcome.

Is the Opportunity Significant?

Desired Outcome #1: Locate a Significant Market Opportunity in the Financial Services Industry. Schwab chose to play in the discount brokerage market. With over $13 trillion in investable assets in banks and brokerage accounts in the United States (in 1997) and with a very high growth rate in discount brokerage, this looked like a very promising market opportunity.

Metrics to Track:

- Discount brokerage firms share of total retail brokerage funds
- Percent growth rate of discount brokerage funds

Is the Target Segment Financially Attractive?

Desired Outcome #2: Locate Financially Attractive Target Segment(s) Within the Financial Services Industry. Schwab's focus at the customer-acquisition stage was on medium- to high-net-worth individuals that exhibited a high level of Internet adoption. Metrics to quantify the impact of these actions include the following:

Metrics to Track:

- Medium- to high-net-worth individuals in segment
- Percent of customers in target segment versus other segments
- Percent of target customers with Internet access

How Intense Is the Competition in the Segment?

Desired Outcome #3: Locate Competitively Attractive Segment. Schwab avoided competing in the crowded low-commission market. Instead, it focused on the underserved market of high-quality online investment information and service, leveraging Schwab's established and trusted brand. Metrics to quantify the impact of these actions include the following:

Metrics to Track:

- Schwab market share relative to competition
- Rate of competitor entry and exit in the market

Business Model. In this category, we establish metrics for the uniqueness of Schwab's value proposition, the attractiveness of Schwab's offering to its customers, the strength of Schwab's capabilities relative to the competition, and the sustainability of Schwab's position.

How Is the Schwab Value Proposition Perceived Versus Competition?

Desired Outcome #4: Schwab Value Proposition Outperforming Competition. Part of Schwab's motivation to fully enter the online discount brokerage market was in response to the churning of its customers. Specifically, Schwab was losing its customer base to existing online brokerage firms offering very low commission rates but low quality of information and service. Schwab responded to this challenge by offering a unique combination of benefits: innovative products combined with high-quality information and service at low prices (albeit higher prices than the highest discount brokerages).

Metrics to Track:

- Number of competitors offering any combination of Schwab's benefits
- Customers' perceptions of Schwab's performance on the four critical benefits versus the competition

Is the Schwab Offer Perceived as Attractive Versus Competition?

Desired Outcome #5: Schwab Offer Perceived as More Attractive Than Competition. Schwab wanted to not only offer customers the benefits that they needed but to enhance customers' perceptions of the attractiveness of Schwab's offering.

Metrics to Track:

- Importance to target customers of innovative products, high-quality information, service, and low price
- Extent to which customers perceived that Schwab was outperforming competition on the stages of the customer decision process (i.e., inner ring of the Egg Diagram)
- Extent to which the site's products, services, and information were viewed as superior to the competition (i.e., outer ring of the Egg Diagram)

Are Schwab's Firm Capabilities and Partnerships Significantly Better When Compared to Competition?

Desired Outcome #6: Market Street Perceives Schwab's Capabilities and Partnerships Superior to Competition's. From the start, Schwab had at least three core capabilities that distinguished it from the competition: leadership in technology, strong brand equity, and extensive online and offline channels. In addition, Schwab strove to improve the quality and effectiveness of its offering through a number of partnerships with, among others, content providers, software developers, mutual funds, and investment banks.

Metrics to Track:

- Dollars invested in technology relative to competition
- Customer brand awareness relative to competition
- Number of distribution channels relative to competition
- Number of strategic alliances (and associated customer base) relative to the competition

How Sustainable Is Schwab's Value Proposition Relative to Competition?

Desired Outcome #7: Factors That Drive Sustainability Are in Excellent Condition. In order to increase the likelihood of a sustainable competitive advantage, Schwab would need to continue to improve the quality of information and tools on its site, increase the number of its branches, increase the number of its partnerships (and, if possible, make them exclusive), and expand into international markets.

Metrics to Track:

- Exclusivity and length of partnership agreements
- Number and remaining duration of patents held for offered products and services
- Average switching cost for customers

Branding and Implementation.

This category involves establishing metrics for the effectiveness of Schwab's branding as well as its implementation (this includes the delivery system and innovation).

How Is the Schwab Brand Perceived in the Market?

Desired Outcome #8: Schwab Maintains Best Brand Associations and Equity in Financial Services Industry. Schwab already enjoyed a reputation of reliability and trust among customers. It would need to leverage its existing brand equity and ensure uniformity between the online and offline brand message.

Metrics to Track:

- Customer-unprompted brand awareness
- Customer associations with the Schwab brand
- Customer perceptions of Schwab brand in online investing (versus the competition)

Does Schwab Have the "Best of Class" in IT Infrastructure?

Desired Outcome #9: To Possess the "Best of Class" IT Infrastructure. A significant part of Schwab's value proposition was associated with technological innovation. In order to maintain its leadership in technology, Schwab would need to take a number of actions on the technology front that included investing heavily on IT, increasing system capacity, enabling mainframes to reroute information to each other quickly in order to minimize downtime, and ensuring system security.

Metrics to Track:

- Trade capacity to volume ratio
- Number of possible simultaneous Web sessions that the system can handle
- Uptime of system (versus competition)
- Cut-over time (time to route information between mainframes)
- Number of security breaches

Does Schwab Have the Best Organization in Place?

Desired Outcome #10: Ability to Deliver on the Brand Promise Versus Competition. A number of actions on the internal organization front would be needed for Schwab to be able to deliver on its value proposition. These include increasing the number of branches and decreasing the number of employees per branch, building and training an IT staff to support Web-based operations, and retaining a sales staff.

Metrics to Track:

- Number of branches
- Average number of staff per branch
- Number of hours of training per year per salesperson
- Average time to respond to and resolve a problem
- Percent of time order not fulfilled or fulfilled inaccurately

Customer Interface and Outcomes.
This category establishes metrics for (a) the customer's perception of the 7Cs of the interface and (b) outcome measures that include the effectiveness of customer acquisition and the degree of customer satisfaction and loyalty.

How Effective and Efficient Is Schwab's New Customer Acquisition?

Desired Outcome #11: Lower Customer Acquisition Costs Versus Competition. Schwab leveraged and built on its existing brand equity to acquire new customers. In addition, it reached out to new customers through online and offline marketing and it encouraged customers to switch to online services.

Metrics to Track:

- Customer acquisition cost
- Dollars spent on marketing (percent offline and online)
- Number of new accounts opened
- Customer churn rate

Can Schwab Transition Customers Online?

Desired Outcome #12: Seamless Transition of Customer Base from Offline to Online Trading. Schwab's across-the-board online offer at discounted commission rates was expected to impact investor behavior in a number of ways. There was an expected increase in the number of online accounts as old customers transitioned online and as new customers were acquired. There was also an expected increase in transaction volume, driven by the lower commission rates. Finally, there was anticipation of an increase in customer service requests driven by the platform change from offline to online.

Metrics to Track:

- Average user account balance
- Number of trades per year per customer
- Total assets in online and offline accounts
- Percent of Schwab customers online and offline

What Is the Perception of the Online Customer Experience?

Desired Outcome #13: Schwab Will Outperform the Competition on Interface and Usability Metrics. One of the essential features of Schwab's online offering was the Schwab website, the interface between the company and its online customers. The success of the user interface could be measured along three dimensions: performance of each of the Cs, overall site usability, and the service recovery.

Metrics to Track:

- Original impression

    Customer evaluation of the 7Cs versus competition

- Site usability metrics

    Goal-based success rate

- Conversion rate
- Number of occurrences of critical failures
- Service recovery metrics
- Number of service requests per user

    Percent of users who leave the site before requesting service

How Satisfied and Loyal Is the Customer Base Versus Competition?

Desired Outcome #14: Maintain the Highest Customer Satisfaction and Loyalty Scores in the Industry. Satisfied and loyal customers are the source of long-term profitability. Schwab was striving toward customer satisfaction and loyalty by offering high-quality, superior products coupled with reliability, security, as well as high-quality service.

Metrics to Track:

- Overall customer satisfaction relative to competition as well as a number of key attributes including quality of information, price, reliability, and quality of service
- Percent of users in frequent trader programs

Financial. In this category, we establish metrics for the financial performance of the company in terms of revenue, profit, and cost.

Are We Outperforming Competition in Financial Metrics That Matter in the Financial Services Industry?

Desired Outcome #15: Schwab Outperforms Competition on Both Top-Line (Revenue Growth) and Bottom-Line (Net or Operating Income) Measures of Financial Performance. Schwab's move to an across-the-board discounted online offering was expected to have some immediate and longer-term financial implications. There was an expected initial revenue hit of around $125 million that would be driven by the decrease in the average commission rate. This hit would be carried almost straight through to the bottom line, leading to an expected profit hit of $100 million. On the other hand, the move to render service online was expected to lead to significant savings, quantified in one report to be the equivalent of 1,500 people and four call centers.

Metrics to Track:

- Revenue

    Total revenue and revenue growth

Revenue breakdown by offering

Total transaction volume

- Profit

    Total profit and profit growth

    Profit breakdown

    Earnings per share and growth

- Cost

    Total cost

    Cost breakdown by department

    Cost per transaction

- Balance Sheet

    Debt to equity ratio

    Corporate credit rating

    Total margin loans

    Margin loans spread

Exhibit 7-11 provides a summary of the desired outcomes. A quick review of the figure reveals that the firm is tracking about 18 desired outcomes. The specific number of metrics includes multiple metrics for each outcome. While it may seem large at first glance, management must be able to track all the relevant business-model metrics, including those that provide early warning signs of strategic problems. We turn to this issue of leading and lagging indicators in the next section.

Exhibit 7-11 SCHWAB DESIRED OUTCOME SUMMARY

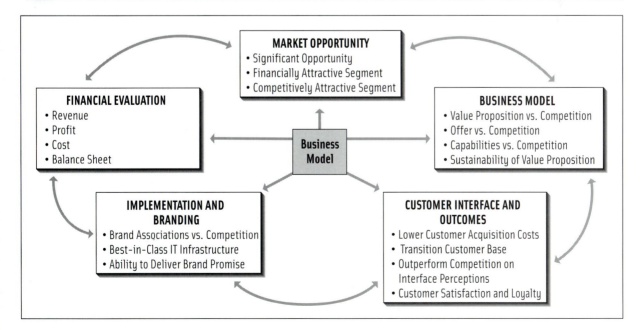

Step Four: Link Metrics to Leading and Lagging Indicators

Now that we have a list of useful metrics to track Schwab's performance, the relevant question is, "How do we link them to each other?" There can be three possible relationships between two metrics, let us call them A and B. A could affect B (A would then be called a leading indicator with respect to B), A could be affected by B (A would then be called a lagging indicator with respect to B), or A and B could not affect each other. In order for management to be able to use these metrics effectively, it needs to understand which metrics (or groups of metrics) are leading or lagging indicators for which other metrics.

Knowledge of this interrelation will help management understand which groups of leading indicators it needs to focus on in order to achieve its target performance on lagging indicators. For example, if a company has a revenue target, then knowledge of the fact that revenue metrics are affected by new customer acquisition, website usability, and high levels of customer service will signal to management that these are the metrics it should focus on in order to achieve its revenue target.

The interrelation between leading and lagging indicators for Schwab is demonstrated in Exhibit 7-12. Let us trace just one flow of leading and lagging indicators in this exhibit.

Metrics to avoid crowded markets and target attractive segments increases the probability that Schwab will provide a unique value proposition. This, in turn, links to an attractive offering. An attractive offering in conjunction with capabilities to deliver the offering leads into a number of implementation metrics that include investing in technology and increasing the number of IT staff. These two groups are causally related to increased system uptime that leads to increased usage and customer satisfaction. Increased customer satisfaction produces increased customer loyalty and eventually increased profit.

Step Five: Calculate Current and Target Performance

Knowledge of the appropriate use of each metric is of little help if management does not know the current and target value of these metrics. A successful strategy needs to be implemented by setting targets and taking actions to reach these targets.

To illustrate the concept of current and target metrics let us consider one category of metrics for Schwab that are publicly available—financial metrics. Table 7-4 demonstrates some actual and target financial figures for Schwab during the time period of this analysis (1997 to 1998). In terms of total revenue, there is a target of 10 percent revenue growth, compared with a current 24 percent growth (in 1997). This drop in the target growth rate reflects management's expectation that the increase in transaction volume due to the online offering will only in part counterbalance the drop in average commission rates. In order to achieve its revenue growth target, management must set corresponding targets for leading indicators to total revenue. In this case, management has set a transaction volume target of 132 million per day compared to 106 million per day in the previous year. Also, management has set a target of $51.41 as the average transaction fee, down from $64.27 in the previous year. In order to achieve these two new targets, management must now move down one more level to leading indicators.

Exhibit 7-12 CHARLES SCHWAB—CUSTOMER ACQUISITION STAGE

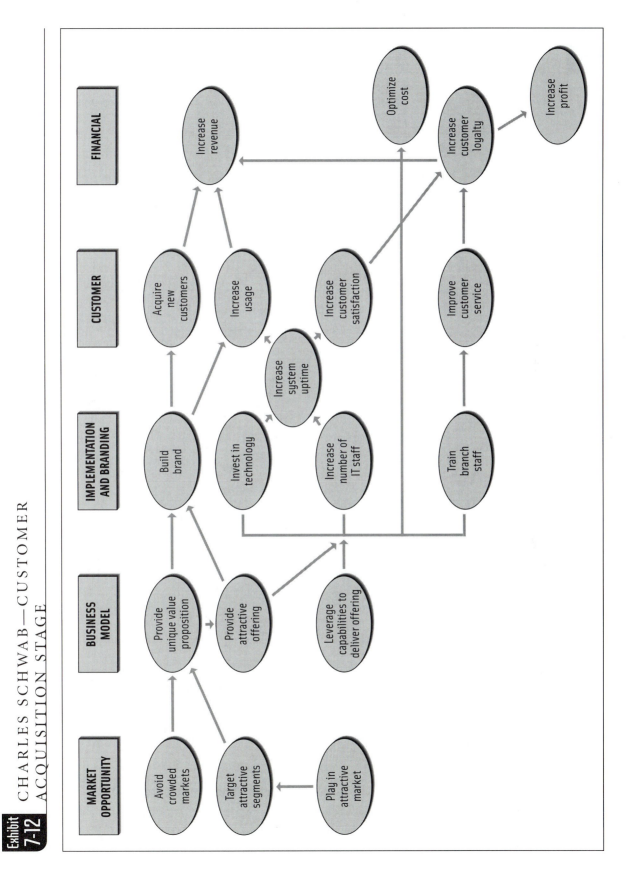

Table 7-4 CHARLES SCHWAB—CUSTOMER ACQUISITION STAGE CURRENT AND TARGET LEVELS FOR SELECT METRICS

Revenue	1997 Actual	1998 Target	Comment
Total revenue	$2,299	$2,529	
Revenue growth	24%	10%	Despite the decrease in Schwab's pricing for trades, increases in the number of accounts and number of trades per account should produce revenue growth, albeit at a reduced rate.
Revenue breakdown	Trading 62% Nontrading 38%	Trading 59% Nontrading 41%	An additional driver of revenue growth will be increases in margin loans to account holders. This will outpace the growth in trading revenues.
Total trading volume	106,000/day	132,000/day	Lower trading prices will result in a 25% growth in trading volume.
Average fee per trade	$64.27	$51.41	1998 will be a year of transition for Schwab as customers migrate toward the Web platform. Average fees per trade will drop by 20%.
Profit			
Posttax profit margin	19.50%	19.50%	Investments in technology will be offset by branch staff reductions and lower trade fulfillment costs.
Pretax profit growth	14%	10%	
Profit breakdown Earnings per share	$0.99	$1.07	Option packages granted to key staff will cause some EPS dilution.
Earnings per share growth	14%	8%	

Source: Tempest, Nicole and Warren McFarlan. 1999. *Charles Schwab Corporation (B)*. Case no. 9-300-507, 13 September. Boston: Harvard Business School Publishing

SUMMARY

1. Why should senior managers be concerned about metrics?

Managers should be concerned about metrics because metrics drive organizational behavior in a number of ways, including helping to define the business model, communicating the strategy, tracking performance, increasing accountability, and aligning objectives.

2. How can we assess the health of New Economy firms?

The Balanced Scorecard assesses the health of a business in four categories of metrics: financial, customer, internal business process, and learning and growth. While this framework may be appropriate for New Economy firms, it is also limited in three respects: it does not offer a definition of strategy, capabilities of the firm are not clearly articulated (rather, the focus is on internal business processes not linked to customer benefits), and partnerships are not explicitly included.

3. What are the steps to implement the Performance Dashboard?

There are five steps to implement the Performance Dashboard. They include (1) articulate the strategy, (2) translate strategy into actions, (3) devise metrics, (4) link metrics to leading and lagging indicators, and (5) calculate current and target performance levels.

4. What are three sources of metrics information that firms can use to chart their progress?

Market-research data sources tend to focus on customer perceptions of sites and site performance. Analyst reports often combine primary data collection along with a strong analyst point of view on the issue at hand. Financial sources focus heavily on the investment community and tend to include in-depth financial information. Each approach has its strengths and limitations, but all are complementary. Firms often need to acquire data from all three areas in order to obtain a complete picture of their markets.

KEY TERMS

metrics

Balanced Scorecard

financial metrics

customer metrics

internal business process metrics

learning and growth metrics

Performance Dashboard

market-opportunity metrics

business-model metrics

customer-interface metrics

customer-outcome metrics

branding and implementation metrics

life cycle of a company

startup

acquisition of customers

monetization

maturity

market research

analyst reports

financial information

Endnotes

[1]Readers are encouraged to review the seminal work of Robert Kaplan and David Norton on the Balanced Scorecard. The starting point should be Kaplan, Robert and David Norton. 1996. *The balanced scorecard.* Boston: Harvard Business School Press.

[2]See: Kaplan & Norton. 1996. Chap. 2 in *The balanced scorecard.*

[3]See: Kaplan & Norton. 1996. *The balanced scorecard,* pp. 10–19.

[4]Day, George. 1994. The capabilities of market-driven organizations. *Journal of Marketing* 58, no. 4 (October): 37–52.

[5]Excerpt from the following: Gurley, J. William. 2000. The most powerful Internet metric of all. *CNET NEWS.COM,* 21 February. URL: *http://www.news.com/Perspectives/Column/0,176,403,00.html?tag5st.ne.*

Valuation

The Internet has created enormous new wealth in the last five years. Yahoo! is one of the most highly valued and established dot-com companies; its valuation is over $50 billion. However, it did not exist before the mid 1990s. To many observers, the enormous valuations of Internet businesses—the majority of which have yet to show a profit—are seen either as a mystery or a sign of the stock market's "irrational exuberance."[1] This chapter attempts to demystify these valuations and to show that a rationale exists for them. We examine some of the approaches that can be used to value companies, such as dot-coms, that are new and growing very rapidly, but have yet to make a profit. Correctly valuing companies is a complex task, and the techniques that we discuss are not straightforward. In this chapter we provide a brief primer on basic valuation techniques for students new to the topic as well as an examination of the most sophisticated techniques for advanced readers. We show that there is in fact a rational explanation for what often seem to be unreasonably high valuations that Internet companies command. Although we believe that many high valuations are justified, there are probably many instances of Internet companies being overvalued. By using the tools contained in this chapter, investors will be able to avoid overvaluations.

QUESTIONS

Please consider the following questions as you read this chapter:

1. **How can one apply discounted-cash-flow analysis for robust growth companies?**

I would like to acknowledge the invaluable contribution in the real options portion of this chapter by my colleague Vladimir Antikarov.

2. How and when is it appropriate to use a real-options methodology for valuing emerging growth companies?

3. How should we think about valuing start-up companies?

4. How do valuation methodologies actually work?

5. When is one methodology more appropriate than others?

In the late 1990s and now in the early years of the new millennium, we have been confronted with what appear to be unreasonably high multiples for companies that did not exist a few years ago. In a *Fortune* magazine article in February 2000, Stern Stewart and Company remarked that America Online would have to grow at 67 percent per year for the next 10 years to justify its multiple of 18 times sales revenues. Professor Ken French of MIT was quoted as saying, "It doesn't make any sense at all. These Internet valuations fly in the face of everything I have ever believed." Warren Buffett claims, "If I were a business school professor in finance, I would assign the following exam: How do you value Internet companies? And I would fail everyone that did not leave the answer sheet blank."

The purpose of this chapter is to demonstrate that many, but of course not all, of the multiples that are being paid in the market do have a rational basis if one applies sound analysis. However, it is important to choose the right analysis for the situation at hand.

Exhibit 8-1 shows the life cycle of most companies. The earliest phase of a company is embryonic. These **embryonic companies** have no track record, a small but rapidly growing sales base, and expect no profit for several years. Yet they sometimes sell for several hundred times their sales revenue. If a company survives its start-up phase without being acquired, or, more likely, without going bankrupt, it makes the transition to an **emerging growth company** which is really a small portfolio of projects with high optionality (growth options that require the use of real-option analysis to understand their multiples). Finally, there is the **robust growth company,** like AOL or Amazon.com, which is large but still growing rapidly and is selling for 15 to 25 times sales. This chapter reviews our experiences valuing all three types of Internet companies. We have an approach for each type that explains the company's range of multiples logically and consistently.

ROBUST GROWTH COMPANIES

The key to valuing companies like AOL and Amazon.com is understanding the market's consensus forecasts for their key value drivers, how their cost of capital changes over time, and the shape that their industry competition will take a decade or more from now. Robust growth companies, as we define them, are already large and are composed of portfolios of literally hundreds of projects. As a result, the optionality of a single effort is not material for valuing the whole company. In what follows, we had no difficulty using the consensus of analysts' forecasts, careful understanding of the long-term industry structure, and discounted-cash-flow analysis to explain the high multiples of robust growth companies.

Exhibit 8-2 summarizes our results and the major assumptions behind them. Both valuations come within plus or minus 10 percent of the actual market values

Exhibit 8-1 FRAMEWORK FOR UNDERSTANDING THE VALUE OF INTERNET COMPANIES

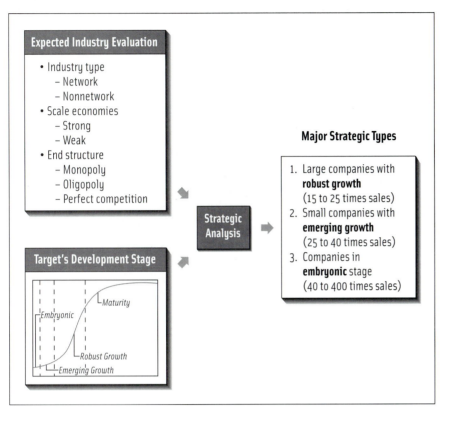

in August 1999, when the analysis was completed. (Note that the completion date is before AOL announced its merger with Time Warner and before Amazon.com had a stock split.) Starting with AOL, we assumed sales growth in the 25.4 percent range for the next five years, declining to 13.2 percent from 2005 to 2009, and then 9 percent for the long run. Our assumptions—and the fact that they fell in the same range as analyst reports of Donaldson, Lufkin, and Jenrette; Robertson Stephens; ING Barings; and Bank Boston—are illustrated in Exhibit 8-3.

Our sales growth assumption was never more than 3 percent per year different from the analyst consensus. We also assumed better operating margins based on a changing business mix. These are shown in Exhibit 8-4. AOL's business mix is projected to shift away from subscription fees, which will decline as a fraction of total revenues because even though the number of subscribers is expected to continue growing, the fee per subscriber will decrease. For successful Internet service providers with large market shares, revenues from advertising and e-commerce will grow quickly to make up for the lost subscription revenue. This is what will drive the change in the revenue mix and with it the improved operating margins.

Next, we took a look at the cost of capital and capital structure of AOL over time. The current **beta** of AOL is quite high—1.69. Furthermore, the company has a low **bond rating** of B1, even though its debt to equity ratio is only 0.3 percent, based on market values. The result is a current **weighted average cost of capital (WACC)** that

Exhibit 8-2

VALUATION OF AOL AND AMAZON.COM

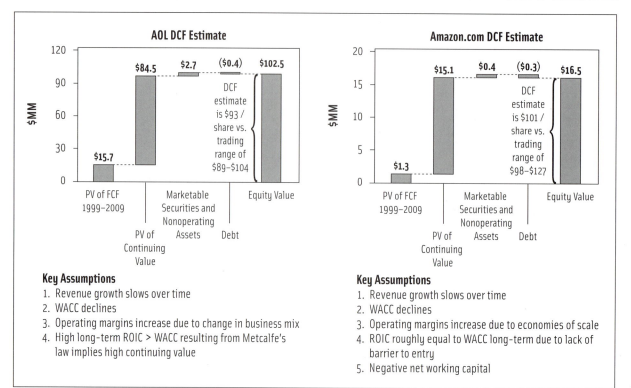

AOL DCF Estimate

$MM — 120, 90, 60, 30, 0

$15.7 — PV of FCF 1999–2009
$84.5 — PV of Continuing Value
$2.7 — Marketable Securities and Nonoperating Assets
($0.4) — Debt
$102.5 — Equity Value

DCF estimate is $93 / share vs. trading range of $89–$104

Amazon.com DCF Estimate

$MM — 20, 15, 10, 5, 0

$1.3 — PV of FCF 1999–2009
$15.1 — PV of Continuing Value
$0.4 — Marketable Securities and Nonoperating Assets
($0.3) — Debt
$16.5 — Equity Value

DCF estimate is $101 / share vs. trading range of $98–$127

Key Assumptions
1. Revenue growth slows over time
2. WACC declines
3. Operating margins increase due to change in business mix
4. High long-term ROIC > WACC resulting from Metcalfe's law implies high continuing value

Key Assumptions
1. Revenue growth slows over time
2. WACC declines
3. Operating margins increase due to economies of scale
4. ROIC roughly equal to WACC long-term due to lack of barrier to entry
5. Negative net working capital

is quite high—15.6 percent according to our estimate (using a market risk premium of 5.5 percent). (WACC is defined as a weighted average of the current marginal costs of debt and equity if the firm were refinanced at today's rates.) A decade from now we expect that AOL will be much more stable, and that its beta will look more like that of a telecom company. We assumed that it would be roughly 1.06 in 2009. Furthermore, AOL's bond rating will improve (we guessed that it will be A3), even though its debt-to-equity ratio in market-value terms could increase to 14.6 percent. As a result, we forecasted that AOL's weighted average cost of capital could fall from 15.6 percent in 1999 to 11.0 percent in 2009.

Finally, we had to make defensible **continuing (or terminal) value** assumptions. Our studies of the Internet-provider industry reminded us of the telecommunications industry. Interconnectivity is very likely to provide a natural barrier to entry. To understand why, it is useful to review a principle called Metcalfe's law, which says that the number of interconnections between users of a system increases as the square of the number of users. For example, there is a single connection between two users, three connections among three users, six among four users, 10 among five users, 15 among six users, and so on. In general, there are $(N^2 - N)/N$ connections among N users. This is illustrated in Exhibit 8-5. Users are represented by dots, and the lines are the two-way connections between them.

Metcalfe's law implies that AOL, with about 18 million subscribers (in the summer of 1999), had roughly 10 times as many subscribers as Microsoft (with around 2 million), but roughly 100 times as many interconnections. Interconnectivity may prove to be even more important in the Internet industry than in telecommunica-

Exhibit
8-3

REVENUE GROWTH ASSUMPTIONS FOR AOL WERE CLOSELY MATCHED TO ANALYST ESTIMATES

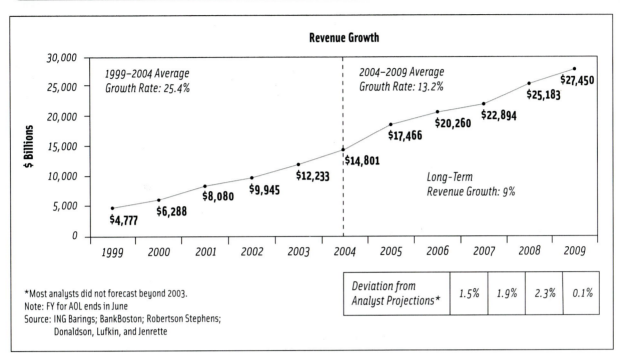

Revenue Growth

1999–2004 Average Growth Rate: 25.4%

2004–2009 Average Growth Rate: 13.2%

Long-Term Revenue Growth: 9%

$4,777 $6,288 $8,080 $9,945 $12,233 $14,801 $17,466 $20,260 $22,894 $25,183 $27,450

Deviation from Analyst Projections*	1.5%	1.9%	2.3%	0.1%

*Most analysts did not forecast beyond 2003.
Note: FY for AOL ends in June
Source: ING Barings; BankBoston; Robertson Stephens; Donaldson, Lufkin, and Jenrette

Exhibit
8-4

OPERATING MARGINS AT AOL BENEFIT FROM BOTH SCALE ECONOMIES AND CHANGES IN REVENUE MIX TOWARD HIGHER MARGIN BUSINESSES

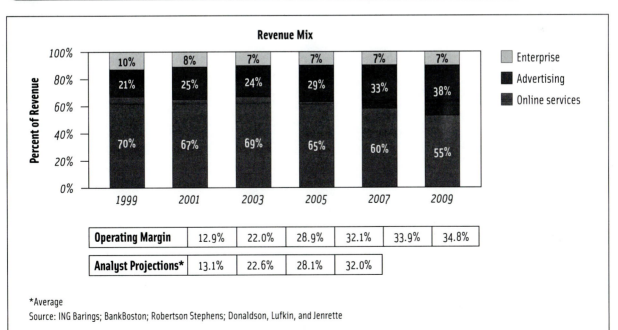

Revenue Mix

Enterprise / Advertising / Online services

	1999	2001	2003	2005	2007	2009
Enterprise	10%	8%	7%	7%	7%	7%
Advertising	21%	25%	24%	29%	33%	38%
Online services	70%	67%	69%	65%	60%	55%

Operating Margin	12.9%	22.0%	28.9%	32.1%	33.9%	34.8%
Analyst Projections*	13.1%	22.6%	28.1%	32.0%		

*Average
Source: ING Barings; BankBoston; Robertson Stephens; Donaldson, Lufkin, and Jenrette

tions. At the margin, subscribers want the easiest access to other subscribers, chat lines, auctions, and information in general. Advertisers and e-commerce merchants also want access to better interconnectivity. For this reason, we believe that the Internet-provider industry will be oligopolistic in nature and will yield AOL a long-term return on invested capital in the 40 percent range. This may seem extraordinarily high, but Coca-Cola earns 50 percent year after year and pharmaceutical companies earn 30 to 40 percent.

It is not hard to understand why AOL's stock price is so volatile. Exhibit 8-6 shows that the current stock price is highly sensitive to small changes in assumptions about the growth in **net operating profit less adjusted taxes (NOPLAT)** or about the **return on new invested capital (ROIC).** For example, a 1 percent decline in NOPLAT growth reduces AOL's value 31.2 percent, and a 5 percent cut in ROIC drops the value by 4.2 percent.

Unlike AOL, there seem to be few if any barriers to entry for companies that choose to compete with Amazon.com. Although there is some interconnectivity, e.g., book reviews posted at Amazon.com, nevertheless we expect that 10 years from now, Amazon.com will earn a return on invested capital approximately equal to its cost of capital, much like Wal-Mart today.

As shown in Exhibit 8-7, our revenue growth assumptions were similar to the consensus forecast, except for the Donaldson, Lufkin, and Jenrette (DLJ) estimate, which was more optimistic. Revenue for the next five years is forecast to grow at 40.5 percent, at 25.9 percent between 2005 and 2009, and at 9 percent thereafter. Our **operating margin** forecasts are also similar to those of analysts—minus 5 percent in the year 2000, 1.4 percent in 2001, 9.1 percent in 2002, and 12.2 percent in the long run. Like AOL, we forecast that Amazon.com's weighted average cost of capital will decline over time and that the company will use more debt.

Exhibit 8-5 METCALFE'S LAW (INTERCONNECTIVITY) MAKES SCALE A SUSTAINABLE COMPETITIVE ADVANTAGE

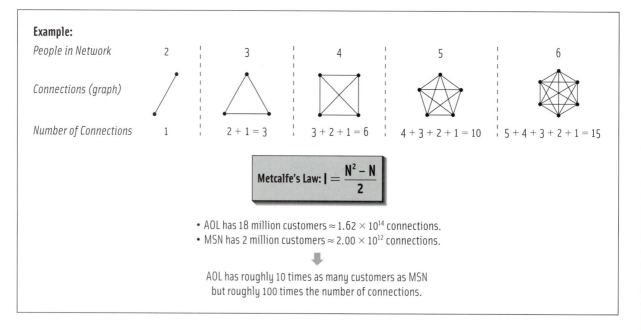

Example:

People in Network	2	3	4	5	6
Number of Connections	1	2 + 1 = 3	3 + 2 + 1 = 6	4 + 3 + 2 + 1 = 10	5 + 4 + 3 + 2 + 1 = 15

Metcalfe's Law: $I = \dfrac{N^2 - N}{2}$

- AOL has 18 million customers $\approx 1.62 \times 10^{14}$ connections.
- MSN has 2 million customers $\approx 2.00 \times 10^{12}$ connections.

AOL has roughly 10 times as many customers as MSN but roughly 100 times the number of connections.

Consequently, its WACC is projected to fall from 16 percent in 1999 to roughly 10 percent a decade later. Amazon.com's continuing value (or terminal value) turns out to be 92 percent of the current stock price—in spite of a ROIC that is only about 1 percent above its cost of capital—because the economic profit created is low or negative during the explicit forecast period. As with AOL, the current stock price is unusually sensitive to changes in the continuing value assumptions. For

Exhibit 8-6

CONTINUING VALUE IS 85% OF AOL'S VALUE AND IS HIGHLY SENSITIVE TO ASSUMPTIONS OF LONG-TERM GROWTH AND ROIC

Continuing Value		Return on Invested Capital (ROIC)		
		35%	40%	45%
NOPLAT Growth	8%	$55,933	$58,038	$59,674
	9%	$80,934	$84,474	$87,228
	10%	$155,025	$162,820	$168,883

WACC = 11% in the Long Run

Exhibit 8-7

REVENUE ASSUMPTIONS FOR AMAZON.COM TRACKED CLOSELY TO ANALYST ESTIMATES

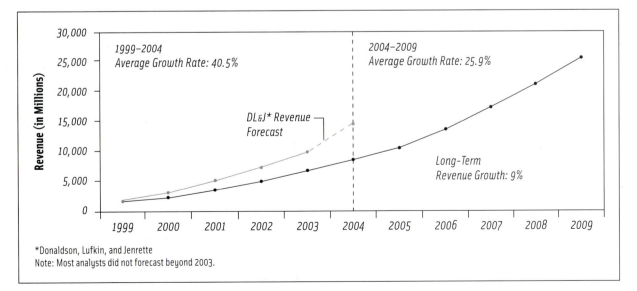

1999–2004
Average Growth Rate: 40.5%

2004–2009
Average Growth Rate: 25.9%

DL&J* Revenue Forecast

Long-Term Revenue Growth: 9%

*Donaldson, Lufkin, and Jenrette
Note: Most analysts did not forecast beyond 2003.

example, if the ROIC forecast in the continuing value increases by only 1 percent, the value of Amazon.com increases by $30 billion—roughly 30 percent.

This chapter's first part shows that typical discounted-cash-flow models with forecasts that (a) are very close to those reported by analysts and (b) are made with careful understanding of the long-term industry structure provide estimates of the market value of equity that are easily in the actual price range in which the stocks are traded—market to sales ratios of 15 to 25. By the start of 1999, AOL was trading for a multiple of 18 times sales and Amazon.com for 23 times sales. Our **discounted-cash-flow (DCF)** model gave similar multiples in August 1999. A decade later however, according to our forecasts, AOL's price-earnings ratio will fall from its current level to 33 and for Amazon.com to about 22. Both multiples are reasonable for what the companies will be by then—mature with more normal business outlooks.

THE BASICS OF DISCOUNTED-CASH-FLOW VALUATION

If you already have experience doing valuations, skip to the next section. If you want more advanced material for a deeper background, take a look at *Valuation: Measuring and Managing the Value of Companies.*[2] If you want the basics, the three components of the DCF valuation of a company and a simple numerical example are described below. We start with the definition of **free cash flows (FCF)**, then move to estimating the rate at which they are discounted back to the present, or the weighted average cost of capital. Finally we provide a discussion of continuing value.

The DCF approach starts by valuing the entire enterprise, i.e., its debt and equity. This is called the entity approach. Once we estimate the entity value, or the value of all operations, we add the value of any excess marketable securities (these provide financial returns but are not part of operations) and subtract debt and other financial liabilities, enabling us to estimate the market value of the firm's equity. Therefore, we are interested in all the firm's operating cash flows on an after-tax basis.

Operating cash flows are *equal* and *opposite* to financial flows. This is an extremely important concept that requires elaboration. Cash flow from operations can be defined as the after-tax cash (provided from the income statement) less the cash needed to grow the balance sheet. These are the firm's free cash flows prior to any financing cash flows. They are sufficient to pay off the financial flows—namely, the interest and principal on debt, the dividends on equity, any repurchase (or issuance) of equity, and the cash flows from investments of cash and marketable securities (income received and money invested).

To calculate the free cash flow from operations (see Table 8-1), we start with revenue ($1,300) then subtract variable costs of operations, depreciation, and selling and administrative expenses ($487.50). (In our example, we have listed the depreciation expense separately. Usually it is included in the cost of goods sold.) The resulting number is called **earnings before interest and taxes**, or **EBIT** (EBIT = $812.50 rounded to the nearest dollar in the table). From EBIT we subtract the taxes the company would have paid if it had no debt (called cash taxes, adjusted taxes, or taxes on EBIT). It is equal to the provision for income taxes ($291) plus the interest tax shield ($0.41 \times \$133 = \$55$) minus the tax on interest income ($0.41 \times \$30 = \$12$). Thus, $333 is the tax that the firm would have paid on EBIT if it had no interest expense or income. Next, add any change in deferred taxes and add back depreciation (because it was a noncash expense).[3] The resulting number is called gross cash flow from operations. From this, we subtract the cash needed to grow the balance sheet. Capital expenditures are the first items to be subtracted, and changes in operating working capital are the second.

The change in operating working capital excludes any financial flow items; therefore, excess marketable securities and notes due (short-term debt) are not included. Our rule of thumb for deciding on the amount of excess marketable securities is to estimate that the cash and securities needed for operations is roughly 2 percent of sales—any extra is defined as excess marketable securities.

Once we have estimated the free cash flows in future years, we need to determine what those flows are worth today; this is done by discounting them at the firm's weighted average cost of capital. The algebraic expression for determining WACC is

$$\text{WACC} = k_b(1 - T_m)(B/V) + k_s(S/V)$$

For the cost of debt, we use the yield to maturity on 10-year bonds of the same credit rating as the company, for example, 8 percent. The tax rate, T_m, is the marginal statutory corporate rate after federal, state, and local taxes, usually about 41 percent. Using market value weights, the debt-to-value ratio is 30 percent; therefore, the equity-to-value ratio is 70 percent. Finally, the cost of equity is equal to the rate on 10-year government bonds (6 percent), plus a market risk premium of 5.5 percent, multiplied by the measure of systematic risk for the company, which is 1.2. Therefore the cost of equity is 12.6 percent and the weighted average cost of capital is 10.236 percent.

The last part of the valuation is to estimate the present value of the cash flows beyond the explicit forecast period (five years in our simple example). To do this, we need to employ the *continuing value formula*, which can be written as follows:

$$\text{Continuing value} = \text{EBIT}_5(1 - T)(1 + g)(1 - g/r)/(\text{WACC} - g)$$

This formula requires that we estimate, in addition to what we have already estimated, the long-term rate of growth, e.g., in the company's EBIT, and the long-run rate of return on new invested capital. Long-term growth is assumed, in this case, to be roughly equal to long-term inflation (3–4 percent) plus demographic growth (about 1.5 percent), which adds up to about 5 percent. The return on invested capital is expected to be equal to the weighted average cost of capital, about 10.236 percent in the long run, due to competition. Given this assumption, the continuing value formula reduces to be what is called the perpetuity formula, or NOPLAT divided by WACC.

By discounting the forecasted free cash flows of the company during the explicit forecast period ($539), by adding the present value of the continuing value ($5,049), and by adding the value of the excess marketable securities ($404), we obtain the value of the entity. Then we subtract the value of all debt liabilities ($1,665), and the remainder is our estimate of the market value of equity ($4,327).

We used the same discounted-cash-flow process to estimate the market values of AOL and Amazon.com. We started with the same set of assumptions that analysts believed were reasonable for forecasting the basic ingredients of free cash flow, added our own assumptions regarding the nature of competition in the long run, and came up with estimates of the current equity values that (although enormously sensitive to changes in any assumptions) were easily within the actual trading range of stock prices for the two companies.

Table 8-1 · A SIMPLE NUMERICAL EXAMPLE OF A DCF VALUATION*

Forecasted Income	2000	2001	2002	2003	2004	Perpetuity
Revenue	1,300	1,430	1,573	1,730	1,903	2,094
– Cost of goods sold	130	143	157	173	190	209
– Depreciation	228	170	187	206	226	249
– Selling, general, and admin.	130	143	157	173	190	209
EBIT	813	974	1,071	1,178	1,296	1,426
– Interest expense	133	143	159	170	193	217
+ Interest income	30	24	25	19	20	18
Earnings before taxes	709	855	937	1,027	1,123	1,227
– Provision for income tax	291	351	384	421	461	503
Net Income	419	505	553	606	662	724
– Dividends	150	175	200	250	300	350
Change in Retained Earnings	269	330	353	356	363	374
Forecasted Balance Sheet	**2000**	**2001**	**2002**	**2003**	**2004**	**Perpetuity**
Assets						
Cash	130	143	157	173	190	209
Marketable securities	300	200	200	100	100	50
Accounts receivable	260	286	315	346	380	419
Inventories	325	358	393	433	476	523
Gross PP&E	6,500	7,150	7,865	8,652	9,517	10,468
Less accum. depreciation	1,700	1,870	2,057	2,262	2,489	2,738
Net PP&E	4,800	5,280	5,808	6,389	7,028	7,730
Total	5,815	6,267	6,873	7,440	8,175	8,932
Liabilities						
Accounts payable	390	429	472	519	571	628
Accruals	260	286	315	346	381	419
Short-term debt	233	251	275	298	327	357
Long-term debt	930	1,002	1,100	1,190	1,308	1,429
Unscheduled debt	502	530	614	636	780	928
Common	3,000	3,000	3,000	3,000	3,000	3,000
Retained earnings	500	768	1,098	1,451	1,807	2,170
Total	5,815	6,267	6,873	7,440	8,175	8,932
ROIC (percent)	10.11	11.02	11.02	11.02	11.02	11.03
WACC	10.24	10.24	10.24	10.24	10.24	10.24

Table 8-1

A SIMPLE NUMERICAL EXAMPLE OF A DCF VALUATION* cont.

Free Cash Flow	2000	2001	2002	2003	2004	Perpetuity
EBIT	813	974	1,071	1,179	1,296	1,426
Tax	291	351	384	421	461	503
Interest exp. tax shield	55	58	65	70	79	89
Interest inc. tax	−12	−10	−10	−8	−8	−7
Tax on EBIT	333	399	439	483	532	585
Depreciation	228	170	187	206	226	249
Gross cash flow	707	745	819	901	991	1,090
Less CAPEX	500	650	715	787	865	952
Less incr. working cap.	21	7	7	8	9	10
Free cash flow from ops.	228	101	111	122	135	148
Discount factors	.9071	.8229	.7465	.6772	.6143	.6143
Present value of FCF	207	83	83	83	83	
Continuing value						8,220
Present value of CV						5,049

Estimate of the weighted average cost of capital		Estimate of the cost of equity	
Before tax cost of debt (k_b)	8.0%	Risk-free rate	6.0%
One minus the marginal tax rate (T_m)	59%	Market risk premium	5.5%
Percent of debt to entity value	.30	Beta	1.2
Cost of equity (k_s)	12.6%	Cost of equity	12.6%
Percent of equity to entity value	.70		
WACC	10.236%		

Valuation Results

Present value of explicit cash flows	539
+ Present value of continuing value	5,049
= Entity value	5,588
+ Value of excess marketable securities	404
− Debt value	1,163
= Equity value	4,829

*All figures are rounded to the nearest whole figure.

EMERGING GROWTH COMPANIES

Emerging growth companies are still small but have broken through to a high-growth track and are full of optionality (flexibility). We recently successfully used a real-option approach to value an emerging growth company, an Internet portal. The company was asking $600 million to be acquired, but a standard discounted-cash-flow valuation indicated a value of only $69 million. We recognized, however, that there were significant options involved. On the up-side, if the company proved successful, its operations could be expanded by investing more (the exercise price of a call option to expand). If things went badly, the company could be sold for a bargain basement floor price (an abandonment put option). When our work was finished, the option pricing approach estimated the value of the emerging growth company at roughly $443 million.

To determine the option pricing, we used the four-step process illustrated in Exhibit 8-8. We started with the standard discounted-cash-flow method to estimate the present value (PV) of the company ($69 million) without any of the flexibility. Next, the uncertainties that affect the value of the company needed to be estimated. For this Internet portal, four variables were believed to be important: the number of e-orders, the average revenue per order, the cost of goods sold as a percentage of sales, and the average acquisition cost per customer.

Exhibit 8-9 shows the modeling of the uncertainty of e-orders as an example. We asked management to begin by estimating the expected number of e-orders each year for the next five years. This forecast is the line that starts at 29,417 and ends five years later at 726,665. Next they were asked to provide an estimate of the 95 percent

Exhibit 8-8 REAL-OPTIONS ANALYSIS— A FOUR-STEP PROCESS

Steps	Compute Base Case Present Value (PV) without Flexibility, Using DCF Valuation Model	Model the Uncertainty, Using Event Trees	Identify and Incorporate Managerial Flexibilities by Creating a Decision Tree	Calculate Real-Option Present Value (ROA)
Objectives	• Compute base case present value without flexibility	• Identify major uncertainties in each stage • Understand how those uncertainties affect the PV	• Analyze the event tree to identify and incorporate managerial flexibility to respond to new information	• Value the total project using a simple algebraic methodology
Comments		• Still no flexibility; this value should equal the value from Step 1 • Explicitly estimate uncertainty	• Incorporating flexibility transforms event trees, which transforms them into decision trees • The flexibility continuously alters the risk characteristics of the project, and hence the cost of capital	• ROA includes the base case present value without flexibility plus the option (flexibility) value • Under high uncertainty and managerial flexibility, option value will be substantial
Output	• Project's PV without flexibility	• Detailed event tree capturing the possible present values of the project	• A detailed decision tree combining possible events and management responses	• ROA of the project and optimal action plan for the available real options

Exhibit 8-9

UNCERTAINTY ABOUT THE
NUMBER OF E-ORDERS

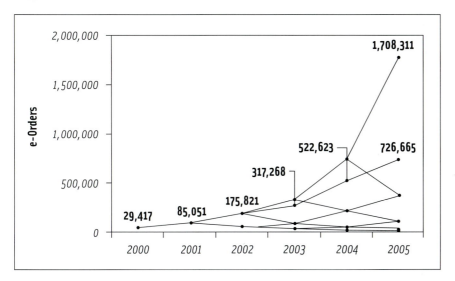

confidence interval for around the mean forecast in 2005. The high end of the range was 1,708,311 and was based on aggressive assumptions about the size of the eventual market and about the portal's share of it. At the low side of the range, orders might fall as low as 4,275, only about 14 percent of current demand. Once we had the expected values and the 95 percent confidence interval, we constructed lognormal probabilities year by year that were consistent with the client's beliefs.

Once the volatility of each source of uncertainty was estimated, then those estimates were combined by running them through a Monte Carlo simulation that ran samples of the four variables through a DCF valuation model.[4] The output was the distribution of present values shown in Exhibit 8-10. The average value is still $69 million, but now we have an estimate of the variance around that average.

The final outcome of the second step of our analysis was an event tree (a lattice) based on percentage changes in the value of the project as reflected in the output of the Monte Carlo simulations. The results are shown in Exhibit 8-11. (Note that the present value is still $69 million, so that if the flexibility is removed, we end up with the DCF result.)

The third step of the real-options analysis was to build the two real options—the right to expand and the right to abandon—into the event tree so that it becomes a decision tree. Both decisions are available at each node, but are exercised only if the act of doing so produces the maximum value at each decision node in the lattice. Our client believed that the right to expand was a real option because, if the Internet portal turned out to be successful, it could be expanded anytime during the next five years. The expected benefit would be to increase the value of the business by 25 percent, and the cost (the exercise price of the option) would be $400 million. There was also a second type of real option—namely, the right to abandon the project at a "floor" price should it get into trouble. The action taken in this case would be to stop further investment and to close the portal. The exercise price paid by this put option was assumed to be zero. In other words, the owners would receive no liquidation value; they would just avoid negative cash flows.

Exhibit 8-10 · MONTE CARLO SIMULATION OF THE PROBABILITY DISTRIBUTION OF PRESENT VALUES

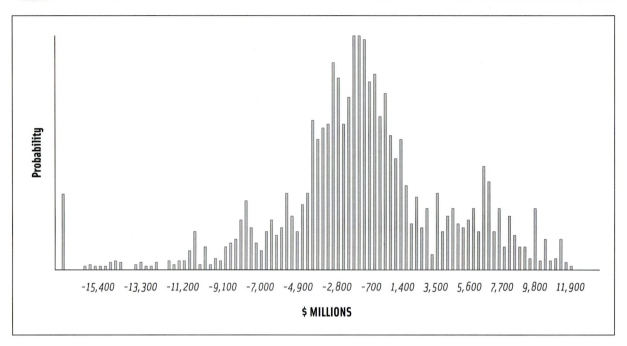

Exhibit 8-11 · PRESENT VALUE (PV) EVENT TREE

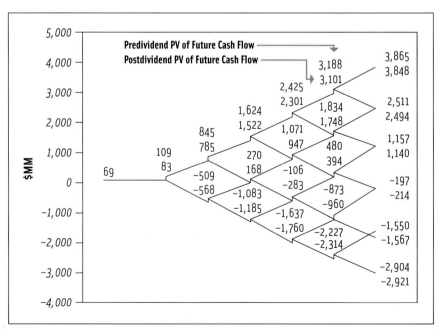

Exhibit 8-12 shows the optimal decisions and their timing, which is dependent on whether the value of the business has gone up or down. (Note that expansion optimally takes place in Year 5 in the two highest states of nature, and that abandonment would take place in Years 3, 4, or 5 if the value of the company falls enough.)

The real options in this case were very valuable—raising the estimated value from a DCF-based estimate of $69 million to a real-options estimate of $443 million. As is often the case, options add significantly to the value when the DCF value without the options is small, or close to zero. This is often true of emerging growth companies, like the Internet portal, that have not yet established a track record, have no current earnings, but could become very successful. Remember, our real-options analysis reduced to the same value as the DCF analysis when flexibility was removed. The added value of the flexibility to expand or to abandon was particularly valuable because of the high volatility in the estimates of future subscription rates, the number of e-orders, acquisition costs, and operating costs as a percentage of revenues.

MORE ON THE VALUATION OF REAL OPTIONS*

It is not possible to become an expert on the valuation of real options in only a few pages, but we can give a simple example that illustrates some of the key differences between DCF and **real-options analysis (ROA)**. Consider a simple two-period investment. The cash flows of a project are $100 right now, but they can go up by 20 percent (and down by 16.7 percent) a year for two years. At the end of the second year, the company has two mutually exclusive alternatives. At a cost of $700, it can lock in the second year cash flow forever or abandon the project.**

OPTIMAL EXECUTION
OF REAL OPTIONS

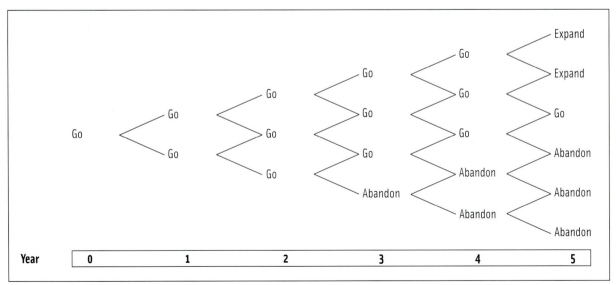

Otherwise, the company can spend an additional $120 at the end of the second year for a test market study. It will last one year with no cash flow and will indicate with 50–50 probability that the perpetual cash flows starting in Year 4 will be either 50 percent higher or $33\frac{1}{3}$ percent lower than the flows in Year 2. As before, at Year 4, the company can lock in the cash flows forever at a cost of $700 or abandon the project. The cost of capital is 10 percent, the risk-free rate is 5 percent, and the project costs $400. We will solve by first using **net present value (NPV) analysis,** then by using ROA. Because NPV analysis cannot capture the flexibility we have to choose from between the two alternatives, each alternative has its own NPV. The free cash flow tree for the first two years is identical for the two alternatives, as shown in Exhibit 8-13.

Based on the cost of capital and on the up and down coefficients (u = 1.2, d = 0.833), we can calculate the probabilities for each point in the tree. In the "go straight to market" alternative, the analysis shows that we never abandon the project at the end of Year 2 and always make the $700 investment to lock in the free cash flows forever (see Exhibit 8-14). Using the objective probabilities, we can calculate the expected free cash flow for each year. Discounted at 10 percent, the present value equals $722. Therefore, the net present value is

$$NPV = 722 - 400 = 322$$

In the "take the additional test" alternative, the objective probability for each point in Year 3 is the same as in Year 2 and then split in half (see Exhibit 8-15).

The analysis shows that we should abandon the project at the end of Year 4 only in one of the possible outcomes (see Exhibit 8-16). Using the objective

Exhibit 8-13 CASH FLOWS AND PROBABILITIES FOR THE FIRST TWO YEARS OF THE PROJECT

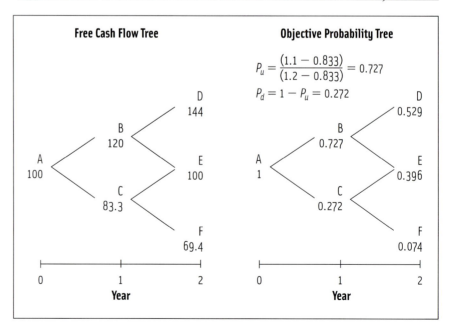

Exhibit
8-14
GO STRAIGHT TO
MARKET ALTERNATIVE

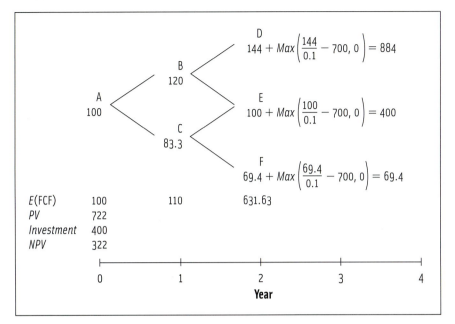

$$D$$
$$144 + Max\left(\frac{144}{0.1} - 700, 0\right) = 884$$

B
120

A
100

$$E$$
$$100 + Max\left(\frac{100}{0.1} - 700, 0\right) = 400$$

C
83.3

$$F$$
$$69.4 + Max\left(\frac{69.4}{0.1} - 700, 0\right) = 69.4$$

E(FCF)	100	110	631.63
PV	722		
Investment	400		
NPV	322		

0	1	2	3	4

Year

Exhibit
8-15
OBJECTIVE PROBABILITIES FOR THE
CASE WITH ADDITIONAL TEST

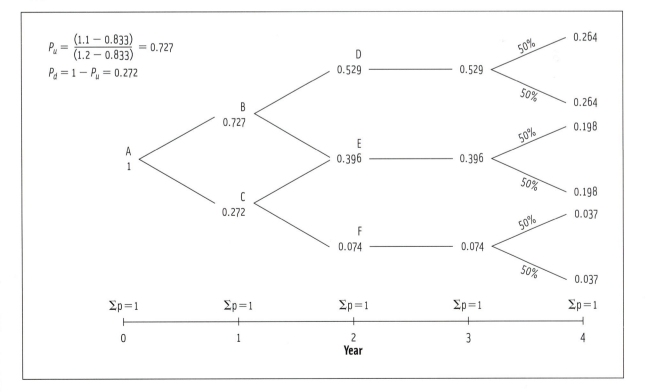

$$P_u = \frac{(1.1 - 0.833)}{(1.2 - 0.833)} = 0.727$$

$$P_d = 1 - P_u = 0.272$$

D
0.529 — 0.529
50% 0.264
50% 0.264

B
0.727

A
1

E
0.396 — 0.396
50% 0.198
50% 0.198

C
0.272

F
0.074 — 0.074
50% 0.037
50% 0.037

$\Sigma p = 1$	$\Sigma p = 1$	$\Sigma p = 1$	$\Sigma p = 1$	$\Sigma p = 1$
0	1	2	3	4

Year

probabilities, we can calculate the expected free cash flow for each year. Discounted at 10 percent, the present value equals $712.55. Therefore, the net present value is:

$$NPV = 712.55 - 400 = 312.55$$

Unable to account for the future flexibility to choose one of the two alternatives—instead, forced to commit to one alternative now, we would select the first, based on its higher NPV.

ROA solves the same problem by using a decision tree (working backward through time) and by using a **replicating portfolio** technique to guarantee that all decisions are valued appropriately. ROA allows us to correctly model the fact that we don't have to choose an alternative now. We can and should wait until the end of Year 2 to make an optimal choice based on the present value that each alternative provides (see Exhibit 8-17).

To illustrate the flexibility at the end of Year 2, we can look at decision node D. We will choose the alternative that has the greater value—either going straight to market or investing in a test marketing study. If we go straight to market, our payoff at the end of Year 2 is $144 plus the present value of $144 forever, discounted at 10 percent and minus the $700 investment, i.e., $144 + $144/0.1 − $700 = $884. In other words, we have a call option on the perpetuity of the cash flow with an exercise price of $700. If we consider the test marketing alternative, our payoffs at the end of the fourth year will be as shown in Exhibit 8-18. After the test, we have the

Exhibit 8-16 FREE CASH FLOW TREE FOR THE CASE WITH ADDITIONAL TEST

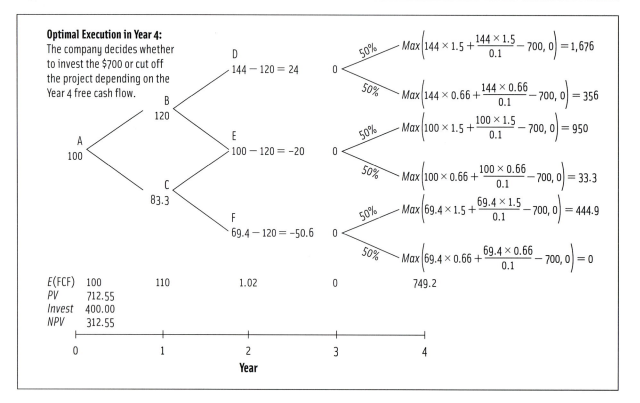

Exhibit 8-17 ROA FREE CASH FLOW TREE

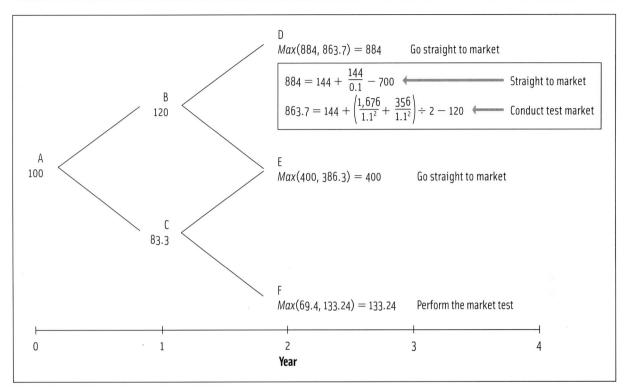

right, but not the obligation, to spend the $700 and lock in the cash flow forever. Here again, we have a call option with a $700 exercise price in Year 4. At the end of Year 2, we have the option to choose between the two alternatives. The present value of the second alternative at decision node D can be shown as follows: $(1,676/1.1^2 + 356/1.1^2)/2 + 144 - 120 = 863.7$. Being rational, we should go straight to market if the project is at node D.

Because of the changing risk profile of the project and depending on which branch of the event tree materializes, we cannot discount the values along each branch at 10 percent of the cost of capital. We will use the value tree of the project for one of the alternatives without flexibility as an underlying risky asset to find its value with flexibility. The value tree of the project with the "go straight to market" alternative is shown in Exhibit 8-18.

To illustrate the use of replicating portfolio to value the option to choose alternatives, let us analyze the value of the project at point C. After this point, the project's value can move either up to point E or down to point F. Without the option, the value of the project (V) at this point is C = 281.7 (after the free cash flow at C), E = 400, and F = 69.4. This means that if the project was "trading" at point C, it would be priced at $281.7 and would be expected to reach $400 or $69.4 a year later at points E and F respectively.

As Exhibit 8-19 clearly shows, we will exercise our right to go straight to market at E and will choose to test market at F. The value of the project with the option at these two points is E = 400 and F = 133.2 . The question we face is: What is the

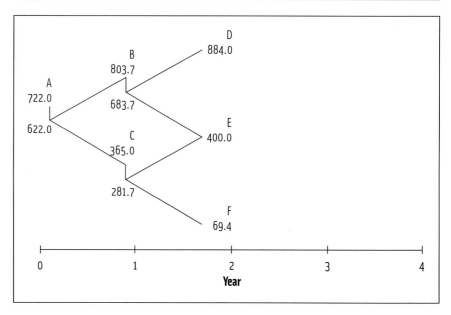

value of the project with this option at point C? We can find this value by creating a replicating portfolio that consists of "m" units of the underlying risky asset and "B" dollars of risk-free bonds. This portfolio will have exactly the same payoffs as the project with the option at the end of the third period—E = 400 and F = 133.2.

$$\text{Replicating portfolio} = mV + B$$

At the end of the period, the replicating portfolio will have the following payoffs:

For point E: $m400 + (1+r_f)B = 400$
For point D: $m69.4 + (1+r_f)B = 133.2$

We have two equations and two unknowns. Solving for m and B, we get:

m = 0.807, and B = –$73.57

The value of the replicating portfolio for point C is as follows:

$0.807 \times (\$440) - \$73.57 = \$300.9$

Because the replicating portfolio has exactly the same end-of-year payoffs (E and F) as the project with the option flexibility, the portfolio's value is equal to the value of the project with the option flexibility at point C. Applying the same approach to the other intermediate point B and then moving backward to point A, we can estimate the present value of the project with a flexibility of 728.84. The NPV of the project with flexibility is as follows:

$$\text{NPV} = 728.84 - 400 = 338.84$$

| Exhibit 8-19 | ROA VALUE OF THE PROJECT WITH FLEXIBILITY |

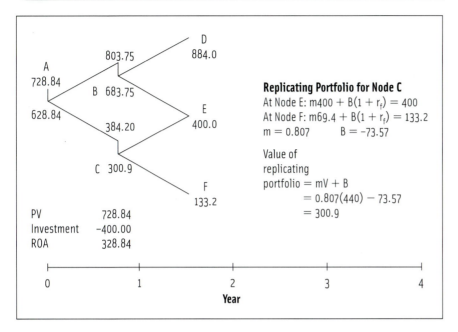

Replicating Portfolio for Node C
At Node E: $m400 + B(1 + r_f) = 400$
At Node F: $m69.4 + B(1 + r_f) = 133.2$
$m = 0.807 \qquad B = -73.57$

Value of replicating portfolio = $mV + B$
$= 0.807(440) - 73.57$
$= 300.9$

PV	728.84
Investment	−400.00
ROA	328.84

There are several lessons to learn from this example. First, the NPV approach must treat the choice of test marketing versus going straight to market as mutually exclusive alternatives with two different valuations, while the real-options analysis provides a single present value result. Consequently, the NPV analysis concluded that one of the alternatives (in our example, it is "going straight to market") is better, while the real-options analysis selects one or the other based on the conditions of the project at the time of the decision. As a result, the value of the project with flexibility is higher than both alternative NPVs.

$$338.84 > 322 > 312.55$$

When a company is small it is really like a single project—its business prospects are highly volatile. Furthermore, options like the option to expand the scale of operations (**expansion option**), to scale down, or to abandon (**abandonment option**), are important—more important than they would be for a robust growth company with a well-diversified portfolio. The optionality of a single project is much less important for robust growth companies.

EMBRYONIC COMPANIES

What about the case of a small company that was founded 18 months ago, has only 20 employees, sales revenues of only a few million dollars, and no profits—and it sells for a billion dollars? Examples are Yahoo!'s acquisition of Geocities and @Home's acquisition of Excite. Both acquisitions took place in January 1999 (see

Exhibit 8-20). Geocities had sales of $13 million, 281 employees, and losses of $14 million, yet it sold for a multiple of 372 times sales—$4.66 billion. Excite had even larger losses of $37 million, on sales of $154 million. It sold for $6.06 billion—a multiple of 39 times sales.

There is no rational basis for paying such high multiples for these companies as stand-alone businesses. No forecast of their free cash flows, even under the most optimistic scenario, would justify such high prices.

Remember though, that the guiding principle of valuation is the value of an asset is its value in its best use. In both cases, the value of the target companies was based not on their stand-alone value, but rather on their value impact on the companies that acquired them. The appropriate valuation is the discounted value of the change in cash flows of the acquiring companies. For the target company to get the maximum price, there should be several potential buyers; otherwise the bargaining power of the much larger acquirer may result in a lower transaction price.

GeoCities was the definitive leader in personal publishing tools and Web-based communities. Its combination with Yahoo! without question enhanced Yahoo!'s position as one of the world's leading globally branded Web networks. Through GeoCities, Yahoo! will be able to integrate and distribute a powerful set of state-of-the-art editing tools and content published through personal homepages in an array of services, e.g., Yahoo! Clubs, Yahoo! Shopping, and Yahoo! Classifieds. The merger facilitates the distribution of Yahoo! Services, including shopping, commu-

Exhibit 8-20 EXAMPLES OF VALUE IN BEST USE

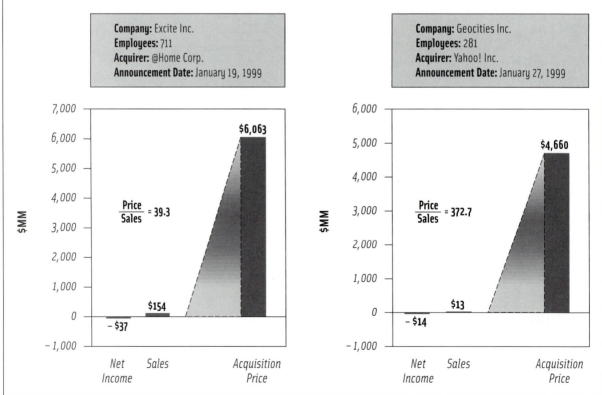

nications, and personalized services to the extensive community of GeoCities members.

The logic behind @Home's acquisition of Excite was equally compelling. The combined company utilizes the high-speed, always-on attributes of cable to provide residential subscribers with multimedia content that goes far beyond current web experiences. Moreover, in the workplace, Excite@Home will deliver advanced data services that will allow businesses using the Internet to cut costs, enhance productivity, and compete globally.

To provide an idea of the kind of value that an embryonic growth company can command, we took the hypothetical case of "Newco," which has a proprietary technology that AOL could use to increase its growth rate by only 1 percent. If this were the case, AOL's revenue, which was $4.8 in 1998, would grow to $29.8 billion by the year 2009, instead of to $27.5 billion (our original forecast). On a graph, this change is hard to grasp. Nevertheless, the present value of Newco amounts to $10.8 billion, the maximum amount that AOL could afford to pay and still hope to create value for its shareholders.

SCHWAB'S VALUATION

Each chapter in this book has had a little to add to the case history of Schwab. What can our valuation methods contribute? Take a look at Exhibit 8-21. It shows the market capitalization–to-sales ratio for Schwab over the last decade, along with earnings growth estimates and the S&P 500 index. Schwab was more or less tracking the S&P until 1998–1999, when it more than doubled from three times sales to eight or nine times sales. By the way, earnings growth estimates did not rise substantially. What happened? The explanation that fits the picture is that Schwab was

Exhibit 8-21 THE RISE IN SCHWAB'S MARKET-TO-SALES RATIO

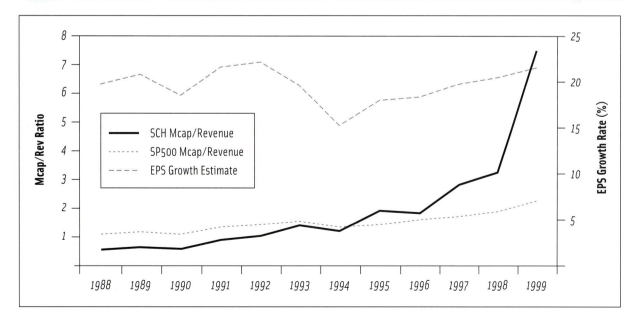

an early entrant into the Internet business, beating its competition to a rapid growth market that would not increase profitability in the short run but had enormous promise for the long run. Is the market's valuation reasonable? We think so, due to the option to expand the e-business if it shows promise of succeeding or to abandon it if it proves to be a disappointment.

SUMMARY

The valuation of Internet companies is not completely irrational. An acquirer who believes that it is could open itself to overpaying. Without a logical anchor, it could become easy to drift into paying any price. We have shown by example that standard discounted-cash-flow valuation works well for large companies with robust growth. We had no difficulty using analyst forecasts, coupled with some careful thought about the logical industry structure a decade from now, to build valuations that were easily within the trading ranges of AOL and Amazon.com at the time of this writing. We also saw that the estimated values were very sensitive to relatively small changes in assumptions about NOPLAT and ROIC.

Next, we examined emerging growth companies, using an Internet portal as an example. These companies are at an inflection point. Either they will break into robust growth, resulting in the valuable option to expand, or they will fail and should be abandoned. We used real options to show how the value of an Internet portal could increase from $68 to $443 million when the value of expansion and abandonment options was considered. The real-options approach applies best to those situations in which the company value depends on the success or failure of a few projects that have wide variability in their possible outcomes. Finally, we discussed how embryonic companies with justified high multiples should be valued based on how they affect the discounted cash flows of the large, high-growth companies that could acquire them.

In all three cases, the valuation can be tied back to logical roots. Therefore, valuations can be understood. Acquirers can estimate a range of prices that is justified and can keep from overpaying. Of course, not all prices that are paid are necessarily justifiable, and it is a safe bet that in most unjustifiable situations, emotion and the magic of smoke and mirrors won the day.

1. How can one apply discounted-cash-flow analysis for robust growth companies?

Robust growth companies may be thought of as portfolios of hundreds of projects, and the optionality on any one project is not usually material to the overall value of the company. Valuing robust growth companies requires three analytical steps. First, forecast future cash flows using data from analysts' reports. Second, calculate a weighted average cost of capital and discount the cash flows to derive the present value. Lastly, calculate and discount a terminal value for the company; this is determined by the company's projected future growth and how much the company makes on new investment compared with the cost of the capital that it invests.

2. How and when is it appropriate to use a real-options methodology for valuing emerging growth companies?

Emerging companies are small, high-growth businesses that have yet to establish a track record of profitability but are highly flexible and may have investment or growth opportunities that could greatly increase their cash flows. These opportunities have an option value that often represents a very significant portion of the company's total value. In these cases, it is most appropriate to use a real-options-based valuation technique. By modeling the value and probability of the growth opportunities and then assuming that management will make rational decisions, it is possible to create a decision tree that shows the value of the company under different scenarios. The net present value of a replicating portfolio gives the value of the company.

3. How should we think about valuing start-up companies?

The value of start-up companies is a reflection of the marginal value that they can create in the acquirer's business, rather than the cash flows that they will create by themselves. Valuations of these types of companies are often based on synergies between two businesses, rather than on the value of the business as a stand-alone company. An acquisition that could increase the growth of a very large and profitable company such as AOL by an increment of just 1 percent per year could be worth billions of dollars to the shareholders of AOL. This explains the huge premiums that are sometimes paid for these companies.

4. How do valuation methodologies actually work?

Valuation methodologies evaluate the amount that the company is worth to its owners, taking into account factors such as the time value of money and the cost of any new capital that must be invested in the business. Sometimes the value of a company is primarily derived from the cash flows that it is expected to generate in the future from its existing business; sometimes it is from the new business opportunities that the company will be able to pursue and that in turn will generate cash flows. Other times, the value of a business is derived from the beneficial effects that the business will have on the cash flows of the buyer's existing business.

5. When is one valuation methodology more appropriate than others?

We have seen that each of our valuation techniques is appropriate for different circumstances. When a company is well established and is either profitable or has a clear path to profitability, it is possible to use a standard discounted-cash-flow forecast based on analysts' forecasts. Valuations of these robust growth companies are usually very sensitive to very small changes in growth or profitability assumptions. When companies are emerging growth companies, most of their value is tied up in the opportunities, or options, that they will have, so a real-options-based valuation, though rather technical, will deliver the best results. Finally, embryonic, start-up companies are best valued by examining the impact that they will have on the acquirer's business, rather than by valuing them as stand-alones.

KEY TERMS

embryonic company	operating margin
emerging growth company	discounted cash flow (DCF)
robust growth company	free cash flows (FCF)
beta	earnings before interest and taxes (EBIT)
bond rating	
weighted average cost of capital (WACC)	real-options analysis (ROA)
continuing (or terminal) value	net present value (NPV) analysis
net operating profit less adjusted taxes (NOPLAT)	replicating portfolio
	expansion option
return on invested capital (ROIC)	abandonment option
	market risk premium

Endnotes

[1]Greenspan, Alan. 1996. Excerpt from a speech given by the Federal Reserve chairman, 5 December.

[2]Copeland, Thomas E., Tim Koller, and Jack Murrin, Valuation: Measuring and Managing the Value of Companies, 3rd ed. (New York: John Wiley, 2000).

[3]To estimate the taxes the company would have paid, start with the provision for income taxes on the income statement, add back the tax rate times interest expenses, and subtract out the tax rate times interest income.

[4]For simplicity, we assumed that the four variables were independent of each other, although it is also possible to assume they are correlated and still use the Monte Carlo model.

*Author's note: I would like to acknowledge the invaluable contribution in the real options portion of this chapter by my colleague Vladimir Antikarov.

**The abandonment of a project with negative NPV, particularly when the project is the company, is usually forced by bankruptcy. In this sense, here we consider the abandonment option as assumed in the NPV calculation.*

9

Network Infrastructure

The purpose of this chapter is to provide a basic understanding of the network infrastructure that allows businesses to compete in the New Economy. We will discuss how the Internet began, how it works, and how future advances in technology and changes in public policy will transform it even further.

In the first section, we will examine the development of the microprocessor, operating systems, and the graphical user interface. We then continue with the Internet's evolution—from its creation as a means to maintain communications in the event of a nuclear attack to its transformation during the 1970s and 1980s into an electronic repository for academic research, to its most recent emergence, at the beginning of the twenty-first century, into a medium for communications, commerce, news, and entertainment.

In the second section, we will illustrate how Internet users are able to connect to one another through the World Wide Web, and how new, cutting-edge technologies, such as broadband and wireless transmission, will impact and enhance both business-to-consumer and business-to-business relationships online in the future.

In the third section, we will show how commercial enterprises are beginning to use the Internet as a foundation upon which to build their information systems by establishing online applications for individual business processes, such as customer service, supply-chain management, enterprise resource planning, and procurement.

Finally, in the chapter's last section, we will review how increased usage of the Internet by both consumers and businesses alike will affect laws governing privacy, taxation, access, patent rights, free speech, and network economics and monopolies.

This chapter was coauthored by Bernie Jaworski, Jeffrey Rayport, and Dickson Louie.

Please consider the following questions as you read this chapter:

1. How was the development of the microprocessor important to the Internet?

2. How was the development of a graphical interface important to the Internet?

3. What are the Internet and the World Wide Web, and why are they important?

4. How do we access the Internet?

5. How can the Internet be used in business processes?

6. How will the increased use of the Internet affect public policy and politics?

Underlying each strategic decision is the **market infrastructure,** or the general industry environment outside the boundaries and largely outside the control of the specific business. This environment, with both opportunities and constraints, can be subclassified into two broad categories: network infrastructure and media infrastructure. Two forms of convergence have been occurring: network and media. Both of these infrastructures are converging independently due to the digitization of information. We have **digital convergence** with the network infrastructure, now fully digital, leading to massive cross-industry competition across telecommunications, satellite, cable, and wireless industries. These heretofore indirect or noncompetitors now are all competing for the same customers. We also find that a second type of convergence—what we term as **media convergence**—is unfolding. In Chapter 10, we explore how the major content players of the twentieth century—radio, television, magazines, film, newspapers, and now the dot-coms—are competing to deliver content to the same target segments.

Network infrastructure is the basic, underlying group of electronic devices and connecting circuitry designed as a system to share information. This infrastructure includes all the various communications systems and networks now in use, such as the telephone, cable television, broadcast radio and television, computer, satellite, and wireless telephone. Network infrastructure refers to the hardware and software used in communication. Computer networks are used wherever any two or more computers are connected for the exchange and sharing of data and system resources. These networks can be characterized by topology, types of signals, type of connection, and type of physical link. Network infrastructure companies and service providers enable the transport of digital information.

The story of the evolution of network infrastructure and the emergence of the digital economy is a tale of two worldwide technological shifts woven together over the past three decades—the increased use of personal computers and the rising popularity of the Internet. To understand the market infrastructure for the New Economy, we first review the beginnings of the digital economy with the development of the microprocessor. Then, we examine the Internet and how it has evolved over the past three decades—its own history interwoven with that of the personal computer—from initially, in the early 1960s, a Cold War communications tool for the U.S. Department of Defense into today's converging mass medium channel for communications, commerce, news, and entertainment for millions of individuals and businesses worldwide (see Exhibit 9-1).

HOW WAS THE DEVELOPMENT OF THE MICROPROCESSOR IMPORTANT TO THE INTERNET?

One fundamental aspect of the New Economy is that there is an expanded presence of technology-mediated screen-to-face interfaces, all of which are powered by embedded microprocessors. The proliferation of screen-to-face interfaces was made possible with the mid-1960s development of the microprocessor—the central processing unit (CPU), made up of several highly integrated circuits on a single silicon chip—which foreshadowed the personal computer revolution in the following decade. Let us briefly review the evolution of the computer from its initial expensive mainframe centralized computing to today's highly decentralized, inexpensively distributed computing using microcomputers.

Early Computers

During Word War II, in 1943, the first electronic computers were developed by the British government to help crack secret German military codes. These first-generation computers were powered by 2,000 vacuum tubes to perform calculations at a rate of 5,000 characters per second. In 1958, Seymour Cray introduced the second generation of electronic computing using transistors that were one-hundredth the size of vacuum tubes when he created the Control Data Corporation CDC 1604.

Exhibit 9-1 NETWORK AND MEDIA CONVERGENCE

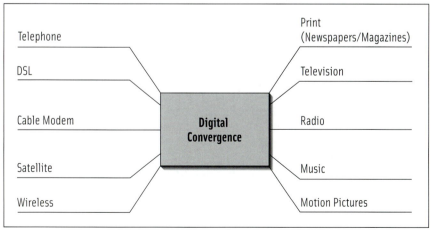

That same year, Jack Kilby of Texas Instruments and Robert Noyce of Intel Corporation each independently developed the first integrated circuits. Seven years later, in 1965, the IBM 360 was introduced as the first mainframe computer using integrated circuits (IC). In that same year, 1965, the Digital Equipment Corporation (DEC) launched the PDP-8 as its first minicomputer.[1] In 1967, DEC introduced the PDP-10, designed for timesharing and real-time operations, which became very popular with university computing centers and research laboratories.

Early **mainframe computers** were extremely bulky in size, typically with a room-sized central processing unit. **Supercomputers** are a class of mainframe computers; this class usually refers to the fastest computing CPU available at the time (at the time of this writing, IBM delivered a computer employing 8,000 microprocessors in parallel, capable of executing over 12 trillion operations per second). The term "super-computer" can also now refer to a very large server. The smaller, refrigerator-sized **minicomputer** became increasingly popular as miniaturization and integration of circuitry continued to reduce the cost and size of computing. Minicomputers are intermediate-size computers between microcomputers (those used for personal computing) and mainframes. Typically, minicomputers are stand-alones, with attached terminals and other peripherals sold for general business applications and department-level operations.

Microprocessors

The first **microprocessors** were based on third-generation integrated-circuit technology. In 1971, Intel Corporation created the 4004, its first microprocessor using integrated circuits with the equivalent of 2,300 transistors. Microprocessors were different from the prior generation of computers in that each contained several integrated circuits on a *single silicon chip* rather than several integrated circuits on a *single circuit board.* The 4004 chip was initially used to power electronic pocket calculators produced by Busicom, a Japanese manufacturer. These calculators weighed about 2.5 pounds and cost about $150. In the calculator's original design, 12 chips were needed, each with a separate function. The 4004 chip unified these functions into a single processor.[2]

In 1972, Intel introduced the 8008, its second microprocessor, which had twice the power of the original 4004 and could be used to power dummy terminals connected to mainframes. A third microprocessor, the 8080, was developed by Intel in 1973. In 1975, using the 8080 microprocessor as its CPU, the MITS Altair 8800 became the first **microcomputer,** a computer designed for personal computing (PC)—one person per computer—a radical new idea.

Five years later in 1978, Intel created its next generation of microprocessors, the 8088 chip, which IBM selected as the CPU for the first business-oriented personal computers and established Intel microprocessors as part of the architecture standard. In 1982, Intel produced the 80286 microprocessor (or the "286" chip), which allowed personal computers to run multiple applications simultaneously for the first time. And in 1985 Intel introduced the 80386 microprocessor (or the "386" chip), with the equivalent of 275,000 transistors and 100 times the processing speed of the original 4004 microprocessor.

The Intel Pentium family of microprocessors, which includes the Pentium, the Pentium Pro, the Pentium II, and the Pentium III, has dominated the manufacturing of microprocessor chips worldwide since 1981. The Pentium processor has enabled the average computer user to easily access the multimedia now prevalent in websites on the Internet.

With each succeeding generation, the transistors found on a microprocessor have become more densely packed. The Pentium microprocessor introduced in 1993 had the equivalent of 3.1 million transistors. The Pentium Pro introduced in 1995 had the equivalent of 5.5 million transistors. The Pentium II introduced in 1997 had the equivalent of 7.5 million transistors. And the Pentium III microprocessor introduced in 1999 had the equivalent of 9.5 million transistors.[3] Between 1993 and 2000, the average cost of a microprocessor dropped from $300 per unit for a Pentium Pro to $193 per unit[4] for a Pentium III. To serve a market of low-cost PC notebooks with a retail price of $1,000 or less, Intel introduced its Celeron processor in March 1998.[5]

In addition to Intel, which has an 82 percent market share[6] of all microprocessor chips produced for the personal computer worldwide, other major manufacturers of microprocessors include Advanced Micro Devices (AMD), the Taiwan-based Via Corporation, and Motorola. During the first quarter of 2000, Intel's closest competitor, AMD, increased market share from 16.6 percent to 17 percent—largely through the introduction of its high-end Athlon chip, which many PC manufacturers sought to use due to a shortage of Pentium III chips.[7]

Motorola introduced the 88000 Power PC Reduced Instruction Set Control (RISC) chip, which would later be developed jointly by Apple, IBM, and Motorola. The first personal computers to use the Power PC RISC chips were the Macintosh Power PCs, beginning in 1994. By the end of 1999, the Power PC chips found on the Apple G4 desktop personal computer had the computing power of one billion operations per second, or about equivalent to the calculating power of the Cray 2 supercomputer introduced in 1985.[8]

Between 1995 and 1999, the number of households in the United States with access to a personal computer increased from 33.2 million to 51.9 million, reflecting a penetration increase from 34 percent to 51 percent of all households nationwide (see Table 9-1).[9] During that same time period, the average per-unit cost of a

Table 9-1 NUMBER OF U.S. COMPUTER USERS AND U.S. INTERNET HOUSEHOLDS— 1994 TO 1999

	Internet Users (Millions)	Percent	Computer Households (Millions)	Percent
1994	–	–	–	–
1995	–	–	33.2	34.0%
1996	8.5	8.6%	38.2	39.1%
1997	14.5	14.5%	44.0	44.0%
1998	24.4	24.2%	47.8	47.3%
1999	28.0	27.5%	51.9	51.0%
2000 estimate	32.0	31.3%	55.1	53.8%
2001 estimate	35.3	34.2%	56.0	–
2002 estimate	44.0	42.5%	57.0	–

Source: U.S. Department of Commerce, 1999. Cited in *The New York Times 2000 Almanac*

personal computer decreased by 20 percent, from \$1,500 to \$1,200 per unit.[10] This cost decrease occurred despite a geometric increase in microprocessor calculating power. Microprocessors gave each personal computer the equivalent computing power of an early-generation mainframe computer. At the end of the second quarter of 1999, the leading manufacturers of personal computers in the United States and worldwide were Dell, Compaq, IBM, Gateway, and Hewlett Packard.[11]

Computing Power and Moore's Law

The decrease in the average price of a personal computer, coupled with a corresponding increase in computing power, reflects **Moore's Law,** a concept developed by Gordon Moore, a cofounder of Intel Corporation. In 1965, Moore predicted that the calculating power of a computer microprocessor would double every 12 months for the next 10 years. Ten years later his prediction had proven true. Moore then forecasted in 1975 that the doubling would occur every 2 years for the next 10 years through 1985. In the late 1980s, Moore again estimated that this doubling would continue for another decade.[12] The important point to note is that the development of the microprocessor, with its rapid growth in computing power, allowed the creation of and wide availability of inexpensive, powerful microcomputers.

At the beginning of the year 2000, the most common way for home access to the Internet was with the use of a PC, a browser, an analog modem, and an analog telephone line. Connectivity to the Internet through digital subscriber lines (DSLs) and cable modems were expected to become more commonplace with the increasing number of Web offerings that assumed broadband access by users.

HOW WAS THE DEVELOPMENT OF A GRAPHICAL INTERFACE IMPORTANT TO THE INTERNET?

The development of the microprocessor, with its rapid growth in computing power (following Moore's Law), allowed microcomputers to run larger and more sophisticated operating systems and applications. The **operating system (OS)** is a set of instructions to a computer on how to operate its various parts and peripherals.[13] Each operating system provides a standard on which to build software applications. Each operating system has inherent design strengths and weaknesses in its approach to providing applications developers the facilities to control computer hardware and, therefore, each creates constraints to software applications development; e.g., MS-DOS was originally designed for text-only display, not graphics, while the Mac OS was designed for graphic display from the beginning. Operating system constraints have profound implications when one begins to consider the evolving nature of screen-to-face interfaces now pervasive within the Internet (i.e., interfaces are increasingly graphical in design).

Operating Systems

In 1999, the Microsoft operating systems—Windows (95, 98, NT, 2000) and Microsoft-Disk Operating System (MS-DOS)—were the most dominant operating systems in the United States with nearly 90 percent market share. Other major

What Is the Difference Between Analog and Digital Information?

We live in an analog physical world, that is, **analog information** is continuously variable in quality. When we speak, our mouths create air pressure changes that are continuously variable that are then captured by our ears, converting air pressure changes to mechanical changes by our eardrums to nerve cell stimulation and transmission to the brain as we hear and perceive sounds as speech. Continuously variable light is reflected off objects in our field of vision, focused by the lens of our eye onto our retina, converted to nerve cell stimulation by the eyes' internal rods and cones, and transmitted to the brain as we see and perceive the varying light in sight as patterns.

With the use of a COder-DECoder (or "codec"), analog signals can be digitized through an analog-to-digital (A-to-D) conversion process, and digital signals can be converted into analog signals through a digital-to-analog (D-to-A) process. A-to-D and D-to-A conversions are done routinely to bring all types of signals in and out of the digital domain for fast, inexpensive, and precise processing or mixing with other digital signals, which are then returned to the analog physical world for our consumption.

Until the recent availability of inexpensive digital signal processing components and subsystems, analog technology was the only means for the processing and transmission of electronic information. Analog technology uses a continuously varied amplitude, frequency, or phase of an electronic signal or carrier to transmit information. We have continued to use analog technology to transmit voices (and now data) over telephone wires and to broadcast AM and FM radio and television (digital television transmission has only just begun and is not yet widely available). However, because of the nature of analog signal processing and its requisite use of various signal filtering techniques to isolate and process the signal, the ability to accurately carry and process multiple types of analog signals through multiple generations becomes greatly limited. The analog signal becomes mixed with background noise until the former is no longer intelligible from the latter. Also, analog technology does not allow easy compression of signals—we cannot easily transform and pack more signals through a given amount of bandwidth. For example, it does not permit efficient videoconferencing or other emerging forms of telephone traffic, a majority of which, by the end of 1999, was not voice-to-voice but computer-to-computer.

Digital information is a series of discrete "bits" represented by a 0 or 1 or any pair of symbols that can represent *on* or *off*—the binary language of computers—which allows for easy generation, processing, and transmission of signals with the assistance of microprocessors. Eight bits make up a byte, usually an alphabetic or numeric character, which is the smallest accessible unit in a computer's memory.[14] With the increased volume of electronic signals and a physical limit of bandwidth for all transmission media, data requirements in the late 1990s strained the usefulness of analog technology and pushed for the convergence and increased use of digital technology across a variety of information products and platforms.[15] Digital technology has become a means to convert analog electronic signals to the digital domain and to process and compress more signals into a given bandwidth while maintaining an acceptable level of signal quality.

operating systems for personal computers at year-end 1999 included Mac OS, Linux, and UNIX (see Table 9-2).

Maintaining the licensing rights and not selling the copyrights to the MS-DOS platform was consistent with the original philosophy of Microsoft's two co-founders, Bill Gates and Paul Allen. Both believed when they founded Microsoft in 1974 that software, not hardware, would drive the personal computer revolution. Ownership of the MS-DOS software would prove to be a tremendous cash cow for

Table 9-2 PC OPERATING SYSTEMS MARKET SHARE IN 1999

Windows 98	49.6%
Windows 95	26.5%
Windows NT/2000	11.1%
Total Windows	**87.2%**
Macintosh	**4.5%**
All Others/Unspecified	**8.3%**
Total	**100%**

Source: *http://www.mycomputer.com.* Cited in Lake, David. 2000. Microsoft dominates PC operating systems. *Industry Standard,* 3 April

Microsoft throughout the 1990s, allowing the software manufacturer to license the operating system to other IBM-PC clone makers, beginning with Compaq's PC-equivalent laptop computer (SLT/286) in 1988.

Despite the early successes of IBM and Apple Computer—the two most dominant computer manufacturers in the early 1980s—the failure of IBM to completely own the MS-DOS system and the failure of Apple to license its Macintosh operating system would ultimately allow other low-cost personal computer manufacturers, such as Dell and Compaq, to emerge as market leaders by the late 1990s. With Microsoft licensing MS-DOS to other personal computer manufacturers, consumers were able to buy much cheaper personal computers that could run the same business software applications as an IBM PC—Lotus 1-2-3, WordPerfect, and Microsoft Office. Meanwhile, Apple Computers maintained the Macintosh operating system as a proprietary system for its own computers and its market share declined over time as fewer and fewer software applications were written for its platform rather than that of MS-DOS and Windows.

Originally developed at Xerox Corporation's Palo Alto Research Center (PARC) in the early 1970s, the **graphical user interface (GUI)** uses a pointing device to navigate among graphical metaphors of windows, icons, and menus on a computer screen. The Apple Macintosh computer, launched in January 1984, popularized GUI. In 1990, Microsoft introduced Windows software to add GUI to the MS-DOS system for personal computers. Windows allowed computers running the MS-DOS operating system to have a similar look-and-feel to the Macintosh, which already had more user-friendly point-and-click on-screen icons that represented key functions instead of requiring the user to enter often-cryptic commands.

Microsoft originally licensed this GUI technology from Apple and was subsequently sued by Apple for including the technology beyond its first version of Windows. Microsoft successfully defended its technology license against Apple and, with each new more-powerful microprocessor developed by the Intel Corporation, launched new successive generations of Windows with added features and functions.

As the number of personal computers in use in the United States soared from 10 million in 1985 to almost 200 million in 1999[16]—almost all using Windows/MS-DOS—so did Microsoft's net sales and profits. Between 1981 and 1998, Microsoft's sales revenue increased almost 140,000 percent from $16 million in 1981 to $22.4 billion in 1999. At year-end 1999, the Microsoft Corporation had a market capitalization of almost $550 billion.

Although Apple's Macintosh icon-based operating system made it the first user-friendly personal computer, Microsoft's introduction of Windows and its continued enhancement of Windows' functions and reliability slowly reduced differences between the two operating systems. The most important point is that regardless of the market share of each operating system, virtually all of the major desktop personal computer operating systems are now graphical by design. With its mature stage of development and general acceptance, the GUI has become the personal computer standard.

WHAT ARE THE INTERNET AND THE WORLD WIDE WEB AND WHY ARE THEY IMPORTANT?

The Internet

Another important New Economy aspect has been the creation of the Internet as a relatively low-cost, easily accessible connection for all users. The **Internet** is a web of hundreds of thousands of computer networks, linked together primarily by telephone lines that can carry data around the world in seconds.[17] Once connected to the World Wide Web with browser software, one can quickly and easily access a vast wealth of information located on servers anywhere in the world.

The concept for the Internet emerged in the early 1960s as a way for the U.S. Department of Defense to maintain communications in the event a nuclear attack wiped out major communication outposts in the United States. In 1962, Paul Barran at the Rand Corporation conceived the underlying packet switching technology that later became the mandatory standard **TCP/IP (Transmission Control Protocol/Internet Protocol)** for the Internet. The TCP/IP allowed for a communication to be broken into packets that were routed separately to their destination as separate packets, then reassembled to the communication's original form (see Exhibit 9-2).

In 1966, Bob Taylor, an official with the Department of Defense's Advanced Research Projects Agency (ARPA), received funding for the first network experiment that would tie together several universities. Three years later in 1969, that experiment led to the creation of ARPANET, which allowed government-contracted scientists to share information over an Internet-based network for the first time. ARPANET first linked together researchers from the University of California at Los Angeles and Stanford Research Institute, then linked researchers at the University of California at Santa Barbara and the University of Utah. Over the next 14 years, ARPANET primarily was used by universities and military personnel, until the defense department split off in 1983 to create its own network, MILNET (Military Network), leaving ARPANET for the civilian sector.

In 1987, the National Science Foundation (NSF) accepted funding and management responsibility of NSFNet, the Internet backbone, as "alt" or newsgroups were being created to generate discussion on Internet bulletin boards. Two years later in 1989, physicists at the Switzerland-based CERN (European Laboratory for Particle

Exhibit 9-2

HOW INFORMATION TRANSFERS
OVER THE INTERNET

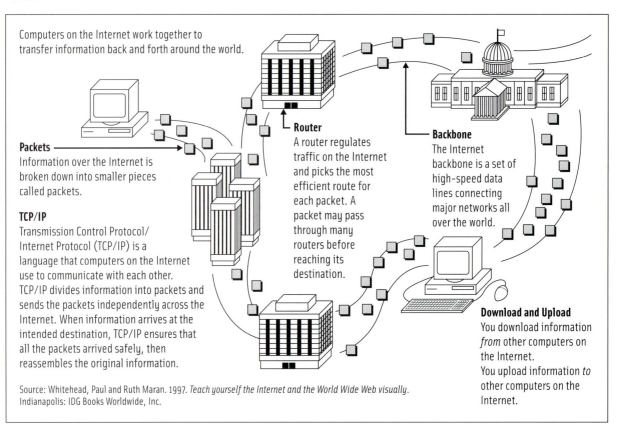

Computers on the Internet work together to transfer information back and forth around the world.

Packets
Information over the Internet is broken down into smaller pieces called packets.

TCP/IP
Transmission Control Protocol/ Internet Protocol (TCP/IP) is a language that computers on the Internet use to communicate with each other. TCP/IP divides information into packets and sends the packets independently across the Internet. When information arrives at the intended destination, TCP/IP ensures that all the packets arrived safely, then reassembles the original information.

Router
A router regulates traffic on the Internet and picks the most efficient route for each packet. A packet may pass through many routers before reaching its destination.

Backbone
The Internet backbone is a set of high-speed data lines connecting major networks all over the world.

Download and Upload
You download information *from* other computers on the Internet.
You upload information *to* other computers on the Internet.

Source: Whitehead, Paul and Ruth Maran. 1997. *Teach yourself the Internet and the World Wide Web visually*. Indianapolis: IDG Books Worldwide, Inc.

Physics), led by Tim Berners-Lee, created a more efficient way for geographically dispersed newsgroups to share information by defining the hypermedia protocol **HTTP (Hypertext Transfer Protocol),** the standard document addressing format **URL (Uniform Resource Locator),** and the programming language **HTML (Hypertext Markup Language).** This standardization allowed users to connect via hyperlinks from one document to another at different sites on the Internet,[18] whether the sites were on the same server or halfway around the world. This technology developed at CERN eventually became the basis of the World Wide Web— now the most popular part of the Internet.

The Browser and the World Wide Web

The **World Wide Web** is a subset of the Internet that is accessible through the use of HTTP to link documents at various URLs that are composed in HTML (and now also XML). By 1991, the World Wide Web allowed computers to access **multimedia,** i.e., computers could link many types of media including text documents, graphics material, video, and audio for the first time through a GUI.

In 1993, Marc Andreessen, a 22-year-old student at the National Center for Superconducting Applications (NCSA) at the University of Illinois, developed a new piece of software that would change the world. Called Mosaic, it was the first GUI Internet browser software. The **Internet browser** was a new class of software that served as the interface that allowed users of Windows-based PCs, Apple Macintoshes, and UNIX operating systems to easily access information published on the Web in HTML. Now the PC could display in graphics format what resembled a magazine page with text, photos, and illustrations.[19] The HTML file does not actually contain the graphics, sound, and multimedia files. Rather, it holds the hyperlinks to those graphics and files. The user's browser uses these hyperlinks to find and load the files from the server, interpret the files, and then display them as the webpage.[20] Not long after, in 1994, Andreessen joined forces with high-tech entrepreneur Jim Clark to cofound and launch Netscape Communications to design the first Netscape Navigator browser.

With the restriction of commercial use of the Internet lifted by the NSF in 1991 and with the commercial introduction of the Netscape Navigator browser based on the NCSA technology in December 1994, Internet use in the United States surged from less than a million individuals in 1991 to 12.5 million in 1996[21] (see Exhibit 9-3).

Within a year after the introduction of the Netscape Navigator, Microsoft entered the software browser market in August 1995 with its release of Microsoft Internet Explorer 1.0. Between August 1995 and September 1997, three subsequent releases of the Internet Explorer browser were distributed at no cost to consumers by Microsoft to build its market share against Netscape. After Microsoft cofounder Bill Gates acknowledged "An Internet Tidal Wave" in the software industry in December 1995, Microsoft fully integrated Internet Explorer 4.0 into the Windows operating system, further blurring the distinction between a user's computer and the Internet. Using Microsoft's Active Desktop, the Windows background could function as an HTML page instead of wallpaper or background color. Web links could now be placed on the desktop background and, with a click, launch the Internet Explorer software and send the user directly to a website.[22]

Exhibit 9-3 GROWTH IN INTERNET HOST COMPUTERS AND MAJOR E-COMMERCE DEVELOPMENTS

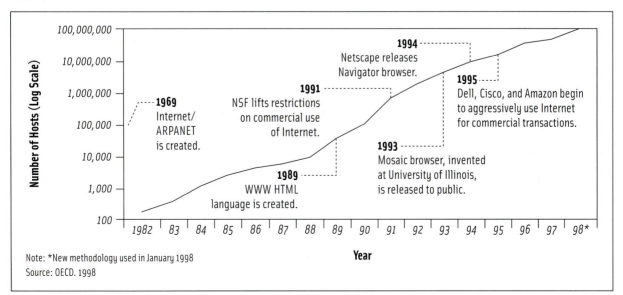

Note: *New methodology used in January 1998
Source: OECD. 1998

Today, browser technology has evolved to where secure communication between a user and a website for private transactions, such as banking, online trading, and electronic commerce, can be achieved through encryption of data using the Secure Socket Layer (SSL) protocol. Encrypted data is sent over the Internet between the user's browser software and the receiving company's servers, which are also protected by software firewalls to prevent hackers from breaking into the secure servers that contain private financial information.

Netscape gradually lost market share in the browser war that started in 1998. After achieving over 80 percent of the browser market by midyear 1996, Netscape fell behind Microsoft in the Web browser market in November 1998 and has remained second ever since. Today Microsoft Internet Explorer has a 70 percent share of the browser market[23] (see Exhibit 9-4).

There were parallels in Apple's battle with Microsoft in Mac OS versus Windows and in Netscape's battle with Microsoft in Navigator versus Explorer. In the latter, Microsoft was able to quickly match Explorer's functions and reliability with Netscape Navigator's and, in a period of three years, reversed Netcape's increasing market share. Similarly, the important point here is that regardless of the market share of each browser, the two dominating Internet browsers were not only graphical but multimedia by design. The graphical user interface had evolved into an easy to use multimedia standard that Internet users were rapidly adopting.

Internet Access More Widespread

As Internet access became more user-friendly, government agencies in the United States were among the first to offer free access to information on the Internet. An increasing number of elected officials, including the president and vice president of the United States, as well as many members of Congress, could be contacted via

 Exhibit 9-4 WEB BROWSER MARKET SHARE (1994–2000)

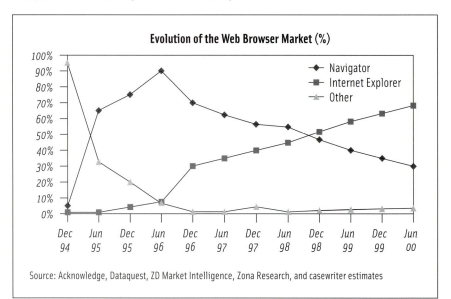

Source: Acknowledge, Dataquest, ZD Market Intelligence, Zona Research, and casewriter estimates

Caffeinating the Web—A Look at Java[24]

by Leo Griffin

In 1990, Sun Microsystems engineer Patrick Naughton decided to quit Sun because he was frustrated with trying to support the hundreds of different APIs (application program interfaces that allow programs to talk to each other) used by the company. Sun CEO Scott McNealy responded by letting Naughton pull together a team of six engineers, code named "Green" to create "something cool" that would solve the problem.

The Green team began taking apart devices such as Nintendo Game Boys and remote controls to try and develop a way to make all of these appliances talk to each other. As a result, the team developed a bare-bones programming language called "Oak." Sun wasn't quite sure what to do with Oak, and the project was adrift until 1993 when the launch of the Mosaic browser heralded the beginnings of the Web. Oak was repositioned as a "language-based operating system" and renamed Java. The group developed a Web browser that could run applications written in Java, then downloaded when needed over the Web.

Today, Java is an object-oriented (which means that programs are structured as a series of modular units or "objects") programming language that can be run on virtually all computer platforms as well as on many devices such as cell phones and set-top boxes. Java applications can run on any machine because Java is an interpreted language (meaning that the machine running it needs to "translate" the code into a native language as it runs). The application that does this is known as a "Java Virtual Machine." As well as interpreting Java code, the virtual machine itself controls permissions, determining whether the application has security clearance to perform actions such as writing to the local hard drive. Netscape built a Java Virtual Machine into Navigator 2.0 and Microsoft quickly followed. Today nearly all browsers can run Java.

The software developer community grew very excited about Java during the late 1990s, and the language was heralded as a "Windows killer" because it was believed that its "write once, use anywhere" capabilities would negate the advantage of the thousands of applications created for Windows. Java did not live up to this overhyped promise—largely because its flexibility makes it much slower than compiled languages. Despite this initial disappointment, Java has continued to evolve and become more powerful. Java applications are now primarily run on Web servers; for example, IBM has ported much of its business software to Java, allowing the applications to run on any of its (or its competitors') platforms.

Web designers have also become more skilled at using Java. Thousands of sites use Java "applets" (very small applications) to create powerful and interactive experiences on the Web. For example, Datek (*www.datek.com*) used Java to create a sophisticated stock streamer that users can personalize with their own "watch list" and run from the Datek website, and Pogo Games (*www.pogo.com*) used Java to offer games such as chess, blackjack, and roulette over the Web.

e-mail through their websites. In February 1994, the U.S. Securities and Exchange Commission (SEC) announced that it would make its EDGAR (Electronic Data Gathering and Retrieval) database available over the Internet at no charge. EDGAR contained SEC filings from several thousand companies at the time of its announcement and would include all SEC-regulated companies by 1996. While this information had been available for a fee from Mead Data Central, Disclosure, and Dow Jones, the SEC decision made it available to all Internet users for free.[25]

The World Wide Web is now regarded as the world's largest communications network. The number of names registered in the domain name systems—websites of commercial enterprises, private and public institutions, and other

POINT-COUNTERPOINT

Should Microsoft Be Broken Up?

In October 1997, the U.S. Department of Justice charged the software manufacturer Microsoft with violating the terms of its 1995 consent decree by tying distribution of the Internet Explorer to Windows 95. According to the court filings, executives at several personal computer manufacturers, including Compaq, Gateway, and Micron Electronics, had claimed that Microsoft had forced their firms to install Internet Explorer as a prerequisite for licensing the Windows 95 operating system. In addition, it was revealed that Microsoft had entered into restrictive agreements with several Internet Service Providers (ISPs), such as EarthLink, that prohibited the ISPs from promoting competing browsers and potentially dropping the ISPs from the Windows 95 desktop directory should their shipments of Internet Explorer fall below a targeted level. In May 1998, the Department of Justice and 20 states filed an antitrust suit against Microsoft, noting that the company had tried to "develop a chokehold" on the market for Web browsers and other Internet products.[26] With Microsoft failing to negotiate a settlement with the Justice Department and the 20 suing states prior to the court's verdict, U.S. District Judge Thomas Penfield Jackson found Microsoft guilty of violating the Sherman Antitrust Act on April 3, 2000. The case is now under appeal.

Possible penalties for Microsoft for violating federal antitrust laws range from paying a stiff monetary fine to breaking up Microsoft into two separate companies—one for the Windows operating system and the other for software applications such as Microsoft Office and Internet Explorer. Proponents of a Microsoft breakup suggested that this would prevent Microsoft from violating antitrust laws in the future, foster innovation among software developers, and increase the number of new products and services. Opponents of a Microsoft breakup, including its cofounder and chairman, Bill Gates, argued that the dominance of the Windows operating system had led to a uniformity among computer users, and this uniformity was a key factor in the increased usage of personal computers. This uniformity also helped support many independent software developers who had worked in partnership with Microsoft. Furthermore, opponents of a Microsoft breakup argued that the company had not engaged in any price-fixing that harmed consumers, and that Netscape itself had benefited by its $4.2 billion acquisition by America Online in December 1998.

major organizations—climbed to over 3 million in 1999.[27] In less than a decade, the Internet and the Web have literally transformed the way millions of people go about their daily lives. Everything from everyday tasks, such as checking on sports scores or purchasing books, to more eventful activities like searching for a job, planning a vacation, or searching for a house mortgage, can all be done sitting in front of a computer.[28]

According to a study released by Jupiter Communications in December 1999, e-mail, news, research, and financial services—all basic narrowband-type applications—were among the top reasons cited by Internet users for going online. In 1999, approximately 28 million households in the United States, or almost 28 percent of the total households, were online.[29] About 55 percent of the Internet users were male, and the average Internet user spent about 7.1 hours per week online—placing third behind the average number of hours spent watching television (15.6 hours) and listening to the radio (12.6 hours), but ahead of reading newspapers (4 hours) and magazines (3.4 hours).[30] Internet usage varied with length of experience. For example, "newbies"—those who had been online less than a year, spent an average of 5.4 hours per week online; "intermediates"—those who had been online for one to two years, spent an average of 6.5 hours per week online; and "veterans"—those who had been online for more than two years, spent an average of 8.2 hours per week online (see Exhibit 9-5 and Table 9-3).

Projected Rapid Online Growth Over the Next Five Years

During the 1999 holiday season, consumers spent an estimated $10 billion to $13 billion shopping online, with a full-year estimate of $25 billion to $30 billion for all of 1999—or less than 1 percent of all retail sales in the United States. Among the top commercial websites during the 1999 holiday season were Amazon.com, e-Toys, ToysRUs.com, BarnesandNoble.com, and Buy.com.[31] Of those who shopped online, 62 percent said that the experience was better than shopping in a store, 25 percent said that it was about the same, and only 8 percent said that it was worse.[32]

Among the factors that users mentioned as things that would increase their overall Internet use were increased transfer speed, more security of personal information, increasing the speed of establishing a connection, greater reliability of technology, and easier navigation (see Table 9-4).[33] Forecasts of increased online usage and commerce are projected to grow rapidly over the next five years. The number of U.S. households with access to the Internet is expected to grow from 28 million individuals in 1999 to 43 million the end of 2003, an increase of 54 percent.[34] The worldwide number of individuals with access to the Internet is expected to grow from 81 million in 1999 to 140 million at the end of 2003.[35]

Business-to-consumer e-commerce is expected to show a similar increase globally, growing from $20 billion in 1999 to $80 billion in 2003, while business-to-business e-commerce is expected to grow at an even faster pace, from $100 billion to $1.1 trillion over the same time period[36] (see Exhibit 9-6 on page 338).

Exhibit 9-5 IDC PREDICTS 179 MILLION AMERICANS ONLINE BY 2003

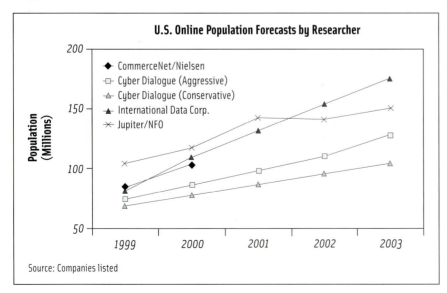

U.S. Online Population Forecasts by Researcher

Source: Companies listed

Table 9-3

WHAT USERS DO ONLINE

Percentage of Users Who Say They Go Online for Each of the Following at Least Once a Month	
e-Mail	96%
Use Search Engine	88%
Research Products/Services	72%
Local Content	58%
Online Directory	58%
e-Greeting/Postcards	55%
Download Free Software	54%
Daily News	51%
Instant Message	51%
Contest Sweepstakes	49%
Travel Research	47%
Online Chat	45%
Health Sites	45%
View Classified	43%
Music Sites	40%
Create or View Personal Web Pages	40%
Work Research	40%
Play Games	38%
Check Stocks/Quotes	37%

Source: *Wall Street Journal.* 1999. A wide net, 6 December

HOW DO WE ACCESS THE INTERNET?

Internet Service Providers

At the end of 1999, many users in the United States accessed the Internet primarily by dialing a telephone number provided by **Internet Service Providers (ISPs).** These ISPs ranged from well-known online services, such as America Online, MindSpring, and the Microsoft Network; to regional telecoms, such as BellSouth, NYNEX, and Pacific Bell; to local ISPs such as Access Internet Communications in Cupertino, California. By the middle of July 1999, there were an estimated 6,000 ISPs in North America.[37] In December 1999, America Online was the largest ISP in the United

Table 9-4

FACTORS USERS SAY WILL INCREASE THEIR OVERALL INTERNET USE

Increased Transfer Speed	65%
More Security of Personal Information	40%
Increased Speed of Establishing a Connection	40%
Greater Reliability of Technology	33%
Easier to Navigate	32%
More Audio/Video	20%
Greater Breadth of Information/Entertainment	18%
Easier to Use	16%
Greater Breadth and Quality of Shopping	8%
Other	12%
Nothing Would Increase My Internet Usage	11%

Source: *Wall Street Journal*. 1999. A wide net, 6 December

States with over 18 million members, followed by EarthLink/MindSpring, the Microsoft Network, AT&T, and NetZero (see Table 9-5).

Prior to the increase in Internet usage during the mid-1990s, online commercial services, such as America Online, CompuServe, and Prodigy, were often closed-end, proprietary systems. Registered members of these online commercial services usually paid an hourly usage fee to access each of the individual service's proprietary features, such as sending e-mail, reading published content online from newspaper and magazine partners, or participating in chat-room discussions. With the increase in Web popularity, however, many Internet users began to seek direct access to the Internet through independent ISPs. By 1997, almost all of the commercial online services also began to offer their users a direct connection to the Internet as part of their online services package as a way to retain their members. Delphi became the first national commercial online service to offer Internet access including e-mail to its subscribers in 1992.[38]

In 1999, 86 percent of the estimated 81 million Internet users worldwide accessed the World Wide Web at home through a telephone line, via an analog modem, to their personal computer.[39] At the time of this writing, analog modems typically have a theoretical maximum speed up to 56 kilobits per second (for illustrative purposes, one page of text is roughly 2.7 kilobytes, and one webpage with graphics is equivalent to 30 kilobytes), although most run at a top speed of 40 to 53 kilobits per second, depending on line quality and the distance from a telephone company's central office.[40] Bits of data are transmitted from a personal computer through a modem (MODulate-DEModulate). The **modem** converts, or modulates, the digital bits into analog signals and sends them over the telephone line as such. When the modem receives analog signals, it converts, or demodulates, the analog signal back into digital form before transferring them into the computer.

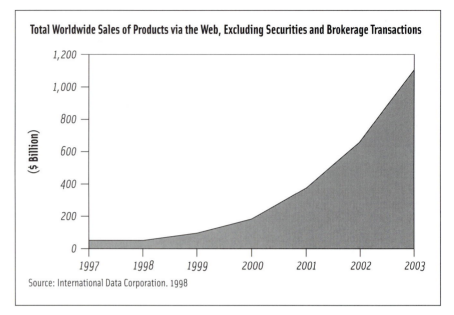

Total Worldwide Sales of Products via the Web, Excluding Securities and Brokerage Transactions

Source: International Data Corporation. 1998

Other methods that allow Web users to connect to the Internet include digital subscriber lines, cable modems, satellite transmission, and two types of wireless transmission. A discussion of each type of Internet connection follows (see Exhibit 9-7).

Digital Subscriber Line

Also known as DSL, a **digital subscriber line** allows for very high speed connections over existing copper telephone wires in homes. DSL service requires that DSL modems be on each end of the connection—in the user's home and at the telephone company's central office. DSL modems are different than traditional modems in that DSL modems send and receive all data as digital data—no translation to analog signals ever takes place—allowing faster data transmission.

One advantage of DSL is that it enables people to talk on the telephone and use the Internet at high speeds simultaneously—all over a single phone line. DSL divides the phone line into three channels: one for receiving data, one for sending data, and one for talking over the telephone. To work properly, a DSL modem must be located within a maximum distance—usually 18,000 feet (the equivalent of just over three miles) or less—from the phone company's answering DSL modem. The exact distance varies according to the DSL service, speed being offered, and even according to the gauge of the copper telephone wire. Speeds on a DSL range from 128 kilobits per second to over 1 megabit per second.

There are several variations of DSL but the most common versions are the high data rate digital subscriber line (HDSL or T-1) or the asymmetric digital subscriber line (ADSL). The HDSL uses a total of four transceivers: two at the subscriber's end and two at the telephone company's central office. Data—both download and upload—can be transmitted across an HDSL at a speed of 1.5 megabits per second.

Table 9-5

TOP INTERNET SERVICE PROVIDERS IN THE UNITED STATES (DECEMBER 1999)

America Online	18.0 Million
EarthLink/MindSpring	3.0 Million
MSN	1.9 Million
AT&T Worldnet	1.6 Million
NetZero	1.1 Million
Prodigy	1.0 Million
WebTV	0.8 Million
@home	0.7 Million
Bell South	0.7 Million

Source: Bloomberg; Jupiter Communications, Dec. 1999

ADSL is more commonly used than HDSL because there is less expense. ADSL uses only two transceivers and is capable of uploading and downloading at different maximum preprescribed speeds. Downloading through an ADSL ranges typically between 1 and 12 megabits per second, while uploading is typically between 160 kilobits and 1.5 megabits per second. Users generally upload only a few characters to select and control the download of webpages with large graphics files. These typically uneven speeds for uploading and downloading are the reason ADSL is labeled asymmetric.

Another form of DSL is the ISDN line (or integrated services digital network). This line can be used to dial into the Internet at higher speeds than regular nondigital phone lines, usually from 64,000 bits per second to 128,000 bits per second. Special ISDN modems must be used with ISDN lines at both a subscriber's location

DRILL-DOWN

Baud Rates

What does baud rate refer to? Named after J. M. Emile Baudot, baud rate initially referred to a unit of telegraph signaling speed where one baud was equal to one Morsecode dot per second. More recently, one baud was equal to one **bit** per second. Early modems were slow and measured on baud rate instead of kilobits per second.[41] When personal computers were first intro-duced in the early 1980s, common baud rates were at 300 baud (or 300 bits per second) or 1,200 baud (1,200 bits per second). Baud rate equaled the number of voltage or frequency changes in a second. But with today's advanced data compression and advanced modulation techniques in data communications, baud rate can no longer be equated with the bit rate of data transmitted.[42]

Exhibit 9-7 POSSIBLE INTERNET
CONNECTION METHODS

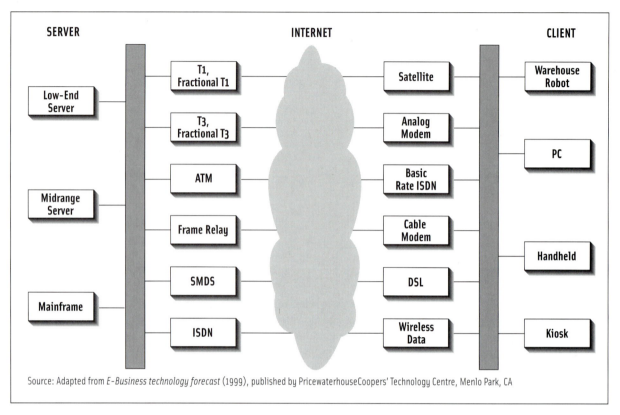

Source: Adapted from *E-Business technology forecast* (1999), published by PricewaterhouseCoopers' Technology Centre, Menlo Park, CA

and at the telephone company's central office. ISDN lines cost more than normal phone lines, so user telephone rates are usually higher. ISDN requires the installation of a second line since it can not be run over the same line as regular telephone lines and, like DSL, must be within 18,000 feet, or three miles, of a central office location.

Cable Modem

With the use of a special cable modem, the Internet can be accessed over some cable TV systems through the coaxial cable that normally carries television signals. Since 1996, most cable operators began to upgrade their plants by installing fiber-optic transmission technology. By replacing the coaxial copper with fiber-optic lines, cable operators could improve signal reliability and reception quality, increase channel capacity, and support the introduction of two-way interactive services.[43] To date, cable operations have spent $10 billion nationwide to transform their aging phone lines from coaxial to fiber optic. Another $20 billion is projected to be spent over the next few years.[44] **Cable modems** may be able to send and receive data at speeds of 2 to 3 megabits per second, or 35 to 52 times as fast as conventional analog modems of 56 kilobits per second.

Satellite Transmission

Three types of satellite systems—geostationary, medium-earth orbit (MEO), and low-earth orbit (LEO)—have been proposed for Internet access. Geostationary satellites will orbit 22,000 miles above the equator at the same speed as the earth's rotation, thus appearing from the ground to be stationary. Geostationary satellites will communicate with fixed-orientation dish antennas attached to customer homes and will use advanced-signal processing to compensate for transmission delays caused by the great distances their signals must travel. MEO satellites and LEO satellites, on the other hand, will circle the globe once every two hours at altitudes between 12,000 and 500 kilometers, reducing the time needed to beam signals to and from the earth's surface. Both MEO and LEO satellite methods, however, will require sophisticated subscriber antennas that will be able to track and communicate with the fast-moving MEO and LEO satellites.

The advantages of satellite transmission include ubiquity, economics, and performance.[45] Its disadvantages are the fact that dozens of satellites are required to service a single downlink station with continuous transmission, and the handoffs from one satellite to the next will often be technically and potentially complex.[46] DirectPC from Hughes Electronics currently offers satellite-based Internet access and data delivery downstream at 400 kilobits per second. Upstream access is only available by modem or other land-line connections through ISPs.[47] By 2003, after the launch of a three-satellite, $1.4 billion Spaceway system, Hughes Electronics hopes to offer Internet service to consumers via satellite at a speed of 1 megabit per second.[48]

LMDS Wireless Transmission

Local multipoint distribution service (LMDS) is a wireless system that can deliver digital data through the air at speeds of up to 155 megabits per second. LMDS uses wireless cells that cover geographic areas typically from two to five miles in radius. Unlike mobile services for cellular phones or personal communications systems (PCS, which are the digital version of cellular phones[49]), which a user can move from cell to cell, the transceiver of an LMDS customer has a fixed location and remains within a single cell. A common design requires that customers' antennas be fixed on rooftops to provide a line of sight to the hub transceiver. A limitation of LMDS is that a fragile band is allotted for its services, which makes transceivers for LMDS quite expensive.

Mobile Wireless Transmission

In addition to the common method of using a personal computer to access the Web, forecasters see **mobile wireless** technology becoming one of the fastest growing alternatives. Worldwide projections for the number of installed wireless devices—whether it be Qualcomm's PDQ (a combination of a Palm Organizer and a cellular phone), a National SemiConductor WebPad, or Nokia WAP phones—connecting users to the Web are projected to grow almost 20-fold, from 3.4 million to 67.4 million between 1999 and 2004.[50]

One technology that enables wireless communication is WAP, an open system (originally advocated by Finnish mobile phone manufacturer Nokia) that allows Internet users to access information from the Web on their cell phones. The key to WAP is a language called eXtensible Markup Language (XML), another open standard. This language tags all the data being distributed wirelessly and makes sure that it is displayed in a comprehensible way to the user's device. In the future, the mantra will be to "give [users] just what they need when they need it," observed Alan Kessler, president of Palm Computing. "That's a lot different than the PC era, when everyone said, 'Give me more memory. Give me more power. Give me more complex software.'"[51]

Palm-size computers are now enabled to receive wireless data through the Internet as well. These computers do everything from serve as an electronic appointment calendar to act as a digital memo pad. The market is dominated by Palm Computers, which has a 76 percent market share in the United States. Palm-size computers[52] using the Windows CE—short for Windows Compact Edition—are second with 10 percent of the market. Sales of the palm-size computers, TV set-top devices, and gaming devices are projected to increase from 5.6 million in 1999 to 20.8 million by 2002.[53]

Excluding LMDS wireless and satellite transmissions—which still have many operational limitations in their transmission of Internet data—cable modems offer consumers the fastest access times of 2 to 3 megabits per second, followed by DSL at an average of 1.5 megabits per second, ISDN at 1 megabit per second, and traditional phone lines at 56 kilobits per second. A 2-megabyte file—approximately the size of this chapter—would take roughly eight seconds to download on a cable system. By comparison, it would take just over 10 seconds to download this entire chapter on a DSL or ISDN line, and six minutes to download on a standard phone line running at a maximum speed of 45 kilobits per second (see Exhibit 9-8).

Broadband

The increased use of **broadband** technology—usually defined as those methods with connectivity speeds exceeding 128 kilobits per second—will allow for more online applications, such as video-on-demand, multiplayer games, streaming of audio and video, and software distribution[54] to be offered over the Internet. Motion picture companies, video game makers, media streaming companies (such as Real Networks), and software companies will all benefit (see Exhibit 9-9).

Exhibit 9-8 RELATIVE SPEED OF VARIOUS TYPES OF INTERNET CONNECTIONS

Cable — 3.0 to 4.0 megabits per second

DSL — 1.5 megabits per second

ISDN — 128.0 kilobits per second

Telephone — 56.0 kilobits per second

At the end of 1999, Forrester Research estimated that only 2.6 million Americans had access to broadband technology. By the end of 2003, Forrester projects that over 27.3 million Americans will have access to broadband, with 16.5 million Americans upgrading their service from dial-up to broadband, and another 7.6 million Internet newcomers starting directly with broadband technology. The total number of dial-up subscribers will grow at a much slower rate, from 41.3 million at the end of 1999 to 45.3 million at the end of 2003[55] (see Table 9-6).

Free-standing ISPs, such as EarthLink or NetZero, do not believe that cable MSOs (multi-system operators) or telecoms will automatically become the leading ISPs of the future. These independent ISPs advocate an "open system" whereby telephone or cable subscribers choose the ISP of their choice regardless of the type of Internet delivery system. These ISPs believe that they can differentiate themselves through pricing or superior customer service. Steve Case, chairman and CEO of America Online, pledged in January 2000 to keep Time Warner's cable system open—or made available for leasing—to free-standing ISPs following the announced $165 billion merger between AOL and Time Warner.

Network Routers and Switches

Once a user accesses the Web through an ISP, he or she can then call up a particular website by typing the site's URL. The URL will then access the site's Internet Protocol (IP) address (every computer connected to the Internet has a unique number, such as 204.71.200.75), which in turn will access the site's homepage. Communication between the user and the site is broken into packets that are sent through the Internet by specialized computers called routers and switches. **Network routers** hold information on the many possible routes between the origination point and destination point; they also direct packets across the Internet through these routes. **Network switches** do the actual moving of the packets

POINT-COUNTERPOINT

Which Is Better—Cable or DSL?

The battle for "the last mile" of transmitting broadband into the household has largely become between the telecoms that provide DSL-type services and cable companies that provide the same services through cable-ready modems. While the monthly costs of $30 to $40 for both types of Internet access service are comparable, cable-modem access has lower installation costs and can download data from the Internet at much faster speeds than DSL.

In the not-so-distant future, with the expected increase in services for video-on-demand and multi-player games (services that require downloading speeds of at least 3 to 4 megabits per second) advocates of cable modems say DSL may quickly become outdated. Supporters of DSL, however, say that while their technology is based upon dedicated phone lines between the home and the phone company, Web access through DSLs is more reliable and more secure than Web access through cable modems because the addition of subscribers to a single neighborhood hub dilutes the quality of cable-modem service. Also, there is less security risk of an outsider hacking into an individual's personal computer system when using a DSL. But some observers, such as the Yankee Group, see potential for Internet access via satellite transmission since an estimated one-quarter of all homes in the United States will not have access to DSL or cable modems by 2004.[56]

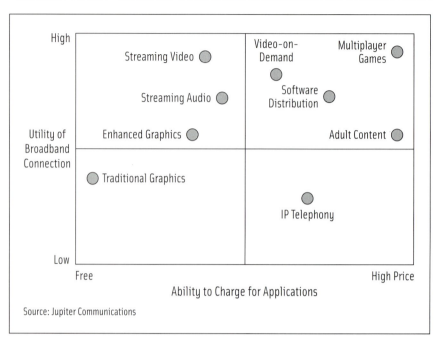

Exhibit 9-9 CERTAIN APPLICATIONS ARE MORE DEPENDENT ON BROADBAND

Source: Jupiter Communications

through an assigned route over the Internet. Among the leading manufacturer of network routers and switches are Cisco (which controls over 85 percent of the market), 3Com, and IBM.[57]

Network Servers

Once data communications from a user is routed to a site, the information goes into one of the site's **network servers** (which can be a computer anywhere in size from a mainframe to a microcomputer), which stores and "serves" the website's information to the connected personal computer. A server usually has a name that indicates what type of information it stores or function it serves, whether it be a Web server, file server, or mail server. For example, the name of a server that stores e-mail messages usually starts with "mail."[58] The server then integrates the information it receives from the user with the company's computerized functions, such as order processing fulfillment or accounting. The leading server manufacturers include IBM, Hewlett Packard, and Sun Microsystems.

The most popular Web server software—programs that allow individual servers to communicate with one another—include Apache, Microsoft NT, and Netscape. Linux can be used as desktop-operating system software, as well as server-operating software. Linux has been gaining in popularity in use to nonmainframe servers, and the number of new unit shipments increased by 93 percent between 1998 and 1999.[59]

Table
9-6

HOW USERS ACCESS THE WEB WORLDWIDE

Technology	1998		1999		2001		2002		2003	
	Installed Base (millions)	Market Share	Installed Base (millions)	Market Share	Installed Base (millions)	Market Share	Installed Base (millions)	Market Share	Installed Base (millions)	Market Share
Analog Modem	55.39	90.8%	69.39	85.7%	79.53	79.5%	87.56	73.0%	93.53	66.8%
Cable Modem	0.57	0.9%	2.12	2.6%	4.25	4.3%	7.26	6.1%	10.76	7.7%
XDSL	0.05	0.1%	0.35	0.4%	1.10	1.1%	3.10	2.6%	6.20	4.4%
ISDN	4.89	8.0%	8.99	11.1%	14.87	14.9%	21.53	17.9%	28.61	20.4%
Wireless Data	0.10	0.2%	0.15	0.2%	0.25	0.3%	0.55	0.5%	0.90	0.6%
Totals	61.00	100%	81.00	100%	100.00	100%	120.00	100%	140.00	100%

Source: IDC 1999

DRILL-DOWN

What Is Linux?

Originally developed by Linus Torvalds, a Finnish student at Helsinki University in 1991, Linux is a Unix-like operating system available for free over the Internet.[60] Since Linux's code is "open source," any developer can gain access to it online and suggest modifications to be incorporated into it. Companies such as Red Hat and VA Linux sell Linux as a bundle of office suite software, utilities, and support services along with the Linux Operating System.

IBM recently announced that it plans to make all its PC and mainframe servers Linux compatible by the end of 2000.[61] Some see Linux as a long-term threat to Microsoft's NT Operating System because of its greater reliability in the multiuser and high-volume transaction environment of the Internet.

The Transformation and Creation of the New Economy

Prior to the personal computer revolution in the 1980s, computer mainframe manufacturers were proprietary systems and vertically integrated. For example, computer manufacturers in 1980, such as IBM, Digital, Sperry/Univac, and Wang, often developed their own application software, operating system, computer hardware, and chips for their mainframes. By 1995, the computer industry—transformed by the personal computer—had been completely redefined into individual horizontal businesses. For example, users of personal computer applications could choose from a menu of individual operating-system providers, application software

Table
9-7

CHANGES IN THE VALUE OF
THE NEW ECONOMY

The 10 Biggest Market Value Losers		The 10 Biggest Market Value Winners	
	(Billions Lost)		(Billions Gained)
Coca-Cola	$52.3	Cisco	$293.3
Bank of America	51.1	Oracle	198.1
Proctor and Gamble	48.6	Intel	192.5
Ford Motor	27.9	Nokia	161.2
Gillette	24.2	LM Ericsson	126.9
Xerox	23.8	Sun Microsystems	123.6
Unilever	17.1	Nortel Networks	120.8
Allstate	14.9	Microsoft	106.5
McDonald's	14.2	Texas Instruments	106.3
Emerson Electric	10.2	EMC	78.2
Total Market Loss	$284.3	Total Market Gain	$1,507.4

Note: Period between May 1, 1999 and March 9, 2000
Source: Byrne, John A. and Debra Sparks. 2000. What's an old-line CEO to do? *Business Week*, 27 March.
URL: *http://businessweek.com/2000/00_13/b3674109.htm*

developers, and hardware manufacturers. In 1999, with the increasing usage of e-business applications, business entities could choose from a greater array of database software manufacturers, financial system software providers, network integrators, and networking infrastructure builders.

Table 9-7 shows the value migration from the Old Economy to the New Economy. Between May 1, 1999, and March 9, 2000, the top 10 losers of market value included blue-chip Old Economy brands, such as Coca-Cola, Bank of America, Proctor and Gamble, and the Ford Motor Company. The top 10 winners of market value largely included those involved in the building of the New Economy. These include Cisco, Oracle, Intel, Nokia, and Ericsson. By comparison, while the top 10 losers of market value had a total market loss of $284.3 billion, the top 10 gainers of market value had a total market gain of $1.5 trillion[62] (see Table 9-7).

HOW CAN THE INTERNET BE USED IN BUSINESS PROCESSES?

During the 1960s, 1970s, and 1980s, corporate information systems were often centralized and mainframe-based (see Exhibit 9-10A). For executives and managers desiring to receive immediate information on inventory, sales, and financial or purchasing data, special programming requests in a computer language such as

COBOL had to be written. Further complicating this data output was the fact that this needed information rarely could be provided in real time.

With the emergence of PC-based information networks and the development of improved graphical user interfaces in the mid-1990s (see Exhibits 9-10B and 9-10C), the concept of enterprise information systems (EIS) was established. Warehousing company data through the use of PC-based networks, EIS, and company intranets allowed users to collect data by almost any category and, along with online analytical processing (OLAP), could provide vital information to a wider range of people in the organization—and often in real time. As a result, organizations could become flatter in their decision-making processes, react more quickly to market changes, and reduce the amount of time devoted to administrative paperwork[63] (see Exhibit 9-11). Bill Gates, Microsoft's cofounder and chairman, called the networking of an enterprise's information system a "digital nervous system" (see Exhibit 9-12). He explained:

> *A digital nervous system comprises the digital processes that closely link every aspect of a company's thoughts and actions. Basic operations such as finance and production, plus feedback from customers, are electronically accessible to a company's knowledge workers, who use digital tools to quickly adapt and respond. The immediate availability of accurate information changes strategic thinking from a separate, stand-alone activity to an ongoing process integrated with regular business activities.*[64]

For example, by implementing a highly integrated information system, a company could link together its information system's applications for customer service, inventory, sales, accounting, and procurement. By doing so, a company would be more able to focus on servicing customer needs. For example, a prospective customer may either call a company's toll-free line or visit its website to order a product. The computer system—either through a customer service representative or a Web screen interface—would then provide information to that customer on his or her individual account, the prices of the individual products to be ordered, and the availability of the product in stock. Managers at the company would know which products are selling well and see the financial results of their daily operations. Both systems—the call center and the Web—would be linked together in real time, and the company's servers would support both customer interfaces.

Enterprise Resource Planning (ERP)

Enterprise resource planning (ERP) allows an entity to establish a digital nervous system within its company, whereby data is shared electronically—using a company intranet—among corporate managers, allowing them to unify key business processes. More than 60 percent of the Fortune 1000 companies have either begun implementing an ERP system or plan to do so over the next few years. Leading ERP vendors such as SAP, Oracle, Peoplesoft, J.D. Edwards, and Baan have become common names. ERP is not a single system but a framework that includes administrative, sales, and service applications, as well as manufacturing resources planning and human resource applications. In short, ERP is the foundation of e-business.[65]

Reasons for pursuing ERP include the need to replace creaky legacy systems, gaining greater control, managing global operations, handling deregulation and regulatory change, and improving the integration of decisions across the enterprise.[66]

Exhibit 9-10A | TRANSFORMATION OF THE COMPUTER INDUSTRY

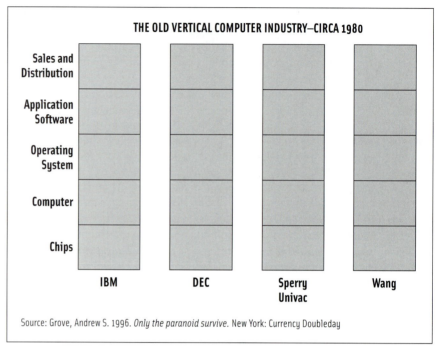

THE OLD VERTICAL COMPUTER INDUSTRY—CIRCA 1980

	IBM	DEC	Sperry Univac	Wang
Sales and Distribution				
Application Software				
Operating System				
Computer				
Chips				

Source: Grove, Andrew S. 1996. *Only the paranoid survive.* New York: Currency Doubleday

Exhibit 9-10B | TRANSFORMATION OF THE COMPUTER INDUSTRY

THE NEW HORIZONTAL COMPUTER INDUSTRY—CIRCA 1996

Sales and Distribution	Retail Stores	Superstores	Dealers	Mail Order

Application Software	Word	Word Perfect	Etc.

Operating Systems	DOS and Windows	OS/2	Mac	Unix

Computers	Compaq	Dell	Packard Bell	Hewlett Packard	IBM	Etc.

Chips	Intel Architecture	Motorola	RISCs

Source: Grove, Andrew S. 1996. *Only the paranoid survive.* New York: Currency Doubleday

THE EXPANDED HORIZONTAL COMPUTER INDUSTRY—CIRCA 1999

Exhibit 9-10C

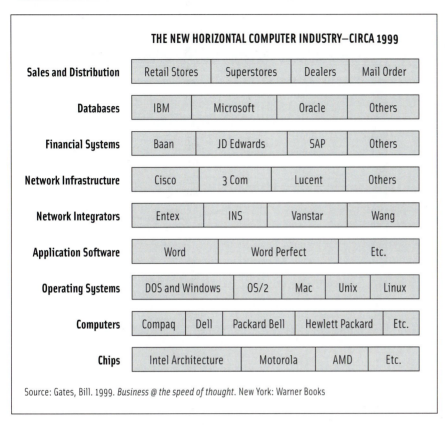

THE NEW HORIZONTAL COMPUTER INDUSTRY—CIRCA 1999

Sales and Distribution	Retail Stores	Superstores	Dealers	Mail Order
Databases	IBM	Microsoft	Oracle	Others
Financial Systems	Baan	JD Edwards	SAP	Others
Network Infrastructure	Cisco	3 Com	Lucent	Others
Network Integrators	Entex	INS	Vanstar	Wang
Application Software	Word	Word Perfect		Etc.
Operating Systems	DOS and Windows	OS/2	Mac	Unix / Linux
Computers	Compaq / Dell	Packard Bell	Hewlett Packard	Etc.
Chips	Intel Architecture	Motorola	AMD	Etc.

Source: Gates, Bill. 1999. *Business @ the speed of thought.* New York: Warner Books

Customer Relationship Management (CRM)

Customer relationship management (CRM) enables a company to provide customer service in real time by focusing on relationship development with each individual customer through the effective use of individual account information. By better understanding a customer's behavior patterns, the lifetime value of a customer's relationship with a company should be more profitable over the long term because it will lead to more sales, better service, and higher retention of individual customers[67] (see Exhibit 9-13).

Successful CRM is defined as an integrated sales, marketing, and service strategy that depends on coordinated actions by all departments within a company rather than being driven or managed by one single, functional department. The goals of effective CRM are to achieve long-running customer dialogue across all customer access points, to provide more effective cross-sell and up-sell, to increase customer retention and loyalty, to increase higher customer profitability, to achieve higher responses to marketing campaigns, and to provide extraordinary service and support. An explanation of each goal follows:

Achieving Long-Running Customer Dialogue Across All Business Functions and Customer Access Points.
Customer inquiries come from various channels such as a call center, the Internet, or the postal service. To manage all of the access points

Exhibit 9-11

OVERVIEW OF BASIC INTERNET
E-BUSINESS ARCHITECTURE

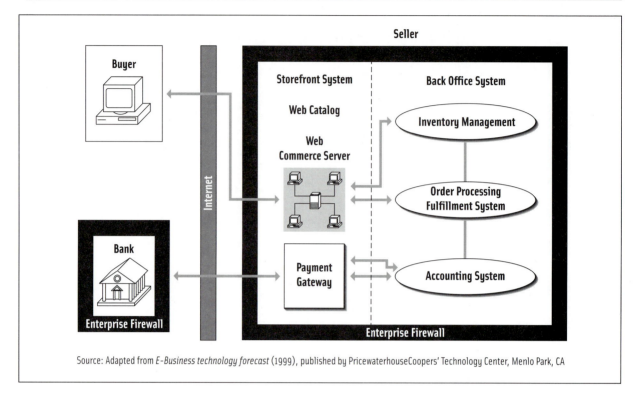

Source: Adapted from *E-Business technology forecast* (1999), published by PricewaterhouseCoopers' Technology Center, Menlo Park, CA

from the customer, a company's effective customer relationship management requires that all customer information be centralized into a single database and available 24 hours a day, regardless of the sales channel.[68] Whatever type of communications channel the customer uses—call center, Internet, or postal system—customers must find it easy to use and its response timely.

More Effective Cross-Selling and Up-Selling. Easily accessible key information on individual customers will increase the opportunities for cross-selling and up-selling of company products. For example, First Direct, a 24-hour direct bank in the United Kingdom that provides most of its services over the phone, uses "active listening" to note information on individual customers in their database. If a customer mentions that his or her family is expecting to have a baby, First Direct customer representatives enter that information into the customer's profile so that they can use it at a later date to cross-sell or up-sell additional financial products such as savings accounts or insurance to the new family.

Increased Customer Retention and Loyalty. Better understanding of customer behavior leads to increased sales and higher retention. For example, through the technology of collaborative filtering offered by both Firefly and NetPerceptions, online companies such as Amazon.com and BarnesandNoble.com can predict the types of books an individual customer may buy based upon other buyers with similar traits. With the knowledge of the types of books an individual customer might be

Exhibit 9-12

DIGITAL NERVOUS SYSTEM

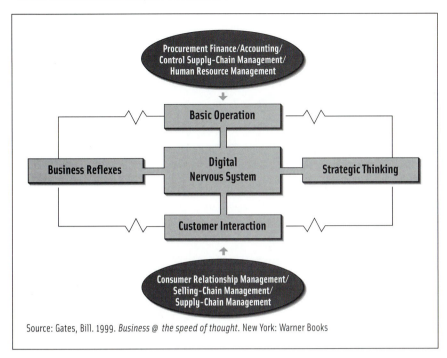

Source: Gates, Bill. 1999. *Business @ the speed of thought.* New York: Warner Books

likely to buy, both Amazon.com and BarnesandNoble.com can increase their sales revenue from each customer. A highly integrated database that provides a company with comparisons of customer purchases makes collaborative filtering possible.

Achieving Higher Customer Profitability.
CRM efforts will enable companies to place a value on customers. In many industries, 20 percent of customers represent 80 percent of a firm's profit—the oft-cited Pareto Principle, or 80–20 rule. In-depth analysis of customer buying habits will allow management to determine which customers should be actively courted and which should be politely dropped.[69]

Achieving Higher Responses to Marketing Campaigns.
In the past, customer contacts from a company's sales and service departments were kept separate. For example, company customer service departments were often unaware of marketing campaigns or the launch of a new product. With an integrated system, both the sales and service departments would be aware of offers and products available to customers. Such integration would not only facilitate communications but would also provide companies with data for further market analysis. This analysis may also identify both potential "bottleneck" problems and further market opportunities.

Providing Extraordinary Service and Support.
Extraordinary customer service is reflected in customer satisfaction surveys. Not only should companies provide assistance to their customers when needed, but they also should provide customers with the technology to help themselves virtually at any time during the day.[70]

CUSTOMER RELATIONSHIP MANAGEMENT

Exhibit 9-13

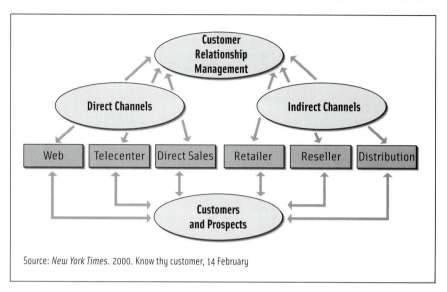

Source: *New York Times*. 2000. Know thy customer, 14 February

Supply-Chain Management

Supply-chain management allows a company to improve its competitive positioning by achieving lower costs and accelerating the time-to-market of new products.[71] Achieving successful chain management requires restructuring the way products are designed, manufactured, and sold. Current efforts by companies to streamline their supply chains are driven by several trends: changes to a customer-driven sales model, consolidation within each segment of the technology supply chain, and the creation of new supply-chain partnerships.[72] An explanation of each trend follows:

Changes to a Customer-Driven Sales Model.
In the past, sales were often vendor-driven; that is, the customer purchased what the selling company offered. Now sales are customer-driven as demand shifts from push to pull models with increased customization. As a result, a company is required to carry significantly less inventory as part of its supply chain. Reduced inventory levels lead to lower pricing, more stable product supply, and an eventual reduction in the severity of traditional boom-bust cycles of many industries.[73]

Consolidation with Each Segment of the Technology Supply Chain.
Consolidation is accelerating within each segment of the economy as companies seek to reduce the number of suppliers with whom they interact. This establishes a few key supplier-partnership relationships and helps the speed-to-market process.

Creation of New Supply-Chain Partnerships.
Reinventing the supply chain for many companies will provide new market opportunities and relationships. For

example, in February 2000, retail giants Sears, Roebuck and Company and France's Carrefour announced that they would team up with Oracle Corporation to set up a global supply marketplace using the Internet. The two retailers will link up with their respective suppliers and distributors in an attempt to cut purchasing costs and will allow network members to buy, sell, trade, or auction goods online. The three major automakers—General Motors, Ford Motor Company, and DaimlerChrysler AG—announced a similar electronic network[74] as well.

Selling-Chain Management[75]

Selling-chain management software enables the development and successful deployment of large-scale field-sales solutions that focus on automating many order-acquisition functions, such as configuration, pricing, quoting, and service. The goals of a selling-chain application framework include the following:

Making It Easy for the Customer.
This goal allows customers to find the products they are looking for quickly and helps them find the solutions that they need for their business rapidly.

Adding Value for the Customer.
Effective selling-chain management should also be solutions-based in offering customers solutions that deliver and meet individual needs rather than the traditional order-taking mode. An example of this would be Amazon.com's gift center, where customers receive a list of customized gift suggestions after identifying key attributes of the intended recipient.

Increasing Sales Force Effectiveness.
Sales made online can help improve a company's sales productivity and effectiveness by reducing overhead and time spent on field sales calls.

Coordinating Team Selling.
Selling-chain management will help provide customer information in a central location and facilitate a team-selling environment, in which various members of a sales team—across different departments—can easily work together to close a deal.

Procurement

Increased **procurement** on the Web will reduce both the amount of paperwork needed to complete purchased items and the turnaround time to deliver the ordered goods. The initial goal of integrating the procurement supply chain was to take apart some traditional, hierarchically structured purchasing organizations. In addition, many companies continue to have multiple layers of approval procedures that often slow procurement without adding any value to the process. What has emerged is an emphasis on an order-to-delivery process rather than individual procurement tasks[76] (see Exhibit 9-14).

At the same time, procurement is migrating from traditional paper-based processes to e-procurement. The benefits of e-procurement fall into two major categories: efficiency and effectiveness. Efficiency includes reduced procurement costs, faster cycle times, less maverick (unauthorized) buying, more highly organized

Exhibit 9-14 E-PROCUREMENT

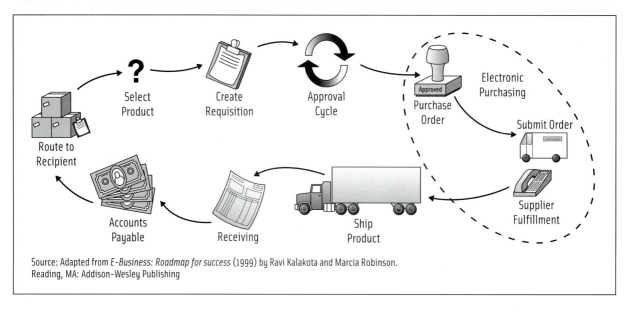

Source: Adapted from *E-Business: Roadmap for success* (1999) by Ravi Kalakota and Marcia Robinson. Reading, MA: Addison-Wesley Publishing

information, and tighter integration of procurement function with key back-office systems. Effectiveness includes increased control over the supply chain, proactive management of key procurement data, and higher-quality purchasing decisions within organizations.[77]

HOW WILL THE INCREASED USE OF THE INTERNET AFFECT PUBLIC POLICY AND POLITICS?

As communications technology and content rapidly shifted in the early 1990s, government and industry alike struggled with the new challenges posed by the rapidly emerging national and global information infrastructure. In particular, over the next few years elected and corporate leaders will continue to struggle with laws governing privacy, taxation, copyrights and patents, access, free speech, and monopolies.

Privacy

Through the use of cookies—software programs that keep a log of where Internet users browse[78]—company databases can track every page visited or every item purchased by a customer. As a result, Web users are becoming increasingly fearful that every keystroke is being monitored and recorded by online retailers or public agencies. In a March 2000 survey conducted by *Business Week*, 78 percent of the respondents indicated that they were very or somewhat concerned that a Web company would use personal information to send unwanted information. This information represented a 20 percent increase in consumer concerns over **privacy** when the question was asked two years earlier, in February 1998.[79]

While Web merchants have taken considerable measures to assure Internet users that individual online consumer information would be secure and never released, an uproar was created in August 1999 when Amazon.com made available "purchase circles," on its website. The circles showed the most popular items purchased at its site by company domain or city. Amazon.com later allowed individual consumers to be excluded from purchase circle tabulations if they wished. Experts suggest that online companies, in order to reduce consumer anxiety over privacy on the Web, display their practices online, give consumers a choice in having their personal information stored in a company's database, allow their customers to see their individual information being collected, and subject themselves to SEC disclosures or third-party audits regarding the reliability of their self-imposed privacy regulations.[80]

Taxation

The question of whether states and local authorities have the right to place sales taxes on merchandise sold by out-of-state retailers has led to enormous debates between the federal government, states, and local municipalities. Advocates of charging no sales taxes on merchandise sold by Web retailers have argued that a continued moratorium would help grow an emerging industry that has been a vital part of the United States' strong economy in the late 1990s. Critics of the policy have argued that the lack of sales taxes on merchandise sold by out-of-state Web retailers provides online merchants with an unfair advantage over in-state, brick-and-mortar retailers and has denied local municipalities sales tax revenue. The 19-member Advisory Commission of Electronic Commerce, created to advise Congress of the implications of sales taxes on the New Economy, voted in March 2000 to extend the moratorium on sales taxes on out-of-state Web merchants for five years after it expires in October 2001.[81] The decision to do so by the commission was quite divided as the members voted according to their affiliation, with representatives of electronic commerce voting for it and representatives of local municipalities voting strongly against it.

Patents

In October 1999 and February 2000, Amazon.com obtained two patents for developing its One-Click system and for sales of merchandise by other online retailers through its affiliate program—prompting complaints within the Web community about the effectiveness of applying century-old patent laws to the New Economy. The One-Click system, introduced in September 1997, allowed returning customers to the site to quickly purchase items on Amazon.com with a single click of a mouse. BarnesandNoble.com, one of Amazon.com's major online competitors, followed with a similar service in June 1998. Upon Amazon.com's securing of a patent for its One-Click system, a court injunction was issued in December 1999 barring BarnesandNoble.com from using the one-click system. Amazon.com was one of many companies that have rushed to patent business processes that use the Internet.

Critics have complained that many of these patents reward trivial innovations, as much of software development is incremental, and that patent examiners do not do a good job of looking for similar existing software on the Internet. Responding to the critics, Amazon.com founder and CEO Jeff Bezos, while not agreeing to surrender his company's patents, did suggest that software and business method patents should be shortened to 3 to 5 years instead of the current 17 years. Bezos also suggested that outsiders be allowed to comment on proposed software patents before they are issued, and he offered to fund a software repository that patent examiners could use to determine if an idea was truly novel and deserving of a patent.[82]

Access

Unlike telephone companies, which must function under regulated pricing and are required to provide service to anyone living within their coverage area, online services and Internet service providers are not regulated. Moreover, while access to the telephone system might require the purchase of a $15 telephone, this new multimedia revolution demands a much higher investment. It is unclear how Americans living near the poverty level might take part in this new era.[83] Without government intervention, it seems the "haves and the have-nots" might evolve into the "wired and unwired," creating a digital divide in the United States. Most of those who do not have access to personal computers or Internet services are often lower-income families living in the inner cities. At the end of 1999, both the government and private companies and foundations began to take steps to address the concerns of a digital divide by making personal computers more accessible in public schools and public libraries.

Free Speech

From the bombing of the Federal Building in Oklahoma City to the shooting of high-school students in Littleton, Colorado, authorities feared that increasing access to the Internet provided disenchanted citizens—hate groups, militia organizations, and other disgruntled outcasts—an easier opportunity to find and communicate with one another and to build online communities counter to that of the public interest. Advocates of free speech argued that the Internet was simply another form of communications protected by the First Amendment.

Network Economics and Monopolies

Media convergence, both among media content providers and information distributors, have raised issues of conflict of interest, antitrust, and concentration of media power. While the Telecommunications Act of 1996 increased competition between providers of telephone, electrical, and cable television services to households, the number of mergers among media companies and information distributors has increased rapidly since then. For example, the recently announced merger of America Online and Time Warner in January 2000—to become the largest media company in the world—provides an example of a company that will be fully integrated in all areas of editorial content and information delivery. While supporters of the merger have applauded the inherent synergies that could be ultimately realized by the marriage of both companies, critics raised the concerns that fewer voices would be heard and that AOL-Time Warner would be most likely to

An Open Letter from Jeff Bezos on the Subject of Patents[84]

I've received several hundred e-mail messages on the subject of our 1-Click ordering patent. Ninety-nine percent of them were polite and helpful. To the other one percent—thanks for the passion and color!

Before I go on, I'd like to thank Tim O'Reilly. Tim and I have had three long conversations about this issue, and they've been incredibly helpful to me as I've tried to clarify in my mind what is the right thing to do. I had previously known Tim as the publisher of the successful and excellent O'Reilly technical books. He off-handedly proved his narrative and editing skills when he took what was our first rambling hour-long conversation and somehow made sense of it all in a posting on his site. My thinking on the topic of business method and software patents has been strongly influenced by Tim's observations, and especially his ability to ask excellent questions. I also read the first four hundred or so responses to Tim's summary of our conversation—these too were helpful.

Now, while we've gotten substantially less e-mail on this issue than we have over several other lightning-rod issues in the past, I've spent a lot more time thinking about this one. Why? Because the more I thought about it, the more important I came to realize this issue is. I now believe it's possible that the current rules governing business method and software patents could end up harming all of us—including Amazon.com and its many shareholders, the folks to whom I have a strong responsibility, not only ethical, but legal and fiduciary as well.

Despite the call from many thoughtful folks for us to give up our patents unilaterally, I don't believe it would be right for us to do so. This is my belief even though the vast majority of our competitive advantage will continue to come not from patents, but from raising the bar on things like service, price, and selection—and we will continue to raise that bar. We will also continue to be careful in how we use our patents. Unlike with trademark law, where you must continuously enforce your trademark or risk losing it, patent law allows you to enforce a patent on a case-by-case basis, only when there are important business reasons for doing so.

I also strongly doubt whether our giving up our patents would really, in the end, provide much of a stepping stone to solving the bigger problem.

But I do think we can help. As a company with some high-profile software patents, we're in a credible position to call for meaningful (perhaps even radical) patent reform. In fact, we may be uniquely positioned to do this.

Much (much, much, much) remains to be worked out, but here's an outline of what I have in mind:

1. That the patent laws should recognize that business method and software patents are fundamentally different than other kinds of patents.

2. That business method and software patents should have a much shorter lifespan than the current 17 years—I would propose 3 to 5 years. This isn't like drug companies, which need long patent windows because of clinical testing, or like complicated physical processes, where you might have to tool up and build factories. Especially in the age of the Internet, a good software innovation can catch a lot of wind in 3 or 5 years.

3. That when the law changes, this new lifespan should take effect retroactively so that we don't have to wait 17 years for the current patents to enter the public domain.

4. That for business method and software patents there be a short (maybe 1 month?) public comment period before the patent number is issued. This would give the Internet community the opportunity to provide prior art references to the patent examiners at a time when it could really help. (Thanks to my friend Brewster Kahle for this suggestion.)

To this end, I've already contacted the offices of several Members of Congress from the committees with primary responsibility for patents to ask if they would be willing to meet with me on this issue. Since some of them have previously expressed an interest in similar issues, I have every expectation that at least

(continued on page 358)

(continued from page 357)

some of them will want to talk about it. I've also invited Tim O'Reilly to attend any such meetings with me. Tim and I are also going to try to pull together some software industry leaders and other people with an interest in this issue and an ability to help.

If done right—and it could take 2 years or more—we'll end up with a patent system that produces fewer patents (fewer people will bother to apply for 3- or 5-year patents, and fewer patents means less work for the overworked Patent and Trademark Office), fewer bad patents (because of the pre-issuance comment period), and even the good patents won't last longer than is necessary to give the innovator a reasonable return (at Internet speed, you don't need 17 years).

Bottom line: fewer patents, of higher average quality, with shorter lifetimes. Fewer, better, shorter. A short name might be "fast patents."

Many have noted, and I too would like to point out, that given the laws they operate under and the resources at their disposal, the Patent Office and examiners are doing a good job and it's unfair to criticize them.

On a related issue, to further try to help with the prior art problem, I've also agreed to help fund a prior art database. This was Tim's idea, and I'm grateful for it. Tim is poking around to find the right people to run with that project.

On an important meta-level, one thing to note is that this episode is a fascinating example of the new world, where companies can have conversations with their customers, and customers can have conversations with their companies. I've been saying for 4 years now that, online, the balance of power shifts away from the merchant and toward the customer. This is a good thing. If you haven't already, read the cluetrain manifesto. If you want the book, well . . . you can get it at several places online . . .

Jeff

Tell us what you think. How would you like to re-invent the patent system? Share your views.

push its own editorial products first, although the management of both companies pledged that they would keep their Internet and cable systems open to all content providers.

SUMMARY

1. How was the development of the microprocessor important to the Internet?

A fundamental aspect of the New Economy is that there is an expanded presence of technology-mediated screen-to-face interfaces, all of which are powered by computers. The proliferation of screen-to-face interfaces was made possible with the mid-1960s' development of the microprocessor, which foreshadowed the personal computer revolution in the following decade.

The microprocessor, with its rapid growth in computing power, has allowed the creation and wide availability of inexpensive, powerful microcomputers. By the end of 1999, the number of households in the United States with access to a personal computer was 51.9 million, reflecting a penetration of 51 percent of all households nationwide. From 1995 to 1999, the average per-unit cost of a personal computer decreased by 20 percent, from $1,500 to $1,200 per unit. This cost decrease occurred despite a geometric increase in microprocessor calculating power. At the beginning of 2000, the most common way for home access to the Internet was with the use of a personal computer, a browser, an analog modem, and an analog telephone line.

2. How was the development of a graphical interface important to the Internet?

The operating system is a set of instructions to a computer on how to operate its various parts and peripherals. Each operating system provides a "standard" on which to build software applications. Each operating system has inherent design strengths and weaknesses in its approach to providing application developers the facilities to control computer hardware; each operating system creates constraints to software applications development, e.g., MS-DOS was originally designed for text-only display, not graphics, while the Mac OS was designed for graphic display from the beginning. Operating system constraints have profound implications when one begins to consider the evolving nature of screen-to-face interfaces now pervasive with the Internet, i.e., interfaces are increasingly graphical in design.

Virtually all of the major desktop personal computer operating systems are now graphical by design. With its mature stage of development and general acceptance, the graphical user interface has become the personal computer standard.

3. What are the Internet and the World Wide Web, and why are they important?

The Internet is a web of hundreds of thousands of computer networks, linked together primarily by telephone lines, by which data can be carried around the world in seconds.

A subset of the Internet, the Word Wide Web is accessible through the graphical user interface (GUI) of Web-browser software that uses HTTP (Hypertext Transfer Protocol) to link documents at various URLs that are composed in HTML (Hypertext Markup Language) (and now also XML [eXtensible Markup Language]). The browser allows computers to link many types of multimedia-based information, including documents, graphics, video, and audio.

As Internet access became more user-friendly, government agencies in the United States were among the first to offer free access to information on the Internet. Today, the World Wide Web is regarded as the world's largest communications network. In less than a decade, the Internet and the Web have literally transformed the way millions of people go about their daily lives. Everything from everyday tasks, such as checking on sports scores or purchasing books, to more eventful activities like searching for a job, planning a vacation, or searching for a house mortgage, can all be done sitting in front of a computer.

Forecasts of increased online usage and commerce are projected to grow rapidly over the next five years. The worldwide number of individuals with access to the Internet is expected to reach 140 million at the end of the year 2003. Business-to-consumer e-commerce is expected to reach $80 billion in 2003 while business-to-business e-commerce is expected to reach $1.1 trillion over the same time period.

4. How do we access the Internet?

Most Internet users worldwide access the World Wide Web at home through a telephone line, connecting via an analog modem, to their personal computer. Other methods that allow Web users to connect to the Internet include digital subscriber lines (DSLs), cable modems, satellite transmission, LMDS wireless transmission, and mobile wireless transmission.

Once a user accesses the Web through an ISP (Internet Service Provider), he or she calls up a particular website by typing the site's URL. The URL accesses the site's Internet Protocol (IP) address. Communication between the user and the site is broken into packets that are sent through the Internet by specialized computers called routers and switches. Routers hold information on the many possible routes between the origination point and destination point and also direct packets across the Internet through these routes. Switches do the actual moving of the packets through an assigned route over the Internet.

Once data communications from a user is routed to a site, it goes into one of the site's servers, which store and "serve" the website's information to the connected personal computer.

5. How can the Internet be used in business processes?

Companies with PC-based information systems can better manage their business processes, such as customer service, supply-chain management, and procurement, by creating an intranet—an internal network on the Web—whereby individual managers can obtain information in real time from a centralized database to analyze customer opportunities or to order supplies. In the past, prior to the establishment of PC-based networks, requests for executive information had to be made through special requests that often required time-consuming mainframe programming. Now, with PC networks and company intranets, company managers can be connected to the same database in real time to derive needed customer or supply information easily and quickly.

6. How will the increased use of the Internet affect public policy and politics?

Laws governing privacy, taxation, access, patents, free speech, and network economies and monopolies in the United States are currently under review as a result of increased usage of the Internet. While many of these issues still need to be resolved, they are being addressed at all levels of government—local, state, and federal.

KEY TERMS

market infrastructure

digital convergence

media convergence

network infrastructure

mainframe computers

supercomputers

minicomputer

microprocessor

microcomputer

Moore's Law

operating system (OS)

analog information

digital information

graphical user interface (GUI)

Internet

TCP/IP (Transmission Control Protocol/Internet Protocol)

HTTP (Hypertext Transfer Protocol)

URL (Uniform Resource Locator)

HTML (Hypertext Markup Language)

World Wide Web

multimedia

Internet browser

Internet Service Providers (ISPs)

modem

digital subscriber line (DSL)

cable modem

mobile wireless

broadband

network routers

network switches

network servers

enterprise resource planning (ERP)

customer relationship management (CRM)

supply-chain management

selling-chain management

procurement

privacy

Endnotes

[1] *The New York Times 2000 Almanac,* s.v. "Chronology of Information Processing," pp. 805–806.

[2] Clark, Diane. 1996. 25th anniversary of the microprocessor. *The Journey Inside Newsletter* 2 (autumn). URL: *http://www.intel.com/education/journey/ji_arch/jif96.*

[3] *ibid.*

[4] Hamilton, David P. 2000. High demand for chips lifts Intel earnings. *Wall Street Journal*, 19 April.

[5] *ibid.*

[6] Reinhardt, Andy. 2000. The new Intel. *Business Week,* 13 March.

[7] Hamilton. 2000. High demand for chips. *Wall Street Journal*, 19 April.

[8] The PowerPC Chip in 1999 was also ten times faster than the original SuperCray computer that was introduced in 1975. The Cray I could process 100 million operations per second.

[9] *The New York Times 2000 Almanac,* s.v. "Personal Computer Households, 1995–2000," p. 809. Citing U.S. Department of Commerce; Jupiter Communications.

[10] *ibid.* (source: Consumer Electronics, Manufacturing Association).

[11] Thompson, Mary Jones. 1999. Dell finally edges out Compaq in U.S. PC sales. *Industry Standard*, 20 September. Citing International Data Corporation.

[12] PricewaterhouseCoopers. 1999. *E-Business technology forecast.* Menlo Park, CA: PricewaterhouseCoopers Technology Centre, p. 36.

[13]*The New York Times 2000 Almanac,* s.v. "Glossary of Computer Terms," p. 808.

[14]*The New York Times 2000 Almanac,* s.v. "Glossary of Computer Terms," p. 808.

[15]Rayport, Jeffrey, George C. Lodge and Thomas Gerace. 1997. *National information structure(A): The United States in perspective*, 20 March. Boston: Harvard Business School Publishing, p. 4.

[16]Markoff, John. 2000. A strange brew's buzz lingers in Silicon Valley. *New York Times*, 26 March.

[17]*The New York Times 2000 Almanac,* s.v. "The Internet," pp. 816–18.

[18]*TIME Almanac 2000,* s.v. "Internet Timeline," p. 556. Citing International Data Corporation, W3C Consortium, Internet Society.

[19]*The New York Times 2000 Almanac,* s.v. "The Internet," p. 816.

[20]Gralla, Preston. 1998. *How the Internet works.* Indianapolis, IN: Que Publishing Corporation, pp. 152–3.

[21]*The New York Times 2000 Almanac,* s.v. "U.S. Online Households and Internet Users, 1996–2002," p. 819.

[22]Gralla. 1998. *How the Internet works,* p. 156.

[23]Lake, David. 2000. *Industry Standard* (online version only), 3 April. URL: *http://www.thestandard.com/article/display/1,1151,13662,00.html.*

[24]This sidebar draws from information from the following sources: java.sun.com—The source for Java™ technology. URL: *http://www.java.sun.com.* Cringely, Robert X. 2000. Have another cup. *I, Cringely/The Pulpit,* 2 March. URL: *http://www.pbs.org/cringely/pulpit/pulpit20000302.html.*

[25]This paragraph adapted from the following: Rayport, Jeffrey F. et al. *National information infrastructure (A): The United States in perspective,* p. 11.

[26]Yoffie, David and Mary Kwak. 1998. *The browsers wars, 1994–1998.* Case no. 9-798-094, 19 April. Boston, MA: Harvard Business School Publishing.

[27]*The New York Times 2000 Almanac,* s.v. "The Internet," p. 816.

[28]*The New York Times 2000 Almanac,* s.v. "Glossary of Computer Terms," p. 816.

[29]*The New York Times 2000 Almanac,* s.v. "U.S. Online Households," p. 819.

[30]*Wall Street Journal.* 1999. A wide net, 6 December.

[31]*Reuters.* 2000. E-Commerce sales tally seen between $10 billion and $13 billion, 3 January.

[32]Hansell, Saul. 1999. Retailers look back and see online shopping is gaining. *New York Times,* 24 December.

[33]*Wall Street Journal.* 1999. A wide net, 6 December.

[34]*The New York Times 2000 Almanac,* s.v. "U.S. Online Households," p. 819.

[35]PricewaterhouseCoopers. 1999. *E-Business technology forecast.* Menlo Park, CA: PricewaterhouseCoopers Technology Centre, 1999, p. 9. Citing International Data Corporation (1999).

[36]PricewaterhouseCoopers. 1999. *E-Business technology forecast.* Menlo Park, CA: PricewaterhouseCoopers Technology Centre, 1999, p. 14. Citing International Data Corporation (1998).

[37]Richel, Matt. 1999. Small internet service providers survive among the giants. *New York Times,* 16 August.

[38]*The Sunday Contra Costa Times.* 1999. Timeline of the Internet, 19 December.

[39]PricewaterhouseCoopers. 1999. *E-Business technology forecast.* Menlo Park, CA: PricewaterhouseCoopers Technology Centre, p. 216. Citing International Data Corporation (1999).

[40]Light, Jay O., Applegate, Lynda M. and Dan J. Green. 2000. *The last mile of broadband access.* Case no. 9-800-076, 25 January. Boston, MA: Harvard Business School Publishing.

[41]*The New York Times 2000 Almanac,* s.v. "Glossary of Computer Terms," p. 807.

[42]Siegel, Allan M., and William G. Connolly. 1999. *The New York Times manual of style.* New York, NY: Times Books, p. 43.

[43]Eisenmann, Thomas R. 1998. *Tele-Communications, Inc.: Accelerating digital deployment.* Case no. N9-899-141, 3 December. Boston: Harvard Business School Publishing, p. 2.

[44]Wallack, Todd. 1999. The need for speed. *San Francisco Chronicle,* 28 March.

[45]Norcross, Richard T. 1999. Satellites: The strategic high ground. *Scientific American* (October).

[46]Light, Jay O. et al. *The last mile of broadband access: technical note.* Case no. 9-800-076, 25 January. Harvard Business School Publishing, p. 15.

[47]PricewaterhouseCoopers. 1999. *E-Business technology forecast.* Menlo Park, CA: PricewaterhouseCoopers Technology Centre, p. 217.

[48]Pollack, Andrew. 2000. Coming soon, downloads from up above. *New York Times*, 27 February.

[49]Light, Jay O. et al. *The last mile of broadband access*. Case no. 9-800-076. Harvard Business School Publishing, p. 13.

[50]Lake, David. 2000. Worldwide Information Appliance Installed Forecast. *Industry Standard* (online version only), 3 April. URL: *http://www.thestandard.com/research/metrics/display/0,2799,13508,00.html.* Citing IDC.

[51]Holstein, William J. 1999. Moving beyond the PC. *U.S. News and World Report*, 13 December.

[52]*The New York Times*. 2000. The news at hand, 10 April, p. C-21.

[53]Ervin, Keith. 1999. Bsquare riding high on success of Windows CE. *Seattle Times*, 8 April.

[54]Pollack. 1999. Coming soon, downloads from up above. *New York Times*, 27 February.

[55]Wigder, Zia Daniell. 1999. Broadband applications. *Jupiter Communications* (June). URL: *http://www.jup.com/sps/research/report.jsp?doc*=bas99-33, p. 3.

[56]Forrester Research. 1999. *From dial-up to broadband* (April).

[57]Bunnell, David. 2000. *Making the Cisco connection*. New York: John Wiley and Sons, Inc., p. xi.

[58]Whitehead, Paul and Ruth Maran. 1997. *Teach yourself the Internet and the World Wide Web visually*. Indianapolis, IN: IDG Books Worldwide, Inc., p. 40.

[59]Lohr, Steve. 2000. A mainstream giant goes countercultural. *New York Times*, 20 March, p. C1.

[60]Castelluccio, Michael. 2000. Can the enterprise run on free software? The Linux OS and the Open Source Revolution. *Strategic Finance* (March): 51–5.

[61]Lohr. 2000. A mainstream giant. *New York Times*, 20 March, p. C1.

[62]Byrne, John A. and Debra Sparks. 2000. What's an old economy CEO to do? *Business Week*, 21 March, p. 38.

[63]Gates, Bill. 1999. *Business @ the speed of thought: Using a digital nervous system*. New York: Warner Books, p. 17.

[64]*ibid.*, p. 15.

[65]Kalakota, Ravi and Marcia Robinson. 1999. *E-Business: Roadmap for success*. Reading, MA: Addison-Wesley Publishing, p. 166.

[66]*ibid.*

[67]Harvard Business School. 2000. A crash course in customer relationship management. In *Management Update* (March): p. 5.

[68]Hopkins, William and Britton Manasco. 2000. The coming customer free-for-all. *New York Times*, 14 February.

[69]*ibid.*

[70]*ibid.*

[71]Kalakota and Robinson. 1999. *E-Business*, p. 228.

[72]*ibid.*

[73]*ibid.*

[74]Carpenter, Dave. 2000. Big retailers to link up with suppliers, distributors online. *Associated Press*, 29 February.

[75]This section draws from Kalakora and Robinson, *E-Business,* pages 140 and 141.

[76]Kalakota. 1999. *E-Business*, pp. 263–64.

[77]*ibid.*

[78]Green, Heather, Mike France and Marcia Stepanek. 2000. Privacy on the Net: What should be done. *Business Week*, 20 March.

[79]*ibid.*

[80]*ibid.*

[81]Anderson, Carl. 2000. E-Commerce panel opposes net taxes. *San Francisco Examiner*, 21 March.

[82]Thrum, Scott. 2000. Amazon.com chief executive urges shorter duration for internet patents. *Wall Street Journal*, 10 March.

[83]Rayport, Jeffrey, George C. Lodge and Thomas Gerace. 1997. *National Information Structure(A): The United States in Perspective,* 20 March. Boston: Harvard Business School Publishing, p. 20.

[84]Bezos, Jeff. 2000. An Open Letter from Jeff Bezos on the Subject of Patents. URL: *http://www.amazon.com/exec/obidos/subst/misc/patents.html/002-5634001-5632807*

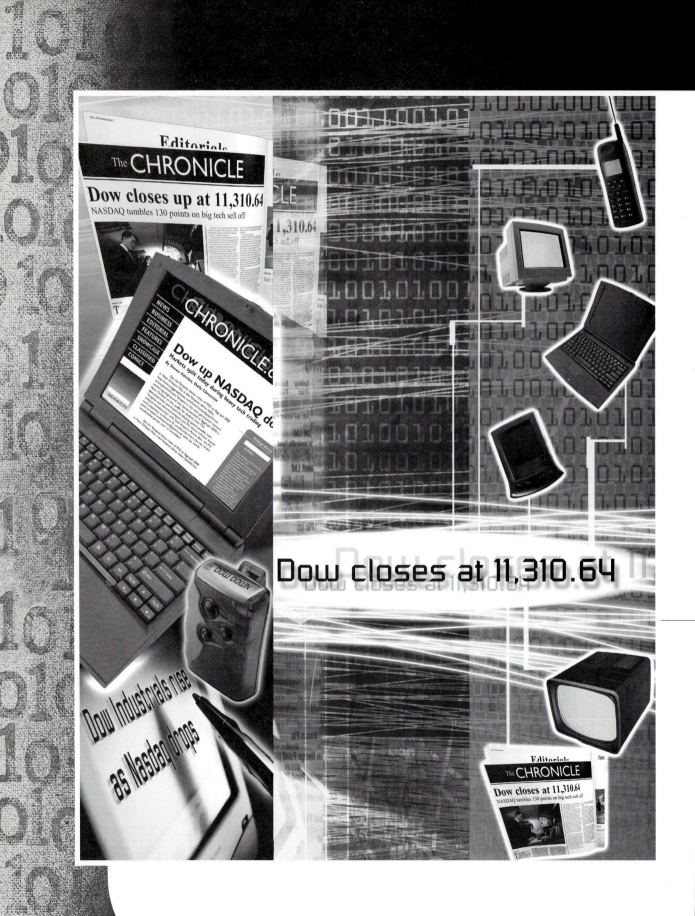

Media Convergence

The purpose of this chapter is to provide an understanding of media convergence. Media convergence and its expected synergistic benefits have been the key drivers behind several recent megamergers of media companies including the marriages of America Online and Time Warner, Viacom and CBS, and The Walt Disney Company and Capital Cities/ABC. With increasingly fragmented media usage in American households, recent changes in federal telecommunications laws, and advances in digital technology—especially with the expected increase in the household use of broadband—media convergence offers much promise and hope for a future of convenient access to new and innovative media services.

QUESTIONS

Please consider the following questions as you read this chapter:

1. **What is media convergence?**

2. **What conditions make media convergence possible?**

3. **How do new media companies leverage off traditional media channels?**

4. **What are reasons for media megamergers?**

5. **What public policy issues must be addressed with digital convergence and media convergence?**

This chapter was coauthored by Bernie Jaworski, Jeffrey Rayport, and Dickson Louie.

In Chapter 9, we reviewed the network infrastructure, which showed how the Internet is evolving as the digital platform of the New Economy. We explained how users connect to websites, how businesses now use the Web as a single digital media base to create an electronic architecture for commercial applications, and how public-policy issues governing privacy, patents, free speech, network economics, and monopolies may be impacted in the future. As discussed, the infrastructure convergence from analog technology to digital involves the conversion of all data streams into bits of zeros and ones—the binary language of computers.

The **media infrastructure** is all the various communications companies and their channels of communication, such as radio, television, newspapers, and magazines, that are used in mass communication with the general public. Whereas the network infrastructure refers to the hardware and software used in communication, the media infrastructure refers to the content of the communication. Media companies produce the content for print-media distribution chains or for programs that are broadcast over a chain or network of radio or television broadcast stations.

Media convergence happens when different types of media content—news, information, and entertainment—found across various types of media forms—text, images, audio, and video—evolve into a single media platform through the Internet. **Media convergence** can be defined as the evolution and migration of the various media content (news, information, and entertainment) from traditional analog media platforms (print, audio, and video) to a digital platform or cross-platform in which all content will be accessible through various digital devices (e.g., wireless telephones, personal computers, handheld Palm Pilots, and interactive television set-tops). Media convergence has been the key driver behind several recent megamergers of media companies, including those of America Online and Time Warner, Viacom and CBS, The Walt Disney Company and Capital Cities/ABC, and the Tribune Company and the Times Mirror Company.

In this chapter, we review the current and potential future impact of media convergence across an array of Old and New Economy media and look at areas of public policy that will need to be addressed. We review the proliferation of media and the fragmentation of media usage for news, information, and entertainment over the past three decades. We explore the beginnings of media convergence with Internet companies that leverage off the media of the Old Economy to build brand awareness and usage for their products and services in the New Economy. We examine how the possibility of media convergence has become a driving force behind several megamergers of various media companies during the past few years. We also review the potential impact of media convergence on various media platforms and their current business models. Finally, we look at the public-policy issues governing media convergence.

WHAT CONDITIONS MAKE MEDIA CONVERGENCE POSSIBLE?

Continued Advances and Decreasing Cost of Digital Technology

Advances and decreased costs in computers and all of the related digital technology make possible a potentially cost-effective common platform for placing all types of media content into binary form. Most media content now begins in digital form, and once text, audio, video, and graphics are in the digital domain, the digital forms of content are easily manipulated, combined, stored, and transmitted with the use of computers across the Internet through such digital devices as a personal computer, a digital television set, or another type of Internet device.

Low-Cost Digital Network Infrastructure

The development of the Internet, with its nonproprietary network protocol (IP), transfer protocol (HTTP), and hypertext language (HTML), allowed hardware and software development to occur in a relatively unencumbered environment. With the ubiquitous Internet as a digital communications backbone, HTTP and HTML allowed development of an easy-to-use, free-to-the-consumer, industry standard Internet browser with a graphical user interface that reduced user navigation to a click of a mouse. Because of this and a lifting of commercial use restrictions, the World Wide Web became a low-cost digital network infrastructure that experienced an explosive growth in number of users and number of sites.

Media Proliferation

At the start of the twentieth century, daily printed newspapers were the single unifying source of news, information, and entertainment. In the 1920s, radio and magazines emerged as additional sources. Then, immediately following World War II, in the late 1940s and throughout the 1950s, many Americans replaced newspapers and radio with network broadcast television as the primary source of news, information, and entertainment.

In the 1960s, most Americans had a choice of one of three networks for news or entertainment. By the 1970s, cable television had emerged and offered additional channels, such as HBO and Turner Broadcasting's TBS Superstation. In the 1980s, the VCR became commonplace, and cable television further exploded with new networks, such as CNN and MTV. In the 1990s, direct-broadcast satellite services found their way into American homes and the number of cable television channels continued to grow.

Media Usage Fragmentation in American Households

To estimate the increasing fragmentation of media usage, the Pew Research Center in Washington, D.C., conducted a survey in April 1996. It showed that while broadcast television news, both network and local, was still the primary source of news and information, newspapers were the secondary source. During a 24-month period between 1994 and 1996, viewership of daily television news programs by most Americans declined by almost 20 percent, from 74 percent to 59 percent.

The study also noted that a dwindling television news audience was apparent in all demographic groups but particularly was most evident among younger people. Network, local, and CNN regular audiences slipped the most among people under 30 years of age, followed by those 30 to 49 years of age. Regular viewing of all three types of news programs was off only slightly, or not at all, among people 50 years of age and older.[1]

While young people cited the "lack of time" for less news viewing, they spent as much time as older people engaging in a variety of other media activities, such as watching entertainment television and reading books and magazines. Young people also spent more time using computers but decidedly less time following the news on television or in the newspapers.

As with television news, audiences for entertainment shows on broadcast television also showed a steady decline largely due to the increased penetration of cable television. For example, during the 1985–86 season, approximately 93 percent of the prime-time viewing audience in the United States watched one of the shows on a network affiliate, an independent television station, or on public television. During prime time only 7 percent had watched a show on cable television. During the 1996–97 season, the percentage of households watching a show on a network affiliate, on an independent television station, or on public television had declined to about 67 percent while those watching a cable television show increased to 33 percent. Over the same 12-year period, the number of subscribers to basic cable had increased from 39.8 million (or 46.2 percent of all households) in 1985 to 67.0 million (or 68.0 percent of all households) in 1997.[2] The number of cable systems showed a similar increase from 6,600 to 10,845. Table 10-1 shows how cable television services have eroded prime-time viewership from the broadcast networks.

Although the amount of time spent watching news and network television entertainment has steadily declined for all age groups over the past two decades, the percentage of households with alternative forms of media entertainment and information has increased, thus contributing to further fragmentation of media usage. For example, as 1999 came to an end, 99 percent of all U.S. households had at least one television set and 98 percent had at least one radio. Ninety-one percent of the

Table 10-1

PRIME-TIME VIEWING SHARES OF FREE AND CABLE TELEVISION NETWORKS (1985–1998)

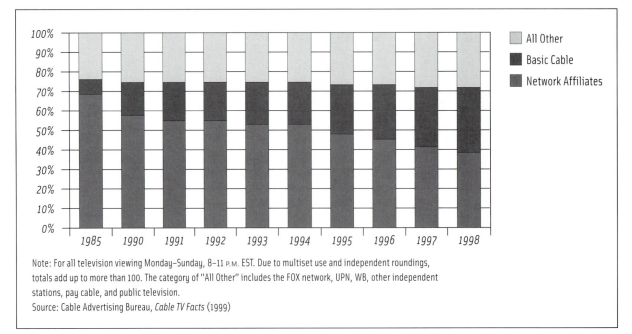

Note: For all television viewing Monday–Sunday, 8–11 P.M. EST. Due to multiset use and independent roundings, totals add up to more than 100. The category of "All Other" includes the FOX network, UPN, WB, other independent stations, pay cable, and public television.

Source: Cable Advertising Bureau, *Cable TV Facts* (1999)

households had a VCR; 51 percent, a personal computer; 44 percent, a video-game unit; and 43 percent had a cellular telephone. Approximately 28 percent of all households had access to the Internet, and 68 percent were wired to cable television.[3] By comparison, 10 years earlier in 1990, only 68 percent of all households in the United States had access to a VCR; 23 percent, a personal computer; 15 percent, a video-game unit; and 59 percent, cable television.[4] Very few households had access to the Internet or owned a cellular phone.

With the increase in the number of multiple media devices and services found in the typical American household, children were found to be immersed in media usage. A November 1999 study, released by the Kaiser Family Foundation, showed that on average American children spent 5.5 hours per day—or just over 38 hours per week—using media. Television viewing accounted for almost half of the usage at 2 hours 46 minutes, followed by listening to music at 1 hour 27 minutes, and then reading, watching videos, and using a computer. The typical American household had three television sets, three radios, two VCRs, two CD players, a video-game player as well as newspapers, magazines, and comic books.[5]

Forecasted Continued Media Proliferation and Media Usage Fragmentation

With the continued proliferation of television channels and services, as well as other media outlets, and the resulting fragmentation of audiences, the sources of news, information, and entertainment were varied for many Americans in the year 2000. Experts predict that over the next 10 years technological advances in wireless, digital compression, two-way networks, and the Internet, along with the introduction of high-definition television, will present consumers with even more media choices and perhaps as many as 300 channels of television at any given moment.[6] See Exhibit 10-1 for a representation of the anticipated explosion in media choices that will drive even more audience fragmentation.

HOW DO NEW MEDIA COMPANIES LEVERAGE OFF TRADITIONAL MEDIA CHANNELS?

While much has been written recently about the Internet as an increasingly important source for news, information, and commerce, the New Economy has actually been quite dependent on the traditional Old Economy news outlets. Online media are using traditional media channels to build audiences for new media. Dot-coms are using newspapers, magazines, and broadcast television to build audiences from the initial stage of attracting "early adopters" into a secondary stage of attracting mainstream users.[7] In 1999, an estimated 28 percent of all American households were online, a threefold increase from almost 9 percent just four years earlier.[8]

To build brand awareness for a rapidly growing mainstream audience of Internet users, dot-com companies spent an estimated $3 to $4 billion in advertising in 1999, with approximately 90 percent of those dollars being spent on traditional media outlets, such as network television, national newspapers, and network radio.[9] Among the top dot-com advertisers in local and national newspapers in 1999 were Value America, E*Trade, Dow Jones, Cheap Tickets.com, Priceline.com, and Charles Schwab's online trading site.[10]

Exhibit 10-1

MEDIA FRAGMENTATION— 1960s TO 2010s

> TV faces the worst audience fragmentation of all. Here, News Corp. tracks and forecasts the explosion of TV viewing choices available in any given hour. Once there were three options; soon there will be 1,000.

1960s	1970s	1980s	1990s	2000s	2010s
Most Americans watch the Big Three networks every night.	UHF stations bring more choices, and the fledgling cable industry introduces a few new channels like HBO and Turner's TBS Superstation.	The VCR becomes commonplace, letting consumers watch recorded shows and movies whenever they want. Cable explodes, with new networks like CNN and MTV.	Direct-broadcast satellites are introduced, offering hundreds of channels. Cable systems are slowly upgraded with more channels.	Digital compression and two-way networks allow cable companies to offer even more channels and services. DBS services grow more entrenched. As TVs are linked to the Internet, new programming delivered via the Internet takes hold. Result: 300 choices at any moment.	Broadcasters may use the high-definition TV spectrum to launch more channels. Internet chat evolves into networked virtual reality games, interactive movies, and other activities being hatched by MIT's media lab and others. News Corp. forecasts 1,000 channels, now called "context windows."

Source: *Business Week*, February 16, 1998

Online companies' use of traditional media channels instead of primarily relying on online banners or button advertisements to build brand awareness is not unexpected. Approximately 32 percent of all Internet users said that they used articles in magazines or newspapers to discover URLs. Twenty-eight percent said that they had relied on word of mouth to find URLs; 27 percent, on products; 26 percent, on print advertisements; 24 percent, on television advertising; 22 percent, on product literature; and 15 percent, on radio advertising.[11]

Aside from using traditional media outlets to build brand awareness, online news users said they still read newspapers and listened to radio news—two traditional sources of news and information—at about the same or at a higher rate since going online. Although this is not surprising given that most Internet users are more interested in current events than non-Internet users, it is interesting to note that the Internet is emerging as a mechanism for supplementing, not replacing, traditional media sources.[12] Furthermore, 75 percent of all online news users indicated they used traditional news outlets *more* often to get their news and information. Furthermore, since going online, 63 percent said they used offline sources about the same as before, and only 11 percent said they had used offline sources less than before.

Case Example: America Online

Originally incorporated in 1985 as Quantum Computer Services to provide an online "Q Link" to Commodore Business Machines, America Online transformed itself in 1989[13]: it expanded the customer base for its proprietary online service by making it available for users of the Apple Macintosh and Apple II computers.[14] To build its brand name against more established online services, such as Prodigy, CompuServe, and Delphi, America Online first sought out partnerships with established media brands (e.g., Apple, MTV, the *San Jose Mercury News,* and NBC) to make their content available online for the first time.

In the early 1990s many newspapers were eager to provide their content to emerging online services. A decade earlier, Times Mirror (the parent company of the *Los Angeles Times* and *Newsday*) and Knight-Ridder (the corporate owner of the *Philadelphia Inquirer, Miami Herald,* and the *San Jose Mercury News*) had both attempted to venture into electronic media. Times Mirror invested in VideoText to introduce online news services, at-home banking, and other electronic activities through interactive television. Knight-Ridder tried to do the same with its ViewTron project by using television and personal computers. Both ventures were well ahead of consumer demand and infrastructure development, and both failed. As a result, many newspapers retreated from electronic media back to print and allowed third-party online services such as America Online, Prodigy, and CompuServe to emerge in the early 1990s in an uncontested market.[15]

By 1995, America Online (see Exhibit 10-2) would surpass both Prodigy and CompuServe as the largest online service company in the United States. In five years, its subscriber base would grow from 1 million in 1994 to over 20 million at the end of 1999. The average time spent per day by each America Online subscriber online would increase fourfold from 15 minutes in September 1996 to almost 60 minutes at the end of 1999, with almost half of the time being spent on commercial services and content.[16] Along the way, America Online achieved a market value of over $138 billion and would also acquire CompuServe, Netscape, and, still pending at the time of writing, Time Warner.

Case Example: Monster.Com

Founded in 1993 by Jeff Taylor, the Massachusetts-based Monster.com (see Exhibit 10-3) has emerged as the leading online career site on the Web, as of January 2000 reaching over 3.5 million unique users, or 5.3 percent of all Internet users in the United States. The size of Monster.com's audience is twice that of its three nearest competitors—Careermosaic.com, Hotjobs.com, and Careerpath.com.[17] Between December 1998 and January 2000, Monster.com was able to build brand awareness and increase its reach from 1.4 percent to 5.3 percent of all Internet users, largely through the combined use of broadcast television commercials, along with the simultaneous creation of content and communities online to encourage visitors to make repeat visits. See Table 10-2 for statistics on Monster.com's phenomenal growth.

Along with its rival, Hot Jobs.com, Monster.com was the first dot-com company to ever advertise in a Super Bowl in January 1999. The Monster.com television ads, featuring mock testimonials of elementary school–aged children aspiring to get dead-end jobs in corporate America, were run for the rest of the year on network television and gradually helped increase Monster.com's share of the online market.

Exhibit 10-2

AMERICA ONLINE
WELCOME SCREEN

Exhibit 10-3

MONSTER.COM
HOMEPAGE

Table
10-2

MONSTER.COM USER STATISTICS

	Monster.com Key Metrics—December 1998 to January 2000				
	December 1998	March 1999	June 1999	September 1999	January 2000
U.S. Internet Users Visiting Monster.com	1.4%	3.4%	4.2%	4.1%	5.3%
Direct Traffic (Nonalliance)	81.0%	90.0%	94.0%	95.0%	NA
Page Views	48 million	82 million	122 million	146 million	158 million
Paid Job Listings	186,000	204,000	252,000	255,000	315,000*
Resume Database	1.0 million	1.3 million	1.6 million	2.0 million	3.0 million
Registered Members	NA	2.5 million	3.6 million	4.2 million	6 million

*as of December 1999
Source: Bean Murray Institutional Research, Monster.com, Media Metrix

Taylor explained the rationale behind launching the television campaign, with the 30-second Super Bowl ad accounting for 15 percent of the company total advertising budget for 1999:

> *In February 1998, about a third of our traffic came through 90 strategic alliances and partnerships with many of the Internet's most popular websites. By August 1998, traffic generated from the alliances had fallen below 15 percent but traffic to Monster.com was going through the roof. With these facts in hand, I decided to change our focus from the three-year strategy of using alliances to build our traffic to going directly to the consumer.*
>
> *In launching the television campaign, we thought that we could go from being the "leader" in our category to becoming the "dominator." It worked; we ended up almost quadrupling our reach.[18]*

Anne Hollows, Monster.com's vice president for branding, explained the urgency behind Monster.com's decision to build its brand quickly using television. "You don't have 20 years," she said. "By any measure, since [the Super Bowl in] January 1999, Monster.com has created a pre-emptive lead against its competitors and an effective barrier to entry."

Case Example: CBS Marketwatch.com

San Francisco-based financial news vertical, CBS MarketWatch.com (see Exhibit 10-4) utilizes the resources of CBS, its minority equity owner and broadcast partner, to build brand awareness nationwide. Established in October 1997 as a joint venture between CBS and Direct Broadcast Corporation, CBS MarketWatch.com has risen to become the fortieth most visited site on the Web as of March 2000, with 5.5 million unique users. By using the entire CBS Network in a promotion-for-equity exchange, the contents of CBS MarketWatch appear nationally each day on CBS News' "Early Show" and on the news shows of CBS television affiliates.[19]

Exhibit 10-4

CBS MARKETWATCH HOMEPAGE

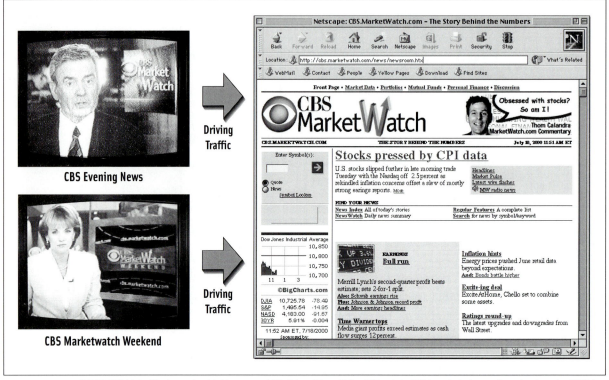

CBS Evening News

Driving Traffic

CBS Marketwatch Weekend

Driving Traffic

In addition, CBS television affiliates can choose to air the syndicated "CBSMarketWatch Weekend" television program, which provides a summary of the week's activity on Wall Street, and CBS radio affiliates can air daily updates of the financial market activities provided by the MarketWatch staff. Larry Kramer, CBS MarketWatch's chairman, cofounder, and CEO, observed:

> The reason we beat people like CNBC and CNNfn on the Web is because they use the Web as a way to only enhance their core business [of financial cable television]. Our mission is to build a great website. I'm not here to be CNBC or a financial cable channel. Our audience is bigger. I have more people coming to our website than they have watching CNBC. The CBS relationship helps build branding, credibility, and drives traffic to our site.[20]

WHAT ARE THE REASONS FOR MEDIA MEGAMERGERS?

With increased fragmentation of media usage, over the past five years media companies have been merging as a way to develop vertical integration for content and distribution across all types of media—print, video, and audio. Over the past three years, the pace for media mergers has increased, especially with the promise of "broadband" technology, through which media users can quickly access over the Internet a variety of media forms, ranging from video-on-demand to software distribution to multiplayer games.

Recent media mega mergers include the following:

- Time Warner and Turner Broadcasting (1995)
- Walt Disney Company and Capital Cities/ABC (1995)
- Westinghouse and CBS Inc. (1995)
- Viacom and CBS Inc. (1999)
- America Online and Time Warner (2000)
- Tribune Company and Times Mirror (2000)

There were several reasons behind each of these mergers; they include changes in the Telecommunications Act of 1996, vertical integration of both content and distribution channels, advances in new digital technologies, and entry into global markets.

Telecommunications Act of 1996

The **Telecommunications Act of 1996** was signed into law by President Bill Clinton on February 8, 1996. This represented the first major overhaul of federal laws regulating the communications industry since 1934. With the passing of this act, emphasis was changed from a regulation-based industry to a market-based industry to allow for increased competition. The law allowed for increased ownership of television stations by a single entity (up to 25 percent of the total U.S. market) and for the convergence of media, whereby telephone service providers, cable television companies, and utility companies could directly compete with one another to provide telephone, cable, and utility services into the home.

Vertical Integration

While the Telecommunications Act of 1996 allowed for increased competition to provide "regulated" media distribution channels into the typical U.S. household, media companies were often at the center of megamergers as part of an overall strategy of the **vertical integration** of media content with media distribution. For example, the merger of Disney with Capital Cities/ABC and Viacom with CBS allowed for traditional content providers of motion pictures and television shows to merge with a television network as a way to distribute content into the households through broadcast television.

The reason often cited for a media merger acquisition was "synergy." Michael Eisner, Chairman and CEO of the Walt Disney Company explained in 1996:

> At Disney, it is our conviction that synergy can be the single most important contributor to profit and growth in a creativity-driven company.
>
> It is simply this. When you embrace a new idea, a new business, a new product, a new film, or TV show, whatever—you have to make sure that everyone throughout the company knows about it early enough so that every segment of the business can promote or exploit its potential in every other possible market, product or context.

[For example, if a film] does well in its initial domestic run, it almost ensures later success in international distribution, domestic and international home video, network, and foreign television, pay-per-view TV, and cable. At Disney [synergy goes further] a well-received film will also provide profitable opportunities in our theme parks—new rides, new characters, new parades, new attractions, and in consumer products for Disney stores, for Sears, and for others.[21]

Advances in New Digital Technologies

Rapid advances in new digital technologies present media companies with the opportunity to put their content online in various forms, ranging from the current streaming technology to play short audio and video clips over a narrowband feed to the future promise of playing movies-on-demand through broadband delivery.

An example of media convergence on the Internet is demonstrated by the ABCNews.com (see Exhibit 10-5) site, which the Walt Disney Company owns through the ABC Television and Radio Network as part of the GO Network. On the ABCNews site, visitors can read, listen to, or view ABC News content from both its television and radio news programs. For example, digitalized technology allows for selected video clips from the television network's branded news shows—"Good

Exhibit 10-5

ABCNEWS.COM HOMEPAGE

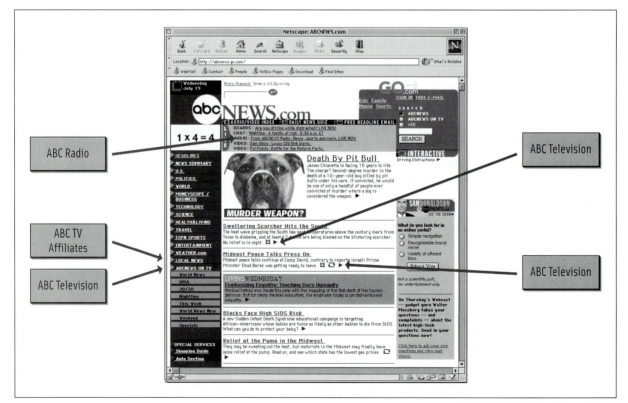

Morning America," "20/20," and "World News Tonight"—to appear both on television through any one of its 215 affiliates or over the Internet on the ABCNews.com site. Hourly audio clips of news and sports reports from ABC Radio are also available on the ABCNews.com site through audio streaming. With broadband technology, longer video and video-audio clips can be added to the site in the future.

Entry into Global Markets

With no geographic barriers to the distribution of digitized content on the Internet, many media companies have sought to create global markets for their content through mergers. Expansion of brand names into overseas markets included CNN International, MTV Overseas, ESPN, and the Disney Channel.

With increased digitization of content and the promise of broadband delivery in the near-future, the personal computer will not be the only receiver of information over the Internet. Other Internet receivers include digital telephones, handheld computers, and video-game player stations. In fact, by mid-2000, many observers noted that the new Sony PlayStation 2 (see Exhibit 10-6), in addition to being a video-game player, also had the potential to become the primary household appliance for converging media applications because of its capabilities to be a DVD player, CD player, and an Internet connection. Howard Stringer, CEO of Sony Corporation of America, observed, "Synergy was forced in the analog world, but in the digital world, people can't get out of the way of each other."[22]

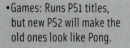

Exhibit 10-6

SONY PLAYSTATION 2

- Games: Runs PS1 titles, but new PS2 will make the old ones look like Pong.

- DVD Player: Can play digital movies right out of the box. Not a bad deal just for that.

- Music CDs: PS2 spins them, too. Pressed for space? Give the old player away.

- Internet: In 2001, Sony says you will be able to add Net connectivity. Browse and buy.

- Download: Also in 2001, store and replay digital music and video from the Web.

How Is Media Content Delivered Over the Internet?

With the Internet, text, photos, graphics, audio, and video can be all broken into bits, transmitted across the Internet in digitized form, and reassembled at an end user's computer. For example, graphic files can be transmitted in various formats, the two most common being **GIF** (Graphics Interchange Format) and **JPEG** (Joint Photographic Experts Group). Both GIF and JPEG files contain binary data that will display an image when viewed with proper software and hardware. A computer graphics card takes the image data and displays it on a computer monitor. The Web browser reads and displays these graphic files without needing any additional software.

Binary multimedia files for sounds, music, and video are also transmitted the same way, although they take much longer over current narrowband transmission speeds of less than 128 kilobits per second. Window sound files, which end in a WAV extension, and Macintosh sound files, are among the most common types of files that one can download to their computer and play through a sound card.[23]

What Is Streaming Media?

Certain sound files, such as those created by Real Audio software, allow a computer user to listen to sounds while the file is still downloading instead of waiting until the file is completely downloaded. This process is called **streaming audio.**

Macintosh QuickTime and MPEG files are common streaming video formats. With a video player, such as Real Player or Windows Media, a computer user can watch the video while the file is downloaded. This process is called **streaming video.**

Currently, streaming audio and video content is possible over a narrowband transmission by using media player software in conjunction with a personal computer.[24]

At the end of November 1999, 16.9 million Internet users (or 22.7 percent of all users) had access to a media player for listening or viewing media content from the Internet. Real Player controlled 53 percent of the market; Macintosh QuickTime, 32.5 percent; and Windows Media Player, 15 percent.[25]

Media Economics

As stated earlier, media companies have been merging over the past five years as a way to develop vertical integration for content and distribution across all types of media. The conditions surrounding these mergers included changes in the Telecommunications Act of 1996, the vertical integration of content and distribution channels, advances in new digital technologies, and entry into global markets. For today's media company, the strategy is to collect and, through media

How Do Digital Cameras Work?

Digital cameras don't use film. The quality of a digital picture is based on resolution, just like traditional photography. But in the digital world, resolution is based on the number of tiny electronic picture elements, or "pixels." The more pixels there are, the better and higher the possible resolution of your picture. When examining the "megapixel" technical specification of a digital still camera, be aware of the horizontal resolution as well as the vertical resolution and that the stated resolution numbers are not equal to that of a display monitor.

The various colors that we see in an image are the result of the varying amounts of red, green, and blue (RGB) light reflected from illuminated objects and detected by our eyes. Similarly, reflected light from objects are focused on the sensor elements of a charged coupled device (CCD) internal to the digital camera. The CCD is designed such that each element detects red, green, or blue light within the image before the lens. Because of this, the actual display resolution is the stated horizontal pixels divided by three by the stated vertical pixels divided by three; e.g., a 2.3-megapixel (million square pixel) digital camera with 1800 × 1200 has an approximate display resolution of 600 × 400.

Expose. Just like a traditional film camera, a digital camera's shutter admits light when you take a picture. (A scanner uses its own light source to illuminate the film or the print that it is scanning.) The subject is reflected onto light-sensitive material composed of the millions of tiny electronic elements of the CCD.

Develop. Even while you're setting up your next shot, the camera is instantly adjusting the light detected by the cells and correcting it for color temperature balance. The press of a button triggers the sampling/quantizing/digitizing process and creates a set of digital data to represent the image.

Record. This code is stored as a picture file in the camera, on a floppy disk, or in a removable memory card. Once your pictures are transferred to a computer you can modify, manipulate, and combine images, using the proper software. The possibilities are endless.[26]

From *Capturing Data, www.kodak.com,* 1999

Do Media Megamergers Work?

Bill Gates, the Chairman of Microsoft Corporation, offered an opposing view of media megamergers, suggesting that joint ventures and minority interest investments provided the same benefits. He noted:

. . . Beware! Mergers that are attempts to bring all aspects of highway expertise should be viewed skeptically. Much of what the press covers about the highway has been concerned with just huge corporate deals. It will be a long time before the corporations making these investments can assess how wise they are.

Instead Microsoft plans to reach out to hundreds of companies, including movie studios, television

networks, and newspaper and magazine publishers. We hope to work with them so that together we can assemble their respective content assets and build applications for CD-ROM, the Internet, and the highway. We believe in alliances and are eager to participate in them.[27]

The alliances that Microsoft participated in include a partnership with NBC News to create an online and cable news channel, as well as investments in AT&T, NEXTEL, and Comcast Cable.

(continued on page 381)

convergence and digital convergence, to create a synergistic combination of once disparate media to produce a direct bottom-line benefit. Each of the media has its own economics and, therefore, a different business model. Content commonly discussed in connection to media convergence includes newspapers, magazines, books, broadcast television, cable television, radio, film, videos, music CDs, and MP3s.

Newspapers. At the end of 1998, there were 1,489 daily newspapers in the United States, with a total daily circulation of approximately 56.2 million and a total Sunday circulation of 60.1 million. Although only half of the daily newspapers were published in the morning, the morning publications attracted 80 percent of the total circulation, or about 45.6 million. The top four newspapers in the United States were *USA Today,* the *Wall Street Journal, The New York Times,* and the *Los Angeles Times*—all with a daily circulation of one million or more.[28]

Since 1987, total daily circulation, or the number of copies sold, for newspapers began to decline after a reading peak of 62.8 million. There were several reasons for this drop-off including the closing of several evening daily newspapers, the increase in the number of alternative weekly newspapers, and the emergence of other electronic news sources. The number of evening newspapers declined from 1,166 in 1987 to 781 in 1998. In that same time period, the number of weekly newspapers increased from 7,600 to 8,193, with total weekly circulation growing from 47.5 million to 72.3 million.[29]

This overall decline in daily newspaper circulation paralleled the continued decline in the percent of adults who read a newspaper daily. In 1970, 78 percent of all adults in the United States said that they read a daily newspaper. Almost 30 years later, by 1998, this percentage had shrunk to 58.6 percent. The drop-off in Sunday readership was less dramatic, declining from 72 percent in 1970 to 68 percent in 1998.[30]

The average newspaper reader is older, more educated, and earns a higher income than the general population. Over 66 percent of all daily newspaper readers have college degrees and two-thirds have household incomes of $50,000 or more, where the median household income in the United States is approximately $37,000.[31]

While circulation revenue from readers and subscribers only generates a portion of a daily newspaper's revenue, approximately three-quarters of a daily newspaper's revenue comes through advertising. Through its readership, a daily newspaper often delivers a well-educated, high-income audience to its advertisers—an audience that advertisers covet. In 1998, advertising in newspapers accounted for $43.9 billion, or 21.8 percent of all advertising expenditures in the United States. The bulk of this advertising came from retail and classified advertising, which, respectively, accounted for 46.2 percent (or $20.3 billion) and 40.7 percent (or $17.9 billion) of the total advertising in newspapers. The balance of newspaper advertising comes from national advertising, or national accounts, such as financial services, airlines, and hotels.[32]

In March 2000, America Online reported that it had more than 23 million subscribers, more than the circulation of the top 20 daily newspapers in the United States combined.[33] Because of the increasing use of the Internet, newspapers have rushed to create a presence there in an effort to capture this audience. At the end of 1999, approximately 1,000 newspapers in North America had an online product of some kind, ranging from classified ads to complete reproduction of the entire newspaper.[34]

Magazines. At the end of 1998, there were over 500 consumer magazines and 2,700 trade publications published in the United States. The top 100 consumer magazines had a combined total circulation of approximately 248 million. Among the top magazines were *Modern Maturity, Reader's Digest, AARP Bulletin,* and *TV Guide,* each with a circulation base greater than 12 million.[35]

Unlike newspapers, consumer magazines ranged from the very specialized, such as *Cooking Light* or *Sunset,* to those of general interest, like *Newsweek* or *People Weekly.*[36] Approximately 82 percent of all consumer magazines were sold through subscriptions, and the remaining 18 percent were sold through retail outlets, such as supermarkets and newsstands.

Trade publications are magazines with a narrow focus in a particular area of business, such as restaurants or computers. Most trade publications are sold either by subscription or are distributed free.

Like newspapers, almost all magazines make money through a combination of circulation and advertising revenue. Magazines often guarantee their advertisers a base circulation of readers. The top magazines by advertising revenue in 1999 were *People Weekly* ($626 million), *Time* ($561 million), *Sports Illustrated* ($554 million), *TV Guide* ($453 million), and *Better Homes and Gardens* ($410 million).

Although magazines are not as directly threatened by the growth of the Internet as newspapers are, many magazines seek to use their sites on the Web as a way to enhance subscriber benefits and to build home-delivery circulation. For example, beginning in 1999, several Time Warner magazines sought to strengthen their presence on the Web and began to offer exclusive services to their subscribers, such as free archival searches and chats with editors and writers.

Books. According to the Book Industry Study Group, which monitors the reading habits of American households, sales of books in the United States increased in 1998 for the eighth straight year. Sales of hardcover books grew by 6 percent while paperback sales increased by 5 percent.[37] The increase in sales came even as the total number of titles published declined. After hitting an all-time high of 68,175 titles in 1996, production dropped slightly to 65,796 in 1997 and dramatically to 56,127 in 1998. While this is a significant decline of over 15 percent, the number produced is

(continued from page 380)
with word of mouth. It may be getting people involved in communities and chat rooms and talking about something and generating interest. In fact the users are creating as much of the content in this new medium as the so-called professional content creators.

Get the full interview at www.marketspaceu.com

POINT-COUNTERPOINT

Will Newspapers Survive?

Doomsayers predicting the demise of newspapers say that inroads made by the Internet as a primary news source as well as the loss of classified advertising revenue to online career sites, such as Monster.com, spell the potential end for newspapers. Supporters of newspapers point out that the websites of local newspapers, such as Boston.com, operated by the *Boston Globe,* are often the leading sites for news and information in many local markets nationwide, instead of a national news site, such as CNN or MSNBC.[38] Proponents add that television was supposedly going to kill the newspaper industry in the 1950s the same way people are predicting that the Internet will today. John Morton, a newspaper industry analyst observed, "We've heard it all before. A newspaper is cheap, easy to use, portable, and a great way to get information out to the masses without straining eyes or a budget."[39]

Growing by Shrinking: The *Wall Street Journal*
How One Web Publisher Is Leading the Charge from PCs to Handhelds

by Peter Meyers, staff writer for tnbt.com

Analysts predict that by 2002, non-PC, Internet-ready "information appliances" such as personal digital assistants (PDAs) and cell phones will represent half of all computing devices sold. No one is working harder to adapt itself to this nascent revolution than the *Wall Street Journal*, which, since early 1999 has been publishing its paper on devices such as PDAs, e-book readers, and even in audio format.

The *Journal*, which has offered its Web-based Interactive Edition since 1996, began its efforts to deliver a daily edition to PDAs by teaming up with a company called AvantGo to prepare the newspaper's content for the PDA market. Like many other leading publishers (including *Business Week* and the *New York Times*), the *Journal* chose the San Mateo, California–based AvantGo because of a popular system it devised for publishing content to almost all PDAs sold today. The system, which is free for publishers to use, relies upon a free mini-browser that PDA users install on their devices.

The browser, which can be used only to view content prepared through AvantGo's system, works in conjunction with the servers of AvantGo and the publisher to display content in a PDA-friendly way. And in a touch that seems fitting for an interactive publication, the *Journal*'s readers played a role in the decision to go with AvantGo. "We were starting to hear from our own customers that they were interested in getting our stuff from AvantGo," says Neil Budde, editor of the *Journal*'s Interactive Edition.

AvantGo has gained a first-mover advantage that's comparable to the one achieved by RealNetworks, the streaming audio and video service that became a leading provider by signing up a critical mass of publishers and end users. Similarly, AvantGo has signed up hundreds of content partners and convinced hundreds of thousands of users to download its proprietary browser. Until all publishers are PDA-enabling their content and there is the equivalent of a universal PDA Web browser (in the same way that, say, Microsoft's Internet Explorer works on all PCs), AvantGo's lead is likely to continue. "They are the ones to beat in that space right now," says Jack Gold, an analyst for the Stamford, Connecticut–based market research firm Meta Group.

(continued on page 383)

still higher than the 46,748 titles in 1990. The most popular subject areas were sociology, fiction, and medicine.[40] Part of the reason for the continued increase in the printed word was the continuing increase in educational attainment among Americans over the past two decades. In 1998, 83 percent of the population had finished high school compared to 68 percent in 1990. Over that same time period, 24 percent of the population had a college degree 1998, compared to only 17 percent in 1980.[41]

With the increased use of the Internet, book publishers are increasingly looking into the possibility of going from a "print-and-distribute" model to a "distribute-and-print" model, similar to the popular distribution in March 2000 of Steven King's 66-page online book, *Riding the Bullet,* which was available for downloading from Amazon.com, BarnesandNoble.com, and from Palm Pilot sites.[42] By early 2000, computer hardware companies such as Hewlett Packard

(continued from page 382)

When it came time to prepare the *Journal*'s content for AvantGo, Budde said that several previous decisions—some technology-related, some editorial—facilitated this new form of publishing. "We have all our content internally stored in XML," said Budde, referring to the data markup language that has become a favorite of publishers looking to deliver their content to a variety of platforms. By using XML, some templates and some scripts, the *Journal* is easily able to publish AvantGo-ready content, explained Budde. The content consists of the summaries that have accompanied every article for years in the print edition's What's News section. They are written by editors who "boil [the articles] down to a really concise sentence," Budde said. The summaries and accompanying headlines are what handheld users see when they use the AvantGo service.

Due to the limited amount of screen space available on a handheld, Budde said that it works out well that these short descriptions provide an almost ideal way of presenting PDA-compatible versions of the articles. Consider, by contrast, a method popular with many other online publishers: providing an article's first sentence to readers so they can decide whether to read the full text.

Meta Group's Gold agrees with the decision not to publish full text articles. "People are going to go blind trying to read the damn thing," he said. That said, the *Journal* does have a program for Internet-surfing Palm VII users that offers the full text of some of the paper's articles. But because the users pay according to how much data they download, the *Journal* decided to offer the content incrementally. Readers are given the options of viewing summaries or full text.

Looking ahead, Budde is optimistic about future non-PC publishing projects, including the *Journal*'s early foray into audio publishing with Audible.com. Audible is one of the Web's leading providers of downloadable spoken text. Currently the partnership with the *Journal* involves preparing digest summaries of content that users can download and play back on a handheld device.

And while Budde thinks the audio *Journal* is a great convenience for commuters who drive each day, he admits that the process—download to PC, transfer to handheld, hook up for playback in car—is "not as convenient" as he thinks it someday will be. What he envisions in the not too distant future is *Journal* content that gets downloaded overnight directly into an Internet-enabled car radio. "I don't think that's that far off," he said. "It's very clear that the world of the near future is going to be a much wider range of devices."

Read more articles about The Next Big Thing at *www.tnbt.com*

---

were exploring how publishing houses could possibly use these new technologies to exploit this business model.[43]

It is the computer that some doomsayers thought would lead to the demise of books that, ironically, has been responsible for the increase in book production since 1990. Computers reduce publishers' production costs and enable the publication of many more titles. The computer has also made possible the superstore, such as Borders and Barnes & Noble, in which computer indexes, rather than humans, keep track of thousands of titles.[44]

Broadcast Television. Unlike most businesses that produce or sell tangible products and services, TV network broadcasting is essentially a programming service. The three major U.S. networks—ABC, CBS, and NBC—each have approximately 200 local television affiliates and generate revenues by creating and delivering audiences to advertisers. On average, each network airs 90 hours of programming a week. The amount of money that a network or a station charges advertisers for commercial spots within a show depends on the size and composition of the program's audiences. The larger the audience is for a particular show, the higher the advertising rates, because advertising is sold on a cost per thousand (CPM) basis. At the same time, CPM rates vary considerably, based upon a particular audience's demographics. In contrast with other media, such as newspapers, magazines, cable television, and a few websites, broadcast television is fully supported by advertising revenue rather than fees.[45]

Cable has changed the television broadcasting landscape, drawing away up to one-third of the total television viewing audience. With many available television channels and the resulting fractured nature of today's television audience, no single broadcast television program will ever reach the kind of viewership numbers achieved during the 1960s and 1970s when viewers usually had only three or four choices. For example, the final episode of "Seinfeld" in May 1998 drew fewer viewers than the regular episodes of the "Beverly Hillbillies" during the 1960s.[46]

The introduction of digital television (DTV) will allow increased network channels and, therefore, increased programming in the future. Digital compression techniques will permit the transmission of several DTV channels of programming over the same bandwidth that is currently required for the transmission of a single, analog standard-definition television (SDTV) channel. However, the transmission of a single, digital high-definition television (HDTV) will require even more bandwidth than that used currently for conventional television. Broadcasters and policy makers will need to determine what is in the public interest.

Digital television is considered by some to be the biggest broadcast innovation since color television was introduced in the 1950s. DTV could provide a lifelike picture with CD-quality sound. All commercial stations will be required to broadcast a digital signal by summer 2003, and all analog broadcasts will stop by spring 2006. Each of the three television networks currently broadcast select programs using high-definition digital technology.[47]

Cable Television. Cable television was originally meant to be a way to improve television reception in rural areas. In the 1960s, cable operators realized that viewers were willing to pay for commercial-free programming, but their efforts were hindered by stringent Federal Communications Commissions (FCC) restrictions. The industry began to boom when RCA launched its first communication satellite into orbit in 1975.[48]

Under the name Home Box Office (HBO), which was later sold to Time Warner, RCA started transmitting programming all around the country to independent operators who relayed the programming to subscribers at a minimum cost. With the 1977 federal court dismissal of most of the FCC's regulations governing cable television, the development of what has become a multibillion dollar industry began.[49]

Currently the number of cable subscribers is increasing by about half a million per year. Despite deregulation and increased competition from direct-satellite service providers, the average cable bill continues to increase. For example, the average bill increased from $7.81 in 1980 to $27.81 in 1998.[50] The cable channels make their revenue through a combination of advertising and subscription fees. By mid-1998, the top six cable channels in the United States were the Discovery Channel, TBS, C-SPAN, the Fox Family Channel, ESPN, and the Cable News Network (CNN)—all available to 65 million or more cable subscribers. The top five pay-cable services were HBO, the Disney Channel, Spice, Showtime, and the Sundance Channel.

In 1997, the nation's largest cable operators were Tele-Communications (TCI), owned by AT&T, with over 14 million basic subscribers; Time Warner cable,

12.3 million subscribers; and the U.S. Media Group, 4.9 million subscribers. With all of the changes brought forth by the Telecommunications Act of 1996, cable companies were allowed to compete directly with telephone and utility companies in providing cable, telephone, and electrical services to households. Because of the increased competition allowed by the act and because of the general anticipation of broadband delivery and media convergence, several megamergers involving cable television systems and regional telephone companies have taken place, including AT&T's acquisition of TCI in 1998 and U.S. West's acquisition of Media One in 1999.

Radio. Ninety-nine percent of all U.S. households had at least one radio in 1999. Of Americans over the age of 12, 95 percent listened to the radio for an average of 3 hours and 20 minutes each workday. There were a total of 576.5 million radios in the United States. They were distributed as follows: 367.4 million (or 63 percent) were in homes; 142.8 (or 24.7 percent) million in cars; 43.7 million (or 7.5 percent) in trucks, vans, and RVs; and the remaining 22.6 million (or 6.1 percent) in the workplace.[51]

Similar to broadcast television, radio generated almost all of its revenue from advertising by delivering a select audience to advertisers. Unlike broadcast television, however, radio channels were highly specific in their targeting of audiences. In 1998 the three most popular radio formats were country, adult contemporary, and news/talk. At the end of 1998, there were 12,641 radio stations on the air, and approximately 81 percent of those were commercial stations.

The Internet now offers net radio, or audio programs, over the World Wide Web. Net radio does not fall under the guidelines of the Federal Communications Commission. Anyone, ranging from relative unknowns such as Dan Schulz and Scott Wirkus to celebrities like Robin Williams (on audible.com), can host their own radio program from their home basement and make it available to the public through the Internet.[52]

Film. The motion picture industry generates close to $7 billion in business each year. The various studios release an average of about 500 films per year. The cost of making movies has escalated dramatically in recent years. In 1988, the average price tag of a motion picture was $18.1 million, according to the MPAA. In 1998, the average cost of making a movie had increased to $52.7 million, largely because of rising actor salaries, increased demand for special effects, and other spiraling costs. On average, in 1998 studios spent $25.3 million on prints and advertising—or almost half of total production costs per film.[53]

Videos. In the 20 years since it was introduced, the videocassette recorder (VCR) has become a common appliance, with 91 percent of American households now owning one. Video releases of movies are now the largest part of a motion picture's revenue stream. In 1995, a film's domestic and foreign theatrical releases accounted for almost 30 percent of its total revenue; by 2000 cash intake from video releases are over 40 percent of total revenue.[54]

With higher-quality digital technology now available to many people at lower costs, aspiring directors can make the motion picture that they always wanted to make, which is what happened in the case of the *Blair Witch Project*. "It's too late for the studios to panic. They've already lost," said director Francis Ford Coppola, whose Zoetrope.com allows filmmakers to read scripts, get feedback, hire directors, and show their work. "The minute artists don't need studios, they'll abandon them."[55]

Music CDs. In 10 years, the digital audio compact disk developed by Sony and Philips Electronics in 1982 has gone from a technological breakthrough to the music format of choice among most consumers. Less than 100,000 CDs were sold the first year they were available, 1983, but the format quickly overtook LPs by 1988 and topped cassette sales in 1992. Almost 75 percent of all music sold is now produced on CDs, followed by cassettes (15 percent) and singles (7 percent). The recording industry's willingness to support the new technology by releasing a large amount of music on disk has no doubt played a large part in the CD's growth. CDs cost no more to manufacture than albums or cassettes, yet consumers are still willing to pay twice as much for the digital format, largely due to the superior sound quality.[56]

The total U.S. dollar value of all music sold was $13.7 billion in 1998, with rock, country, R & B, and pop accounting for the top four categories. About one-third of all consumers of musical devices were 24 years old or younger.

MP3. The music industry has been thrown into turmoil recently by the emergence and mainstreaming of digital music technologies. At the center of the current firestorm is Michael Robertson and his activities as chairman and CEO of MP3.com, which is one of the most visited music sites on the Internet. MP3 technology offers musicians and listeners a community and an experience that is revolutionizing the way music is consumed. Members of MP3.com gain online access to over 45,000 CDs. The Recording Industry Association of America (RIAA) says that for no charge MP3 music seekers copy music file recordings off the MP3.com site onto their computer hard drives, individuals can then listen to the files that feature near-CD-quality sound. Because digital music does not vary with subsequent copying, a fiftieth generation copy is the same quality as a second generation copy.[57] MP3.com's activities have attracted the attention—and the ire—of many in the traditional music industry. The RIAA, along with a consortium of major record labels, has filed a major lawsuit against MP3.com. However, Robertson, a vocal proponent of listener's rights to content, believes that consumers have the right to do what they want with music after it has been purchased and that current copyright laws won't prevent further piracy in the future with upcoming advances in compressed digital technology.

Adding more fire to the MP3 controversy is the use of Napster software. This software allows an individual to easily search and swap MP3 musical files with other individuals. Napster has become so popular among college students that several universities have banned its use altogether. The schools have done this because the simultaneous transfer of large numbers of MP3 files can overload a computer system so much that it becomes effectively useless. As with MP3.com, the RIAA has also filed a lawsuit against Napster charging that it "is operating a haven for music piracy on an unprecedented scale."[58]

What Is MP3?

 MP3 is the acronym for the standard specifications to the MPEG-1 Audio Layer-3. MPEG is the acronym for the Motion Picture Experts Group. **MPEG-1** is a computer file format and compression specification for motion video with audio. It should not be confused with JPEG (Joint Photographic Experts Group), which is a computer file format and compression specification for photographs (static single frame with no audio). MP3 is one in a series of audio encoding standards developed under MPEG and formalized by the International Organization for Standardization (ISO).

For hi-fi-quality sound reproduction, the frequency response to human hearing is usually referenced as from 20 Hz to 20 kHz; i.e., humans can typically hear sounds with frequencies between 20 cycles per second through 20 thousand cycles per second.

Nyquist's theorem states that to accurately capture an analog signal digitally, one must use a sample rate at least twice the highest frequency desired. Therefore, to capture 20 kHz sounds as well as a few harmonics above, standard CD-quality digital audio is typically created by taking 16-bit samples at 44.1 kHz of the analog sound signal. This means CD-quality stereo sound requires 2 channels $\times$ 16 bits $\times$ 44,100 times per second, or approximately 1.4 million bits per second (some 180 kilobytes of data for one second of stereo audio!).

MP3 includes a compression algorithm to reduce data around sounds that most listeners cannot perceive. MP3 allows the compression of any sound sequence into a small file (typically a 10:1 compression ratio) while mostly preserving the original sound quality. MP3 files are usually downloaded and played through free MP3 player software.

WHAT PUBLIC POLICY ISSUES MUST BE ADDRESSED WITH MEDIA AND DIGITAL CONVERGENCE?

Media Concentration

In an attempt to ensure multiple editorial voices in the same market, existing FCC regulations disallow the mutual ownership of newspapers and television and radio stations in the same market unless a waiver is accepted by the commission. These regulations were established in the early 1970s in order to prevent undue **media concentration.** At the time, public policy makers felt that it could harm the public interest if a single company sought to own multiple media outlets in the same market.

Some of the potential legal issues confronting the increased concentration of media ownership include fewer editorial voices and potential conflicts of interest. Proponents of media mergers believe that the laws limiting cross-ownership of media companies (e.g., newspapers and television stations) are outdated and should be eliminated. These proponents believe that with the growth of new media, more sources of news and information are now readily available and that media usage is now highly fragmented.

Does Cross-Media Ownership Matter?

The increase in the number of media mergers over the past five years has raised concerns about media concentration and the possibility that only a few companies could end up controlling the majority of media businesses. Critics have charged that with fewer media companies to choose from, there will be will be fewer voices, less competition, and potential conflicts of interest. Proponents of the media mergers argue that concerns about media concentration are unfounded, considering the increase in the number of media outlets now available to the public and the increasing fragmentation of media usage by the general public. Some have even argued that the current communications laws prohibiting cross-ownership of newspapers and television or radio stations in a single market are now outdated and should be eliminated, owing to the large variety of sources of information now available. "It just doesn't make any sense," observed John W. Madigan, chairman and CEO of the Tribune Company, after the company had acquired Times Mirror in March 2000. "It's there for what must be non-economic reasons. I believe in good logic prevailing."[59]

Do Copyright Laws Matter?

The right for authors and artists to earn income from their work is protected by the U.S. Constitution, as provided in ARTICLE I, SECTION 8, CLAUSE 8, which gives Congress the "power to promote the Progress of Science and useful Arts, by securing for limited Times to Authors and Inventors the exclusive Right to their respective Writings and Discoveries."[60] The **copyright** protection to "authors" is for their original works, such as photographs, musical compositions, and books. Among the protections that copyright owners have are the exclusive right to (1) make copies of the work, (2) prepare other works based on the original, and (3) distribute copies of the work to the public by sale, rental, lease, or lending.

The general rule is that a copyright lasts the lifetime of an author plus 50 years. If the copyright work was done as "work for hire," then the copyright lasts for 75 years from the date of the first publication or 100 years from the date of creation, whichever expires first.[61]

Proponents of extending copyright laws to digital assets argue that individuals continue to have the right to earn a commission for each incremental copy of their work, regardless of media, as allowed by the Constitution. If an individual's work is allowed to be freely distributed, it would diminish that person's creative value.

Those who are against extending copyright laws to digital assets counter that the consumer should have the right to distribute an artist's work, at no incremental cost, to anyone they choose once they have paid the initial fee. They also argue that copyright laws cannot realistically be enforced in a digital age.

Copyright Issues

Digital technology is both a blessing and a curse for media companies. It is the digital convergence that is the basis for media convergence. On the plus side, digital technology enables the possibility of media convergence and allows for both movies and music to be easily transmitted across a variety of platforms. On the negative side, digital technology can allow for increased piracy, once the digital codes are broken. Enterprising individuals can easily copy content, especially of movies on DVDs and MP3 music files. This raises the issue of how to protect and enforce the copyrights of artists and studios in the future.

The **Digital Millennium Copyright Act of 1998,** which goes into effect in October 2000, allows for the criminal prosecution of any individual who tampers with a digital watermark or offers a download of any digital property without a watermark. **Digital watermarks** were to be embedded into all music files beginning in spring 2000.[62] Critics of the new copyright act note that these laws would be hard to enforce and that consumers have the right to copy or trade intellectual property once they have paid for it.

SUMMARY

1. What is media convergence?

Broadly defined, media convergence is the concept that states that media content across various media platforms—print, audio, and video—will ultimately become available through a single Internet platform. With the emergence of broadband, traditional graphics, streaming video, and streaming audio will become available on one platform, as will video-on-demand, software distribution, books-on-demand, and multiplayer games.

2. What conditions make media convergence possible?

The continued advances and decreasing cost of digital technology, the existence of a low-cost digital network infrastructure, media proliferation, media usage fragmentation in American households, and the forecasted continued media proliferation and media usage fragmentation all allow for media convergence through digital convergence and make the media environment attractive for consolidation and vertical integration.

3. How do new media companies leverage off traditional media channels?

While the Internet is an increasingly important source for news, information, and commerce, the New Economy has been quite dependent on the traditional news outlets of the Old Economy. Online media are using traditional media channels to build an audience for new media. Dot-coms are using newspapers, magazines, and broadcast television to build audiences from the initial stage of attracting "early adopters" into a secondary stage of attracting mainstream users.

To build brand awareness for a rapidly growing mainstream audience of Internet users, dot-com companies spent an estimated $3 to $4 billion in advertising in 1999, with some 90 percent of those dollars being spent on traditional media outlets, such as network television, national newspapers, and network radio.

4. What are reasons for media megamergers?

While the Telecommunications Act of 1996 allowed for increased ownership of television stations by a single entity and for the convergence of media through direct competition among telephone companies, cable television companies, and utility companies, media companies were at the center of media megamergers as part of an overall strategy to vertically integrate media content with media distribution. With rapid advances in new digital technologies, media companies have the opportunity to put their content online in various forms over narrowband feeds with the future promise of playing movies-on-demand through broadband delivery. With no geographic barriers to the distribution of digitized content on the Internet, many media companies have sought to create global markets for their content through mergers. With increased digitization of content and the promise of broadband delivery in the near-future, the personal computer will not be the only receiver of information over the Internet. For today's media company, the strategy is to collect and, through media convergence and digital convergence, to create a synergistic combination with what were once disparate media to produce a direct bottom-line benefit.

5. What public policy issues must be addressed with digital convergence and media convergence?

Some of the potential public policy issues confronting the increased concentration of media ownership include fewer editorial voices and potential conflicts of interest. Proponents of media mergers believe that current laws limiting cross-ownership of media companies such as newspapers and television stations are outdated and should be eliminated. These proponents believe that more sources of news and information are now readily available with the growth of new media and that media usage is now highly fragmented.

The use of digital technology represents both a blessing and a curse for moviemakers and the recording industry. On the plus side, digital technology enables the possibility of media convergence and allows for both movies and music to be transmitted across a variety of platforms. On the negative side, digital technology can allow for increased piracy once the digital antipiracy codes are broken. This raises the issue of how copyrights to artists and studios can be protected and enforced in the future.

KEY TERMS

media infrastructure	streaming video
media convergence	MP3
Telecommunications Act of 1996	MPEG-1
vertical integration	media concentration
GIF	copyright
JPEG	Digital Millennium Copyright Act of 1998
streaming audio	digital watermarks

Endnotes

[1] *Pew Research Center*. 1996. TV news viewership declines. Press release, 13 May.

[2] *The New York Times 2000 Almanac*, s.v. "Primetime Viewing Shares of Free and Cable TV Networks, 1995–98," p. 408. Citing from Cable Advertising Bureau, *Cable TV Facts* (1999).

[3] *The New York Times 2000 Almanac*, s.v. "Sales Penetration of Telecommunications Products in U.S. Homes," p. 811. Citing from 1999 Electronics Industries Assoc.

[4] *The New York Times 2000 Almanac*, s.v. "Basic and Pay Cable TV Systems and Subscribers, 192-99," p. 408. Citing from Television Association, *Cable TV Developments* (Spring 1999), Nielsen Media Research; *The New York Times 2000 Almanac*, s.v. "Sales Penetration of Telecommunications Products in U.S. Homes," p. 811. Citing from 1999 Electronics Industries Association.

[5] Haddock, Vicki. 1999. How media saturates American kids' lives. *San Francisco Examiner*, 17 November.

[6] Stevens, Elizabeth Lesly. 1998. The entertainment glut. *Business Week*, 16 February.

[7] Modahl, Mary. 2000. *Now or Never: How companies must change to win the battle for the internet consumer.* New York: Harper Business.

[8] *The New York Times 2000 Almanac*, s.v. "U.S. Online Households and Internet Users, 1996–2002," p. 819. Cited from the U.S. Dept. of Commerce, eStats.

[9] Drewry, William. 1999. *Newspapers.com*. Newsletter, 8 November, p. 6. Citing the *Advertising Age Interactive Special Report* (1 November 1999); Lake, David and Stacy Lawrence. 2000. Two Years of Change. *Industry Standard*, 1 May, pp. 296–7.

[10] Drewry, William. 1999. *Newspapers.com*. Newsletter, 8 November. Citing the *Advertising Age Interactive Special Report* (1 November 1999).

[11] Reents, Scott. 1998. Expert insight: Leveraging TV-Net synergies. *Industry Standard*, 28 October.

[12] *Pew Research Study*. 1998. The Internet news audience goes ordinary, 15 December.

[13] *San Jose Mercury News*. 2000. Historic dates for AOL, 11 January.

[14] Swisher, Kara. 1998. *AOL.com*. New York: Times Books.

[15] Louie, Dickson. 1997. *The New York Times Electronic Media Company.* Case no. 897-051. Boston: Harvard Business School Publishing.

[16] Harmon, Amy. 2000. How blind alleys led old media to new. *New York Times*, 16 January.

[17] Louie, Dickson. 2000. *Monster.com*. Case no. N9-800-304. Rev. 4 April. Boston: Harvard Business School Publishing, p. 2.

[18] *ibid.*, pp. 8–9.

[19] CBS MarketWatch is also branded each night on "The CBS Evening News with Dan Rather," but the content is produced by the CBS News staff. A verbal or visual prompt promotes the CBS MarketWatch website.

[20] Louie, Dickson. *CBS.MarketWatch.com*. Case no. 9-800-303. Boston: Harvard Business School Publishing.

[21] Eisner, Michael. 1996. Speech to Chicago Executives Club, 19 April.

[22] Levy, Steve. 2000. Here comes Playstation 2. *Newsweek*, 6 March, p. 57.

[23] Gralla, Preston. 1998. *How the Internet works*. Indianapolis, IN: QUE books, p. 27.

[24] *ibid.*

[25] Richtel, Matt. 2000. Microsoft aims at real network in MediaPlayer software duel. *New York Times*, 10 January.

[26] *Capturing digital*. 1999. From *www.kodak.com*

[27] Gates, Bill. 1996. *The road ahead*. New York: Penguin Books, p. 248.

[28] *Newspaper Assoc. of America's Facts about Newspapers*, s.v. "Top 20 Daily Newspapers by Circulation." Citing *Editor and Publisher*. URL: http://www.naa.org/info/facts99/14.html.

[29] *Newspaper Assoc. of America's Facts about Newspapers*, s.v. "Number of U.S. Daily Newspapers." Citing *Editor and Publisher Yearbook 1999*. URL: http://www.naa.org/info/facts99/11.html.

[30] *Newspaper Assoc. of America's Facts about Newspapers*, s.v. "U.S. Daily and Sunday/Weekend Newspaper Reading Audience." Citing NAA; W.R. Simmons & Associates Research, Inc. 1970–1977; Simmons Market Research Bureau, Inc. 1980–1994; Scarborough Research—Top 50 DMA Market Report, 1995–1998. URL: http://www.naa.org/info/facts99/02.html.

[31] *The New York Times 2000 Almanac*, s.v. "General median income of households with selected characteristics, 1997," p. 333. Citing Bureau of the Census, *Current Population Reports: Money Income*

in the U.S.; Newspaper Assoc. of America's Facts about Newspapers, s.v. "U.S. Daily and Sunday Newspaper Readership Demographics." Citing Scarborough Research—Top 50 DMA Market Report, 1998 (Release 1).

[32]*Newspaper Association of America's Facts about Newspapers,* s.v. "U.S. Daily Newspapers Advertising Expenditures." Citing U.S. Dept. of Commerce, NAA. URL: http://www.naa.org/info/facts99/08.html.

[33]*The New York Times 2000 Almanac,* s.v. "The Print Media," p. 401.

[34]*Newspaper Association of America's Facts about Newspapers,* s.v. "Newspaper Voice and Online Services." Citing NAA. URL: http://www.naa.org/info/facts99/18.html.

[35]*The New York Times 2000 Almanac,* s.v. "Top 100 U.S. Magazines by Circulation, 1998," p. 402. Citing *Magazine Publishers of America.*

[36]*The New York Times 2000 Almanac,* s.v. "The Print Media," p. 403.

[37]Drewry, William. 1999. *Newspapers.com.* Newsletter, 19 August. Citing the *Advertising Age Interactive Special Report.*

[38]Anderson, James A. 2000. Newspaper investors may have the last laugh. *Business Week,* 17 April, p. 212. URL: http://www.businessweek.com/2000/00_16/b3677133.htm?scriptFramed.

[39]*The New York Times 2000 Almanac,* s.v. "The Print Media," p. 403.

[40]R.R. Bowker Co. 1999. *The Bowker Annual: Library and Book Trade Almanac.* Cited in *The New York Times 2000 Almanac,* s.v. "New Books and Editions Published, by Subject, 1980–98," p. 403.

[41]*The New York Times 2000 Almanac,* s.v. "The Print Media," p. 404.

[42]Ratnesar, Romesh and Joel Stein. 2000. Everyone's a star.com. *Time,* 27 March. URL: http://www.time.com/time/everyone/magazine/main.html.

[43]Hardy, Quinten, 1999. Balancing the need for speed with a respect for HP's past. *Forbes,* 13 December, p. 141.

[44]*The New York Times 2000 Almanac,* s.v. "Books," p. 403.

[45]Louie, Dickson. 1999. *CBS evening news.* Case no. 9-898-086. Rev. 11 March. Boston: Harvard Business School Publishing.

[46]*The New York Times 2000 Almanac,* s.v. "Cable Television," p. 408.

[47]Best Buy Co. 1999. *Change the way you look at TV.* Brochure.

[48]*The New York Times 2000 Almanac,* s.v. "The Print Media," p. 407.

[49]*The New York Times 2000 Almanac,* s.v. "Cable Television," p. 407.

[50]*ibid.,* pp. 409–10.

[51]*The New York Times 2000 Almanac,* s.v. "Radio," p. 410.

[52]Winters, Rebecca. 2000. Live from your basement. *Time,* 27 March. (http://www.time.com/time/everyone/magazine/sidebar_dj.html).

[53]*The New York Times 2000 Almanac,* s.v. "Film/movie budgets," p. 412.

[54]Vogel, Harold. 1998. *Entertainment industry economics.* Cambridge, England; New York: Cambridge University Press. 4th ed., p. 55.

[55]Ratnesar, Romesh and Stein, Joel. 2000. Everyone's a star.com. *Time,* 27 March.

[56]The New York Times 2000 Almanac, s.v. "The Recording Industry," p. 410.

[57]Tucker, Chris. 2000. Online pirates beware. *Southwest Spirit Magazine* (April).

[58]Greenfield, Karl Taro. 2000. The free juke box. *Time,* 27 March.

[59]Fitzgerald, Mark. 2000. The team riding the tiger. *Editor and Publisher,* 27 March, p. 22.

[60]Lessig, Lawrence. 2000. *Code and other laws of cyberspace.* New York: Basic Books, p. 133.

[61]Kodak, Inc. 2000. *Customer copyright information for our Walgreen customers.* Pamphlet.

[62]Tucker, Chris. 2000. Online pirates beware. *Southwest Spirit Magazine* (April).

APPENDIX
AND INDEXES

APPENDIX
Contributing Authors

Jennifer Barron joined Monitor Company in 1985 as a strategy consultant. Barron has a broad range of experience in helping clients solve business problems, with a particular focus on competitive positioning and marketing strategies. She has worked with executives across many industries, including financial services, technology, and consumer packaged goods.

Barron is a principal and founder of Monitor Company's Strategic Marketing and Research (SMR) division. She has been instrumental in driving the growth of the group, overseeing product development and new business development initiatives. Currently, Barron is actively involved in helping clients with their brand design and delivery issues.

Barron graduated from Dartmouth College with an honors degree in Economics. She received her Masters of Business Administration from Harvard Business School.

Thomas E. Copeland is Chief Corporate Finance Officer at Monitor Company, where he is leader of the office of Finance Practice. A leading authority on valuation and risk management, Tom has been a consultant to over 200 companies in 34 countries around the world. He has participated in cases involving restructuring companies, mergers and acquisitions, joint ventures, performance measurement and value-based management, privatizations, and changes in the trading rules at a major stock exchange. He has assisted a developing stock exchange with the design of its rules and with automation of trading, clearing, and settlement. He has also participated in valuing financial institutions, developing a risk management system for an investment bank, developing hedging programs for commodity and FX risks, managing dividend policy and share repurchases, determining the optimal capital structure for major corporations, and using option pricing to evaluate major project decisions.

Before joining Monitor, Tom was Director of Corporate Financial Services at McKinsey & Company (1987–1998) and was a tenured full professor of finance at UCLA (1973–1987), where he served as chairman of the Finance Department and Vice Chairman of the Graduate School of Management. He received his B.A. in Economics from Johns Hopkins University in 1968 and in 1969 his M.B.A. in Finance from the Wharton School, where he graduated second in his class. His Ph.D. in Applied Economics was granted by the University of Pennsylvania in 1973.

With J. Fred Weston, Tom is coauthor of *Financial Theory and Corporate Policy,* a widely used advanced-level finance text, and of *Managerial Finance,* the well-known intermediate-level corporation finance text. With Tim Koller and Jack Murrin of McKinsey & Company, Tom coauthored *Valuation: Measuring and Managing the Value of Companies,* a book that shows how top management can take an action-oriented approach to enhancing shareholder value and that instructs staff on the methodology of doing valuations. *Valuation* has sold over 250,000 copies and is used as a textbook at over 100 universities.

Tom's books have been translated into eleven languages. His publications include articles about stock splits, market trading activity, receivables policy, leasing, exchange offers, bid-ask spreads, nonprofit organizations, spin-offs, pension fund management, portfolio performance measurement, corporate recapitalizations, foreign exchange hedging, capital productivity, asset options, growth through acquisition, LBOs, and experimental economics. A member of the editorial board and Board of Directors of *The Journal of Financial Management,* Tom has served as chairman of the practitioners Board of Directors.

Yannis Dosios is a consultant at the Marketspace Center in Los Angeles. He received a Bachelor of Science in Mathematics from Harvard University. Since he joined Monitor in August 1997, Yannis has worked in a number of industries, including e-business, telecommunications, entertainment, high tech, consumer products, and the nonprofit sector. His work has focused primarily on market analysis; corporate strategy; streamlining of activities, processes, and systems; and identification and development of new business concepts. Outside of work, Yannis enjoys traveling, playing tennis, and watching international movies.

Leo Griffin is a consultant at Monitor Marketspace Center's Los Angeles office. Leo received a B.Sc. (Econ) in Industrial Economics at the London School of Economics and received his M.B.A. with distinction from Kellogg. During his career he has worked in the United States, the United Kingdom, Spain, Italy, Canada, and Russia. Prior to joining Monitor, Leo worked for an Internet start-up. When not at work, he enjoys biking in the nearby Santa Monica mountains.

Ellie Kyung is a consultant with Monitor Marketspace Center's New York Office. Since joining Monitor in 1998, she has focused primarily on the development of marketing and branding strategy, working closely with Monitor's Strategic Market Research group. Ellie's work has been focused in the health care and e-commerce industries. She graduated from Yale University with a degree in Economics and International Studies (B.A., cum laude).

Dickson Louie is principal of Louie & Associates, a San Francisco Bay area–consultancy that provides business development, marketing research, and competitive analysis to media companies. Clients of Louie & Associates include the *San Francisco Chronicle,* the Monitor Company, and the Maynard Institute.

Prior to establishing his own consulting practice in February 1999, Louie spent 13 years in the newspaper industry. From 1984 to 1995, he was a member of the management team of the *Los Angeles Times* and its parent company, Times Mirror.

As a member of the circulation department's senior management, Louie was responsible for management reporting, subscriber retention analysis, and department operational reviews. In November 1989, Louie drafted the initial business plan that helped make the *Los Angeles Times* the largest metropolitan daily newspaper in the United States. More recently, Louie served as business development and planning manager for the *San Jose Mercury News.* He was responsible for the development of several new product and revenue initiatives, including the launch of *Viet Mercury,* a Vietnamese-language newspaper, to serve the growing Vietnamese-American community in the Silicon Valley. In 1996, Louie was appointed as a research associate at the Harvard Business School, where he has authored over 20 case studies for the Marketspace course, including those on Amazon.com, CBS Evening News, New York Times Electronic Media Company, QVC, and Monster.com.

Louie is a graduate of California State University, Hayward, where in 1980 he received his bachelor's degree in business administration with a minor in journalism, and of the University of Chicago, where in 1984 he received his M.B.A. degree.

Nancy Michels has been a consultant with Monitor Company since 1992. Over the course of her career at Monitor, she has worked in health care, technology, financial services, and industrial manufacturing. Her work in these areas has focused primarily on marketing strategy, including customer segmentation, market assessment, competitive analysis, and brand positioning. Nancy also has experience in distribution analysis, new product development, process design, and organizational change management. As part of Monitor's Marketspace Center, Nancy has concentrated on online branding. She is currently working with the marketing department of a large biotechnology company on a new product launch.

Nancy also has been a faculty member in Monitor's internal marketing training program for new consultants and is a professional development advisor for other consultants. She graduated magna cum laude from Brigham Young University with a B.A. in Economics and received her M.B.A. from Harvard Business School. Currently Nancy resides in San Francisco with her husband David and daughter Elise.

Rafi Mohammed has been a consultant with Monitor Company since 1998. He has worked in areas of the New Economy, broadband, and online service marketing and development strategy. Prior to joining Monitor, Mohammed had his own media strategy consulting practice in Los Angeles and worked on deregulatory issues at the Federal Communications Commission in Washington, D.C.

Mohammed holds economics degrees from the London School of Economics and Boston University and has a Ph.D. in Economics from Cornell University. His academic research has focused on media and business strategy topics.

Mark W. Pocharski is an Officer and Global Account Manager in Monitor Company's Marketing Strategy group (SMR). Pocharski works with B-to-B and B-to-C clients in a variety of industries, including consumer packaged goods, consumer financial services, pharmaceuticals, beverages, business telecommunications, health insurance, and natural gas. He has managed client relationships in North America, Europe, and Asia.

Pocharski's recent projects include developing an integrated online/brick-and-mortar new business offering for a major U.S. consumer products company, turning around the growth trend for a leading consumer financial services company with online and brick-and-mortar marketing initiatives, devising a growth of strategy for a major beverage brand, and refreshing the brand personality for a leader in skin care products. He also has been involved in creating a set of innovative product offerings for and introducing a new product development process to a major U.S. telecommunications player, designing and implementing a segment-based marketing strategy for a major U.S. health insurance company, creating an account management program for a national energy company, and redesigning the roles and service offerings of market research groups for global leaders in consumer packaged goods and pharmaceuticals. In addition to client project work, Pocharski designed and teaches a strategic marketing course for clients.

Pocharski graduated cum laude from Dartmouth College, with a major in economics and government. He received his M.B.A. from Harvard Business School.

Marco Smit is a Senior Project Manager in Monitor Company's Cambridge, Massachusetts, office. He has more than five years of consulting experience in Europe, Asia, and the United States. Since joining Monitor in 1998, Smit has worked in a variety of industries, including biotechnology, high technology, consumer products, financial services, and the nonprofit sector. Within these industries, he has worked on market segmentation, organizational design, competitive strategy, new business development, private/public partnerships, and mergers and acquisitions. Recently, Smit's work has focused on biotechnology and e-business strategy, including business plan development, partnership strategy, implementation, organizational strategies, and growth path development.

Smit holds a Masters Degree in Economics from the Erasmus University in Rotterdam (Netherlands), where he studied Economic Integration with a specialization in Financial Derivatives. He also studied strategy at the post-graduate school of management of ESSEC in Paris (France). He is a fluent speaker of French, German, Dutch, and Bahasa-Indonesian.

Tobias H. A. Thomas is an Officer and Global Account Manager in Monitor Company's Marketing Strategy group (SMR). Thomas is a cofounder and leader of SMR's Web-based marketing services group. In addition, Thomas is the head of SMR's GrowthPath® Application Group, which enables Monitor's clients to systematically identify and capture new growth opportunities.

Thomas is one of the primary developers of the GrowthPath®, Customer Portrait®, and Action Segmentation™ frameworks, as well as many of the other core technologies used in SMR's Web-based marketing services group and Monitor client engagements. He has advised clients on their e-commerce strategies as well as starting up SMR's own Web-based business.

In addition, Thomas has developed impactful marketing, business unit, and corporate strategies for clients in a variety of B-to-B and B-to-C contexts including consumer packaged goods, financial services, telecommunications, chemicals, metals, travel, and beverages industries, often doubling their historical rate of growth. Thomas's most recent client work includes developing detailed local and national consumer, brand, and channel strategies and frameworks for a global beverage company; creating targeted-offers channel strategies for a telecommunications client; and building the internal marketing capabilities of a leading investment bank.

Thomas received a B.Sc. in Chemical Engineering, with Honors, from Queen's University in Canada and an M.B.A. from Harvard Business School, where he was an honors student.

Michael Yip joined the Monitor Marketspace Center in January 2000 as a member of the R&D team and serves as project manager and writer for the development of this textbook and its companion casebook, *e-Commerce* and *Cases in e-Commerce*.

From 1992 to 1999, Yip worked in international treasury and finance at Sony Pictures Entertainment, where he developed foreign exchange hedge strategies and managed all company-wide foreign exchange transactions, cross-border funds transfers, and international lines of credit and letters of credit.

Yip has also worked in film and television production. He has been a studio engineer and a production manager of national television commercials, as well as a producer for Jim Henson, where Yip developed interactive video and game controller devices. He was also a faculty head and taught graduate and undergraduate courses in television production and new technologies at New York University's Tisch School of the Arts.

Yip is a graduate of the University of California at Berkeley, where he received his bachelor's degree in psychology, and of New York University, Tisch School of the Arts, Institute of Film and Television, where he received his B.F.A. degree.

NAME INDEX

COMPANY INDEX

SUBJECT INDEX WITH GLOSSARY

A

abandonment option The right to abandon or sell a business for a predetermined value (even zero), 313

actionable segmentation, 41–43, 45, 58, 60

advertising, 12, 35, 123, 184, 295
    banner ads, 172–174, 176, 232
    conversion rates, 268
    media convergence, 369, 371, 373–374, 380, 383–385
    revenue, 86, 88
    on the Web, 86, 88

affiliate program Directs users to affiliated websites through links or links embedded in site banners or other advertising materials, 153, 154 *il.*, 175–178

analyst reports Refer to data sources that are a blend of primary market data on a particular topic and an analyst's view of the market, 272, 274 *il.*

applications service providers (ASPs), 16

assets, 75, 80, 81

auction-exchange, 4, 20, 88, 92 *il.*, 218
    pricing, 132, 157
    reverse, 91

auction pricing Where buyers bid against each other and the highest bidder wins supplier products or services, 157

B

backward-integrated user, 101–102, 101 *il.*

Balanced Scorecard Introduced by Kaplan and Norton in response to their perception that managers overwhelmingly focus on short-term financial performance. To address this concern, they argued that firms must balance their financial perspective by analyzing other domains of the business that include internal business processes and customer responses, 261–263, 262 *il.*, 264

banking, electronic, 2

banner ads The boxlike ads that are displayed on webpages. These ads usually display a simple message that is designed to entice viewers to click on the ad, 172–174, 176, 232

baud rate, 339

bazaar, online, 136–137 *il.*

benefits
    core, 74–75, 82
    customer, 71, 75
    identification of capabilities, 82

beta (valuation) A measure of the sensitivity of a security price to the market portfolio of all securities, called the systematic risk, and usually estimated as the slope of a linear regression of the total returns of a security versus the total returns on an equally weighted market portfolio of all securities, 295–296

bond rating The quality of bonds is rated by agencies such as Moody's and Standard & Poor's. High-quality bonds are able to pay lower interest rates, and therefore have a lower cost of debt than low-quality bonds, 295, 296

books, 16, 381–383

brand equity, 14, 186–188

branding Concerns the consumer's perception of the offering—how it performs, how it looks, how it makes one feel, and what messages it sends to others, 14, 17, 21, 169–170, 185–204, 206–208
    implementation, 214, 219, 220, 233
    metrics, 264, 269, 284
    ten-step branding process, 189–192

branding and implementation metrics These metrics focus on supply-chain performance, organizational dynamics, and marketing communication effectiveness (including branding), 258, 264, 266–267

broadband Usually defined as those methods with connectivity speeds exceeding 128 kilobits per second, 326, 342, 344 *il.*, 377, 385

browsers, 331, 332, 332 *il.*, 378

businesses. *See also* Companies
    alliances of, 29
    assets, 81
    benefit offerings, 74
    capabilities, 81
    classification schemes, 97–102
    delivery, capability of, 82
    demand-side classification, 11
    forward-integrated producers, 100, 101 *il.*, 102
    horizontal plays, 33–34
    infrastructure, 12
    network. *See* Network infrastructure
    offline, 2, 13
    operations, 33–34
    opportunities online, 26
    resource systems, 73–74, 79–87
    start-ups, failure rates of, 26
    strategy, implementation of, 14, 85
    supply-side classification, 11
    valuation calculations, 8, 14
    valuation of online, 8
    vertical plays, 33–34

business models, 14, 17, 21, 69–108, 71 *il.*, 221, 259, 263–264, 267, 269, 282–284
  backward-integrated user, 101–102, 101 *il.*
business-model metrics Metrics that capture the subcomponents of the business model: the value proposition, Egg Diagram, resource system, and financial metrics, 258, 264, 265–266
business-to-business (B2B) The full spectrum of e-commerce that can occur between two organizations, including purchasing and procurement, supplier management, inventory management, channel management, sales activities, payment management, and service and support, 3–4
business-to-business (B2B) delivery systems, 8, 12, 20, 29, 91
    activities and categories of, 3–5, 4 *il.*
    functional hubs, 98–100
    implementation, 226–228
    projected growth of online activities, 10
    statistics of use, 9 *il.*
    vertical hubs, 98–100
business-to-consumer (B2C) Exchanges between businesses and consumers; e.g., Amazon.com, Yahoo.com, and Schwab.com, 4
business-to-consumer (B2C) delivery systems, 4, 4 *il.*, 10, 20, 98
    implementation, 222–226
    network infrastructure, 335
buyer groups, 4, 20

C

cable modem May be used on some cable television systems to send and receive data at speeds of two to three megabits per second, or 35 to 52 times as fast as conventional analog modems of 56 kilobits per second, 7, 326, 340, 342–343, 345 *il.*
cafe, 139, 141 *il.*
capitalization-to-sales ratio, 315
cash flow, 8, 89, 300, 308 *il.*, 310 *il.*, 311 *il.*
catalog pricing Where the price of goods and services is preset by the seller. Users select items from displayed catalogs and pay the associated prices, 157
category killer, 128, 130 *il.*
category switchboard, 91–92, 92 *il.*
CD (digital audio compact disk), 386
central processing unit (CPU), 323, 324
chat, online, 135
changing the basis of competition Involves using innovations that create a new competitive position or niche in a market, 234, 235
circuit board, 324
clickographics, 42–43
click-stream information, 39, 42, 184
click-through, 7, 172–174, 176, 181, 184
click-through-based data, 39
click-through shopping, 157
clothes, purchases of online, 115–117
club online (online community archetype), 137, 139 *il.*
COder-DECoder (or "codec"), 327
commerce The sale of goods, products, or services on the site, 116–117, 163
communication Communication refers to the dialogue that unfolds between the site and its users, 116
communications. *See also* E-mail; Market communications
    across time zones, 11
    affiliate programs, 153, 154 *il.*, 175–178
    broadcast, 143, 145
    direct, 171, 173 *il.*, 174 *il.*, 182–183, 205–206

general online, 171–175, 178–179
    hybrid, 146
    interactive, 145
    multimedia, 330, 331
    networks, 322
    personalized online, 171–172, 173 *il.*, 174 *il.*, 179–181, 183 *il.*, 205
    traditional mass media, 171–172, 173 *il.*, 174 *il.*, 182, 205
    Web-based, 4
    website, 162–163
community The interaction that occurs between site users, 115
community online, 33, 115, 133–140
    archetypes of, 136–139, 140 *il.*, 141 *il.*
    bazaar, 136, 137 *il.*
    benefits of, 135
    cafe, 139, 141 *il.*
    club, 137, 139 *il.*
    dimensions of, 135–136
    elements of, 133
    participation within, 134
    shrine, 138
    theater, 138–139, 140 *il.*
    theme park, 137, 138 *il.*
companies. *See also* Businesses
    customer acquisition of, 267
    embryonic companies, 294, 295 *il.*, 313–315
    emerging growth companies, 294, 295 *il.*, 304–313, 316
    life cycle and maturity of, 267
    monetization of, 267
    robust growth companies, 294–300, 296 *il.*, 316
    spin-out, 13
    startup of, 267
competition, 217
    adjacent, 52
    advantages of, 79–80
    behavior of, 20
    "co-opetition," 29
    cross-industry, 16, 28, 70, 322
    direct, 29, 51–52, 64
    dynamics of, 51
    environment of, 217
    hyper-, 5
    identification of, 51–52
    indirect, 29, 51–52, 64, 322
    intensity of, 51–54
    maps, 52–54, 53 *il.*
    microeconomics of, 51, 55
    monitoring, 191
    price information of, 74
    response of, 28
    speed-based, 5
    substitute producers, 52
    technology vulnerability, 51, 55, 62–64
    weak or nonexistent, 72
computers and computer operations. *See also* Modems; Network infrastructure; Operating systems (OS)
    cable modem, 326, 340, 342, 343, 345 *il.*
    central processing unit (CPU), 323, 324
    circuit board, 324
    mainframe computers, 323–324, 326, 340 *il.*, 344, 346–347
    microcomputer, 324, 344
    microprocessor, 323–326, 328

resource system from a conceptual structure into a concrete configuration of resources, processes, and supply chains, 219–233, 246–249, 284. *See also* Business-to-business (B2B) delivery systems; Business-to-consumer (B2C) delivery systems; Supply chain models of delivery systems
    components of, 221–222
    consumer-to-business (C2B), 4, 4 *il.*, 20, 228–229
    consumer-to-consumer (C2C), 4, 4 *il.*, 20, 229
    customer support/handling processes, 222
    drop shipping, 225
    fulfillment intermediaries, 225–226
    human-resource management processes, 221
    manufacturing and distribution processes, 221
    outsourcing warehousing, 225
    payment/billing processing, 221–222
    resource allocation process, 221
    stock-it-yourself, 224–225
demand aggregations pricing Pricing in which buyer demand for specific products is aggregated in order to achieve economies of scale, 157–159
demand-side
    aggregators, 101, 101 *il.*, 102, 157–159
    classification of businesses, 11
    focus, 80–81
destination site Provides almost exclusively site-generated content with very few links to other sites, 151, 152 *il.*
Developer-Driven Development Type of innovation that occurs when a firm develops a new way of meeting an existing consumer need, 241–242
dial-up connection, 16
digital audio compact disk (CD), 386
digital cameras, 379
digital convergence Refers to the convergence of the network and media infrastructures due to the digitization of information, 17 *il.*, 322
digital information A series of discrete bits represented by a 0 or 1 or any pair of symbols that can represent "on" or "off"—the binary language of computers. The series allows for easy generation, processing, and transmission of signals with the assistance of microprocessors, 327. *See also* Network infrastructure; Signal, electronic transmission
    exchange of, 20
Digital Millennium Copyright Act of 1998 Goes into effect in October 2000. Allows for criminal prosecution of any individual tampering with a digital watermark or offering a download of any digital property without a watermark, 389
digital satellite, 11
digital subscriber line (DSL) Digital subscriber lines allow for very-high-speed connections over existing copper telephone wires in homes, 7, 11, 326, 338–340, 339 *il.*, 342, 343
digital watermark Are to be embedded into all music files beginning in Spring 2000 to deter copyright infringement, 389
direct broadcast satellite (DBS), 16
direct communications Can take many forms, including the use of the classic business-to-business sales rep calling on accounts, retail sales clerks, and telephone customer sales reps, as well as the use of direct marketing and telemarketing, 171, 182–185
direct competition, 29, 51–52, 64
direct marketing, 183
direct offline communications Examples include monthly statement inserts and specially targeted mailings or telephone calls made to investors who could potentially be having difficulty

(e.g., investors who have been inactive for long periods of time), 182–185
discounted cash flow (DCF) The present value of expected future free cash flows that have been converted from their future values into a current equivalent value by discounting them at the weighted average cost of capital, 296 *il.*, 300–305, 307, 314, 316
disruptive technologies Innovations that create an entirely new market through the introduction of a new kind of service or product, 239–240
distributed innovation model Is a step away from the classical funnel process. This process model puts the purpose of continuously maintaining a fit between the organization and the evolution of the online domain at the very heart of the innovation process, 244–246
distribution centers, 15
Dorothy Leonard innovation framework Framework that categorizes five types of innovations: User-Driven Enhancement, Developer-Driven Development, User-Context Development, New Application or Combination of Technologies, and Technology/Market Coevolution, 241–242
drop shipping Requires e-commerce companies to depend on their manufacturers or distributors to pack and ship their retail Web orders, 225
DSL (digital subscriber lines), 7, 11, 326, 338–340, 339 *il.*, 342, 343

E

earnings before interest and taxes (EBIT), 88, 300, 302 *il.*, 303 *il.*
e-commerce Technology-mediated exchanges between parties (individuals or organizations) as well as the electronically based intra- or interorganizational activities that facilitate such exchanges, 3
    access, level of, 5
    activities and categories of, 3–4
    decision-making process, 12
    definition of, 3
    difference from traditional commerce, 5–7
economics
    of information, 8
    of scale, 88, 157
EDGAR (Electronic Data Gathering and Retrieval), 333
EDI (electronic data interchange), 2
efficiencies
    sales force efficiency, 226
    service efficiency, 226
Egg Diagram, 171
    business models, 79–81, 83, 84 *il.*, 103–105
    metrics, 265, 266, 280, 281 *il.*, 283
EIS (enterprise information systems), 347
Electronic Data Gathering and Retrieval (EDGAR), 333
electronic data interchange (EDI), 2
e-mail Messages sent and received electronically via telecommunication links, such as between microcomputers or terminals, 136, 174–175, 177, 198, 333
    newsletters, 143
    spam, 174–175, 177
embryonic company Has no track record, a small but rapidly-growing sales base, and no profit expected for several years, 294, 295 *il.*, 313–315
emerging growth company Company that is really a small portfolio of projects with high optionality (growth options that require

innovation by design Occurs when the manager and a subset of his staff cull ideas from the brainstorming session for those ideas that are cost effective and show promise in consumer acceptance. As a team, they reduce the initial set of ideas into a smaller, commercially viable set, 235–236

innovation by direction Occurs when, working from the commercially viable set, the staff undertakes market research and test runs and further tests implementation viability. After reviewing the results of these tests, the staff further narrows the commercially viable idea set into a final set of marketing concepts to fully implement into the market, 235–236

innovation by doodling Occurs when a manager knows that his or her staff has a great deal of experience, knowledge, and interesting ideas. He or she gathers them into a conference room and announces that he or she wants to learn from the staff and wants to create a free-form brainstorming session where no idea is dumb. At the end of the brainstorming session, the manager has several pages full of innovative marketing ideas, 235–236

innovation funnel process Process in which the offline world innovates using three distinct and successive phases: innovation by doodling, innovation by design, and innovation by direction, 235–236

instant messaging services, 20, 135
interaction, customer controlled, 6, 20
interchange, scientific, 11
interface
    customer. *See* Customer interface
    graphical user interface (GUI), 328–331
    screen-to-face, 6, 323

internal business process metrics Metrics that focus on operations inside the company. In particular, this set of metrics focuses on the critical value-adding activities that lead to customer satisfaction and enhanced shareholder value, 262–263

Internet A web of hundreds of thousands of computer networks, linked together primarily by telephone lines through which data can be carried around the world in seconds, 2
    access to, 17, 33, 356
    advertising, 86, 88
    commodization of products by, 74, 74 *il.*
    community building enabled by, 33, 115, 133–140
    connection methods, 16, 340 *il.*
    definition of, 2, 329
    free speech of, 356
    as indispensable utility service, 12
    information transfer, 330 *il.*
    legal concerns of, 17
    network infrastructure, 322
    number of users, 9 *il.*, 20
    politics of, 354–358
    privacy and security of, 17, 354–355
    projected growth of, 10
    public policy of, 17, 354–358
    reasons for using, 334–335
    relation to other mass media, 10 *il.*
    speed of, 342 *il.*
    statistics of use, 9 *il.*, 20, 334–335, 335 *il.*–337 *il.*
    stocks, 88
    taxes, 17, 355
    usage, 369
    World Wide Web, 329, 330, 333–334, 367

Internet browser A new class of software that serves as the interface to allow users of Windows-based PCs, Apple Macintoshes, and UNIX operating systems to easily access information published on the Web in HTML to display in graphics format what resembles a magazine page with text, photos, and illustrations, 331, 332, 332 *il.*, 378

Internet Service Provider (ISP) Provider that allows users access to the Internet, 16, 336–344, 339 *il.*
    broadband, 326, 342, 344 *il.*, 377, 385
interorganizational activities, 3, 20
intra-organizational activities, 3, 20
investment advice, online, 103–108
investments in e-commerce, 85
ISPs. *See* Internet service providers

J

Java, 333

JPEG (Joint Photographic Experts Group) Joint Photographic Experts Group is a graphic file format that contains binary data that will display an image when viewed with the proper software and hardware. A computer graphics card takes the image data and displays it on a computer monitor. The Web browser reads and displays these graphic files without any additional software, 378

L

LAN (local area networks), 16

learning and growth metrics Learning and growth metrics broadly capture the employee, information systems, and motivation, 263
legal issues, media, 17, 387
    copyright laws, 388–389
    Digital Millennium Copyright Act of 1998, 389
    Digital Watermarks, 389
libraries, public, 12, 356

life cycle of a company There are four stages of development in the life cycle of a company. These stages are identified as startup, acquisition of customers, monetization, and maturity, 267

line extensions One of three types of innovation, line extensions are innovations that are incremental advances to an existing product, 234
linking structures, 119
Linux, 327, 344, 345
LMDS (local multipoint distribution service), 341
local area networks (LAN), 16
local multipoint distribution service (LMDS), 341
log-in registration, 141

M

Macintosh operating system (MacOS), 326, 328, 328 *il.*, 331, 332
magazines, 16, 381

mainframe computers Extremely bulky computers, typically with a room-sized central processing unit, 323–324, 326, 340 *il.*, 344, 346–347

manufacturing and distribution processes Also known as supply chains—how a company manufactures and distributes its goods, 221, 222–229
market. *See also* Branding; Market communications; Market opportunity
    assessment, technological, 28
    attractiveness, 21, 72
    boundaries, existing, 33, 90–91

opportunity metric, 258

Performance Dashboard, 261, 263–267, 264 *il.,* 270 *il.,* 277–288, 289 *il.,* 290 *il.*

resource-system metrics, 266

shareholder value, 90

value proposition or cluster metrics, 265

microcomputer Computer designed for personal computing, 324, 344

microprocessor Known as the central processing unit (CPU) and made of several highly integrated circuits on a single silicon chip, the microprocessor foreshadowed the personal computer revolution in the following decade, 323–326, 328

Microsoft-Disk Operating System (MS-DOS), 326–329

middleware

commerce enabling, 12

providers, 16

minicomputer, 324

mobile wireless Technology that is becoming one of the fastest growing ways to access the Web, 341–342

mobile wireless transmission, 341–342

models. *See also* Business models; Delivery systems

assortment, 93–95

classification of approaches, 100–102, 102 *il.*

emergent valuation model, 7

financial, 87, 107, 280

growth, 87, 96–97, 107, 108 *Il.*

profit, 89

revenue, 87, 88, 94 *il.,* 107, 260

shareholder value, 89–96

value, 107

modem Converts (or MODulates) the digital bits into analog signals and sends them over a telephone line as such. When the modem receives analog signals, it converts (or DEModulates) the analog signals back into digital form before transferring them into the computer, 326, 337, 338, 345 *il.*

cable modems, 7, 326, 340, 342–343, 345 *il.*

monetization Third stage in the life cycle of a company. Its goal is to increase revenues and customer lock-in by developing new revenue streams, 267

Moore's Law A concept developed by Gordon Moore that predicted that the calculating power of a computer microprocessor would double every 12 months for the next 10 years, 55, 326

motion picture film industry, 385

MPEG files, 378

MP3 The acronym for the standards specifications to the MPEG-1 Audio Layer-3, 7, 29, 93, 380, 386–387

Digital Watermarks, 389

MPEG-1 A computer file format and compression specification for motion video with audio, 387

MS-DOS (Microsoft-Disk Operating System), 326–329

multimedia When multiple types of media, including text documents, graphics material, video, and audio, are linked together, 330, 331

N

NAICS codes, 11

NASDAQ, 8, 58

National Center for Superconducting Applications (NCSA), 330–331

National Science Foundation (NSF), 329, 331, 331 *il.*

navigation tools, 119

browsers, 331, 332, 332 *il.,* 378

NCSA (National Center for Superconducting Applications), 330–331

needs of customer. *See* Customer needs

net operating profit less adjusted taxes (NOPLAT) Earnings before interest and taxes less taxes on EBIT (adjusted taxes), 298 *il.,* 299, 301, 316

network economics The theory that the New Economy is driven by networks, rather than scale, so a company's (or website's) value is highly dependent on how many users are using that company's network and/or technology, 7

network infrastructure The basic, underlying group of electronic devices and connecting circuitry designed as a system to share information. In the current context, the network infrastructure can be thought of as the hardware and software to run the Internet, 15, 17, 21, 321–363

analog information, 327, 338

baud rate, 339

broadband, 326, 342, 377, 385

cable modem, 326, 340, 342, 343, 345 *il.*

COder-DECoder (or "codex"), 327

digital convergence, 17 *il.,* 322

digital information, 327

digital subscriber lines (DSL), 7, 11, 326, 338–340, 339 *il.,* 342, 343

Electronic Data Gathering and Retrieval (EDGAR), 333

Hypertext Markup Language (HTML), 330, 331, 331 *il.,* 367

Hypertext Transfer Protocol (HTTP), 330, 367

implementation, 214

internet browser, 331, 332, 332 *il.,* 378

internet service providers (ISP), 16, 336–344, 339 *il.*

Local Area Networks (LAN), 16

local multipoint distribution service (LMDS), 341

media convergence, 322, 323 *il.*

mobile wireless transmission, 341–342

multimedia, 330, 331

routers, 330 *il.,* 343–344

satellite transmission, 16, 341

Secure Socket Layer (SSL) protocol, 332

server, 340 *il.,* 344

switches, 343–344

Transmission Control Protocol/Internet Protocol (TCP/IP), 329, 330 *il.*

Uniform Resource Locator (URL), 330, 343, 370

Wide Area Networks (WAN), 16

network router Holds information on the many possible routes between the origination point and destination point and directs packets across the Internet through these routes, 343

network server A computer that stores and "serves" the website's information to the connected personal computer, 344

network switch Facilitates the actual moving of the packets through an assigned route over the Internet, 343–344

networks. *See also* Network infrastructure

computer, 16

economics, 7, 8, 20, 30, 31, 356, 358

effects, 20

global communications, 16

protocol, 16

returns, increasing, 7

New Application or Combination of Technologies Part of the Dorothy Leonard innovation framework. Innovation occurs when an established technology is applied to a new industry, 241–242

new industries A category of offline innovation. New industry innovations are innovations that can create a new industry, 234–235

newspapers, 16, 380–381

new-to-the-world value New offerings that create value for customers. Examples include: customizing offerings, radically extending reach and access, building community, enabling collaboration among multiple people across locations and time, and introducing new-to-the-world functionality or experience, 32–34, 54, 58, 63, 85, 194

NOPLAT (net operating profit less adjusted taxes), 298 *il.*, 299, 301, 316

NSF (National Science Foundation), 329, 331, 331 *il.*

O

"the offering," 48, 103, 214, 265
    category-specific dominance, 76–77
    cross-category dominance, 77
    customization of, 7
    products, 76–78
    scope of, 76–78
offline companies, 13
one-click shopping, 157
online advertising, 86, 88
online auction-exchange, 4, 20, 88, 91, 92 *il.*, 132, 157, 218
online bazaar, 136–137 *il.*
online brokerage service, 58–63, 88
online business opportunities, 26
online cafe, 139
online chat, 135
online club, 137, 139 *il.*
online commerce companies, 88
online communications. *See* Communications
online community. *See* Community online
online content providers, 88
online implementation process The online implementation process can be divided into two phases. First, the firm is concerned with the delivery of the offering. In the second phase, the firm is concerned with the extent to which the offerings and infrastructures are modified to fit the evolution of the market, 214–219, 264, 269
online information providers, 88
online investment advice, 103–108
online market research, 272, 274 *il.*, 275–277
online shopping, statistics of, 335
online shrine, 138
online "stickiness" of a site, 261
online theater, 138–139, 140 *il.*
online theme park, 137, 138 *il.*
operating margin Earnings before interest and taxes divided by sales revenues, 296 *il.*, 297 *il.*, 299
operating system A set of instructions to a computer about how to operate its various parts and peripherals, 326–329, 328 *il.*, 348 *il.*, 349 *il.*
    graphical user interface (GUI), 328–331
    Java, 333
    Linux, 327, 344, 345

    Macintosh operating system (MacOS), 326, 328, 328 *il.*, 331, 332
    Microsoft-Disk Operating System (MS-DOS), 326–329
    Unix, 327, 331
    Windows operating system, 16, 326–329, 328 *il.*, 331, 332
opportunity. *See also* Market opportunity
    assessment, 50–51, 64
    attractiveness, 28, 51–56
    identification of, 27
    microeconomics of, 51
    nucleus, 27, 35, 63
    resource based, 28
    seed opportunity, 27, 63
opportunity nucleus A set of unmet or underserved need(s), 35
option pricing, 304–305, 307, 310–311
organizational activities, 3, 20
organizational hierarchy, 13
OS. *See* Operating systems
outsource warehousing Generally involves the use of logistics specialists like Federal Express or UPS to stockpile and ship Web orders, 225
outsourced content Content that has been generated by third parties. Third-party suppliers can often create content of higher quality, greater appeal, or at a lower cost than the website operation, 153, 155 *il.*

P

partners and partnerships, 50–51, 178, 264–265, 353
    anchor tenant agreements, 86
    benefit matrix, 107 *il.*
    business, 14, 64, 79, 82, 178, 264–265
    capability, 50–51
    communication of, 218
    complementor, 50, 64, 73
    firms, 73
    identification of, 82
    media, 82
    portal agreements, 86
    promotion agreements, 87
    role of, 86–87
    strategic partnering, 263
patents, e-commerce, 355–358
payment/billing processing It is important that online companies have an efficient system for payment/billing processing so they don't lose money, 221–222
PC (personal computer), 324–329, 325 *il.*, 331, 337, 340 *il.*, 344, 345
Pentium processor, 324–326
Performance Dashboard Standard that reflects the health of a business, it is comprised of five categories of metrics: opportunity, business model, customer interface and outcomes, branding and implementation, and financial, 263–267
permission marketing When customers agree a priori to share personal information in exchange for receiving targeted market communications. Presumes successful marketing campaigns can be created by establishing a mutually beneficial and trusting relationship between the firm and its customers, 180
personal computer (PC), 324–329, 325 *il.*, 331, 337, 340 *il.*, 344, 345
personalization by user of website, 115, 141–143, 144 *il.*
politics of e-commerce, 354–358
portals, 12, 52, 88, 181, 185
    implementation, 239–240

metrics, 272
partners of, 86

portal site Consists almost exclusively of absolute links to a large number of other sites, 123, 139, 151, 153 *il.*, 175, 181, 239–240, 272

Porter Generic Strategy Model, 98

portfolio, replicating, 310

postindustrial period, 2

procurement The purchasing, leasing, renting, or selling of materials, services, equipment, or construction, 353–354

present value (PV), 304–305, 306 *il.*, 307, 308

pricing
 auction, 132, 157
 demand aggregations, 157–159
 haggle pricing, 159
 sensitivity, 74

print media, 16, 380–383

privacy and public policy, 354–358

procurement, 353–354, 354 *il.*

product offering, 77

programs, affiliate, 153, 154 *il.*, 175–178

project optionality, 313

public policy, privacy and, 354–358

public schools, 12, 356

PV (present value), 304–305, 306 *il.*, 307, 308

R

radio, 367, 385
 broadcast, 15, 16, 322
 online stations, 42

Rayport, Jaworski, and Siegal Model, 99–102

real-options analysis (ROA) A discounted-cash-flow valuation approach that captures the present value of flexibility in decision making and includes the DCF value as a special case assuming that there is no flexibility in decision making, 304, 304 *il.*, 305, 307, 307 *il.*, 310, 311, 311 *il.*, 313 *il.*, 316

real value options, 8

replicating portfolio A portfolio of assets whose value is known, constructed to provide exactly the same payoffs in every state of nature as a portfolio whose present value is not known. By the law of one price, the value of the replicating portfolio is the same as the value of the risky asset that is being priced, 310

report, analyst, 272, 274 *il.*

resources. *See also* Resource system
 activities, 81
 "back office," 15
 enterprise resource planning (ERP), 347
 internal, 50
 links within, 85

resource allocation process Formalization of the trade-offs and prioritization that the company uses when making choices about which opportunities to pursue, 221

resource system A unique combination of resources within and outside the firm that delivers promised benefits, 50, 64, 79–87, 220–222, 258, 264–266, 280
 capabilities and benefits, 85
 construction of, 82
 model of, 83
 quality of, 83
 sustainable advantage, 86

uniqueness of, 83–84

responsiveness
 real-time competitive, 5, 8, 20
 strategic/tactical, 5

return on invested capital (ROIC) Defined as earnings before interest and taxes times one, minus the cash tax rate, and all divided by the amount of invested capital, it is the rate of return on money invested in the company and should be higher than the weighted average cost of capital in order to create shareholder wealth, 296 *il.*, 298 *il.*, 299–300, 302 *il.*, 316

revenue
 advertising, 86, 88
 growth, 87
 new, 85
 streams, 88

reverse auction pricing Pricing in which sellers bid against each other and the lowest bid wins buyer business, 157

ROA (real-option analysis), 304, 304 *il.*, 305, 307, 307 *il.*, 310, 311, 311 *il.*, 313 *il.*, 316

robust growth company A company, like AOL or Amazon.com, that is large but still growing rapidly, selling for 15 to 25 times sales, 294–300, 296 *il.*, 316

ROIC (return on invested capital), 296 *il.*, 298 *il.*, 299–300, 302 *il.*, 316

S

salesforce efficiency Extent to which the salesforce operates in the most time-effective manner; has been increased on the Internet because fewer transactions need to be routed through the salesforce, which results in salesforce efficiencies. Also, salesforce personnel who handle calls originating from the website have a higher "close" rate, 226

sales rep, traditional, 183

satellite transmission, 341

Sawhney and Kaplan Model, 98–99

schools, public, 12, 356

scientific interchange, 11

screen-to-customer interface, 14, 20, 326

screen-to-face interface, 2, 6, 323

search process, customer control of, 6

Secure Socket Layer (SSL) protocol, 332

SEC (U.S. Securities and Exchange Commission), 333

seed opportunity, 27, 63

segmentation The process of dividing the diverse population of target customers into homogenous segments, any of which may be selected as the one to be reached with a distinct marketing mix, 39, 265, 282
 actionable, 41–43, 45, 59–60, 72
 behavioral, 40, 44, 46 *il.*, 47 *il.*, 60
 beliefs and attitudes, 40
 benefits, 40
 choice of, 72, 75
 customer variables, 43
 demographics, 40, 42, 44, 46 *il.*, 47 *il.*, 60, 72, 114
 firmographics, 40
 geographics, 40
 interaction, 54, 64
 mapping, 54 *il.*
 of markets, 40
 meaningful, 41–43, 45, 59–60, 72

microeconomic variables, 43
occasion, 40
purchase occasion, 42
pyschographics, 40
success of, 48
target, 53, 64, 71, 72
seller, control of buying process by, 6
selling-chain management Enables the development and successful deployment of large-scale, field-sales-automation solutions in order to automate many of the order acquisition functions, such as configuration, pricing, quoting, and service, 353–354, 354 *il.*
service efficiency Extent to which service operations operate in the most time-effective manner; has been increased on the Internet because many inquiries can be handled by an automated system instead of by person-to-person contact, 226
service providers, 12. *See also* Internet service providers (ISPs)
applications service providers (ASPs), 16
services, personal, 4, 20
7Cs Framework Framework for customer interface. The 7Cs are context, content, community, customization, communication, connection, and commerce, 114–117, 266, 285
shareholder
value focus, 90
value model, 89–96, 94 *il.*
shopping cart, 156
shrine (online community archetype), 138
SIC codes, 11
signal, electronic transmission
analog information, 327, 338
COder-DECoder (or "codex"), 327
digital information, 327
silicon chip, 324
site. *See also* Websites
destination, 151, 152 *il.*
hub, 131, 151, 152 *il.*
portal, 123, 139, 151, 153 *il.*
security of, 156
spam, 174–175, 177
specialty store, 129, 130 *il.*
spin-out businesses, 13
SSL (Secure Socket Layer) protocol, 332
stand-alone value, 314
startup Beginning cycle in life cycle of a company. The goal is to develop a platform for rapid growth by building a strong team and creating a flexible site, 267
start-up business, failure rates of, 26
stock-it-yourself Generally involves an automated warehouse that can directly fulfill online orders, 224–225
strategy, 13–15, 17
business of, 14, 21
evaluation of, 17
implementation of, 17
online and offline, 85
streaming audio Sound files that allow a computer user to listen to a file while it is still downloading, instead of waiting until the file is completely downloaded to listen, 378
streaming technology, 376–378, 382
audio, 7, 342, 344 *il.*, 378, 382
MPEG files, 378
video, 120, 378

streaming video Audio files that allow a computer user to watch a file while it is still downloading, instead of waiting until the file is completely downloaded to watch, 378
strength of association, 187–188
supercomputers Supercomputers are a class of mainframe computers that have the fastest-computing CPUs available at the time (at the time of this writing, IBM had a computer that employed 8,000 microprocessors in parallel and was capable of executing over 12 trillion operations per second). Supercomputer can also mean a very large server, 324
superstore, 127–128, 129 *il.*
supply-chain management Allows a company to improve its competitive positioning by achieving lower costs and accelerating time-to-market of new products, 352–353
supply-chain models Supply-chain models in the New Economy focus on rapidly changing structures in B2C, B2B, C2B, and C2C markets. These new supply-chain options have significantly changed the manner in which customers and suppliers interact with manufacturers, 222–229
supply chain models of delivery systems, 4, 4 *il.*, 20, 221–229, 258, 263, 267. *See also* Business-to-business (B2B) delivery systems; Business-to-consumer (B2C) delivery systems
management, 352–353
partnerships, 352–353
supply-side
aggregators, 101, 101 *il.*, 102
classification of businesses, 11
focus, 80–81
switching costs of customers The costs—both financial and personal—of switching from one business or product to another, 216–217

T

tailoring by site Form of customization that enables the site to reconfigure itself based on past behavior by the user or by other users with similar profiles. These sites can make recommendations based on past purchases, filter marketing messages based on user interests, and adjust prices and products based on user profiles, 115, 140, 142–143, 144 *il.*
taxation of e-commerce, 17, 355
TCP/IP (Transmission Control Protocol/Internet Protocol) Underlying packet switching technology that became the mandatory standard. TCP/IP (Transmission Control Protocol/Internet Protocol) allowed for communications to be broken into packets, routed to their destination as separate packets, and then reassembled as the original communication, 329, 330 *il.*
Technology/Market Coevolution Occurs when neither the customer base is clearly known nor is the technology well-established. These products sometimes appear to have a more or less accidental growth path but can be the beginning of entire new markets, 242
Telecommunications Act of 1996 Signed into law in 1996, this represented the first major overhaul of federal laws regulating the communications industry since 1934. With the passing of this act, emphasis was changed from a regulation-based industry to a market-based industry to allow for increased competition, 379
telemarketing Marketing by a salesforce over the telephone, 183
telephone, 15, 31
companies, 13, 16
lines, 11

marketing, 183

Telecommunications Act of 1996, 379

television

broadcast, 16, 383–384

cable, 11, 15, 16, 367–369, 370 *il.,* 384–385

Ten-Step Branding Process Branding framework that includes 10 steps: clearly identify the brand audience, understand the customer, identify key leverage points in customer experience, continually monitor competitors, design compelling and complete brand intent, execute with integrity, be consistent over time, establish feedback systems, be opportunistic, and invest and be patient, 189–192

the offering The specific product or service a company offers to its customers, 48

theater (online community archetype), 138–139, 140 *il.*

theme park (online community archetype), 137, 138 *il.*

time zones, communication across, 11

topology of computer networks, 16

traditional mass media Consists of television (network, cable, and local), print media (including high circulation newspapers and magazines), and national and local radio, 182

traditional sales rep Uses a face-to-face sales process between a salesperson and a customer; this type of process is reemerging as a result of the Web. When properly managed, the Web can paradoxically lead to increased effectiveness of sales reps rather than making sales reps obsolete, 183

transactions

companies, of, 88

technology-enabled, 3, 20

technology-mediated, 3, 20

Transmission Control Protocol/Internet Protocol (TCP/IP), 329, 330 *il.*

trapped value Can be unlocked by creating more efficient markets, creating more efficient value systems, enabling easier access, or disrupting current pricing power, 32–34, 48, 58, 58 *il.,* 63–64

twenty-four seven (24X7), 5, 29, 280

U

underserved needs of customer, 26–28, 34, 36–37, 56, 59, 63, 72

Uniform Resource Locator (URL), 330, 343, 370

uniqueness (customer, strength of association), 187–188

Unix, 327, 331

unmet needs of customer, 26, 27, 34, 36–37, 56, 59, 63, 72

URL (Uniform Resource Locator) Specifies a transmission protocol and an Internet identifying number, 330, 343, 370

U.S. Department of Defense, 329

U.S. Securities and Exchange Commission (SEC), 333

User-Context Development Occurs when firms develop products to meet a previously unexpressed need. In many cases, careful market research revealed these needs and firms have built products to meet these needs, 241–242

User-Driven Enhancement No-risk improvements to a product. Common types of user-driven enhancements include lowering product price, low-cost, high-value feature enhancements, and cost-efficient quality improvements, 241

V

valence (customers), 187–188

valuation, 88, 293–317

beta, 295–296

bond rating, 295, 296

calculations of, 8, 14

capitalization-to-sales ratio, 315

continuing (or terminal) value, 296, 298 *il.,* 299, 301

discounted cash flow (DCF), 296 *il.,* 300–305, 307, 314, 316

earnings before interest and taxes (EBIT), 88, 300, 302 *il.,* 303 *il.*

emergent valuation model, 6

entity, of, 300

free cash flows (FCF), 300, 308 *il.,* 310 *il.,* 311 *il.*

market value of equity, 300

net operating profit less adjusted taxes (NOPLAT), 298 *il.,* 299, 301, 316

online companies, of, 8

operating margin, 296 *il.,* 297 *il.,* 299

option pricing, 304–305, 307, 310–311

present value (PV), 304–305, 306 *il.,* 307, 308

projected, 8

real-options analysis (ROA), 304, 304 *il.,* 305, 307, 307 *il.,* 310, 311 *il.,* 313 *il.,* 316

replicating portfolio, 310

return on invested capital (ROIC), 296 *il.,* 298 *il.,* 299–300, 302 *il.,* 316

weighted average cost of capital (WACC), 295–296, 296 *il.,* 298 *il.,* 299, 301, 302 *il.,* 303 *il.*

value

assortment, 93–95

best experience, 94 *il.,* 95–96

best information, 93

broadest user network, 94 *il.,* 95

chain, 29, 31, 33–34

cluster, 71–73, 82, 103, 191, 258, 259

company derived, 94 *il.*

creation, 28, 31, 63

lowest prices, 94 *il.,* 95

most personalized, 94 *il.,* 96

proposition, 103, 105, 191, 220, 221, 259, 265, 266, 271, 280, 283–284

propositions, 70, 71–76, 79

stand-alone value, 314

system, 27, 32–34, 39–40, 49, 56, 63

value chain According to Michael Porter, a value chain represents the collection of activities that are performed to design, produce, market, deliver, and support a product. A firm's value chain and the way it performs individual activities are a reflection of its history, strategy, approach to implementing its strategy, and the underlying economics of the activities themselves, 26–28

value system An interconnection of processes and activities within and among firms that creates benefits for intermediaries and end consumers, 27

VCR (videocassette recorder), 385–386

vertical hubs, 98–100

vertical integration Occurs when a company deepens its position in a particular market by acquiring complementary firms in a value system (e.g., Amazon acquiring/building warehouses to distribute books), 378, 379–380

vertical plays, business, 33–34

videocassette recorder (VCR), 385–386

viral marketing Company-developed products, services, or information that is passed from user to user. It is analogous to how a viral infection is passed between two people, 175

virtual connection, 16
virtual storefront, 15

W

WACC (weighted average cost of capital), 295–296, 298 *il.*, 299, 301, 302 *il.*, 303 *il.*
WAN (wide area networks), 16
WAP devices, 6
warehouses, offline physical, 15
waterfall concept of new product innovation Also known as the innovation funnel process, the purpose of this is to make internal choices about innovations that the company should pursue and to launch only the innovations with the highest chance of succeeding, 235
wealth creation of e-commerce, 9, 12, 14
websites
    aesthetics, 121–124, 124 *Il.*
    commerce, 116–117, 155–159, 163
    communication, 116, 143–149, 162–163
    community, 115, 133–140
    connection, 116, 149–155, 163
    content, 115, 126–132, 159
    context, 115, 119–126, 159
    customization of, 115, 140–143, 161–162
    design, 113–159
    fit, 117
    form *vs.* function, 119–126

    function, 119–122, 124 *il.*
    markup languages, 120, 330, 331, 331 *il.*, 367
    performance, 120
    personalization by user, 115, 141–143, 144 *il.*
    reinforcement, 118
    tailoring by site, 115, 140, 142–143, 144 *il.*
weighted average cost of capital (WACC) The opportunity cost of funds employed in a company—the marginal after-tax cost of debt multiplied by the market value of debt as a percent of the value of the firm, plus the marginal cost of equity multiplied by the percent of equity financing used by the firm, 295–296, 298 *il.*, 299, 301, 302 *il.*, 303 *il.*
wide area networks (WAN), 16
Windows operating system, 31, 326–329, 331, 332
word-of-mouth (WOM), 7
World Wide Web A subset of the Internet that is accessible through the use of HTTP to link documents at various URLs that are composed in HTML (and now also XML), 329, 330, 333–334, 367. *See also* Internet

X

XML (markup language), 120

Z

Zaltman Metaphoric Elicitation Technique (ZMET), 38
ZMET (Zaltman Metaphoric Elicitation Technique), 38

Media Convergence to a Digital Platform

	1964	1970			1980
eCommerce					
Television			1975 HBO begins satellite transmission		1980 CNN formed
Radio/Music					1983 First CDs launched
Print					1982 *USA Today* launched, satellite printing used 1983 *New York Times* completes conversion from letterpress to offset
Video Games		Early 70s Nolan Bushnell creates Pong			
Wireless					
Online Services					
Internet/Browsers	1966 First funding to establish the Internet 1969 Internet established by U.S. Department of Defense				
Servers					
Personal Computers	1965 IBM 360, first integrated-circuit computer & PDP-8, first minicomputer introduced by Digital	Early 70s Graphical User Interface developed by XEROX PARC 1970 First floppy disk created 1971 Texas Instruments creates its first pocket calculator	1975 MIT's Altair 8800, first personal computer, introduced; Cray supercomputer created 1977 Apple II, first widely sold PC, introduced; Microsoft founded 1978 Hayes introduces first microcomputer-compatible modem		1981 IBM introduces its personal computer 1984 Apple introduces the Macintosh 1984 Dell founded
Microprocessors		1971 Intel introduces first microprocessor, the 4004 chip	1973 Intel introduces the 8080 microprocessor	1978 Intel introduces the 8088 chip	1982 Intel introduces the 80286 chip
Legal		Mid-70s FCC prohibits cross media ownership of newspapers and television	1977 Federal court lifts FCC restrictions on cable television		1984 U.S. Court orders breakup of AT&T into 8 regional "Baby Bells"